Prologue:
A Gathering of Beasts

Bela Lugosi's dead, and so am I. But what's left of Bela is rotting in a pine coffin somewhere, while I have the opportunity to sit here on the balcony, enjoy my drink and look at you. Correct me if I'm being presumptuous, but I suspect that I have the better end of the deal.

I can tell by looking at you that you're not comprehending. Of course you're not — these are cynical, rational times, and you're not going to believe that I'm a dead man just because I say so. A century ago it would have been different — well, it was quite different the last time I had this little talk with someone — but this is the age of *facts*. And the facts are that corpses don't move, don't walk, don't talk. I'm terribly sorry, my dear, but I have a surprise for you: This corpse does.

So sit down. Please, I insist that you make yourself comfortable. Pour yourself something to drink, preferably from the bottle on the left — the stuff on the right is an acquired taste. It's going to be a long evening, and you're going to need a stiff drink or two, I suspect. After all, in the next few hours I'm going to explain to you in excruciating detail why everything you think you know about life and death is wrong. In other words, you don't know a blessed thing about the way the world really works, and I'm going to open your eyes.

But I'm afraid, my dear, that you're not going to like what you see.

What I Am

Before we go any further, allow me to tell you that you're getting an unprecedented opportunity here. My kind doesn't talk about itself to your kind — not now and, for the most part, not ever. We've spent five centuries weaving a stage curtain that we call the Masquerade to hide the real show from you, but in the end it comes down to one simple fact: We vampires don't want you mortals knowing we're out there. It's for the same reason the wolf doesn't want the sheep knowing he's around. It makes our work *so* much easier. And so, for example, though we do indeed possess the sharpened canines with which dime novels and the cinema have branded us, you mortals will not see them unless we choose to reveal them. Like *so*.

You're looking pale, my dear. That will never do if we're going to be seen later — allow me to take care of looking pale for both of us. Still, I must admit I'm disappointed that you seem so disturbed by the notion of my being a vampire. Take a moment and compose yourself, if you can. Truth be told, I'm afraid that's the least of the shocks waiting for you tonight. Please, don't waste time trying to come up with a rational, scientific explanation, because there isn't one. It's just what I am. What many, many of us are — too many, by some accounts.

Damnation, are you truly that much of a fool? Sit back down. I said *sit*. Now watch. *Hush*, stop screaming. No one will come to rescue you, and no one will call the police — not in this building. Discreet neighbors are a blessing to one in my condition. It's positively Victorian the way they ignore anything not directly in front of them.

So, at last you have your proof. Now do you believe me? Yes, it is blood in the other decanter; served cold like that, of course, the stuff loses much of its taste. You can try it if you like, but I don't recommend it, no. You're not set up to enjoy such things, at least not as presently configured.

Don't get ahead of yourself guessing my intentions, my dear. If I were going to act according to your beloved clichés, you would be dead right now. I am a predator, after all, and you and your entire species are my prey.

BEGINNINGS

I suppose we should begin with the basics of the whole thing. I am in fact a vampire, brought into this state of existence in the Year of Our Lord 1796 by a woman who was introduced to me as a quote-unquote "lady of the evening." The gentleman who introduced us — one of her servants, I later discovered — had an odd sense of humor.

But I digress. Yes, I do drink human blood. Without the nourishment it provides, I will wither away; with it, I will live forever. Yes, forever. Unless destroyed — and destroying one of the Damned is no mean feat, I can assure you — we vampires are every bit as immortal as the legends say. Only the sun, and the emotions it engenders, remain forever foreign to us; we Kindred can drink in the nights of countless ages, can remain unchanging while all that we know crumbles to dust around us and is replaced by another stage-set that in turn crumbles to dust, and so on....

Ah, once again, I lose the way. Blood, yes, blood. I can get by on the blood of animals — most of us can, except the true elders of our kind — but such a diet is unpleasant. Unpalatable. No, we all want to feed on the best vintages, otherwise one goes around all the time with a dull ache in one's gut that just never goes away. It gets worse the hungrier one gets, I might add; a vampire who goes too long without feeding is liable to demonstrate a regrettable lack of self-control.

There are other tell-tale physiological signs of my condition. My heart does not beat; the strength of my will alone suffices to force the blood through my body. My internal organs, by all accounts, have long since atrophied into vestigial husks, but that won't matter to a coroner, as once I am truly killed I will rapidly decompose into dust. In the meantime, however, I'm not troubled by such trifles as breathing, extremes of temperature and the like. My skin is cold, unless I take the effort to warm it. Doing so takes effort, though, and the expenditure of precious blood. Regular food is an abomination unto me, and it doesn't sit for more than a few seconds in what remains of my stomach. Even with eternity stretching before me, my dear, I have better things to do with my time than to crouch over toilets, heaving ashes and gobbets into the bowl.

In layman's terms, then, I am no longer human. For all intents and purposes, I am simply a blood-drinking, ambulatory cadaver, indistinguishable from any body in a morgue unless I am moving about. I save the niceties like warming my flesh and remembering to blink for company, such as yourself.

Say thank you, dear. Keeping myself fresh and rosy-looking for you is costing me more than you know.

Ah, we return to the drinking of blood, the defining act, as it were, of my state. Yes, I am afraid it is a necessity, though one can leave one's prey alive. All that requires is a little self-control and a touch of effort to close the wound — and no, we don't all drink from the neck. You can cross another cliché off your list. The problem with leaving one's prey alive, however, is that unless one has certain…protections, she remembers. Such breaches of the Masquerade are not looked on kindly by the vampiric powers that be. Oftentimes, it makes more sense simply to kill.

My Drinking Problem

The crux of the matter, really, is that drinking blood not only allows me to perpetuate my existence, but also provides a sensation unlike anything else this world has to offer. What is it like? My dear, words cannot describe it. Imagine drinking the finest champagne and the sensation of the most sensual lovemaking you've ever experienced. Overlay that with the rush the opium fiend feels as he takes that first breath on the pipe, and you begin to have some sense, some tiny, infinitesimal sense of what it feels like to drink the blood of a kine — excuse me, a living human being. Your modern-day addicts will lie, steal, cheat and kill for their little tickets to Heaven. Mine is better, and it makes me immortal besides. Can you imagine the deeds I might commit to feed that hunger? Don't bother speaking possibilities; the truth is worse than you can

imagine. And I am considered to be a gentleman of my kind. Now imagine, if you will, some of my relatives, the ones who aren't so nice as I.

They can — and do — commit acts that even I don't wish to consider.

And here you are, poor little mortal, learning how fragile your whole existence is.

Are you starting to be afraid yet? You should be.

THE FIRST FATAL SIP

In most cases, one receives one's first drink of blood on the night one becomes a vampire — one of the "Kindred," as we like to call ourselves. The process is called "The Embrace," and has two distinct and rather difficult phases. The first is simple: The vampire who wishes to create progeny drinks every last drop of blood he can from his intended "childe." This is no different from normal feeding, save that one doesn't need to worry about erasing the memory or disposing of the corpse afterward, and that one gets a very full meal indeed. The difference comes afterward.

Once the last bit of blood has pulsed its way out, the "parent" vampire — the technical term is "sire," not that you care yet — then returns some of his ill-gotten gains. He bites his lip, or wrist, or whatever, and allows some of his blood to pass his victim's lips. Assuming that the mortal does not actively and successfully resist the process — few do, believe me — and assuming that the sire has not delayed too long in granting this gift, then the blood trickles down the victim's throat and revives her, albeit as a vampire.

It sounds simple, does it not? The truth is, as truth is always wont to be, more complicated. My own Embrace would seem to be the epitome of the lushly romantic gloss your age has put on my kind, and even so I shudder in retrospect at the memory. All of the ingredients of romance were there — the candlelit boudoir, the half-drunk goblets of wine, milady's pale heaving bosom — one would think we'd retreated from the party into the pages of a novel. And so we tumbled onto the bed, and, at the height of passion, she plunged her fangs into my neck. Between the pleasure of the moment and the pleasure of her feeding — yes, it is quite pleasurable for mortals, to the point of addiction for some — I was quite content to drift away. I remember distinctly thinking that my mother had been right about me after all, and that loose women would be the death of me, and I even recall laughing as my sire drank my life.

And then, as I lay there watching that shimmering door open before me, as my soul took its first faltering steps toward Heaven, she calmly slit her wrist and poured the vitriol of eternal life down my throat. You can mock me for not rejecting what she offered, but even in the face of Grace, life is sweet. Her blood seared as it trickled past my lips and down my throat, and I found myself wanting to live. The pain the blood brought was proof that I was alive. And, when it became clear that I would not be ascending, the shining door vanished with a feeling of ineffable sadness, leaving me with my sire and a murderous hunger. Fortunately, my sire was kind enough to see me through the change; she'd seduced my best friend prior to stalking me, and cached him in an adjoining room like a shrike stocking its larder. While I felt my body dying cell by cell, he lay senseless, waiting for my hunger.

Ah, yes, the hunger of creation. That little bit of blood that one's sire uses to bestow the Embrace isn't much — a few drops with more mystical than nutritional significance. They certainly don't provide enough sustenance to satisfy the hunger of a newborn vampire. So the newborn childe had better pray her sire has laid in a few bottles or, better yet, a few bodies for the moment, so that there's something to feed on right after the change. I've witnessed the horror of newly Embraced Kindred giving in to that uncontrollable hunger and ripping to shreds whoever was nearest in their madness. When that first thirst is upon you, you will do whatever you must to feed. You will kill your lover, your child, your parent or your priest to sate that thirst, and you will be glad to do so — for as long as the frenzy lasts.

There, my dear, is the rub. Because no matter how long you're in that state of frenzy, no matter what triggered it — fear or hunger or pain or rage — no matter how long you give in to the animal inside you, you can't control what you do and *you always come down*. And that's when you must deal with the consequences of what you did when that animal wearing your skin was in control. And the first frenzy is never the last. One would think it gets easier to deal with that loss of control as one grows more experienced. One who thought that would be quite wrong.

The Beast

A vampire's animalistic side is called the Beast, in what is, I suspect, an attempt to demonize it by dissociation. Alas, merely giving the monstrous urge a different name is not enough to tame it. In the end the Beast always wins, I'm told. If one survives long enough as a vampire, one is forced by one's own nature to do some obscene things. And eventually, one gets acclimated to committing those atrocities and moves on to new ones, and whatever was human in that vampire dies. When the last bit of humanity in a vampire dies — and once you watch enough friends, loved ones and descendants pass into the dust of ages, it does die, rest assured — then the Beast takes over once and for all. The vampire becomes an animal. If you ever reach that stage, the odds are you won't even notice when you get put down like a mad dog.

If your will is strong, and you've got a decent sense of self, you can hold out for decades. Centuries, even — I have spoken to a Kindred who is over two millennia old. But you are never, ever free of the fear that the Beast will one night triumph, and that fear is what the Beast will use to bring you to bay.

Of course, the best way to fight the Beast is to keep oneself in fighting trim, and that means eating regularly. Then again, eating regularly usually means that sooner or later, you start killing kine — mortals, pardon me again — and the more kine you kill, the easier the killing gets. So the Beast wins that way, as well. Even if you don't mean to, even if the process begins with an accident, sooner or later you get inured to the sight of a brand-new corpse that you're responsible for, lying dead at your feet. After the tenth, hundredth, thousandth or whatever corpse, it stops being a person and becomes an object, a vessel. A footnote in your history of the ages. And you, at that moment, cease to be remotely human.

A Return to Blood

But there's more to blood than just food, a lot more. There's power to it, so much so that some vampires call it *vitae* — "of life." Blood above and beyond what is needed to survive can be put to a variety of uses. The legendary vampiric strength or speed? A product of the proper application of blood. Invulnerability to mortal woes? Another draught from the same well. I've had pistols emptied into my belly and not slowed down a whit. Blood powers many of the "magical" talents ascribed to us as well; you've witnessed one. And of course, I can flush blood to my skin so as to appear, well, almost human.

There is a price to be paid, of course. The more blood I spend on such parlor tricks, the more quickly I exhaust what is in my belly. The more quickly I empty my gut, the sooner I need to feed — and hunt — once again.

You would prefer me to cease the charade of warmth, then? I am in your debt. It is so refreshing to meet a young person who is willing to look past appearances, don't you think? Hmm? My dear, were you six times your current age you'd be a child to me. "Young" is a relative term.

Tsk. I'm feeling a bit hungry. Would you care to escort me out on the town? The other option is that I leave you here as a prisoner, and I'd prefer not to do that. No doubt you'd try to get inventive and escape, and I'd lose some antiques as you smashed things in the process. You, my dear, are replaceable. My possessions are not. It's that simple.

The Lies

I am quite glad you decided to come along after all. Lucky, wasn't it, that I had something appropriate for you in the guest bedroom's closet. No, not from a previous victim, if that's what you're worried about; it's just that when the same situations pop up over and over across a dozen decades, you learn to prepare for them. Surely you don't think you're the first woman I've strolled with since my Embrace? You are lovely, but don't allow it to go to your head, my dear.

It *is* cold tonight, isn't it? I see you're staring at my breath — yes, it is steaming like yours. That's another use of blood, one that's quite useful for disguising myself in the presence of vampire-hunters and other unpleasant souls. You'd be amazed at how many of my kind have met their ends over the years because they forgot a tiny detail. The devil is in fact in the details, and he's just as happy to turn on his putative servants as he is on those who think themselves divinely inspired.

In the meantime, this wolf likes to blend in with the flock, yes.

Hmm. Hunters. They're nasty, nasty people, full of fire and drive for their self-appointed mission. Most of them never come within a half-mile of destroying one of my kind; of the rest, the vast majority do their causes more harm than good. They cull the weak and the stupid from this state of unlife, leaving better, smarter, stronger vampires. Many hunters are self-employed, a ragtag rabble toting shotguns and stakes as they stomp blindly through the gardens of the night. Others work for branches of your government, convinced we're part of some enemy's conspiratorial attempts to bring down The American Way. Imbeciles.

The most dangerous hunters are tied up with the Catholic Church and something called the Society of Leopold. Don't be fooled: It's the Inquisition in modern guise. They, and others like them, have learned just enough of the truth about the Kindred to draw all the wrong conclusions. According to your basic vampire-hunter, we are all evil pawns of Satan, sent to Earth to wreak havoc and serve our Infernal Master.

That, contrary to what one might think, is unequivocally *merde*. I hold as master no man, vampire or devil; I serve no will save my own. Vampires simply have…appetites and goals that diverge from what your average Inquisition adherent thinks is normal. Then again, I'm told they run to hair shirts and self-flagellation, which is hardly well-socialized behavior either.

There are a great many other half-truths and misconceptions out there, most of which serve our purposes. Do you see the church across the way? You will notice that I am standing *in media crucis* — right where the shadow of the cross falls on the street — and it's not doing a blessed thing to me. Nor will any other crucifix, Star of David or other religious apparatus, unless the person holding it has some faith of her own. That sort of faith is really quite rare these days, I assure you. Nine times out of ten you can walk up to a priest (if so inclined), rip the cross out of his hands, and then kill him while he's still asking God what precisely went wrong.

Not that I've done such a thing, of course.

Most of the other folderol they sell you in the movies is exactly that. Garlic? Worthless. A stake? Only if it catches you right in the heart, and even then it only immobilizes you. Running water? I do bathe, thank you very much. Sunlight? Well, that does hurt, but it takes more than a single sunbeam to turn you to ash. The same for open flame — it burns you, but takes more than a second to do so.

Am I in fact using "you" in all of these examples? I'm terribly sorry about that. I have no idea what came over me.

As for where we're going right now, well, we're going to a nightclub. More precisely, we're going to a watering hole where the kine have gathered, not realizing there are predators about. You're also going to meet a few others of my kind, of different families. Don't worry, you're perfectly safe from them as long as you remain in my company. I have no intention of letting anyone hurt you tonight.

FLAVORS OF THE BLOOD

Here we are: Xero, the latest blip on what passes for a nightlife in this dungheap metropolis. The hot spots come and go — dance halls fade into speakeasies turn into swing clubs and burger joints, which meld into coffeehouses, discos and eventually…this. The details don't matter; there are always places where the young can come to show how rebellious they are, at least until that night's money runs out. They want the taste of danger, you see, while we're just looking for the taste of blood. The intersection of our interests is natural, but the irony of the situation is lost to them.

No, we are not going to have to wait in line. The bouncer at the door is one of ours, you see. He is what we call a ghoul. Every so often he drinks some vampire blood and in exchange gets a few of the perks of being a vampire. Just a few, mind you — ghouls are most assuredly still mortal. The benefits to the arrangement are limited; ghouls don't get the full range of our powers, but in exchange they are still capable of fathering children, feeling the sun on their shoulders, and accidentally drowning.

Yes, ghouling is yet another property of the Blood. There are a great many things about the Blood I haven't told you; I'm not being paid to tutor you, after all. Still curious? Well, how's this: Drink a vampire's blood three times, and you're hopelessly enthralled with him. The resultant feeling of affection is called the blood bond, and if the vampire responsible for it reinforces it, the bond can last *forever*. After all, it's not like one can even die to escape it.

Can you imagine that, by the way? Being forced to love someone, forever? Knowing that the love you have for them — which is so strong you'll kill or die for this person — is a lie, a damnably induced lie? Hating them and loving them at the same time, and not being able to do a damned thing about it?

Yes, it does sound like I'm speaking from personal experience, doesn't it? Funny how that works. Mind your step here; management keeps forgetting that not all of the patrons can see in the dark.

A Breed Apart

Now, here's a little primer on family relations before I introduce you around. According to vampire legend, we are all descended from Caine, son of Adam and Eve. Supposedly God punished Caine for killing Abel by turning him into a vampire; the "mark" God placed upon Caine was in fact the curse of vampirism. Caine discovered he could pass his curse on through the Embrace, and created childer to ease his loneliness. Unfortunately, the process did not stop there. Each of Caine's childer made childer, and they made childer, and so on. Caine realized his mistake, forbade the further creation of vampires, and vanished.

Of course, with the cat away the mice did play. The younger vampires listened about as well as one might expect, which is why I'm here. Of course, each step away from Caine — each generation of vampires — is a little weaker, a little closer to mortal. Caine himself is the First Generation, his childer are second, and so on down the line. The 13th generation is about the last one worth the oil it will take to roast them in Hell; I am led to believe that 14th-generation vampires are all mules anyway.

Never ask someone her generation. Doing so is considered fatally rude.

That's not all there is to it — can you hear me over this din? Why *do* mortals insist on dancing to this, this *noise* at such high volume, anyway? In any case, we're not all like Caine. Heaven help the world if we were! Instead, each of Caine's grandchilder — Antediluvians, we call these mythical beings, for they are presumed to predate Noah's little Flood — supposedly bore unique mystical gifts and curses, and all vampires descended from that particular Kindred kept those characteristics. We became specialized, bred like hounds or racehorses, and those specialized lineages became known as clans. Thirteen great clans are known to us, each distinct in powers and purview. Those powers, by the way, we call "Disciplines." For all intents and purposes, they're magical. You've seen me use one of mine. Pray you don't see some of the others.

Oh, and then there is the Jyhad, of course. Yes, Jyhad. The Eternal Struggle, The Great Game, or whatever poetic sobriquet one wishes to attach to it. Most Kindred would say the Jyhad, like the Antediluvians, is but a myth, and yet many believe in it, deep in their cold, dead hearts. As the stories go, during the first nights, the eldest childer of Caine began fighting amongst themselves, using their own childer and the kine as pawns to be sent to and fro against the minions of their rivals. Naturally, since we vampires are immortal, the ancient feuds never quite died out, and so the game of feint and thrust, parry and counter continues — so they say — to this very night, with most participants entirely unaware of their part in the struggle. Kindred versus Kindred, clan versus clan, mortal nation versus mortal nation, all at the strings of hidden puppetmasters. A silly notion, really. And yet, I have seen many strange things in the night, and I occasionally wonder whether my actions are indeed my own…. Ah, well. Existentialist piffle.

Anyway, please allow me to introduce you around. Do you see that woman over there in the black lace skirt and top hat? No, not her, the *other* one. Her name is Jillian. She's one of us, but from a different clan than I. Specifically, she is of Clan Toreador, the "Clan of the Rose," as they call it. Art, beautiful boys, imagining themselves to be characters out of Keats or Shelley — all these things are meat and drink to the Toreador. Or that is what conventional wisdom would have one believe. I put little stock in stereotypes, particularly the noble ones.

The gentleman in the charcoal suit and collarless shirt who's trying to be inconspicuous in watching Jillian and her flock? He's Paolo, a Tremere. The Tremere are sorcerers, quite nasty and secretive. Anger one and you'll have the whole pack of them expressing

their disapproval all over you. And over in the corner, the ruffian in the biker jacket looking all harsh and brooding? Devin. He's a Brujah, a rabble-rouser, and he's actually hunting. Sooner or later, his Byronic demeanor is going to draw some female attention, he'll allow himself to be cheered up and taken home, and then…well, you know what comes then.

Don't even think about trying to interfere, or I'll kill you myself. Think of yourself as watching a nature documentary. That's what's going on here, really. Survival of the fittest. The herd of humanity loses one or two animals, but most get to move on, unharmed. It's balance between predator and prey.

That's what the Camarilla is all about, by the way, maintaining the balance. Making sure that we don't run amuck through the herd, and that you don't learn that there are hunters among you.

What's the Camarilla? Not much, according to some vampires. In theory, it is the umbrella organization of all vampires dedicated to providing order and maintaining the Masquerade. In reality, it has only seven of the great clans, plus assorted hangers-on. A

couple of the other clans style themselves independent, and the rest are in a beastly cult called the Sabbat. The Sabbat makes Devin over there look like a nursery-school teacher; they're a lot closer to what the Inquisition thinks it's looking for than we Camarilla types are.

Don't make the mistake that we in the Camarilla are *nice*, though. We're not. We just realize that at this point, it is a great deal safer to coexist and try to work through you than it is to try to fight you. Never, ever be fooled into thinking we're the "good guys."

We just have more use for you alive than dead.

No good prospects tonight, I think — Devin is hogging the spotlight. Let's get out of here. You look like you could use some air, and this place is beginning to bore me.

No, I'm not going to kill you and drink your blood in the alley. The act of granting the Embrace should be done in comfort, in luxury. Besides, by now my ghouls should have garnered sufficient nourishment for your first Hunger; I'm a generous sort of sire.

Please, don't act shocked. Ingenuousness doesn't suit your complexion. I've been dropping hints all night, and you've been dutifully picking them up. Besides, you couldn't

have thought I was going to tell you all of this and then let you just walk away? Oh, *most of the world* would think you were crazy if you repeated the story I've given you, but just enough people wouldn't. They'd believe, and they'd tell other people. And the whole thing would come tumbling down like a house of cards.

So, my dear, there's no way I can let you walk out of this alive.

You can walk out of it dead, though. You know what I'm offering you. You know that deep down, you want it, too. If you didn't, you would have tried to escape hours ago. But here you are.

So, lovely lady, am I going to make you live forever? Yes? I'm glad.

Take my arm, my dear. Are you afraid yet?

You should be.

A STORYTELLING GAME
OF PERSONAL HORROR

CREDITS

Vampire: The Masquerade Creators: Mark Rein•Hagen with Steven C. Brown, Tom Dowd, Andrew Greenberg, Chris McDonough, Lisa Stevens, Josh Timbrook, Stewart Wieck

New Edition Authors: Justin Achilli, Andrew Bates, Phil Brucato, Richard E. Dansky, Ed Hall, Robert Hatch, Michael B. Lee, Ian Lemke, Jim Moore, Ethan Skemp, Cynthia Summers

Third Edition Developer: Robert Hatch

Editor: Cynthia Summers

Art Director: Lawrence Snelly with Richard Thomas

Layout and Typesetting: Aileen E. Miles

Interior Art: John Bolton, Mark Chiarello, Mike Danza, Guy Davis, John Estes, Richard Kane Ferguson, Darren Frydendall, Michael Gaydos, Rebecca Guay, Pia Guerra, Fred Harper, Mark Jackson, Leif Jones, Brian LeBlanc, Paul Lee, Vince Locke, Greg Loudon, Larry MacDougall, Jon J. Muth, William O'Connor, George Pratt, Andrew Ritchie, Matt Roach, Christopher Shy, Bill Sienkiewicz, Lawrence Snelly, Ray Snyder, Ron Spencer, Richard Thomas, Joshua Gabriel Timbrook, Karl Waller, Kent Williams, Matthew Wilson

Front and Back Cover Design: Aileen E. Miles

735 PARK NORTH BLVD.
SUITE 128
CLARKSTON, GA 30021
USA

© 1998 White Wolf Publishing, Inc. All rights reserved. Reproduction without the written permission of the publisher is expressly forbidden, except for the purposes of reviews, and for blank character sheets, which may be reproduced for personal use only. White Wolf, Vampire the Masquerade, Vampire the Dark Ages, Mage the Ascension and World of Darkness are registered trademarks of White Wolf Publishing, Inc. All rights reserved. Werewolf the Apocalypse, Wraith the Oblivion, Changeling the Dreaming, Werewolf the Wild West, Trinity, and Kindred of the East are trademarks of White Wolf Publishing, Inc. All rights reserved. All characters, names, places and text herein are copyrighted by White Wolf Publishing, Inc.

The mention of or reference to any company or product in these pages is not a challenge to the trademark or copyright concerned.

This book uses the supernatural for settings, characters and themes. All mystical and supernatural elements are fiction and intended for entertainment purposes only. Reader discretion is advised.

Check out White Wolf online at
http://www.white-wolf.com; alt.games.whitewolf and rec.games.frp.storyteller

PRINTED IN CANADA.

DEDICATION

To you, fans old and new, who have helped us get to this point. May the beginning of the new millennium be as good to you as the passing of the old has been to us.

THE INEVITABLE DISCLAIMER

Vampire: The Masquerade is a game. It's a game that requires imagination, effort, creativity and, above all, maturity. Part of maturity is realizing that **Vampire** is only a game and that the situations depicted in these pages are strictly imaginary. If you beat somebody at *Monopoly*™, you don't go out and foreclose on their house. If you sink someone's *Battleship*™, you don't go down to the Navy Yard and start throwing Molotovs at the boats. The same principle applies to any roleplaying or storytelling game.

In other words, you are not a vampire. When a game session ends, put away the books, pack away the dice, enjoy the rest of your life and let other people enjoy theirs.

For the 99.9999+% of you who are sufficiently well-adjusted not to need such a ridiculous disclaimer, have fun.

Contents

INTRODUCTION

Vampires.

Bloodsucking corpses returned from the grave to feast on the blood of the living. Monsters damned to Hell who avoid their punishment through life unlawfully stolen. Erotic predators who take their sustenance from innocent, struggling — or, perhaps, willing? — men and women.

Since time's beginning, humanity has spoken of the vampire — the undead, the demonic spirit embodied in human flesh, the corpse risen from its grave possessed of a burning hunger for warm blood. From Hungary to Hong Kong, from New Delhi to New York, people throughout the world have experienced chills of delicious terror contemplating the deeds of the night-stalking vampire. The vampire has haunted novels, movies, TV series, video games, clothing, even breakfast cereal.

But these stories are mere myths, right?

Wrong.

Vampires have walked among us from prehistoric times. They walk among us still. They have fought a great and secret war since the earliest nights of human history. And this eternal struggle's final outcome may determine humanity's future — or its ultimate damnation.

STORYTELLING

The book you hold is the core rulebook of **Vampire: The Masquerade**, a storytelling game from White Wolf Publishing. With the rules in this book, you and your friends can take the roles of vampires and tell stories about the characters' triumphs, failures, dark deeds and glimmerings of goodness.

In a storytelling game, players create characters using the rules in this book, then take those characters through dramas and adventures, called (appropriately enough) stories. Stories are told through a combination of the wishes of the players and the directives of the Storyteller (see below).

In a lot of ways, storytelling resembles games such as *How to Host a Murder*. Each player takes the role of a character — in this case, a vampire — and engages in a form of improvisational theatre, saying what the vampire would say and describing what the vampire would do. Most of this process is freeform — players can have their characters say or do whatever they like, so long as the dialogue or actions are consistent with the character's personality and abilities. However, certain actions are best adjudicated through the use of dice and the rules presented in this book.

Whenever rules and story conflict, the story wins. Use the rules only as much — or preferably as little — as you need to tell thrilling stories of terror, action and romance.

PLAYERS AND STORYTELLERS

Vampire is best played with a group, or troupe, of two to six participants. Most of these people are to be players. They create vampire characters — imaginary protagonists similar to those found in novels, cinema and comics. In each troupe, however, one person must take the role of the Storyteller. The Storyteller does not create one primary character for herself. Rather, she acts as a combination of director, moderator, narrator and referee. The Storyteller invents the drama through which the players direct their characters, creating plots and conflicts from her imagination. The Storyteller also takes the roles of supporting cast — allies with whom the characters interact and antagonists against whom the characters fight. The Storyteller invents the salient details of the story setting — the bars, nightclubs, businesses and other institutions the characters frequent. The players decide how their characters react to the situations in the game, but it is the Storyteller (with the help of the rules) who decides if the characters actually succeed in their endeavors and, if so, how well. Ultimately, the Storyteller is the final authority on the events that take place in the game.

Example: Rob, Brian, Cynthia and Alison have gathered to play **Vampire**. Rob, Brian and Cynthia are players: Rob is playing Baron d'Havilland, a Ventrue aristocrat; Brian is playing Palpa, a Nosferatu sewer-dweller; and Cynthia is playing Maxine, a Brujah street punk. Alison is the Storyteller, and she has decreed that the characters have been brought before the vampire prince of the city to face judgment for feeding in a forbidden area of the city.

• Alison (describing the scene): The room into which you are dragged is large, opulent, and filled with mementos from eras ranging from the Italian Renaissance to the Harlem Renaissance. A great iron chandelier, filled with candles, throws dim light on alcoves filled with paintings and statuary. Still, you don't have too much time to look, for at the prodding of the prince's enforcer, Lord Maxwell, you are rudely shoved before a great oaken chair — almost a throne. The shadows seem to cluster more deeply about the imposing figure that sits in state, commanding, unmoving, and gazing at you with burning eyes.

• Alison (again, now speaking as the prince): "For over a century have I kept order in my domain. Like a careful gardener, I have watched this city grow from a rural town to a thriving metropolis. I have bested anarchs and squelched the plots of the Black Hand. Through what temerity do you newborn whelps now choose to flout my rule? Speak quickly and well, lest I personally stake you and leave you for the sun's kiss!"

The players may now decide what to do:

• Rob (speaking as Baron d'Havilland): "Milord, clearly there has been a misunderstanding, as my colleagues and I…"

• Cynthia (speaking as Maxine): "Don't presume to speak for me, you weak-blooded toady! To hell with your rules, you fascist prick! This is the 20th century, and I'll go anywhere I damn well choose!"

• Alison (playing the prince's none-too-amused reaction): The prince's fingers noticeably tighten on the arms of the throne, and a low hiss rises in his throat.

• Brian (describing his character's action): Brilliant, Maxine! I avoid the prince's gaze and look around. Is there any sort of pillar, shadow or other place that I can unobtrusively slip behind? If so, I'm going to use my Obfuscate (a magical invisibility power) to get the hell out of here.

What happens next is decided by the actions of the players and the decisions of the Storyteller. As you can see, each player is the arbiter of his or her own character's actions and words. Ultimately, though, it is Alison, the Storyteller, who determines the prince's reaction to the characters' words or actions; it is Alison, speaking as the prince, who roleplays the prince's reaction; and it is Alison who determines whether the characters' actions, if any, succeed or fail.

What Is a Vampire?

Storytelling and roleplaying games may feature many kinds of protagonists. In some games, players assume the roles of heroes in a fantasy world, or superheroes saving the world from villains' depredations. In **Vampire**, appropriately enough, players assume the personas of vampires — the immortal bloodsuckers of the horror genre — and guide these characters through a world virtually identical to our own.

The vampires who walk the earth in modern nights — or Kindred, as they commonly call themselves — are both similar to and different from what we might expect. It is perhaps best to begin our discussion of the undead as if they were a separate species of being — sentient, with superficial similarities to the humans they once were, but displaying a myriad physiological and psychological differences.

In many ways, vampires resemble the familiar monsters of myth and cinema. (There is enough truth in the old tales that perhaps they were created by deluded or confused mortals.) However — as many an intrepid vampire-hunter has learned to his sorrow — not all of the old wives' tales about vampires are true.

• **Vampires are immortal.** True. While they can be killed (a very difficult process), they do not age or die from natural causes. They need no food such as humans eat, and they do not need to breathe.

• **Vampires are living dead and must sustain themselves with the blood of the living.** True. A vampire is clinically dead — its heart does not beat, it does not breathe, its skin is cold, it does not age — and yet it thinks, and walks, and plans, and speaks…and hunts, and kills. To sustain its artificial immortality, the vampire must periodically consume blood, preferably human blood. Some penitent vampires eke out an existence from animal blood, and some ancient vampires must hunt and kill others of their kind to nourish themselves, but most vampires indeed consume the blood of their former species.

Vampires drain their prey of blood through the use of retractable fangs, which are magically gifted to vampires when they first become undead. Each vampire can also magically lick closed the wounds made by their fangs, thus concealing the evidence of their feeding.

Blood is all-important to the Kindred, for it is both the crux of their existence and the seat of their power. Mortal food, mortal air, mortal love — all of these things are meaningless to a vampire. Blood is the Kindred's only passion, and without it, they will quickly wither and fall dormant. Moreover, each vampire can use its stolen blood to perform amazing feats of healing, strength and other magic.

• **Anyone who dies from a vampire's bite rises to become a vampire.** False. If this were true, the world would be overrun with vampires. Vampires feed on human blood, true, and sometimes kill their prey — but most humans who die from a vampire's attack simply perish. To return as undead, the victim must be drained of blood and subsequently be fed a bit of the attacking vampire's blood. This process, called the Embrace, causes the mystical transformation from human to undead.

• **Vampires are monsters — demonic spirits embodied in corpses.** False…and true. Vampires are not demons *per se*, but a combination of tragic factors draws them inexorably toward wicked deeds. In the beginning, the newly created vampire thinks and acts much as she did while living. She does not immediately turn into an evil, sadistic monster. However, the vampire soon discovers her overpowering hunger for blood, and realizes that her existence depends on feeding on her species. In many ways, the vampire's mindset changes — she adopts a set of attitudes less suited to a communal omnivore and more befitting a solitary predator.

At first reluctant to kill, the vampire is finally forced into murder by circumstance or need — and killing becomes easier as the years pass. Realizing that she herself is untrustworthy, she ceases to trust others. Realizing that she is different, she walls herself away from the mortal world. Realizing that her existence depends on secrecy and control, she becomes a manipulative user of the first order. And things only degenerate as the years turn to decades and then centuries, and the vampire kills over and over, and sees the people she loved age and die. Human life, so short and cheap in comparison to hers, becomes of less and less value, until the mortal "herd" around her means no more to her than a swarm of annoying insects. Vampire elders are among the most jaded, unfeeling, paranoid — in short, monstrous — beings the world has ever known. Maybe they are not demons exactly — but at that point, who can tell the difference?

• **Vampires are burned by sunlight.** True. Vampires must avoid the sun or die, though a few can bear sunlight's touch for a very short period of time. Vampires are nocturnal creatures, and most find it extremely difficult to remain awake during the day, even within sheltered areas.

• **Vampires are repulsed by garlic and running water.** False. These are myths and nothing more.

• **Vampires are repulsed by crosses and other holy symbols.** This is generally false. However, if the wielder of the symbol has great faith in the power it represents, a vampire may suffer ill effects from the brandishing of the symbol.

• **Vampires die from a stake through the heart.** False. However, a wooden stake — or arrow, crossbow bolt, etc. — through the heart will paralyze the monster until it is removed.

• **Vampires have the strength of 10 men; they can command wolves and bats; they can hypnotize the living and heal even the most grievous wounds.** True and false. The power of a vampire increases with age. Young, newly created vampires are often little more powerful than humans. But as a vampire grows in age and understanding, she learns to use her blood to evoke secret magical powers, which vampires call Disciplines. Powerful elders are often the rivals of a fictional Lestat or Dracula, and the true ancients — the Methuselahs and Antediluvians who have stalked the nights for thousands of years — often possess literally godlike power.

The Embrace

Vampires are created through a process called the Embrace. Some vampire clans Embrace more casually than others, but the Embrace is almost never given lightly. After all, any new vampire is a potential competitor for food and power. A potential childe is often stalked for weeks or even years by a watchful sire, who greedily evaluates whether the mortal would indeed make a good addition to the society of the Kindred.

The Embrace is similar to normal vampiric feeding — the vampire drains her chosen prey of blood. However, upon complete exsanguination, the vampire returns a bit of her own immortal blood to the drained mortal. Only a tiny bit — a drop or two — is necessary to turn the mortal into an undead. This process can even be performed on a dead human, provided the body is still warm.

Once the blood is returned, the mortal "awakens" and begins drinking of his own accord. But, though animate, the mortal is still dead; his heart does not beat, nor does he breathe. Over the next week or two, the mortal's body undergoes a series of subtle transformations; he learns to use the blood in his body, and he is taught the special powers of his clan. He is now a vampire.

The Hunt

When all is said and done, the most fundamental difference between humans and vampires lies in their methods of sustenance. Vampires may not subsist on mortal food; instead, they must maintain their eternal lives through the consumption of blood — fresh human blood.

Vampires acquire their sustenance in many fashions. Some cultivate "herds" of willing mortals, who cherish the ecstasy of the vampire's Kiss. Some creep into houses by night, feeding from sleeping humans. Some stalk the mortals' playgrounds — the nightclubs, bars and theaters — enticing mortals into illicit liaisons and disguising their predation as acts of passion. And yet others take their nourishment in the most ancient fashion — stalking, attacking and incapacitating (or even killing) mortals who wander too far into lonely nocturnal alleys and empty lots.

The Nocturnal World of the Vampire

Vampires value power, for its own sake and for the security it brings — and they find it ridiculously easy to acquire mundane goods, riches and influence. A mesmerizing glance and a few words provide a cunning vampire with access to all the wealth, power and servants he could desire. Some powerful vampires are capable of implanting posthypnotic suggestions or commands in mortals' minds, then causing the mortals to forget the vampire's presence. In this way, vampires can easily acquire legions of unwitting slaves. More than a few "public servants" and corporate barons secretly answer to vampire masters.

Though there are exceptions, vampires tend to remain close to the cities. The city provides countless opportunities for predation, liaisons and politicking — and the wilderness often proves dangerous. The wilds are the home of the Lupines, the werewolves, who are vampires' ancestral enemies and desire nothing more than to destroy vampires outright.

The Jyhad

Many vampires seek to have nothing to do with their kind, choosing instead to exist and hunt in solitude. However, the civilization of the undead is a manipulative and poisonous dance, and few vampires are left entirely untouched. Since the nights of antiquity, the Kindred have struggled for supremacy, in an ancient and many-layered struggle known as the Jyhad. Leaders, cultures, nations and armies have all been pawns in the secret war, and vampiric conspiracies have influenced much (though by no means all) of human history. Few things are as they seem in the vampires' nocturnal world; a political coup, economic crash or social trend may be merely the surface manifestation veiling a centuries-old struggle. Vampire elders command from the shadows, manipulating mortals and other vampires alike — and the elders are often

manipulated in turn. Indeed, most combatants may not even realize for whom they fight, or why.

Reputedly begun millennia ago, the Jyhad rages even today. Though skyscrapers take the place of castles, machine-guns and missiles replace swords and torches, and stock portfolios substitute for vaults of gold, the game remains the same. Kindred battles Kindred, clan battles clan, sect battles sect, as they have for eons. Vampiric feuds begun during the nights of Charlemagne play themselves out on the streets of New York City; an insult whispered in the court of the Sun King may find itself answered by a corporate takeover in Sao Paolo. The ever-swelling cities provide countless opportunities for feeding, powermongering — and war.

Increasingly, vampires speak of Gehenna — the long-prophesied night of apocalypse when the most ancient vampires, the mythical Antediluvians, will rise from their hidden lairs to devour all the younger vampires. This Gehenna, so the Kindred say, will presage the end of the world, as vampires and mortals alike are consumed in an inexorable tide of blood. Some vampires strive to prevent Gehenna, some fatalistically await it, and still others consider it a myth. Those who believe in Gehenna, however, say that the end time comes very soon — perhaps in a matter of years.

How to Use This Book

This book is divided into several chapters, each of which is designed to explore and explain a specific area of the game. Remember, though, that in a storytelling game, the most important "chapter" is your imagination. Never let anything in this book be a substitute for your own creativity.

Chapter One: A World of Darkness describes the Kindred and the world in which they hunt.

Chapter Two: Clans and Sects describes the 13 great "clans" of Kindred and the organizations to which they hold allegiance.

Chapter Three: Character gives step-by-step instructions for creating vampire characters.

Chapter Four: Disciplines delineates the magical powers of the undead.

Chapter Five: Rules provides the basic means of resolving the characters' various actions.

Chapter Six: Systems describes a plethora of ways to simulate everything from gentle seduction to brutal combat.

Chapter Seven: A History of the Kindred recounts the ancient history and bloody feuds among the Children of Caine.

Chapter Eight: Storytelling tells Storytellers how to build entertaining stories in which to involve the characters.

Chapter Nine: Antagonists gives notes on the Kindred's (few) friends and (many) enemies.

Finally, the **Appendix** provides addenda and rules for advanced players.

Live-Action

Most **Vampire** games take place around a tabletop, and the players describe what their characters say and do. However, games can also be conducted through Live-action play.

This exciting form of gaming bears similarities to improvisational theatre, in that players actually dress as their characters and act out their characters' scenes as though they were actors in a play. Thus, rather than saying, "My character walks over to the table and picks up the ancient document," you, the player, would actually get up, walk over to a properly decorated table, and pick up the "ancient document" (probably a prop created by the Storyteller — for example, a piece of parchment that's been scorched around the edges to give it the appearance of age with a little flour "dust").

A Storyteller still guides the action and directs the plot; the Storyteller describes special features of the setting, oversees challenges the characters undergo, and may interrupt the action at any time.

Live-action roleplaying does not typically use dice; alternate systems, such as those presented in White Wolf's **Mind's Eye Theatre** line of products, take the place of dice when determining the results of challenges. Most situations are resolved simply through acting and the Storyteller's decisions.

SAFEGUARDS

Some rules are necessary to ensure that live-action is safe and enjoyable for all participants and bystanders. Unlike any other rules in this book, these rules *must* be followed.

• **No Touching:** Period. All combat and physical interaction must be handled through dice or other abstract systems. Players must never strike, grapple or otherwise touch anyone during the game. It is the Storyteller's responsibility to call a time-out if one or more players get overly rambunctious.

• **No Weapons:** Props such as hats, period dress and canes are great in a live-action game. Weapons aren't. Period. No knives, no swords and nothing that even remotely resembles a firearm. Don't even bring fake swords, squirt guns, or foam-rubber weapons. If your character must carry a "weapon," take a 3" x 5" card and write "Gun" or "Sword" or whatever on it; during combat challenges, present the card to the Storyteller, who will adjudicate its use in play.

• **Play in a Designated Area:** Live-action is meant to be played in the home or other predesignated spot. Don't involve bystanders in the game, and make sure everyone in the area, or who passes through the area, understands exactly what you're doing. A game can look disturbing, even frightening, to those who aren't aware of what's going on. Don't try to shock or intimidate passersby; this is not only immature, but could also lead to well-deserved prosecution.

• **Know When to Stop:** If the Storyteller calls for a time-out or other break in the action, stop immediately. The Storyteller is still the final arbiter of all events in the game. Likewise, when the game is over for the night, take out your fangs and call it a night.

• **It's Only a Game:** Live-action is for having fun. If a rival wins, if a character dies, if a plan goes awry, it's not the end of the world. Sometimes folks like to get together outside the game and talk about it — say, a group of players who form a neonate coterie gathers to complain about their sires over pizza — and there's nothing wrong with that. But calling your clanmate up at four in the morning to ask for her assistance in your primogen bid is taking things too far. Remember, everyone's doing this to have fun!

The Bottom Line: Live-action can be one of the richest and most satisfying storytelling experiences, if handled maturely and responsibly. We're not kidding about that "maturely and responsibly," folks. In live-action, you are the prop, so it is imperative that you treat yourself and others with utmost care, dignity and respect. This game is emphatically *not* about "real" blood-drinking, hunting, fighting or erotic activities. You are not a vampire, you only play one in the game.

SOURCE MATERIAL

Vampire, of course, pays homage to a long-standing and thriving genre. The vampire/goth subculture waxes and wanes in the public eye, but is perennially alive (or undead) and kicking. The following are a few important influences on **Vampire: The Masquerade** and the World of Darkness.

Recommended literature includes: *Dracula*, by Bram Stoker; *Interview with the Vampire*, *The Vampire Lestat*, and *The Queen of the Damned*, by Anne Rice; *Lost Souls*, by Poppy Z. Brite; Brian Lumley's *Necroscope* series; *The Hunger*, by Whitley Streiber; and *I Am Legend*, by Richard Matheson. The vampire plays a role in the Romantic poetry of Byron, Shelley and Baudelaire. As well, cruise on down to a public or university library and read some of the scary old myths and legends of vampires around the world.

The vampire has also played a role in film. Bela Lugosi's *Dracula* and Murnau's silent *Nosferatu* are the granddaddies of the genre. Other good (or at least amusing) films include *The Hunger*, *Near Dark*, *Vamp*, *The Lost Boys*, *Salem's Lot*, the Cristopher Lee Hammer Horror films, and the anime flick *Vampire Hunter D*. Coppola's *Dracula* is not the best in terms of plot, but does have lush cinematography. For camp, *Buffy the Vampire Slayer* and *From Dusk Till Dawn* provide some entertaining moments.

In terms of capturing the ambience of the World of Darkness, try *Blade Runner*, Tim Burton's *Batman* (first film only), *The Silence of the Lambs*, *Trainspotting*, *New Jack City*, and most Hitchcock films.

"So we are agreed that one of us is to assume Father's name and titles?"

Seven heads bowed in assent. There were seven men in the room, all remarkably similar in build and appearance. Each had a strong chin and an aristocratic face; each was dressed in finery far too warm for the Castilian night. Outside, voices cried out in Spanish and Portuguese — merchants hawking their wares, their wines, their women. The voices floated in through a single window, as did the light of the sliver of moon to the west.

"If it becomes common knowledge that our sire has been destroyed, the consequences will be…unpleasant. It will give hope to the anarchs and their puppetmasters. It will cause some of our younger brethren to defect to their cause for fear of our weakening. And it will cause division in the councils of our father's peers, delaying the unification of the clans. I find all of these to be undesirable results." The speaker was, perhaps, the eldest of the seven gathered. He sat in a tall chair cushioned in red, its legs carved like lions' claws and gilded. The others sat in smaller, lower seats. One of those, seated closest to the window, spoke.

"But which? And what steps to ensure the secrecy of the matter? Should the charade be exposed, the damage will be worse than if we just admit to Father's destruction."

The eldest shrugged slightly. "I had thought that, being closest to Father in age and power…" — there were some murmurings at this — "…that I would become him, so to speak. And that I would rely on our bond of shared lineage to ensure your silence."

The others looked around, eyes meeting as each silently tested his brothers' resolve to mount a challenge. Then came the babble of reassurances that yes, of course, they would be a part of this plan.

"Your show of solidarity is touching, brothers. If you will excuse me for a moment?" And the eldest childe of Hardestadt rose and walked to the door of the library, which a ghoul servant once in the service of the Knights Templar held open for him. Behind him, he heard the clatter of metal goblets against the wooden tabletop as his brethren reached for the refreshments he'd had set out hours past. Each cup contained a mix of the vitae of various powerful and ancient Cainites, all long since destroyed by Hardestadt the Younger. Each also contained some of Hardestadt's own vitae, masked by the headier flavors of elder blood. This was not the first time Hardestadt had assayed such a subterfuge; bending a wine steward's will was an easy matter for one of Hardestadt's power.

Silence would be assured, yes.

Chapter One: A World of Darkness

The world of **Vampire: The Masquerade** is not our own, though it is close enough for fearsome discomfort. Rather, the world inhabited by vampires is *like* ours, but through a looking glass darkly. Evil is palpable and ubiquitous in this world; the final nights are upon us, and the whole planet teeters on a razor's edge of tension. It is a world of darkness.

Superficially, the World of Darkness is like the "real" world we all inhabit. The same bands are popular, violence still plagues the inner city, graft and corruption infest the same governments, and society still looks to the same cities for its culture. The World of Darkness has a Statue of Liberty, an Eiffel Tower and a CBGB's. More present than in our world, though, is the undercurrent of horror — our world's ills are all the more pronounced in the World of Darkness. Our fears are more real. Our governments are *more* degenerate. Our ecosystem dies a bit more each night. And vampires exist.

Many of the differences between our world and the World of Darkness stem from these vampires. Ancient and inscrutable, the Kindred toy with humanity as a cat does with a trapped mouse. The immortal Kindred manipulate society to stave off the ennui and malaise that threaten them nightly, or to guard against the machinations of centuries-old rivals. Immortality is a curse to vampires, for they are locked in stagnant existences and dead bodies.

This chapter examines the vampires' world. The World of Darkness reflects the passion and horror of its secret masters, and the hope of redemption is the only thing that lets most denizens of this cursed place go on living — or unliving.

The World of Darkness

The greatest difference between our world and that of **Vampire: The Masquerade** is the presence of immortal monsters pulling the strings of humanity. Violence and despair are more common here, because they need to be in order for the Kindred to continue their existences. The world is bleak, but escape is an ever-present commodity — perhaps too present. The setting of **Vampire** is a composite of its populace and their despair.

Gothic-Punk, and Portents of the Future

"Gothic-Punk" is perhaps the best way to describe the physical nature of the World of Darkness. The environment is a clashing mixture of styles and influences, and the tension caused by the juxtaposition of ethnicities, social classes and subcultures makes the world a vibrant, albeit dangerous, place.

The Gothic aspect describes the ambience of the World of Darkness. Buttressed buildings loom overhead, bedecked with classical columns and grimacing gargoyles. Residents are dwarfed by the sheer scale of architecture, lost amid the spires that seem to grope toward Heaven in an effort to escape the physical world. The ranks of the Church swell, as mortals flock to any banner that offers them a hope of something better in the hereafter. Likewise, cults flourish in the underground, promising power and redemption. The institutions that control society are even more staid and conservative than they are in our world, for many in power prefer the evil of the world they know to the chaos engendered by change. It is a divisive world of have and have-not, rich and poor, excess and squalor.

The Punk aspect is the lifestyle that many denizens of the World of Darkness have adopted. In order to give their lives meaning, they rebel, crashing themselves against the crags of power. Gangs prowl the streets and organized crime breeds in the underworld, reactions to the pointlessness of living "by the book." Music is louder, faster, more violent or hypnotically monotonous, and supported by masses who find salvation in its escape. Speech is coarser, fashion is bolder, art is more shocking, and technology brings it all to everyone at the click of a button. The world is more corrupt, the people are spiritually bankrupt, and escapism often replaces hope.

As if this weren't fearful enough, the last few years have seen a quiet but pervasive dread grip the Kindred community. Many Kindred whisper of the Jyhad, the eternal war or game said to consume the most ancient vampires. This struggle has been waged since the dawn of time, but many vampires fear that, as one millennium passes to the next and the curse of undeath grows weaker, an apocalyptic endgame is at hand. Signs and portents, many recorded in the prophetic *Book of Nod*, trouble vampires of all clans and lineages, even those who profess not to believe. Whispers in Sabbat covens and Camarilla salons alike speak of turmoil in the East, of armies of Clanless rabble, of vampires whose blood is so thin that they cannot Embrace, of meetings with mysterious elders whose vast power betrays no discernible lineage, of black crescent moons and full moons red as blood. All, say the believers, are omens that the Final Nights are approaching, and that the end of all things is nigh.

Some Kindred believe that a Reckoning is at hand, that the powers of Heaven are preparing at last to judge the vampires and what they have made of the world. Others speak of the Winnowing, or *Gehenna*, the night when the most ancient vampires will rise to consume their progeny, taking their lessers' cursed blood to sate their own hunger. Few admit to such superstitions, but most feel a palpable tension in these nights. Elder vampires play their hands in one fell swoop, negating centuries-long schemes in a single mad flurry of action. The war packs of the dread Sabbat hurl themselves at the fortresses of their enemies, for they fear they might not get another opportunity. Cells of Assamite cannibals, formerly held in check by a great curse, hunt other vampires and ravenously drink their blood. Vampires of uncertain lineage are hunted down and destroyed by paranoid elders, who fear them as harbingers of Gehenna. Though patience is a special virtue among the immortals, it is practiced less and less, and the whole Kindred world teeters on the verge of a great collective frenzy.

Gothic-Punk is a mood and setting conveyed during the course of the game. The greatest share of creating this ambience falls upon the Storyteller, but players should consider their characters' stake in it as well. The ambience is also a matter of taste. Some troupes may prefer more Gothic than Punk, while others may want equal amounts of both elements, or little of either. In the end, it's your game, and you are free to make of it what you will. Simply bear in mind that experiencing the world is a shared endeavor, and everything the players and Storyteller do helps make that world more believable. Actions, settings, characters and descriptions all convey the Gothic-Punk aesthetic.

CITIES

Vampires are inherently creatures of the city, though some claim this is a matter of decision rather than nature. Urban landscapes offer everything a Kindred could want: near-infinite supplies of blood, enough contact to satisfy the most social of vampires (and enough seclusion to satisfy the most isolationist), and refuge from the werewolves who linger in the rural lands beyond the city lights.

Unfortunately for the Kindred, cities are breeding grounds for the events of the *Jyhad*, the great cannibalistic war that has raged among the undead for longer than the eldest vampires remember. The night is as capricious as the Kindred themselves are, and long periods of relative peace can erupt into bloodshed with little or no warning. As vampires cling to the cities for protection and sustenance, juxtaposition with other Kindred is inevitable.

In the nights of old, when humans were fewer and cities not so congested, Kindred often stalked their hunting grounds alone, never seeing another of their kind. In the modern era, contact with other predators is nearly unavoidable, and so some balance of power usually exists within a city. Elder vampires control their own territories, the princes of the undead govern with iron talons, lawless anarchs clash on the streets of the slums, and wild vampiric *fêtes* take place far from the eyes of mortals. Even the gravest Kindred conflicts occur behind the veil of the *Masquerade*, the code of silence that prevents the Kindred from revealing themselves to the humans around them.

Ironically, the cities are both prisons and paradises to the Kindred. By leaving, they risk losing their unlives to starvation or the claws of werewolves. By staying, they may indulge their passions, but inevitably clash with others of their kind. It is a tense, tenuous existence, and one devoted to staving off the myriad curses of immortality: depression, futility and maddening boredom.

A rough ratio of vampires to mortals has evolved in the last century. Many vampire princes enforce a limit of one vampire per 100,000 mortals, in the interests of keeping the existence of the Kindred a secret. Nonetheless — and particularly in the last few years — some cities exceed this ratio, and the ever-growing population of Kindred is becoming a very dire concern. In cities that do not slavishly heed the Masquerade, such as those under Sabbat control, the ratio may soar to two or three times the acceptable level. Overpopulation is not an easy problem to address; arbitrarily deciding which vampires may stay and which must suffer the Final Death is a matter of policy no prince wishes to decide, except in the most critical of circumstances.

Some vampires, though, feel that the situation will be addressed forcibly. Young vampires of weak blood appear with increasing frequency in the elders' cities, and many Kindred whisper that the time of the "grazing," when the hidden masters of the Jyhad will arise and devour the rest, is nigh.

THE KINDRED

Vampires have long been feared as rapacious monsters of the night — terrible black forms sweeping out of the darkness to steal infants from their cribs and ravish the blood of innocents. Vampires are also creatures of deadly beauty, immense passion and predatory sensuality.

Each vampire is unique, and each has her own fascinating story to tell. The most important characteristic all vampires share, though, is their damnation. More important than any lineage, clan, sect or cause is the fact that all vampires are undead predators. Fealties and duties fall second to the inescapable urge of hunger. Without exception, vampires are parasites, cursed by fate to prey upon those from whom they originated.

Vampire emphasizes this theme over all others. Vampires are monsters. How does it feel to leave a dead, bloodless child in a dumpster? To manipulate mortals like pawns on a chessboard? To suspect that the elders wield you as an unwitting weapon against their ancient foes? To eke out an unlife of secrecy and bloodshed? To succumb to the wiles of the Beast and tear innocent victims to shreds?

In response to their environment, the Kindred have evolved a complex society that exists just out of sight of the mortals who surround them. Age, clan, sect, sire, power, influence and many other aspects of unlife make the Kindred who they are. Part of any Kindred's being is membership in a number of social castes that grace vampire society. By creating and enforcing divisions and roles for themselves, no matter how artificial, the Kindred seek to escape the Beast that roils within them. **Vampire: The Masquerade** is, in fact, a double entendre. Not only do vampires hide from mortals, they hide from themselves as well, pretending they are not the horrors they have truly become.

One way the Damned distinguish themselves is through a combination of age and *generation*, or how far removed a Kindred is from the progenitor vampire, Caine. Young vampires must prove themselves to their elders to be afforded any bit of status, and Kindred society is often as stagnant and stultifying as the immortal Damned themselves. There is a small degree of mobility, however, as elder Kindred are always looking for assets and allies who may aid them against their rivals in the Jyhad.

The greatest status is accorded to the Antediluvians, vampires of the Third Generation. Most vampires consider these Kindred to be legendary — certainly, none has been verifiably seen in the modern nights. The lowest rung of status is held by rank neonates and the clanless Caitiff, those claimed by no clan or with blood too weak to trace a proper lineage.

• **Antediluvians:** These ancient vampires, if they exist at all, are likely the most powerful creatures in the world. Members of the Third Generation, the *Antediluvians* are only two steps removed from the First Vampire, Caine. Antediluvians, when they choose to rise from their long sleep, affect all with whom they come in contact; according to the few fractured accounts of their doings, they possess virtually godlike power. According to Kindred legend, there were 13 original Antediluvians, though some have allegedly been destroyed. Their eternal struggle, the Jyhad, touches all Kindred, and innumerable layers of manipulation and deception make the plots of these Ancients almost imperceptible.

• **Methuselahs:** If the Antediluvians are the Kindred's gods, the terrible *Methuselahs* are demigods and avatars. At a point between a vampire's thousandth and two thousandth year, a grave change overtakes the Kindred. Sometimes the change is physical, while at other times it is mental or emotional. Whatever the nature of the change, the end result is that the vampire no longer bears any semblance of humanity. Having truly moved from the earthly into the realm of the supernatural, the Methuselahs often retire into the earth, where they may slumber away from the thirsty fangs of younger vampires. Their powers

are so great, however, that they continue to direct their inscrutable plans mentally, communicating magically or telepathically (and almost always invisibly) with their minions.

Kindred greatly fear the Methuselahs, who are accorded any number of horrifying characteristics. Rumors speak of Methuselahs whose skin has become stone, of everything from hideous disfigurements to unearthly beauty that cannot be looked upon. Some are believed to drink only vampire blood, while others control the fates of entire nations from their cold tombs.

• **Elders:** *Elders* are Kindred who have existed for hundreds of years, and typically range from sixth to eighth generation. With centuries of accumulated cunning and a terrible thirst for power, elder Kindred are the most physically active participants in the Jyhad — they do not suffer the long fits of torpor that hamper the Methuselahs and Antediluvians, but they are not so powerless or easily manipulated as the younger Kindred are. The term "elder" itself is a bit subjective; a Kindred who qualifies as an elder in the New World might be just another ancilla in Europe or older corners of the Earth. Elders keep a stranglehold on the Kindred power structure, preventing younger vampires from attaining positions of influence by exercising control they have maintained for decades, if not centuries.

• **Ancillae:** *Ancillae* are relatively young vampires (between one and two hundred years of unlife) who have proved themselves as valuable members of Kindred society. Ancillae are the lackeys to greater Kindred, and — if they're clever or lucky — tomorrow's elders. Ancilla is the rank between neonate and elder, signifying that the Kindred has cut her teeth (so to speak), but lacks the age and experience to become a true master of the Jyhad. Because the world's population has grown so in the last

two centuries, the vast majority of vampires are ancillae or neonates (see below).

• **Neonates:** *Neonates* vary from newly released fledglings to indolent Kindred of a hundred years or more. Marked by the stigma of not yet having proved themselves to the elders, neonates are inexperienced vampires who might one night make something of themselves — but, more likely, will fall as pawns in the schemes of the other undead.

• **Fledglings:** Also known more loosely as *"childer"* (although every vampire except Caine is someone's childe), *fledglings* are newly reborn vampires still under the tutelage and protection of their *sires*, the vampires who created them. Fledglings are not considered full members of Kindred society and are often treated disrespectfully or as the sire's property. When her sire decides her childe is ready, the fledgling may become a neonate, subject to the prince's approval.

OTHER DISTINCTIONS

• **Anarchs:** *Anarchs* are vampires who reject the Traditions of Caine and the dictates of the elders who enforce them. Ironically, elders grudgingly afford anarchs some degree of status, due to the anarchs' ability to obtain power in spite of the elders' opposition. Anarchs are also respected for their passion and drive, which few elder Kindred, mired as they are in their age and dissatisfaction, can muster. Ultimately, however, most Kindred see anarchs as jackals, scavenging their unlives from what slips through the elders' fingers.

• **Caitiff:** The *Caitiff* are the clanless vampires, outcast by other Kindred and despised by those who bother to notice them at all. Vampires may become clanless either by having no idea of

their sires' identities (and thus having no sense of lineage) or by being of such a weak generation that no identifying clan characteristics are discernible. Caitiff are almost universally regarded as bastard children and orphans, though some rise to a degree of prominence among the anarchs. Once there were few Caitiff, but the post-WWII period has seen a sharp increase in their numbers. Some elders whisper direfully of the "Time of Thin Blood" that signifies the imminence of Gehenna.

The Embrace

Not every victim of the vampire's Kiss rises to become Kindred herself — making a new vampire requires a conscious effort, and often permission. The *Embrace* is the term for the act of turning a mortal into a vampire. When a vampire wishes to sire progeny, her hunts take on a new characteristic. No longer does the Kindred simply search for sustenance; instead, she becomes more aware and cunning, looking for the perfect combination of personal behaviors that warrant immortality.

The reasons for Embracing new Kindred vary from vampire to vampire. Some sires feel great remorse over their undying curse of vampirism, and select mortals who might "give something back" to the depraved race of Kindred. A few vampires look for great artists, thinkers, creators or just compassionate souls whose talents should be preserved forever. These Kindred often suffer greatly when they see what their selfishness wreaks upon those brought into the fold, for the Embrace often destroys the spark of creativity. Kindred lack the ability to truly innovate — they ride human trends rather than set them, and even their most inspired works are nothing more than pale imitations of mortal work that has gone before. It is an irony that those Kindred who would preserve a childe's gift forever actually do more damage to their progeny's talent than simply allowing it to age naturally ever would.

Other Kindred are vindictive and spiteful with the Embrace, choosing mortals whom they wish to see suffer. Some particularly cruel Malkavians delight in bringing the truly and pitiably insane into their ranks, hoping to glean some new insight from a fledgling's madness as she sinks into despair. The hideous Nosferatu also delight in Embracing the vain or beautiful into their clan, enjoying the anguished shrieks of the childe as she becomes a malformed horror. Even the Toreador, in their degeneracy, sometimes select childer for the purpose of asserting their superiority over those who had been spoiled in life.

Most Kindred, however, Embrace out of loneliness or desire. These vampires are invariably the worst off as, after the culmination of their lust or anguish, they are left not with soulmates, but with monsters every bit as callous and predatory as they are.

Kindred rarely Embrace capriciously — the right to create a childe is seldom granted, and those who observe the Traditions are loath to squander an opportunity that they may not receive again for a thousand years. Some vampires, though, are flighty, negligent or simply heedless of a prince's right to destroy them and their progeny. The ranks of the Caitiff swell with Kindred who do not know their lineage, accidentally rose after being left for dead by careless vampires, or otherwise left sires who cared little for them.

The physical act of creating a Kindred is not complex, though many sires refuse to instruct their childer in the process. The vampire

first drains his victim's blood to the point of death — which is not difficult, for once the Kiss is administered, the victim is usually too lost in the agonizing rapture to resist her attacker. After removing all of her prospective childe's mortal blood, the sire places a quantity of her own blood in the childe's mouth. This amount varies, as some vampires literally suckle their childer at their own wrists while other Kindred place the tiniest drop on their childer's lips and watch as the Beast takes over thereafter. Vampires of the Sabbat reputedly Embrace their childer and then bury them, forcing the progeny literally to dig themselves out of their own graves.

Whatever course is taken, the childe then dies a mortal and spiritual death, only to rise unnaturally afterward. Most of the time, dying is a period of great pain and anguish; the childe suffers spasms and shock as her body sloughs off the mortal coil.

The instant of rebirth, by comparison, is perhaps the greatest pleasure a Kindred may ever feel, and is likely the last true ecstasy the vampire will ever know. As the mystical process transforms the now-dead corpse of the childe, it evens out imperfections and often makes the body beautiful, albeit in a surreal manner. Such beauty is frightening to behold, a predatory grace like that of a shark or venomous snake. The childe's senses also hone to an uncanny level, revealing sounds she has never before heard or heeded, tactile stimuli never appreciated with touch, panoplies of color imperceptible to the human eye, and myriad individually distinguishable smells.

The vampire's sense of taste heightens as well, though toward a single, terrible flavor. Only one substance satisfies the vampire: human blood. From the moment she rises, the vampire is a slave to the passion of her Hunger, and every night from her Embrace to eternity she will experience a starvation that can be sated only by preying upon members of her former species.

After the Embrace, the childe is known as a fledgling, under the protection and guidance of her sire until that sire deems her ready to face the night alone. It is the sire's responsibility to educate the childe in the ways of the Kindred, though such education is rarely formal, often spotty, and always tainted by the sire's jealousies and prejudices. Many sires, desiring conspirators, sycophants or outright dupes, poison the minds of their childer against their enemies or intentionally leave out important bits of information, the better to rein in the childe later.

First Nights

As the childe slowly enters the world of the Damned, she learns about the society of the undead through her sire's tutelage and accumulated experience. Should the sire introduce her to other Kindred, the fledgling may gain a firsthand knowledge of the pomp and ritual associated with the vampires' society. Most sires, however, sequester their childer from other Kindred, fearing that exposure to other vampires may sway their younglings' knowledge away from what the sires wish them to learn.

Many of these first nights are spent learning what it means to be undead. The childe inevitably meets her Beast, and either falls to frenzy or learns early on how to subjugate its wild call. The sire may offer aid and guidance in thwarting the Beast, or he may watch as it overtakes his childe, then admonish her for weakness afterward. It is now that the childe learns that undeath is indeed a curse — despite the power brought by the Embrace, she is no longer entirely herself, and must forever be wary of the Hunger that burns inside her.

Also at this time, the childe learns — too late! — to appreciate the emotional capacity possessed by mortals. As a vampire, the childe's heart has died, leaving her a cold corpse incapable of truly feeling anything. Most vampires compensate by *making* themselves feel, conjuring up memories of emotions long dead. Desperation is all that remains in the hearts of many vampires, as they realize what they have lost as their mortal selves died.

The first nights are a time of bleak revelations. Many fledglings cannot cope with the terrible new world of night into which they have been reborn, and choose to meet the obliterating rays of the sun rather than continue their existences.

Hunting

The most important lesson a newly Embraced Kindred learns is how to hunt for human prey. The sire inevitably takes an important role in this process, either instructing the childe in the art of feeding or leaving her to her own devices and offering criticism afterward.

The malice in a Kindred's personality tends to come to the fore when instructing a childe how to hunt. Many vampires offer no "weaning period" to their childer, whereby the vampire may subsist on the blood of animals. In fact, many sires fail to inform their childer that animal blood may sustain a vampire. They turn the childer upon humankind immediately, forcing them to prey upon what they once were.

A childe soon learns that the hunt is the crux of a vampire's existence. Of all the practices to which the sire introduces his childe, feeding is the only one absolutely mandatory to the existence of a vampire. Thus, many sires guide their childer into savoring the hunt, stoking their passions on their prey's terror or basking in the anticipation of a draught of blood even before it courses over their lips. The vampire's feeding, known as the *Kiss*, engenders great ecstasy in the *vessel*, the person upon whom the vampire feeds. Needless to say, the Kindred feels physical bliss as well, as nourishing vitae rushes in to fill the void in the vampire's soul.

Kindred feed in numerous manners, as best befits their personalities. Some Kindred prefer the brutality of feeding from whomever they choose, roughly handling their vessels and leaving them broken afterward. Others go to great lengths to increase the sensuality of the Kiss, concocting elaborate seductions and gathering veritable harems of mortal lovers from whom they can feed. Still other Kindred steal their vessels' vitae without their knowledge, feeding from the sleeping or the oblivious. Kindred also experience the aftereffects of drinking from vessels who have peculiarities of blood — the vitae of an ill individual tastes poorly and may have an adverse effect on the vampire, while a Kindred who feeds from a drunken or drugged vessel will feel as if she herself is drunk or high. A few Kindred enjoy this vicarious debauchery, and select their vessels specifically for such intoxication.

In the end, each vampire cultivates her own particular style and preferences when feeding. Learning to feed gives the vampire an opportunity to find these preferences, and the sire often enjoys watching his childe take the first few fumbling steps toward becoming a true predator. Kindred must remember, though, to observe the Masquerade when feeding. To this end, they typically lick the puncture wounds made by their fangs, magically sealing them shut and leaving no traces of their presence.

HAVENS

As a fledgling grows more and more knowledgeable in the ways of the Kindred, she must establish her own haven. Although her early nights are likely spent in the company of her sire and the safety of his haven, the time inevitably comes to leave the nest.

Selecting a haven is a very personal process, much as selecting a mortal dwelling is. A vampire must consider certain requirements when deciding upon her haven, however, that most mortals need not pay heed to.

Obviously, the haven must be secure from the rays of the sun. Even the slightest lick of sunlight can cause a Kindred to burst into flame. A haven must also offer reasonable isolation — curious neighbors who observe the nocturnal comings and goings of the person in the apartment next door may prove bothersome. Finally, the haven should offer physical security; during the daylight hours, vampires slumber unstirringly, and even should they manage to rouse themselves, they act sluggishly and with great lethargy. Foes who find a vampire's lair have a great advantage on that Kindred, for she is at their mercy.

For these reasons, many Kindred prefer inaccessible or highly guarded havens. The Nosferatu prefer the secrecy offered by the sewers, while no self-respecting Ventrue would think of keeping anything less than lavishly appointed apartments. Some Kindred keep their mortal homes as havens, while others choose locations where no one would even consider to look, to discourage unwelcome visitors.

DOMAIN

Although only the most powerful vampires claim regions of domain, most vampires tacitly claim small areas of personal influence. Of course, many princes allow vampires to claim only their havens and immediate surroundings as domains.

A vampire's *domain* is the area in which she is the authority — king of the castle, as it were. This does not necessarily mean that she has any "control" or vested interest in the domain, merely that it is nominally her "turf." Other Kindred who wish to visit must ask permission of the Kindred who claims it as domain.

Few young vampires claim domain other than their havens; elders have already taken the city's prime areas under their own aegis. This is a great bone of contention among many cities' Kindred, as the increasing numbers of undead must make do with the dwindling resources offered by the finite area in which they find themselves. Sometimes, open revolt or subtle usurpation is the only way to acquire new domain.

KINDRED SOCIETY

Vampires are first and foremost solitary predators. A Kindred might go years or even decades without seeing another vampire, preferring to hunt in solitude or walk among a select group of mortals. Nonetheless, most Kindred choose or are

forced to interact with their fellows at some point in their unlives; the movements of the Jyhad rarely leave even the most detached Kindred entirely untouched.

The society of the Damned is as structured as any mortal institution, if not more so. Numerous offices, titles and responsibilities circulate among the upper echelons of a city's Kindred, and these positions confer great power — albeit with an accompanying peril, as those who would shake the foundations of a Kindred power structure often come looking for obvious title-holders.

The following societal tableaux apply primarily to Kindred of the sect known as the *Camarilla*. As the upholder of the Masquerade and preserver of the ancient traditions of power, the Camarilla sets the standard of vampiric interaction. Vampires may adhere to the Camarilla's model or defiantly deviate from it, but they cannot simply ignore it. Kindred entirely outside the Camarilla's aegis often follow very different customs and mores, but we will speak of these things later.

THE PRINCE

For time out of mind, vampires followed Darwin's law: Only the strong survive. Those who had the mettle to seize power and the strength to hold it would rule, and so it was. Vampires styled themselves as warlords and nobles, controlling whatever territory they could hold, living in uneasy truce with their mortal and Cainite neighbors, and ever seeking to expand their holdings and herds. In the cities of the ancient world, this often proved disastrous, as vampires battled for trade and feeding grounds.

In the elder nights, the strongest vampire in each city or region claimed domain over it and used whatever means necessary to keep his control over it. As time went on, traditions sprang up around this claiming and controlling, and certain responsibilities were either tacitly assumed or forcibly taken by the one in power. The Camarilla set down and enforced these ideals over the centuries following the Renaissance. In 1743, a London anarch published a pamphlet decrying the elder society of Kindred, breaking the Masquerade in a most flamboyant manner. The Camarilla responded quickly, first by covering up the incident ("A most remarkable work of fantastical fiction!") and destroying the anarch, and then by formally acknowledging the position of prince. The office is still held by many vampires in these nights.

The *prince* is, to put it simply, the vampire who has enough power to hold domain over a city, codify the laws for that city and keep the peace. Such a position is typically held by an elder, for who but an elder has the necessary personal charisma and power to take and hold domain in a metropolis? In some small towns, younger vampires may be able to claim domain in the same way, but their claims are rarely respected by the coteries of the cities. On occasion, strange circumstances have placed younger vampires in a position to rule cities, but few such upstarts manage to hold their titles when the elders appear.

The title "prince" is simply that — a title given to formalize a role, whether that role is held by a man or a woman. There are no dynasties of vampires holding their cities for centuries on end, no hereditary ascensions. Sometimes a prince may be called by a title native to the land he rules, such as "baron," "sultan," "count" or a less formal title such as "boss." Kindred scholars tracing the origins of the term believe that it had its roots in the Dark Ages, in reference to the lord of the manor, becoming a solid term of address after the publishing of Machiavelli's *The Prince.*

A prince does not "reign" over a city. His role is more like that of an overseer or magistrate than that of a monarch. He is the judge who settles disputes between Kindred, the ultimate authority on the Traditions as they relate to his city, and the keeper of the peace. Above all, his concern is the Masquerade and its preservation. Whether this means he regularly scours his city for Sabbat or keeps a stranglehold on the wilder elements is up to him. Not every prince realizes or cares that his power is meant to be so informal; indeed, some demand that they be treated like the kings of old, holding "court" and requiring that their "subjects" within the domain attend them as they pass royal pronouncements. Such arrogance can rankle the populace, both disenfranchised youth and irritated elders.

The vampire denizens of a city owe their prince no oaths of loyalty or vassalage. Their obedience depends on their cowardice, and most princes make certain to have some means of reinforcing that cowardice. If a prince's rule is questioned or thwarted, he may call in force to maintain control. However, if there is not enough force for the problem, or he finds himself without allies, his reign ends.

Having followed the protocol demanded by the Traditions, most vampires ignore their prince, or give him half an ear at best to make sure they don't miss anything that might pertain to them. On the whole, Kindred have plenty of diversions to occupy themselves with besides listening to their "leader." Some elders, Inconnu and those in a position not to care (such as justicars) find princely announcements alternately amusing and arrogant, the blustering of a youngster still impressed with the gaudy trappings of power.

When all is said and done, however, the prince is nothing to brush off. A prince wields vast amounts of temporal power to achieve and maintain her position. Not only does she manage the Kindred affairs of a city, she usually has quite a bit of sway over mortal business. The police, the fire department, construction companies, hospitals, the mayor's office — all are extremely useful for putting down one's enemies or securing one's hold on a particular sphere of influence. If the prince wishes to squash a gang of particularly troublesome anarchs, she can have a construction company bulldoze their haven in the middle of the day. A Church-sponsored hunter operating out of a local cathedral may find the mayor's office calling to inquire about his church's tax-exempt status. Such influences usually capture the attention of those who might otherwise be inclined to thumb their noses at a prince. It is unwise to anger the one who could have your haven condemned by the zoning board or your phone line "accidentally" cut while a gas main is being dug.

BECOMING PRINCE

As was mentioned earlier, there are no dynasties or royal families from which princes are selected (though some clans would argue that point). Traditionally, the eldest vampire of a city rules, although this is no longer true in every city. It is one thing to say that the eldest traditionally rules the city, but any vampire may challenge for domain and princedom. A prince reigns freely only when her claim is unchallenged. If she finds herself squaring off with one or more other claimants, then things get messy. There is a mad scramble for the crown, and whoever is left standing will rule. "Coronation," if it can be truly called that, can be anything from a bloodless, elder-backed coup to a violent usurpation led by a bloodthirsty coterie. Normally, the current regime is overthrown brutally and mercilessly, serving the dual purpose of dealing with the old prince and providing a graphic demonstration of the new prince's power. Whoever the new prince and however she takes the throne, though, she needs the support of the elders if she wishes to hold the crown for more than a night. Most importantly, the council of elders known as the primogen must sanction the reign of a prince; without this acknowledgment, the reign will be a remarkably short one.

Combat for the princedom is not simply a matter of pistols at midnight on a deserted street, or for that matter any kind of direct combat. Like everything about the Children of Caine, subtlety in all things counts, and the war for the crown takes place entirely in the shadows. The city's vampires — elders, coteries, individuals — choose their sides as the rivals cultivate allies and determine enemies. Many things can drive a Kindred to choose a particular claimant — promise of reward, loyalties to the vampire or her clan, concessions guaranteed upon ascension, personal beliefs, or threats — but once she has chosen, changing loyalties can be extremely dangerous, particularly if she has backed the wrong claimant when the fighting is done. Mortal institutions under vampiric influence — banks, industry, high society, education, police, the underworld — are brought to bear on the rival. Anything that can be done to give an added edge can, will, and has been tried. When the smoke clears, there is usually one claimant left standing, and the prize is in her grasp. Rarely is a new prince generous enough to leave her rival alive; even if she were, the primogen would never allow it to happen. Revenge, particularly that of fallen rivals, is a dish best not served at all.

Cleaning House

Sometimes a group of anarchs or ancillae decides to bring down a prince once and for all. Coups are dangerous to attempt unless one is very secure in one's allies. Princes rarely get their seats on charm alone, and most have broods of childer for protection. Taking on the prince can also mean taking on the primogen, who can readily crush any potential insurrection in the name of the city's stability.

A coup usually results in a political vacuum, and in the Kindred world, vacuums can have far-reaching consequences. A city in turmoil means instability; coteries battle for a place in the new order, elders war to ensure their survival, and sometimes the turmoil attracts the unwelcome presence of Sabbat, werewolves or witch-hunters. The resulting threat to the Masquerade can occasionally mean setting up any likely vampire to temporarily stabilize the city, but such solutions are rarely effective and often result in further chaos.

Most elders, and indeed the majority of vampires in a city, will support a prince in the name of a stable city. War is never pleasant and, for elders concerned with their survival, war means the potential for Final Death. Unless a prince has become completely unmanageable — through insanity, supernatural corruption or excessive tyranny — the Cainites of her city can count on being stuck with her for a good while.

Abdication can, and occasionally does, happen. Indeed, in recent nights, a number of strange, sudden abdications and uncanny disappearances of ruling figures have rocked the ancient power structures. If one or more primogen choose to make unlife miserable for their prince for whatever reason, she may be driven from office. A vote of no confidence is also possible, but rare in the extreme, owing to the potential chaos that can arise when a prince is forced out of office or leaves under bitter circumstances.

Advantages of Princedom

Some vampires believe that only the insane or vain seek out the position of prince. After all, as the symbol of Cainite power in a city, the prince is the likeliest target for anarchs, Sabbat and other perils. Add to this the political squabbling and jockeying for position within a prince's "court," and perhaps the critics are right. However, princedom must come with advantages to entice even the lowest to dream, and it does in spades.

• Right to progeny — Only the prince may freely create progeny. Other vampires who wish to sire must first obtain his permission or risk the destruction of themselves and their new childer. The prince may deny a Kindred who has offended him permission to sire a childe; conversely, he may sire as he chooses, in order to have more loyal followers. Most princes are reluctant to allow their subjects to sire. This stems partly from paranoia, partly from simple space considerations; after all, an overcrowded city risks the Masquerade.

• Protection of the elders — The primogen generally support their prince so long as he maintains order, preserves the Masquerade, and protects the city during times of trouble, such as werewolf incursions or Sabbat attacks.

• Political power — Among the Camarilla, a prince can expect to be heard by most elders and enjoys greater status than the ruck and run of Kindred. In almost any gathering, he is typically accorded great respect.

• Control over domain and those who enter — Under the Fifth Tradition, the prince may extend his reign to those who enter his domain, which is the entire city or region. New vampire arrivals, whether travelers or hopeful residents, are expected by the same Tradition to present themselves to him. The prince may punish Kindred who fail to introduce themselves.

• Feeding — The prince may restrict or limit the feeding grounds of other vampires for any number of reasons, chief among them the preservation of the Masquerade. This most often affects where Kindred may feed (e.g., "Not in the red-light district" or "Avoid the Clermont Hotel") and from whom (e.g., "Clergy and children are forbidden"). Disobeying orders regarding feeding can be very dangerous, as the prince may punish violators on grounds of breaking the Masquerade.

SHY
98

• Domain over enemies — By the Sixth Tradition, the prince may call a blood hunt against those who cross her too many times. She may not destroy at will (the elders' protection can run out inconveniently if she oversteps her bounds), but if she determines her enemies to have broken one or more Traditions, she is perfectly within her rights to punish them. Naturally, what constitutes a violation of the Traditions can be stretched quite far in the name of power.

THE NIGHTLY GAME

The powerplays and intrigues that swarm around any prince are rarely dull. When several elders jostle for greater position and access to the prince, unlife can get downright exciting. Each Cainite has her own way to attempt to sway her ruler to her side, whether through cajolery, flattery, trickery or even threats if the stakes are high enough. Through it all, the players practice studied disinterest in the whole messy business, but only a fool would believe it. Pushing matters to the point of a *coup d'etat* or abdication is ill advised — power vacuums can mean blood in the streets — but the elders play more than one game in the corridors of power.

Most princes are "advised" by a group of elders called the primogen. Collectively, the primogen can be considered among the most powerful vampires in a city, and can rival the prince for influence of the city's Kindred. Individually, however, they are either not as powerful as the prince himself or do not care to devote themselves to the duties of maintaining a city (beware these last, for if they become discontented, they can influence a coup by merely stretching). The primogen usually serve as check and balance against the power of the prince, while seeking to advance their own or their clan's agendas. The bickering of the primogen can bog down the simplest of decisions and cause as much or more trouble than a prince's high-handed pronouncements.

The struggle between and among prince and primogen is by no means the sole component of the Kindred's political game. The prince versus the elders, clan versus clan, elder versus neonate, traditionalist versus anarch — add in personal vendettas, revenge, greed, alliances and powermongering, and one has a very unsettled mix that can change from night to night.

OTHER KINDRED OF IMPORTANCE

Over the centuries, certain positions have sprung up in the cities. Some assist the prince in keeping order; others began more as "vanity" positions, but became more solidified and codified as time went on.

• The Primogen — The *primogen* are the assembled elders of each clan in a city. Most often, each clan has a representative primogen, but in some cities a prince refuses to allow a given clan to place a member on this council of elders. In theory, primogen represent their clans among the political body of elders, but in practice the primogen are more often an "old vampires' club" and an incestuous nest of treachery and favor-currying. Primogen — the term refers to individual members as well as the collected body — convene at the prince's discretion. In cities with powerful or despotic princes, the primogen may be nothing more than a figurehead, while in other cities princes govern solely at the whim of the elder council.

It is worth noting that the prince is often not the primogen for his clan. Although some Kindred claim that having duplicate clans involved in the political structure weighs matters in favor of that clan, no one is really in a position to change it.

• The Sheriff — Most sheriffs are appointed by the prince and approved by the primogen. While the job description may vary from city to city, the *sheriff's* prime job is to be the prince's "enforcer," the vampire who hauls offenders into court, keeps order on the streets, and generally stands ready to assist with the "muscle" aspects of ruling. Sheriffs may select deputies, who occasionally require the prince's approval.

• The Harpies — These Kindred pride themselves on being the social managers of Elysium. They traffic in gossip and social maneuvering, and status is their coin. With the right or wrong word to a prince, they can make or break a vampire's place in the city. This position is rarely appointed outright; over time, those with the skills to be harpies tend to rise to the top. Most are unimpressed with displays of bluster and demonstrate remarkable insight into vampire nature. Bucking a harpy will assure one a place at the bottommost rung of the ladder of power for years to come.

• The Whip — Primogen occasionally keep whips as assistants. Not much different from the whips in mortal government, the *whip's* job is to goad and encourage discussion and decision-making during clan meetings, and to keep the clan updated on their primogen members' doings. Whips are selected by the primogen.

• The Seneschal — This is one position that many princes would like to do without, but which occasionally is necessary. One prince described the filling of this position to be akin to choosing which knife to put at her throat. A *seneschal* is meant to be a chamberlain, a second-in-command and an advisor to the prince. At any time, he may be asked to step into the prince's place if she leaves town on business, abdicates or is slain. Naturally, a prince wishes to have final authority on such an important position, and many have fought endlessly with their primogen over the subject. This is a dangerous position in more ways than one — familiarity with the subject can give one ideas….

• The Keeper of Elysium — The *keeper* is in charge of what goes on in Elysium. A Toreador wishing to display her latest work, a Tremere wanting to give a lecture, or a Brujah scheduling an open debate on princely policies — all must clear things with the keeper, who can cancel or approve an event on the grounds of preserving the Masquerade. The keeper is responsible for ensuring that mortals do not enter the area during Elysium and that events run smoothly. Most keepers are appointed by the prince, often with the stipulation that their appointment is conditional until their qualifications are assured.

• The Scourge — As the nights grow more and more violent and the cities fill with unknown Kindred, some princes have resurrected this ancient position. Essentially, the *scourge* patrols the borders of a princedom, seeking out and often destroying newcomers who have failed to present themselves. Caitiff, as well as the fledglings of the 13th, 14th and 15th generations, have much to fear from the scourge. In some cases, even vampires who have followed protocol fall victim to the scourge, as princes reflexively react to fears of overpopulation and espionage. A few scourges are Assamite assassins under contract to a prince.

THE TRADITIONS

A vampire living in a prince-ruled city must accept certain responsibilities for the privileges of security and stability. This stability is maintained only when the Kindred within behave in a proper manner, one dictated by a near-universal set of rules. These rules are known by the gentle-sounding name of the *Six Traditions*, although they are hardly polite suggestions. For Camarilla Kindred, and the princes who enforce them, they are the law. A vampire may be assured that wherever she travels, the Traditions will be in force. They may be interpreted differently, but they remain. It is through the enforcement of these laws, and through the laws themselves, that princes receive much of their power. Obviously, then, princes are among the most zealous of the Traditions' enforcers.

The Six Traditions that form the laws of vampire society are believed to have been passed down since the wars that slew the Second Generation. They are rarely written down, but they have never been forgotten, and they are known by all Kindred in some form. Even vampires who scorn the Traditions know them; though their specific wordings may vary, the intent behind them never falters.

It is a popular Camarilla conceit that a sire recite the Traditions to his childe before that childe is recognized as a neonate. Some princes stage grand spectacles to honor new childer's transition from fledgling to neonate, while others need not even witness the release, trusting the sire with the proper execution. Almost all childer learn the Traditions well before this recitation, but the act is accorded great symbolism and gravity in Camarilla affairs. Staunch supporters of the Camarilla and the Traditions maintain that a newly Embraced Kindred has not truly become a vampire until her sire speaks the Traditions to her. Obviously, the Traditions are quite a serious matter, and the sire is held accountable for the childe until, by speaking them to her, he makes her responsible for upholding the code herself.

Some vampires believe that Caine himself created the Traditions when he sired his childer, and that what modern vampires follow are their progenitor's original wishes for his descendants. Others, however, think that the Antediluvians created them to maintain control over their childer, or that they were simply a set of common-sense ideas that were upheld over the millennia because they worked. The Tradition of the Masquerade, for example, is thought to have existed in some form since the nights of the First City, but it changed in response to the Inquisition.

A number of young vampires, children of the modern world, see the Traditions as being merely a tool of the elders to maintain their stranglehold on Kindred society, and an antique tool at that. The times that produced the need for the Masquerade are over and done, ancient history. Caine, Gehenna, the Antediluvians — all myths with about as much substance as the Flood or the Tower of Babel, and all for the sake of controlling the younger generations. It's time to drop the Traditions and live in the modern age. The vampires of the Sabbat rabidly adhere to this reasoning, and their scorn for the Traditions is one of the primary motivations behind their constant attacks on the ancient power structures.

Most elders see the young as temperamental adolescents who think they know everything but who lack the wisdom and experience of age. As many of the rebels are anarchs and neonates, mostly powerless and without voice in Kindred society, it should come as no great surprise that they are so wild. However, not every elder takes such an indulgent viewpoint. Many feel that the reckless whelps who demand the Traditions be dropped may get their wish when they bring mortal society down on their heads. Natural selection takes care of a few of these, but such selection has occasionally been "assisted" by a prince exasperated beyond patience with a particularly recalcitrant young vampire.

What follows is the most common wording of the Traditions. Bear in mind that this is the phrasing used by elders and on formal occasions. The wording may change according to the clan, the age of the vampire speaking, or simple circumstance. During a childe's presentation to the prince, she may be required to recite the Traditions as proof that her sire has taught them to her.

THE FIRST TRADITION: THE MASQUERADE

Thou shalt not reveal thy true nature to those not of the Blood. Doing so shall renounce thy claims of Blood.

THE SECOND TRADITION: THE DOMAIN

Thy domain is thy concern. All others owe thee respect while in it. None may challenge thy word in thy domain.

THE THIRD TRADITION: THE PROGENY

Thou shalt sire another only with permission of thine elder. If thou createst another without thine elder's leave, both thou and thy progeny shalt be slain.

THE FOURTH TRADITION: THE ACCOUNTING

Those thou create are thine own childer. Until thy progeny shall be released, thou shalt command them in all things. Their sins are thine to endure.

THE FIFTH TRADITION: HOSPITALITY

Honor one another's domain. When thou comest to a foreign city, thou shalt present thyself to the one who ruleth there. Without the word of acceptance, thou art nothing.

THE SIXTH TRADITION: DESTRUCTION

Thou art forbidden to destroy another of thy kind. The right of destruction belongeth only to thine elder. Only the eldest among thee shall call the blood hunt.

The Tradition of the Masquerade

This has become the foundation of modern Kindred society and the basis for the Masquerade that hides vampires from mortal eyes. To reveal vampires to the mortal world would be disastrous to both. While most people do not believe in vampires, there are enough who do that revealing vampiric existence would place all Kindred at risk. In older nights, during the Dark Ages and more superstitious ages, this Tradition was less strictly enforced, and vampires rode through the night with few cares for the mortal eyes who saw them. The Inquisition and Burning Times changed this drastically, however, as those vampires who could be seen were slain and tortured into revealing their secrets. While the youth may prattle about the Inquisition as ancient history, it is still very fresh in the minds of the elders who survived it. This is one of the greatest points of contention between the Camarilla and the Sabbat — the Sabbat sees no need to hide itself from the feeble kine, while the Camarilla knows the opposite to be true.

A breach of the Masquerade is the most serious crime a vampire can commit, and one of the easiest for a prince to fabricate if she wishes to punish an enemy. Depending on how strictly the prince upholds the Masquerade, anything from using vampiric powers in public to having mortal friends may constitute a breach.

To stave off their immortal boredom, many vampires skirt the Masquerade as closely as they can, taking thrill from the forbidden rush that places their unlives in jeopardy. The world has acknowledged many artists, poets, writers, musicians, models, club habitués, actors and fashion designers who, unbeknownst to the populace, were vampires. Of course, many of these vampires saw their unlives come to abrupt ends, as other Kindred decided that their continued existences were threats to the Children of Caine as a whole.

The Masquerade is a dangerous balance; ironically enough, the elders who support it most strongly are sometimes the ones who threaten it (albeit indirectly and without their recognition). An apocryphal story tells of a pair of vampire-hunters — a new recruit and her patron — on vigil in a nightclub. The patron said to his charge, "There is a vampire in this establishment. Find him," whereupon the charge immediately selected the thin, pale gentleman in 18th-century velvet and brocade. Sure enough, that was the vampire — a Ventrue envoy from a neighboring city.

The Tradition of Domain

Once, vampires staked claims to specific areas to use as hunting grounds, bases of power, or because they wished to take care of them. This Tradition was then used to enforce the idea of "domain," and a vampire could be justified in killing another because her domain was violated. Over the years, as societies changed, this became unacceptable. For the past 200 or so years, a city or region ruled by a prince became the domain of the prince upon his taking the throne, or at least in theory. The truth is, a number of vampires maintain domain, many times from the sheer weight of custom ("The sewers have *always* been the domain of the Nosferatu," or "A Ventrue has ruled this bank since its founding"). Of course, in modern nights, with some cities hosting vampire populations of 30, 50, even 100 or more, concessions must be made. As such, many vampires hunt where they will, in the communal hunting grounds of the city's bars, theaters and nightclubs, which are known collectively as "The Rack" in Kindred slang.

Younger vampires, and a number of older ones, often still attempt to hold bits of territory, protecting and using them as private feeding grounds. Some anarchs claim that these mini-fiefdoms are granted by the prince as reward, proof that only the lapdogs get the treats. This is incorrect — the Kindred who hold their bits of turf are violating the Second Tradition, and the prince need not stand for it. He often lets violations go, however, in the name of expediency; there are more important concerns than chasing after every petty would-be anarch who stakes out turf. He may entrust certain trusted allies with guardianship of particular areas, and grant them a few privileges for the burden of the job, but in the end, he holds domain over the city. This allows him to keep order, for he may, by the Second Tradition, punish interlopers with impunity.

For solitary vampires or small groups staking out their territory, domain holds immense value to them, even if the territory is an urban wasteland. Few princes actually grant territory, but they occasionally allow "squatters," provided the vampires there support them and uphold the law there. The downside to this is the turf battles that can arise between gangs of anarchs or coteries. These can spill over into the mortal world and threaten the Masquerade. Some princes have gone so far as to encourage such conflict, regardless of the danger, in order to set the troublemakers at each other's throats and distract them from the business of the city.

If nothing else, each Kindred may claim her haven as domain, making her responsible for the activity in and around the area. Some vampires take an active interest in their environment to ensure a secure haven, while others merely want a room where they can get away from the sun and to hell with the rest.

The question of what exactly constitutes domain is debated nightly. Does domain mean the physical territory and its concerns (such as hunting and haven), or does a domain also grant a vampire access to and influence over the mortal spheres within? Most princes argue that domain is strictly an issue of physical "turf," but wisely realize that influence over mortal affairs comes with the territory, no matter how they might attempt to curb it otherwise. A vampire who keeps up domain at the docks cannot help but become involved in the nightly mortal business of shipping and unions, if for no other reason than to keep her haven secure (after all, a labor strike could be very inconvenient, particularly if her bolthole is on the other side of the picket line). Very few vampires stake a domain encompassing mortals they cannot affect in some way, which can be a help or a headache to their princes. A prince does, however, become inclined to step in when a particular vampire's power within and stemming from her domain threatens to eclipse his own.

As the nights progress and omens of Gehenna permeate Kindred society, more and more vampires fortify individual domains, holing themselves away in spite of princely prohibition. Only in this manner, these paranoid creatures reason, do they have a chance of surviving the Jyhad.

The Tradition of Progeny

Most princes insist that they are the "elder" of this Tradition's wording and, as such, require that any vampire wishing to create a childe obtain their permission before the creation. Most vampires obey more out of fear than respect; after all, the unlife of a childe is at risk. If a childe has already been created without permission, the prince may claim the childe to be of his brood, declare sire and childe outcast and throw them out of the city, or have both slain outright. At the prince's discretion, childer who are created and abandoned without being taught of their existence may be "adopted" by other vampires, who accept full responsibility no differently than if they had created the childer themselves. The Camarilla recognizes the prince's right to restrict creation, out of concern for overpopulation. Indeed, such is the Camarilla's concern for the increasingly strained vampiric population that, at a recent conclave, its leaders resurrected the institution of the scourge. Scourges patrol princely domains, finding Kindred created without permission and either expelling or destroying them.

In the Old World, this Tradition has several corollaries. The would-be sire's sire must be consulted, as must the prince who holds domain over the sire's haven (if there is one). European Kindred are noted for their complete lack of tolerance for those who transgress against this Tradition. Failure to gain the permission of any of these undead can result in the outright slaying of the childe, and possibly the sire as well. Disregard and lack of respect may be appropriate for American rabble, but they certainly do not belong in the Old World.

The Tradition of Accounting

If a vampire creates a childe, she is responsible for that childe, no differently than a mortal parent is for her child. If the childe cannot handle the burdens of vampirism, the sire must take care of the matter one way or another. If the childe threatens the Masquerade, either through ignorance or malice, the sire must prevent it. The sire must ensure that the childe is taught the Traditions and the ensuing responsibilities, and see to it that the childe will not constitute a threat to herself or the Masquerade upon her release. The sire is also responsible for protecting the childe. A prince is under no obligation to recognize a childe, and other vampires may kill or feed from a childe with impunity.

Before siring, a wise vampire considers the maturity of the childe-to-be. Will she be able to endure the changes to her body and soul? Will she understand what is being asked of her when the Traditions are recited? No sire wishes to be responsible for a childe forever (although a long childhood is not unknown), but releasing a childe before she is ready courts destruction.

Releasing a childe typically involves the sire introducing the childe to the prince who holds domain where the sire and childe live. The childe may be asked to recite the Traditions or provide other proof that she has been taught and understands them. If the prince, for whatever reasons, does not accept a childe, then the childe must find a new city. On occasion, a sire must also introduce the childe to his own sire, but this is not always required.

After release, the childe (now a neonate) is permitted to live in the city with full rights as accorded by the prince's law and the Traditions. The release is considered a major rite of passage, much like a coming of age for mortals, for the neonate is responsible for his own actions. He will be watched carefully in the coming months; his actions determine whether he will be considered an "adult" and treated as one.

The Tradition of Hospitality

Some call this the Tradition of "politeness": Knock before entering. This was done even before princes ruled cities, and continues to be done even if there is only one other Kindred in a domain. Simply put, a vampire traveling to a new city should present herself to the prince or other elder in charge in that city. This process can be frightfully formal, with a prince demanding some form of surety regarding the newcomer's status, politics and lineage, or as casual as meeting at Elysium and introducing oneself politely. Some princes require guests to announce their arrivals immediately, while others accept presentations weekly or within the lunar month. Certain very liberal princes even permit visitors to come and go unannounced as they please, requiring that a guest present herself only if she wishes to take up permanent residence in a city.

Those who choose not to present themselves take dangerous chances. If a city is currently facing Jyhad, a newcomer risks being mistaken for an enemy. A prince may invoke the Second Tradition to punish an unintroduced vampire with impunity. By the Fifth Tradition, a prince's right to question all who enter her domain is unchallenged, even if her power to expel may be thwarted occasionally. A prince also has the right to refuse entry to any who enter, particularly in the case of newcomers whose poor reputations precede them or who bring cumbersome baggage in the form of blood hunts, enemies or other potential threats to the city and Masquerade.

Such individual denials have become quite common in the modern nights, as princes grow paranoid and xenophobic in light of looming Gehenna. Some princes, when presented with a group of Kindred visitors, permit entry to certain members of the coterie while denying it to others, reasoning that, if the group is on some sort of sinister errand, its potential to harm will be lessened by dividing its numbers. Certain notorious Kindred may also find themselves unwelcome in some cities, while their companions are welcomed without reservation.

Not every vampire chooses to present herself. Vampires such as Inconnu, Methuselahs and even some elders refuse on the grounds that they do not acknowledge the prince's right and power over them, even if they are in her domain. Vampires of independent clans (such as the Ravnos or Giovanni) may prefer not to have a prince's eye scrutinizing them. Autarkis and anarchs simply sneer at the prince; they aren't part of the party, so why should they bother knocking? And vampires who were made, then abandoned — an increasingly common phenomenon — may be unaware of the necessity.

The Tradition of Destruction

The Tradition of Destruction is perhaps the most easily abused and the most hotly contested aspect of Caine's code. Few other laws have caused so much controversy in the halls of power, and this Tradition is forever under reinterpretation.

Most believe that the original meaning gave a sire right of destruction over his progeny (which is upheld by Kindred law). However, if "elder" is interpreted to mean "prince," the Tradition covers its modern meaning, and one many princes claim gladly: Only the prince may call for the destruction of another Kindred in the city. The Camarilla has upheld this claim for the extra security it provides a prince's reign. It is a right which many princes cling to, and they enforce it with brutal strength if need be.

Murder of another Kindred by one who is not granted the Right of Destruction is not tolerated. If the vampire is caught in the act, it usually means the destruction of the murderer herself. Investigation of such murder is usually swift and thorough, although the status of the victim does have some impact on this. Generally, the higher the rank of the victim, the swifter and more thorough the investigation. While the murder of two neonates may cause consternation in a community, it might take the death of an elder before the wheels turn in a more timely fashion. Some ancillae have taken this to mean that anarchs may be slaughtered with impunity. This is dangerous to assume; if nothing else, the prince may order the murderer slain for attempting to usurp her Tradition-given right.

Turmoil in the streets is considered by many to be one of the best covers for kinslaying, but the punishment for getting caught is still severe. The only time when a vampire ranked lower than an elder might receive sanctioning to kill another is during a blood hunt.

The Lextalionis

The ancient law of "An eye for an eye, a tooth for a tooth" is as true for Kindred as it is for kine. The precept is simple: Those who break the laws are slain. A vampire who violates the Traditions and brings the wrath of the elders on his head is hunted down and destroyed. All who hear the call are expected to participate and assist. The most common name for this action is the *blood hunt*.

Only the eldest in a city may call the blood hunt. "Eldest" is considered most times to be the prince. Other elders or even ancillae may call a hunt, but they would have few takers; overstepping one's bounds into princely territory is unwise. Only a foolish prince would openly call a hunt for personal reasons; even the lowest Kindred know what the hunt is meant for, and a prince who uses it without proper justification of the charges loses respect in the eyes of his subjects.

Aiding and abetting the quarry can be a sure ticket to suffer a blood hunt oneself. At least nominal participation is recommended on the grounds of survival, even if the Kindred does not agree with the hunt or its charges. A powerful prince may charge that all vampires in a city are required to participate in a hunt, on pain of being declared accomplices. This decree is reserved for the most serious of crimes.

A blood hunt is not a hunt in the sense of an English fox-hunt, which is what comes to the minds of many young vampires. The hunters spread out across the city like a net to track their quarry, calling in flanks when the prey is in sight. Like all things vampiric, the Masquerade is observed, and mortals rarely realize that anything is happening around them, except perhaps some strange incidents that they will either forget or read about in next morning's paper. Many times, influences in the mortal world are brought to bear on the hunted; he may find that every airline is suddenly booked full, the police have an APB on him, Church-sponsored witch-hunters have been called in, his bank accounts

are tapped out before he can touch them, etc. Disturbingly, more and more princes are resorting to calling in Assamite trackers from outside the domain, using them as vampiric bloodhounds against the hunted.

The blood hunt is not called lightly, though it has been called more often in the last decade than in entire centuries of yore. The Camarilla reserves the right to examine the prince's judgment in conclave, hearing evidence for and against the accused. The threat of a conclave has been deterrent enough to keep a hunt from being declared. A prince who is determined to have called the hunt without cause rarely suffers formal punishment (unless he has made a habit of this), but he often suffers a great loss of status. Unfortunately, even if the accused is found to be innocent, it is often after the fact, and tradition dictates that once a blood hunt is called, it cannot be stopped.

A hunted may attempt to flee the city and seek a new haven, an option occasionally offered by princes who are being forced to exile someone in the name of stability or when the offense does not warrant death. However, by tradition, the hunt remains in effect in that city, no matter who rules in the future. The hunted should never attempt to return unless she wishes to court Final Death.

Blood hunts are typically the business of the cities in which they originate. In the case of truly horrendous crimes, word is spread to other cities, requesting that the hunt be called against the offender there as well. Kindred who have committed some crime that affects the Camarilla as a whole (such as a spectacular breach of the Masquerade on national television) are an example of such.

Elysium

Though most younger vampires consider the tradition of Elysium a stuffy, outdated custom, it is one of the more honored of the Kindred's traditions. A prince may declare portions of domain to be *Elysium*, places free from violence. It is here that many vampires come to pass the nights, debating, politicking and conducting intrigues among themselves for long hours. This is also where the Kindred business of the city takes place, and just about every vampire will have at least one occasion to visit Elysium, if only to speak with the prince or an elder. However, it is certainly an elders' playground, and the young who venture here are expected to remember that.

Elysium is said to be under the "Pax Vampirica," meaning that no violence of any sort is permitted to take place and that Elysium is neutral ground. While tempers may flare and heated words may be exchanged, rivals are expected to keep a leash on their tempers. When apologies don't work, offenders are usually shown the door and told to correct their behavior. If things do get out of control on the premises, the prince may punish the offenders through the invocation of the First Tradition.

Most areas of Elysium tend to be spots conducive to artistic or intellectual pursuits, such as opera houses, theaters, museums, galleries, university halls and the like. Occasionally, nightclubs or even certain Kindred havens are declared Elysium. Wherever one goes, one is expected to have some semblance of proper dress and manners, if for no reason other than the Masquerade.

Elysium rules are simple:

1) No violence is permitted on the premises. (Many princes take this a step further and demand that no weapons be brought into Elysium, to prevent hot tempers from having ready means.)

2) No art is to be destroyed on pain of Final Death. ("Art" has been expanded to include the artist on occasion, making the vampires of Clan Toreador some of the greatest proponents of Elysium.)

3) Elysium is neutral ground. (With relation to Rule One; what happens off Elysium grounds is another thing, however, and the upstart neonate who insults an elder during Elysium had best have reliable transportation back to her haven when she leaves.)

4) Remember the Masquerade at all times. (This includes such matters as entering and leaving, taking a heated argument outside to cool, or hunting.)

It is also considered bad manners to show up to Elysium hungry. While refreshments are sometimes provided, often they are not, and hunting around Elysium grounds can draw suspicion. If a Kindred brings a guest to Elysium, she is responsible for that guest's behavior.

Sects

Sects are groups of vampires and clans that supposedly share a common ideology. They are a modern contrivance, but an important one. Sects as they are known in these nights first surfaced after the Great Anarch Revolt, a continent-wide upheaval which took place in Europe during the 15th century. Many elders accept sect membership grudgingly, deriding sects as "foolishness — the Blood is all that matters." In nights before the Great Anarch Revolt and the Inquisition, these elders claim, there were no sects at all. Other vampires argue that this is still true — a vampire in a sizable city may go a decade or more without ever seeing another Kindred, so of what use is a sect?

Regardless, most vampires belong to one sect or another; others claim independence, no preference, or that they are affiliated with their clan, not a sect. The sect known as the Camarilla is arguably the largest and most prevalent, though its rival the Sabbat has recently made considerable inroads against it and still opposes the Camarilla at every turn. The secretive Inconnu, when it may be reached for comment, maintains that it is not a sect, although it seems to be organized and manages to steer clear of the other sects. On the opposite side of the coin, the anarchs make much show of pretending to be a sect, though they are the first to enlist Camarilla aid when the Sabbat appears at a city's borders. Thus, the Camarilla considers the anarchs to be under its purview.

The Camarilla

The largest sect of vampires in existence, the Camarilla concerns itself with the Masquerade, thereby hoping to maintain a place for Kindred in the modern nights. The Camarilla is an open society; it claims all vampires as members (whether they want to belong or not), and any vampire may claim membership, regardless of lineage.

According to the often-contradictory history of the Kindred, the Camarilla came to be at the end of the Anarch Revolt, sometime in the 15th century. The Kindred of Clan Ventrue loudly claim to have been instrumental in the sect's formation, to which many Kindred owe their unlives. With the enforcement of the Masquerade, Kindred had a means of foiling the *Inquisition*, a Church office sworn to the destruction of supernatural creatures.

Though the Camarilla is the largest sect, just over half of the 13 known vampire clans actively participate in its affairs. The sect holds meetings attended by active clans' representatives; these gatherings are known as *convocations*. It also calls periodic *conclaves*, which are open to any and all members of the sect, to discuss matters of imminent sect importance. Only *justicars*, officers elected by the Inner Circle to attend to matters of the Traditions, may call conclaves. Justicars are always of great age, and rightly feared; as such, their interpretations of the Traditions are heeded out of self-preservation. Coteries of vampires known as *archons* attend the justicars; meeting an archon is usually a portentous event.

Officially, the Camarilla does not recognize the existence of the Antediluvians or Caine. It reasons that these vampires, if they ever existed at all, have long since suffered the Final Death, and those who allude to them are publicly derided.

THE SABBAT

Rumored to have its origins in a medieval death cult, the *Sabbat* is greatly feared by Kindred who do not belong to it. The sect is monstrous and violent, and no longer clings to any trappings of human philosophy or morality. Members instead revel in their vampiric unlives. Sometimes referred to as the *Black Hand*, the Sabbat actively seeks the overthrow of the Traditions, the destruction of the Camarilla, and the subjugation of humankind.

GEHENNA CULTS

As the fear of Gehenna grips the Kindred community, more and more *Gehenna cults* form. These groups, which resemble secret societies or cliques, are most common among the Camarilla, though some Gehenna cults pervade the Sabbat and even the independent clans. Due to the stigma of belonging to a Gehenna cult, cult business is always conducted in secret, and the cults are officially derided as foolish rumor. In recent nights, though, they have proliferated, and certain vampires of great power and influence secretly belong to Gehenna cults.

Gehenna cults exist to prepare for, or prevent, the end of the world. Fearing the culmination of the Jyhad and the return of the Antediluvians, the cults prepare either to serve the Ancients (thus hopefully averting their own destruction when the end comes) or to discover the Antediluvians' hidden havens (thus striking preemptively against them and averting Gehenna outright).

The Sabbat recruits wherever it takes hold, spreading like a poisonous weed and tearing down the established institutions around it. Unlike the Camarilla, the Sabbat recognizes the existence of the Antediluvians, though it rabidly opposes them. According to Sabbat propaganda, the Antediluvians pull the strings of the entire world, and it is this malignant control they oppose. They see the Camarilla as pawns of the Ancients, and oppose its members politically as well as physically. Most Sabbat express bilious contempt for the vampires of the Camarilla, whom they see as cowardly wretches unable to accept their predatory natures.

Outsiders know little about the Sabbat's inner workings. Some Camarilla Kindred even doubt its existence, believing it to be a rumor created by elders to keep troublesome childer in line — an undead boogeyman. Lurid tales about the sect spread like wildfire, including claims that its members indulge in ceaseless diablerie, worship demons, hunt and kill other vampires, and possess the ability to break blood bonds. The only consistent rumor attributed to the Sabbat is its members' apparent love of fire — the sect has a fearsome reputation for leaving burning wakes behind it.

THE INCONNU

The *Inconnu* are not a sect so much as they are a disparate group of like-minded vampires. No longer wishing to be the puppets of those older than they, and tired of the

incessant maneuvering of those younger than they, the Inconnu seem to have dropped out of the Jyhad altogether. This is what distinguishes an Inconnu vampire from those of other sects — the Inconnu distance themselves from other vampires and their contemptible machinations.

The Inconnu are rumored (as no one ever really goes *looking* for them) to be of great age and potency. Many reportedly spend much time in torpor or otherwise sleeping, the better to avoid the Jyhad. Some Kindred liken the Inconnu to the Antediluvians, claiming that they have grown away from the world and into a timeless, inhuman mindset. Other Kindred believe that the Inconnu all pursue or have attained Golconda, a fabled state of vampiric transcendence.

Kindred who deal with the Inconnu typically leave the encounter with a sense of profound mystery and awe. Although the Inconnu seem to be informal and loosely organized, they communicate very well among themselves. Inconnu know when to avoid Kindred, when to hide from them and when to unleash their significant power to turn vampires away. Their agenda, if they even have one, is unknown.

THE CLANS

If the myth of the Antediluvians is to be believed, Caine sired a number of progeny, who then sired childer themselves. These childer, accordingly of the Third Generation, were the progenitors of the modern *clans*, and all vampires descended from them shared common traits and characteristics. Certainly this is true to some degree, as each clan has a set of vampiric powers its members learn more readily than others, and each clan also has a distinguishing weakness or character flaw by which its members may be identified.

Lineage is important to the Kindred. Though they are loners and typically shun each other's company by nature, the Damned place great value on their heritage. The honor a vampire is due stems from clan as much as generation, and even the most dull-witted Kindred is afforded some modicum of respect if his legacy demands it.

There are 13 known clans, each supposedly spawned by one of the Antediluvians, but whispers circulate through the Kindred world about "lesser" clans or *bloodlines* that branched off

from their parent genealogies somewhere in the nights of history. Few vampires have ever met Kindred claiming to hail from these mysterious bloodlines, and few of these have turned out to be anything other than Caitiff with delusions of self-importance. It is widely accepted, however, that of the 13 "great" clans, seven claim membership in the Camarilla, two belong to the Sabbat, and the remaining four abstain from sects entirely.

THE CLANS OF THE CAMARILLA

The Camarilla claims that all vampires are under its purview, whether they wish to be so included or not. The Camarilla realistically comprises seven clans, though any Kindred may be recognized as a member if she so declares.

BRUJAH

As the *Brujah* tell the tale, they were once philosopher-kings of Mesopotamia, Persia and Babylon. They controlled an empire that spanned from the cradle of civilization to northern Africa, and collected lore and knowledge from around the world. In their pursuit of freedom and enlightenment, however, they killed their founder. For this, Caine cast them out from the First City. Since then, the Brujah have suffered inescapable decline. Now they are perceived as little more than spoiled childer who have no sense of pride or history. One of the mainstays of the Great Anarch Revolt, the Brujah were barely brought to heel by the founders of the Camarilla, and the clan as a whole still resents the elders. Though nominally in the Camarilla, the Brujah are the sect's firebrands and agitators, testing the Traditions and rebelling in the name of whatever causes they hold dear. Many Brujah are outright anarchs, defying authority and serving no prince.

GANGREL

The night-prowling *Gangrel* are feral

vampires and possess disturbing animalistic tendencies and features. Rarely staying in one place, Gangrel are nomadic wanderers, satisfied only when running alone under the night sky. Their founder is whispered to have been a barbarian, unlike the other clan progenitors, and for this reason, Gangrel often Embrace outsiders. Distant, aloof and savage, Gangrel are often tragic individuals; although many hate the cities' crowds and constrictions, the presence of hostile werewolves prevents most Gangrel from living outside their confines. Gangrel vampires seem to support the Camarilla solely because it intrudes upon their unlives less than the Sabbat. Some members of Clan Gangrel think that independence would be better than their nominal Camarilla involvement, however, and the clan's continued membership in the sect is uncertain.

MALKAVIAN

Clan *Malkavian* has suffered throughout history, and continues to do so to this very night. Every member of this clan is afflicted with madness, and all are slaves to their debilitating lunacy. The Malkavian clan founder is rumored to have been one of the most important vampires of

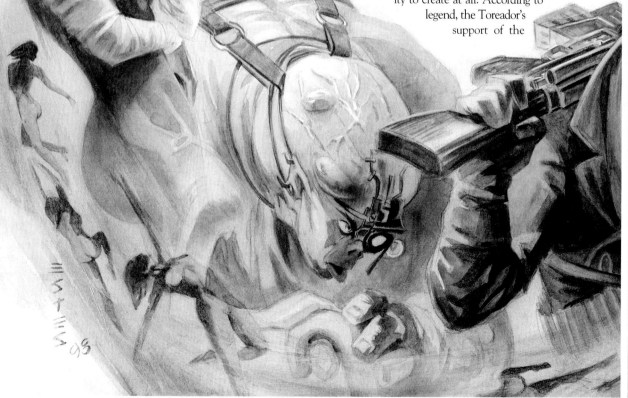

old, but in committing some grievous crime, Caine cursed him and his descendants with insanity. Throughout Cainite history, Malkavians have been alternately feared for their bizarre behavior and sought out for their even more bizarre insight. Kindred who have regular dealings with the Malkavians report that the clan is now more morbidly unstable than ever, spreading madness in its wake like a contagious disease. Though the Malkavians have historically been fragmented and disorganized, recent migratory waves and inexplicable gatherings have many elders questioning — and fearing — the possible future of the lunatic clan.

NOSFERATU

The members of Clan *Nosferatu* suffer the most visible curse of all. The Embrace hideously deforms them, twisting them into literal monsters. Legends say that the Nosferatu were blighted as punishment for their founder's degeneracy and his childer's wicked behavior, but in the modern nights, Clan Nosferatu is known for levelheadedness and calm in the face of adversity. Nosferatu have reputations as information brokers and harvesters of secrets, as their horrid appearances have forced them to perfect their mystical ability to hide, sometimes in plain sight. At present, the clan claims that it has distanced itself from its founder and no longer serves him. Some Kindred whisper that the clan is on terrible terms with its progenitor, and that he actively seeks their destruction.

TOREADOR

Prodigals of the Kindred, Clan *Toreador* indulges in excess and degeneracy, all while claiming to maintain patronage of the arts. To a great degree, this patronage is true, as the clan claims many talented artists, musicians, writers, poets and other gifted creators. On the other hand, the clan possesses just as many "poseurs," those who fancy themselves great aesthetes but lack the ability to create at all. According to legend, the Toreador's support of the arts dates back to the clan founder's Embrace of a pair of twins. The twins pursued unlives of beauty and indolence while their sire, Arikel (if the tale is to be believed), doted on them, protecting them from the ravages of plague, famine and parricide that swallowed the First City. Further, darker rumors circulate that one of the twins eventually grew depraved in her immortality and slew her brother and sire. Clan Toreador vehemently denies this, and those who bring up the subject suffer the clan's wrath.

TREMERE

No clan is so shrouded in deliberate mystery as the *Tremere*. The inventors and practitioners of terrible blood magics, the secretive Tremere have a tightly knit political structure based on the acquisition of power, as well as a fanatical clan loyalty practically unknown to any other Kindred. Because of the veil of secrecy that surrounds the clan, disturbing stories have surfaced as to the nature of their vampirism. Some Kindred claim that the Tremere are not truly vampires at all, but rather mortal wizards who cursed themselves for eternity while studying the secret of immortality. One of the most rampant rumors, spread by a Gypsy visitor to their chantry-house in Vienna, is that the clan founder, Tremere himself, is undergoing a horrid metamorphosis into *something* else. Clan Tremere is silent on the matter, and looks askance upon those who would presume to know its secrets.

VENTRUE

The nominal leaders of the Camarilla, the *Ventrue* claim to have created and supported the organization of the sect since its inception. The

clan suspects that its founder was slain by a member of the Brujah clan, which is a great blow to its members' pride. In any event, the clan almost certifiably has no founder any longer, and has thereby achieved untold independence from the Antediluvians. Nonetheless, Ventrue actively involve themselves in the Jyhad, in which they exercise their formidable influence over the doings of the kine. Much curiosity exists among the Kindred as to the inner workings of this well-organized clan, as rumors of dark mysteries and slumbering Ancients sometimes slip out from under the Ventrue's austere façade.

THE CLANS OF THE SABBAT

Like the Camarilla, the Sabbat welcomes any Kindred who wishes to become a member — provided the vampire in question subscribes to the sect's inhuman philosophy. Indeed, almost every Camarilla clan has an *antitribu*, or "anti-clan" analog, in the Sabbat; these rebels reject the tenets of

the mainstream clan in favor of the monsters' way of thinking. The Sabbat's two leading clans both claim to have destroyed their Antediluvian founders, and are said to pursue the annihilation of the other Antediluvians as well.

Lasombra

The *Lasombra* are masters of darkness and shadow, and possess a knack for leadership as keen as that of Clan Ventrue. Indeed, many Kindred see the Ventrue and Lasombra as twisted reflections of each other. Once, the Lasombra were nobles, but the chaos of Kindred history and the formation of the Sabbat have caused most of them to turn their backs upon their origins. Now, the Lasombra give themselves wholly over to the damnation of being vampires. The Sabbat has affected this clan as profoundly as the Lasombra have affected the Sabbat, and without the rulership of these fallen aristocrats, the Sabbat would likely disintegrate.

Tzimisce

Formerly the tyrants of Eastern Europe, the *Tzimisce* (zhi•mee•see) have been uprooted from their Old Country manses and relocated into the clutches of the Sabbat. Possessed of a peculiar nobility, coupled with an evil that transcends mortal perception, Clan Tzimisce leads the Sabbat in its rejection of all things human. Certain Kindred apocrypha claims that the Tzimisce was once the most powerful clan in the world, but that history and other Kindred conspired to bring its members down to their current state. More so than any other vampires, the Tzimisce revel in their monstrousness. They practice a "fleshcrafting" Discipline that they use to disfigure their foes and sculpt themselves into beings of terrible beauty.

The Independents

The independent clans claim membership in no sect, instead following the legendary tenets of their mythical founders. Independent clans tend to be the most cohesive and sociable Kindred of all, as their clan duties ensure that they interact with other vampires almost nightly.

In elder nights, the independent clans held domains far from the havens of the rest of the Kindred and did not participate overmuch in the upheavals of the Inquisition and Anarch Revolt. As a result, they were rarely seen, their members considered more legend than fact. The past few years have changed that. As the world shrinks and the kine speak of "geopolitics" and "global economy," the clans of the Camarilla and Sabbat find their herds and spheres of influence conflicting more and more with those of the independents. Independent Kindred cross Camarilla and Sabbat domains with increasing frequency, and the sect-affiliated clans are beginning to realize that the four "neutral" clans have networks, concerns and goals far greater than they had previously imagined.

Assamite

The *Assamites* are feared assassins from lands far to the east. No other clan has earned such a deserved reputation for diablerie, though they also sell their murderous services to other Kindred, acting as contract killers. According to the Assamites' own teachings, they drink the blood of other Kindred on the command of their founder, in an attempt to purify their own taint. So dreaded were the Assamites that, during the nights of the Great Anarch Revolt, the Tremere cursed them, making them unable to drink the blood of other Kindred. However, the Assamites have recently thrown off this curse, and so they hunt other Kindred for their blood once more. Kindred who regularly deal with the clan have noticed an increased bloodthirstiness on the part of the Assamites, as well as a disregard for their former codes of honor. Some Kindred believe that the Assamites now act at the behest of older powers, perhaps preparing to play their preordained part in the Jyhad's final moves.

Followers of Set

Originally hailing from Egypt, the serpentine *Setites* are said to worship the undead vampire-deity Set, serving him in all their efforts. The Setites seem intent on "corrupting" others, enslaving victims in snares of their own weakness, but for what inscrutable purpose, none can guess. Other Kindred despise the Followers of Set, and the clan claims no allies. Nonetheless, many vampires seek out the Setites, as the clan is whispered to possess arcane gifts and secrets from elder nights. Inevitably, sin and debasement follow in the Setites' wake, and many princes refuse to allow them in their cities. Some sinister purpose unites the Followers of Set, and they are one of the few clans rumored to have consistent contact with their founder. Many Kindred rightly fear these fork-tongued vampires, for their very presence is often enough to set a Kindred down the road to ruin.

Giovanni

Reviled almost as much as the Setites, the *Giovanni* is a clan of financiers and necromancers. Trafficking in the commodity of souls has given this clan a disproportionate amount of power, while trafficking in world finance has made the clan sickeningly rich. Other Kindred are loath to trust the mercenary Giovanni, who seem to be using their influence toward some unknown end. Part of Clan Giovanni's unhealthy reputation stems from the fact that it is a very insular clan, drawing almost all its members from its incestuous mortal family. Further damaging the Giovanni's reputation is the pervasive rumor that its members usurped their Kindred status from the vampire who originally Embraced them. Soon after becoming a vampire, the Giovanni clan leader destroyed his sire and the bloodline, reinventing the clan in his own image.

Ravnos

Descendents of the Gypsy Rom and their forebears in India, the *Ravnos* vampires lead nomadic unlives. Like the Gypsies of history, the Ravnos are spurned due to their reputations as thieves and vagrants. Many princes and Sabbat leaders persecute the Ravnos because of the chaos that follows these Kindred. The Ravnos return the scorn of their peers manyfold, holding Camarilla and Sabbat in equal contempt. The Ravnos are also known for their ability to create amazing illusions, the better with which to trick their marks. Recently the movements of the Ravnos have become even more erratic than usual; whispers have begun to circulate among the cities of Europe and Asia, speaking of Ravnos Methuselahs who have risen from torpor to direct their younglings' games.

Coteries

At heart, the vampire is a solitary creature. No longer able to see the light of day or interact with others save with the intent of sucking their blood, vampires often cloister themselves, stealing forth at night only to claim sustenance.

Nonetheless, loneliness takes its toll on the isolationist Kindred. This is particularly true of younger Kindred — neonates and fledglings — who also band together for protection from their own elders. As such, gatherings of Kindred, known as *coteries*, have been a staple of Kindred society for at least the past hundred years.

Elders deride the coteries, as they themselves exist in antiquated havens far from the deadly hands of mortals. Likening the groups to bands of lesser animals on the hunt or, more derogatorily, the brutal packs of Sabbat vampires, elder vampires fail to realize that younger, weaker vampires often have no option other than Final Death. A solitary neonate may eke out a wretched existence for a while, but sooner or later, without someone to watch his back, he will likely fall to one of the innumerable other predators of the city. In truth, many elders *fear* the neonates' coteries, though they would never admit it. Established vampires undermine the growing power of the coteries at every turn, frightened as they are by the versatility and modern savvy the groups possess.

Coteries are here to stay. Though unnatural, inconvenient, often inefficient and almost always tense, coteries provide the only recourse for vampires who wish more than subsistence from their unlives.

Purpose

The main reason vampires form coteries, other than the underlying need for security, is a common interest: blood ties, similar ideologies, gang affiliation, practical inclination or even simple convenience. Coteries are as wide and varied as the Kindred who compose them.

Clan Coteries

One of the most common types of coteries, the clan coterie is composed exclusively of members of one clan. Brujah broods are one of the best examples of this coterie, as vampires with the same sire often cling to each other long after their sire has grown bored and left them on their own. Young Ventrue sometimes form consortiums, pooling their resources to better usurp their elders' power bases. Cabals of Tremere are also known to pool resources; these cabals often maintain close connections with the clan as a whole, due to the structured nature of the Warlocks. Horrific nests of Nosferatu dwell under the streets of the cities, away from the judgmental eyes of Kindred and kine. Clutches of Malkavians, united under the charismatic leadership of one of their number, often resemble cults or Manson Family-esque assemblies of unhealthy minds. Even the independent and territorially catty Toreador sometimes band together to form salons or "art movements" composed of a few inspired Kindred. Family groupings of Giovanni vampires are sometimes classified as coteries, though these are usually led by clan elders or ancillae, as are Assamite assassin cells and Setite cults. Essentially, any group of Kindred with a common lineage may have reason to stick together, though this is less true among the rugged individualists of Clans Gangrel and Tzimisce.

Gang Coteries

Common among the streetwise and less well-to-do Kindred, gang coteries are true urban terrors. Composed of a group of vampires, their ghouls, and any hangers-on who somehow convince the vampires not to eat them, gang coteries are the scourge of the inner city. Their ranks include brutal vampires, commonly of the Brujah, Gangrel, Malkavian and Ravnos clans, with Caitiff sometimes thrown in for good measure. Gang coteries are violent and ruthless, though some defend the rights of drifters and the homeless (who usually end up as members of the gang or its herd). Gang coteries may be nomadic, like bike gangs or Gypsies, or static, like chapters of nationwide gangs or locals-only outfits. Gang coteries are often involved in local drug scenes and almost invariably spend as much time fighting other gangs and gang coteries over "distribution rights" as they do police.

Anarch Coteries

While the violent tactics, styles of dress and clan makeups of anarch coteries sometimes cause them to be mistaken for gang coteries, the fundamental ideologies differ. Anarch coteries oppose elders' scheming and stranglehold on power, arguing that every vampire should have a fair, equitable claim to domains and hunting rights. Anarch coteries typically comprise members of the Brujah, Gangrel, Malkavian and Nosferatu clans, but a few resentful Ventrue and disillusioned Tremere have joined the cause. If a Toreador is seen among anarch company, she's likely slumming or trying to annoy her sire. Anarchs tend to be younger Kindred, and these coteries are often short-lived, as the group accomplishes enough to gain a prince's notice and is then destroyed or disbanded by a city's elders and their minions. The anarchs have proved remarkably successful on the U.S. West Coast, though their power erodes nightly under an influx of Cathayans from the East.

Wartime Coteries

The Camarilla is efficient in its opposition of the Sabbat, and one of its best tactics is the establishment of wartime coteries. When a city becomes contested territory between the two sects, the Sabbat often sends waves of newly Embraced vampires against its opponents. The Camarilla, with its better organization and greater resources, has found that an effective manner of repelling these attacks is to create teams of neonates and ancillae, who gain the opportunity to impress their elders by turning the tide. These coteries are often composed of diverse members — Brujah and Gangrel warriors, Malkavians and Nosferatu scouts, Tremere magicians and Ventrue and Toreador diplomats. Although normally of finite duration, these coteries sometimes see bonds of camaraderie form among their members, who maintain relations following the repulsion of the Sabbat threat.

Diplomatic Coteries

Sometimes a prince needs a matter of policy enforced or a matter of urgency attended to, but lacks the resources to address it herself. In this case, she entreats the elders of her city to recommend Kindred to handle the task. After much boon-exchanging and promise-swearing (or the cancellation thereof),

the prince has a pool of vampires upon which to draw. These are often cosmopolitan coteries, assembled in much the same manner as wartime coteries, but often with less threat of physical violence. Diplomatic coteries often enjoy the endorsement of elders, the prince and the primogen, but this may work against them if offenders are predisposed against the current regime.

CRIMINAL COTERIES

Criminal coteries resemble Mafia families, Yakuza *gumi*, Seoulpa rings, drug cartels or Chinese tongs. Essentially collections of vampires who want to make money "outside the system," criminal coteries run rackets, extortion, numbers, prostitution, drug distribution (often with the aid of lesser criminal coteries or gang coteries), "distressed goods" liquidation, car-parts scams, large-scale theft, union strikes, gambling, bookmaking and protection operations. If it's illegal, they do it; vampires' power and influence allow criminal coteries to create a highly profitable mixture of blue-collar and white-collar crime. Criminal coteries frequently degenerate into hotbeds of distrust as various prospects atrophy or change in profitability. Clans involved with criminal coteries tend to be more refined Brujah, Toreador, Ventrue, Giovanni and the odd Caitiff, though one of the Gambino street gangs in New York is rumored to have a Nosferatu at the head.

ENTREPRENEURIAL COTERIES

Like criminal coteries, but legal.

INTELLIGENCE COTERIES

A prince cannot typically gather her own intelligence, but rather sends agents to do it for her. The prince or one of her ministers hand-picks a group of Kindred, then dispatches them to a different city, or sometimes to a faction within the same city, and awaits their report. Elder Kindred thrive on this sort of espionage, carefully moving their pawns and agents to inconvenience their rivals. Spies are dealt with harshly, and Kindred in such coteries are advised to tread lightly and make as many contacts as possible.

ENTERTAINMENT COTERIES

Some Kindred associate with each other in the interests of performing for others. Entire bands composed of vampires move through vampire society, touring across the country like mortal musicians and playing for prestigious princes and appreciative Toreador patrons. Likewise, dramatic troupes of vampire actors also band together to enact popular plays or even the works of Kindred playwrights. "Movements" of performance artists and other artisans come and go, challenging social issues or working for commissions. Obviously, Toreador vampires lend themselves well to this sort of coterie, but Brujah thrash bands, Malkavian actors and Nosferatu shock acts are not unheard of. Even certain Gangrel like the opportunity afforded by touring.

QUESTING COTERIES

The Jyhad stretches back through thousands of years, and many secrets have been hidden over the ages. Questing coteries are mystical archaeologists, determined to uncover not only

Kindred artifacts but the secrets of Kindred history as well. Questing coteries often form of their own volition, pursuing their concealed knowledge out of desire rather than edict. Some report directly to princes or patrons, while others operate independently. Questing coteries often have Tremere, Toreador and Ventrue members, though many Brujah are quick to join the cause, and more than one Follower of Set has been reluctantly admitted to a questing coterie. Questing coteries are typically nomadic, traveling wherever their search leads them.

SOCIAL COTERIES

Birds of a feather flock together, and this is particularly true with social coteries. United by ties of social prominence or simple common enthusiasms, social coteries are common in Camarilla cities and Sabbat cities alike. Some social coteries unite under gothic, club or other countercultures, sharing similar tastes in music and fashion. High-society coteries share common interests in influence, art, fashion and/or whatever else takes their whim, while Sabbat social coteries often pursue grotesque pastimes indeed. Mortal societies like the Fabians and the Algonquin Round Table are examples of kine social coteries, while the harpies are an excellent example of a Kindred social coterie. Members of any clan may join social coteries, as they are very rarely dependent upon skill or productivity, inclined as they are toward discourse and fraternity.

BLOOD CULTS

A recent resurgence triggered by the coming of Gehenna, blood cults are almost universally despised by princes and formally condemned as violations of the Masquerade. Blood cults are groups of Kindred who entice mortals to partake in "religious" rituals, then feed blood to or enslave the "worshippers." Combining the most heinous aspects of ghouldom and cult membership, blood cults prey upon desperate mortals who are searching for something to give their lives value. Obviously, these cults are breaches of the Masquerade, as the vampire openly reveals her supernatural (if not vampiric) nature to her coven, and risks exposing all of Kindred society to the wrath of outraged mortals.

DIABLERIST COTERIES

Diablerist coteries are another reaction against Gehenna's imminence. Many young Kindred, frustrated by the elders' unshakable grip on power, take the short, direct route to that power, and actually *hunt* the elders, killing them and drinking their essences. In addition to the thrill of patricide and the rush of mystical power, diablerie provides these coteries with a weapon against their foes — destruction. Although not every coterie exists for this purpose, packs of diablerists represent one of the reasons elders truly fear younger Kindred and the coteries they form. Most terrifying of all are the Assamite *falaqi*, or war cells, who stalk and bring down elders in the manner of wolves dragging down game.

SABBAT PACKS

Exclusive to the Sabbat, the *pack* is the basic social unit of the Black Hand. Composed of several Sabbat vampires, packs ensure their members' loyalty through a requirement that each vampire regularly drink a mixture of all the other members' blood. Thus mystically bound, Sabbat packs are among the tightest and most

CHARACTER COTERIES

Players should pay particular attention to their coterie's focus, and select a unifying cause that satisfies all of their characters' concepts. As undying creatures, Kindred don't just band together for the hell of it. Characters stuck in coteries toward which they have either apathy or antagonism don't work very well in the long term. During character creation, players should take the opportunity to make sure their characters have some reason to fraternize. **Vampire** is a game of horror, secrets and manipulation, and the mood is easily ruined by an overabundance of petty bickering.

Be responsible. Play a character who won't ruin the game for everyone else.

vicious groups of vampires in existence. Each pack is unique, with its own name, membership requirements, customs, style of dress and rites. Some packs have existed for centuries; these packs have "illustrious" (or depraved) histories, legends of departed members, and bitter rivalries with other packs.

This list of coteries is by no means exhaustive — vampires have any number of reasons to band together, though their cause should be enough to keep them unified despite their natures. Coteries are like the cliques of the undead, and very rarely fit a stereotype completely. After all, each vampire's reasons for joining a particular coterie are as unique as he is. As such, coteries are seldom unified fronts, more often being vehicles for individual vampires to advance their own agendas.

WITCH-HUNTERS AND OTHER MORTALS

Kindred prey on the kine; this is the way of things. As the elders are painfully aware, though, they may be preyed on as well. Vampires must step lightly and be ever mindful of the Masquerade; were the human race as a whole ever to turn its attention to the Kindred, the Children of Caine would be quickly wiped out. Superstition is the vampires' best weapon. By enforcing mortals' disbelief, by cultivating a smug belief in reason, by dismissing vampires' presence as the fancies of children and lunatics, the Kindred allow the mass of kine to do the work of shielding them from the few mortals who do know that vampires walk the night.

And there are, indeed, a few. Ignored or scoffed at by the bulk of their fellows, these mortals choose to delve into the Kindred's hidden world. Some do it out of curiosity, or for a forbidden thrill; others fear the Kindred and seek to exterminate them outright. The Children of Caine take no chances; their elders remember the Inquisition of old, when the race of vampires was nearly extinguished in a tide of fire and blood. Thus, all mortals "in the know" are commonly referred to as *witch-hunters*, the term Kindred gave to their pious tormentors.

The Inquisition itself still exists today, though no official Church records speak of it. The Inquisition of the modern world is known as the *Society of Leopold*. Many of its members are researchers and occultists, but some are fanatic vampire-hunters who, in true Torquemada-esque fashion, mercilessly root out and destroy the "spawn of Satan."

Most Inquisitors are fanatic but spottily educated and trained, seldom posing any real threat. What they know of the Kindred tends to come from old records and poorly translated manuscripts. This, of course, leads to mistakes in hunting, and it is unwise to make mistakes when dealing with vampires. Likewise, most Inquisitors are mere mortals, with none of the supernatural powers attributed to saints. Though such a hunter might hold up a crucifix and frantically wave it in a vampire's face, the holy symbol would be a mere object to be contemptuously swatted aside. A few Inquisitors, though, actually manifest sufficient Faith to repel or even wound the Damned with their holy auras.

On a secular level, the Kindred often move in the higher echelons of mortal power. Though they act furtively and cunningly, enough traces of their presence exist to arouse the suspicions of certain members of the world's intelligence agencies. In these nights of DNA testing and computer databases, the Masquerade is stretched thin indeed.

Other mortal groups find themselves on the periphery of the Damned's world. A mystic secret society known as the *Arcanum* seeks to uncover traces of the paranormal. Kindred tend to dismiss the Arcanum as a comic organization of garden-variety "ghostbusters" and dilettantes, but it occasionally — and increasingly — stumbles across events of interest. Additionally, various criminal organizations find themselves pawns in — or disrupters of — Kindred plots.

For more information on witch-hunters, see Chapter Nine.

THE OTHERS

The Kindred are not the only monsters to stalk the streets of the World of Darkness. Behind many a looming shadow lurks a pair of eyes belonging to something…else. The Kindred share the night with many other inhuman presences. When Kindred come into contact with these "others," the results are rarely pleasant, as the world's supernatural denizens have vied for supremacy for millennia. Many Kindred suspect that, not unlike themselves, these others have societies of their own. Unfortunately, few vampires have been able to get close enough to the others to tell, and even fewer have escaped to warn others.

The fabled *Book of Nod* speaks of the others, warning the Kindred that as the Final Nights approach, these creatures will rise up in preparation for the end of the world. Certainly, recent nights have seen Kindred come into more frequent — and often hostile — contact with these mysterious beings.

LUPINES

Outside the protective streets of the city, the land belongs to the *Lupines*, monsters who have been the dire enemies of the Kindred since time immemorial. Also known as werewolves, the Lupines seem to travel in packs, much as normal wolves do. Werewolves are universally feared by vampires as ruthless, efficient killers, and more than one vampire claims to have witnessed a single angered Lupine bring down an entire coterie of Kindred. Insular and xenophobic, the werewolves despise the Kindred; the precise reason behind this loathing is unknown, but a vampire caught by a werewolf is assuredly in dire peril. Wise Kindred know to keep to the cities, and that to leave their protection is to invite disaster in the form of a cloud of fur and fangs. On nights when the full moon is high and white, Kindred can hear the howls of the Lupines and smell their ferocity on the wind.

Recent years have seen a greater aggressiveness on the part of the Lupines. Formerly reluctant to leave their wilderness domains, werewolf packs have in the last few years begun pursuing Kindred into the cities, or even raiding the vampires' formerly impregnable domains outright. The vampires of Clan Gangrel, who know more of the Lupines' ways than any other Kindred, fear that a great war may be at hand, and that the first stroke of the Jyhad endgame will be made not by a vampire, but by a werewolf.

MAGES

Practicioners of arcane arts, the mages resemble humanity even more than Kindred do. In fact, the Tremere maintain that mages are humans themselves, though ones who know the secrets of ancient magic. Though not overtly hostile to vampires, mages seem to prefer solitude and will not hesitate to eliminate a bothersome Kindred. Few vampires know much about this group's powers, but strange events tend to happen in the presence of mages. It is rumored that mages may evoke truly fantastic effects, but they evidently maintain a practice similar to the Masquerade, one which likewise protects them from a fearful populace.

GHOSTS

It would seem that some spirits linger on after death, either to haunt the living or to resolve things they could not accomplish in life. As ghosts apparently exist on the "other side," very few vampires have any dealings with them, though Giovanni vampires are known to be able to converse with them. Some ghosts claim to be the souls of victims killed by vampires, and return to plague those vampires' nights with wailing and torment.

FAERIES

Few vampires know *anything* about the faeries, and it would seem that the "Good Folk" either fear vampires or otherwise avoid them as anathema. Whatever the reason, faeries are by turns attributed with fanciful, wondrous powers or the ability to inflict terrible curses. Those who have opinions on the matter maintain that the "wild ones" are not to be trifled with.

GHOULS

Kindred in need of powerful servitors often cultivate *ghouls*. Created by giving a mortal or animal a sip of vampiric vitae without first draining their blood, ghouls most commonly serve as minions of their vampiric masters, known as *domitors*. Although not so powerful as Kindred, ghouls may use the ingested vitae to become preternaturally strong and resilient.

Most ghouls are fanatically loyal to their masters, for ghouls are just as susceptible to the blood bond (p. 218) as Kindred are. As the ghoul requires the blood of her domitor to maintain her status, she often has cause to drink repeatedly from the same vampire.

Frightening rumors abound, however, of ghouls gone rogue, rebelling against their Kindred masters, killing them, and seeking out the precious vitae from other vampires. These marauding ghouls do not serve new masters; rather, they strike at unwary or weak Kindred and take the blood by force, often destroying the hapless vampire in the process. Many Kindred scoff at these rumors, but others know all too well the power of ghouls and keep their eyes on their own entourages.

THE CATHAYANS

The Children of Caine have spread throughout the world, but they find themselves thwarted in the Far East by the mysterious *Cathayans*, non-Kindred vampires native to the Orient. The Cathayans, or "Kindred" of the East, seem to have very little in common with their Western brethren. Rumors of demonic powers surround these Asian visitors, and their enigmatic behavior and foreign mindset leave many Western Kindred ill at ease. Making matters worse are the increasingly frequent reports of the "Hooded Mandarin," a formidable Cathayan vampire, and his presence at disastrous Kindred events.

ENIGMAS

As if these disturbing reports weren't enough, some Kindred claim to have dealt with even stranger creatures of the night. Meetings with demons, immortal mummies, zombielike walking dead, mystical spirits, shapeshifting animals, sentient gargoyles, angels and less definable entities have been claimed and sometimes documented. The only certainty to emerge from these statements, however, is that the World of Darkness is as terrifying as it is cosmopolitan.

GENERATIONS AND CAINITE MYTHOLOGY

According to the most widely accepted history of the Kindred, the race of vampires issued from the progenitor vampire, Caine. Banished into the land of Nod after killing his brother Abel, Caine was cursed by God and thereby became the first vampire. Thereafter, Caine sired three childer, who in turn sired their own childer, and on and on.

An oft-referenced collection of Kindred lore known as *The Book of Nod* contains numerous illustrations of the Kindred's creation myth. Unfortunately for those who wish to know it all, the book engenders more questions than it answers, and even forms the basis for one of the other theories of Kindred origin, the Lilith Cycle (which is decried and suppressed as heresy by the Camarilla).

In the end, there are no immediately forthcoming answers. Indeed, there may be no answer to the mystery at all.

CAINE

Reputedly the "father of all vampires," Caine is more myth than reality in the modern nights. Some of the Fourth Generation, as well as certain members of the Sabbat, claim to have met a being who referred to himself as Caine, but the story has filtered through so many individuals and layers of the Jyhad that no one can precisely tell where truth ends and fabrication begins.

ANCIENT LORE

The verbal history of the Kindred — though some insist that it is more legendry than history — occupies a position of great reverence in vampire society. The most popular and widely accepted myth is that of Caine, the First Vampire and slayer of his brother. An elusive text known as *The Book of Nod* chronicles Caine's exile and his subsequent journeys eastward. Much of what is "known" about Caine originates in various passages of *The Book of Nod*, though little exists to corroborate the book or its validity.

> In the beginning there was only Caine.
> Caine who sacrificed his brother out of love.
> Caine who was cast out.
> Caine who was cursed forever with immortality.
> Caine who was cursed with the lust for blood.
> It is Caine from whom we all come,
> Our sire's sire.
> For the passing of an age he lived in the land of Nod,
> In loneliness and suffering.
> For an eon he remained alone.
> But the passing of memory drowned his sorrow.
> And so he returned to the world of mortals,
> To the world of mortals,
> To the world his brother and his brother's children had created.

As Caine returned to the Children of Seth (the name that vampires came to call the kine), many believe that he went about the construction of a great city, in which vampires coexisted with mortals. Some Kindred historians speak of this period as an idyllic time of harmony, though more cynical Cainites say that the vampires inflicted themselves upon the Children of Seth like a plague. It is believed that the 13 clans came into existence at this time, as Caine's childer sired childer of their own. Breaks in the narrative suggest that there may have been more than 13 members of the Third Generation, or more than three members of the Second Generation. Cainite cults dedicated to the progenitor's myth claim that there may have been as many as 100 members of the Third Generation, but no evidence is forthcoming.

> Though he became ruler of a mighty nation, he was still alone,
> For none was as he. His sorrow grew once again.
> Then he committed another great sin, for he begat progeny,
> [Of whom there were only three.]†
> But from them came more progeny, Caine's grandchilder,
> And then Caine said, "An end to this crime. There shall be no more."
> And as Caine's word was the law, his brood obeyed him.
> The city stood for many ages,
> And became the center of a mighty empire.

The city's nights were numbered, the tales continue, and God sent the Great Flood to erase the wickedness Caine's childer brought to the world. Mortal Biblical accounts place this event as the one in which Noah built his ark to escape the fate humanity had brought upon itself. The vampires who survived became known as the Antediluvians, for they had received the Embrace before the Flood.

> But then came the Deluge, a Great Flood that washed over the world.
> The city was destroyed,
> And its people along with it.
> Again Caine fell into a great sorrow and went into solitude,
> Becoming as a dog amidst the wastes,
> And leaving his progeny to their own ends.
> They came to him and begged him to return,
> To help them rebuild the city.
> But he would not come with them,
> Saying the Flood had been sent as punishment
> For his having returned to the world of life
> And subverting the true law.

Without their father Caine, the vampires fell to petty bickering and warring among themselves. Murder and avarice became the rule for Kindred, and though they tried to re-create the glory of their First City, the resulting Second City was a den of intrigue, treachery, bloodlust and diablerie.

> So they returned alone to what mortals were left
> And announced that they were the new rulers.
> Each created a brood,
> In order to claim the glory of Caine,

Yet they did not have his wisdom or restraint.
A great war was waged, the elders against their children,
And the children slew their parents.

It was these kinslayer vampires who gave rise to what are commonly referred to as clans, siring the Fourth and lesser generations. Their lack of wisdom, however, prevented them from seeing that their childer would rise against them as they had against their sires. As this became obvious, the Ancients adopted the great game, their war of supremacy, the Jyhad, and went into hiding to direct their movements from secret havens.

Inevitably, this terrible war resulted in the collapse of the Second City, and the Kindred and the Children of Seth scattered to the ends of the Earth, where they could exist relatively free from the monstrous influence of the Antediluvians. This belief was folly, however, as the power and influence of the Third Generation know no bounds. Thus, the stories say that to this very night the Jyhad continues to rage, with all Kindred but pawns in the cannibalistic war of the elders.

The rebels then built a new city
And brought to it [13] tribes.††
It was a beautiful city and its people worshipped them as gods.
They created new progeny of their own,
The Fourth Generation of Cainites.
But they feared the Jyhad,
And it was forbidden for those childer
To create others of their kind.
This power the elders kept for themselves.
When a childe was created, it was hunted down and killed,
And its sire with it.
Although this city was as great as Caine's, eventually it grew old.
As do all living things, it slowly began to die.
The gods at first did not see the truth,
And when they last looked about them it was too late.
Their city was destroyed and their power extinguished,
And they were forced to flee, their progeny along with them.
But many were killed in the flight, for they had grown weak.
With their authority gone, all were free to create their own broods,
And soon there were many new Cainites,
Who ruled across the face of the Earth.
But this could not last.
Over time, there came to be too many of the Cainites,
And then there was war once again.
The elders were already deep in hiding,
For they had learned caution.
But their childer had founded their own cities and broods,
And it is they who were killed in the great wave of war.
There was war so total, that there are none of that generation
To speak of themselves any longer.
Waves of mortal flesh were sent across continents
In order to crush and burn the cities of the Cainites.
Mortals thought they were fighting their own wars,
But it is for us they spilt their blood.
Once this war was over,
All of the Cainites hid from one another
And from the humans who surrounded them.
In hiding we remain tonight,
For the Jyhad continues still.

† Several Kindred historians believe this line to have been mistranslated through the millennia between the First City and the modern nights. The notes of early vampire historians indicate this line has been interpreted as "Of whom there were as few as three" in some transcriptions of The Book of Nod.

†† Most Kindred accept this number as 13, seeing as how there are 13 clans known in existence, but at least one of the fragments of The Book of Nod alludes to "three by 10" instead of "three and 10" with reference to the Third Generation. This indicates, to some Kindred, that there once may have been as many as 30 distinct "clans," if indeed they have passed into extinction at all.

Skeptical Kindred have noted a lapse in the myth of Caine: If Caine's first childer are of the Second Generation, and thereby two steps removed from Caine, what, if anything, was the First Generation? Certainly, Caine himself is not "First Generation," as he can hardly be one step removed from himself. The question will likely go forever unresolved.

SECOND GENERATION

According to Kindred texts of unknown authenticity, Caine sired three childer. Created to ease Caine's sorrow, Caine's childer (some accounts agree on the names Zillah, Irad and Enosch, though the last is frequently referred to as Enki) carried out their unlives in the First City of Enoch.

Little is known of the Second Generation — presumably they sired the Third Generation, but nothing is known of them after their childer rose up against them in the nights of the First City. Likely, the Second Generation perished in the Great Flood or at the hands of their childer.

THIRD GENERATION

The Third Generation, vampires known as Antediluvians (for they predate the Great Flood), supposedly gave rise to what are called clans in the modern idiom. Recently, tales of active Antediluvians have become rampant, and new accounts of their movements, while dubious, arise nightly. Although the Camarilla scoffs at the notion of surviving Antediluvians, four Antediluvians have been observed with varying degrees of credibility. Lucian and Mekhet, obviously pseudonyms for clan founders wishing to remain anonymous, are the only widely known names of active Third Generation vampires. Clan Giovanni and its founder reportedly confer regularly, while an inhuman creature some say is the founder of the Tremere has been seen recently in Mexico City. Certain Antediluvians are said to have been destroyed, but none can corroborate these statements.

The Antediluvians are the true players of the Jyhad, an ancient and terrible game predicated upon the thwarting of the other members of the Third Generation. The turns of the Jyhad are inscrutable, but the Antediluvians have pawns in every corner of the Earth, carrying out the directives of their sleeping masters. The rules are as unknowable as the players themselves are, and everything from outright war to centuries-long games of espionage seems to be de rigueur.

Whether or not the game has always been one of movement and counterattack is likewise unknown — are these the rules, or has the Jyhad degenerated into petty hamstringing? Some vampires, noting the origin of the word Jyhad, also wonder if there are other factors at play. It is possible that some of the Kindred involved in the Jyhad have attained the fabled peace of Golconda, and may be trying to aid — or hinder — others in attaining that state of transcendence. Certainly, they are counteracted as well by foes who do not wish this to come to pass.

Antediluvians are almost divine in their scope of ability, and possess powers unimaginable by those not of their caliber. Jyhad scholars have hypothesized that the Third Generation are the last vampires to have true mastery over life and death, and may be destroyed only if they so choose or if one of equal power bests them. These same Kindred wonder if perhaps the Jyhad is a contest, with the last Antediluvian left without suffering the Final Death named as winner.

FOURTH AND FIFTH GENERATIONS

These powerful vampires are known as Methuselahs. They are millennia old, exceedingly rare, and almost as powerful as the Third Generation. Few of these generations remain active participants in the Jyhad, as their potent blood is craved by Kindred younger than they. Many Methuselahs take refuge in hidden torpor, where they may avoid attempts at diablerie by lesser Kindred and control their own forces in the Jyhad. In recent years, a number of powerful Methuselahs are whispered to have risen in far corners of the Earth, and the most influential members of the Camarilla's Inner Circle and the Sabbat's regent and prisci are rumored to be Methuselahs.

SIXTH, SEVENTH AND EIGHTH GENERATIONS

Most of the powerful, *visible* masters of the Jyhad are members of generations six through eight. Kindred of these ages have concentrated areas of influence and wield significant quantities of power (enough to make them prime pawns in the Jyhad, though these vampires find it inconceivable that they themselves may be manipulated). Princes, powerful primogen and justicars tend to hail from these generations, though it should be noted that European holders of these titles tend to be of lower generation and greater power than their American counterparts.

Members of these generations are commonly referred to as elders. The Eighth Generation is certainly the lowest generation at which one may be considered an elder, though this seems largely arbitrary. Most members of the Eighth Generation and below were sired long before the modern nights, and are thus accustomed to power and high station.

NINTH AND TENTH GENERATIONS

Kindred of the ninth and tenth generations play a dangerous game. Often too old and experienced to be associated with the lesser neonates and ancillae, but too raw and weak to hold their own among the elders, the Ninth and Tenth Generations find themselves left to their own devices. They do not require the governance that the wilder, younger Kindred do, and so they meet the night on their own terms. Much like mortal adolescents, the Ninth and Tenth Generations are getting a taste for the power and influence they may soon come to possess.

11TH, 12TH AND 13TH GENERATIONS

Neonates and young ancillae, members of these generations are relatively new to the curse of vampirism. Although they are powerful creatures in and of themselves, at least compared to the mortals upon whom they prey, their newfound powers are nothing compared to Kindred hundreds of years their elders. Most **Vampire** players' characters will be of these generations.

14TH AND 15TH GENERATIONS

A woeful modern development, these thin-blooded Kindred have appeared in recent years. The blood of Caine is so weak in them that some are rumored to be able to bear the light of the sun and partake of mortal food. Many Kindred scholars look upon the influx of these vampires with fear, remembering passages in The Book of Nod that make reference to the "Time of Thin Blood." This time is said to presage the coming of Gehenna.

THE MODERN NIGHTS

Much has come to pass recently in the World of Darkness, and many Kindred are convinced that the Final Nights have arrived. Numerous events portend the movement of the Antediluvians; the world has undergone significant changes, as have the Kindred themselves.

Varying accounts of Antediluvians, most unreliably accredited, have become common, and it would seem that as the world spirals toward its presumed destruction, some subtlety has been lost in the Jyhad. Whether these sighting are actual or not, they reveal an unsettling paranoia and a sense of urgency previously unknown. Stories of encounters with a being who claims to be Caine are also circulating like never before. Whereas it was once fashionable to mock such preposterous conversation, many Kindred wonder if there may be some legitimacy to the matter.

The Sabbat has recently increased its activity, actively vying for power in Chicago, Atlanta, Washington, DC, and other elder-controlled cities. Animalistic and monstrous, the sect has swarmed like locusts over the East Coast and southern borders of the United States. Its influence in Canada has also increased, and it appears as if the Sabbat is realizing a grand enfilade, surrounding the United States and cutting off all access except that which it grants. Many Kindred *en route* to Europe from the United States or *vice versa* have been destroyed or disappeared altogether as the Sabbat exerts its influence where it can: at the borders.

It would seem that the West Coast is relatively free of Sabbat presence, but this is true only because an influx of Cathayans from Asia has taken root. The anarch holdings of California have become battlegrounds, and the proud anarchs have even begged the Camarilla's Inner Circle for aid in turning back the Asian peril. The Kindred of the East have made significant advances into the United States from the West Coast, and their presence may soon shift the balance of power among the Children of Caine.

The Camarilla as a whole seems less and less dominant, its influence eroding by the night. Years ago, it seemed as if the sect virtually owned North America. As millennial hysteria rises, more and more slips through the ever-tightening grip of the sect, leaving its members consistently losing ground. Indeed, one of its greatest members, the mighty justicar known as Petrodon, was struck down and destroyed in Chicago by parties unknown.

The Sabbat has suffered its own losses, however, and may hardly be said to have the upper hand. Recently, all the Tremere of the Sabbat were destroyed in a great conflagration in Mexico City. Add to this the fact that the Sabbat Malkavians have communicated their terrible madness to their Camarilla and anarch brethren, and the Sabbat no longer has the edge it once did. Both sides suffer from incursions of independent Kindred, particularly the Assamites, who pursue their murderous ways anew. Even the formerly carefree Ravnos have begun to act with greater purpose and malevolence, and some elders wonder if, in dismissing the Deceivers, they have ignored fangs long poised at their throats.

Thus, the World of Darkness decays and crumbles more each night. With less and less to be sure of, and many more ominous portents becoming plainly visible, many Kindred wonder what the immediate future holds, and it seems that immortality may not mean much if the end of the world is nigh.

GEHENNA

Central to Kindred myth is the idea of Gehenna. The Kindred believe that this approaching apocalypse bears down ever more each night upon the world. When Gehenna arrives, the Antediluvians shall arise and make a wasteland of the world, consuming Kindred and mortal alike in the culmination of their horrendous Jyhad.

Although few Camarilla Kindred would admit it, many vampires see the world on a downward plummet and believe that Gehenna will occur soon — perhaps even within the next few years. Frantically piecing together the signs from whatever Cainite histories and mythological fragments they can compile, the Kindred seek to learn the true nature of Gehenna, and possibly avert it. Elder vampires know, however, of the implacable wills of the Antediluvians. Should they so will it, Gehenna shall come and overwhelm the world, destroying every mortal and vampire in a tide of blood and fire.

PROPHECIES OF DOOM

"The Chronicle of Secrets," a revelatory section of *The Book of Nod*, speaks of the imminent Gehenna. The revelations are cryptic and couched in mysticism, but many Kindred believe that the world of tonight reflects the signs portended in the Chronicle. Indeed, a few Kindred believe that Gehenna has already begun.

> And the world will turn cold
> and unclean things will boil up from the ground
> and great storms will roll, lightning will light
> fires, animals will fester and their bodies,
> twisted, will fall.
> So, too, our Grandsires will rise
> from the ground
> They will break their fast on the
> first part of us
> They will consume us whole…
> And you will know these last times by the
> Time of Thin Blood, which will mark vampires
> that cannot Beget,
> you will know them by the Clanless,
> who will come to rule
> you will know them by the Wild Ones,
> who will hunt us even in the strongest city
> you will know them by the awakening
> of some of the eldest…
> and those who eat heart's blood will flourish
> and the Kindred will crowd each to his own,
> and vitae will be as rare as diamonds…
> Shine black the sun!
> Shine blood the moon!
> Gehenna is coming soon.

Even so, the Kindred attempt to foil or aid the Jyhad as they see their roles coming to critical culmination. The millennial tension that plagues the planet is certainly a precursor to the coming apocalypse, and the Final Nights are upon us. Unless….

LEXICON

The Kindred have their own dialect of specialized words and phrases. Vampires have a tremendous capacity for double-talk; what they say often means something other than its literal interpretation, or something in addition to its simple meaning. Certain words have evolved new connotations among the Damned, while others are unique to vampires and their society. The Kindred, set in their ways as they are, are loath to adopt new manners of speech or slang, and one can often determine a rough estimation of a vampire's age by listening to the individual words she chooses.

COMMON PARLANCE

These words are in common use among all echelons of Kindred society.

Anarch: A Kindred rebel who opposes the tyranny of elders. Anarchs wish to redistribute the wealth and resources of a city equitably among the vampires therein. Naturally, the elders oppose this, having cultivated their influence for centuries.

Barrens, The: The areas of a city unfit for life, including graveyards, abandoned buildings, industrial wastelands and areas of irreversible urban blight.

Becoming, The: The moment one passes from being a fledgling into "full" vampire status. One may not Become until her sire deems her ready and gains the prince's approval.

Book of Nod, The: A loose collection of Kindred legendry and history. *The Book of Nod* chronicles the origin of the Kindred, though it has never been published in its entirety. Fragments of the document and its many partial transcriptions circulate among certain strata of Kindred society.

Beast, The: The inchoate drives and urges that threaten to turn a vampire into a mindless, ravening monster.

Blood: A vampire's heritage; that which makes a vampire a vampire. Usage: *I doubt her claims to such esteemed Blood.*

Blood Bond: A mystical power over another individual engendered by partaking of a particular vampire's blood thrice; accepting blood from a vampire is an acknowledgment of her mastery.

Caitiff: A vampire of unknown clan, or of no clan at all. Caitiff are typically of high generation, where Caine's blood dilutes too greatly to pass any consistent characteristics.

Camarilla, The: A sect of vampires devoted primarily to maintaining the Traditions, particularly that of the Masquerade.

Childe: A vampire created through the Embrace — the childe is the progeny of her sire. This term is often used derogatorily, indicating inexperience. Plural *childer*.

Clan: A group of vampires who share common characteristics passed on by the Blood. There are 13 known clans, all of which were reputedly founded by members of the Third Generation.

Coterie: A small group or "pack" of Kindred, united by the need for support and sometimes common interests.

Diablerie: The consumption of another Kindred's blood, to the point of the victim's Final Death. Vampires of high generation may lower their generation through this practice; particularly old Kindred have such rarefied tastes that mortal blood no longer sustains them, and they *must* consume vampire blood.

Domain: An area of a particular vampire's influence. Princes claim entire cities as their domains, sometimes allowing lesser vampires to claim domain within.

Elder: A vampire who has experienced three or more centuries of unlife. Elders are the most active participants in the Jyhad.

Elysium: A place where vampires may gather and discourse without fear of harm. Elysium is commonly established in opera houses, theaters, museums and other locations of culture.

Embrace, The: The act of transforming a mortal into a vampire. The Embrace requires the vampire to drain her victim and then replace that victim's blood with a bit of her own.

Fledgling: A newly created vampire, still under her sire's protection.

Generation: The number of "steps" between a vampire and the mythical Caine; how far descended from the First Vampire a given vampire is.

Gehenna: The imminent Armageddon when the Antediluvians will rise from their torpor and devour the race of Kindred and the world.

Ghoul: A minion created by giving a bit of vampiric vitae to a mortal without draining her of blood first (which would create a vampire instead).

Haven: A vampire's "home"; where she finds sanctuary from the sun.

Hunger, The: The urge to feed, as with any living creature. For vampires, however, the Hunger replaces all other drives with its own powerful call.

Inconnu: A sect of vampires who have removed themselves from Kindred concerns and, largely, the Jyhad. Many Methuselahs are rumored to exist among the Inconnu.

Jyhad, The: The secret, self-destructive war waged between the generations. Elder vampires manipulate their lessers, using them as pawns in a terrible game whose rules defy comprehension.

Kindred: The race of vampires as a whole, or a single vampire. According to rumor, this term came about in the 15th or 16th century, after the Great Anarch Revolt. Sabbat vampires scorn the term.

Kiss, The: To drink blood, especially from a mortal. The Kiss causes feelings of ecstasy in those who receive it.

Lupine: A werewolf, the natural and mortal enemy of the vampire race.

Lush: A vampire who typically feeds from drugged or drunk mortals in order to experience their inebriation.

Life, The: A euphemism for mortal blood. Many Kindred regard this term as affected and effete.

Man, The: The mote of humanity that a vampire maintains; the spark of mortality that distinguishes him from the Beast.

Masquerade, The: The habit (or Tradition) of hiding the existence of vampires from humanity. Designed to protect the Kindred from destruction at the hands of mankind, the Masquerade was adopted after the Inquisition claimed many Kindred unlives.

Prince: A vampire who has claimed a given expanse of domain as her own, particularly a city, and supports that claim against all others. The term can refer to a Kindred of either sex.

Rogue: A vampire who feeds upon the vitae of other Kindred, out of necessity or depravity.

Sabbat, The: A sect of vampires that rejects humanity, embracing their monstrous natures. The Sabbat is bestial and violent, preferring to lord over mortals rather than hide from them.

Sect: A group of Kindred arguably united under a common philosophy. The three most widely known sects currently populating the night are the Camarilla, the Inconnu and the Sabbat.

Sire: A vampire's "parent"; the Kindred who created her.

Vessel: A source of vitae for sustenance or pleasure, primarily mortal.

OLD FORM

The elders typically use these turns of phrase, which have existed since long before the modern nights. One is advised to use these words carefully — in some company, their use may be seen as humorously anachronistic, while in the company of anarchs, for example, they may be misconstrued as the elders' propaganda.

Amaranth: The act of consuming another Kindred's blood (q.v. *Diablerie*).

Ancilla: A "proven" vampire, between the elders and the neonates.

Antediluvian: A member of the dreaded Third Generation, one of the eldest Kindred in existence.

Archon: A vampire in the retinue of a justicar. Archons are generally nomadic in nature, frequently pursuing Kindred who have fled to avoid persecution at the hands of the Camarilla.

Autarkis: A Kindred who remains outside the larger vampire society of a given city and often refuses to acknowledge the claim of a prince.

Blood Oath: The blood bond (*vide*).

Cainite: A vampire; a member of the race of Caine.

Canaille: The bovine masses of humanity, especially the uncultured and unsavory. The Canaille are viewed primarily as a source of sustenance.

Cauchemar: A vampire who feeds exclusively on sleeping victims.

Consanguineous: Literally, "of the same blood," especially with reference to lineage. Usage: *That vampire is consanguineous of Hardestadt the Elder, his childe.*

Cunctator: A vampire who avoids killing when delivering the Kiss; one who takes so little blood as to avoid bringing about her prey's death.

Domitor: A ghoul's master; one who feeds her blood and issues her commands.

Footpad: One who feeds from derelicts and other chaff of society. Footpads are frequently debased and may not maintain permanent havens.

Gentry: A Kindred who preys at nightclubs, bars and other establishments of the "red-light district," where mortals engage in reverie.

Golconda: A fabled state of vampiric transcendence; the true mastery of the Beast and balance of opposing urges and principles. Rumored to be similar to mortal Nirvana, Golconda is greatly touted but rarely achieved.

Humanitas: The extent to which a Kindred still maintains her humanity.

Kine: A term for mortals, largely contemptuous. The phrase *Kindred and kine* refers to the world at large; everything.

Leech: A human who drinks vampire blood, yet acknowledges no master.

Lextalionis: The code of the Kindred and the system for punishing transgression. It suggests Hammurabian or Biblical justice — an eye for an eye, and punishment in keeping with the grievance.

Lineage: A vampire's bloodline; the Kindred's sire, sire's sire, etc.

Methuselah: A vampire who has existed for a millennium or more; an elder who no longer exists among the greater whole of Kindred society. Methuselahs are rumored to hail from the Fourth and Fifth Generations.

Neonate: A young Kindred, recently Embraced.

Osiris: A vampire who builds a mortal cult around himself, in the interests of gaining sustenance. As the millennium approaches and passes, Osiris cults become increasingly common.

Papillon: The red-light district; the area of town punctuated by drinking establishments, brothels, gambling houses and other locales of ill repute. The prime hunting grounds of a city, where the disappearance of mortals goes hand in hand with the area's general seediness.

Progeny: All of a given vampire's childer, collectively. Less formal, and less flattering, is *Get*.

Praxis: The right of princes to govern; the prince's claim to domain. This term also refers to the prince's matters of policy and individual edicts and motions.

Primogen: The leaders in a given city; its ruling body of elders, typically composed of one member from each clan present in a city.

Regnant: A Kindred who holds a blood bond over another.

Retainer: A human who serves a vampiric master. This term is almost archaic, referring to a time when vampires kept vast entourages of mortal servants as part of their estates.

Siren: A vampire who seduces mortals in order to drink from them, and then only takes a small quantity of blood, so as to avoid killing them.

Suspire: The rumored epiphany experienced just prior to the attainment of Golconda.

Third Mortal: Caine, who was cast out and became the First Vampire.

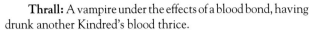

Thrall: A vampire under the effects of a blood bond, having drunk another Kindred's blood thrice.

Vitae: Blood.

Whelp: A derogatory term for a young Kindred, originally used with exclusive reference to one's own progeny.

Wight: Human; man; a mortal.

Witch-hunter: A mortal who searches out and destroys vampires.

Whig: A contemptuous term for a vampire who possesses an interest in mortal trends and fashions.

Vulgar Argot

These terms are slang, the modern equivalents of older turns of phrase which have fallen out of favor due to their association with the elder ranks. These words carry great connotation, as they are associated with the younger Kindred, who seek to establish their own vampiric cultures.

Alleycat: A vampire who keeps no permanent haven, but sleeps in a different location each night. This term also refers to a Kindred who feeds exclusively from the homeless, vagrants and other elements of low society.

Banking: The practice of "withdrawing" blood from blood banks and hospital reserves. This blood has little taste, though it will sustain a vampire, and elder Kindred eschew this base indulgence. A Kindred who engages in this practice is known as a *Banker*.

Black Hand: Another name for the sect known as the Sabbat.

Blister: A vampire "Typhoid Mary" who contracts a mortal disease and spreads it to each vessel upon whom he feeds.

Bloodline: A vampire's heritage (q.v. *Lineage*).

Blood Doll: A mortal who freely gives her blood to a vampire. Most blood dolls gain a perverse satisfaction from the Kiss, and actively seek out vampires who will take their vitae.

Butterfly: One who mingles among the mortal high-society element and feeds exclusively from the famous and wealthy.

Casanova: A vampire who seduces mortals to take their blood, but does not kill them. Casanovas typically erase the memory of their presence from their vessels' minds (q.v. *Cauchemar*).

Change, The: The moment an individual ceases to be a mortal and becomes one of the Kindred.

Damned, The: The race of Kindred; all vampires.

Donor: A sarcastic term for a vessel, typically human.

Farmer: A term of mockery for vampires who refuse to feed on human blood, instead taking sustenance from animals.

Fief: A sarcastic term for a vampire's domain or claim thereof, most commonly used in reference to a prince.

Head: A Kindred who feeds upon those who have imbibed alcohol or drugs, so as to vicariously experience the same sensations. Those Kindred who prefer individual drugs have their "poison" prefixed to the term head (e.g., crackhead, dopehead, smackhead).

Headhunter: A vampire who hunts and feeds from other Kindred (q.v. *Rogue*).

Juicebag: A contemptuous term for mortals, indicating that their sole use is for sustenance. Even more irreverent is the term *Bag*.

Lick: A vampire; one of the race of Kindred.

Rack, The: The hunting ground of choice, including bars, nightclubs, drug dens, whorehouses and other bacchanalian locales, where mortals go missing all the time (q.v. *Papillon*).

Rake: A habitual visitor to the Rack, especially in the interests of feeding (q.v. *Gentry*).

Sandman: A vampire who feeds upon sleeping victims only.

Slumming: The practice of feeding from derelicts, the homeless and other dregs of society; one who does this regularly is known as a *Slummer*.

Stalker: A mortal who hunts down and destroys Kindred (q.v. *Witch-hunter*).

Tease: A term for a female Casanova (*vide*).

Turf: A modern affectation used in reference to a domain; it may also refer to the area under a given gang's influence.

Vegetary: A term of contempt for one who drinks exclusively from animals (q.v. *Farmer*).

Lucita:

Well, the trail is hot again. Anatole went out-of-body again — in some ways it was a relief, because he swears he has to fast for a week before trying it, and that means fewer bodies to dispose of — and this time he claims he's got a lead.

Supposedly — and I'm just transcribing what Anatole said when he came out of it and finished eating, so don't kill the messenger, sweetheart — he's found where the Setites have set up shop. There's a warehouse down along Manayunk that's serving as a temple. He claims to have seen at least three Snakes, including one with a quote-unquote "angelic aura," and about eight ghouls. Most of the ghouls seem to have been created in accordance with the usual Setite philosophy of giving vitae to dumb muscle for protection. They're loaded for bear but hooked on the blood, not the Serpents' philosophy.

Oh, and Anatole also claims that the temple's centerpiece is a severed head on a stick that speaks in tongues and gives prophecies.

Stop laughing, woman, it's better than anything you or I have come up with in the past year. Besides, that description might match one of the Noddite artifacts I've been chasing after for a few hundred years — an item called a vathi.

In any case, I think this is worth checking out. I'm going to give Anatole a couple of nights to rest up and eat properly, then we're going to case the warehouse. You can meet us in Camden on Thursday at the usual place — entry routes are safer across the river.

Until then, watch out for Daddy.

Beckett

Chapter Two:
Clans and Sects

In the first nights, so sires tell their childer, the 13 grandchilder of Caine who survived the strife of the First City begot progeny in their own images, passing on their mystic arts and magical curses. Thus were founded the 13 great clans of Kindred that haunt the world to this very night.

Century followed century, and each clan developed its own history, traditions and lore. As the Jyhad raged and the Antediluvians retreated into the wastelands, the childer of the clans assumed lordship of the night for themselves.

Certainly, all has not been peaceful through the ages. The clans of the Sabbat are whispered to have slain their founders in vile acts of patricide. Over the course of history, some clans, such as the Giovanni, have undergone considerable internecine turmoil, and one clan — the reclusive Salubri — was destroyed outright, its mystic gifts usurped by upstart mortals.

This chapter presents the 13 clans, each claiming descent from a mythical Antediluvian, that comprise the majority the Children of Caine. Because the clans align themselves by sect, we group the clans under the descriptions of the sects to which they adhere. First is covered the Camarilla, keeper of tradition, along with those clans (Brujah, Gangrel, Malkavian, Nosferatu, Toreador, Tremere, Ventrue) who pay it real or fatuous homage. Next is presented the Camarilla's archenemy, the monstrous Sabbat, along with its Lasombra and Tzimisce founders. Finally the four independent clans — Assamite, Followers of Set, Giovanni and Ravnos — stand revealed.

Players may select their characters' clans from one of these 13 templates, or may choose to be Clanless (Caitiff). Each clan has certain distinguishing powers and weaknesses, which a member of that clan automatically adopts.

Bloodlines

Lineage is very important to the Damned. Vampires descended from particularly illustrious sires often display peculiar characteristics, and a few vampires have deviated from their clan in noteworthy fashion. Most such things can be simulated through simple roleplaying, or through Merits and Flaws (p. 295); for example, while the childer of the mighty Hardestadt might all display the same feeding restriction or obsessively focus on control, they do not differ significantly from Ventrue as a whole. In a few cases, bloodlines actually manifest different Disciplines or weaknesses; these are noted in the "Bloodlines" entry under each clan.

THE CAMARILLA

The Camarilla came about in an attempt to hold vampire society together against the power of the Inquisition in the 15th century. Under its iron guidance, the Tradition of the Masquerade grew from a cautious suggestion to the guiding principle of Kindred unlife. Even today, the Camarilla concerns itself with the enforcement of the Masquerade, maintaining harmony between Kindred and kine, and battling the Sabbat, which it views as its direct opponent.

The Camarilla touts itself as *the* society of the Kindred, and it is partially correct. It is the largest sect of undead on the planet. Almost any vampire, regardless of lineage, may claim membership in the Camarilla. In truth, the Camarilla asserts that all vampires are already under its aegis, regardless of the wishes of the vampires in question.

Over the years, the sect has attempted to extend its influence over other areas of vampire life, and each time has had its hands roundly slapped for its insolence. Princes brook no interference in the affairs of their cities, while the ancient Methuselahs scoff at the temerity of the younglings who think they can play at Jyhad. In the end, the Camarilla's influence begins and ends with protecting the Masquerade and ensuring Kindred-kine coexistence.

The Camarilla claims to allow membership to any interested vampires, regardless of bloodline, but the vast majority represent the seven founding clans. It was their members who founded the sect, and only these clans regularly make up the Camarilla's governing Inner Circle. Other vampires of different bloodlines may attend conclaves and meetings, but their voices frequently go unheard.

After the Anarch Revolt, the Camarilla placed itself squarely against the Sabbat, seeing itself as the only means to hold the war packs at bay. The Camarilla alone upheld the Masquerade and protected its own, while the Sabbat would as soon throw away the Traditions and everything sacred to sustain its paranoid dreams of Gehenna. Dissent is a luxury that cannot be afforded during times of war, and the Camarilla believes quite firmly that those who are not with the sect must be against it. However, for the frightened elders who make up the higher echelons, the Camarilla has quite a few enemies.

In these modern nights, the Camarilla is hardly the monolith that its proponents advertise it to be. Elders cling to their positions, refusing to relinquish them to those who have reached the age of consideration. Younger vampires feel left out of an organization they are expected to uphold, but which offers little to no reward for their efforts save the threat of punishment if they fail. Ancillae are trapped in the middle, unable to turn to either the younger or older vampires; taking up with the neonates means relegation to the lower strata of power, while attempting to fall in with the elders risks the appearance of overstepping boundaries and being crushed for insolence.

Many elders in the Camarilla's upper echelons find themselves in the position of relics. A good many are unwilling or unable to pick up the new technology that the young ones have mastered — cellular phones, laptop computers, Kevlar, phosphorus grenades, sun lamps, Dragonsbreath rounds — and in the modern world, being barely able to use a telephone or radio leaves these elders at a distinct disadvantage. Should they relinquish their positions and find themselves outside the halls of power, they become targets as their personal might lessens without the Camarilla behind it. A few gangs of ancillae with diablerie on their minds and the latest technology in their hands, and an elder might well find himself becoming obsolete in more ways than one. Therefore, in preemptive strikes of paranoia run rampant, the elders kill the best and brightest who could some night pose a threat. The result is an organization that is cannibalizing itself, and one night it might regret the mistake.

THE JUSTICARS

These seven mighty vampires are the judges appointed by the Inner Circle to be the Camarilla's eyes, hands and, if necessary, fists. Justicars have the only true authority across the Camarilla and all Kindred, with the exception of the Inner Circle. They alone have the ultimate power to adjudicate matters regarding the Traditions. No one is considered to be above them in this. It is justicars who decide the punishment for those who have violated the Traditions on a widespread level; the one being judged may not expect mercy. Justicars are supposed to call for a conclave when they wish to pass judgment, but over the years this lapsed as they grew in power. Justicars have the authority to call a conclave at any time, either to

---

THE VIEW FROM WITHOUT

The Sabbat

Camarilla? The relic of frightened elders who prey upon their childer and cling to dreams of glory that are long gone.

— Polonia, Archbishop of New York

The Independents

Their overwhelming ideal of "for the good of Kindred" leads them to sweep you along with their plans, and if you don't want to go, then you must be the enemy. There's a reason why we prefer to stay on our own side of the street.

— Ambrogino Giovanni

---

confirm a ruling or to make certain decisions that one justicar alone does not wish to burden himself with.

A justicar serves for 13 years, and her actions may be challenged only by another justicar. If things grow heated, a conclave may be called by the combatants or by another justicar to resolve the dispute. When rival justicars decide to start battling it out, few Kindred are safe from being used and abused in the ensuing struggle.

Many vampires, elders and younglings alike, resent the power the justicars wield, and certainly none care for the abuses that can come with it. However, very few would dream of openly taking them on, due to their immense age and resources. A shocking exception occurred in 1997, as the mighty Nosferatu justicar Petrodon was murdered by parties unknown. What movement of the Jyhad lay behind this assassination, or whether it is a precursor of further strikes against the justicars, is unknown.

The Archons

Each justicar selects a number of minions, known as archons, to act in his name as suits his purposes. If the justicars are the hands of the Inner Circle, then the archons are the fingers on those hands. No justicar can be everywhere he might need, or wish, to be, and archons can often make certain his presence is felt if not seen. Archons, although they are part of the Camarilla hierarchy of power, are not so far removed from typical Kindred unlife that they cannot observe it or gain the trust of other Kindred outside the hierarchy; this makes them ideal watchers. Some Kindred attempt to gain favorable attention from an archon, in the hope that she will mention them to her master. Such attempts often backfire, as continued efforts to curry favor are more likely to encourage suspicion.

Archons are typically chosen from the upper ranks of ancillae and occasionally elders of lesser station. Such a prestigious appointment can make or break a Kindred's career in the halls of power. Justicars occasionally choose archons to carry out specific missions, and sometimes prefer political savvy, insight and skill over recognizability.

An archon's position typically lasts for as long as a justicar wishes to retain her, or the length of the justicar's tenure. It is not unheard of for a new justicar to retain an archon who served with his predecessor, provided the archon understands to whom she now owes allegiance. Most times, though, a justicar prefers to select an entirely new staff, particularly if the last one left under strange or bitter circumstances.

Conclaves

Conclaves are the greatest events in Camarilla politics — at least the greatest events to which every vampire can be privy. One American Kindred described conclave to his childe as "a House Committee session, the Supreme Court and a tent revival all rolled up into one." A conclave serves as the highest court of Camarilla Kindred, a legislative session for considering and deciding future Camarilla policy, and a reaffirmation of the Camarilla as the guiding principle behind the Masquerade and Kindred-kine relations.

Any and all Kindred who hear the call to conclave are welcome to attend. These events can last anywhere from a few hours to several weeks. A city hosting a conclave may never be aware of what is occurring, except that many hotels are suddenly booked up. Naturally, conclaves are perilous undertakings; so many vampires (many of them potent-blooded elders) in a single location presents a tempting target for Sabbat or diablerists. Many attendees might not know where the conclave will be held until a few nights before the event itself.

Only justicars may call conclaves, and only when needed, due to logistical concerns. The conclave is usually held in the geographic region most concerned with the issue at hand, or more centrally if the problem is widespread. The vampires who attend the conclave are referred to as the assembly, and any may speak, provided they are supported by at least two other members. Each member of the assembly receives a single vote regarding the issue.

Conclaves are typically called with regard to powerful individuals, such as princes, or serious breaches of the Traditions. Any Kindred may bring a grievance to the conclave and expect to have it addressed. A prince may request more leeway regarding the Traditions to deal with Sabbat or anarchs, or to have a destructive quarrel between two powerful elders mediated. The conclave may call blood hunts against individuals, including princes, or have particularly powerful princes removed from office. The right to depose princes is one the Camarilla keeps a tight leash on, and while a justicar may not remove a prince, she may call a conclave for the sole purpose of forcing a prince's abdication.

Any actions that would result in a serious breach of the Traditions must be discussed and agreed upon by the conclave to avoid punishment in the future. The conclave interprets the Six Traditions and may add amendments or enact precedents. Many princes have come to demand that certain powers, which could be breaches of Tradition, be given them in dealing with unruly Kindred.

A Kindred on trial at a conclave may challenge the ruling by requesting an ordeal. These ordeals can be quite literally almost any exacting task or quest, with a time limit for completion. If the ordeal is not completed to satisfaction, the justicar may impose any penalty. Should the crime be considered too heinous to allow the accused an ordeal, she may be challenged to ritual combat by one of her accusers. As with the ordeal, almost anything can happen: ritual weapons, both opponents blindfolded, forbiddance of Disciplines, etc.

After a conclave, princes often reward those who voted in their favor and punish those who did not. Some vampires, in anticipation of a prince's anger, settle their affairs and seek out new living arrangements at the conclave. Others take the opportunity to curry as much favor as possible, hoping that their "loyalty" will be rewarded.

Not every conclave called is an emergency meeting. Some justicars arrange for annual conclaves allowing all Kindred who choose to attend an opportunity to meet and talk over the year's business. For the past decade, the Toreador justicar has called a

conclave on the weekend closest to Halloween, while another takes place in New Orleans every three years. These are opportunities for Camarilla vampires to discuss business that relates to the sect as a whole, to fraternize with others of their station and clan, and simply to socialize with new faces and old acquaintances. However, with the increasing boldness of the sect's many enemies, many Kindred fear that one of these conclaves will provide a perfect target for a retaliatory strike.

The Inner Circle

The true hub of the Camarilla, this group meets in Venice once every 13 years to plan out the business and direction of vampire society — as much as any group can presume to dictate the doings of a race of immortal predators. Every clan is permit-

ted one representative, usually the eldest member of the clan, as only the eldest may cast the clan's vote. Others may be brought to the meeting and allowed to speak, but in the end only the elders may vote.

One of the Circle's main purposes is the appointment of justicars, one for each of the seven Camarilla clans. Appointment is a long, drawn-out process, as each clan seeks to get its best in the plum spots. Often, when the shouting is over, the losers end up with young or relatively weak justicars who are ignored for their 13-year stints. Those who are eventually appointed are most often compromise candidates, or even obscure Kindred who the Circle believes can be manipulated. These latter types sometimes display a surprising amount of initiative, and may even bite the hand that feeds them.

BRUJAH

Clan Brujah is largely composed of rebels, both with and without causes. Individualistic, outspoken and turbulent, Brujah hold social change near to their undead hearts, and the clan's ranks contain some of the most violent of the Camarilla Kindred. Most other vampires perceive the Brujah as nothing more than punks and miscreants, but the truth of the matter is that genuine passion lies behind their polemics.

Brujah Kindred adopt pet passions and causes, which they support with volume and vitriol. Some Brujah follow charismatic members of their clan, while others prefer stances of blatant, defiant individualism. The clan claims a history rich with warrior-poets, and it has adapted this concept into the modern night; many Brujah are glad to have an opportunity to speak their minds, then indulge in a bit of destruction afterward to illustrate their points.

The Rabble's espousal of change unites them, albeit tenuously, in their nightly crusades. Given a common enemy, Brujah with vastly differing ideals will join side by side to oppose their foe. After that foe is defeated, however, all bets are off and it's back to business as usual. A common Brujah theme involves the foundation of a Kindred "Utopia," or the re-creation of a mythical one from nights past, though each Brujah vampire has a different idea of what said Utopia *is*.

Brujah rely on chaotic behavior and upheaval to get their ideas across, and the Rabble are allowed a certain leeway that other clans do not have. In fact, Brujah are almost *expected* to be incoherent and bellicose; this stereotype works to the advantage of many eloquent, well-spoken members of the clan, who have no need to resort to violence when making their arguments.

Respected for their martialry and readiness to rally under a banner, the Brujah are the physical strength of the Camarilla. Of late, however, many Rabble neonates see their role in the Camarilla as an institution unto itself, and more than a little unrest circulates among the clan. Other Kindred believe that the Brujah would be the first to leave the Camarilla. The Brujah believe it, too....

Nickname: Rabble

Sect: Rhetoric aside, most Brujah are in the Camarilla. Brujah Kindred also support the anarchs, arguably more so than the Camarilla. Indeed, the anarchs have more Brujah than members of all other clans combined.

Appearance: Brujah vary widely in appearance, though many adopt radical styles and bold looks. If dismissive stereotypes are to be believed, the typical Brujah wears a biker jacket, tattered jeans, combat boots and a fearsome array of high-maintenance hair. In truth, few Brujah fit this image. Youthful, fashion-forward dress and noteworthy hairstyles are indeed found among many Brujah, but others favor tasteful ward-robes that encourage others to take them seriously. In the end, a Brujah's appearance often suggests his attitudes: A skinhead bravo is likely an open rebel or anarchist, while a bespectacled pedant in a tweed suit is probably a reformationist or liberal. It should be noted, however, that given the Brujah penchant for nonconformity, any assumption of ideals based on appearance could be potentially dangerous. Brujah look how they want.

Haven: Wherever they damn well please. Are *you* going to tell them to leave?

More so than any other clan, the Brujah keep the company of other vampires, and one haven might house an entire brood. Brujah Kindred also keep multiple safehouses and boltholes, as their conflict-driven existences often make single locations inhospitable. Some Brujah neonates even carry on the urban practice of the home invasion, Dominating or killing a home's occupants and taking over. Like other pursuits, however, home invasions rarely sustain the Rabble's interest, and the vampires often move on once they grow bored with the locale.

Background: Brujah prefer those who espouse change in one form or another, and often recruit from college campuses, political groups or oppressed minorities. Young Brujah may hail from any background and often have a pet cause or issue of burning personal importance. All types of dissidents find their way into the ranks of the Brujah, from bomb-throwing biker anarchists to vociferous fascists to nihilistic radicals. This is, of course, part of the reason the clan is so disorganized — hatred between Brujah is often more bitter than hatred for those whom they mutually oppose.

Character Creation: Brujah often have violent, criminal concepts, but they are as likely to be intellectual or socially adept. Natures and Demeanors tend to be aggressive and similar, as Brujah wear their emotions on their sleeves (when they *have* sleeves…). Physically predisposed characters are predominant among the clan, but some favor Mental Attributes. Likewise, Skills are favored, with Knowledges running a close second. Any Backgrounds may be appropriate to a Brujah character, though many in the clan cultivate Contacts, Allies and Herd. Very few Brujah claim Mentors.

Clan Disciplines: Celerity, Potence, Presence

Weaknesses: Fiery passion is at once the Brujah's blessing and curse. Though they are quick to adopt a cause, they are equally as quick to fall to frenzy. Of course, the Brujah rabidly deny this penchant for excitement, and become quite hostile when the issue is raised. The difficulties of rolls to resist frenzy (p. 228) are two higher than normal for members of Clan Brujah.

Organization: Clan Brujah is far too fractious and torn by internecine conflict to have true organization, and the clan never meets formally. Two conventions the clan does support universally are the Rant and the Rave. Rants are just that: informal meetings of Brujah (and other insurgents, Kindred and kine) at which anyone who can scream loudly enough can have her opinions heard. Raves, named after the all-night techno dance parties started in England, are social gatherings in the guise of huge-scale musical or entertainment events. One usually leads to another, and clues to the locations of the events are often hidden in the media of the gathering in progress. These meetings

almost invariably degenerate into riots, further eroding the organizational base of the clan.

Bloodlines: Brujah *antitribu* of the Sabbat are, ironically, almost bastions of stability. In a sect devoted to chaos and destruction, the Brujah are the most dependable of the monsters who populate the Sabbat. They are viewed less as impassioned rebels and more as brutal shock troops. Sabbat Brujah tend to be less intelligent and discerning than their Camarilla brothers and sisters. Their causes fall by the wayside at the promise of new havoc to wreak.

Quote: *Think for yourself, or you're better off dead. Either way, I'm satisfied.*

Gangrel

Of all vampires, the Gangrel are perhaps closest to their inner nature. These nomadic loners spurn the constraints of society, preferring the comfort of the wilderness. How they avoid the wrath of the werewolves is unknown; perhaps it has something to do with the fact that the Gangrel are themselves shapeshifters. When a mortal speaks of a vampire changing into a wolf or a bat, she is probably speaking of a Gangrel.

Like the Brujah, Gangrel are fierce warriors; unlike the Brujah, Gangrel ferocity does not stem from anarchic rage, but from animalistic instinct. They are among the most predatory Kindred, and love to lose themselves in the thrill of the hunt. Gangrel have a keen understanding of the Beast in their souls, and prefer to spend their nights in communion with the animals whom they so emulate. Indeed, Gangrel are so attuned to their Beasts that, after losing themselves to frenzy, animalistic features often appear on their bodies.

The clan itself has little contact with, or regard for, the rest of the Kindred. This might be due to a desire to avoid the snares of the Jyhad, but is more likely the product of simple disinterest. Certainly, Gangrel are popularly viewed as quiet, taciturn and reclusive. Although there is no more truth to this than there is to any other stereotype, the clan as a whole displays little of the ostentation found among lines such as the Toreador or Ventrue.

Gangrel are closely tied to the Rom, or Gypsies, adopting much of that culture's speech patterns and mannerisms. Rumors speculate that the Rom are in fact descended from the Antediluvian who founded the Gangrel line. As such, say the rumors, any Kindred who harms or Embraces a Gypsy will suffer the wrath of the Ancient. Obviously, the vampires of Clan Ravnos ignore this

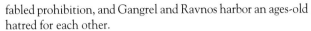

fabled prohibition, and Gangrel and Ravnos harbor an ages-old hatred for each other.

Nickname: Outlanders

Sect: Clan Gangrel is nominally in the Camarilla, though a fair number of Sabbat Gangrel exist as well. Most Gangrel care little for sect, and rumblings of outright secession from the Camarilla have made the rounds at recent Gangrel Gathers.

Appearance: Gangrel's harsh unlifestyle and lack of interest in fashion often make them seem rugged and wild. Couple this with the animal features common among the clan, and Gangrel sometimes appear downright frightening. Some mortals and Kindred find a certain predatory beauty in the Gangrel, though this can lead to a dangerous misjudgment of the Gangrel's intentions.

Haven: Gangrel often make no permanent havens, sleeping wherever they can find shelter from the sun. Gangrel with sufficient mastery of the Protean Discipline sleep in the very earth, lairing in parks and other spots of natural terrain. Although many Gangrel prefer to lair in the wild or travel from place to place, they are as vulnerable to attack by werewolves as other Kindred are, and so they are often forced to remain in the city's confines.

Background: Gangrel Embrace for a variety of reasons, as do most Kindred, but do not pass on the Curse lightly or commonly. If a generalization must be made, it could be said that Gangrel prefer to Embrace loners, those who have the physical and emotional resiliency to survive the shock of the Change. The sire's training, what little there is, tends to be gruff and harsh; most Gangrel must discover the vagaries of unlife largely on their own.

Character Creation: Gangrel often have similar Natures and Demeanors, as they rarely rely on subterfuge to get their way. Physical Attributes and Talents or Skills are common among Gangrel. They often have Allies (Gypsies) or Mentor as Background, but rarely have high levels of Influence or Resources.

Clan Disciplines: Animalism, Fortitude, Protean

Weaknesses: Gangrel are very close to the Beast Within; as they succumb to it, it leaves its mark on their bodies. Every time a Gangrel frenzies, she gains an animalistic feature. This feature is determined by the player and Storyteller; it might be tufted ears, a pelt, a tail, catlike eyes, a snarling voice, tusks, even scales or feathers. Every five such features acquired permanently reduce one of the Gangrel's Social Attributes by one.

Organization: Gangrel have no true organization to speak of. Vampires of great age and great deeds are typically shown respect, though the young are by no means subservient. Out-

landers occasionally meet in groups known as "Gathers"; at these festivals, vampires dance, feast and tell stories of their travels. Disputes between Gangrel are often settled through ritual combat to first blood or submission; while savage, these fights rarely result in the loser's Final Death. Gangrel commonly hunt alone, though occasionally two or more Gangrel unite in a coterie of sorts (a "pride" or "pack").

Bloodlines: Two bloodlines exist among the Sabbat: the Country Gangrel (similar in most ways to the main branch of the clan) and City Gangrel (whose Disciplines are Celerity, Obfuscate and Protean). Both types are found only among the Sabbat.

Quote: *You provided worthy sport, mortal. Now, though, the chase is ended.*

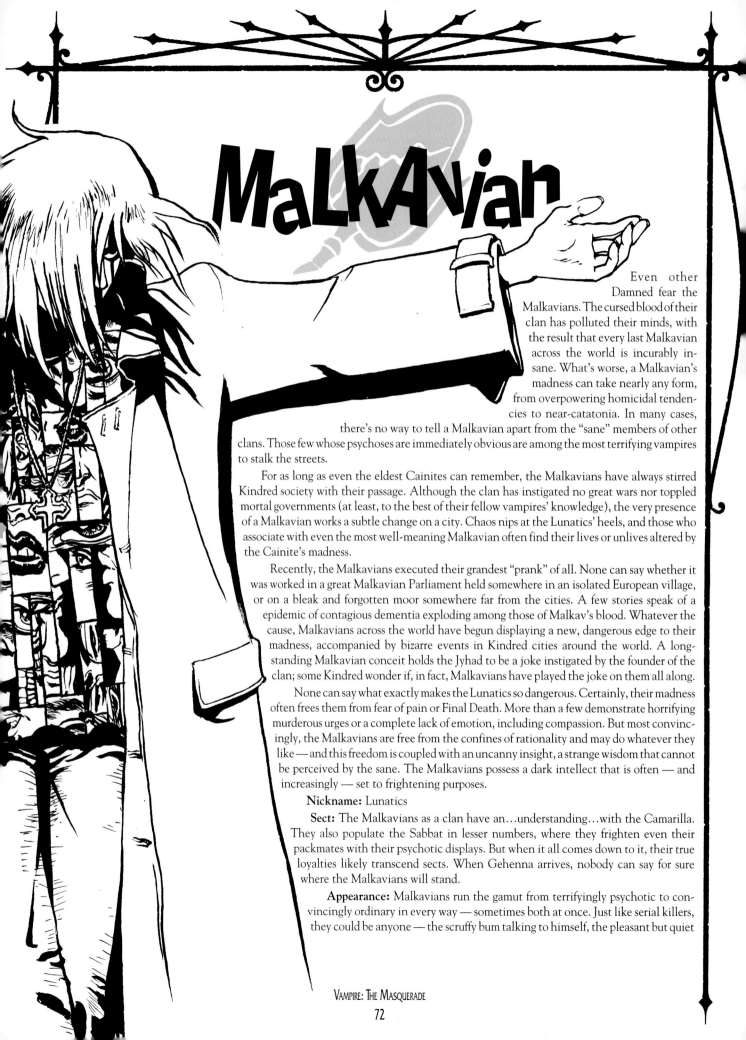

MALKAVIAN

Even other Damned fear the Malkavians. The cursed blood of their clan has polluted their minds, with the result that every last Malkavian across the world is incurably insane. What's worse, a Malkavian's madness can take nearly any form, from overpowering homicidal tendencies to near-catatonia. In many cases, there's no way to tell a Malkavian apart from the "sane" members of other clans. Those few whose psychoses are immediately obvious are among the most terrifying vampires to stalk the streets.

For as long as even the eldest Cainites can remember, the Malkavians have always stirred Kindred society with their passage. Although the clan has instigated no great wars nor toppled mortal governments (at least, to the best of their fellow vampires' knowledge), the very presence of a Malkavian works a subtle change on a city. Chaos nips at the Lunatics' heels, and those who associate with even the most well-meaning Malkavian often find their lives or unlives altered by the Cainite's madness.

Recently, the Malkavians executed their grandest "prank" of all. None can say whether it was worked in a great Malkavian Parliament held somewhere in an isolated European village, or on a bleak and forgotten moor somewhere far from the cities. A few stories speak of a epidemic of contagious dementia exploding among those of Malkav's blood. Whatever the cause, Malkavians across the world have begun displaying a new, dangerous edge to their madness, accompanied by bizarre events in Kindred cities around the world. A long-standing Malkavian conceit holds the Jyhad to be a joke instigated by the founder of the clan; some Kindred wonder if, in fact, Malkavians have played the joke on them all along.

None can say what exactly makes the Lunatics so dangerous. Certainly, their madness often frees them from fear of pain or Final Death. More than a few demonstrate horrifying murderous urges or a complete lack of emotion, including compassion. But most convincingly, the Malkavians are free from the confines of rationality and may do whatever they like — and this freedom is coupled with an uncanny insight, a strange wisdom that cannot be perceived by the sane. The Malkavians possess a dark intellect that is often — and increasingly — set to frightening purposes.

Nickname: Lunatics

Sect: The Malkavians as a clan have an…understanding…with the Camarilla. They also populate the Sabbat in lesser numbers, where they frighten even their packmates with their psychotic displays. But when it all comes down to it, their true loyalties likely transcend sects. When Gehenna arrives, nobody can say for sure where the Malkavians will stand.

Appearance: Malkavians run the gamut from terrifyingly psychotic to convincingly ordinary in every way — sometimes both at once. Just like serial killers, they could be anyone — the scruffy bum talking to himself, the pleasant but quiet neighbor, the borderline-suicidal musician. These vampires are capable of great subtlety, and rarely show anyone a face other than the one they want people to see.

Haven: The Lunatics by and large take whatever shelter they like, although more than a few find aging hospitals and poorly funded asylums to their tastes. Many seem to enjoy the company of desperate mortals, and prefer slums and institutions to more secluded havens.

Background: Malkavians take their childer from all walks of life and for all number of reasons. Anyone can be chosen to further a sire's twisted purposes, although most Lunatics prefer Embracing those already close to (or subject to) madness. Most other vampires believe that the Malkavians Embrace their childer on a whim; however, virtually all Lunatics discover themselves subtly championing some barely perceptible "purpose," the full extent of which none — not even their sires — can properly fathom.

Character Creation: Malkavians come in all shapes and flavors, but many have primary Mental Attributes, befitting the clan's reputation for wisdom and insight. Apart from that, it's anyone's guess just what Traits a Malkavian may manifest — with the diversity of their concepts and backgrounds, these mad vampires could be anyone. Anywhere.

Clan Disciplines: Auspex, Dementation, Obfuscate

Weaknesses: Every last vampire of Malkav's blood is irredeemably insane in some form or another. Some attribute this to a curse of the blood, while other Lunatics actually call it a special blessing, a gift of insight. When a Malkavian character is created, the player must choose at least one derangement (see p. 222) for that character at the time of the Embrace; this derangement can be temporarily fought with Willpower, but can never be permanently overcome.

Organization: The hierarchy of the Malkavians, if it exists at all, defies description. Most are usually content to let one another do as they like from night to night. But now and again, in times of great need, Malkavians demonstrate an uncanny ability to act in unison, even without any apparent leadership — and sometimes even without any apparent communication. As one, they arise from their desolate haunts; as one, they fall on the problem at hand. And when it is a problem no longer, they drift back to their usual routines. If the Malkavians indulge in any form of machinations as a clan, they are incomprehensible to outsiders — which may be a blessing.

Bloodlines: Before the Dementation Discipline spread contagiously throughout the clan (in 1997 or so), a great number of Malkavians expressed their mind-warping talents through the use of the Dominate Discipline. A few Malkavians weren't caught in the redoubled tide of insanity that swept the clan, and still possess that power in lieu of

Dementation. The rest of the clan pays these offshoots no particular notice; indeed, with only a few exceptions, Malkavians don't differentiate between this bloodline and the clan proper at all.

Quote: *Laugh if you like. Doesn't matter. Assume that you're so much smarter than the poor, broken lunatic. Doesn't matter. But think about this: You're a dead thing, same as me. You died and were reborn...as this. What makes you and me different? Simple — I remember what I saw when I was full and truly dead. You'd be mad, too.*

NOSFERATU

Caine's childer are called "The Damned," and no vampires embody this more fully than the wretches of Clan Nosferatu. While other vampires still look human and may travel in mortal society, Nosferatu are twisted and deformed by the curse of vampirism. Other Kindred speak shudderingly of Caine placing a mark upon the entire clan for the monstrous deeds of its Antediluvian founder. As such, Nosferatu find themselves loathed and ostracized by the other Children of Caine, who consider them disgusting and interact with them only when they must.

Following the Embrace, Nosferatu childer suffer an agonizing transformation as, over the subsequent weeks, they warp from humans into hideous monsters. The horror of the physical devolution often produces an accompanying psychological trauma. Unable to walk among the kine, Nosferatu must dwell in subterranean sewers and catacombs forever after.

Nosferatu often choose physically or emotionally twisted mortals for the Embrace, seeing in the curse of vampirism a possible means of redemption for the mortals. Amazingly, there seems to be some merit to this belief. Many Nosferatu are surprisingly levelheaded and practical, avoiding the obsessions, fits and rages of their fairer brethren. Not that this makes the Sewer Rats particularly pleasant to be around; indeed, some Nosferatu come to delight in the shock and horror their grotesque appearances inspire in others.

Nosferatu are survivors *par excellence*. Few creatures, mortal or vampire, know a city's back alleys and dark corners like the Nosferatu do. Additionally, Nosferatu have mastered the crafts of sneaking and eavesdropping; they make a point of keeping up with current gossip and affairs, not merely for pleasure, but for survival. Information brokers without peer, they can command high prices for their knowledge. Using their Obfuscate Discipline, Nosferatu make a point of listening to others' conversations from hiding, or sitting in on "secret" meetings. If a Kindred wishes to learn about the doings and denizens of the city, she would do well to consult the Nosferatu.

Finally, millennia of shared deformity and abuse have fostered strong bonds among the monsters. Nosferatu forego the squabbling and feuds ubiquitous to the other clans, preferring to work in unison. They treat each other with meticulous politeness and freely share information among themselves. To mess with one Nosferatu is to mess with them all — and that can get messy indeed.…

Nickname: Sewer Rats

Sect: Surprisingly, the clan as a whole belongs to the Camarilla, despite obvious difficulties with upholding the Masquerade. Perhaps they value the safety of membership; perhaps they simply want the other clans within observing distance. Still, a fair number of Nosferatu are in the Sabbat or simply consider themselves *autarkis* (of no sect).

Appearance: No two Nosferatu look precisely alike, but all are hideous. Gaping fang-filled maws, discolorations, tumors, holes in place of noses, batlike ears, sloping bald heads, twisted spines, claws, wrinkled hides, pustulent sores and webbed fingers are just a few possible deformities possessed by Nosferatu. An existence in sewers and crypts tends to ensure that most Nosferatu smell about as good as they look.

Haven: Their disfigurement forces most Nosferatu to take havens far from the eyes of mortals, in graveyards, abandoned warehouses and cellars. In large cities, entire broods of Nosferatu lair in sewers and subway systems. These "kingdoms," particularly the older ones, are often much more extensive than mortals or Kindred are aware — subterranean labyrinths stretching deep into the darkness and guarded by monstrous ghouls. Even princes treat warily with the Nosferatu kingdoms.

Background: Nosferatu choose their progeny from society's castoffs: derelicts, the mentally ill and the hopelessly antisocial. Occasionally, a vindictive Nosferatu chooses to Embrace a beautiful, vain mortal, then watch gleefully as the Curse takes hold.

Character Creation: Nosferatu can have any concept, but often come from loner, outsider or drifter stock. Physical or Mental Attributes are often primary (Social are rarely anything other than tertiary!). Stealth is highly prized among the clan, while Survival allows a Sewer Rat to find shelter in the blighted zones Nosferatu favor. Nosferatu occasionally have retainers in the form of ghoul animals, or even a human ally or two, but Backgrounds are rarely predominant among the clan.

Clan Disciplines: Animalism, Obfuscate, Potence

Weaknesses: As mentioned, Nosferatu are absolutely loathsome to look at. All Nosferatu have Appearance ratings of zero — cross the automatic dot right off the character sheet. Nor may they improve Appearance with experience points. Most Social actions based on first impressions, except intimidation and the like, fail automatically.

Organization: While Nosferatu do not have the rigid protocols that mark clans such as the Tremere and Ventrue, their shared deformity creates an exceptional clan unity. Shunned and reviled by other creatures, Nosferatu stick together out of equal parts necessity and loneliness.

Bloodlines: Like many other clans, Nosferatu has an *antitribu* analog in the Sabbat, though this branch does not differ greatly from the ruck and run of the clan save in ideology. Descendants of certain sires sometimes bear "signature" deformities, but few differ in any significant fashion.

Quote: *Come here, little boy, howsabout a kiss?* [phlegmy, wheezing hack] *Whazza matter? Big bad gangbanger's scared now? Don't so much like being a victim, heh? Well, get used to it, 'cuz you ain't seen the half of it!*

STEREOTYPES

Assamite: This is bad. This is straight-up, fucked-up bad. Roll around in sewage; maybe they won't wanna bite you.

Brujah: They talk a lot about equality and egalitarianism and other bullshit, but they flinch like the rest.

Followers of Set: What have they got that we need? Money? Hah. Fancy clothes? Hah. A comfortable apartment? Hah. Lovers?!? *Hah!!!* Can't corrupt what's already filthy, gardenslugs.

Gangrel: They understand — more than the others do, at any rate. We don't talk much, and the silence speaks volumes.

Giovanni: You know that odor that comes off my skin after a good rain? That Giovanni I met had that coming from the inside. I smelled it coming out of her mouth when she sucked up to me about "partnership."

Lasombra: Mean, mean bastards. Can't even trust the shadows when you're around 'em. They won't go down first or easy, I'll tell ya that now.

Malkavian: There's a nasty smell on the wind, and it's not us. Watch 'em, observe what they do. When you can't see 'em anymore, run or hide.

Ravnos: Easily dismissed. Way, *way* too easily dismissed. I'm beginning to think we may have made a bad, bad mistake here....

Toreador: These pusbags sure make themselves easy to hate, don't they?

Tremere: You really thought abracadabras and eye of newt would let you dive in the deep end of the Jyhad? Idiots. Have fun in Hell.

Tzimisce: In theory, I can appreciate their conceit of being monsters through and through. Unpretentious, in a way. In practice, they're fucked-up bitches, and I hate 'em.

Ventrue: Little Lord Fauntleroy sat on a throne, Little Lord Fauntleroy died there alone.

Caitiff: Kick or be kicked, Lickboy. I know which one I'm going to do.

Camarilla: Come on down here and give me that order again, Mr. Prince. Yeah, didn't think so.

Sabbat: Do they really think that what they do is *liberating*?

TOREADOR

The Toreador are called many things — "degenerates," "artists," "poseurs" and "hedonists" being but a few. But any such lumpen categorization does the clan a disservice. Depending on the individual and her mood, Toreador are alternately elegant and flamboyant, brilliant and ludicrous, visionary and dissipated. Perhaps the only truism that can be applied to the clan is its members' aesthetic zeal. Whatever a Toreador does, she does with passion. Whatever a Toreador is, she is with passion.

To the Toreador, eternal life is to be savored. Many Toreador were artists, musicians or poets in life; many more have spent frustrating centuries producing laughable attempts at art, music or poetry. Toreador tout themselves as cultivators of all that is best about humanity. Occasionally, a particularly gifted or inspired creator is Embraced into the clan, to preserve her talent for eternity. In this manner, Clan Toreador has inducted some of humanity's greatest artists, poets and musicians into its ranks; of course, if one thing can be said about the Toreador, it is that no two of them agree on precisely what "gifted" or "inspired" means.

Of all clans, Toreador are the vampires most connected to the mortal world. While other vampires view the kine as pawns or simple sustenance, Toreador glide gracefully and effortlessly through the society of the Canaille, sampling the delights of each age as a gourmand savors rare delicacies. Toreador are the Kindred most likely to fall in love with mortals, and they surround themselves with the best, most elegant and most luxurious things — and people — that the world has to offer. It is, thus, acutely tragic when a Toreador succumbs to ennui and discards aesthetic pursuits in favor of pointless hedonism. Such Kindred become decadent sybarites, concerned only with indulging personal whims and vices.

Toreador are committed to the Camarilla and share the Ventrue's love of high society, though not for them the tedium of actually *running* things — that's what functionaries are for, after all. Toreador know that their place is to captivate and inspire — through their witty speech, graceful deeds and simple, scintillating existence.

Nickname: Degenerates

Sect: Most Toreador are in the Camarilla, as only that august organization promotes "culture" and allows the Toreador to live among the mortals they so favor. Those in the Sabbat pursue bizarre "artistic" pastimes, such as torture and blood-painting, or are the rulers of the most decadent underground movements.

Appearance: Toreador Embrace out of passion as much as any other reason; accordingly, many Toreador are creatures of surpassing beauty. Of all Kindred, Toreador are the vampires most attuned to human fashion trends; centuries-old Degenerates are often more stylish than some 30-year-old mortals. If it's in, chances are that at least one Toreador will adopt it.

Haven: Toreador take care to ensure that their havens are comfortable, convenient for socializing and — above all — conform to their aesthetic tastes. Vampires of a more artistic bent might maintain spacious lofts to display their works, while their "poseur" counterparts love opulent suites perfect for hosting parties.

Background: Toreador range across a spectrum of concepts, from lonely, tortured artists to debauched jetsetters. Some Toreador are Embraced for no reason other than their beauty or personal style, as a passionate sire decides that they simply must be "preserved" for eternity.

Character Creation: Social Attributes and Abilities are prized among the clan, though Toreador are typically concerned less with outright control than with making a good impression. Perception is also favored, both for creation and for critiquing. Artistes favor Abilities such as Expression and Performance, often enjoying very high levels in these aesthetic Traits; their poseur brethren must make do with Abilities like Subterfuge and Etiquette. Toreador are very social creatures, and love adoration from both Kindred and kine; as such, Backgrounds like Allies, Contacts, Fame, Herd, Resources and Status are common.

Clan Disciplines: Auspex, Celerity, Presence

Weaknesses: Toreador are preternaturally attuned to the aesthetic and beautiful, but this sensitivity can prove dangerous. When a Toreador views, hears or even smells something that is truly beautiful — a person, a painting, a song, a particularly lovely sunrise — he must make a Self-Control roll (difficulty 6) or become entranced by the sensation. The Toreador will stand in rapt fascination for a scene or until the beautiful thing withdraws. Enraptured Toreador may not even defend themselves if attacked, though being wounded allows them to make another Self-Control roll to "break the spell."

Organization: Toreador have little practical organization, though their cliquishness and social networks are legendary. The clan meets frequently, but more as an excuse to host lavish parties and showings than to accomplish anything. Status among the Toreador is a tempestuous whirlwind in which one subtle smile or catty critique can lead to fortune or disaster; a prodigy may be adored one night, commit a barely perceptible *faux pas*, and be ostracized the next.

Bloodlines: Toreador put a fair degree of stock in lineage; a vampire fortunate enough to descend from a favored sire is lavished with adoration (to her face, anyway), while childer of a sire "on the outs" suffer social humiliation. Few of these lines deviate from the main clan in any significant way. The Toreador *antitribu* of the Sabbat are a notable exception, for they take equal aesthetic delight in great beauty or great ugliness.

Quote: *Oh, yes, isn't she exquisite? Yes, she's my newest find — I'm her muse, the sweet little creature. Imagine! And what of — oh, Thomas? Why, I could hardly say — after all, he had his "15*

STEREOTYPES

Assamite: There is beauty in what they do, make no mistake, but it is a beauty best observed from a distance.

Brujah: On the first night, their passion terrifies. On the second night, their passion fascinates. On the third night, their passion inflames. After that…frankly, their passion begins to bore.

Followers of Set: It is inevitable, of course, that persons of epicurean refinement will in the course of eternity engage in dealings with those of…unsavory character. Record well any transactions made, and repay all favors promptly.

Gangrel: As charmingly untamed as a tiger; as worthy of consideration as a housecat.

Giovanni: They dress splendidly and are charmingly mannered. Why, then, do they frighten me so?

Lasombra: Their Miltonian conceit is dreadfully provocative, or provocatively dreadful, but they take it all so seriously.

Malkavian: The fractured kaleidoscope of their thoughts is enchanting at first glimpse. Gaze at it too long, though, and one grows prone to terrible headaches.

Nosferatu: Odious beasts! And to think that they are allowed in the halls of culture! Oh, how gauche….

Ravnos: The subjects of many delightful stories — well, delightful so long as one does not also feature in the tale.

Tremere: One deals with the butcher and the bureaucrat because they provide useful conveniences. One graciously acknowledges services efficiently performed. One does not, though, invite the hired help to the soiree, nor take kindly to party-crashers.

Tzimisce: To experience this clan's alien fruits would be almost worth the price. Remember well that "almost," dear.

Ventrue: Every masterwork must have its frame; every bust must have its pillar. This the Ventrue understand, and they perform their functions admirably.

Caitiff: Really. Who let *them* in?

Camarilla: Through its auspices may Kindred and kine harmoniously coexist, each benefiting from the other's presence.

Sabbat: Why would I wish to spend eternity wallowing in gore?

minutes," as they say, but it just wasn't going to last, and it all became so very tedious, so I had to say adieu. Suicide? Really? Silly boy — he should thank me, then, that I didn't give him the Embrace. It would have made things so difficult, after all….

TREMERE

Whether dreaded, mistrusted, feared or reviled, the insular vampires of Clan Tremere are anything but ignored. Those who have heard of the clan's doings are typically suspicious of the Tremere, and with good reason — for the Warlocks are aptly named. Through their own artifice, they have mastered a form of vampiric sorcery, complete with rituals and spells, that is as potent — if not more so — than any other power of the Blood. Paired with the clan's rigid hierarchy and the smoldering ambition so common among Warlocks, this power is an unsettling thing indeed to those who know what the Tremere are capable of doing.

According to some Kindred records, the Tremere came into being as a clan very recently, at least by an immortal's standards. Legend has it that, during Europe's Dark Ages, a cabal of human wizards enacted a great ritual over the slumbering body of an Antediluvian and thereby wrested for themselves the gift of vampirism. War followed soon thereafter — the fledgling clan found itself besieged by enraged Kindred on every side. But the Tremere are nothing if not survivors. Their human magicks lost, they nonetheless managed to alter their rituals and wardings to utilize the power of their vitae. These magical skills, now practiced as the Discipline of Thaumaturgy, have ensured the Tremere's place among the Kindred ever since.

The Warlocks gladly play the games of diplomacy and intrigue with their newfound brethren. However, their dealings are always tinged with a touch of paranoia, for the Tremere know that the elders of no fewer than three clans bear them a terrible grudge that has yet to be repaid. Therefore, the Tremere work to cultivate what allies they can, even as they strive to heighten their magical mastery. No less is required for their survival. As a result, the childer of Clan Tremere are among the most driven and learned of all Cainites; few cross these undead sorcerers and escape unscarred.

The Tremere are vampires of the Old World, but have traveled across the continents to establish footholds elsewhere. The clan's seat of power lies in Vienna, where the Tremere elders convene in council and discuss the clan's future direction. But many larger cities across the globe house Tremere "chantries" — well-defended houses that are equal parts university, monastery and stronghold. There the Warlocks gather to exchange information and study their vampiric witchcraft, safe from the attentions of their rivals.

Nickname: Warlocks

Sect: The Tremere were more than glad to join the fledgling Camarilla when the sect was forming, and they quickly made themselves invaluable there. In fact, the Tremere are one of the linchpins of the sect. They have a marked interest in keeping the Camarilla strong, of course — with their hated Tzimisce enemies directing their Sabbat minions against any Tremere they find, the Warlocks require allies. And with the valuable magical power they offer, the Tremere find the Camarilla glad to provide the support they require. With the Camarilla's protection, the Tremere are free to pursue the arcane mastery they so avidly desire.

Appearance: The sorcerous Tremere are typically imposing or sinister in mien. Some favor classic suits; others prefer a slightly more antiquated look, dressing in 1940s-cut suits, Edwardian finery or the simple black turtlenecks of the Beat era. Many wear charms or amulets inscribed with cabalistic or other arcane symbols, as a sign of their learning. Although individual Warlocks may run the gamut from immaculately precise to disheveled and eccentric, the vampiric sorcerers' eyes always gleam with hidden insight and frightening acuity.

Haven: While Warlocks may maintain their own individual havens (often complete with extensive libraries), the clan maintains a chantry in every city that harbors a strong Tremere presence. A chantry is open to any of Tremere's bloodline and absolutely forbidden to all others. The Warlocks are infamous for their well-guarded havens; almost all boast mystical wards that even other Tremere would find difficult to circumvent.

Background: Many Tremere dabbled in occult or other scholarly pursuits in life. However, a fascination with the unknown is hardly enough to draw a Warlock's attention; clan members seek "apprentices" with aggressive natures and clear thinking, and care little for muddle-headed New Agers or befuddled conspiracy theorists. Clan Tremere has an unspoken tradition of sexism, and most of its elders are male. Tremere ancillae have become rather more open-minded of late, though, and draw ample numbers of suitably ambitious and persistent acolytes from both sexes.

Character Creation: Tremere typically have strong Mental Attributes and a high Willpower to match; dilettantes and churls cannot meet the grueling demands of sorcery. Many have Knowledges as their primary Abilities, although Skills are also highly in demand. Although a few Tremere specialize in one particular area of excellence, many more prefer a more well-rounded approach to personal aptitudes; after all, a Warlock can typically rely on no one other than himself.

Clan Disciplines: Auspex, Dominate, Thaumaturgy

Weaknesses: By clan law, all neonate Tremere must drink the blood of the clan's seven elders when they are created. All Tremere are at least one step toward being blood bound to their elders, and therefore usually act with great clan loyalty — in order to avoid having such loyalty forced on them. What's more, this arrangement means that Tremere are hard-pressed to resist the will of their elders; the difficulty of any Dominate attempt from a clan superior is one less.

Organization: No tighter internal structure exists among the clans. No clan binds its neonates so strictly. And no clan acts with such unity of purpose as the Tremere. Although younger clan members generally are free to do more or less as they wish, occasionally they receive instructions from their elders that they may not ignore. Paranoia keeps the clan well-oiled and unified.

Of course, the Tremere do encourage individual achievement among the group, seeing it as a Darwinian method of ensuring the clan's strength. With such ambitious, powerful young vampires cooperating with such commendable clan unity, it's no wonder the Warlocks have plenty of envious and spiteful enemies among the Kindred.

The Tremere's pyramidal hierarchy contains several ranks, each divided into seven mystical "circles" that an aspirant must master if he desires to advance in rank (and nearly every Tremere desires that very thing). The lowest rank, that of apprentice, belongs to neonates. Above the apprentices are the regents, each one the master of a chantry; then the lords, whose domains include several chantries each. Forty-nine Tremere hold the title of pontifex, each bearing great responsibilities. And at the top of the pyramid sits the Inner Council of Seven, some the masters of entire continents, and all whispered to be in constant mental communication with the others.

Bloodlines: The strict organization of the Tremere, as well as their insistence on obeying one's elders, offers few freedoms. No variants of the Tremere bloodline have been allowed to survive to the

present night. A small group of Tremere rebels once made its home in the Sabbat, but recent events have seen to that group's destruction.

Quote: *We are more than vampires. We are the next step in Cainite evolution. We will direct the others if they allow us to do so, or we will stand alone if we must. But we will survive.*

Ventrue

The Kindred of Clan Ventrue have a reputation for being honorable, genteel and of impeccable taste. From time out of mind, Ventrue has been the clan of leadership, enforcing the ancient traditions and seeking to shape the destiny of the Kindred. In nights of old, Ventrue were chosen from nobles, merchant princes or other wielders of power. In modern times the clan recruits from wealthy "old money" families, ruthless corporate climbers, and politicians. Whatever their origin, Ventrue vampires preserve stability and maintain order for the Camarilla. Other Kindred often mistake this for arrogance or avarice, but to the Ventrue, their shepherd's role is more burden than honor.

Ventrue support the Masquerade wholeheartedly, feeling that under its auspices the best existence for all vampires may be obtained. To the Ventrue mind, other clans are brash and impetuous. Too concerned with their short-term comfort, other vampires gladly give up an eternity tomorrow for a bit of vitae tonight. Without the Ventrue, there would be no Masquerade; without the Masquerade, there would be no vampires. Thus, the Ventrue have the weight of Atlas upon their shoulders. They bear their burden with a stiff upper lip and just a hint of *noblesse oblige*. No other clan could lead the Children of Caine in the nights of imminent Gehenna — or so the Ventrue are apt to say. After all, their reputation rests on it.

Ventrue see themselves as nobles in the classical sense of the word, fighting to uphold the station of those below them. They are the kings, knights and barons of the modern night. Although the struggle has moved from battlefields to boardrooms and from jousting lists to voting districts, Clan Ventrue continues the duel. Young Ventrue rally and lead the troops with their cellular phones and limousines, while the clan elders watch the horizons for threats that loom like storm clouds. Many holdings under Camarilla control are overseen by Ventrue, and the Blue Bloods are loath to relax their grip over endeavors they so desperately struggle to maintain. Reputation and achievement take a Kindred far in the Ventrue clan, but none of that counts if the vampire cannot maintain his influence.

Other vampires often cast aspersions on the Ventrue, vilifying them as sanctimonious, pompous or even tyrannical — and yet it is the Blue Bloods to whom those other vampires turn when something goes wrong. Ventrue cultivate, influence and — when they can — control the kine's media, police, politics, health and medicine, organized crime, industry, finance, transportation and even the Church. When another vampire requires aid, the Ventrue can often provide it — for a price.

Naturally, Ventrue gravitate to the upper crust of kine society, where their sophistication serves them in good stead. Although Ventrue move in the same social circles as the Toreador, they do not fritter away their existences in frivolity and idle chatter. The Ventrue proudly wear the privileges of leadership, and stoically bear its burdens. Thus has it always been; thus shall it always be.

Nickname: Blue Bloods

Sect: Elegant, aristocratic and regal, the Ventrue are the lords of the Camarilla. It was Clan Ventrue that provided the cornerstone of the Camarilla, and it is Clan Ventrue that directs and coaxes the Camarilla in its darkest hours. Even in the modern age, the majority of princes descend from Clan Ventrue. The Ventrue would, of course, have things no other way.

Appearance: Ventrue cultivate classical, traditional appearances. Set in their ways, Ventrue vampires often affect the styles of their breathing days, and one may frequently guess a Ventrue's age by determining from which period of history her clothing dates. Young members of the clan tend toward fashions ranging from "preppy" styles to omnipresent suit-and-tie wardrobes. Ventrue are elegant and stylish, but rarely on the cutting edge of couture or haberdashery trends. After all, one must stand out, not stick out.

Haven: Only the best will do. Ventrue commonly make their havens in mansions or valuable estates. Ventrue vampires often come from wealthy families, and their havens may even be ancestral homes. An old Ventrue tradition holds that any member of the clan may take sanctuary with any other member of the clan, and cannot be refused. This tradition is rarely invoked, for the vampire seeking refuge subsequently owes a great debt to the vampire who provided succor. Nonetheless, the custom has saved the unlife of more than one Blue Blood.

Background: Ventrue traditionally hail from professional or high-society stock, though in modern nights the clan may claim any noteworthy person. Age, wisdom and experience play great parts in Ventrue Embraces, and a Blue Blood never Embraces capriciously. Some Ventrue create neonates exclusively along family lines, in a twisted progression of gentrification. Other Kindred joke that the Ventrue are inbred, while the Ventrue themselves maintain that only the cream of the crop is suitable for membership in their clan.

Character Creation: Social and Mental Attributes are equally important, and illustrious members of the clan cultivate both aspects. Skills and Knowledges share similar importance, as the clan places great emphasis on being well-rounded and capable. Ventrue Kindred greatly prize Backgrounds, and high levels of Fame, Influence, Mentor, Resources, Retainers and Status go far toward establishing a Blue Blood's precedence.

Clan Disciplines: Dominate, Fortitude, Presence

Weaknesses: Ventrue taste is rarefied to the point of exclusivity, and each Blue Blood may partake of only a certain type of mortal blood. This type is chosen at character creation. For example, a particular Ventrue might feed exclusively from virgins, blond men, naked children or clergy. The character will feed on no other type of blood, even if starving or under duress. Ventrue may feed on vampire blood normally.

Organization: The Ventrue in a given region meet often, though their convocations resemble salons or debates and tend to result in more talk than action. Of course, this ponderous discourse is the only "civilized" way to resolve an issue, and impulsive or rash Kindred often chafe under the clan's rigidity. Younger, impatient Ventrue have been known to mount direct challenges to an "old boy's" holdings and position, which is considered the height of treachery and rudeness — unless, of course, the upstart wins.

STEREOTYPES

Assamite: Nobility once belonged to this clan, but they have cast aside their honor in pursuit of wanton diablerie.

Brujah: Old wounds scar the Rabble. These hotheads cultivate buried hatreds better than the harpies do. Still, we must be tolerant — centuries of failure must surely be difficult to bear.

Followers of Set: Their association with serpents is more than appropriate, for their poison infects all whom they taint with their presence. Do not allow them in your domain.

Gangrel: They are as trustworthy and useful as well-bred dogs. We send them forth when it is time for hunting, then call them back to the kennel when more subtle tasks beckon. In this way does everyone fulfill their appointed role.

Giovanni: There are none so base as those who would raze the pillar of stability to further their own twisted interests.

Lasombra: For time out of mind have we dueled with these self-styled Keepers. It is a small comfort to see they cannot achieve for their Sabbat what we have garnered for the Camarilla. All the capering and blood-sports in the world cannot disguise inadequacy.

Malkavian: The price they pay for their supposed enlightenment far exceeds its benefice. Still, learn from them what you may.

Nosferatu: These pitiful creatures still pay the debt earned by their sires so many nights ago, though through no fault of their own.

Ravnos: Exercise the wisdom of the ancient kings when dealing with these vulgar deceivers.

Toreador: Truly, their great passion must be a curse, for Kindred lack the ability to create what they may only impotently observe.

Tremere: It is good that they favor stability, otherwise their depredations might outweigh their utility.

Tzimisce: Are there any left? How quaint!

Caitiff: One can choose neither one's parents nor one's sire, so bear them no ill will unless they earn it.

Camarilla: This is both our honor and our penance.

Sabbat: Infantile and unruly, the Sabbat abandons any hope of redemption.

Bloodlines: Heritage is prized among the clan, and the childer and grandchilder of luminaries are held in esteem (or envy) by the rest of the clan. On a darker note, the Ventrue *antitribu* of the Sabbat have no foes so hated as the Kindred of their parent clan. Sabbat Ventrue are dark knights of that sect, sworn to atone for their line's failings by upholding the tenets of the Sabbat. They are most commonly found among the Sabbat's templars and paladins.

Quote: *The guidance of the Damned is my burden to bear, not yours. You would do well, however, to ask yourself whether your unlife is one of benefit to the Children of Caine, or a detriment. I have already made my judgment.*

THE SABBAT

The Camarilla's archenemy is the monstrous sect known as the Sabbat. Perceived as mindless savages and bloodthirsty fiends by the Camarilla and independent clans alike, the Sabbat is vilified among the society of the Damned, and for good reason. They're just not the reasons other Kindred claim. While the "Kindred" of the Camarilla espouse concealing themselves among mortals and maintaining the tattered vestiges of their Humanity, the Sabbat favors a different philosophy. Not content to cower like beaten dogs from humans, nor to act as pawns in the schemes of their elders, Sabbat vampires instead prefer to revel in their undead nature.

As the Sabbat reasons, vampires are a cut above mortals, who are merely food or diversion. Isn't Kindred vitae more powerful than mortal blood? Don't vampires have unnatural powers with which to assert themselves over the bovine masses? Who needs petty mortal morality when one is a blood-drinking, immortal monster? The Sabbat, though, involves far more than a simple *carte blanche* to behave as abominably as one chooses. Sabbat vampires are inherently alien, and their behavior reflects this.

Sabbat vampires wish no place among humans or those who pretend to be humans. They loathe humankind except as sustenance, and they lack the ability to relate to vampires who cannot accept their natures. They even rebel against their own solitary unlives, traveling in wild nomadic packs instead of eking out secretive, isolated existences. For this reason, tensions run high in the Sabbat, and the sect's surroundings often suffer for it. Cities held by the sect are some of the most violent places in existence, challenged for this dubious honor only where Sabbat and Camarilla vie for supremacy. Mexico City, Detroit, Miami and Montreal are all under the purview of the Sabbat. Cities in contention include New York; Washington, DC; Buffalo; and Atlanta. A city under Sabbat control or conquest is an explosive, volatile place; murders occur nightly, and rape and robbery are to be expected at every turn. In the World of Darkness, these cities have themselves grown toward the alien and away from the human, abandoned as they are to the depredations of the monsters who prowl their alleyways.

Thus, the Sabbat threatens every city it touches, creeping like a cancer into communities that remain oblivious until the war packs tear the city down around them. Though it is arguably no more "evil" than the degenerate elders of the Camarilla, the Sabbat is almost universally more blatant, terrorizing the kine populace with insidious games and premeditated destruction.

Now more than ever before, the Sabbat has the Camarilla on the ropes. Many Camarilla neonates, frustrated by the unattainable power and stagnant ineffectiveness of their elders, have joined the Sabbat in open protest. Numerous cities that were once bastions of Camarilla strength now exist in stalemate or contention. Camarilla princes fear the swelling tide of the Sabbat, and with good cause: Their unlives and those of the Kindred in their cities are on the line. Accordingly, Sabbat members in a Camarilla city can expect no quarter if exposed, as princes and primogen ruthlessly quash agents of the infernal insurrectionist sect. Many neonates, still wishing to please their sires and build a place for themselves in the Camarilla, aid their elders in Sabbat persecution. It would seem they prefer the evil they know to the one they've heard so many horror stories about.

PRACTICES AND ORGANIZATION

Sabbat culture revolves heavily around the twin principles of loyalty and freedom. Vampires, as superior beings, are free to do as they please, but they must also remain true to the Sabbat, lest their freedom be jeopardized by the machinations of the elders. Above all, the Sabbat refuses to be placed under the yoke of the Antediluvians; many of the sect's schemes involve means of frustrating, or at least surviving, Gehenna. The sect's two founding clans, the Lasombra and Tzimisce, are said to have diablerized and destroyed their progenitors, and the other Sabbat vampires follow their lead, hoping that they may one night do the same.

Internal rivalries, power plays and ancient vendettas rend the sect from within, however, and the Sabbat often takes two steps back for every three it takes forward. The sect has no true, all-encompassing guidance; it is a hydra, doubling back to bite itself and its foes even as it gains in membership and influence.

Sabbat vampires themselves, with the exception of the Lasombra and Tzimisce shepherds of the sect, mockingly claim to be "anti-clans," or *antitribu*, of their parent clans. Some Sabbat vampires openly involve themselves in Satanism, paganism or other deviant faiths to spite the propriety of those who stand against them. Perversion and brutality are the Sabbat's tools, and the sect uses them with merciless cunning.

The nucleus of the Sabbat's organization is the "pack," a loose confederation of vampires nominally united toward a single goal. Sabbat packs may be nomadic, traveling from city to city leaving death and fire in their wakes, or they may settle in one location on a permanent basis. Because vampires are primarily solitary predators, forcing themselves into each other's company for prolonged periods of time certainly takes its toll on the individual Kindred who make up the packs.

RITUALS

Sabbat vampires, upon their Embrace, are unceremoniously buried in the ground. The subsequent rite of having to claw her way out of the cold, blind earth after having her head dashed open with a shovel strips away much of a Sabbat neonate's

Humanity. She is then ready to join her Sabbat sectmates as a monster rather than as a feeble, mewling kine.

The Sabbat corrupts and distorts many conventions of the institutions that stand against it. Many of the rituals and practices of the sect stem from the Catholic Church, including partaking of the *Vaulderie*, a corruption of the Eucharist in which vampires drink from a chalice of their commingled vitae to strengthen loyalty.

The vampires of the Sabbat also participate in numerous other rituals, of which there are a seemingly endless number. The sect regularly makes use of fire, serpents, violence and blood at its rituals, which may take the form of fire dances, snake-handling, torture, ceremonial killing or other debased practices. The rituals' purpose is to create solidarity in the packmates, who lead tense, hostile unlives and are prone to fractiousness and mistrust.

OFFICES

The Sabbat, for all its disorganization, maintains numerous positions for its members. Each pack usually has a *priest*, who leads the pack in its rituals and sometimes its other affairs. The offices of *archbishop* (the vampire who oversees Sabbat activity in a given city) and *bishop* (a vampire who assists the archbishop and carries out her will) command great respect among vampires in a city where these Kindred are encountered. Above these offices are those of the *cardinal*, who coordinates Sabbat influence over a given region; and the *prisci* (singular *priscus*), who act as advisors

---

THE VIEW FROM WITHOUT

The Camarilla

I heard that the Sabbat drink each other's blood and burn their sires to cinders at their coven meetings. I've been to Sabbat cities before, and they're the most rundown, violent hellholes in the First World. Did you know they handle snakes, practice black magic and bury each other alive? As if being a vampire isn't curse enough — these guys have to raise the Devil on top of it!

— Pentangellis, Tremere neonate

The Independents

They're insidious, those Sabbat. At least with the Camarilla, you know they're going to stab you in the back. Those maniacs in the Sabbat sell you insurance while they're setting your haven on fire and hanging your sister upside down in the basement. Don't give an inch, though, because if they respect you, they're more likely to burn down someone else's house.

— Zander, Ravnos black marketeer

---

to the "supreme" leader of the sect, the *regent*. The martial arm of the governing body comprises the *templars* and *paladins*, who serve as assassins and bodyguards for the regent, prisci and cardinals. Worrisome references are made to a "sect within the sect" known as the Black Hand, but these are often simply confused references to the sect itself, which has used that moniker before.

LASOMBRA

The Lasombra clan has fallen from grace — and its members enjoy it. Simultaneously graceful and predatory, the Lasombra guide — and, when necessary, whip — the Sabbat into an implacable force. Turning their backs upon the humans they once were, Lasombra give themselves wholly over to the dark majesty of the Embrace. Murder, frenzy, predation: Why fear these things, many Lasombra ask, if one is meant to be a vampire? In contrast to the Tzimisce, though, Lasombra generally seek not to reject all things mortal, but to shape them for their own pleasure.

The Lasombra have been involved with the Church since its inception, and some Kindred whisper that the clan was instrumental in the spread of the Christian faith. In modern nights, however, Lasombra have turned their backs on that divine institution. There are exceptions, of course, but for the most part, Clan Lasombra bears only contempt for the notion of salvation. In fact, the Lasombra brought many of the Church's rites and rituals into the Sabbat sect, twisting them into mockeries of Christian doctrine. The Lasombra ordained many of the sect's *auctoritas* and *ignoblis ritae*, so that the vampires of the Sabbat might never forget who and what they are.

Lasombra are best known for their Discipline of Obtenebration, a means by which they call forth a tangible "living" darkness, manipulating it at their whim. Clan doctrine holds that this "darkness" is in fact the stuff of the vampiric soul, which has been simultaneously strengthened and corrupted by the Embrace. Through the Curse of Caine, some Lasombra believe, God has cast them out, and thus it is their duty to build a new order on Earth via the Sabbat. More scientific Lasombra scoff at this superstition, but even they tend to believe that, as vampires, they represent a new and more advanced breed of sentience, one unconcerned with petty human notions of ethics. Let the milksops of Clan Ventrue burn in the solar fires of martyrdom; the Lasombra are happy with what they are.

Naturally, this villainous outlook is not universal among the clan, but many newly Embraced Sabbat Lasombra take great glee in the wanton destruction and vulgar depravity that such a philosophy allows. In striking contrast, some elder Lasombra still maintain their ties to the Church, though even they seem to consider themselves "tools of the Devil." The two groups do see eye to eye on one matter:

Members of Clan Lasombra, as consummate manipulators themselves, adamantly refuse to submit to the antiquated whims of the Antediluvians. They fight the Jyhad proudly, but unlike many Kindred, they firmly believe they can win.

The typical Lasombra possesses a gift for manipulation, as well as keen leadership skills. Lasombra are the most common leaders of Sabbat packs, as their motivational and Machiavellian natures make them ideal for orchestrating the movements of the sect. Unfortunately, pride goes hand in hand with this dark nobility, and very few Lasombra acknowledge other vampires as equal, let alone superior.

Nickname: Keepers (as in "my brother's...")

Sect: The Lasombra are the ruling clan of the Sabbat, as much as any clan can be said to "rule" that chaotic body. A few elder Lasombra hold membership in the Camarilla or Inconnu, but such creatures lead lonely and perilous existences.

Appearance: Many Lasombra of elder generations hail from Spanish or Italian stock, and some still show their Moorish or Berber heritage. Lasombra neonates and ancillae, however, run the gamut of cultures and ethnicities. Almost all Lasombra are reasonably attractive, with well-bred, aristocratic features — blue-collar Lasombra are rare, and one hardly sees the callused hands or broken noses of the working class among the Keepers.

Haven: Many young Lasombra disdain private havens, sleeping with the pack and maintaining communal lairs "for the good of the sect." Old habits die hard among the Keepers, though; certain elders maintain ancestral manses or other ostentatious havens.

Background: Lasombra may come from any background, but are typically professionals, politically inclined or well educated. Lasombra tend to be aggressive, both physically and socially; the clan has little interest in weaklings and does not hesitate to cull unworthy vampires from its ranks. Lasombra are universally skilled at social discourse and pulling the strings of others — coarse manners are viewed poorly, for the Lasombra are refined monsters.

Character Creation: A Lasombra may have any Demeanor (the better to hide her true Nature!). Most Lasombra favor Social Attributes, though Mental Attributes are prized almost as greatly. Many Keepers cultivate extensive Influence, Status (Sabbat) or Resources, and favor Backgrounds more than additional Disciplines or Abilities. Lasombra founded the Path of Night, and this Path has a number of followers in the Keepers' clan (though many choose to follow other Paths of Enlightenment, and some Lasombra keep vestiges of Humanity).

Clan Disciplines: Dominate, Obtenebration, Potence

Weaknesses: Lasombra vampires cast no reflections. They cannot be seen in mirrors, bodies of water, reflective windows, polished metals, photographs and security cameras, etc. This curious anomaly even extends to the clothes they wear and objects they carry. Many Kindred believe that the Lasombra have been cursed in this manner for their vanity. Additionally, due to their penchant for darkness, Lasombra take an extra level of damage from sunlight.

STEREOTYPES

Assamite: Useful tools, though a bit too...independent of late.

Brujah: Their fiery passion, once harvested, makes a wonderful means through which to use them toward your own ends.

Followers of Set: Hmm...How best to keep them in Egypt?

Gangrel: Easily excited; terrible, monstrous foes. Agitate them and turn them loose on your enemies.

Giovanni: The tree that does not branch hides rot within.

Malkavian: Madness sometimes offers insight, but usually simply obstructs those who would glean its benefit.

Nosferatu: Useful as flies on the wall when you need them, but Nosferatu tend to draw too many flies themselves.

Ravnos: Rather than deal with them directly, it's best to goad them somewhere else and let whoever dwells there address the problem.

Toreador: They possess the most tortured of unlives, and devious minds often lurk under their flighty façades.

Tremere: Inelegant, yet effective in their own way. Their continued existence certainly keeps the Fiends' attentions constructively channeled.

Tzimisce: Valorous allies and venomous rivals, often simultaneously.

Ventrue: Their potential is dissipated by their weakness. They squander their curse by lurking among mortals.

Caitiff: I find it unimaginable that any of these survive past the initial disappointment of learning what they are.

Camarilla: Acceptable, if you're talking about a kine institution. If you're a blood-sucking devil of the night, though, why hide from those upon whom you prey?

Sabbat: If it would merely listen a little better, it would almost be worth the effort we invest in it.

Organization: Clan Lasombra's structure is simultaneously formal and open. Respect and homage are afforded to the elder warriors who helped found the Sabbat, but younger members operate with almost no guidance from the clan as an entity. Quarterly meetings, known as conventicles, serve to keep the Lasombra informed as to each other's status, and blood-drinking rituals are performed at these meetings. While no Lasombra is ever told "You may not do that" (at least not publicly), almost all Keepers have a profound respect for tradition. A secret Lasombra coterie known as *Les Amies Noir* is rumored to hand down "death sentences" on those Keepers who bring undue shame, attention or ignominy to the clan or its members.

Bloodlines: Lasombra *antitribu* are among the staunchest supporters of the Camarilla, though the sect largely distrusts them. Some of the eldest members of Clan Lasombra hold the Sabbat Lasombra in contempt. Naturally, the Sabbat Lasombra greatly fear these powerful Kindred who oppose them, and nothing rallies rival Lasombra like the rumor of an *antitribu* in their midst.

Quote: *Shadows? Hah! I wield Darkness itself, not mere shadows! Tell me — could a shadow do this?*

Tzimisce

(ZHI-MEE-SEE)

If Clan Lasombra is the heart of the Sabbat, Clan Tzimisce is the soul. Even other vampires grow uneasy around these eerie Kindred, and the clan's nickname of "Fiends" was given to it in nights past by horrified Kindred of other lines. The Tzimisce's signature Discipline of Vicissitude is the subject of particular dread; tales speak of crippling disfigurements inflicted on a whim, of ghastly "experiments" and tortures refined beyond human — or vampiric — comprehension or endurance.

This fearsome reputation often seems unwarranted at first. Many Tzimisce are reserved and perspicacious beings, a far cry from the howling war packs that compose much of the Sabbat. Most Tzimisce appear to be rational creatures, formidably intelligent, possessed of an inquisitive and scientific bent, and unstintingly gracious to guests.

Kindred who treat with the Tzimisce, though, realize that the Fiends' human traits are the merest veneer over something…else. For millennia the Fiends have explored and refined their understanding of the vampiric condition, bending their bodies and thoughts into new and alien patterns. Should it prove necessary, enlightening or simply enjoyable, Tzimisce do not hesitate to bend victims in similar fashion. While younger Fiends might be described as merciless or sadistic, elders of the line simply fail to comprehend mercy or suffering — or perhaps they do comprehend, but no longer consider the emotions relevant.

In nights past, the Tzimisce was among the most powerful clans in the world, dominating much of the region now known as Eastern Europe. Potent sorcerers, the Fiends dominated the region's mortals as well, in the process inspiring many of the horror stories about vampires. Clan after clan conspired to uproot the Tzimisce, but it was the sorcerous Tremere who finally succeeded. Indeed, as some tell the tale, the Tremere used captured Tzimisce vitae in their experiments to become immortal. For this, the Tzimisce hate the Tremere unrelentingly, and Tremere who fall into the Sabbat's clutches typically suffer a hideous end at the talons of the Fiends.

During the Great Anarch Revolt, the Tzimisce clan turned on itself, as younger members of the clan discovered mystic means of breaking the blood bonds ensnaring them in the service of their elders. In the ensuing struggle, the younger Fiends destroyed many of their elders and demolished what was left of their power bases. Certain Sabbat whisper that the clan managed to find and destroy its own Antediluvian progenitor, though the Fiends will neither confirm nor deny this tale.

Now the Tzimisce serve the Sabbat as scholars, advisors and priests. Many of the sect's practices originated in the customs of the clan. By exploring the possibilities and limits of vampirism, the clan hopes to discover the greater purpose of the Kindred as a whole. If this means the wholesale destruction of the archaic Antediluvians, the razing of the Camarilla, and the vivisection of millions of kine victims, well, all experiments have their consequences.

Nickname: Fiends

Sect: Most Tzimisce serve the Sabbat. A few powerful Tzimisce elders retain their independence; these are believed to be Inconnu. Almost no

Tzimisce are in the Camarilla; even those Fiends unsympathetic to the Sabbat find the Camarilla's skulking among the masses to be distasteful.

Appearance: As masters of the Vicissitude Discipline, Tzimisce often have striking appearances — whether strikingly beautiful or strikingly grotesque depends on the whim of the Fiend in question. Younger Tzimisce, seeking to explore their inhuman natures, perform all manner of body modifications on themselves. Their elders, though, often affect flawless, symmetrical forms; the body is merely a passing useful machine, after all. Tzimisce faces often resemble masks of blank perfection, and the Fiends typically laugh little, though some have been known to chuckle during particularly elaborate experiments.

Haven: Tzimisce are exceedingly private beings, placing great value on the sanctity of the haven. In fact, the clan has an entire series of elaborate protocols based around hospitality. Guests invited into a Fiend's haven are protected with the host's unlife; trespassers are pursued to the ends of the Earth and punished in gruesome and lingering fashion. Surprisingly, Tzimisce havens, or "manses," are not necessarily comfortable or well-kept in the manner of Ventrue or Toreador dwellings. The amenities of mortals matter little to the Fiends.

Background: Tzimisce rarely Embrace capriciously; choice of childer reflects on the sire, and thus Fiends choose only those mortals who they feel have the capacity to improve the clan as a whole. "Brilliance" and "insight" are particularly prized; whether a childe's brilliance and insight manifest in scientific theory or serial murder is a trifling distinction.

Character Creation: Mental Attributes are most prized among the clan. Although descended from a background of nobility, the typical Sabbat Fiend is unconcerned with petty social interplay; thus, Social Attributes (with the notable exception of Appearance) are rarely primary. Knowledges are favored, and Tzimisce are as likely to follow a Path of Enlightenment (see p. 286) as they are to retain Humanity. Tzimisce often have Status (in the Sabbat), Resources and Retainers (ghouls).

Clan Disciplines: Animalism, Auspex, Vicissitude

Weaknesses: Tzimisce are very territorial creatures, maintaining a particular haven and guarding it ferociously. Whenever a Tzimisce sleeps, she must surround herself with at least two handfuls of earth from a place important to her as a mortal — perhaps the earth of her birthplace or the graveyard where she underwent her creation rites. Failure to meet this requirement halves the Tzimisce's dice pools every 24 hours, until all her actions use only one die. This penalty remains until she rests for a full day amid her earth once more.

Organization: Despite the Tzimisce's pride in their heritage and customs, little organization exists among the clan. Sires and childer remain closer than most Sabbat vampires do, but in general each Fiend makes her own way in the world. One among the Fiends' number bears the ancestral title of *Voivode*; the *Voivode* is nominally the clan leader, though in practice he acts more as a "priest" or rite leader than a temporal ruler.

Bloodlines: Many Tzimisce are descended from specialized "ghoul families" who have long served the clan as minions.

Tzimisce descended from the ghoul family Bratovitch replace Auspex with the Clan Discipline of Potence, but suffer +1 difficulty on any roll to avoid frenzy. Certain Tzimisce are *koldun*, or sorcerers. These Kindred replace the clan Discipline of Vicissitude with Thaumaturgy, but suffer +1 difficulties to resist magic as well.

Quote: *Welcome; a thousand welcomes! I am honored that we could put aside the Jyhad's foolish rivalries for a night, that you might come under my eaves in the spirit of — eh? You start? Ahh — that noise! A trifle! Nothing that need concern you, sweet guest!*

THE INDEPENDENTS

Since the close of the Middle Ages, the dangerous pavanne danced by Camarilla and Sabbat has shaped the face of Kindred society. The bloody conflict has broken millions of human lives and shaped the secret history of cities across the world.

Of course, there are some clans that watch both sects leap at one another's throats in the name of the Jyhad — and prefer to have none of that, thank you very much. Although they certainly have the pedigree of true clans (as opposed to the mongrel bloodlines that occasionally surface), the four independent clans share a powerful disinclination to "take sides" in the Jyhad. Of course, some of the younger members of each clan can be found in both Camarilla and Sabbat. However, the elders of the independent clans plot toward their own inscrutable purposes, purposes that would be delayed by such nonsense as sect allegiance.

It would be foolish to assume that the average member of an unaligned clan is somehow possessed of an absolute allegiance to her clan's ideal. Like all other Kindred, the independents are vampires first and clan members second. Most of these Cainites are concerned with their personal goals first and foremost, whether or not they coincide with (or serve) those of their clans. This fact serves only to aggravate outside observers further; an independent vampire is often a true wild card, with neither sect politics nor clan law as a guideline for predicting her behavior.

And yet…

And yet, rumor has it that the elders of the independent clans are awake in greater numbers than those of any other bloodline. One clan has thrown off an ancient spell that kept it in check, presumably due to the direct intervention of its forebears. Another, the youngest of the clans, allegedly has enjoyed the unceasing patronage of its founder since the Renaissance. The terrible and merciless Methuselahs of a third are said to be throwing off the earth of the ages and summoning their childer to them. And the fourth…

But despite such talk, the childer of each independent clan continue their activities as if all is well, offering as much loyalty to their clans as they did before. If they are indeed pawns of their Antediluvian sires, they are apparently ignorant of the fact — or worse, fully cognizant, and quite acquiescent.

THE UNALIGNED CLANS

The four independent clans have little in common, save their disdain for sects. Each pursues its own goals, and each defines its role in the Jyhad differently. Diffident even to each other, they keep their own laws amid the Camarilla's Traditions and the Sabbat's chaos.

• The **Assamites** are a predatory clan of vampires based in the Middle East. For ages, they have served as independent contractors, assassins for hire to any who provided them with blood. Now, with an ancient curse lifted again, they are proving themselves enemies of all clans as they seek to slake their bottomless thirst for Cainite vitae.

Of all the independents, the Assamites are most feared by the others. Their role in the Jyhad, formerly that of mercenaries alone, has abruptly changed. None can say where the Assamites' loyalty will lie in the next decade or so — or how their new practices will alter the Jyhad itself.

• The **Followers of Set** disdain sects for different reasons. They claim to be heirs to a tradition far older than both Camarilla and Sabbat, and scorn the idea of setting aside their hereditary tasks for a passing fad of mere centuries or so. The tenets of the clan's shadowy faith allegedly date back to the first nights of civilization, and this ancient pedigree takes precedence over matters of mere politics.

The "Setites," as they also call themselves, aren't above playing a fairly mercenary role between the two sects. The clan offers hoarded knowledge and sinister favors to any vampire… for a price. Many elders of other clans look askance on the Setites' bartering; it seems all too possible that with every deal struck, the Clan of the Serpent takes another step to whatever goal its Antediluvian founder has set for it.

• The **Giovanni** are as much a family as they are a clan; the majority of their neonates are Embraced from clan members' mortal descendants. The insular Necromancers avidly pursue two goals: accumulating material wealth and power, and learning the secrets of Death itself.

The Giovanni, frankly, see no need for sects. They effectively police their own ranks, and managed to survive the Inquisition quietly, without requiring the help of other Kindred. They have all the allies they need in the form of their family, and can sternly enforce such aid when necessary. All they require is to be left alone to achieve their own ends — and the prospect of their success is frightening indeed.

• Finally, the **Ravnos** are driven by a clanwide compulsion for larceny and deception, as well as a powerful wanderlust. These masters of illusion, primarily of Indian and Gypsy stock, owe allegiance to themselves first, their clan second, and to no one else at all. Certainly the most loosely organized of the unaligned clans, the nomadic Ravnos are scattered across the world. They travel freely between Camarilla and Sabbat territory, for most princes have learned that it is more trouble to attempt to keep a Ravnos from one's city than to wait for the wastrel vampire to become bored and move on.

The Ravnos are flatly indifferent to sect politics, and most vampires have dismissed them as incapable of playing any great role in the Jyhad. They seem too chaotic and undisciplined to be of any use even to Methuselahs — and the Ravnos enjoy that reputation. The clan has happily lasted the past millennium or so without responsibility or duty, and sees no reason to change. However, the near future may see the Ravnos working toward a common purpose after all....

THE VIEW FROM WITHOUT

The Camarilla

As if we didn't have enough to worry about, these vipers insist on playing both sides against one another. It's certain they're up to no good; what else could convince them they could survive without allies? They are perfectly capable of shifting the balance of the Jyhad, and they know that full well. I would pray that they make the proper choice — if I believed anyone would listen to me.

— Anne Bowesley, Prince of London

The Sabbat

They are too weak to threaten our power — but also too strong to crush easily beneath our boots. Sometimes we lose a pack, or more, to idiocy; only a fool tries to wrest a Serpent from its den, or beat one of those damn Giovanni at his own game. But we learn from such things. We learn where the so-called "free clans" are strong, and where they are not so strong. And they will be not so strong when the earth cracks open and the sun goes red. That I guarantee.

— Cicatriz, Bishop of Tijuana

Assamite

From the desert wastes of the East come the Assamites, and they bring with them a miasma of terror. The Assamites are known throughout vampire society as a clan of murderous assassins, working for whoever can pay their price. The price they charge for their work is the vitae of other Kindred; for the Assamites, diablerie is the greatest sacrament.

Assamites tend to avoid the affairs of the Camarilla and the Sabbat, working for either or both sides in pursuit of their goals. They do circulate among sect-held cities; other Kindred find them useful for slaying rivals, enforcing blood hunts, scourging undesirable childer, and infiltrating rivals' power bases. However, Assamites rarely form true alliances with other Kindred, for they consider other Children of Caine to be of inferior stock. Unlike the other clans, the Assamites do not claim to have a founder of the Third Generation. Rather, they believe their founder to be a member of the *Second* Generation, making all other Cainites flawed copies of themselves.

In nights prior to the formation of the Camarilla and the Sabbat, the Assamites practiced diablerie widely, always looking to bring themselves closer to "the One," as they referred to their mythical founder. As the Anarch Revolt ensued, and the Sabbat and Camarilla rose from the ashes, many powerful elders grew uneasy at the cannibal assassins stalking their ranks. Calling upon the Tremere to curse the Assamites' blood, the Camarilla placed a yoke on the clan that rendered its members unable to consume the vitae of other Kindred. Unable to face the unified front the Camarilla represented, the Assamites submitted to this indignity. Those few who did not accept the curse went into hiding and joined the Sabbat.

Those who deal regularly with Assamites have sensed great upheaval among the clan. The greatest sign of this is the clan's recent circumvention of the Tremere blood curse. Freed from the mystic shackles preventing it from engaging in diablerie, the clan has begun a campaign of murder and cannibalism once again. Assamites now kill other Kindred without provocation — indeed, without sanctioned contracts.

The clan as a whole has assumed a more aggressive disposition. Whereas once the Assamites would take no further contracts on a victim who bested their assassins, the clan may now pursue that victim, and often does with unparalleled fervor. Similarly, Assamites no longer honor the age-old custom of tithing to their sires. In these nights of impending Gehenna there is no place for lazy Assamites who rest on their laurels.

Precisely what the Assamites want, though, is unknown. Certainly, Assamites have flexed their muscle in both the physical and the political arenas, and hidden agents of the clan have come out of cover in cities where the ruling vampires have become lazy and fatuous. Their hold in the cities of India and the Middle East is much stronger than other Kindred had previously guessed. Whereas other Kindred once viewed the Assamites as honorable (i.e., relatively impotent), useful functionaries, they now hold the clan in dread.

Nickname: Assassins

Sect: The Assamites hold Sabbat and Camarilla in equal contempt. Some Assamites remain among the Sabbat, and a scattered few exist as loners in the Camarilla.

Appearance: Assamites tend to dress stylishly but practically. Aquiline noses, dark hair and slim, graceful builds dominate the clan's membership, though African members obviously bear more Nubian characteristics. Recently, a number of Westerners have been introduced into the clan, though they remain in the minority. These individuals may have almost any appearance, as they are chosen for their skill, not their looks. Also, Assamites' skin grows darker as they age (as opposed to other vampires, whose skin gets paler with age); particularly ancient Assamites are almost ebony in complexion.

Haven: Most clan elders make their homes at Alamut, the clan stronghold, which is located high atop a mountain thought to be somewhere in modern Turkey. Neonates and operatives abroad typically select remote, inaccessible locations to ensure that they receive no unexpected guests.

Background: Many Assamite *fida'i* (newly Embraced apprentices) hail from Asia Minor or northern Africa. Most members of the clan have been involved with assassination, wet work or terrorist activities for some portion of their mortal lives, though this is less true among the Assamite vizier bloodline. Recently, the clan has Embraced many neonates from the Western stock among which it moves, particularly soldiers, criminals and street gangsters.

Character Creation: Assamites favor Physical Attributes, with Mental Attributes a close second. The Assassins favor Skills and Talents equally. Assamites typically have similar Natures and Demeanors, as subterfuge isn't their style, but rarely are they the exact same. Popular Backgrounds include Mentor, Contacts and, of course, Generation.

Clan Disciplines: Celerity, Obfuscate, Quietus

Weaknesses: In light of their recent circumvention of the Tremere blood-curse, the Assamites have reacquired their appreciable taste for vitae, particularly that of other Kindred. Having been forced to rely on alchemical blood potions for much of its modern history, the clan is easily addicted to the blood of other vampires. Any time an Assamite drinks or even tastes the blood of another Kindred, she must make a Self-Control roll (difficulty equal to the number of blood points ingested +3). If this roll is failed, she is addicted, and she must make another Self-Control roll the next time she comes in contact with Kindred vitae. Failing this roll sends the vampire into a sanguinary frenzy, in which she will do anything physically possible to partake of as much blood as possible. When (not if) the character's addiction manifests, the consuming need for blood should be roleplayed — Clan Assamite no longer sees the need to hide its vampiric nature.

Organization: Elders of the clan still orchestrate the Assassins' movements from the Eagle's Nest at Alamut, but more and more Assamites have been dispatched throughout the world, killing Kindred with or without sanction or contracts. Many of the clan's former "rules of engagement" — such as the prohibition against hunting an opponent who'd already bested another Assamite — have been discarded. To those outside the clan, it appears as if the Assamites are running rampant.

Assamites organize themselves into units similar to Sabbat packs; these bands are known as *falaqi*. A *falaqi* typically consists of two or three Kindred who infiltrate a city and gain a foothold there. Assamites in a city engage in activities common to many Kindred (establishing power bases, cultivating herds), but also weaken rival Kindred through selective assassinations, for they do not see the Sixth Tradition as applying to them.

Bloodlines: The Assamite vizier bloodline specializes in the study of Thaumaturgy and Middle Eastern magic. Viziers almost never leave the confines of Alamut, and certainly never engage in assassination activities. They instead refine their — and accordingly, the clan's — knowledge of blood magic. Assamite viziers forsake Celerity, instead learning Thaumaturgy as a clan Discipline, but must spend an extra blood point on all Thaumaturgical invocations. Assamite *antitribu* of the Sabbat differ very little from their

IN NIGHTS PAST

Storytellers who wish to set their games in nights prior to 1998 should make a few adjustments to Clan Assamite as presented. As they have only recently shaken off the blood curse, pre-1998 Assamites bear a different clan weakness. Assamites must tithe 10 percent of the blood they garner in contract payments to their sires. Additionally, they may not imbibe the vitae of Kindred. Should an Assamite ingest vampire blood, each point so taken inflicts one automatic health level of lethal damage to the Assamite.

STEREOTYPES

Brujah: Whatever gods we shared in the past, we have nothing in common now.

Followers of Set: To sup with snakes is to invite their poison to your table.

Gangrel: I would almost forsake the tainted blood of animals, but my need is great.

Giovanni: Let them traffic with their dead, but never suffer them to stain your domain with their debased presences.

Lasombra: Untrustworthy and vulgar — but they are nonetheless some of our best employers.

Malkavians: Their blood brings madness when it stains our lips. Avoid them, lest you be tainted with their derangement.

Nosferatu: Their hideousness hides a semblance of honor and, thus, they are fools.

Ravnos: I find the sounds of their exsanguination more musical than their ugly Gypsy songs.

Toreador: A pursuit of beauty is luxury and, therefore, wasteful.

Tremere: We shall never again bear the indignity of their sorcery. The only good Tremere is the one you kill on the road back to Haqim's bosom.

Tzimisce: I am surprised that our mutual hatred for the Warlocks doesn't make us better bedfellows. It is irrelevant, however, as these relics mean nothing to the modern night.

Ventrue: Though they give us leave to practice our rites in cities they control, it was nevertheless the Blue Bloods who contrived to place us under Clan Tremere's curse.

Caitiff: Worthless chaff, fit only to be separated from the wheat. They are rarely missed, though their weak blood does us little long-term good.

Camarilla: Their nights are numbered, and we shall never forget the shackles they placed upon us.

Sabbat: Too callous and classless, and so dead-set against heeding their elders' advice that they remind one of adolescent children.

independent counterparts, their only variance being their nominal allegiance to the sect. Assamites and their *antitribu* relate very well, particularly since the parent clan's breaking of the Tremere curse.

Quote: *Save your breath, weak one — no one will hear your screams. Now aid me on my journey back to Haqim's grace....*

Followers of Set

The Followers of Set, more commonly referred to as "Setites," are mistrusted perhaps more than any other clan. Their ties with the archetypal Serpent of myth are well-known, and bolstered by their disturbing powers. They are custodians of knowledge that, according to their claims, predates even the First City. When they enter a city, the Cainite power structure almost inevitably erodes. But most unnerving of all, they share a dark and powerful faith as a clan — a faith that the blood of gods pulses in their cold veins.

Of course, the clan's very name is proof of such faith. According to most Setites, their clan founder was none other than the dark god of ancient Egypt, a hunter without equal in the desert night. Other tales state that Set was an Antediluvian — at *least* — who enshrined himself as a god among the Egyptians. In either case, Set's rule went unquestioned until he was challenged by a being named Osiris — whom some call a vampire, and others something else. Their war lasted for centuries, but ultimately Set was cast out of Egypt, into the darkness. And yet, his followers claim, it was in the darkness that wise, ancient Set began his rule in earnest. Although great Set has vanished from the world, his childer work to ensure that the world will be in a suitable state for his return — advancing their own schemes in the process, of course.

To achieve their goals, Setites master several potent tools. To their thinking, the weapons of addiction, seduction and decay are the oldest and finest of means to an end. Setites use drugs, sex, money, power — even vitae and supernatural lore — to draw others into their coils. To date, the Followers' methods have proved terribly effective. Kindred and kine alike succumb to the Setites' charms, gladly doing whatever their new masters bid in return for the Serpents' reptilian patronage. Indeed, in some cities, entire subcultures and economic strata are under one or more Setites' sway.

The Followers of Set cryptically refer to themselves as the "eldest among clans," whatever that phrase may mean to them. Cainite historians dismiss this as groundless braggadocio, citing Set's rise as well past the time of the First City. However, those who listen carefully to the Setites' whispering are somewhat less flippant, as the Snake Clan seems to have access to hoary lore that, some worry, might date back to the first and longest nights of all. A few Serpents have even hinted that Set was thrown into the darkness before Caine himself received his own curse — a theory that most Kindred dismiss, but one with frightening implications nonetheless.

Whatever the clan's origins, it is a fact that its influence is widespread indeed. Although they are rare in "traditional" vampiric haunting grounds such as Europe, the Followers of Set prowl many other areas of the world. They have a potent presence in Africa, particularly in Cairo and the sub-Saharan area of the continent. They nest in India, just on the edge of the Cathayan hunting grounds, pursuing the wisdom of destroyer gods and gathering cults to themselves. They sleep under Middle Eastern sands and rule the Caribbean night. And they go unafraid into the worst urban hellholes in America. Their web stretches from continent to continent, and the other clans have yet to realize just how much of the world the Setites have in their clutches.

Nickname: Serpents

Sect: Neutrality is far too valuable for the Followers of Set to bother with sects. They find the Camarilla pretentiously idealistic, and the Sabbat exactly the same. Setites prefer to barter their secrets to both sides, but reserve their truly significant finds for the clan's exclusive use.

Appearance: Most elder Setites are of Egyptian, North African or Middle Eastern blood. However, the Snakes have adopted a more egalitarian approach in recent years, and have Embraced men and women of all ethnicities. Red hair is considered a mark of Set's favor, and some neonates are not above hennaing their hair nightly to prove their devotion. Setites usually have impeccable taste in clothing and accessories, and have an inviting, commanding demeanor that transfixes onlookers.

Haven: Although many younger Setites aren't above snatching the most practical crashspaces possible, the elders of the clan treat haven-building as a reverential process. Many use ancient alchemical rituals to consecrate their havens, be they temples, hidden libraries or simple crypts. Most train cadres of ghouls for the "sacred duty" of guarding the master's haven, and some are fond of letting various snakes roam the interior of their lairs. Their havens are often decorated in ancient Egyptian fashion, but the Followers of Set have become quite multicultural in recent years. An individual Setite may adorn his haven with Ghanan sculpture, Moroccan rugs or Hopi kachinas — whatever suits his tastes or background.

Background: Many Setites served as retainers to other Followers of Set prior to receiving the Embrace. In former nights, the clan chose only those of Egyptian descent, but pragmatism has led them to include those from all ethnicities of late. The Serpents tend to select childer who prove themselves manipulative and mentally resilient — the former to better sway mortals into the clan's service, the latter so that the childe can safely learn the knowledge kept by the Followers. The Setites choose only the best; those who are anything less cannot hope to rise above the status of pawn.

Character Creation: Setites tend to focus on Social and Mental Attributes, but their Abilities vary with the character concept. The Occult Knowledge is common among the clan. Their Natures can be scholarly or bestial, while their Demeanors are whatever they find appropriate for the occasion. Many have great networks of Contacts, Herd (cultists), Retainers and other pawns willing to do their bidding; exactly what the Setite offers for such service may vary greatly, from blackmail to simple friendship.

Clan Disciplines: Obfuscate, Presence, Serpentis

Weaknesses: The Setites, as creatures of the most ancient darkness, have a severe allergy to bright lights of all sorts, and sunlight in particular. Add two health levels to any damage inflicted by exposure to the sun. Followers of Set also subtract one from all dice pools while in overly bright light (spotlights, magnesium flares, etc.).

Organization: Individually, Followers of Set act much like other vampires, maintaining herds, acquiring power and suborning rivals. Nor is one Setite automatically immune to the predation of a rival — the clan takes a Darwinian approach even among its own ranks. Communally, though, Serpents usually organize themselves into temples where they can exchange lore and practice their rites. Their hierarchy tends to be organized by age, with the eldest and wisest among them officiating. Rumor has it that somewhere in Africa exists the Grand Temple of Set, the dwelling place of the clan's Dark Hierophant. This Methuselah is said to be the most powerful of Set's personal childer and the first vampire Embraced into the clan; if rumor is correct, his knowledge has no equal, and his authority over the clan is absolute.

Bloodlines: The Serpents have several offshoot bloodlines, most of which derive from alternate interpretations of the dark faith of Set. The Path of the Warrior is one of the most dramatic; these stalkers

STEREOTYPES

Assamite: It seems that our brothers have forgotten all their teachings at the merest taste of a drop of vitae. And what implications this has….

Brujah: They have forgotten more lessons than they've learned. Once worth a touch of respect, now…nothing, really.

Gangrel: Cunning in a savage sort of way, but lacking even the common sense of a wild dog. They have nothing we require, and are valuable only as an object lesson in control.

Giovanni: Dangerous rivals, although they balance such crassly material priorities along with their search for enlightenment.

Lasombra: Children of the void, though still fresh from the mother's teat and new-weaned on stolen vitae. Only the eldest among them have any idea of exactly what power they evoke.

Malkavian: Dangerous. They are the keepers of truths perhaps even older than we. Fortunate that the other clans are foolish enough to dismiss the mad ones' prophesying as delusion and rambling; were they wise enough to listen, Set's time might well have come before we were ready.

Nosferatu: A not-so-subtle reminder of what we all are, and why it is pointless to play at anything else.

Ravnos: Concern yourself not with the wandering adolescents of this clan; they are foolish and ignorant of their true lineage. It is the head of the rakshasa that bears watching, and its eyes have opened again.

Toreador: Such ardor is…admirable. I could become drunk on a Toreador's passion, and might drain him dry trying to fill myself with it.

Tremere: How like a precocious child, with spectacles perched so seriously on his nose and a heavy book in his lap! Ah, but this little darling might eventually prove dangerous, and so requires a parent's gentle guidance….

Tzimisce: Self-titled dragons who nonetheless crawl nightly on their bellies and feast on dust. They are crafty, but not so crafty as we.

Ventrue: They dislike us and spread slander against us, for they cannot accept that we are elder and of greater birth than they. Abide a while yet, and their rule will stop persecuting us soon enough.

Caitiff: Like the others, save more easily led. Their thin blood betrays the Cainites' essential weakness.

Camarilla: For all its skill at crafting Masquerades, it cannot see through its own veils.

Sabbat: A frightful mask does not a monster make. It simply makes a victim easier to spot.

glorify Set as hunter and warrior, and learn Potence in lieu of Obfuscate. Similarly, the Path of Ecstasy glorifies the pleasures of the flesh offered by the Serpent itself; such vampires seek to master Presence above all other Disciplines. Finally, the Serpents of the Light are a splinter bloodline that nests among the Sabbat. These Cainites differ from other Setites only in outlook, but practice a code of conduct that the rest of the clan considers heresy punishable by Final Death.

Quote: *Please. I'd thought you above such abysmal Judeo-Christian fallacies. "The serpent is not to be trusted." "Knowledge is the source of all evil." Why do you think parents instill such beliefs in their children — or that your sire reared you in like fashion? Why would they balk at sharing wisdom? Ah. You begin to understand. Would you like to sit and speak with me now?*

Giovanni

The Giovanni are respectful, genteel and well-mannered. Affluent beyond imagination, Clan Giovanni traces its roots back to before the Renaissance, to a family of merchant princes. The clan still maintains its original home in Venice, in a thousand-year-old *loggia* just outside the heart of the city. No other clan makes such a spectacle of humility and propriety as does the Giovanni. And no other clan hides its blasphemous secrets as well.

According to tales whispered in Camarilla salons and Sabbat esbats, the Giovanni's money spoiled the family, and the Venetians turned to *nigrimancy* out of perverse boredom. Surprisingly enough, the family demonstrated a great aptitude for trafficking with the dead, and their newfound abilities caught the eye of a forgotten Antediluvian. The vampire Embraced the head of the family, Augustus Giovanni, and brought him into the world of the Damned. This particular Antediluvian, the legends say, had a profound interest in death, and the Embrace of Giovanni and his family was intended to further the vampire's knowledge of what lay beyond the wall of mortality.

The Ancient's plan worked better, albeit differently, than he'd intended. Augustus, a cutthroat and mercenary merchant, saw the opportunity to seize his doddering sire's power and did so, hunting and killing all of the Antediluvian's descendants as well. After drinking the Ancient's blood, Augustus became a member of the Third Generation and founded his own clan, the Giovanni.

Other vampires reacted in horror, and, for a century, the "Devil Kindred" Giovanni were rooted out and destroyed wherever they went. Finally, the Giovanni sat down with the newly formed Camarilla and formed a mutual truce. This truce guaranteed the Giovanni would not participate in the Jyhad and would leave other vampires to their affairs. The Giovanni agreed, thus averting the genocide they surely would have otherwise met.

Taking advantage of other vampires' lack of involvement with them, the Giovanni quietly continued to amass wealth and power, practicing their Discipline of Necromancy all the while. Few believe the clan is engaging in either practice for altruistic purposes, and recent global movements by the Giovanni have many Kindred worried. With all that money and all those harvested souls, something is on the horizon; it is an ill wind that blows out of Venice.

Members of the Giovanni clan are also members of the Giovanni family, and those not Embraced often serve their Kindred relations as ghouls. This familial tie — members of the clan are related by blood *twice* — ensures complete loyalty on the part of the Giovanni. While concentrated primarily in Europe, the Giovanni have recently been expanding into the world market, and the clan seems to be more prolific in recent nights.

Nickname: Necromancers

Appearance: Giovanni vampires typically maintain airs of presentability and respectability. Most Giovanni, hailing as they do from the Italian branch of the clan, bear European features, including fair-to-dark complexions, dark hair and solid statures. Giovanni tend to dress well but not lavishly, preferring subtle accouterments of affluence to ostentatious displays.

Haven: Giovanni favor havens befitting their wealth. Mansions, palatial homes and well-appointed apartments suit the Giovanni best, though uncommon is the Necromancer who doesn't keep a backup haven in a sewer or graveyard. Some Giovanni involve themselves in medical power structures and make their havens in hospitals, where plenty of cover exists and precious blood may be taken at a whim.

Background: Most Giovanni come from the ranks of the Venetian family and have spent much of their mortal lives as ghouls in service to another family member. As closely knit as the family is, rivalry and treachery are rampant among the clan, as each member tries to assert his superiority over others. Amazingly versatile for having such a finite pool from which to draw new Kindred, the Giovanni may Embrace any individual who shows particular promise, but only after a "trial period" of ghouldom known as the Proxy Kiss.

Character Creation: Giovanni typically have professional concepts, the better to fund the clan's endeavors. Their Natures and Demeanors tend toward the crafty and selfish, though perversity festers in the incestuous family, and many are Deviants. Mental Attributes and Knowledges are primary, and Backgrounds are greatly prized. Almost all Giovanni possess a comfortable level of Resources, and many claim Retainers, Contacts and Influence.

Clan Disciplines: Dominate, Necromancy, Potence

Weaknesses: The Giovanni Kiss causes excruciating pain in mortals who receive it. In fact, the bite of a Giovanni vampire often kills its mortal victim from shock before the poor soul has a chance to die from blood loss. The Necromancers do twice as much damage as any other vampire to mortals (and *only* mortals) who suffer their Kiss. Thus, if the Giovanni in question took one blood point from a mortal vessel, that vessel would suffer *two* health levels of damage. As such, Giovanni vampires are quite likely to feed from already dead corpses or from resources like hospital blood reserves.

Organization: Giovanni clan affairs are handled in Venice, in a vast *loggia* colloquially known as the Mausoleum. As is to be expected, the clan has a familial structure. Incest, necrophilia, favor-currying, ancestor worship and carefully cultivated guilt riddle the family; by the time most Giovanni Kindred are Embraced, they've seen more than enough to inure them to the vagaries of undead existence. The clan's nonintervention in the Jyhad allows members to focus on their own vendettas and better their knowledge of Necromancy. The Giovanni Antediluvian, Augustus Giovanni, reportedly still maintains direct control over the clan, though none outside the clan is known to have seen him in the past 400 years.

Bloodlines: The Giovanni do not have *antitribu* — they are all loyal to the family as a whole, if not individual members. However, the clan has brought several other families into its fold. These include the Pisanob (Central and South American witches), the Dunsirn (Scottish bankers who practice cannibalism), the Milliners (a prominent New England family dating back to the turn of the 20th century) and a host of minor families. Not all Giovanni are surnamed Giovanni.

Quote: *Consider taking a different tone with me. You are, after all, worth as much to the Giovanni dead as you are undead.*

Ravnos

If ever a clan was renowned for a wickedly black sense of humor, the Ravnos would be that clan. These Cainites are deceivers of the first order, weaving illusion and lies into elaborate schemes to part the foolish from whatever it is the Ravnos might fancy — be it wealth, blood or even their victims' freedom. Like Mephistopheles or Old Scratch, the Ravnos ply their devil's deals with whomever they choose, be it human or Kindred, and woe to those who wind up unable to pay the hidden costs.

Although many Ravnos see themselves as great tricksters, the generally benevolent tricks of Coyote and Raven aren't so much their style. Instead, they draw on a tradition of illusion and deceit inherited from the rakshasas and *ghuls* of the Middle and Far East. A Ravnos is a highly dangerous being with whom to sup or bargain. And *these* devils have been making their wagers and bargains for a long time indeed.

The Ravnos are nomadic to the core and care little for permanent havens or positions in a city's established power structure. Even those who have chosen a given city for their home tend to establish and abandon havens as the mood strikes them, taking whatever lairs they like, doing as they please, and moving on when bored. This habit infuriates princes across the world, who resent the Ravnos' disregard for the Tradition of Hospitality. Few punish violators, though, for fear drawing the malice of the clan as a whole.

Although the clan has long-standing ties with the Gypsies, few Ravnos enjoy the hospitality of their mortal kin. Perhaps the Gypsies know these vampires' true natures too well, and are loath to offer friendship to the undying. Perhaps the Ravnos themselves alienate their mortal families through their dangerous tricks. Whatever the reason, a Ravnos typically has no allies he can rely on regularly. His charm may win him a few temporary companions, and clan loyalty may draw fellow Ravnos to his side in times of dire need, but the vampire's path ultimately lies alone.

Naturally, the princes of many cities are leery of allowing such tricksters free rein in their domains. The Ravnos' eccentric code of honor is strong, but rarely coincides with another Kindred's definition of the term. A Ravnos may break her word at will, unless she's spit in her palm and shaken on the deal. She'll defend her "good name" for all it's worth — depending on what she considers slander. And she'll usually come to the defense of a clanmate, and *vice versa*; the Ravnos may take advantage of one another, but they consider it their privilege. Outsiders aren't allowed the same.

Perhaps the most worrisome thing about the Ravnos is that as a clan, they managed to survive for centuries in Asia, where most Kindred are quickly hunted down and devoured by the ruthless Cathayans. No other Cainites know exactly how they managed this — but now a possible reason is emerging. Rumors filter back to Europe and the Americas of elder things awakening, of ancient vampires shrugging off the earth of millennia and throwing the Cainite courts into disorder. These elder Ravnos — if rumor speaks correctly — have demonstrated terrifying mystical powers, including a talent for illusions so powerful they can affect the physical world. Time can only tell what part the reemergence of these "demon kings" will play in the Jyhad.

Nickname: Deceivers

Sect: The Ravnos go where they will and deal with whomever they will, and sects be damned. The elders of the clan, particularly those centered in India, scoff at the Camarilla and Sabbat as temporary social clubs at best, hollow institutions where paranoid vampires can gather in numbers and reassure themselves that they are the apex of the food chain. The younger ones simply reject the idea of giving any outsider even a fraction of authority over them. Most Ravnos look at the Sabbat's promises of freedom and the Camarilla's offer of protection as nothing more than honeyed bait for the trap, and politely (or not so politely) decline.

Appearance: Many younger Western Ravnos are of Gypsy descent, usually of dark complexion, with darker hair and eyes. Slightly rarer are those with Asian, African or Nordic features, and rarer still are those without even a trace of Gypsy blood. In fact, European Ravnos do not Embrace *gorgio* (non-Gypsies) at all.

The Eastern half of the clan is mostly of Indian blood, although members have Embraced promising men and women of other ethnicities. Like their Western cousins, they favor colorful and beautiful clothing, and enjoy practicing their allure on mortals.

Haven: Ravnos are nomadic by nature; even their Eastern childer feel the wanderlust upon them from time to time. Members of the clan often travel in vans or RVs, taking shelter wherever they may. Those with mortal relatives, particularly Gypsies, often stay with their families for a while. But when the local Kindred start getting uncomfortably curious, the Ravnos are on the road again.

Background: These nomadic vampires Embrace few childer, despite the swelling herds of humanity. The youngest Ravnos, however, are fairly indiscriminate in siring childer, and the latest generations have seen Ravnos from all cultures and ethnicities. Those Ravnos neonates without Indian or Gypsy blood typically demonstrated great facility for misdirection, barter and mischief in life. The Devil has a sharp eye for his own.

Character Creation: Ravnos typically have nomadic concepts, and their Demeanors can change as required by the situation. They tend toward primary Social Attributes, as well as primary Talents. Many have high Resources, either in the form of ancestral treasures or as accumulated hoards of ill-gotten rare goods and objects of art.

Clan Disciplines: Animalism, Chimerstry, Fortitude

Weaknesses: The Ravnos have indulged in their particular vices so long that they have become addicted to them. Each Ravnos has a weakness for some form of trickery, deceit or mischief, whether it be gambling, lying, theft, blackmail or even cleverly framed murder. When the opportunity to indulge presents itself, a Ravnos must make a Self-Control roll (difficulty 6) or succumb to her compulsion.

Organization: Most Ravnos trust nobody, not even their own clanmates, but work together when necessary to bilk, rob or topple an outsider enemy. They often make grandiose pledges of family loyalty to one another, although neither party expects very much to come of the vows.

The recently awakened clan elders, however, are beginning to contact Ravnos on all continents. Although the typically chaotic clan structure has yet to see any real change, it may be only a matter of time before the Ancients' will becomes manifest through the younger Ravnos.

Bloodlines: The Ravnos are divided among family lines, mimicking the family lineages of their Gypsy kin. Among their families are the Phuri Dae, who often focus on Auspex rather than Fortitude; the Urmen, who claim their blood is more eldritch than most and focus primarily on Chimerstry; and the Vritra and Kalderash, who are said to maintain black pacts with the deadly Cathayans.

Quote: *If it'd been me stealing the sun, I wouldn't have given it to the humans to keep them warm. I'd have drowned it in the ocean and started buying the kine's souls by selling them fire.*

STEREOTYPES

Assamite: They've become even worse *ghuls* than ever before. The only good thing about them is that now the other clans hate and fear them so much that you can easily get plenty of cold bodies between yourself and one of these devourers.

Brujah: Go ahead and let them rattle their cages. If they bend the bars, we'll follow them out — and if the zookeeper shows up, they're the first to go.

Followers of Set: What is everyone so afraid of? Even a deal with the Devil isn't so bad if you read the fine print. Snakes can't poison me, and I don't have a soul to lose. Then again, if everyone thought the same as me, I wouldn't have "preferred customer" status. So let 'em cringe.

Gangrel: Our poor cousins, if that's possible. They dig themselves holes in the mud and drag their matted asses into the city only when the Camarilla whistles 'em up. Lapdogs gone feral, and who needs that kind of pet?

Giovanni: A family as much as a clan, same as us. Give 'em space, and maybe they'll do the same. If they don't, pack 'em off to hell. They'll be happiest there, anyway.

Lasombra: They look pretty soft, but these are some hard bastards, that's for sure. They ain't the new kid on the block, and they don't play kid games. (shrug) You gotta respect that.

Malkavian: They see too damn much and don't buy into anybody's delusions but their own. Don't like them, not one bit.

Nosferatu: Their eyes and ears are just too damn sharp for their own good. Be a shame if something…happened to those catacomb crawlers.

Toreador: Poet shirts, wine and roses, leather jackets, artsy tattoos. Kill me if I ever start acting like one of those limpdicks.

Tremere: Our fellow sorcerers, conjuring up solid results to our shadows. Of course, they haven't half the edge we do — I'd be more afraid of my cousin's ghost-fire than the clumsy pyrotechnics of a Warlock.

Tzimisce: There are some real impurities in these bitches' blood. I say Caine took a shine to a monster some time ago, and the Tzimisce are the result.

Ventrue: Bow if you have to, scrape if you must, and slit their throats for the blood if you can.

Caitiff: Like suckers, there seems to be one born every minute.

Camarilla: Everything we need, boxed up like a Christmas present.

Sabbat: They claim to love their existence. Amazing, then, how much their actions smack of self-loathing.

There's blood on the windowsill. That wouldn't be too bad, if the window in question weren't nine stories up, but as things stand, it might be a bit of an oddity. The police are going to look at that, notice the distinct lack of a fire escape and of a body in the alley below, and start asking questions. Then, when the coroner reports that the body on the sofa has been sucked dry, more questions are going to be asked. Someone will eventually put two and two together, and get fangs, and then my ass is going to be in a sling because it's my childe who's responsible for this whole mess. So I've got to be the one to clean it up, otherwise Prince "I've got a stick shoved so far up my ass it ought to paralyze me" LeClercq is going to use this as an excuse to turn both my kid and me into ash. And while at this point I could give a rat's ass about what happens to my errant Embracee, I sure as hell don't want to get crucified because he's a binge eater.

So first things first. I smash the place up as quietly as I can. There's some blood left in the body, so I splash that around as evenly as possible, taking care not to leave bootprints. Whatever valuables I find in the process, I scoop up — hopefully some bored homicide detective will write this off as another case of a crackhead knocking over an apartment and finding the resident home. The fix won't hold up to intense scrutiny, but at least it will take the cops down the wrong road if they actually mount an investigation.

Then I take the body and toss it out the window. I wait a second for that wet "thump" I know and love from way too many of these cleanup jobs, then I concentrate for a second and slough off my human shape like — well, screw the metaphor. If anyone's looking for where the body in the alley came from, all they're going to see is a bat heading up into the night.

Mind you, I'm one very pissed-off bat, but it's hard to tell that kind of thing from a distance.

CHARACTER AND TRAITS

As a player of **Vampire: The Masquerade**, you must create a character — an alter ego through which you interact with the game world and take your part in the story. Like a character in a novel or movie, this character becomes a protagonist in the stories you tell. Rather than making up a new character for each session, you create a single richly detailed character, then assume the role of that character every time you play. As your troupe tells its stories, you watch your character grow and develop. Ultimately, the character you create becomes as real and as timeless as a great hero (or villain) in a literary work.

This chapter describes how to create a vampire character, beginning with a general concept and translating that concept into the Traits and statistics that are used in the game. Though the process is relatively simple, and players can undertake it on their own, it is best to create characters under the Storyteller's supervision, so that she can answer questions and guide the creation process.

TRAITS

Much of a character's life comes from the way you describe and roleplay him. For example, your vampire's general disposition and attitude toward feeding, as decided by you, might all contribute toward his overall role in the story. However, certain aspects of a character — his physical prowess, his looks and his vampire powers, for example — are described in numerical terms and used in conjunction with the systems of the game. These features are called *Traits*. Traits quantify your character's particular strengths and weaknesses, which guide the character in his interactions with other players' characters and the characters the Storyteller creates. For example, your character might have high Mental Traits, making him invaluable when brains and cunning are required. However, he might have low Physical Traits, forcing him to rely on a friend's character when violence or brute force is called for.

Traits are commonly described in numerical terms with ratings between 1 and 5. (Humanity/Path scores and Willpower are exceptions to this guideline, and some particularly ancient and powerful vampires are rumored to have *other* Traits exceeding 5....) These numbers represent the quantity and quality of the character's prowess with a given Trait. One dot is considered a poor rating, while five dots indicate superiority. Think of Trait ratings as similar to the stars with which restaurants and hotels are rated — one is dismal, while five is excellent. Trait ratings become important when rolling dice to perform actions (see Chapter Five for specifics).

Common Traits and Terms

Vampire characters comprise the following Traits:

Name: The character's name — this may be anything from the character's birth name to a pseudonym. Some ancient vampires are known by many names, while others are no longer known by names at all.

Player: This is the name of the player portraying the character in question.

Chronicle: This is the series of linked stories in which the character participates. Your Storyteller will provide you with the name of the chronicle (though he may need your help in deciding!).

Attributes: Attributes define your character's inborn aptitudes and potential.

Advantages: A catchall term for the numerous benefits a vampire has over "normal" folk, Advantages refers to a collection of three other Traits. **Disciplines** refer to the vampiric powers a character possesses as a result of her Embrace. **Backgrounds** define the character's material assets and social network. **Virtues** show the character's spiritual and moral fiber — or lack thereof.

Willpower: This Trait reflects your character's inner drive and desire to succeed at tasks she undertakes.

Blood Pool: Your character's blood pool dictates how well-fed she is, or, conversely, how hungry.

Experience: Your character's Experience Trait represents how much she has learned since her Embrace. All characters begin the game with an Experience Trait of zero. Experience is spent to purchase new Traits.

Nature: This is the "true" personality of your character — who she is deep down.

Demeanor: This is the personality your character presents to the world. More often than not, Nature and Demeanor are different, especially given the deviousness of the vampire mind.

Clan: Your character's clan defines her lineage and her relationship to Caine, the progenitor vampire. Clan dictates your character's vampiric powers and weakness.

Generation: Closely related to clan, your character's generation defines the potency of her blood and how many steps removed she is from Caine.

Concept: Your character's concept is a one- or two-word "sketch" of who your character was prior to the Embrace — anything from Crazed Vigilante to Porn Star.

Abilities: Abilities are those proficiencies your character possesses intuitively or has learned.

Humanity/Path: These Traits define your character's outlook on unlife. A character has either a Humanity rating or a rating in a specific Path, never both (though a character may pretend...). Humanity is the "default" Trait, but Paths are presented in the Appendix.

Health: Although a vampire is no longer "alive," her corpse-body may still suffer sufficient trauma to incapacitate her, and a sufficient quantity of damage can even "kill" the vampire anew (forcing you to create a new character). The Health Trait measures how much injury the character has suffered.

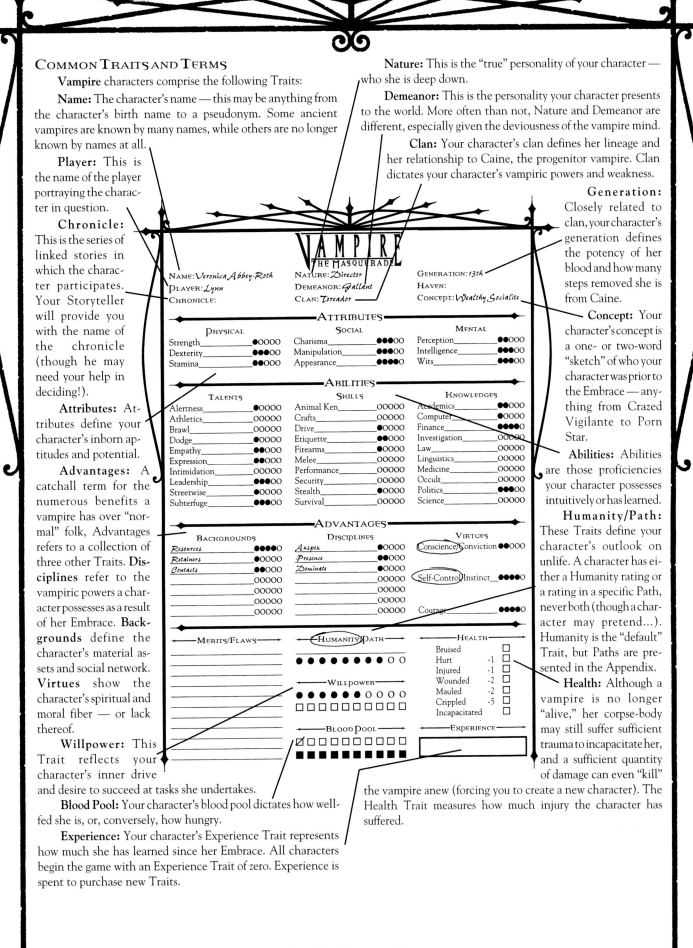

VAMPIRE THE MASQUERADE

NAME: *Veronica Abbey-Roth* NATURE: *Director* GENERATION: *13th*
PLAYER: *Lynn* DEMEANOR: *Gallant* HAVEN:
CHRONICLE: CLAN: *Toreador* CONCEPT: *Wealthy Socialite*

Attributes

Physical		Social		Mental	
Strength	●○○○○	Charisma	●●●○○	Perception	●●○○○
Dexterity	●●○○○	Manipulation	●●●○○	Intelligence	●●●○○
Stamina	●●○○○	Appearance	●●●●○	Wits	●●●○○

Abilities

Talents		Skills		Knowledges	
Alertness	●○○○○	Animal Ken	○○○○○	Academics	●●○○○
Athletics	○○○○○	Crafts	○○○○○	Computer	●○○○○
Brawl	○○○○○	Drive	●○○○○	Finance	●●●●●
Dodge	●○○○○	Etiquette	●●○○○	Investigation	○○○○○
Empathy	●●○○○	Firearms	●○○○○	Law	○○○○○
Expression	●●○○○	Melee	○○○○○	Linguistics	○○○○○
Intimidation	○○○○○	Performance	○○○○○	Medicine	○○○○○
Leadership	●●●○○	Security	○○○○○	Occult	○○○○○
Streetwise	●○○○○	Stealth	●○○○○	Politics	●●●○○
Subterfuge	●●●○○	Survival	○○○○○	Science	○○○○○

Advantages

Backgrounds		Disciplines		Virtues	
Resources	●●●●●	*Auspex*	●○○○○	Conscience/Conviction	●●○○○
Retainers	●○○○○	*Presence*	●●○○○		
Contacts	●●○○○	*Dominate*	●●○○○		
	○○○○○		○○○○○	Self-Control/Instinct	●●●●●
	○○○○○		○○○○○		
	○○○○○		○○○○○		
	○○○○○		○○○○○	Courage	●●●●●

Merits/Flaws

Humanity/Path

● ● ● ● ● ● ● ○ ○

Willpower

● ● ● ● ● ● ● ○ ○ ○
□ □ □ □ □ □ □ □ □ □

Blood Pool

☑ □ □ □ □ □ □ □ □ □
■ ■ ■ ■ ■ ■ ■ ■ ■ ■

Health

Bruised		□
Hurt	-1	□
Injured	-1	□
Wounded	-2	□
Mauled	-2	□
Crippled	-5	□
Incapacitated		□

Experience

CHAPTER THREE: CHARACTER AND TRAITS

101

Getting Started

The **Vampire: The Masquerade** character-creation system is designed around five basic precepts. Keep these in mind while generating the persona you will assume in the World of Darkness.

• You may create a character of any age, from any culture and from any nation, subject to the Storyteller's approval. However, all characters begin the game as neonate vampires who have only recently left the safety of their sires' protection. All players' characters are assumed to have no more than 25 years of experience as Kindred. They know relatively little of Kindred society, other than what their sires have told them. This allows characters to experience the World of Darkness as it unfolds before them in all its malignancy and mystery, rather than having the lore of ages already under their belts. A character's apparent age is the age at which she was Embraced and became one of the Kindred.

• The character-creation system is intended more as a persona development device than as a strict system of mechanical codification. Who wants more rules at the expense of an interesting character or a good story? The character cannot exist as mere dots on a page — roleplaying is always more important than numbers.

• Players have a certain number of points to spend on Traits they would like their characters to have. Players also get "freebie points" at the end of character creation; they may spend these to round out their characters, add personality and further differentiate their characters from those of other players.

• A Trait score of 1 is poor, while a score of 5 is excellent. Thus, a character with a single dot in a Trait is either not very good with that Trait *or* is a beginner. Don't think that your character sucks because she's only got one dot in Manipulation. The experience system presented on p. 141 allows characters to grow and improve their Traits. Traits are rated according to a human scale (except vampiric Traits like Advantages and blood pool, which are rated on a Kindred standard).

• It is your responsibility to take on a role not endemically detrimental to the coterie. Vampires are solitary creatures, so there has to be some reason you've joined up with your Kindred companions (the other players' characters). Despite the fact that the hostile World of Darkness forces coteries together, Kindred don't just hang out for the hell of it.

The Storyteller and Character Creation

The Storyteller must guide the players through character generation, not only to ensure their understanding of the process, but also to get a feel for the characters they're creating. Character creation can provide Storytellers with some wonderful plot ideas — ones they would likely never have considered on their own. Likewise, if the players are unfamiliar with the rules, the Storyteller should use character generation as an introduction to the game as a whole, informing the troupe how the rules work and giving them examples based on the personas they're creating.

As the Storyteller, start by photocopying and handing out the character sheet from the back of the book. Take the players on a "tour" of the sheet, explaining what each section is for. Let

CHARACTER CREATION PROCESS

- **Step One: Character Concept**

  Choose concept, clan, Nature and Demeanor.

- **Step Two: Select Attributes**

  Prioritize the three categories: Physical, Social, Mental (7/5/3). Your character automatically has one dot in each Attribute.

  Rate Physical Traits: Strength, Dexterity, Stamina.

  Rate Social Traits: Charisma, Manipulation, Appearance.

  Rate Mental Traits: Perception, Intelligence, Wits.

- **Step Three: Select Abilities**

  Prioritize the three categories: Talents, Skills, Knowledges (13/9/5).

  Choose Talents, Skills, Knowledges.

  No Ability higher than 3 at this stage

- **Step Four: Select Advantages**

  Choose Disciplines (3), Backgrounds (5) and rate Virtues (7). Your character automatically has one dot in each Virtue.

- **Step Five: Finishing Touches**

  Record Humanity (equal to Conscience + Self-Control), Willpower (equal to Courage) and Blood Pool.

  Spend freebie points (15).

SAMPLE CONCEPTS

- **Criminal** — jailbird, Mafioso, drug dealer, pimp, carjacker, thug, thief, fence
- **Drifter** — bum, smuggler, prostitute, junkie, pilgrim, biker, gambler
- **Entertainer** — musician, film star, artist, club kid, model
- **Intellectual** — writer, student, scientist, philosopher, social critic
- **Investigator** — detective, beat cop, government agent, private eye, witch-hunter
- **Kid** — child, runaway, outcast, urchin, gangbanger
- **Nightlifer** — clubgoer, skinhead, punk, barfly, raver, substance abuser
- **Outsider** — urban primitive, refugee, minority, conspiracy theorist
- **Politician** — judge, public official, councilor, aide, speechwriter
- **Professional** — engineer, doctor, computer programmer, lawyer, industrialist
- **Reporter** — journalist, news reporter, paparazzo, talk-show host, 'zine editor
- **Socialite** — dilettante, host, playboy, sycophant, prominent spouse
- **Soldier** — bodyguard, enforcer, mercenary, soldier of fortune, Green Beret
- **Worker** — trucker, farmer, wage earner, manservant, construction laborer

CLANS

- **Assamite** — (Independent) Dreaded killers and diablerists on a terrible quest for Kindred vitae, the *Assassins* have perfected the art of the silent kill.
- **Brujah** — (Camarilla) The *Rabble* are rebels and insurgents, fighting passionately for their disparate causes. The Brujah dream of a perfect society — for vampires.
- **Followers of Set** — (Independent) Corrupting and deadly, the *Serpents* are feared for their evil, yet sought out for their arcane knowledge and sinister gifts.
- **Gangrel** — (Camarilla) The nomadic *Outlanders* are feral and wild. These solitary wanderers are the source of much of the lore that likens vampires to dark beasts.
- **Giovanni** — (Independent) Insular and incestuous, the *Necromancers* ply their trade in blood, money and the souls of the dead.
- **Lasombra** — (Sabbat) The shadowy, wicked *Keepers* nominally lead the Sabbat. Clan Lasombra serves itself first and its inner darkness second.
- **Malkavians** — (Camarilla) Dangerously deranged and psychotic to a member, the *Lunatics* nonetheless possess uncanny insight.
- **Nosferatu** — (Camarilla) Disfigured and skulksome, the hideous *Sewer Rats* are forever barred from human society, but gather secrets from the darkness that hides them.
- **Ravnos** — (Independent) The nomadic *Deceivers* are masters of illusion and guile, malevolently working their tricks as they travel from city to city.
- **Toreador** — (Camarilla) Lovers of art and the aesthetic, the *Degenerates* are trapped in the stagnancy of undeath. The Toreador are passionate and decadent, surrounding themselves in excess to stave off their encroaching malaise.
- **Tremere** — (Camarilla) A clan of sorcerous blood magicians, the *Warlocks* are widely distrusted…and just as widely feared.
- **Tzimisce** — (Sabbat) A clan of fallen nobles from the Old Country, the brilliant but monstrous *Fiends* now serve the Sabbat. They wield the fearsome Discipline of fleshcrafting.
- **Ventrue** — (Camarilla) The reluctant aristocracy of the Kindred, the *Blue Bloods* atone for their damnation by enforcing the Traditions and the Masquerade.

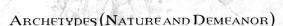

ARCHETYPES (NATURE AND DEMEANOR)

- **Architect** — You build a better future.
- **Autocrat** — You need control.
- **Bon Vivant** — Unlife is for pleasure.
- **Bravo** — Strength is all that matters.
- **Caregiver** — Everyone needs nurturing.
- **Celebrant** — You exist for your passion.
- **Child** — Won't somebody be there for you?
- **Competitor** — You must be the best.
- **Conformist** — You follow and assist.
- **Conniver** — Others exist for your benefit.
- **Curmudgeon** — Nothing is worthwhile.
- **Deviant** — You exist for no one's pleasure but your own.
- **Director** — You oversee what must be done.
- **Fanatic** — The cause is all that matters.
- **Gallant** — You're not the showstopper, you're the show!
- **Judge** — The truth is out there.
- **Loner** — You make your own way.
- **Martyr** — You suffer for the greater good.
- **Masochist** — You test your limits every night.
- **Monster** — You're Damned, so act like it!
- **Pedagogue** — You save others through knowledge.
- **Penitent** — Unlife is a curse to atone for.
- **Perfectionist** — Nothing is good enough.
- **Rebel** — You follow no one's rules.
- **Rogue** — Those who can, win. Those who can't, lose. You can.
- **Survivor** — Nothing can keep you down.
- **Thrill-Seeker** — The rush is all that matters.
- **Traditionalist** — As it has always been, so it shall be.
- **Trickster** — Laughter dims the pain.
- **Visionary** — There is something beyond all this.

DISCIPLINES

- **Animalism** — Supernatural affinity with and control of animals.
- **Auspex** — Extrasensory perception, awareness and premonitions.
- **Celerity** — Supernatural quickness and reflexes.
- **Chimerstry** — The Ravnos ability to create illusions and hallucinations.
- **Dementation** — The ability to pass madness on to a victim.
- **Dominate** — Mind control practiced through the piercing gaze.
- **Fortitude** — Unearthly toughness, even to the point of resisting fire and sunlight.
- **Necromancy** — The supernatural power to summon and control the dead.
- **Obfuscate** — The ability to remain obscure and unseen, even in crowds.
- **Obtenebration** — Unearthly control over shadows.
- **Potence** — The Discipline of physical vigor and strength.
- **Presence** — The ability to attract, sway and control crowds.
- **Protean** — Shapechanging, from growing claws to melding with the earth.
- **Quietus** — The Assamites' arts of assassination.
- **Serpentis** — The reptilian Discipline of the Followers of Set.
- **Thaumaturgy** — The study and practice of blood-sorcery.
- **Vicissitude** — The Tzimisce art of flesh-shaping.

BACKGROUNDS

- **Allies** — Human confederates, usually family or friends.
- **Contacts** — The number of information sources the character possesses.
- **Fame** — How well-known the character is among mortals.
- **Generation** — How far removed from Caine the character is.
- **Herd** — The vessels to which the character has free and safe access.
- **Influence** — The character's political power within mortal society.
- **Mentor** — The Kindred patron who advises and supports the character.
- **Resources** — Wealth, belongings and monthly income.
- **Retainers** — Followers, guards and servants.
- **Status** — The character's standing in undead society.

FREEBIE POINTS

Trait	Cost
Attribute	5 per dot
Ability	2 per dot
Discipline	7 per dot
Background	1 per dot
Virtue	2 per dot
Humanity	1 per dot
Willpower	1 per dot

players ask questions along the way, and help them through the process rather than letting them fend for themselves.

After the players are familiar with the character sheet, give them a few guidelines as to what types of characters will be appropriate for the chronicle. For example, Storytellers running games in Camarilla-held cities might forbid Sabbat or independent vampires outright. Sometimes a player will attempt to portray a character wholly unacceptable to your plotline, and you should feel free to disallow this in favor of a character who won't disrupt the game.

Storytellers are advised to spend an entire session simply creating characters and running preludes (see p. 108) with the players. Exceptionally complex characters or secretive chronicles might even warrant an entire session for each individual player. Spending an adequate amount of time on character generation ensures that the players create realistic characters and not vapid, colorless laundry lists of Traits. After the mechanics of creation are done, take each player aside and lead him through a prelude. This one-on-one storytelling is the player's introduction to the chronicle as well as the means by which the player adds final details to her character, so use it to its greatest effect.

STEP ONE: CHARACTER CONCEPT

Concept is the birthing chamber for who a character will become. It need only be a general idea — brute; slick mobster; manic Malkavian kidnapper — but it should be enough to ignite your imagination. If you choose, a concept may be quite complex — "My character is a streetwise Tremere, Embraced as a child but with a precocious level of maturity. Being a Kindred scares him, but he knows that the alternative is Final Death and he's not ready for that yet." This stage involves the selection of the character's concept, clan, Nature and Demeanor.

CONCEPT

A character's concept refers to who the character was before becoming a vampire. Many Kindred cling desperately to any salvageable aspects of their former selves — their self-image, their occupation, how they lived, what was unique about them. In their new nocturnal world, echoes of their mortal lives are all that stand between many Kindred and madness.

Concept is important because it helps a vampire relate to the world. It's not a numerical Trait, and it has very little mechanical effect on the game. Its benefit is that it allows you to formulate a personality for your character, and it provides an anchor for a vampire who wishes to preserve her dwindling Humanity — or to rail against it.

Some sample concepts are presented on p. 103. *If you don't see a concept you like, make one up!* Who are we to tell you who you can or can't be?

CLAN

A character's clan is her vampire "family," the undead legacy into which she was Embraced. Vampires are always of the same clan as their sires, the vampires who Embrace them. Go back to Chapter Two, look at the templates, and decide which clan you'd like your character to be. As previously mentioned,

the Storyteller may disallow members of certain clans based on the sect the chronicle involves. Many beginning chronicles, for example, allow only vampires from the seven Camarilla clans.

If a player wishes, she need not choose a clan at all. Many vampires in these modern nights have blood so diluted that they can truly claim no clan. Unwanted and scorned, these clanless "Caitiff" are increasingly common. If you wish to play such a character, simply write "Caitiff" under the Clan heading on the character sheet.

NATURE AND DEMEANOR (ARCHETYPES)

After choosing concept and clan, a player should choose her character's Nature and Demeanor. These behavioral Traits, known as *Archetypes*, help players understand what kind of people their characters are. Nature and Demeanor are not required to play **Vampire: The Masquerade**, but they sometimes help players pin down their characters in their minds.

Demeanor is the way a character presents herself to the outside world. It is the "mask" she wears to protect her inner self. A character's Demeanor often differs from her Nature, though it might not. Also, Demeanor refers to the attitude a character adopts most often — people change Demeanors as often as they change their minds. Demeanor has no effect on any rules.

Nature is the character's "real" self, the person she truly is. The Archetype a player chooses reflects that character's deep-rooted feelings about herself, others and the world. Nature need not be the *only* aspect of a character's true personality, merely the most dominant. Nature is also used to determine a character's ability to regain Willpower points (see p. 136).

For a complete list of Archetypes from which to select Nature and Demeanor, see pp. 112-115.

STEP TWO: SELECT ATTRIBUTES

Players must now assign numbers. The first step in determining a character's numeric Traits is to prioritize his Attributes. *Attributes* are the natural abilities and raw "stuff" a character is made of. How strong is a character? How attractive? How quick? How smart? Attributes take all these questions and more into account. All **Vampire** characters have nine Attributes, which are divided into three categories: Physical (Strength, Dexterity, Stamina), Social (Charisma, Manipulation, Appearance) and Mental (Perception, Intelligence, Wits).

First, the player must select which group of Attributes is his character's strong suit (primary). The player then selects the group in which the character is average (secondary). Finally, the remaining group is designated as the character's weak point (tertiary). Is your character tough but antisocial, or gorgeous but a complete airhead? Character concept and clan may suggest certain ranks for these priorities, but feel free to decide upon any scheme you please. Nothing's worse than playing a boring stereotype. Playing an interesting stereotype, though….

All **Vampire** characters start with one dot in each Attribute, reflecting the basic capabilities of the mortals from which they're drawn. (The exception is the Nosferatu, who have zero dots in their Appearance Attribute.) A character's priorities determine how many dots the player may allocate to that cluster of Attributes. A player may distribute seven additional dots to his character's primary group, five additional dots to the secondary group and three dots to the tertiary group. For example, a tough, athletic character will likely allocate seven dots to his Physical category, while a clever, wise character will place seven dots in her Mental category.

Step Three: Select Abilities

Abilities are also divided into three categories: Talents, Skills and Knowledges. *Talents* are intuitive Abilities that are inherent or learned "in the field." *Skills* are Abilities learned through rigorous training or determination. They may be learned with careful practice, but can also be studied or learned through training. *Knowledges* are just that — "book learning" and the like. Knowledges are typically mental pursuits or studies learned through schooling or books.

Like Attributes, Ability groups are also prioritized during character creation. Players should select primary, secondary and tertiary groups for their Abilities. The primary group receives 13 dots, the secondary group gets nine and the tertiary group receives five. Note that, unlike Attributes, characters do not begin the game with automatic dots in any Ability. Note further that no Ability may be purchased above three dots during this stage of character creation — even among the undead, experts in a field don't grow on trees. You may raise Abilities higher with freebie points, but that comes later.

Step Four: Select Advantages

Now comes the part of character generation during which the vampire truly becomes unique. *Advantages* are Traits that make the vampire a contender in the hierarchy of the night. Advantages are not prioritized; a set number of dots may be allocated to each category. Though this number is fixed, additional Advantage dots may be purchased with freebie points.

Disciplines

When vampires are Embraced, their sires teach them certain blood-based mystical powers, known as *Disciplines*. Each character begins with three dots of Disciplines, which may be allocated as the player chooses. For example, she may spend all three dots on one Discipline or spend a dot each on three Disciplines. Disciplines purchased with Advantage dots must be from the three clan Disciplines all clans possess. Each clan description in Chapter Two lists the Disciplines practiced by that clan, along with bloodline variations, if any. If the character is a clanless Caitiff, she may purchase whatever Disciplines she wants, subject to Storyteller approval. (**Note:** Disciplines purchased with freebie points need not be clan Disciplines.)

Backgrounds

A beginning character has five dots worth of *Backgrounds*, which may be distributed at the player's discretion. Background Traits should fit the character concept — a destitute Gangrel street preacher isn't likely to have Resources, for example — though the Storyteller may disallow, or encourage players to take, certain Backgrounds for their characters.

Virtues

Virtues are very important to **Vampire** characters, for they provide the moral backbone for the characters and determine how readily they resist the temptations of the Beast. A character's emotional responses are very closely tied to her Virtues; these Traits define how well the character resists frenzy and how keenly she feels remorse. Virtues are essential in resisting the urges of the Beast and the Hunger, and most vampires lose points in their Virtues as they grow older and more callous.

A **Vampire** character has three Virtues. *Conscience* governs a character's sense of right and wrong, while *Self-Control* determines how readily she maintains her composure and contains her Hunger. *Courage* measures the character's gumption and ability to withstand the proximity of fire, sunlight and other things that vampires dread.

Every character starts out with one dot in each Virtue, and the player may then distribute seven additional dots among the Virtues as she sees fit. These Virtues play instrumental roles in determining a character's starting Humanity and Willpower levels, so be careful how you spend the points.

Step Five: Last Touches

At this stage, the player may spend 15 freebie points to personalize his character. First, however, a bit of bookkeeping needs to be done.

Humanity

A character's starting Humanity score equals the sum of her Conscience + Self-Control Traits, yielding a score between 5 and 10. Players are also encouraged to increase their Humanity scores with freebie points, as too low a score indicates that the Beast lies in close proximity.

Note: Characters on Paths other than Humanity may use different Virtues to determine their initial Path scores. Consult the Appendix (p. 286) to determine which Paths use which Virtues.

Willpower

A character's beginning Willpower score equals her Courage rating, and thus ranges from 1 to 5. Players are encouraged to raise

---

ALTERNATIVE VIRTUES: CONVICTION AND INSTINCT

Vampire: The Masquerade is fundamentally about coming to grips with one's monstrous nature and, hopefully, overcoming it. As such, we strongly encourage beginning players to select the Virtues of Conscience and Self-Control for their characters. However, certain Kindred, particularly the vampires of the Sabbat, adhere to different ethical outlooks. For these vampires, the Virtues of Conviction and Instinct may replace the Virtues of Conscience and Self-Control, respectively. (All vampires have the Courage Virtue.)

Conviction and Instinct are presented on p. 287. If you decide that your character is sufficiently inhuman to warrant these Virtues, and if the Storyteller permits you to take them, you may circle the appropriate Virtues on the character sheet. Be warned that in taking these Virtues, you have effectively designated your character as a monster.

their starting Willpower scores with freebie points, as the Trait is critical to dealing with a Kindred's dangerous emotional situations. Willpower is also used to resist frenzy (p. 228), undertake especially daunting tasks and power certain Discipline effects.

Blood Pool

The crowning touch to character creation is determining the vampire's starting blood pool. This part is simple — roll a 10-sided die. The number is the number of blood points a character has in his system at the beginning of the game. This is the only die roll that is made during character creation.

Freebie Points

The player may now spend 15 *freebie points* to purchase additional dots in Traits. These points may be spent however the player chooses — thus the term "freebie." Each dot has a variable freebie-point cost based on which type of Trait it is — consult the chart on p. 104 for freebie-point costs of Traits. Remember that Disciplines purchased with freebie points need not come from the character's clan Disciplines (although purchase of some Disciplines may require explanation about how she acquired them).

Spark of Life

If you go through the motions above, you will have a character — at least in the purely technical sense. All the dots are on the paper; you can interact your piece of paper with the mechanics of the game, and roll all the right combinations of dice at the appropriate times.

Frankly, though, for your trouble, you might as well play checkers, because at this point your character's not much more detailed than a featureless piece on a gameboard. Now's the time to take the skeleton you've mechanically built with the rules and flesh it out into a living, breathing (well, *formerly* living and breathing) person. Take a good long look at your Traits and numbers. Why are they there? How will they come across in the story? What parts of the character *don't* you know yet? Like a novelist building a literary figure, decide on all the physical, psychological and background details that make your character one of a kind, even among the undead.

Sure, your character has an Appearance of 3 — but what does that mean? Does she have a smile that could launch a thousand ships, or does she simply exude a challenging self-confidence? What color are her eyes and hair? If she's skilled in Performance, or Etiquette, or Firearms, how did she acquire her skill? Did she always want to be a movie star? Is her polished veneer a reaction against growing up in a trailer park? Did she just, for whatever bizarre reason, walk onto a firing range and discover a natural aptitude for plugging holes in targets? Is her Ally actually her ex-lover, who works for the FBI and with whom she maintains an uneasy, tension-laced friendship? Does he suspect what she's become, but help her out for now in an effort to observe her more closely?

This last phase of character creation, while the least "necessary," is the most important. Otherwise, your Brujah with the Strength 4, Dexterity 3, Stamina 3 will be just like all the other

Brujah with Strength 4, Dexterity 3, Stamina 3 — and believe us, there are a lot of such cardboard "characters" out there. And that's a shame, because characters — especially vampires — should be unique, fascinating, passionate and memorable.

The Prelude

A person's past is the foundation on which his personality is built. For that reason, you should have some idea of your character's life before the Embrace, the better to understand who he is. The prelude is something of a one-on-one mini-story — just you and the Storyteller, roleplaying events from your character's life before the actual start of the chronicle. This serves as a storytelling device that can help detail his mortal existence and personality up until the point that the first story begins.

You roleplay out a prelude much as you would a normal game session, except that years of life are compressed into an evening of rapid-fire decisions. Romantic relationships, school, work, family, outside threats — these are all things that you might have to address, for better or worse, over the course of the prelude. When the prelude is complete, you should understand your character's personal history in detail, and you may find that elements of his past actually foreshadow his existence as a vampire.

A prelude offers a frame of reference for everything else that happens to your character, and how he reacts to such events, during the chronicle. Without it, a character just won't be as complete. The prelude is fairly quick and dirty, just like the page or so of personal background that a novelist would give a major character entering the story. It's essential to understanding the character, but needn't go on for 100 pages.

A Storyteller's Guide to the Prelude

"You meet your old boyfriend for lunch at the old café you used to visit. The place has gone downhill since then — or maybe you just romanticized it in your memory. He's wearing a nice suit — apparently the law profession's paying off well for him — but he looks ragged around the edges, like he hasn't been getting much sleep. Halfway through lunch, he admits to having problems with his wife. How do you respond?"

Each player undergoes the prelude alone with the Storyteller; the one-on-one format helps concentrate the feeling that the prelude is very personal, the character's past and his alone. It's possible for two characters to share part of a prelude, but this should be done only if they were friends and spent a lot of time together before the Embrace. Don't worry too much about neglecting the other players during the prelude; although you should certainly make every effort to involve everyone when the game proper begins, a little anticipation can whet the appetite for what's to come.

It's okay to take a much heavier hand in controlling the action. Give the player plenty of decisions to make, and don't spread them out over a long period of time — make him think quickly, so that he goes for the instinctive reaction. Unless you want to spend an entire evening on each character's prelude (which makes for more detailed characters), you should compress things so that the character gets a more concentrated feel of what his life was like. It's certainly potent that way.

Let the player explore both the setting and the rules during his prelude. He probably shouldn't get involved in any combat during the prelude; if it seems to be necessary, then simply describe the results of any fights. It won't do to kill the character before the game begins!

"It's a November afternoon, but it's already sliding into twilight. You were supposed to meet your sister at the park, but it's been half an hour and she still hasn't shown up. You hear a dog bark somewhere in the distance, and the sound suddenly makes you realize that you're all alone — there isn't another human being anywhere within view. Except one, maybe — a derelict, stumbling down the walk toward you. What do you do?"

You want to let the player explore the setting as well as the rules. Have him try out a few rolls. Let him swap a few Traits around if it becomes clear during the prelude that his Traits don't accurately reflect the character (although you shouldn't allow this if the player is just trying to create an unstoppable super-character). Explore the character's environment in detail. Find out why he has the Backgrounds that he does — introduce his allies as characters, or visit his job (if any) to reinforce how he gets rent money.

It may seem odd to be playing through perfectly mundane scenes in the prelude, but these actually build a sense of normalcy that can be shattered when the supernatural takes the stage. Once you juxtapose the tedium of mortal life with the suddenly horrific attack, Embrace and subsequent rebirth as a vampire, the dramatic tension of becoming one of the undead is exhilarating.

Even as you describe things, let the player interrupt with his own ideas and details concerning the events as they occur. Remember, you're telling this story together; the player is your partner in this. You can also throw in details that provoke the player's emotions — "Your girlfriend has tears in her eyes as she tells you that she's pregnant." Of course, once the character becomes a vampire, he can't really be there for her or their baby anymore. **Vampire** is a horror game at heart, and the player must feel a profound sense of loss to truly understand what it's like to be one of the Damned.

"The shabby man shoves you against the subway doors. You try to scream, but there's nobody in the car to hear you. The lights flicker overhead. The noise of the train pounds in your ears, and the terrible reek of your attacker makes you want to faint. Then you feel his teeth in your neck, and the world starts to fade away."

Finally, don't forget that a character's Embrace should be roleplayed to the hilt — this moment, more than anything else, can define how he will be changed by existence as a vampire. Play up the sensation of being watched. Build the tension of an unseen predator stalking the unwitting character. Although the player knows what's coming, he shouldn't know exactly how; describe the attack in great detail so that it seems all the more real and frightening. Carefully play through the transformation. Let the player feel the trauma of the change. Although you may still want to play out some details of the character's existence as a vampire before the chronicle opens, you want the player to remember the Embrace for a long time to come.

Questions and Answers

The following questions are meant to be used as a springboard to fill out the character's background as much as possible. Even if there isn't time for a detailed prelude, you should try to answer as many of these questions as possible — write them out if you like, or talk about them with your Storyteller. The more you know about your character, the more real she'll seem when the game begins.

• How old are you?

When were you born? How old were you when you were Embraced? How long have you existed as a vampire? How old do you look? Are you more mature than you seem? Less?

• What was unique about your childhood?

How did you spend your early years? How were your basic motivations and attitudes forged? Where did you go to school? Who were your immediate family? What is your clearest childhood memory? Did you go to high school? Did you have a hometown, or was your family constantly on the move? Did you go to college? Did you run away from home? Did you play sports? Did any of your childhood friendships last to adulthood?

• What kind of person were you?

Were you a decent person, or were you an asshole? Were you popular? Did you have a family? How did you earn a living? Did you have any real friends? What kept you going from day to day? Will anyone miss you?

• What was your first brush with the supernatural?

When did you realize you were being stalked? Did you believe in the occult before your Embrace? When did you first meet a vampire? Were you afraid? Disbelieving? Angry? What frightened you most?

• How did the Embrace change you?

How did your sire catch you? Was the Embrace painful? Did you get a kinky pleasure out of it? Did the Hunger tear at you? Did it frighten you? Did it feel right? Are you grateful to your sire? Do you want to kill him for what he did to you?

• Who was your sire, and how did he treat you?

What do you know of your sire? Was he abusive, arrogant, cryptic or open? Why do you think he chose you? Did you even know your sire at all? How long did you stay with your sire? Did he teach you anything at all? How long was your "apprenticeship"? Where did you stay? Where did you go? Did you meet any other vampires during that time? Do you judge other vampires in general by your opinion of your sire? When did he teach you the Traditions?

• Were you presented to the prince?

Did the prince welcome you? Was she reluctant to accept you? Did she need to be bribed or threatened? Did your sire have permission to create you? Are you on the run from the prince? What do you think her opinion of you is?

• How did you meet the others in your coterie?

Were you brought together by chance or design? Are you all of one sect? Are you united in purpose and attitude? How long have you been together in the city? Did you know any of the others before the Embrace? Are your sires in cooperation, or are they rivals? What holds your coterie together when things get their worst?

• Where is your haven?

Where do you hide during the day? Do you have a permanent home at all? Do you stay in the place you inhabited in your mortal life? Do you hide in an abandoned building? The sewers? Do you have anyone to protect you during the day?

• Do you retain any connections to your mortal life?

Are you presumed dead? Do you still watch over relatives from afar? Do you pretend to be still alive? Did you abandon your mortal existence entirely?

• What are your habitual feeding grounds?

Whom do you feed upon, and where? Do you have a territory that you consider exclusively yours? Is your favorite hunting ground used by others? Do you compete with others? What is your preferred prey? Do you ever kill when you feed? Do you have a specific herd? Do you seduce your prey? Kidnap them? Assault them on the street? Do they come to you?

• What motivates you?

Do you seek revenge on any enemies? Do you long to return to your mortal life? Do you have ambitions in Kindred society? If you could achieve anything in the world, what would it be?

A Final Note

A character without motivation might as well not have survived the Embrace. Knowing what drives your character is central to understanding who she is. A vampire's values are often very different from those of a normal human; the death and rebirth of the Embrace can work a great change on an individual's personality. Think about where your character has been and where you'd like to see her go (or where she would like to go). Consider her Nature and Demeanor — do they suggest an ultimate goal? Once you have an idea of what it is your character wants to achieve, you're one step closer to making her a full-fledged personality of her own.

Example of Character Creation

Lynn plans to participate in Justin's new **Vampire: The Masquerade** chronicle. Justin tells Lynn that the chronicle centers on the affairs of the Camarilla in Chicago a few years after a devastating werewolf attack that resulted in the Final Deaths of many Kindred. He informs Lynn that characters in the chronicle should be Camarilla or friendly independents (though Justin's not opposed to having a Sabbat spy in deep cover as a part of the coterie), and hands her a copy of the character sheet.

Looking at the outline, Lynn kicks around a few ideas and begins the process of turning those ideas into a full-fledged character.

Step One: Concept

Lynn's first responsibility is to come up with a concept for her character. She loves the intrigue and high-society aspect of the Camarilla, and decides that she wants to play a female vampire who rubs elbows and curries favor with Chicago's influential Kindred and kine. Having a flair for the tragic, Lynn decides that her character is the last scion of a once-prominent family that has slowly but inexorably slid into decline. Envisioning a modern twist on the '20s flapper socialite archetype, Lynn also decides that her character is quite keen at business and finance. Clan Ventrue is the obvious choice, but Lynn decides that her character is a Toreador, to add another twist.

Only a real crackpot would name his character after himself (talk about Freudian…), so Lynn decides that her character goes by the moniker of Veronica Abbey-Roth.

Lynn considers Veronica's Nature and Demeanor. She decides that her character is outgoing, amiable and superficial — all of which hide the cunning deep beneath the surface. Her Demeanor — the face she presents to the world — is Gallant, to reflect an unlife spent largely in Camarilla salons and parties. Lynn decides that Veronica's business acumen necessitates an inner drive and take-charge manner of handling affairs; she chooses Director for the character's Nature. She also sees the opportunity for some excellent roleplaying in choosing a headstrong Archetype — imagine how all those influential Kindred with whom she hobnobs will respond to a brash young industry queen!

As a Camarilla vampire, Lynn's character defaults to the moral code of Humanity. Lynn sees no problem with this, and circles the Humanity Trait on her character sheet.

Step Two: Attributes

Lynn must now prioritize and assign Veronica's Attributes. Social Attributes make the most sense for a primary category, Lynn reasons, as much of her contact with people will be in diplomatic and civil conversation. As Veronica's secondary category, Lynn chooses Mental, reflecting her knowledge and wisdom with matters financial. This leaves Physical Attributes as tertiary, which suits Veronica's concept just fine — she's a lover, not a fighter.

Lynn has seven dots to divide among Veronica's Social Attributes. Deciding Veronica's quite a looker, Lynn puts three dots in Appearance for a Trait rating of 4 (remember the one "free" point every character has in all Attributes). Veronica has quite a gift for getting others to do what she wants — two dots go toward her Manipulation Attribute, giving her a score of 3. Veronica's also likable, for the most part; Lynn puts the remaining two dots into Charisma, giving her a 3 in that Trait.

With five dots to assign to Mental Attributes, Lynn decides Veronica is a savvy, shrewd businesswoman. Putting two dots each into Intelligence and Wits gives Veronica scores of 3 in both these Traits. The remaining point goes into Perception, yielding a score of 2.

Determining Physical Traits is all that's left to finish Veronica's Attributes. Lynn sees Veronica as slim, willowy and lithe, so she adds nothing to the character's Strength, leaving it at 1, and assigns two dots to Veronica's Dexterity, resulting in a score of 3. Finally, Lynn places the remaining Physical dot into Stamina, for a score of 2.

Step Three: Abilities

Like Attributes, Abilities must also be prioritized. Lynn decides that Veronica is well-versed in Talents, nominally familiar with Knowledges and the least accomplished in Skills. This reflects Veronica's ease with social situations and aptitude in the cutthroat world of business while still leaving room to refine her graces.

With 13 dots to spend in Talents, Lynn jumps right in and sinks three dots into Subterfuge — Veronica's no stranger to smooth-talking underhandedness. Three more dots go toward Leadership, as Veronica's guidance keeps her family's company afloat. Two dots each go into Expression and Empathy, signifying Veronica's eloquence and feel for people. Lynn assigns one dot each to Alertness (the oblivious don't make it amid the Darwinian society of the Kindred), Dodge (nor do those who can't get out of the way) and Streetwise (because everyone should know someone who can get things done on the streets).

Lynn has nine dots to allocate among Veronica's Knowledges, and assigns three dots to Finance immediately. Likewise, Veronica receives three dots in her Politics Trait, because one must know whose back to scratch. Lynn puts two dots in Veronica's Academics score, to represent her general knowledge of the world. The last dot Lynn places in Computer, to give Veronica a modern edge over some older, more traditional vampires.

Only five dots may be assigned to Veronica's Skills at this point, but Lynn sees no immediate need for any more (though she may later choose to augment these Traits with her freebie points). Not wanting Veronica to be a boor, Lynn assigns two dots to the Etiquette Trait — apparently, finishing school paid off. One dot goes toward the Drive Skill, and the last two dots go into Firearms (a woman's got to protect herself) and Stealth (sometimes it's better *not* to be seen), resulting in scores of 1 each.

Step Four: Advantages

Lynn has now arrived at the part of character creation that truly makes her character a vampire. She must now figure out Veronica's Advantages, the Traits that distinguish her from the rest of the crowd.

First come Veronica's Disciplines, the mystical powers that vampires possess through their unnatural state of existence. Lynn has three dots to allocate among Veronica's Disciplines, and, as the character is a Toreador, Lynn may distribute those dots among Auspex, Celerity and Presence. Veronica is not a very physically inclined character, so Lynn chooses to pass on Celerity. She is, however, more likely to sway the emotions of those around her, so Lynn places two dots in Veronica's Presence Discipline. The remaining dot goes toward Auspex, granting her preternaturally heightened senses.

Veronica's Backgrounds, which she receives five dots to purchase, would best be spent building a power base, according to Lynn's concept. Lynn passes up Mentor entirely, as she sees a bit of a falling out with her sire as part of Veronica's character history (though a mentor need not be a character's sire). She knows that Resources fit Veronica's concept nicely, so she allocates four dots to that Background. Her last dot goes into Retainers: Veronica employs a chauffeur, whom she plans to turn into a ghoul one of these nights, "when she gets around to it."

As the last part of defining Veronica's Advantages, Lynn must assign dots to the character's Virtues. As Veronica's moral code is Humanity, she has the Virtues of Conscience, Self-

Control and Courage. Veronica is cool and levelheaded; Lynn allocates three dots to Self-Control, for a score of 4. Lynn also assigns one dot to Conscience, giving the character a rating of 2; Veronica's not totally heartless, but doesn't mind doing what's necessary in order to achieve a goal. The remaining three dots go toward Courage, bringing the Trait to 4; Veronica is quite sure of herself and dedicated to her causes.

Step Five: Finishing Touches

Now Lynn gets to round out her character and add a spark of unlife. First and foremost, she must figure Veronica's Humanity and Willpower scores (this is done *before* any freebie points are added to Virtues). Adding Veronica's Conscience of 2 and Self-Control of 4, Lynn sees that the character's Humanity score is 6 — she's no saint. That's a little more monstrous than Lynn is comfortable with (she wants to roleplay Veronica's damnation, not start out already in the hole…), so she makes a mental note to dope it up with some freebie points. Willpower is equal to a character's Courage, so Lynn fills in four dots on the Willpower section of the character sheet. Finally, Lynn casts a 10-sided die: a 1. Justin smirks at her, and she returns a knowing look. (Vampires expend a blood point each night, and Justin's the kind of Storyteller who makes new characters spend that point on the first night of their existences. It appears as if Veronica will begin the game by going into a hunger frenzy.) Lynn marks one box on the character sheet's blood pool section.

All that remains to do is spend the 15 freebie points that may be used to increase the character's Traits. Lynn spends two freebie points to increase Veronica's Humanity to 7, making her less bestial (at least for now…). Spending another two points, Lynn raises Veronica's Finance Ability to 4. Knowing that Veronica will need to network in Chicago's financial world, Lynn spends two points on Contacts (old family acquaintances who admire Veronica's ambition). Two more points go toward raising Veronica's Willpower to 6 (she's determined, but has yet to face any true trials). Lynn would like to purchase an additional Discipline with Veronica's last seven points, and asks Justin if the character can have a Tremere lover who taught her the rudiments of Thaumaturgy. Justin says Veronica can have a Tremere lover if she wants, but rules that no Tremere is likely to have taught the secrets of the clan's blood magic to Veronica at this stage of her unlife. Lynn agrees, and instead purchases a dot of Dominate with Justin's approval (Dominate is more common than Thaumaturgy, and not so closely guarded).

Because Lynn spent no points on the Generation Background, she notes that Veronica is 13th generation, listing that under the appropriate heading. Although her Blood is not so potent as many Kindred's, Veronica also is less likely to be seen as a threat — or a meal — by power-hungry vampires.

Lynn, having finished all of the mechanical details of character creation, decides to flesh out her character a bit more completely. Although the specifics may change during or after the prelude, they give Lynn and Justin some common ground upon which to begin play.

Lynn decides that Veronica grew up in genteel poverty, in the nadir of her family's prominence, and determined early on to do everything in her power to build it back up. In the process she met a few of the wrong people, one of whom took a shine to Veronica and Embraced her. Though she knows many people, she hasn't yet accumulated enough influence over them to be a true power player like the surviving elders in Chicago. Her ambition is enough to turn a profit, but it seems that attempts to rejuvenate her family name are being stifled by mysterious forces. Precisely who or what is causing these events is a matter of mystery and consternation to Veronica, and she wonders if perhaps her sire or one of his acquaintances is behind them.

Veronica maintains her haven in a converted carriage house at her family's estate. Her parents, very advanced in age now, never leave the house and have no knowledge of Veronica's vampiric nature or her nocturnal comings and goings. Her faithful chauffeur Marcus is a skilled driver and knows how to use a pistol and a tire jack with equal precision. Veronica's money is largely tied up in the estate and the business, but if she liquidated her assets she'd be quite well-off. Not that she's ever short on cash or credit.…

Veronica wears a stylish wardrobe of designer sports- and eveningwear, and always draws looks wherever she goes. She carries a snub-nosed revolver in her handbag, though she's never yet had occasion to use it. She owns a vintage German sedan, kept in remarkable repair, as well as a small convertible two-seater for times when she doesn't require Marcus' escort.

Veronica's nightly concerns revolve around the restoration of her family to a position of influence. Failing that, she would be happy to elevate *herself* to a position of influence and build a new legacy over the foundation of the old. In these interests, she has made numerous acquaintances among the vampires and mortals alike of Chicago, and plans on cultivating those relationships so that they may best achieve her ends (this also leaves the door open to acquire allies or additional contacts in the future…). Though emotionally strong and self-sufficient, Veronica realizes that in these nights of tumultuous Kindred events, there is safety in numbers, and she is looking for individuals with whom she can form a protective coterie. Veronica's sire, estranged by the woman's odd fiduciary (and almost un-Toreador) interests, Lynn leaves in Justin's hands to detail.

And that's it. Lynn could choose specialties for Veronica's Traits with four dots (Appearance and Finance), but she chooses to see what shakes out of the prelude. Veronica is ready to take on whatever the World of Darkness can throw at her.

PERSONALITY ARCHETYPES: NATURE AND DEMEANOR

Everyone plays a role, often several, every day. Every individual displays multiple layers of personality, varying from the contrived to the sincere. Each of these roles defines how we interact with the people and places around us, and we choose which parts of ourselves we wish to show.

It is the same with Kindred. The concept of Nature and Demeanor corresponds directly to the different masks we wear when we interact. A **Vampire** character's Nature is her true self, her innermost being — the person she truly *is*. It is dangerous to show this, though, as it lets others know who we are and what is

important to us. Thus, characters also have Demeanors, faces they show to the world. By choosing how we relate to the world, we are able to choose how it relates to us as well, as we guide the responses others give us.

Philosophy aside, personality also has an effect on the mechanics of **Vampire**. A character may regain her drive and sense of purpose by acting in accordance with her Nature. Every time a character fulfills the requirement of her Nature Archetype (see below), that character becomes eligible to regain a point of spent Willpower (see p. 136). If the Storyteller allows, the character regains the point.

Archetypes allow players to build a sense of personality for their characters, and to define a bit of what makes the character "tick." It is worth noting that Archetypes are not rigid; characters need not slavishly devote themselves to their Natures and Demeanors. Rather, the character should act as the player reasonably or emotionally believes she *would* act in a given situation. Eventually, players and Storytellers should come up with their own Archetypes that more closely define how the character in question responds to her surroundings. After all, every character is an individual, and customized Archetypes should be a logical outgrowth of a well-rounded character.

Here are some basic character Archetypes, suitable for beginning play.

ARCHITECT

The Architect has a sense of purpose even greater than herself. She is truly happy only when creating something of lasting value for others. People will always need things, and the Architect strives to provide at least one necessity. Inventors, pioneers, town founders, entrepreneurs and the like are all Architect Archetypes.

— Regain a point of Willpower whenever you establish something of importance or lasting value.

AUTOCRAT

The Autocrat wants to be in charge. He seeks prominence for its own sake, not because he has an operation's best interests at heart or because he has the best ideas (though he may certainly think so). He may genuinely believe others are incompetent, but ultimately he craves power and control. Dictators, gang leaders, bullies, corporate raiders and their ilk are Autocrat Archetypes.

— Regain a point of Willpower when you achieve control over a group or organization involving other individuals.

BON VIVANT

The Bon Vivant knows that life — and unlife — is shallow and meaningless. As such, the Bon Vivant decides to enjoy her time on Earth. The Bon Vivant is not necessarily irresponsible. Rather, she is simply predisposed to having a good time along the way. Most Bon Vivants have low Self-Control scores, as they are so given to excess. Hedonists, sybarites and dilettantes are all examples of the Bon Vivant Archetype.

— Regain a point of Willpower whenever you truly enjoy yourself and can fully express your exultation. At the Storyteller's option, a particularly fabulous revelry may yield multiple Willpower points.

BRAVO

The Bravo is a tough and a bully, and often takes perverse pleasure in tormenting the weak. To the Bravo's mind, might makes right; power is what matters, and only those with power should be respected. Naturally, physical power is the best kind, but any kind will do. The Bravo sees overt threats as a perfectly reasonable means of gaining cooperation. The Bravo is not incapable of pity or kindness, he just prefers to do things his way. Robbers, bigots, thugs and the insecure are all Bravo Archetypes.

— Regain a point of Willpower any time you achieve your agenda through brutishness or intimidation. This need not be physical, as many Bravos verbally or socially cow their victims.

CAREGIVER

Everyone needs comfort, a shoulder to cry on. A Caregiver takes her comfort in consoling others, and people often come to her with their problems. Vampires with Caregiver Archetypes often attempt, as best they may, to protect the mortals on whom they feed. Nurses, doctors and psychiatrists are examples of potential Caregivers.

— Regain a point of Willpower whenever you successfully protect or nurture someone else.

CELEBRANT

The Celebrant takes joy in her cause. Whether the character's passion is battle, religious fervor, foiling her rivals or reading fine literature, it gives the Celebrant the strength to withstand adversity. Given the chance, the Celebrant will indulge in her passion as deeply as possible. Unlike the Fanatic (p. 114), the Celebrant pursues her passion not out of duty, but out of enthusiasm. Crusaders, hippies, political activists and art enthusiasts are Celebrant Archetypes.

— Regain a point of Willpower whenever you pursue your cause or convert another character to the same passion. Conversely, lose a point of temporary Willpower whenever you are denied your passion or it is badly lost to you.

CHILD

The Child is still immature in personality and temperament. He wants what he wants *now*, and often prefers someone to give it to him. Although he can typically care for himself, he would rather have a caretaker-type cater to his bratty desires. Some Child Archetypes are actually innocent rather than immature, ignorant of the cold ways of the real world. Children, spoiled individuals and some drug abusers are Child Archetypes.

— Regain a point of Willpower whenever you manage to convince someone to help you with no gain to herself, or to nurture you.

COMPETITOR

The Competitor takes great excitement in the pursuit of victory. To the Competitor, every task is a new challenge to meet and a new contest to win. Indeed, the Competitor sees all interactions as some sort of opportunity for her to be the best — the best leader, the most productive, the most valuable or whatever. Corporate raiders, professional athletes and impassioned researchers are all examples of Competitor Archetypes.

— Regain one point of Willpower whenever you succeed at a test or challenge. Especially difficult victories may,

at the Storyteller's discretion, allow you to regain multiple Willpower points.

CONFORMIST

The Conformist is a follower, taking another's lead and finding security in the decisions of others. She prefers not to take charge, instead seeking to throw in with the rest of the group and lend her own unique aid. The Conformist is drawn to the most dynamic personality or the individual she perceives to be the "best." Being a Conformist is not necessarily a bad thing — every group needs followers to lend stability to their causes. Groupies, party voters and "the masses" are Conformist Archetypes.

— Regain a point of Willpower whenever the group achieves one of its goals due to your support.

CONNIVER

Why work for something when you can trick somebody else into getting it for you? The Conniver always tries to find the easy way, the fast track to success and wealth. Some people call him a thief, a swindler or less pleasant terms, but he knows that everybody in the world would do unto him if they could. He just does it first, and better. Criminals, con artists, salespeople, urchins and entrepreneurs might be Connivers.

— Regain a point of Willpower whenever you trick someone into doing something for you.

CURMUDGEON

A Curmudgeon is bitter and cynical, finding flaws in everything and seeing little humor in life or unlife. He is often fatalistic or pessimistic, and has very little esteem for others. To the Curmudgeon, the glass is always half-full, though it may be damn near empty when other people are involved. Many elder vampires and Generation Xers are Curmudgeons.

— Regain a point of Willpower whenever someone does something stupid, just like you said they would. You must predict this failure aloud (though you may simply whisper it to the Storyteller if you wish).

DEVIANT

The Deviant is a freak, ostracized from society by unique tastes that place her outside the mainstream. Deviants are not indolent rebels or shiftless "unrecognized geniuses"; rather, they are independent thinkers who don't quite fit in the status quo. Deviant Archetypes often feel that the world stands against them, and as such reject traditional morality. Some have bizarre tastes, preferences and ideologies. Extremists, eccentric celebrities and straight-out weirdoes are Deviant Archetypes.

— Regain a point of Willpower any time you are able to flout social mores without retribution.

DIRECTOR

To the Director, nothing is worse than chaos and disorder. The Director seeks to be in charge, adopting a "my way or the highway" attitude on matters of decision-making. The Director is more concerned with bringing order out of strife, however, and need not be truly "in control" of a group to guide it. Coaches, teachers and many political figures exemplify the Director Archetype.

— Regain a point of Willpower when you influence a group in the completion of a difficult task.

FANATIC

The Fanatic has a purpose, and that purpose consumes his existence. The Fanatic pours himself into his cause; indeed, he may feel guilty for undertaking any objective that deviates from his higher goal. To the Fanatic, the end justifies the means — the cause is more important than those who serve it. Players who choose Fanatic Archetypes must select a cause for their character to further. Revolutionaries, zealots and sincere firebrands are all examples of Fanatic Archetypes.

— Regain a point of Willpower whenever you accomplish some task that directly relates to your cause.

GALLANT

Gallants are flamboyant souls, always seeking attention and the chance to be the brightest stars. Gallants seek the company of others, if only to earn their adoration. Attention drives the Gallant, and the chase is often as important as fulfilling that pursuit. Nothing excites a Gallant so much as a new audience to woo and win. Performers, only children and those with low self-esteem are often Gallant Archetypes.

— Regain a Willpower point whenever you successfully impress another person. Ultimately, the Storyteller is the arbiter of when you dazzle someone, even in the case of other players' characters.

JUDGE

The Judge perpetually seeks to improve the system. A Judge takes pleasure in her rational nature and ability to draw the right conclusion when presented with facts. The Judge respects justice, as it is the most efficient model for resolving issues. Judges, while they pursue the "streamlining" of problems, are rarely visionary, as they prefer proven models to insight. Engineers, lawyers and doctors are often Judge Archetypes.

— Regain a point of Willpower whenever you correctly deduce a mystery by assembling the clues presented, or when one of your arguments unites dissenting parties.

LONER

Even in a crowd, the Loner sticks out, because he so obviously does not belong. Others view Loners as pariahs, remote and isolated, but in truth, the Loner prefers his own company to that of others. For whatever reason, the Loner simply disdains others, and this feeling is often reciprocated. Criminals, radicals and free thinkers are all Loner Archetypes.

— Regain a point of Willpower when you accomplish something by yourself, yet which still benefits the coterie in some way. For truly impressive success, or achievement in spite of strong opposition, the Storyteller may choose to let you regain *two* Willpower points.

MARTYR

The Martyr suffers for his cause, enduring his trials out of the belief that his discomfort will ultimately improve others' lot. Some Martyrs simply want the attention or sympathy their ordeals engender, while others are sincere in their cause, greeting their opposition with unfaltering faith in their own beliefs. Many Inquisitors, staunch idealists and outcasts are Martyr Archetypes.

— Regain a point of Willpower when you sacrifice yourself or your comfort for your ideals or another's immediate gain.

MASOCHIST

The Masochist exists to test his limits, to see how much pain he can tolerate before he collapses. He gains satisfaction in humiliation, suffering, denial and even physical pain. The Masochist defines who he is by his capacity to feel discomfort — he rises each night to greet a new pain. Certain extreme athletes, urban tribalists and the clinically depressed exemplify the Masochist Archetype.

— Regain two points of Willpower whenever you experience pain in a way you never have before.

MONSTER

The Monster knows she is a creature of darkness and acts like it. Evil and suffering are the Monster's tools, and she uses them wherever she goes. No villainy is below her; no hurt goes uninflicted and no lie remains untold. The Monster does not commit evil for its own sake, but rather as a means to understand what she has become. Many Sabbat, degenerate Kindred elders and unstable individuals display characteristics of the Monster Archetype.

— Malignant deeds reinforce the Monster's sense of purpose. Monster characters should pick a specific atrocity, regaining Willpower whenever they indulge that urge. For example, a tempter regains Willpower for luring someone into wickedness, while an apostate earns back Willpower for causing another to doubt her faith. Pick a destiny and fulfill it.

PEDAGOGUE

The Pedagogue knows it all, and desperately wants to inform others. Whether through a sense of purpose or a genuine desire to help others, the Pedagogue makes sure his message is heard — at length, if necessary. Pedagogue Archetypes may range from well-meaning mentors to verbose blowhards who love to hear themselves talk. Instructors, the overeducated and "veterans of their field" are all examples of Pedagogue Archetypes.

— Regain one point of Willpower whenever you see or learn of someone who has benefited from the wisdom you shared with them.

PENITENT

The Penitent exists to atone for the grave sin she commits simply by being who she is. Penitents have either low self-esteem or legitimate, traumatic past experiences, and feel compelled to "make up" for inflicting themselves upon the world. Penitent Archetypes are not always religious in outlook; some truly want to scourge the world of the grief they bring to it. Repentant sinners, persons with low self-esteem and remorseful criminals are examples of the Penitent Archetype.

— Regain a point of Willpower whenever you feel that you have achieved absolution for a given grievance. This redemption should be of the same magnitude as the transgression — the greater the crime, the greater the penance. The Storyteller is the ultimate arbiter of what constitutes a reasonable act of reparation.

PERFECTIONIST

Perfectionist Archetypes simply demand the best. A half-hearted job gives the Perfectionist no satisfaction, and she expects the same degree of commitment and attention to detail from others that she demands from herself. Although the Perfectionist may be strict and exacting, the achievement of the end goal drives her — and often those for whom she is responsible. Prima donnas, artists and conceptual designers exemplify the Perfectionist Archetype.

— Regain a point of Willpower whenever you accomplish your goal without any demonstrable flaw or impediment.

REBEL

The Rebel is a malcontent, never satisfied with the status quo or the system as it is. He hates authority and does everything in his power to challenge and undermine it. Perhaps the Rebel truly believes in his ideals, but it is just as likely that he bears authority figures some ill will over a misunderstanding or "wrong" done to him in the past. Teenagers, insurrectionists and nonconformists all exemplify the Rebel Archetype.

— Regain a point of Willpower whenever your actions adversely affect your chosen opposition. Rebels may oppose the government, the Church, a vampire prince, whatever. The player should choose whom or what his character rebels against when he adopts this Archetype.

ROGUE

Only one thing matters to the Rogue: herself. To each his own, and if others cannot protect their claims, they have no right to them. The Rogue is not necessarily a thug or bully, however. She simply refuses to succumb to the whims of others. Rogues almost universally possess a sense of self-sufficiency. They have their own best interests in mind at all times. Prostitutes, capitalists and criminals all embody the Rogue Archetype.

— Regain a point of Willpower when your self-centered disposition leads you to profit, materially or otherwise. At the Storyteller's discretion, accumulating gain without exposing your own weaknesses may let you regain two points of Willpower.

SURVIVOR

No matter what happens, no matter the odds or opposition, the Survivor always manages to pull through. Whether alone or with a group, the Survivor's utter refusal to accept defeat often makes the difference between success and failure. Survivors are frustrated by others' acceptance of "what fate has in store" or willingness to withstand less than what they can achieve. Outcasts, street folk and idealists may well be Survivor Archetypes.

— Regain one point of Willpower whenever you survive a threatening situation through tenacity, or when another persists in spite of opposition due to your counsel.

THRILL-SEEKER

The Thrill-Seeker lives for the rush brought on by danger. Unlike those of arguably saner disposition, the Thrill-Seeker actively pursues hazardous and possibly deadly situations. The Thrill-Seeker is not consciously suicidal or self-destructive — he simply seeks the stimulation of imminent disaster. Gangbangers, petty thieves and exhibitionists are all examples of the Thrill-Seeker Archetype.

— Regain a point of Willpower any time you succeed at a dangerous task that you have deliberately undertaken. Thrill-Seekers are not stupid, however, and the Storyteller may choose not to reward a player who heedlessly sends her character into danger for the sole intent of harvesting Willpower.

TRADITIONALIST

The orthodox ways satisfy the Traditionalist, who prefers to accomplish her goals with time-tested methods. Why vary your course when what has worked in the past is good enough? The Traditionalist finds the status quo acceptable, even preferable, to a change that might yield unpredictable results. Conservatives, judges and authority figures are all examples of Traditionalist Archetypes.

— Regain a point of Willpower any time the proven ways turn out to be the best. Also, regain a point of Willpower any time you successfully resist change for its own sake.

TRICKSTER

The Trickster finds the absurd in everything. No matter how grim life (or unlife) may become, the Trickster always uncovers a kernel of humor within it. Tricksters cannot abide sorrow or pain, and so they strive to lighten the spirits of those around them. Some Tricksters have even higher ideals, challenging static dogma by exposing its failures in humorous ways. Comedians, satirists and social critics are examples of Trickster Archetypes.

— Regain a point of Willpower any time you manage to lift others' spirits, especially if you are able to deny your own pain in the process.

VISIONARY

The Visionary is strong enough to look beyond the mundane and perceive the truly wondrous. Visionaries test accepted societal limits, and seek what few others have the courage to imagine. The Visionary rarely takes satisfaction in what society has to offer; she prefers to encourage society to offer what it *could* instead of what it *does*. Typically, society responds poorly to Visionaries, though it is they who are responsible for bringing about progress and change. Philosophers, inventors and the most inspired artists often have Visionary Archetypes.

— Regain a point of Willpower each time you are able to convince others to have faith in your dreams and follow the course of action dictated by your vision.

ATTRIBUTES

Every **Vampire** character has Attributes; they represent the basic potential of every person in the world, as well as most other living (and unliving) things. Most people have Attribute scores between 1 (poor) and 3 (good), though exceptionally gifted individuals may have scores of 4 (excellent) or even 5 (peak human capacity). Some vampire elders, those of strong Blood, are rumored to have scores higher still.

PHYSICAL

Physical Attributes define the condition of a character's body. They indicate how strong, agile and resilient a character is. Physical Attributes should be taken as the primary category for an action-oriented character.

Vampires may use ingested blood to supernaturally augment their Physical (and *only* their Physical) Attributes. For more on this, see p. 138.

STRENGTH

Simon winced as blow after blow landed on the other side of the hotel door. His sire was right: The war packs of the Sabbat were terribly tenacious. Unless he managed to keep the door held against them while Josephine called the police, Simon was as good as gone. Envisioning himself and Josephine torn to ribbons under the Sabbat's talons, Simon braced himself against the door for another hail of blows.

Strength is the raw, brute power of a character. It governs how much weight a character can lift, how much he can physically push and how hard he can hit another character or object. The Strength Trait is added to a character's damage dice pool when he hits his opponent in hand-to-hand combat. It is also used when a character wishes to break, lift or carry something, as well as when a character tries to jump a distance.

Specialties: Iron Grip, Powerful Arms, Reserves of Strength, Fists Like Anvils

- • Poor: You can lift 40 lbs.
- •• Average: You can lift 100 lbs.
- ••• Good: You can lift 250 lbs.
- •••• Exceptional: You can lift 400 lbs.
- ••••• Outstanding: You can lift 650 lbs. and crush skulls like grapes.

DEXTERITY

A sheer layer of blood-sweat glistened on Serina's forehead. Her prey knew he was being followed, so her ability to strike quickly and with surprise was paramount. Serina managed to climb the fire escape almost silently, knowing that the man would seek refuge in this alley. Ah, there he was! Baring her fangs and claws, Serina erupted from her ill-lit perch as her prey panted for what would soon be his last breath.

The Dexterity Attribute measures a character's general physical prowess. It encompasses the character's speed, agility and overall quickness, as well as indicating the character's ability to manipulate objects with control and precision. Also included under Dexterity's heading are hand-eye coordination, reflexes and bodily grace.

Specialties: Lithe, Swift, Feline Grace, Lightning Reflexes

- • Poor: You are clumsy and awkward. Put that gun down before you hurt yourself.
- •• Average: You're no clod, but you're no ballerina, either.
- ••• Good: You possess some degree of athletic potential
- •••• Exceptional: You could be an acrobat if you wished.
- ••••• Outstanding: Your movements are liquid and hypnotic — almost superhuman.

STAMINA

Simon awoke to find himself bound to a chair with heavy chains, the prince's enforcer looming over him.

"It seems your little Sabbat friends left you high and dry, no?"

"They're not my friends. They came after me and Josephine," Simon spat through tattered lips.

"Why would you lie to me, Simon?" crooned his captor. "Just tell me the truth, and this will all be over…." The brute pushed up his sleeve and hammered Simon in the face, cracking bone and spattering blood.

Hang in there, *Simon thought to himself. They can't beat it out of you if you don't let them.*

VAMPIRE: THE MASQUERADE

116

SPECIALTIES

Some characters are especially good at particular applications of their Traits. For example, a painter might be particularly good at portraits, a baseball player might be adept at catching fly balls, and a brawler might be infamous for his low blows. To represent this, characters with scores of 4 or higher in Attributes or Abilities may choose specialties for those Traits.

A *specialty* is a particular subcategory of an Attribute or Ability — thus, a character with a Strength 5 might choose to be especially adept in "deadlifting," while a character with Investigation 4 might be a whiz at "ballistics." Whenever a player makes a die roll involving an activity in which her character has specialized, she may take any die that comes up "10," tally the success normally, then reroll that die in an attempt to accumulate extra successes. If the rerolled die also comes up "10," she may continue to reroll for still further successes. This process continues until no further "10s" are rolled.

Example: Victoria has Performance 4 with a specialty in singing love songs. She is performing in front of a live audience, and she begins her hit song "4Ever 1." To gauge the audience's reaction, the Storyteller has Victoria's player, Katie, roll Victoria's Charisma (4) + Performance (4) versus difficulty 6. The dice pool is 8, and Katie scores three successes — but two of those successes are "10s." Katie takes the two "10" dice and rolls them, scoring 9 and 7 — two extra successes. She may not continue to try for further successes, but the five-success total indicates that the crowd absolutely loves Victoria's rendition.

The Stamina Trait reflects a character's health, toughness and resilience. It indicates how long a character can exert herself and how much punishment she can withstand before suffering physical trauma. Stamina also includes a bit of psychic fortitude, indicating a character's grit and tenacity not to give up.

Specialties: Tireless, Determined, Tough as Nails, Resolute

- • Poor: You bruise in a stiff wind.
- •• Average: You are moderately healthy and can take a punch or two.
- ••• Good: You are in good shape and rarely fall ill.
- •••• Exceptional: You can run — and perhaps win — any marathon you choose.
- ••••• Outstanding: Your constitution is truly Herculean.

SOCIAL

Despite their solitary predilections, vampires use human society like building blocks to advance their schemes. Social Attributes delineate a character's appearance, charm and ability to interact with society. These Traits are paramount in determining a character's first impressions, personal dynamics and relations with other individuals.

CHARISMA

The prince pushed the curtain aside and walked out before the assembled council of the city's primogen. Their petty side conversations and guarded whispers stopped as the prince took his place at the head of the table, smiling at them with the look of a predator. Despite their differences of opinion, personal vendettas and centuries-old hatreds, they still accepted the prince as their superior. None could contest the ancient vampire's overwhelming force of personality.

"See how they love me, even in their hate?" commented the prince to his childe, who stood behind the chair next to him. "Let them know who's in charge, and you'll have them drinking out of your hand."

Charisma is a character's ability to entice and please others through her personality. Charisma comes into question when a character tries to win another character's sympathies or encourage others to trust her. Charisma does not indicate necessarily a silver tongue or a skill with bullying. Rather, it is the simple power of a character's charm and influence. Charisma delineates a character's ability at convincing others to see her point of view.

Specialties: Smooth Talker, Genteel, Urbane, Witty, Eloquent Speaker, Graceful

- • Poor: Stop picking your nose.
- •• Average: You are generally likable and have several friends.
- ••• Good: People trust you implicitly.
- •••• Exceptional: You have significant personal magnetism.
- ••••• Outstanding: Entire cultures could follow your lead.

MANIPULATION

Daphne looked at Lucasz as if he were the only Kindred in the city who could help her. He already trusted her, the fool, and now all she had to do was convince him that he needed to go talk to that bastard Barzeski.

"Lucasz, you're the only one who can do it. I'm on such bad terms with them that Barzeski won't even listen to me anymore. Plus, if you start leaning on them now, they'll be too intimidated to come after you later."

Lucasz' face softened a bit — she had him! Now, with any luck, he and Barzeski would kill each other while they were at the table, and she'd be rid of two thorns in her side.

Manipulation measures a character's ability for self-expression in the interests of getting others to share her outlook or follow her whims. In short, it's getting others to do what she wants. Manipulation comes into play when a character tries to influence or subtly guide another's behavior. Manipulation is used to trick, bluff, fast-talk and railroad other characters. Whether or not the characters in question actually *like* the manipulator is irrelevant (this is why Manipulation differs from Charisma); a skilled motivator can even employ the talents of people who hate her.

Manipulation is a dangerous affair, especially among the Kindred (though it is their coin of the realm). Failed attempts at manipulation often earn the ire of the would-be patsy. Botching a Manipulation roll may add a name to the character's list of enemies.

People are manipulated every day, and typically ignore it. ("Would you run to the store for me?") If the fact is brought to their attention, however, most people get quite defensive. Manipulation can be the most powerful tool in a Kindred's repertoire, but failure can be disastrous. Characters with high Manipulation ratings are often distrusted by those around them.

Specialties: Persuasive, "Damn I'm Smooth," Seductive, Well-Reasoned

- • Poor: A person of few (often ineffectual) words.
- •• Average: You can fool some of the people some of the time, just like anybody else.
- ••• Good: You never pay full price.
- •••• Exceptional: You could be a politician or cult leader.
- ••••• Outstanding: "Of course I'll tell the prince it was *I* who tried to stake him!"

APPEARANCE

"Well, Harrick, let's see who the Toreador have pulled from the bottom of their collective shoe to discuss this matter with us, shall we?" Jervis Graves pulled a fat Cuban cigar from his desk drawer and struck a match, flinching instinctively from the tiny flame. "Bring them in!" Graves bellowed at his attendant, ashes tumbling from the cigar's tip.

The cigar hit the table at the same time Graves' jaw hit the floor. In walked the ugliest woman Jervis had ever seen — and he'd even seen some of the Nosferatu.

"Caine's blood, creature, that face could send me into torpor."

"Yes, sir," replied the Kindred calmly. "And now shouldn't we discuss the matter of—"

"No, not at all," Graves cut her off. "Tell the 'artistes' that if they want to do business with Jervis Graves, they need to send someone who still looks human."

The Appearance Attribute is a measure of a character's attractiveness. More than simple looks, however, Appearance is the sum of a character's visible grace, beauty and the indefinable *je ne sais quoi* that makes people desirable.

Appearance is both more and less than words — it appeals to the lower levels of the psyche, so it shapes first impressions and the nature of memories thereafter. No matter how open-minded a person is, no matter how vehemently he claims, "Her personality is more important than her looks," a person still thinks of another in relation to the subject's appearance.

This Trait is used for more than getting potential vessels to heed your beckon across a crowded dance floor. In situations in which first impressions are paramount, or that involve people who view Appearance as very important, a character may have no more dice in a Social dice pool than her Appearance score. Thus, it is critically important to either look your best or get to know people before you start trying to convince them to fire-bomb the justicar's haven.

- • Poor: Ugly as a mud fence.
- •• Average: You don't stand out in a crowd, for better or for worse.
- ••• Good: Strangers offer to buy you drinks at bars.
- •••• Exceptional: You are appealing enough to be a model, and people often go out of their way to tell you so.
- ••••• Outstanding: People react to you with either insane jealousy or beatific awe.

MENTAL

Mental Attributes define a character's cerebral capacities, including such aspects as memory, intelligence, awareness of one's surroundings and the ability to think, learn and react.

PERCEPTION

Lucasz sat on the leather divan, jacket unbuttoned, hands in his lap, waiting for his odd host to enter the room. Above the musky scent of the leather, Lucasz caught a whiff of…poppies?…and heard the clink of glass on glass.

A stooped man with a beaklike nose — probably Barzeski's ghoul servant — limped into the room, a fluted glass on a service in his hand. "An aperitif while the lord dresses, sweet guest?" the ghoul rasped.

"If it's all the same to you, I prefer my vitae without laudanum," answered Lucasz.

The ghoul blanched.

Perception measures a character's ability to observe his environment. This may involve a conscious effort, such as searching an area, but it is more often intuitive, as the character's keen senses notice something out of the ordinary. Perception is a sensitivity to the character's surroundings, and is seldom present in the cynical or jaded (who have seen it all before).

Perception is used to determine whether or not a character understands a given situation or detects an environmental stimulus. It can warn a character of ambushes, help a character identify a metaphor, distinguish a clue from a pile of refuse or uncover any other hidden or overlookable detail, whether physical or otherwise.

Specialties: Attentive, Insightful, Careful, Discerning, Experienced

• Poor: Perhaps you are absurdly self-absorbed, perhaps merely an airhead; in any event, even the most obvious details elude you.

•• Average: You are oblivious to the very subtle, but aware of the bigger picture.

••• Good: You perceive moods, textures and minuscule changes in your environment.

•••• Exceptional: Almost nothing evades your notice.

••••• Outstanding: You instantly observe things almost imperceptible to human senses.

INTELLIGENCE

Aisling stared at the fragile manuscript, wondering why it refused to make sense. The symbols were all in order, the invocations were clearly defined, and the motions were even illustrated correctly. Why wouldn't the damn thing work, then? It was as if whatever backward magician had scrawled this thing had left out some basic but vital element.

Backward…

Aisling laughed aloud as she held the book before a mirror. There were the symbols. Working through the alphabet in reverse, she transcribed the proper verses from the page, and practiced the motions in opposite order. She had broken the primitive code.

The Intelligence Attribute refers to a character's grasp of facts and knowledge. More importantly, however, it governs a character's ability to reason, solve problems and evaluate situations. Intelligence is almost a misnomer, as the Attribute also includes critical thinking and flexibility of thought.

Intelligence does not include savvy, wisdom or common sense, as those are properties of the character's personality, not Traits. Even the smartest character may be too foolish to keep her mouth shut or too daft to assume the thugs who want her car keys are up to no good.

Characters with low Intelligence aren't necessarily stupid (though they might be), they are just uneducated or simple thinkers. Likewise, characters with high Intelligence aren't all Einsteins; they may be better at rote memorization or have particularly keen judgment.

Specialties: Book Knowledge, Creative, Analytical, Problem Solver, Subject Authority

• Poor: Not the sharpest knife in the drawer (IQ 80).

•• Average: Smart enough to realize you're normal (IQ 100).

••• Good: More enlightened than the masses (IQ 120).

•••• Exceptional: You're not just bright, you're downright brilliant (IQ 140).

••••• Outstanding: Certified genius (IQ 160+).

WITS

Fire!

Lucasz leaped from the divan as the first waves of hot smoke wisped through the floorboards. First poison, and now this!

Looking to the door, Lucasz figured it must be braced from the outside. The window overlooked the bay, and using that exit would mean a fall of a few hundred feet. The ventilation ducts were far too small for Kindred to crawl through.

Lucasz looked up. The crawlspace. The Fiend surely couldn't have compartmentalized the thin gap between the floors. Simply crawl up there, burst back through above the hallway, and bolt out the front door.

Lucasz turned the divan on its side, climbed atop and hammered his way through the plaster ceiling with his fists. Now it was only a question of what remained outside.

The Wits Trait measures the character's ability to think on her feet and react *quickly* to a certain situation. It also reflects a character's general cleverness. Characters with low Wits scores are thick and mentally lethargic, or maybe gullible and unsophisticated. By contrast, characters with high Wits Traits almost always have a plan immediately and adapt to their surroundings with striking expedience. Characters with high Wits also manage to keep their cool in stressful situations.

Specialties: Getting the Jump on Others, Snappy Patter, Changes in Strategy, Ambushes

• Poor: Pull my finger.

•• Average: You know when to bet or fold in poker.

••• Good: You are seldom surprised or left speechless.

•••• Exceptional: You're one of the people who make others think, "Ooh, I should have said…" the next day.

••••• Outstanding: You think and respond almost more quickly than you can act.

ABILITIES

As mentioned before, Abilities are the Traits used to describe what you know and what you've learned to do. Whereas Attributes represent your raw potential, Abilities represent the ways you've learned to use that potential. You may not need anything but brute strength to smash through a door — but if you're trying to use sheer muscle power to force an engine part into place without breaking anything, you'd better know something about mechanics. When rolling dice, you'll probably have to pair an Ability with an appropriate Attribute, in order to properly depict the combination of potential and know-how that's necessary for getting things done.

There are 30 Abilities: 10 Talents, 10 Skills and 10 Knowledges. Each Ability typically covers a broad range of aptitudes. For certain Abilities (Expression, Crafts, Performance, Academics, Science), it is best to pick a specialty (p. 117), even if the character's rating in the Ability is not yet 4 or higher. Thus, a character with the Crafts Skill is generally versed in handiwork of all sorts, but might be particularly adept at auto mechanics.

TALENTS

Talents describe what you intuitively know, what you can do without coaching or instruction. The only way to improve your Talents is through direct experience — with the exception of a very few cases (such as studying a text on Jeet Kune Do to learn a dot or so of Brawl), these things can't be learned from a book or mail-order course. If you try an action involving a Talent your character doesn't possess, there's no penalty to your basic Attribute dice pool; these Abilities are so intuitive that virtually everyone has some degree of capacity in each one.

ALERTNESS

Kincaid held up a finger, and the other vampires whispering in the darkened foyer immediately fell silent. "Lady Anna is coming," he murmured. He cupped one hand to his ear, then nodded. "She's maybe two blocks away, and there's no other traffic on the street." He smiled a smile with razored edges. "That custom Rolls of hers, there's no mistaking it. Now shut up and get ready to welcome her in, you idiots."

This is your basic knack for noticing things that go on around you, even when you're not actively looking for them. Alertness describes the attention you pay to the outside world, whether otherwise occupied or not. This Talent is typically paired with Perception, and is best used when sensing physical stimuli (as opposed to moods or clues).

- •　　Novice: You're no mindless drone.
- ••　　Practiced: Habitual eavesdropper
- •••　　Competent: You keep a sharp eye on your surroundings.
- ••••　Expert: Whether from paranoia or good sense, you are rarely caught off guard.
- •••••　Master: Your senses are on par with those of a wild animal.

Possessed by: Hunters, Bodyguards, Security Personnel, Journalists, Burglars

Specialties: Noises, Eavesdropping, Ambushes, Hidden Weapons, Crowds, Forests, Animals

ATHLETICS

Ronnie took a running leap and hit the chain-link fence climbing. He could still hear the hooting and laughter of the gang behind him, and the sound shot more adrenaline into his aching muscles. But he'd done this a thousand times, and he was over the fence in record speed. As he raced further down the alley, he tried to clear his head, reassuring himself that there was no way those muscleheads could climb as quickly as he could. He'd bought himself a little more time; it was just a matter of putting it to use.

Then he heard the gut-wrenching sound of metal wire being torn apart....

This Talent represents your basic athletic ability, as well as any training you might have had in sports or other rigorous activities. Athletics concerns all forms of running, jumping, throwing, swimming, sports and the like; however, it doesn't cover basic motor actions such as lifting weights, nor does it govern athletic feats covered by another Ability (such as Melee).

- •　　Novice: You had an active childhood.
- ••　　Practiced: High-school athlete
- •••　　Competent: Professional athlete
- ••••　Expert: Top-notch in your sport
- •••••　Master: Olympic medalist

Possessed by: Athletes, Enthusiasts, Park Rangers, Jocks, Kids

Specialties: Swimming, Rock Climbing, Acrobatics, Dancing, Endurance Running, specific sports

BRAWL

Lucita neatly snapped her knuckles into the prince's neck — one — then plunged her fingers precisely into his eyesockets — two. One-two, quicker than a child could draw breath and harder than any mortal could strike.

She smiled tautly as the formerly regal Cainite clawed in panic at his ruined eyes and crumpled windpipe. No sight, no voice — and no chance to invoke his otherworldly, hypnotic majesty. Now she could do the rest at her leisure.

The Brawl Talent represents how well you fight in tooth-and-nail situations. This Talent represents skill in unarmed combat, whether from formal martial-arts training or simply from plenty of experience — either type can make you a dangerous adversary. Effective brawlers are coordinated, resistant to pain, quick, strong and *mean*; the willingness to do whatever it takes to hurt your opponent wins plenty of fights.

- •　　Novice: You were picked on as a kid.
- ••　　Practiced: You've seen the occasional barroom tussle.
- •••　　Competent: You've fought regularly and routinely, and generally walked away in better shape than your opponents.
- ••••　Expert: You could be a serious contender on a boxing circuit.
- •••••　Master: You can kill three men in four seconds.

Possessed by: Military, Police, Roughnecks, Thugs

Specialties: Boxing, Wrestling, Dirty Fighting, Kicks, Karate, Judo, Muay Thai, Throws, Submission Holds

DODGE

Beckett cursed as the bullets struck the wall over his head, sending hot chips of brick into his hair. He launched himself sideways, rolling behind the dumpster just as the rounds cut into where he had been standing. Typical, he thought. Saguryev's minions are as subtle as he is. He flexed his fingers and growled as the black talons glided out of his fingertips. Let's see if they're slower.

As it turned out, they were.

The first rule of self-preservation, this Talent covers your ability to avoid blows, missile fire or even oncoming cars. Dodge

entails taking cover, ducking punches or any other methods of getting out of harm's way.

- • Novice: You can reflexively duck and cover your head.
- •• Practiced: You've weathered a self-defense class.
- ••• Competent: You can evade thrown rocks, maybe even knives.
- •••• Expert: It'd take a skilled brawler to land a punch.
- ••••• Master: You can virtually sidestep bullets on open ground.

Possessed by: Police, Criminals, Brawlers, Boxers, People in Bad Neighborhoods

Specialties: Cover, Sidestep, Footwork, Leap

EMPATHY

"I mean," the young woman gesticulated, "how the hell was I supposed to take care of that baby? How could I?" She dabbed at her eyes with her napkin, then stared guiltily into her cup. "Oh my God. Look at me, breaking down right in the coffeehouse. You've got to think I'm so stupid."

"No, no," her companion said gently. "Please, don't. Here." He stood and offered her his hand. "Why don't we go somewhere a little less public, and you can get it all off your chest there?" She looked up and smiled a little at that, and the smile he returned her was nothing short of dazzling.

You understand the emotions of others, and can sympathize with, feign sympathy for, or play on such emotions as you see fit. You are an easy hand at discerning motive, and might be able to pick up on when someone's lying to you. However, you may be so in tune with other people's feelings that your own emotions are affected.

- • Novice: You lend the occasional shoulder to cry on.
- •• Practiced: You can sometimes literally feel someone else's suffering.
- ••• Competent: You have a keen insight into other people's motivations.
- •••• Expert: It's almost impossible to lie to you.
- ••••• Master: The human soul conceals no mysteries from you.

Possessed by: Social Workers, Parents, Actors, Psychologists, Detectives, Seducers, Mediums, Best Friends

Specialties: Emotions, Personalities, Motives, Gaining Trust

EXPRESSION

"By the Blood, Laveaux, compose yourself. Victoria's little ditty hardly merits consideration, let alone a blood hunt — notwithstanding lyrics which could indeed be interpreted as...satirical. A bit...tawdry for my tastes," the prince sniffed, "but scarcely a violation of the Masquerade."

"Billboard #8?!? Millions of kine are mocking me — in their automobiles, in their nightclubs, on their damnable electronic phonographs. I shall be a laughingstock in—"

"Elysium, Laveaux. Elysium. Hardly the place for such histrionics. Remember where you are! Anyway," the prince said airily, the faintest of smiles creasing his visage, "it can hardly be true, can it? That stanza about you and the—"

Laveaux stormed away, gnashing his fangs in fury, as the harpies tittered behind him.

This is your ability to get your point across clearly, whether through conversation, poetry or even email. Characters with high Expression can phrase their opinions or beliefs in a manner that cannot be ignored (even if their opinions are misinformed or worthless). They might also be talented actors, skilled at conveying moods or feigning emotion with every gesture. Additionally, this Talent represents your ability for poetry, creative writing or other literary art forms.

- • Novice: Your talent has matured past crude poetry on notebook paper.
- •• Practiced: You could lead a college debate team.
- ••• Competent: You could be a successful writer.
- •••• Expert: Your work is Pulitzer material.
- ••••• Master: A visionary such as yourself comes along only once in every generation.

Possessed by: Actors, Writers, Poets, Politicians, Journalists, Instructors, Rabble-Rousers

Specialties: Acting, Poetry, Fiction, Impromptu, Conversation

INTIMIDATION

Lucita audibly drew a breath, and something seemed to gather around her. Something…palpable. Her gaze settled on one of the black-clad bodyguards, then the other, but lingered for no more than a second on each. Both men grew very pale; one tried weakly moving his hand toward his shoulder holster, but stopped almost instantly at the sound of her voice.

"I said this conversation was private. Leave. Now."

Intimidation takes many forms, from outright threats and physical violence to mere force of personality. You know the right method for each occasion, and can be very…persuasive.

- • Novice: Crude teenage bully
- •• Practiced: Mugger
- ••• Competent: Drill sergeant
- •••• Expert: Your air of authority cows casual passersby.
- ••••• Master: You can frighten off vicious animals.

Possessed by: Bullies, Executives, Military Officers, Thugs, Bouncers, Gangsters, Sabbat

Specialties: Veiled Threats, Pulling Rank, Physical Coercion, Blackmail

LEADERSHIP

Kincaid stomped across the makeshift stage and shook one fist above his head. "Are you going to go to one knee and offer your neck to your butcher, just because he says Father Knows Best? Are you going to pour your heart's fire between the decayed lips of the ancients?" Enthusiastic, powerful cries of "No!" shook the stage, but Kincaid went on as if he couldn't hear them. "Who will inherit this world, this night, this future? Those who have already seen a millennium or two — or those who can do something with their immortality? ARE YOU WILLING TO FIGHT FOR YOUR FREEDOM?"

The answer was a chorus of bone-rattling shouts. Kincaid screamed more fiery words into the crowd, but his heart was cold as ice, except for a growing flame of gloating satisfaction — and anticipation.

You are an example to others and can inspire them to do what you want. Leadership has less to do with manipulating people's desires than it does with presenting yourself as the sort of person they want to follow. This Talent is usually paired with Charisma rather than Manipulation.

- • Novice: Captain of your Little League team
- •• Practiced: Student body president
- ••• Competent: An effective CEO
- •••• Expert: Presidential material
- ••••• Master: You could be the lord and master of a nation.

Possessed by: Politicians, Princes, Managers, Executives, Military Officers, Police

Specialties: Oratory, Compelling, Friendly, Open, Noble, Military, Commands

STREETWISE

In full daylight, the spraypaint would have had a distinctly neon glare. In the dim light of the streetlight's periphery, it was dull and heavy. Nonetheless, the young man in gang colors was studying it intently. "Yeah, I know that tag," he finally said. He shook his head. "That's a badass marker. The Green Nails. Vietnamese. The kind of gang you never hear about on the damn cop shows, but the ones nobody in their right mind fucks with."

The older man, his impeccable suit very out of place in the alleyway, merely nodded. "Yes, precisely. And very, very suitable for our purposes."

The streets can provide a lot of information or money to those who know the language. Streetwise allows you to blend in unobtrusively with the local scene, pick up gossip, understand slang or even dabble in criminal doings.

- • Novice: You know who sells drugs.
- •• Practiced: You're accorded respect on the street.
- ••• Competent: You could head your own gang.
- •••• Expert: You have little to fear in even the worst neighborhoods.
- ••••• Master: If you haven't heard it, it hasn't been said.

Possessed by: Criminals, Homeless People, Reporters, Detectives, Vice Squads, Sabbat

Specialties: Fencing, Illegal Drugs, Illegal Weapons, Rumors, Gangs, Pickpocketing, Local Slang

SUBTERFUGE

"I mean — I can't promise anything, and I have too much respect for you to give you the usual BS. Who can tell what the future holds?" David looked up, met Linda's gaze across the low table. "But it is different when I'm with you. To be honest—" David's voice almost cracked with emotion, "I don't know if I ever have been in love, really, but this feels like it could, well…."

Wordlessly, Linda slid across the couch, took David's hand in hers, and pressed her forehead to his shoulder.

Ah, the kine are even more unchanging than we, despite their vaunted "progress." David — Dar-Inku in another time — recalled other, similarly meaningless phrases, spoken in Greek, in Aramaic and Chaldean, in the baths of Rome and among the pillars of ruined Nineveh. A true master of the Jyhad, he mused, needs no mind-tricks to beguile a vessel.

You know how to conceal your own motives and project what you like. Furthermore, you can root out other people's motives, then use those motives against them. This Talent defines your talent for intrigue, secrets and double-dealing; mastery of Subterfuge can make you the ultimate seducer, or a brilliant spy.

- •   Novice: You tell the occasional little white lie.
- ••   Practiced: Vampire
- •••   Competent: Criminal lawyer
- ••••   Expert: Deep-cover agent
- •••••   Master: You're the very last person anyone would suspect.

Possessed by: Politicians, Lawyers, Vampires, Teenagers, Con Men, Pick-up Artists

Specialties: Seduction, Impeccable Lies, Feigning Mortality

SKILLS

Skills are Abilities learned through training, apprenticeships or other instruction. If you try to perform an action involving a Skill in which you have no rating, your difficulty is increased by one. An unskilled worker just isn't as effective as someone who might have lower Attributes but an understanding of what the procedure entails.

ANIMAL KEN

The two men by the limousine were engrossed in their conversation, and never saw the movement in the shadowy alley behind them. They didn't see the hideous creature in the tattered trenchcoat kneel by the sewer grating, nor did they hear the low, susurrant call that drifted down below the street.

But when the rats came boiling out of the alley by the hundreds, they noticed.

You can understand an animal's behavior patterns. This Skill allows you to predict how an animal might react in a given situation, train a domesticated creature, or even try to calm or enrage animals.

- •   Novice: You can get a domesticated horse to let you pet it.
- ••   Practiced: You can housebreak a puppy.
- •••   Competent: You could train a seeing-eye dog.
- ••••   Expert: Circus trainer
- •••••   Master: You can tame wild beasts without benefit of supernatural powers.

Possessed by: Farmers, Animal Trainers, Zookeepers, Park Rangers, Pet Owners, Domitors

Specialties: Dogs, Attack Training, Big Cats, Horses, Farm Animals, Falconry

CRAFTS

Jules gestured with unconcealed pride at the wall hanging. "Look there. The original Bayeux Tapestry, stolen away from Britain and replaced with a common forgery. Oh, how the mortals would panic, if we let them discover the truth!"

"Yours is the forgery," Carmelita said quietly, hiding all but a hint of her smile. Jules' normally ashen face paled into eggshell-white, but she continued. "Double-check the edges, Jules. The threads are tied in several places in knots that are distinctly 13th-century, and the dyes have been chemically faded." Then she looked at his stricken expression, and laughed. "Oh, poor dear! I'm so sorry. Here, pretend I didn't say anything."

This Skill covers your ability to make or fix things with your hands. Crafts allows you to work in fields such as carpentry, leatherwork, weaving or even mechanical expertise such as car repair. You can even create lasting works of art with this Skill, depending on the number of successes you achieve. You must always choose a specialization in Crafts, even though you retain some skill in multiple fields.

- • Novice: High-school wood shop
- •• Practiced: You're starting to develop your own style.
- ••• Competent: You could make a living at your work.
- •••• Expert: Your work might be featured in college-level textbooks for your field.
- ••••• Master: Your artistry is virtually without peer.

Possessed by: Mechanics, Artisans, Artists, Designers, Inventors, Back-to-the-Land Types

Specialties: Pottery, Sewing, Home Repair, Carpentry, Appraisal, Carburetors

DRIVE

Karl slammed hard on the brakes, twisting the wheel around as he did so. The Thunderbird's tires squealed as the vintage car slid into the classic bootlegger's reverse — thankfully, they didn't blow out in the process. The black cars behind him weren't so lucky; as Karl poured on the gas, he could hear the passengers' threats turn into screams, followed by the grinding percussion of crumpling metal.

So far, so good....

You can drive a car, and maybe other vehicles as well. This Skill does not automatically entail familiarity with complicated vehicles such as tanks or 18-wheelers, and difficulties may vary depending on your experience with individual automobiles. After all, helming a station wagon doesn't prepare you for controlling a Lotus at 100 miles per hour.

- • Novice: You know how to work an automatic transmission.
- •• Practiced: You can drive a stick shift.
- ••• Competent: Professional trucker
- •••• Expert: NASCAR daredevil or tank pilot
- ••••• Master: You can make a Yugo do tricks out of a James Bond movie.

Possessed by: Cabbies, Truckers, Race Car Drivers, most 20th-century residents of affluent Western nations

Specialties: Off-road, Wheelies, Curves, Stick Shift, Sudden Stops, Heavy Traffic

ETIQUETTE

Carmelita waited until the two men had turned the corner two blocks down, then clutched at her companion's arm. "Those two — Hesha, were they...?"

"Yes, dear. Assamites." His face was expressionless basalt under the street lamps. "And they have agreed to leave us to our affairs while they scrutinize Vlados' chantry instead." He affably patted her hand. "You see, my dear? Clan matters little — theirs, or mine. So much rests on mere civility."

You understand the nuances of proper behavior, in both mortal society and Kindred culture. Your specialty is the culture with which you are most familiar. This Skill is used during haggling, seduction, dancing, dinner etiquette and all forms of diplomacy.

- • Novice: You know when to keep your mouth shut.
- •• Practiced: You've been to a black-tie event or two.
- ••• Competent: You know your way around even obscure silverware.
- •••• Expert: Her Majesty would consider you charming.
- ••••• Master: If the right people came to dinner, you could end wars — or start them.

Possessed by: Diplomats, Travelers, High Society, Executives

Specialties: Formal Dinners, Business, Street Culture, Kindred Society

FIREARMS

Valentine hissed a low, contemptuous sigh. His hand flickered ever so briefly — and instantly a gun appeared in his fingers, a lusterless, heavy revolver. Before the hired security could even gasp for breath, the room shook with four thunderclaps, one right after the other.

Valentine neatly stepped over the nearest spreading pool of scarlet, proceeding directly for the oak door.

Executing a mortal with a sword starts investigations. Clawing someone to ribbons shakes the edges of the Masquerade. So Cainites adapt, and many have devoted their energies to learning how to kill with guns. This Skill represents familiarity with a range of firearms, from holdout pistols to heavy machine guns. Of course, this Skill doesn't include heavy artillery such as mortars or tank guns. However, someone skilled in Firearms can clean, repair, recognize and, of course, accurately fire most forms of small arms. This Skill is also used to unjam guns (Wits + Firearms).

- • Novice: You had a BB gun as a kid.
- •• Practiced: You while away the occasional hour at the gun club.
- ••• Competent: You've survived a firefight or two.
- •••• Expert: You could pick off people for a living.
- ••••• Master: You've been practicing since the debut of the Winchester.

Possessed by: Sabbat, Policemen, Military Personnel, Survivalists, Hunters

Specialties: Fast-Draw, Gunsmithing, Pistols, Sniping, Revolvers, Shotguns

MELEE

Even as the .44 round tore through her shoulder, Fatima pivoted like a ballerina, bringing the Damascene scimitar directly down on the gunman's neck. The carefully honed blade sheared neatly through collarbone, dead flesh and vertebrae, and the head came free almost instantly.

Her expression was aloof as she shifted her gaze to the gunman's panicking partner. "What do they teach you childer these days?" Her English was as flawless as the grace with which she shifted her grip. "Guns against Kindred? No, no. You must do things in the proper fashion." Her grip tightened. "Like so."

As the Kindred maxim runs, *Guns mean nothing to a lifeless heart.* A blade is often worth far more, as is the skill to use it properly. Melee covers your ability to use hand-to-hand weapons of all forms, from swords and clubs to esoteric martial-arts paraphernalia such as sai or nunchaku. And, of course, there is always the utility of the wooden stake....

- • Novice: You know the right way to hold a knife.
- •• Practiced: You may have been in the occasional street fight.
- ••• Competent: You could make a college fencing team.
- •••• Expert: You could keep order in the prince's court.
- ••••• Master: Your enemies would rather face a SWAT team than your blade.

Possessed by: Assassins, Gang Members, Martial Artists, Police, Duelists, Medievalist Buffs

Specialties: Knives, Swords, Improvised Clubs, Stakes, Disarms, Axes

PERFORMANCE

There was nothing but silence around the bonfire as the last notes of Nikos' tune drifted off into the pine forest and night sky. Then there was cheering, whistling, laughing. Nikos, with a laugh of his own, looked over to the stranger. "How's that, hey?" He proffered the fiddle, and the stranger quietly accepted it. "I tell you," Nikos continued, "the man hasn't been born that can outplay me. Go ahead and try, but...." He let his words trail off into a chuckle.

The stranger lifted the fiddle to his shoulder, tucked it neatly under his pointed chin, smiled like a cat, and began to play. And in that moment, Nikos' laugh died in his throat, for he knew he'd lost the wager — and far more than that.

The Performance Skill governs your ability to perform artistic endeavors such as singing, dancing, acting or playing a musical instrument. You are almost certainly specialized in one field, although true virtuosos may be talented in many forms of performance. This Skill represents not only technical know-how, but the ability to work an audience and enrapture them with your show.

- • Novice: You could sing in the church choir.
- •• Practiced: You could get a leading part in a college production.
- ••• Competent: You're in demand at the local clubs.
- •••• Expert: You have the talent to be a national sensation.
- ••••• Master: You are a virtuoso without peer.

Possessed by: Musicians, College Students, Actors, Ballerinas, Mimes

Specialties: Dancing, Singing, Rock and Roll, Acting, Guitar Solos, Drunken Karaoke

SECURITY

The orderlies burst out of the front door, then skidded as a group to an unruly halt. Just ahead of them was John Doe #244, absent-mindedly wandering the lawn, his discarded straitjacket lying crumpled on the walk. "What?" hissed the newest among them. "How'd he…?"

"Never mind that," replied the shift overseer in a low, worried tone. "Just hope he doesn't have anything sharp with him this time."

This Skill entails familiarity with the tools and techniques for picking locks, deactivating car or burglar alarms, hot-wiring automobiles or even safecracking, as well as countless forms of breaking and entering. Security is useful not only for theft, but also for setting up "the unbeatable system" or deducing where a thief broke in.

- •   Novice: You can pick a simple lock.
- ••   Practiced: You can hot-wire a car.
- •••   Competent: You can bypass or disable house alarms.
- ••••   Expert: You can crack a safe.
- •••••   Master: You could get a bomb out of — or into — the Pentagon.

Possessed by: Burglars, Security Consultants, Policemen

Specialties: Safecracking, Hot-wiring, Electrical Alarms, Pressure Plates, Deadbolts, Cars

STEALTH

Lucita suddenly froze — then threw herself down and to the right. There was a sudden, dull noise as the book she'd been holding was bisected by the razored metal blade that sliced through the air. She came up in a roll, muscles bunched, and growled — or was it a purr? — one word: "Fatima."

The woman facing Lucita grinned, her teeth startlingly white against her dark skin. "Lucita. It seems I still give myself away to your ears." Her voice was smooth as the silks she wore, and her hands shifted their grip on the scimitar. "I suppose this will be a challenge, then. As always."

This Skill is the ability to avoid being detected, whether you're hiding or moving at the time. Stealth is often tested against someone else's Perception. This Ability is, for obvious reasons, highly useful in stalking prey.

- •   Novice: You can hide in a darkened room.
- ••   Practiced: You can shadow someone from streetlight to streetlight.
- •••   Competent: You have little difficulty finding prey from evening to evening.
- ••••   Expert: You can move quietly over dry leaves.
- •••••   Master: Nosferatu elder

Possessed by: Burglars, Assassins, Kindred, Spies, Reporters, Commandos

Specialties: Hiding, Silent Movement, Shadowing, Crowds

SURVIVAL

"Here, kid," Emmett grunted, tossing a reeking bundle into the ditch. The ragged Caitiff flinched away at first, then gratefully accepted the noisome wad of blankets. "You wanna get most of the way into that culvert," Emmett continued, "'cause the sun's gonna be mostly on this side for the day. Go fetal, too, 'cause you'll be able to cover more of yourself that way."

The skinny vampire blinked back up at Emmett. "But wouldn't it be safer in the sewers? I mean, there's no—" He stopped short when he saw the look on Emmett's hideous face. "Oh. I see."

"Ain't no sunlight down there," Emmett scowled as he straightened up and turned away. "Don't mean it's safe."

Although vampires have little to fear from starvation and exposure, the wilderness can still be dangerous to a Cainite. This Skill allows you to find shelter, navigate your way to civilization, track prey and possibly even avoid werewolves (although this last is exceedingly difficult). When you use Stealth in the wilderness, you cannot roll more dice for your Stealth rating than you have in Survival.

- •   Novice: You can survive a five-mile hike.
- ••   Practiced: You "roughed it" on a regular basis.
- •••   Competent: You know poisonous mushrooms from edible ones.
- ••••   Expert: You could live for months in the wilderness of your choice.
- •••••   Master: You could get dropped naked into the Andes and do all right for yourself.

Possessed by: Scouts, Soldiers, Outdoors Enthusiasts, Survivalists, Hunters, Park Rangers

Specialties: Tracking, Woodlands, Jungle, Trapping, Hunting

KNOWLEDGES

Knowledges involve the application of the mind, not the body; consequently, Knowledge Abilities are most often paired with Mental Traits. (It's possible to roll Charisma + Academics, or even Stamina + Medicine, but such things are pretty rare.) The following descriptions speak of Knowledge levels in collegiate terms, although formal schooling is just one way to improve a Knowledge.

If you don't have any dots in a Knowledge, you cannot even attempt a roll involving it unless the Storyteller gives explicit permission (such as where common trivia is concerned). If you don't know Spanish, you can't try holding a conversation in *español* on your wits alone.

ACADEMICS

"Little fool," Hesha hissed in disgust. "You babble of your ruined 'Carthage,' yet the term means no more to you than a parroted lyric from one of your shrill, oh-so-important 'alternative' screeds. What do you know of Carthage — or of Rome, for that matter? Did your sire tell you of the Sabines' sacrifices to Tanit and Moloch? Of the screams in the streets as infants vomited forth their blood for the Brujah's sustenance? Of women and children dragged naked to the block and given over to the caresses of foreign mercenaries — who yet defended the 'Utopia' when your noble line was too blood-glutted to stir?

"Go away, whey-blooded Iconoclast. Speak to me again in a century, when your vitae is less tainted with heroin and ignorance." Hesha waved a finger in dismissal.

The anarch's frenzy was sudden and, as the attack was a clear violation of the Sixth Tradition, Hesha suffered no repercussions for the subsequent slaying. Naturally, taking over Morningside Homes was the simplest of matters thereafter.

This catchall Knowledge covers the character's erudition in the "humanities": literature, history, art, philosophy and other "liberal" sciences. A character with dots in Academics is generally well-rounded in these fields, and at high levels may be considered an expert in one or more areas of study. Not only can this Knowledge impress at salons and other Elysium functions, but it can also offer valuable clues to certain past — and future — movements in the Jyhad.

- • Student: You're aware that 1066 is something more than a Beverly Hills area code.
- •• College: You can quote from the classics, identify major cultural movements, and expound on the difference between Ming and Moghul.
- ••• Masters: You could get a paper published in a scholarly journal.
- •••• Doctorate: Professor emeritus
- ••••• Scholar: Scholars worldwide acknowledge you as one of the foremost experts of your time.

Possessed by: Professors, Literati, Trivia Buffs, Elders

Specialties: Poststructuralism, Impressionist Painting, Imperial Rome, American Realism

COMPUTER

Emmett couldn't resist a phlegmy chuckle. It had taken some time to rig up his system in the sewer, to say nothing of getting a power line set up. But it was all about to be worth it.

It wasn't tricky, hacking into Laveaux's S&L institution. It would've been simple to rewrite a few numbers. But Emmett was a pro, and that meant he played hardball. Once the IRS got through checking Laveaux's artfully embellished numbers, there wouldn't be enough left of the self-righteous nancyboy's money or credentials to buy a Taco Bell combo meal. So much for "superior influence."

This Knowledge represents the ability to operate and program computers, as well as the savvy to keep up with the latest technology.

- • Student: Point and click.
- •• College: You can process data with relative ease.
- ••• Masters: You can design software.
- •••• Doctorate: You can make a very comfortable living as a consultant.
- ••••• Scholar: You're on the bleeding edge.

Possessed by: Hackers, Office Workers, Programmers, Data Processors, Students

Specialties: Computer Languages, Internet, Codebreaking, Viruses, Data Retrieval

FINANCE

The vampire set down the newspaper with a deliberate cough. "Were you under the impression that undeath brings effortless, unending power? Did you suppose that our influence and wealth are magically granted to us at the moment of the Embrace? I did not select you for your naiveté, childe." He drummed long, exquisitely manicured nails on the mahogany desktop. "I entered this century with nothing more than a handful of coins. I shall see the millennium turn with billions to my name. And all that I have, I achieved through my own savvy and determination."

He touched one finger to his cheek, and his burning gaze grew pensive. *"It seems you need a practical lesson in how to make money do your bidding. I will apply my skills to bringing about the financial ruin of a person, and you will watch me — and then demonstrate what you've learned."* The corner of his mouth crooked upward. *"What was your ex-husband's name again?"*

You know the ins and outs of commerce, from evaluating an item's relative worth to keeping up with currency exchange rates. This Knowledge can be invaluable when brokering items, running numbers or playing the stock market. Sufficiently high levels in Finance allow you to raise your standards of living to a very comfortable level.

- • Student: You've taken a few business classes.
- •• College: You have some practical experience and can keep your books fairly neat.
- ••• Masters: You'd make a fine stockbroker.
- •••• Doctorate: Corporations follow your financial lead.
- ••••• Scholar: You could turn a $20 bill into a fortune.

Possessed by: Executives, Upper Class, Stockbrokers, Accountants, Fences, Drug Dealers, Smugglers

Specialties: Stock Market, Laundering, Appraisal, Foreign Currencies, Accounting, Fencing, Corporations

INVESTIGATION

Lucita and Anatole walked calmly into the darkened office, then stopped and quietly scanned the opulent surroundings. No more than a minute had passed before Anatole spoke: "There — the right bookend, three shelves down on the south wall."

Lucita strode to the bookcase and lifted the grotesque Olmec statue from the shelf. She turned it over to inspect the base, nodded, then sank her fingers into the stone and pulled. The statue split apart with a crack, and a tiny phial tumbled to the floor in a shower of rock dust and broken hingework.

You've learned to notice details others might overlook, and might make an admirable detective. This Knowledge represents not only a good eye for detail, but also an ability to do research and follow leads.

- • Student: You've read your share of Agatha Christie.
- •• College: Police officer
- ••• Masters: Private detective
- •••• Doctorate: Federal agent
- ••••• Scholar: Sherlock Holmes

Possessed by: Detectives, Mystery Buffs, Policemen, Stalkers

Specialties: Forensics, Shadowing, Search, Discolorations

LAW

"What did you expect me to do?!?" The chained vampire's voice rose in a desperate shriek, almost falsetto at the very end. "My pack was slaughtered! They tore Diego to ribbons without breathing hard!" His eyes snapped to one side, to the metal brewing vat half-visible in the shadows. "I had to warn you!"

"The law is the law," intoned the robed creature before him. "Cowardice is unforgivable." The older Cainite's vestments rustled as he extended his palm in mock benediction. "The sentence is as it must be. Death by acid."

The chained vampire screamed at that, and didn't stop screaming for some time.

With all the lawyers and lawmakers out there, this Knowledge can prove very useful. Law can be useful for filing suit, avoiding lawsuits or getting out of jail. What's more, even the Kindred keep their own laws, and more than one vampire has saved his own unlife by deftly exploiting a loophole in one of the Traditions.

- • Student: You've watched your share of courtroom dramas.
- •• College: You're either studying for or just passed the bar exam.
- ••• Masters: Ambulance chaser
- •••• Doctorate: Major public figures have your number — just in case.
- ••••• Scholar: You could find the loopholes in the Devil's contract.

Possessed by: Lawyers, Police, Judges, Detectives, Legislators

Specialties: Criminal, Suits, Courts, Contracts, Police Procedure

LINGUISTICS

As Anatole raised his face to the broken rose window, his voice lifted into song, echoing in the corners of the chapel. "Pange, lingua, gloriosi/Corporis mysterium/Sanguisque pretiosi...."

Lucita shook her head, artfully drawing one finger across her wine-dark lips to daub away an errant drop of blood. "'Of the Blood, all price exceeding.' How appropriate."

Anatole finished the stanza, then slowly turned to face her. "'O wondrous gift indeed! The poor and lowly may/Upon their Lord and master feed.'" He chuckled, wiping his mouth with the back of his hand. "Communion is a sacred business. It joys me that you have always understood this."

You begin play with the native language of your choice for free, but if you want to speak any other languages, whether modern or ancient, Linguistics is a must. This Ability allows you to understand additional languages, but at high levels also offers a more general understanding of linguistic structure. Linguistics may allow you to recognize accents or decipher word puzzles.

- • Student: One extra language
- •• College: Two extra languages
- ••• Masters: Four extra languages
- •••• Doctorate: Eight extra languages
- ••••• Scholar: 16 extra languages

Possessed by: Diplomats, Ambassadors, Travelers, Ancient Vampires, Cryptologists, Scholars

Specialties: Romance Languages, Kanji, Idioms, Hieroglyphics, Written Expression, Ciphers

MEDICINE

"Yaroslav! Idiot!" The horribly distorted ghoul cowered as his master spoke, shrinking back against the stone wall in abject terror. Shaking its head in contempt, Vykos knelt over the bleeding man and began molding his wounds closed. "This one must be kept intact for a time," the vampire coldly continued. "I shall punish you tomorrow evening."

Vykos shook its head, ignoring the now-piteous whimpering of the ghoul in the corner. Finally, its hands stopped moving. "There," it crooned to the unconscious man. "I have granted you life again. Come, let us see what you are willing to make of it."

You have an understanding of how the human body, and to a lesser extent the vampiric body, works. This Ability entails knowledge of medicines, ailments, first-aid procedures, and diagnosis or treatment of disease. Medicine is of great use to those Kindred with an interest in repairing, damaging or reworking the human body.

- • Student: You've taken a CPR course.
- •• College: Premed or paramedic
- ••• Masters: General practitioner
- •••• Doctorate: You can perform transplants.
- ••••• Scholar: You are respected by the world's medical community as a modern-day Aesculapius.

Possessed by: Med Students, Doctors, Lifeguards, Parents, Paramedics, Tzimisce

Specialties: Organ Transplants, Emergency Care, Poison Treatments, Pathology, Pharmaceuticals

OCCULT

"'Of the mad ones, the wild ones, I say first, drink not of their blood!'" Beckett opened his eyes and sat up straighter in his chair. "That's the first part of that passage in The Book of Nod, *and I can cite plenty of Kindred since then who've voiced more or less the same sentiment. The fae, if that's what you want to call them, are probably very real and likely very dangerous." He frowned. "I hope you know what you're doing, Anatole."*

The Malkavian only smiled.

You are knowledgeable in occult areas such as mysticism, curses, magic, folklore and particularly vampire lore. Unlike most other Knowledges, Occult does not imply a command of hard, factual information; much of what you know may well be rumor, myth, speculation or hearsay. However, the secrets to be learned in this field are worth centuries of sifting legend from fact. High levels of Occult imply a deep understanding of vampire lore, as well as a good grounding in other aspects of the occult; at the very least, you can discern what is patently false.

- • Student: You've paged through the New Age section of a Waldenbooks.
- •• College: There seems to be some unsettling truth to some of the rumors you've heard.
- ••• Masters: You've heard a lot and actually seen a little for yourself.
- •••• Doctorate: You can recognize blatantly false sources and make educated guesses about the rest.
- ••••• Scholar: You know most of the basic truths about the hidden world.

Possessed by: Occultists, The Superstitious, New Agers, Tremere

Specialties: Kindred Lore, Rituals, Infernalism, Witches

POLITICS

Hesha's skin shone like mahogany in the candlelight as he shook his head and spoke into the receiver. "I think you overestimate Bianca's strength in this situation. The recent embarrassment she suffered from her childe's actions has called the harpies' attention to her, and she dare not risk further loss of status. Further, her soldiers — what few she has — are largely occupied in the defense of Lighton Ferry. No. She won't make a move."

He nodded, and a small light came into his eye. "Of course. You have my number if there's anything else you require."

You are familiar with the politics of the moment, including the people in charge and how they got there. This Knowledge can aid you in dealing with or influencing mortal politicians, or even offer some insight into the local Cainite power structure.

- • Student: Activist
- •• College: Political science major
- ••• Masters: Campaign manager or talk-radio host
- •••• Doctorate: Senator
- ••••• Scholar: You could choose the next President of the United States.

Possessed by: Activists, Politicians, Lawyers, vampires of all sorts

Specialties: City, State, Federal, Bribery, Dogma, Radical, Camarilla

SCIENCE

"Douglas, look here!" The young ghoul's eyes shone as she backed away from the microscope. "The circulatory damage is considerable, but there are some signs of repair — clotting, even cell regeneration as usual."

Dr. Netchurch stared through the microscope lenses for a full minute before replying. "Yes. You're right, the deceased most definitely made a conscious attempt to repair the hemotoxin's damage — but to no avail." His smile was taut and without humor. "It seems I've succeeded beautifully."

You have at least a basic understanding of most of the physical sciences, such as chemistry, biology, physics and geology. This Knowledge can be put to all forms of practical use.

- • Student: You know most of the high-school basics.
- •• College: You're familiar with the major theories.
- ••• Masters: You could teach high-school science.
- •••• Doctorate: You're fully capable of advancing the knowledge in your field.
- ••••• Scholar: Your Nobel Prize is waiting for you.

Possessed by: Scientists, Students, Researchers, Teachers, Engineers, Technicians, Pilots

Specialties: Chemistry, Biology, Geology, Physics, Astronomy

BACKGROUNDS

These Traits describe advantages of birth (or rebirth), circumstance and opportunity: material possessions, social networks and the like. Backgrounds are external, not internal, Traits, and you should always rationalize how you came to possess them, as well as what they represent. Who are your contacts? Why do your allies support you? Where did you meet your retainers? How exactly do you make enough money to justify your four dots in Resources? If you've put enough detail into your character concept, selecting appropriate Backgrounds should be easy.

Although it's uncommon to make rolls involving Background Traits, your Storyteller might have you do so to see if you can obtain information, goods or favors. For example, you might have to roll Wits + Resources to keep your stock options healthy, or Manipulation + Contacts to wheedle that extra favor from your smuggler "associate."

ALLIES

"Damn." The middle-aged man set down his fork and dabbed at his lips with his napkin. "I had no idea that the Nash girl was related to you. And your family wants it kept pretty hushed up?" He stifled a belch, then sipped at his wine. "Well, I dunno if I can get away without printing updates, but…"

His companion, who hadn't touched a bite of her linguine, raised a hand to cut him off. "Please, there's no need to endanger your position. I'm not asking you to deny her disappearance, or even to ignore it — simply run your case updates in a less conspicuous area of the paper." Her half-smile was a masterpiece of struggling with grief. "Keeping the affair less public…for the family's sake."

Allies are humans who support and help you — family, friends or even a mortal organization that owes you some loyalty. Though allies aid you willingly, without coaxing or coercion, they are not always available to offer assistance; they have their own concerns and can do only so much in the name of friendship. However, they might have some useful Background Traits of their own, and might provide you with indirect access to their contacts, influence or resources.

Allies are typically persons of influence and power in your home city. They can be of almost any sort, pending your Storyteller's permission; you may have friends in the precinct morgue, or perhaps even the mayor's ear, depending on how many dots you spend on this Trait. Your allies are generally trustworthy (although they probably don't know that you're a vampire, or even that vampires exist). However, nothing comes for free; if you wind up drawing favors from your friend in the *Cosa Nostra*, he'll probably ask you to do him a favor in kind in the future. This often leads to the beginning of a story….

- •   One ally of moderate influence and power
- ••   Two allies, both of moderate power
- •••   Three allies, one of whom is quite influential
- ••••   Four allies, one of whom is very influential
- •••••   Five allies, one of whom is extremely influential

CONTACTS

"Hey, my friend. No offense meant, okay?" The dreadlocked man spread his hands wide. "Can't blame me for being a little curious. You just picked up two crates of some very sweet AK action, and pay so generously for the Dragonsbreath ammo that I know you ain't about to resell it to someone else. No way would some sucker pay so much that you'd turn a profit on this stuff." He tapped a finger under his nose speculatively. "I never hear tell of you doing this kind of dirty, brother. What, are you just stowing things away for a rainy day?"

Kincaid's smile was electric as he gently placed the automatic rifle back in the crate. "Not at all. I never buy things I don't intend to use."

You know people all over the city. When you start making phone calls around your network, the amount of information you can dig up is almost terrifying. Contacts are largely people whom you can bribe, manipulate or coerce into offering information, but you also have a few major contacts — friends whom you can rely on to give you accurate information in their fields of expertise. You should describe each major contact in some detail before the game begins.

In addition to your major contacts, you also have a number of minor contacts spread throughout the city; your major contact might be in the district attorney's office, while your minor contacts might include beat cops, DMV clerks, club bouncers or even hot-dog vendors. You need not detail these various "passing acquaintances" before play; instead, to successfully get in touch with a minor contact, you should roll your Contacts rating (difficulty 7). You can reach one minor contact for each success; of course, you still have to coerce them into telling you what you need to hear.

- •   One major contact
- ••   Two major contacts
- •••   Three major contacts
- ••••   Four major contacts
- •••••   Five major contacts

FAME

"Jesus, I'm sorry if I'm getting in your face, but I just had to come over here and say, uh…well, Jesus! What a show!" The teenager's grin split her face almost in half. "I mean, I drove all the way out from Alabama to see you play, and I just wanted to say it was worth it. Really, man!"

Karl feigned sipping from his beer, the better to keep from bursting out laughing. "Yeah? That's really great of you." He looked around, then leaned forward with a conspiratorial air. "Tell you what. Me and the guys are having a little bash back at my place after the show. Why don't you get directions from Renee — the redhead in the bustier over there — and drop by?"

You enjoy widespread recognition in mortal society, perhaps as an entertainer, writer or athlete. People may enjoy just being seen with you. This gives you all manner of privileges when moving in mortal society, but can also attract an unwanted amount of attention now that you're no longer alive. The greatest weapon fame has to offer is the ability to sway public opinion — as modern media constantly proves.

This Background is obviously a mixed blessing. You can certainly enjoy the privileges of your prestige — getting the best seats, being invited to events you'd otherwise miss, getting appointments with the elite — but you're also often recognized when you'd rather not be. However, your enemies can't just make you disappear without causing an undue stir, and you find it much easier to hunt in populated areas as people flock to you (reduce the difficulties of hunting rolls by one for each dot in Fame). Additionally, your Storyteller might permit you to reduce difficulties of Social rolls against particularly starstruck or impressionable people.

- •   You're known to a select subculture of the city — local clubgoers or the Park Avenue set, for instance.
- ••   A majority of the populace recognizes your face; you're a local celebrity such as a news anchor.
- •••   You have statewide renown; perhaps you're a state senator or minor star of local interest.
- ••••   Nationally famous; everybody knows something about you.
- •••••   You're an internationally famous media icon.

GENERATION

Ruyter took a step back, baring his ivory teeth in a grimace. His brow was furrowed, but no sweat came. "Damn you!" he hissed. "I know your lineage, creature! You are the childe of that weak-blooded fool Pierre L'Imbecile! How is it that you—" He broke off abruptly, and leaned back as if trying to find shelter. But his neck would not shift away, and his gaze remained locked with — almost impaled by — the Malkavian's cold stare.

"Communion brings one closer to our Dark Father," Anatole said in a quiet tone. His eyes flared with a shrouded glow. "Through his Blood, steadfastness—and insight. Here, allow me to share such glory with you."

Plain and simple, this Background represents your generation — the purity of your blood, and your proximity to the First Vampire. A high Generation rating may represent a powerful sire or a decidedly dangerous taste for diablerie. If you don't take any dots in this Trait, you begin play as a 13th-generation vampire. See p. 139 for further information on generations and what part they play.

- •   12th generation: 11 blood pool, can spend 1 blood point per turn
- ••   11th generation: 12 blood pool, can spend 1 blood point per turn
- •••   10th generation: 13 blood pool, can spend 1 blood point per turn
- ••••   Ninth generation: 14 blood pool, can spend 2 blood points per turn
- •••••   Eighth generation: 15 blood pool, can spend 3 blood points per turn

HERD

The susurrant chanting slowly grew louder as the candles burned lower. Finally, as if responding to some inaudible cue, the indigo-robed man kneeling at the head of the throng rose to his feet and turned to face the other supplicants. "Hear us, Mother Without Mercy, Dark Lady of the Envenomed Fang, Moon of the Earth! Come to us and choose thy consort! Our will is thine!"

Then the packed-earth floor cracked, and crumbled, and a dark-skinned woman literally rose through the soil, welcomed by an ecstatic cry from the gathering.

You have built a group of mortals from whom you can feed without fear. A herd may take many forms, from circles of kinky clubgoers to actual cults built around you as a god-figure. In addition to providing nourishment, your herd might come in handy for minor tasks, although they are typically not very controllable, closely connected to you or even highly skilled (for more effective pawns, purchase Allies or Retainers). Your Herd rating adds dice to your rolls for hunting; see Chapter Six for further details.

- •   Three vessels
- ••   Seven vessels
- •••   15 vessels
- ••••   30 vessels
- •••••   60 vessels

INFLUENCE

"Don't think this story won't get out if I disappear, either." The pudgy, sweating reporter did his best to look smug, but fear shone in his eyes nonetheless. "You can't just kill people and expect the American justice system to sit on its ass, buddy."

Hesha chuckled over steepled fingers. "I believe you overestimate your fellow mortals' integrity, Mr. Laurent. Calls have already been made." He shook his head, an expression of grave sorrow in place on his features. "I'm afraid your autopsy will reveal a sudden but fatal heart attack — how tragic." Serpentine shadows began uncoiling from the corners of the room, and a low hissing began echoing in the chamber. "We are nothing if not thorough. Wouldn't you agree?"

You have pull in the mortal community, whether through wealth, prestige, political office, blackmail or supernatural manipulation. Kindred with high Influence can sway, and in rare cases even control, the political and social processes of human society. Influence represents the sum of your political power in your community, particularly among the police and bureaucracy.

Some rolls may require you to use Influence in place of an Ability, particularly when attempting to sway minor bureaucrats. It is, of course, always easier to institute sweeping changes on a local level than a worldwide scale (e.g., having an "abandoned" building demolished is relatively easy, while starting a war is a bit more difficult).

- •   Moderately influential; a factor in city politics
- ••   Well-connected; a force in state politics
- •••   Position of influence; a factor in regional politics
- ••••   Broad personal power; a force in national politics
- •••••   Vastly influential; a factor in global politics

MENTOR

Ramon bounded through the woods, dropping at times to all fours in his haste. "Tibur!" His voice was raised, but not yet a shout. "Tibur!" His nails gouged the soil, sending tiny showers of dirt into the evening air. "Please, sire, I need your help! Tibur, are you here?"

At last he was answered by a voice that seemed to well up out of the earth, a voice with the growl of a bear and the age of worn stone. "I am here, Ramon. What would you know? Speak quickly, for I am hungry and would hunt."

This Trait represents an elder — or possibly even more than one — who looks out for you, offering guidance or aid once in a while. A mentor may be powerful, but his power need not be direct. Depending on the number of dots in this Background, your mentor might be nothing more than a vampire with a remarkable information network, or might be a centuries-old creature with tremendous influence and supernatural power. He may offer advice, speak to the prince (or archbishop) on your behalf, steer other elders clear of you or warn you when you're walking into situations you don't understand.

Most often your mentor is your sire, but it could well be any Cainite with a passing interest in your well-being. A high Mentor rating could even represent a group of like-minded vampires, such as the elders of the city's Tremere chantry.

Bear in mind that this Trait isn't a "Get out of Jail Free" card; your mentor won't arrive like the cavalry whenever you're endangered. What's more, she might occasionally expect something in return for her patronage (which can lead to a number of interesting stories). A mentor typically remains aloof, giving you useful information or advice out of camaraderie, but will abandon you without a thought if you prove an unworthy or troublesome "apprentice."

- •   Mentor is an ancilla of little influence.
- ••   Mentor is respected; an elder, for instance.
- •••   Mentor is heavily influential, such as a member of the primogen.
- ••••   Mentor has a great deal of power over the city; a prince or archbishop, for example.
- •••••   Mentor is extraordinarily powerful, perhaps even a justicar or Inconnu.

RESOURCES

Kincaid smiled as he turned the key, enjoying the shudder of the Porsche's engine as it turned over flawlessly. It suited the others to take whatever they needed and discard it once they were done. Not him. In a half-remembered, long-gone life he'd thirsted for all the trappings of wealth, and it amused him no end to regularly shuck his "champion of the Sabbat" duties and dabble in the upper-class circles for all they were worth. Certainly, he couldn't enjoy the food and drink, and the savor of a beautiful woman had changed entirely — but luxury is luxury, even to the unliving.

Besides, he mused to himself as he roared out of the garage and into the night street, a car like this makes hunting so much easier.

This Trait describes your personal financial resources, or your access to such. A high Resources rating doesn't necessarily reflect your liquid assets; this Background describes your standard of "living," your possessions and your buying power. No dots in Resources is just that: You have no permanent haven and no possessions save a few clothes and possibly a weapon or pocketful of coins.

You receive a basic allowance each month based on your rating; be certain to detail exactly where this money comes from, be it a job, trust fund or dividends. After all, your fortune may well run out over the course of the chronicle, depending on how well you maintain it. You can also sell your less liquid resources if you need the cash, but this can take weeks or even months, depending on what exactly you're trying to sell. Art buyers don't just pop out of the woodwork, after all.

- •   Small savings: a small apartment and maybe a motorcycle. If liquidated, you would have about $1,000 in cash. Allowance of $500 a month.
- ••   Middle class: an apartment or condominium. If liquidated, you would have at least $8,000 in cash. Allowance of $1200 a month.
- •••   Large savings: a homeowner or someone with some equity. If liquidated, you would have at least $50,000 in cash. Allowance of $3000 a month.
- ••••   Well-off: a member of the upper class. You own a very large house, or perhaps a dilapidated mansion. If liquidated, you would have at least $500,000 in cash. Allowance of $9000 a month.
- •••••   Ridiculously affluent: a multimillionaire. Your haven is limited by little save your imagination. If liquidated, you would have at least $5,000,000 in cash. Allowance of $30,000 a month.

Retainers

Vykos clutched the edge of its fluttering cloak with one long-fingered hand, drawing it closer around itself. It strode quickly from the study, and the misshapen creatures in the hallway scurried quickly to its side as it walked. "No," Vykos hissed, glaring at the hideously resculptured monsters. "No, no, no. I require none of you. Where is Anya? Bring me Anya."

"I am here, lord." The voice was pure velvet, and yet the woman's face and form put it to shame. She slid from the shadowy arch of an antechamber, dropping to one perfect knee and bowing her angelic head before her domitor. "What, or on whom, would you have me perform this evening?"

Not precisely allies or contacts, your retainers are servants, assistants or other people who are your loyal and steadfast companions. Many vampires' servants are ghouls (p. 275) — their supernatural powers and blood bond-enforced loyalty make them the servants of choice. Retainers may also be people whom you've repeatedly Dominated until they have no free will left, or followers so enthralled with your Presence that their loyalty borders on blind fanaticism. Some vampires, particularly those with the Animalism Discipline, use "hellhounds" (ghouled dogs) or other animal ghouls as retainers.

You must maintain some control over your retainers, whether through a salary, the gift of your vitae or the use of Disciplines. Retainers are never "blindly loyal no matter what" — if you treat them too poorly without exercising strict control, they might well turn on you.

Retainers may be useful, but they should never be flawless. A physically powerful ghoul might be rebellious, inconveniently dull-witted or lacking in practical skills. A loyal manservant might be physically weak or possess no real personal initiative or creativity. This Background isn't an excuse to craft an unstoppable bodyguard or pet assassin — it's a method to bring more fully developed characters into the chronicle, as well as to reflect the Renfieldesque followers for which the Kindred are notorious. Don't abuse it.

- •   One retainer
- ••   Two retainers
- •••   Three retainers
- ••••   Four retainers
- •••••   Five retainers

Status

Silence greeted the newcomer as she entered the chamber. The sole movement, apart from hers, was the flutter of thin cloth blown by the ventilation currents — cloth that outlined, shroudlike, the lean forms of the vampires who stood motionless in the gloom. Only their eyes moved, and even then just to follow the newcomer as she strode to stand, fists on hips, before the master of the manse. At last, it was the prince who spoke.

"Lucita."

She bowed her head only a millimeter, enough to let one midnight lock fall across her face. Her smile was that of a shark circling its prey. "I see my reputation precedes me."

You have something of a reputation and standing (earned or unearned) within the local community of Kindred. Status among Camarilla society is often derived from your sire's status and the respect due your particular bloodline; among the Sabbat, status is more likely to stem from the reputation of your pack. Elders are known for having little respect for their juniors; this Background can mitigate that somewhat.

High status among the Camarilla does not transfer to Sabbat society (and will most likely make you a notorious target for your sect's rivals), and *vice versa*. Similarly, anarchs can be considered to have zero Status, unless they have somehow garnered so much power and attention that they must be taken seriously. You may have occasion to roll your Status in conjunction with a Social Trait; this reflects the positive effects of your prestige.

Note: Caitiff characters may not purchase Status during character creation. Caitiff are the lowest of the low, and any respect they achieve must be earned during the course of the chronicle.

- •   Known: a neonate
- ••   Respected: an ancilla
- •••   Influential: an elder
- ••••   Powerful: a member of the primogen (or bishop)
- •••••   Luminary: a prince (or archbishop)

Virtues

The Virtue Traits define a character's outlook on unlife — they shape a character's ethical code and describe his commitment to his chosen morality. Virtues exist to help give a character a sense of being, not to force players to portray their characters in a given way. However, Kindred are passionate creatures, and sometimes an act or situation may force a character to consider exactly how she should react to a given stimulus. Virtues come into play when a character faces an impending frenzy, does something ethically questionable (according to the character's morality), or confronts something that terrifies or disturbs her.

A vampire's Virtues are determined by his Path, the particular code of ethics he follows. Most Camarilla Kindred maintain their mortal values and follow the Path of Humanity (referred to simply as "Humanity"), but other vampires often subscribe to radically different philosophies. These alternate Virtues and Paths are detailed in the Appendix, while Humanity is covered below.

Conscience

Conscience is a Trait that allows characters to evaluate their conduct with relation to what is "right" and "wrong." A character's moral judgment with Conscience stems from her attitude and outlook. Conscience is what prevents a vampire from succumbing to the Beast, by defining the Beast's urges as unacceptable.

Conscience factors into the difficulty of many rolls to avoid committing a transgression. Additionally, Conscience determines whether or not a character loses Humanity by committing acts that do not uphold her moral code (see "Degeneration," p. 221). A character with a high Conscience score feels remorse for transgressions, while a character with a lower Conscience may be a bit more callous or ethically lax.

Some vampires replace the Conscience Virtue with the Virtue of Conviction (p. 287); unless your Storyteller tells you it's desirable to do this, assume Conscience is used.

- •   Uncaring
- ••   Normal
- •••   Ethical
- ••••   Righteous
- ••••• Remorseful

SELF-CONTROL

Self-Control defines a character's discipline and mastery over the Beast. Characters with high Self-Control rarely succumb to emotional urges, and are thus able to restrain their darker sides more readily than characters with low Self-Control.

Self-Control comes into play when a character faces her Beast in the form of frenzy (p. 228). Self-Control allows the character to resist the frenzy. **Note:** A character may never roll more dice to resist or control a frenzy than she has blood pool — it's hard to deny the Beast when one's mind clouds with hunger.

As with Conscience, Self-Control can be replaced, in this case by the Virtue of Instinct (p. 287). Again, unless the Storyteller specifically says it's all right to do so, assume Self-Control is used.

- •   Unstable
- ••   Normal
- •••   Temperate
- ••••   Hardened
- ••••• Total self-mastery

COURAGE

All characters have a Courage Trait, regardless of the Path they follow. Courage is the quality that allows characters to stand in the face of fear or daunting adversity. It is bravery, mettle and stoicism combined. A character with high Courage meets her fears head-on, while a character of lesser Courage may flee in terror.

Kindred use the Courage Virtue when faced with circumstances they endemically dread: fire, sunlight, True Faith. See the section on Rötschreck (p. 229) for mechanical systems dealing with character fear.

- •   Timid
- ••   Normal
- •••   Bold
- ••••   Resolute
- ••••• Heroic

HUMANITY

The Trait of *Humanity* is integral to the underlying theme of **Vampire: The Masquerade**. It is a moral code that allows Kindred to retain their mortal sensibilities in the face of their transformation into parasitic monsters. In essence, it is what keeps a vampire from becoming a mindless animal, enslaved by her thirst for vitae.

Humanity, unlike most other Traits, is rated on a scale of 1 to 10, as it is more complex than a 1-to-5 quantification allows for. Also, just because a Kindred follows the Path of Humanity doesn't mean she is a friendly, congenial saint. Vampires are

predators by nature, and Humanity only gifts them with the ability to pretend they're not. It is an inward charade that protects a vampire from herself, much as the Masquerade protects vampires from the mortals outside.

Unfortunately, the very nature of existence as a vampire is anathema to one's Humanity. As the centuries wear on, the Beast takes hold, and Kindred become less and less concerned with the well-being of mortal "kine" (after all, they'll die eventually, anyway). As such, characters are likely to lose Humanity over the course of the game.

Mortals also typically follow the Path of Humanity, though this is largely out of ignorance: They don't know they can be anything else. As such, this mechanical system for morality rarely comes into play for them. Certainly, some mortals — rapists, murderers and the like — have low Humanity scores, but they have no Beasts roiling within them, as do the Kindred. It is possible for a vampire with a high Humanity score to be more human than some mortals are!

X	Monstrous
•	Horrific
••	Bestial
•••	Cold
••••	Unfeeling
•••••	Distant
••••••	Removed
•••••••	Normal
••••••••	Caring
•••••••••	Compassionate
••••••••••	Saintly

EFFECTS OF HUMANITY

A Kindred's Humanity score reflects how much of a character's mortal nature remains despite the curse of Caine. It influences how well a character may deny her vampiric state, as well as how closely she may pass for mortal.

• Vampires sleep unnaturally deeply and are loath to rise even if presented with danger. Vampires with higher Humanity rise earlier in the evening than vampires with lower Humanity scores. Also, if a Kindred is forced to act during the day, the maximum dice pool he may employ for any action equals his Humanity score.

• Humanity also affects a character's Virtues. Whenever a certain Virtue is called into question, a player may not roll more dice for a Virtue than her character has dots in Humanity. Obviously, as the character sinks ever more deeply into the arms of damnation, questions of morality and self-preservation mean less and less. As Humanity depletes, the character creeps slowly toward the night when she loses all self-control.

• The length of time a Kindred spends in torpor (p. 216) relates directly to his Humanity score. A vampire with low Humanity remains in torpor for a longer time than a vampire with a higher Humanity score.

• Humanity determines how, well, *human* a character appears and how easily she may pass for human among the populace. Vampires with low Humanity acquire unnatural and disturbing features like sunken eyes, perpetual snarls and bestial countenances.

• If a character's Humanity score ever drops to zero (what kind of game are you *playing*?), that persona is no longer suitable

for use as a player's character. Completely controlled by his Beast, the character is a mindless force of unnature, and falls under the Storyteller's control.

Humanity scores fluctuate based upon the Hierarchy of Sin — if a vampire accidentally or purposefully commits an act rated lower than her Humanity score, she must roll her Conscience Trait to see whether she accepts the act (and thus loses Humanity) or feels remorse and maintains her current level. Humanity may be *raised* only by spending experience points on it. See the Degeneration section (p. 221) for more information on Humanity loss and the Hierarchy of Sin.

THE DOWNWARD SPIRAL

Vampires are monsters, have no doubt, and even a Kindred with the highest of Humanity scores is nothing more than a wolf in sheep's clothing. Nonetheless, as Humanity erodes, vampires not only become capable of, but also actively pursue, ever more depraved acts. It is in a vampire's nature to hunt, and to kill, and eventually every vampire finds himself holding the corpse of a vessel he had not intended to murder.

It is important, then, to know how vampires change as their Humanity scores deteriorate. Vampires' behavior, even under the auspices of Humanity, may become so utterly depraved and alien that the very thought of her causes discomfort in others. After all, a low Humanity score indicates that very little connects the Kindred with her mortal origins.

Humanity 10-8

Kindred with Humanity scores this high are, ironically, more human than human. Many fledgling vampires sometimes adhere to codes more rigorous than they ever held in life, as a reaction against becoming a predator. Older Kindred scoff at this practice, taking great mirth at the thought of newly whelped neonates cowering beneath fire escapes and subsisting on the foul blood of rats, vainly rebelling against their murderous natures. Oh, the humanity!

In truth, vampires who *maintain* high scores in Humanity are rare, as every Kindred must kill sooner or later. Vampires with high Humanity are almost unbearable by their peers, who find frustration in their perceived naiveté and self-righteousness; most Kindred prefer to suffer the slings and arrows of unlife without belaboring themselves. High Humanity scores indicate aversion to killing and even distaste for taking more vitae than is necessary. Though not necessarily passive or preachy, Kindred with high Humanity uphold excruciatingly exacting standards, and often have very clearly defined concepts of moral right and wrong.

Humanity 7

Most human beings have Humanity scores of 7 or so, so vampires at this level of Humanity can usually manage to pass for mortals. Vampires with 7 Humanity typically subscribe to "normal" social mores — it's not acceptable to hurt or kill another person, it's wrong to steal something that another person owns, but sometimes the speed limit is just too damn slow. The vampire is still concerned with the natural rights of others at this stage of morality, though more than a little selfishness shines through. Just like everyone else in the world....

Humanity 6-5

Hey, people die. Stuff breaks. A vampire below the cultural human norm has little difficulty with the fact that she needs blood to survive, and she does what needs to be done to get it. Though she won't necessarily go out of her way to destroy property or end a victim's life, she accepts that sometimes that's what fate has in store for some folks. Not automatically horrid, Kindred at this stage of Humanity are certainly at least mildly unpleasant to be around. Their *laissez-faire* attitudes toward others' rights offend many more moral individuals, and some minor physical eeriness or malformation may show up at this stage.

Humanity 4

Hey, some people *gotta* die. The vampire begins an inevitable slide into urge indulgence. A Humanity of 4 indicates that killing *is* acceptable to this Kindred, so long as his victim is deserving (which is, of course, quite subjective). Many vampire elders hover around this level of Humanity, if they haven't adopted some other moral code. Destruction, theft, injury — these are all tools, rather than taboos, for a vampire with Humanity 4. Also, the vampire's own self and agenda become paramount at this point, and devil take whoever gets in the way. Physical changes become quite evident at this stage; while not hideous in the sense of the Nosferatu or certain Gangrel, the vampire acquires a pallid, corpselike and noticeably unwholesome aspect.

Humanity 3-2

The lives and property of others are irrelevant to a Kindred this far gone. The vampire likely indulges twisted pleasures and aberrant whims, which may include any manner of atrocity. Perversion, callous murder, mutilation of victims and wickedness for its own sake are the hallmarks of a Kindred with very low Humanity. Few vampires maintain scores this low and lower for very long — their damnation is all but certain at this point. Vampires at this stage may be physically *mistaken* for human, but don't bet on it.

Humanity 1

Only nominally sentient, Kindred with Humanity 1 teeter on the edge of oblivion. Little matters at all to vampires this far gone, even their own desires outside of sustenance and rest. There is literally nothing a vampire with Humanity 1 won't do, and only a few tattered shreds of ego stand between him and complete devolution. Many who attain this stage find themselves no longer capable of coherent speech, and spend their nights gibbering blasphemy among their gore-spattered havens.

Humanity 0

Must sleep. Must feed. Must kill. Players may not run characters with Humanity 0. Vampires at this stage are completely lost to the Beast.

WILLPOWER

Willpower measures a character's inner drive and competence at overcoming unfavorable odds. Unlike other Traits, Willpower has both a permanent "rating" and a temporary "pool." The rating is rolled or tested, while the pool is "spent." When a player spends a point of a character's Willpower, she should cross off the point from the Willpower pool (the squares), not the Willpower rating (the circles). The *rating* stays constant — if a character needs to roll Willpower for some reason, she bases the roll on the permanent rating. The *pool* is used up during the story.

A character's Willpower pool will likely fluctuate a great deal during the course of a story or chronicle. It decreases by one point every time a player uses a Willpower point to enable his character to do something extraordinary, like maintain self-control or gain an automatic success. Eventually, the character will have no Willpower left, and will no longer be able to exert the effort he once could. A character with no Willpower pool is exhausted mentally, physically and spiritually, and will have great difficulty doing *anything*, as he can no longer muster the mettle to undertake an action or cause. Willpower points can be regained during the course of a story (see below), though players are advised to be careful and frugal with their characters' Willpower pools.

Like Humanity, the Willpower Trait is measured on a 1-10 scale rather than a 1-5 scale.

- •   Spineless
- • •   Weak
- • • •   Unassertive
- • • • •   Diffident
- • • • • •   Certain
- • • • • • •   Confident
- • • • • • • •   Determined
- • • • • • • • •   Controlled
- • • • • • • • • •   Iron-willed
- • • • • • • • • • • Unshakable

Other Paths

Not all vampires follow the principles of the Path of Humanity. Many Kindred outside the Camarilla, particularly the vampires of the Sabbat, see no need to continue to subscribe to moral codes akin to Humanity. These vampires do, however, have different ethical systems in place, as complete amorality is an open door for the Beast.

The "default" morality for **Vampire** characters is Humanity, as control and the Beast are such major themes of the game. *It is best that beginning players run characters adhering to this Path.* Players may, however, choose different Paths should they so wish (at the Storyteller's discretion). After all, it just doesn't make sense to play a malicious Tzimisce torturer who can't hurt people without suffering crippling pangs of conscience.

If a player chooses a vampire clan that has a different moral outlook from that of Humanity, he should select the Path that makes the most sense for the character. Otherwise, the player should circle Humanity on the character sheet and continue the character-creation process.

For more information on the following Paths, see the Appendix.

• **Path of Blood** — Followed almost exclusively by Assamites, the Path of Blood governs revenge, diablerie and bringing oneself closer to the First Vampire.

• **Path of the Bones** — This code governs the study of death and its relation to the vampiric state. The Giovanni are its most ardent supporters.

• **Path of Metamorphosis** — This uniquely Tzimisce Path operates on the principle that, as vampirism lies beyond humanity, *something* lies beyond vampirism.

• **Path of Night** — The Path of Night opens the vampire's soul to eternal darkness. It is predominantly practiced by Lasombra.

• **Path of Paradox** — The Ravnos code of ethics, the Path of Paradox centers upon changing reality for the betterment of oneself.

• **Path of Typhon** — Corruption and sin pave this Path's way. It is supported by the Followers of Set.

Spending Willpower

Willpower is one of the most active and important Traits in **Vampire: The Masquerade**. Because there are so many ways to expend, regain and use Willpower, it fluctuates more than any other Trait (besides blood pool) in the game. Willpower is a very versatile Trait, so make sure you understand how to use it.

• A player may spend one of her character's Willpower points to gain an automatic success on a single action. Only one point of Willpower may be used in a single turn in this manner, but the success is guaranteed and may not be canceled, even by botches. By using Willpower in this way, it is possible to succeed at a given action simply by concentrating. For extended rolls, these extra successes may make the critical difference between accomplishment and failure.

Note: You must declare that you are spending a Willpower point *before* you make an actual roll for a character's action; you can't retroactively cancel a botch by spending a Willpower point at the last minute. Also, the Storyteller may declare that a Willpower point may not be spent on a given action.

• Sometimes, the Storyteller may rule that a character automatically takes some action based on instinct or urge — for example, stepping back from a chasm or leaping away from a patch of sunlight filtering through a window. The Storyteller may allow a player to spend a Willpower point and avoid taking this reactive maneuver. It should be noted that the instinct may return at the Storyteller's discretion; a player may need to spend multiple Willpower points over the course of a few turns to stay on task. Sometimes the urge may be overcome by the force of the character's will; at other times, the character has no choice but to follow his instinct (i.e., the character runs out of Willpower points or no longer wishes to expend them).

• A Willpower point may be spent to prevent a derangement from manifesting, with the Storyteller's permission. Eventually, if enough Willpower points are spent (as determined by the Storyteller), the derangement may be overcome and eliminated, as enough denial of the derangement remedies the aberration. Malkavians may never overcome their initial derangement, though Willpower may be spent to deny it for a short period of time.

• By spending a Willpower point, wound penalties can be ignored for one turn. This allows a character to override pain and injury in order to take one last-ditch heroic (or villainous) action. However, an incapacitated or torpid character may not spend Willpower in this manner.

Regaining Willpower

Willpower may be recovered as well as spent. The following situations earn the character back a point or more of Willpower, though a character's Willpower pool may never exceed her Willpower rating. The only way to increase a character's Willpower *rating* is through experience-point expenditure.

Generally, a character's Willpower pool may be replenished whenever the character fulfills a goal or has an opportunity to restore her self-confidence. Ultimately, specific instances of Willpower restoration are up to the Storyteller. For this reason, Storytellers are advised to be prudent in allowing characters to regain Willpower; it is a powerful and versatile Trait, and permitting players to rely on it too much strips much of the challenge from a story.

• Characters' Willpower pools replenish fully at the end of a given story (and that's *story*, not *session*). The Storyteller may restrict this by requiring that the characters achieve (or partially achieve) a goal or otherwise boost their self-esteem. For example, if the story ends in a stalemate for the characters, who didn't destroy a powerful and corrupt elder, but did manage to obstruct his immediate plans, allow them to replenish their Willpower pools.

• (Storyteller's Option) Characters regain one Willpower point each night when they first rise. This is easy on the bookkeeping, and allows a steady stream of Willpower replenishment (not to mention the fact that players are already writing on that part of the character sheet when they mark off their nightly blood consumption). By way of example, when the players rise for the evening in a communal haven, they all replenish a Willpower point then and there.

• (Storyteller's Option) If a character attains some extraordinary goal or fulfills an outstanding objective, the Storyteller may reward her with a point of Willpower pool. For example, if a character manages to deter a team of vampire-hunters from her sire's haven, the Storyteller may award a Willpower point to that character.

• (Storyteller's Option) If a character behaves in a manner that fulfills her Nature Archetype, the Storyteller may reward the character with one to three Willpower points (as stated in the Archetype descriptions). For example, if a Rebel character rabidly opposes a powerful elder, and that elder is later revealed to be a Sabbat spy, that character may be given a point of Willpower.

Storytellers are encouraged to create their own systems or modify our systems to suit their troupe's style of play. Indeed, the manner in which a Storyteller allows, or refuses to allow, Willpower replenishment can determine the overall mood of the chronicle. A word of caution: Give Willpower rewards judiciously, as Willpower can destroy a story if the Storyteller lets the Trait fall to abuse.

Blood Pool

A character's *blood pool* measures how much vitae the vampire has in his system. The blood pool comprises a number of individual blood points. Each blood point corresponds roughly to one-tenth of the blood in an average adult mortal.

The maximum number of blood points a vampire may ingest is dictated by his generation, as is the number of blood points he may spend in a single turn. A vampire with zero blood points in his system is ravenously hungry and likely in the throes of frenzy.

Vampires must subtract one blood point from their blood pools every night, whether they rise for the evening or not, as the unnatural magics animating their dead bodies consume the vitae they have taken from their prey. Blood points may also be spent in a variety of ways, and may be replenished only by consuming — you guessed it — blood.

Blood pool also affects Self-Control (or Instinct) rolls, which come into play when a character's frenzy becomes imminent. A player may never roll more dice for a Self-Control or Instinct roll than the character has blood pool. For example, if a character has only two blood points left, her player may roll only two dice for a Self-Control roll, even if the character's Self-Control score is 4. Voracious vampires just don't fight the Beast very well….

Spending Blood Pool

As previously mentioned, every vampire expends one blood point each night when she awakens, whether or not she actually goes out and about. Characters may also use blood points in a variety of other ways. A vampire may spend only a certain number of blood points per turn; this number depends on the vampire's generation. See the Generation Chart (next page) to determine this number.

• A vampire may spend one blood point to heal one normal (bashing or lethal) health level of damage. Characters must be resting and relatively inactive for this healing to take place, though this recovery is rapid: One blood point per turn may be spent to heal one health level, though vampires of lower generations may heal as many health levels per turn as they can spend blood points. See the Generation Chart for details on this.

Note that blood expenditure is the *only* way that vampires can heal wounds. Just as their immortality prevents the Kindred from aging and dying naturally, so it also inhibits the recuperative processes natural to a living body.

• A player may spend one blood point to increase a single Physical Attribute (Strength, Dexterity, Stamina) by one dot for the duration of the scene. The player must announce, at the beginning of the turn, that he is doing this. A player may spend as many blood points on increasing Physical Attributes as the vampire may use in a turn (based upon generation), but may only freely increase these Traits up to *one higher* than their generational maximum (i.e., a 10th-generation vampire may increase Traits to a maximum of 6). With effort, a character may increase a Physical Attribute to above even this limit, but each dot above the limit lasts for only three turns after the character stops spending blood. This enables vampires to perform truly amazing physical feats, such as throwing cars, moving preternaturally quickly and withstanding blows that would fell trees.

Example: Jerome, an 11th-generation Brujah, has a Strength of 5. Knowing that he's about to get into a fight, he spends blood to increase his Strength. He spends one blood point to raise Strength to 6 (this enhanced Strength will last for the duration of the scene). Wanting to be even stronger, Jerome begins spending blood, at one blood point per turn, to increase his Strength to 9. Once he "levels out," Jerome may maintain his heightened Strength for three turns before dropping to 6 (though his Strength will remain at 6 for the duration of the scene).

Note: No character may increase Physical Attributes above 10.

• A vampire may give a number of blood points to another Kindred, thereby enabling the recipient to use the blood as if it were her own. This is often a grisly prospect, as the "donor" must open his own vein and physically deliver the blood to the needy Kindred. Of course, if a vampire is ever in a situation in which she *needs* blood, she's likely all out of it herself, and may frenzy and take too much from the donor. Blood gifts should be given with care.

If a vampire (or mortal) partakes of another Kindred's blood three times, she becomes bound to that vampire through the mystical properties of Cainite vitae. This is known as the blood bond. For more on blood bonds, see p. 218.

• A vampire may gift a mortal or animal with a dose of his vitae, allowing the mortal in question to inject or ingest it. For so long as the mortal retains the Kindred vitae in her system, she is considered a ghoul (p. 275).

• Though most vampires (with the exception of Nosferatu) appear much as they did in life, they still display certain corpselike features; for example, their skin is unnaturally cold and ashen, and they do not breathe. By spending a variable number of blood points, a vampire may will himself to appear more human for a scene: flushing his skin, drawing breath, even becoming capable of engaging in sexual intercourse (this last, while helpful in certain types of feeding, in no way means that the vampire may inseminate a mortal or become pregnant; a corpse is still a corpse, after all). Performing these actions for a scene requires an expenditure of blood points equal to (8 minus Humanity); thus, Kindred with Humanity scores of 8 or higher may accomplish these feats automatically, while vampires with low Humanity find the process exceedingly arduous.

Only vampires with Humanity may use blood in this manner; vampires on a Path have forsaken their human sides entirely.

• Blood may be spent to fuel certain vampiric Disciplines. Consult Chapter Four to see which individual powers require blood expenditure.

EARNING BLOOD POOL

Vampires replenish blood pool by taking it from others. "Others" need not be human, though a vampire who is too squeamish to take sustenance from the kine is often ridiculed by his peers — the Kindred are predators, after all, no matter how unnatural.

Drinking blood is a risky proposition. As vampires gorge on the vitae of their victims, there is always the chance that they may take too much. Unhygienic vampires may communicate disease by exposing a vessel to bacteria and viruses carried in other blood that still stains their fangs. A vampire may take only 20 percent of a vessel's blood and leave it relatively safe. Taking half of a vessel's blood necessitates hospitalization for that vessel. Obviously, taking all a vessel's blood will kill it.

A vampire may take up to three blood points from a given vessel in a turn. The shorter the turn, the more forcefully the Kindred steals the vitae. It is generally impossible to take more than three blood points from a vessel in three seconds (the shortest a turn gets), though some Nosferatu with hideously distended mouths are able to take more through sheer surface area bled. Most vampires drink their victim's blood slowly, so as to savor the luscious fluid and draw as much pleasure as possible out of the experience.

Once the Kindred breaks her vessel's skin with her fangs, that vessel no longer resists the vampire (if he did in the first place…). Indeed, the ecstasy caused by the vampire's bite is called the Kiss, and it engenders as much exquisite, subtly painful pleasure in vampires as it does in mortals. Exceptionally strong-willed mortals (9+ Willpower) may continue to resist, but even these vessels eventually succumb to the pleasure. Some Kindred and kine even develop lusts for the Kiss and actively seek out those who will drink their blood.

Note: While Kindred find the Kiss pleasurable, they may resist it more readily than mortals can. Any Kindred, regardless of Willpower, may make a Self-Control roll (difficulty 8) to

BLOOD POOL CHART	
Vessel	**Blood Pool**
Vampire	10-???
Werewolf	25
Average human	10
Child	5
Cow	5
Dog	2
Cat	1
Plasma bag	1
Rat	1/2
Bat/Bird	1/4

GENERATION CHART			
Generation	Max. Trait Rating	Blood Pool Max.	Blood Points/Turn
Third	10	???	???
Fourth	9	50	10
Fifth	8	40	8
Sixth	7	30	6
Seventh	6	20	4
Eighth	5	15	3
Ninth	5	14	2
Tenth	5	13	1
Eleventh	5	12	1
Twelfth	5	11	1
Thirteenth +	5	10	1

Max Trait Rating: This indicates the highest permanent Trait rating (excluding Humanity/Path scores and Willpower ratings) a vampire of the given generation can have. This is especially important with regard to Disciplines and Attributes.

Blood Pool Max: The maximum number of blood points a vampire may keep in her system. Remember that elder vampires concentrate their blood — while the *volume* of blood in their bodies is no greater than any other vampire's, each pint of blood is *worth* more than one point.

Blood Points/Turn: This indicates how many blood points a vampire can spend in a single turn.

avoid succumbing to the Kiss. This enables vampiric victims of diablerie (p. 224) to have a chance at fighting back.

Wounded characters typically have less blood than healthy characters. Assume that a normal-sized human has one fewer blood point in his system for each health level of damage he currently suffers. Mortals regain one blood point per day (unless, of course, they are infused with vitae from some other source). Vampires do not lose blood points to wounds in this manner, though they often spend blood to heal wounds they have suffered.

The blood of nonhuman creatures — livestock, wild animals and the like — is not as nourishing as the blood of humankind. Though an animal may physically have a greater volume of blood than a man, vampires draw less sustenance from it. Hence, animals have fewer blood *points*, even if they have more blood.

Old blood is never as nourishing as fresh blood. In fact, many vampires refuse to drink old blood, whether it comes from human corpses, blood banks, or a vampire's private reserve. However, the blood of other vampires, particularly elders, is quite potent. When drinking from elder vampires, each blood point taken may be so concentrated that it is actually worth two — or more! — normal blood points in use. Thus it is possible to obtain a vast amount of blood points by partaking of elder blood, though such prized vitae is rarely available to neonates or even ancillae. Essentially, elders have greater blood pools not because they are bodily larger than younger vampires, but because the blood they ingest is more concentrated in their ancient veins. Werewolf blood is rumored to be similarly potent.

HEALTH

The Health Trait measures a character's physical condition, from perfect health to death. As characters are wounded or otherwise impaired, they lose health levels, then regain them as they heal. A character's Health Trait comprises seven different "health levels," and each level applies a different dice pool penalty to any actions taken by the person in question. A character who is Hurt subtracts one die from her action dice pools, while a Crippled character subtracts five dice from her action dice pools. If health level penalties leave a character with no dice in a given dice pool, the character cannot take that action. However, a point of Willpower can be spent to ignore wound penalties for one turn.

A character at the Incapacitated health level is utterly immobilized and can take no action of any kind except healing himself with blood points (if the character is a vampire or ghoul) or swallowing blood that is offered to him. A mortal who reaches this stage is a breath away from death; if she takes any more damage, she dies. If a Kindred suffers an *aggravated* wound (see p. 218) after being Incapacitated, he dies the Final Death. A vampire at the Incapacitated health level with no more blood in his body immediately sinks into torpor.

Note: Dice pool penalties from health level loss apply only to *actions*. They do not apply to purely reflexive dice pools, such as soak dice, most Virtue checks, or Willpower rolls to abort to another action. If a character is Wounded and suffers more nonaggravated damage, he may still soak

HEALTH LEVELS

Health Level	Dice Pool Penalty	Movement Penalty
Bruised		Character is only bruised a bit and suffers no dice pool penalties due to damage.
Hurt	-1	Character is superficially hurt and suffers no movement hindrance.
Injured	-1	Character suffers minor injuries and movement is mildly inhibited (halve maximum running speed).
Wounded	-2	Character suffers significant damage and may not run (though he may still walk). At this level, a character may not move, then attack; he *always* loses dice when moving and attacking in the same turn.
Mauled	-2	Character is badly injured and may only hobble about (three yards/turn).
Crippled	-5	Character is catastrophically injured and may only crawl (one yard/turn).
Incapacitated		Character is incapable of movement and is likely unconscious. Incapacitated vampires with no blood in their bodies enter torpor.

with his full Stamina (+ Fortitude, if he has it). The health level penalties do apply to damage rolls for Strength-based attacks, but not for mechanical weapons like firearms. Ultimately, this rule must be adjudicated by the Storyteller and common sense.

EXPERIENCE

During the course of a chronicle, characters — much like players over the course of their lives — learn from their mistakes and grow. Change is inevitable, even for the eternal undead. Over years and centuries, vampires hone their Disciplines, learn (and forget) the ins and outs of cultures and languages, and refine their skills at Jyhad.

A great deal of what characters learn is beyond the scope of any game system to reflect. In many cases the more mundane aspects of growing older — and, one would hope, wiser — are reflected in the players' increased confidence and perspicacity. Learning to lock your car when you leave it in a public parking place is simply common sense, not really a skill that can be purchased. Emotional transformations are roleplayed, not bought.

Sometimes, though, characters improve themselves in skills magical or mundane. A system of rewards, called experience points, is used to reflect these more drastic changes. Experience points reflect the Traits that a vampire hones as time passes.

At the end of each story, the Storyteller awards experience points to each character. The players then write down how many experience points the character has earned. Between stories, players may spend their characters' experience points to purchase or increase Traits.

Experience points can be used to improve Attributes, to acquire new Abilities or enhance ones the character already has, to raise existing Disciplines or purchase new ones, or to increase Virtues. Backgrounds may not be purchased through experience points, though they may be acquired through roleplaying if, for example, the character makes a new friend, acquires a windfall, or commits foul diablerie. The costs for all of these different changes vary greatly, as shown on the following chart.

The Storyteller is the final arbiter of how many experience points each character receives, as well as which Traits may be raised. Accordingly, the Storyteller should oversee where experience points are spent. Players may wish to put points into areas that don't honestly reflect what the character has learned during the story or chronicle, in which case the Storyteller can veto their actions. For example, if a character did not use his Dominate Discipline at all during a story, he could not have improved it, and thus the Storyteller should not allow him to increase the number of dots in that Discipline. The same stands for improving Virtues: A character who just killed three children and diablerized her sire has no logical grounds for increasing her Humanity rating. (Note that a character does not have to use his Traits *successfully* to be eligible for an increase; we often learn more from failure than from success, and the undead are no different.)

As Storyteller, try to be fair about experience-point expenditure, and never take things to the point at which the player feels he has no control over the character any longer. Ask the players what they feel their characters learned before awarding any points, and use that as part of the basis for giving them experience points. These limitations are put forth to add a level of reality to the game. If the changes in the character are completely random, the impact is lost. Weave the changes into the course of events; make the changes reflect what has occurred. That's what roleplaying is all about.

Virtues increased by experience have no impact on the character's Humanity or Willpower. Once the character-creation process is finished, that's the end of the matter. A character who, during a story, manages to act in spite of his fear of fire is eligible for a Courage increase, but increasing Courage does not automatically increase Willpower.

No Trait may be increased by more than one point during the course of a story. Vast changes in Traits take time, and the game should reflect that limitation.

NEW TRAITS

Increasing existing Traits can be done fairly readily, so long as the character uses or practices the Trait in question. Learning new Traits, however, is a little more difficult. Even a vampire can't simply pick up a new language or learn to fight if he doesn't know even the basics (to say nothing of learning a new Discipline!). Thus, learning an entirely new Ability or Discipline requires some tutoring and study, in addition to the required experience-point expenditure. This study can be simple (a night-school course to learn Computer 1) or brutally difficult (months or even years of mind-bending rituals, formulas and blood manipulation to learn the first dot in Thaumaturgy), but it must always be accomplished. Having the Mentor Background helps, but even a mentor can teach only what she herself knows.

Storytellers: Do not allow players to neglect this requirement! Particularly for more esoteric arts such as Disciplines, pursuit of new knowledge — and payment for same — can lead to all manner of incredible stories.

Awarding Experience Points

Storytellers: Awarding experience points is a double-edged sword. You can hurt your chronicle by giving away too many, and you can cause just as much of a problem by giving away too few. If you give more to some players than you do to others, you might seem as if you're playing favorites, and you also risk unbalancing the game. However, the characters who do the most, who take the risks and learn from their mistakes instead of simply sitting on the sidelines, deserve the experience points to reflect the changes they're going through. The rules below should help you avoid most problems, but you should feel free to experiment and fine-tune them to fit your needs.

End of Each Chapter

At the end of each game session, or chapter, you should award the characters between one and five experience points. One point is awarded automatically, simply because the character experienced the chapter's events. Despite ourselves, we tend to learn from the follies of others as well as we do from our own.

One Point — Automatic: Each player gets one point at the end of each chapter.

One Point — Learning Curve: Ask the player what his character learned in the course of the night's events. If you agree with the answer, give the player one experience point.

One Point — Roleplaying: The player carried out the role of her character well, not only entertainingly but appropriately. The player performed as the character should in the circumstances. Truly inspired roleplaying might merit two experience points.

One Point — Heroism: On rare occasions even vampires can truly behave as heroes, risking all to let friends or even strangers escape from certain death. If a character acts heroically and manages to survive, he should be rewarded. Some player might try to take advantage of this idea. Don't let them. Stupidity and suicidal behavior should not be mistaken for heroism.

The End of the Story

You might decide to give extra experience points at the end of a story, if the players have done their part and the

EXPERIENCE COSTS

Trait	Cost
New Ability	3
New Path (Necromancy or Thaumaturgy)	7
New Discipline	10
Attribute	current rating x 4
Ability	current rating x 2
Clan Discipline	current rating x 5*
Other Discipline	current rating x 7*
Secondary Path (Necromancy or Thaumaturgy)	current rating x 4
Virtue	current rating x 2**
Humanity	current rating x 2
Willpower	current rating

    * Caitiff have no clan-based Disciplines, just as they have no clan. For them, the cost of raising Disciplines is the current rating x 6 for all Disciplines. This is both a curse and a blessing of being Clanless.

    ** Increasing a Virtue through experience does not increase Traits based on that Virtue (Humanity, Willpower).

characters have faced down substantial trials. Only a few points should be given this way, as they are effectively "bonus points" for a job well done.

    One Point — Success: The characters achieved all or part of the goals they set out to accomplish. Even minor victories can be rewarded if they pushed the game forward.

    One Point — Danger: The characters survived against harsh odds and grave dangers.

    One Point — Wisdom: The player, and thus the character, came up with a brilliant plan or even a spontaneous strategy that enabled the coterie to survive when it would likely have failed otherwise.

    More points can be awarded if you decide they should be, or if you want the characters to advance more quickly than they currently are.

The kid shot me twice, then pissed his pants when he saw me keep on coming. It was a nice gun he had, one of those TEC-9s that are all the rage among street-level dealers these days, but it had absolutely no stopping power. The slugs stung a little bit when they hit, but they didn't pack enough to break anything loadbearing. So I kept on coming after I felt the bullets go out my back, because if you take a shot at me you are going to die, simple as that.

He was a skinny little kid who looked Puerto Rican. He was wearing a white T-shirt and jeans with a big wet stain along one leg, and he'd been toting the gun around in his hand without the slightest attempt to conceal it. He'd mouthed off and waved the gun around, and when I called him on his attitude he laughed and put a couple of caps in me.

I am very happy to say that his attitude changed immediately, at least for the next 10 or 15 seconds. I came over his cover — a rusted-out Chevy Impala — while he was turning to run and after that, it was easy. It took one swipe to knock the gun out of his hand, another to bury my fist inside his gut, and his face took on that "O" expression that I've seen on so many gutshot soldiers. He dropped then, with a wet sucking noise as my fist came out. It was coated in equal parts blood and whatever crap he'd had for lunch, and that put me off the idea of feeding from him before he croaked. So I shook the crud off my hand and leaned in close to his face. He was shivering with shock already, as if I cared.

"Listen up, pobrecito," I said. "You're dead. The gut wound's going to kill you, even if you don't bleed to death. But I'll make you a deal. I used to be a good Catholic, so I'm gonna give you a few seconds to make some kind of confession, then I'm going to stick my finger through your left eye and put you out of your misery. Comprende?"

He nods, and starts praying. Me, I start counting.

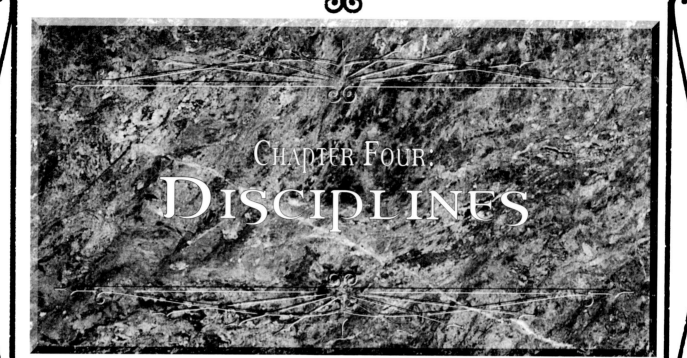

Chapter Four:
Disciplines

All vampires possess Disciplines, supernatural powers granted by the Embrace. These powers separate the undead from mortals, providing vast physical and spiritual might. With Disciplines, a vampire can display the strength of 10 men, bend another being to her will, or transform into an animal. Elders, who have not only learned several Disciplines but mastered them as well, are truly beings to be feared.

No vampire knows exactly whence Disciplines originate. Some Kindred claim that Disciplines are gifts from Caine, or Lilith the Dark Mother; others believe they are simply innate supernatural abilities intrinsic to the vampiric form. Regardless, it is mastery of the Disciplines, more than any other factor, that enables a vampire to play at Jyhad and survive to tell of it.

Like other Traits, Disciplines are rated from 1 to 5. A score of 1 indicates that the Discipline in question has barely been awakened, while a score of 5 indicate mastery of the highest powers. As a character increases her score in a Discipline, she gains access to the powers listed next to the appropriate number of dots, and of course retains access to lesser powers as well. Certain elders are rumored to have Discipline levels of higher than 5, but such beings are assuredly potent in Blood.

Players begin the game with three dots to spend on their characters' clan Disciplines, which are listed with each clan description in Chapter Two. Caitiff may place their three dots on any Disciplines they like, subject to the Storyteller's discretion. Characters may also acquire Disciplines other than those commonly taught by their clan, provided they spend the proper freebie or experience points and have access to a vampiric teacher.

Note: Unless stated in the description, Disciplines cost no blood or Willpower points to activate.

Animalism

The Beast resides within all creatures, from lice-ridden rats to powerful Kindred elders. The Discipline of Animalism allows the vampire to develop a close, intense connection with his primordial nature. He not only communicates empathically with the lower beasts, but also projects his own force of will upon them, directing the animals to do his bidding. Additionally, as the vampire grows in power, he can use Animalism to control the Beast within mortals and even other supernaturals.

A vampire who lacks this Discipline or the Skill of Animal Ken is repellent to animals. Beasts grow distinctly agitated in the presence of such a Kindred, often to the point of fleeing from or attacking the vampire. In contrast, Kindred with Animalism present a soothing aspect to lower creatures — indeed, animals are often attracted to them.

The Gangrel are especially renowned as the masters of Animalism, although the Nosferatu, Ravnos and Tzimisce clans show a talent for the Discipline as well.

The Traits of Manipulation and Charisma are key to Animalism powers. The stronger the vampire's force of personality, the better able he is to influence lesser creatures.

• Feral Whispers

This power is the basis from which all other Animalism abilities grow. The vampire creates an empathic connection with a beast, thereby allowing him to communicate or issue simple commands. The Kindred locks eyes with the animal, transmitting his desires through sheer force of will. Although it isn't necessary to actually "speak" in chirps, hisses or barks, some vampires find that doing so helps strengthen the connection with the animal. Eye contact must be maintained the entire time; if it's broken, the Kindred must look into the beast's eyes once again to regain contact.

Since Feral Whispers requires eye contact, animals that cannot see are not affected. Further, the simpler the creature, the more difficult it becomes to connect with the animal's Beast. Mammals, predatory birds and larger reptiles are relatively easy to communicate with. Insects, invertebrates and most fish (with the possible exception of larger ones like sharks) are just too simple, their Beasts too weak, to connect with.

Feral Whispers provides no guarantees that an animal will want to deal with the vampire, nor does it ensure that the animal will pursue any requests the vampire makes of it. Still, it does at least make the creature better disposed toward the Kindred. The manner in which the vampire presents his desires to the animal often depends on the type of creature. A Kindred can probably cow smaller beasts into heeding commands, but he's better off couching orders for large predators in terms of requests.

If the vampire successfully uses the power, the animal performs the command to the best of its ability and intellect. Only the very brightest creatures understand truly complex directives (orders dealing with conditional situations or requiring abstract logic). Commands that the animal does understand remain deeply implanted, however, and may affect it for some time.

System: No roll is necessary to talk with an animal, but the character must establish eye contact first. Issuing commands requires a Manipulation + Animal Ken roll. The difficulty depends on the creature: Predatory mammals (wolves, cats, insectivorous/vampire bats) are difficulty 6, other mammals and predatory birds (rats, owls) are difficulty 7, other birds and reptiles (pigeons, snakes) are difficulty 8. This difficulty is reduced by one if the character speaks to the animal in its "native tongue," and can be adjusted further by circumstances and roleplaying skill (we highly recommend that all communication between characters and animals be roleplayed).

The number of successes the player achieves dictates how strongly the character's command affects the animal. One success is sufficient to have a cat follow someone and lead the character to the same location, three successes are enough to have a raven spy on a target for weeks, and five successes ensure that a grizzly ferociously guards the entrance to the character's wilderness haven for some months.

The character's Nature plays a large part in how he approaches these conversations. The character might try intimidation, teasing, cajoling, rationality or emotional pleading. The player should understand that he does not simply play his character in these situations, but the Beast Within as well.

•• BECKONING

The vampire's connection to the Beast grows strong enough that he may call out in the voice of a specific type of animal — howling like a wolf, cawing like a raven, etc. This call mystically summons creatures of the chosen type. Since each type of animal has a different call, Beckoning works for only a single species at a time.

All such animals within earshot are summoned, but may choose individually whether or not to respond. While the

---

STORYTELLING ANIMALS

It's challenging for the Storyteller to present animals as more than just plot devices when a character communicates with them. Many Storytellers have beasts speak in monosyllables and allow the characters to direct them easily.

Animals are, indeed, simple creatures. They live always in the present and are directed by basic instincts, seldom understanding the complex rationales that motivate vampires. This doesn't mean they're stupid, however; beasts must be cunning to survive in forest wilds and urban landscapes. Younger vampires are often surprised by how perceptive animals can be — since animals don't play mind games, they're often quite good at cutting through lies and deception.

Bearing these things in mind, the Storyteller can make animals as dynamic and interesting as any other Storyteller characters the troupe encounters.

Statistics for certain animals are found in the Appendix, p. 302.

---

vampire has no control over the beasts who answer, the animals who do are favorably disposed toward him and are at least willing to listen to the Kindred's request.

System: The player rolls Charisma + Survival (difficulty 6) to determine the response to the character's call; consult the table below. Only animals that can hear the cry will respond. If the Storyteller decides no animals of that type are within earshot, the summons goes unanswered.

The call can be as specific as the player desires. A character could call for all bats in the area, for only the male bats nearby, or for only the albino bat with the notched ear he saw the other night.

1 success	A single animal responds.
2 successes	One-quarter of the animals within earshot respond.
3 successes	Half of the animals respond.
4 successes	Most of the animals respond.
5 successes	All of the animals respond.

••• QUELL THE BEAST

As the supreme predators of the natural world, Kindred are highly attuned to the bestial nature that dwells within every mortal heart. A vampire who develops this power may assert his will over a mortal (animal or human) subject, subduing the Beast within her. This quenches all powerful, assertive emotions — hope, fury, inspiration — within the target. The Kindred must either touch his subject or stare into her eyes to channel his will effectively.

Mortals who lack the fire of their inner Beasts are quite tractable, reacting to even stressful situations with indifference. Even the most courageous or maddened mortal becomes apathetic and listless, while an especially sensitive individual may suffer from a phobic derangement while under the power's influence.

Different clans evoke this power in different ways, although the effect itself is identical. Tzimisce call it Cowing the Beast, since they force the mortal's weaker spirit to cower in fear before the Kindred's own inner Beast. Nosferatu refer to it as Song of Serenity, since they soothe the subject's Beast into a state of utter complacency, thus allowing them to feed freely. Gangrel know

the power as Quell the Beast, and force the mortal spirit into a state of fear or apathy as befits the individual vampire's nature.

System: The player rolls Manipulation + Intimidation if forcing out the Beast through fear, Manipulation + Empathy if soothing it into complacency. The roll is made versus difficulty 7 in either case. This is an extended action requiring as many total successes as the target has Willpower. Failure indicates that the player must start over from the beginning, while a botch indicates that the vampire may never again affect that subject's Beast.

When a mortal's Beast is cowed or soothed, she can no longer use or regain Willpower. She ceases all struggles, whether mental or physical. She doesn't even defend herself if assaulted, though the Storyteller may allow a Willpower roll if the mortal's life is threatened. To recover from this power, the mortal rolls Willpower (difficulty 6) once per day until she accumulates enough successes to equal the vampire's Willpower. Kindred themselves cannot be affected by this power.

•••• SUBSUME THE SPIRIT

By locking his gaze with that of a beast, the vampire may psychically possess the animal. Some older Kindred believe that since animals have no souls, only spirits, the vampire can move his own soul into the animal's body. Most younger vampires think it is a matter of transferring one's consciousness into the animal's mind. In either case, it's agreed that the beast's weaker spirit (or mind) is pushed aside by the Kindred's own consciousness. The vampire's body falls into a motionless state akin to torpor while his mind takes control of the animal's actions, remaining this way until the Kindred's consciousness returns.

Tzimisce seldom use this power, considering it debasing to enter the body of a lesser creature. When they do stoop to using it, they possess only predators. Conversely, Gangrel revel in connecting to the natural world in this fundamental way. They delight in sampling different animals' natures.

System: The player rolls Manipulation + Animal Ken (difficulty 8) as the character looks into the animal's eyes (only beasts with eyes can be possessed). The number of successes obtained determines how thoroughly the character overrides the animal's spirit. Fewer than three successes means the character must use Willpower points to take any action that directly violates the instincts of the animal in question. With fewer than five successes, the possessing character behaves much like the animal — his soul is clouded with needs and impulses from the animal's spirit and body. Multiple successes allow the character to utilize some mental Disciplines while possessing the animal, as noted on the chart below.

1 success	Cannot use Disciplines
2 successes	Can use Auspex
3 successes	Can also use Presence
4 successes	Can also use Dementation, Dominate
5 successes	Can also use Chimerstry, Necromancy, Thaumaturgy

This power entwines the character's consciousness closely with the animal's spirit, so much so that the character may continue to think and feel like that animal even after breaking the connection. This effect continues until the character spends a total of seven Willpower points to resist and finally overcome the animal nature. This should be roleplayed, although to a lessening degree as Willpower is spent.

At the end of any particularly exciting incident during possession, the player rolls Wits + Empathy (difficulty 8) for the character to retain his own mind. Failure indicates that the character's mind returns to his own body, but still thinks in purely animalistic terms. A botch sends the character into frenzy upon returning to his own body.

The character may travel as far from his body as he is physically able while possessing the animal. The character retains no conscious connection with his vampire body during this time, though. The vampire may also venture out during the day, albeit in the animal's body. However, the character's own body must be awake to do so, requiring a successful roll to remain awake (see Chapter Six). If the character leaves the animal's body (by choice, if his body falls asleep, after sustaining significant injury), the vampire's consciousness returns to his physical form instantaneously.

Although the vampire has no conscious link to his body while possessing the animal, he does form a sympathetic bond. Anything the animal feels, the vampire also experiences, from pleasure to pain. In fact, any damage the animal's body sustains is also applied to the character's body, although the Kindred may soak as normal. If the animal dies before the vampire's soul can flee from the body, the character's body falls into torpor. Presumably this is in sympathetic response to the massive trauma of death, although some Kindred believe that the vampire's soul is cast adrift during this time and must find its way back to the body.

●●●●● DRAWING OUT THE BEAST

At this level of Animalism, the Kindred has a keen understanding of the Beast Within. Whenever this predator spirit threatens to overwhelm the vampire's soul and send him into frenzy, he may instead release his feral urges upon another creature. The recipient of the vampire's Beast is instantly overcome by frenzy. This is an unnatural frenzy, however, as the victim is channeling the Kindred's own fury. As such, the vampire's own behavior, expressions and even speech patterns are evident in the subject's savage actions.

Gangrel and Tzimisce are especially fond of loosing their Beasts on others. Gangrel do so to stir their ghouls into inspired heights of savagery during combat. Tzimisce care less for who receives their Beast than they do for retaining their own composure.

System: The vampire must be in frenzy or close to it to use this power. The player must announce his preferred target (since it must be someone within sight, Drawing Out the Beast cannot be used if the vampire is alone), then roll Manipulation + Self-Control (difficulty 8). Refer to the table below for the results:

1 success	The character transfers the Beast, but unleashes it upon a random individual.
2 successes	The character is stunned by the effort and may not act next turn, but transfers the Beast successfully.
3 successes	The character transfers the Beast successfully.

If the attempt fails, the intensity of the frenzy actually increases. As the character relaxes in expectation of relieving his savage urges, the Beast takes that opportunity to dig deeper. In this case, the frenzy lasts twice as long as normal and is twice as difficult to shrug off; its severity also increases exponentially. Botching this roll is even more catastrophic; the heightened frenzy grows so extreme that not even expending Willpower curbs its duration or effects. The character is a hapless victim to the terrible fury of his Beast.

If the character leaves the target's presence before the frenzy expends itself, the vampire loses his Beast, perhaps permanently. While no longer vulnerable to frenzy, the character cannot use or regain Willpower and becomes increasingly lethargic. To recover the Beast, he must find the person who now possesses it (who likely isn't enjoying herself very much) and retrap the Beast. The most effective way to do so is to behave in ways that make the Beast want to return — however, this isn't a guarantee that it will wish to do so. Alternatively, the character can simply kill the host (thus causing the Beast to return to the vampire immediately), but such an act costs at least one point of Humanity.

AUSPEX

This Discipline bestows uncanny sensory abilities upon the vampire. While Auspex initially heightens all of the Kindred's senses significantly, that is merely the beginning. As she grows in power, the vampire can perceive the psychic auras that flow around her and even project her mind into another being's thoughts. Furthermore, Auspex can pierce the disguises that Obfuscate creates; see "Seeing the Unseen," p. 152, for more details.

Such sensory command gives the vampire a distinct advantage over mortals and even many supernaturals. Whether these talents let her view a distant haven, sense the prince's mood or pluck secrets from a rival Kindred's ghoul, Auspex is a powerful tool.

Still, the vampire must be careful lest this heightened sensitivity cause her to be distracted by beautiful things, startled by loud noises or overwhelmed by foul smells. Sudden or dynamic events can disorient an Auspex-using character unless she makes a Willpower roll (difficulty 4) to block them out. The more potent the source of distraction, the higher the difficulty. Failure overwhelms the character's senses, making her oblivious to her surroundings for a turn or two.

Malkavians and Toreador are most susceptible to such distractions. Kindred from the Tremere and Tzimisce clans seem better able to regulate their sensory input, but they are not immune to the occasional distraction.

A high Perception Trait is a great boon to using Auspex powers. The better the roll, the greater the degree of sensory information the character gains.

● HEIGHTENED SENSES

This power sharpens all of the vampire's senses, effectively doubling the clarity and range of sight, hearing and smell. While her senses of taste and touch extend no farther than normal, they likewise become far more acute; the vampire could taste the hint of liquor in a victim's blood, or feel the give of the board concealing a hollow space in the floor. The Kindred may magnify her senses at will, sustaining this heightened focus for as long as she desires. At the Storyteller's option, this may make hunting easier.

Occasionally, this talent provides extrasensory or even precognitive insights. These brief, unfocused glimpses may be odd premonitions, flashes of empathy or eerie feelings of foreboding. The vampire has no control over these perceptions, but with practice can learn to interpret them with a fair degree of accuracy.

Expanded senses come at a price, however. Bright lights, loud noises and strong smells present a hazard while the vampire uses this power. In addition to the possibility for distraction mentioned above, an especially sudden stimulus — like the glare of a spotlight or a clap of thunder — can blind or deafen the Kindred for an hour or more.

System: This power doesn't normally require the use of dice, instead being defined through the Storyteller's descriptions and the player's imagination. In certain circumstances, use of this power requires a die roll: for a normal Perception roll (the Storyteller may reduce the difficulty by the character's Auspex rating), to notice a subject using Obfuscate (see p. 166), or to perceive a threat (the Storyteller privately rolls the character's unmodified Auspex rating, applying whatever difficulty he feels best suits the circumstances). For example, in the last instance, sensing that a pistol is pointed at the back of the character's head may require a 5, while the sudden realization that a rival for primogen is planning her assassination may require a 9.

This power does not let characters see in pitch darkness, as does Eyes of the Beast (p. 173), but it does reduce difficulty penalties to act in pitch darkness from +2 to +1, and the character may make ranged attacks in pitch darkness if she can hear, smell or otherwise detect her foe.

•• AURA PERCEPTION

Using this power, the vampire can perceive the psychic "auras" that radiate from mortals and supernatural beings alike. These halos comprise a shifting series of colors that take practice to discern with clarity. Even the simplest individual has many shifting hues within his aura; strong emotions predominate, while momentary impressions or deep secrets flash through in streaks and swirls.

The colors change in sympathy with the subject's emotional state, blending into new tones in a constantly dancing pattern. The stronger the emotions involved, the more intense the hues become. A skilled vampire can learn much from her subject by reading the nuances of color and brilliance in the aura's flow.

Aside from perceiving emotional states, vampires use Aura Perception to detect supernatural beings. The colors in Kindred auras, while intense, are quite pale; mage auras often flare and crackle with suppressed power; werebeasts have strikingly bright, almost frantic, halos; ghosts have weak auras that flicker fitfully like a dying flame; and faerie creatures' radiance is shot through with rainbow hues.

System: The player rolls Perception + Empathy (difficulty 8); each success indicates how much of the subject's aura the character sees and understands (see the table below). A botch indicates a false or erroneous interpretation. The Storyteller may wish to make this roll, thus keeping the player in the dark as to just how good (or bad) the character's interpretation is.

1 success	Can distinguish only the shade (pale or bright).
2 successes	Can distinguish the main color.
3 successes	Can recognize the color patterns.
4 successes	Can detect subtle shifts.
5 successes	Can identify mixtures of color and pattern.

The Aura Colors chart offers examples of some common colors and the emotions they reflect.

The character may view a particular subject's aura only once with any degree of clarity. Any subsequent attempts that result in failure should be considered botches. It is very easy for the character to imagine seeing what she wants to see when judging someone's intentions. After a full month, the character may try again at no penalty.

It is possible, though difficult, to sense the aura of a being who is otherwise invisible to normal sight. Refer to "Seeing the Unseen," p. 152, for more information.

AURA COLORS

Condition	Aura Colors
Afraid	Orange
Aggressive	Purple
Angry	Red
Bitter	Brown
Calm	Light Blue
Compassionate	Pink
Conservative	Lavender
Depressed	Gray
Desirous or Lustful	Deep Red
Distrustful	Light Green
Envious	Dark Green
Excited	Violet
Generous	Rose
Happy	Vermilion
Hateful	Black
Idealistic	Yellow
Innocent	White
Lovestruck	Blue
Obsessed	Green
Sad	Silver
Spiritual	Gold
Suspicious	Dark Blue
Confused	Mottled, shifting colors
Diablerist	Black veins in aura
Daydreaming	Sharp flickering colors
Frenzied	Rapidly rippling colors
Psychotic	Hypnotic, swirling colors
Vampire	Appropriate color is pale
Magic Use	Myriad sparkles in aura
Werebeast	Bright, vibrant aura
Ghost	Weak, intermittent aura
Faerie	Rainbow highlights in aura

••• THE SPIRIT'S TOUCH

When someone handles an object for any length of time, he leaves a psychic impression on the item. A vampire with this level of Auspex can "read" these sensations, learning who handled the object, when he last held it and what was done with it recently.

These visions are seldom clear and detailed, registering more like a kind of "psychic snapshot." Still, the Kindred can learn much even from such a glimpse. Although most visions concern the last person to handle the item, a long-time owner leaves a stronger impression than someone who held the object briefly.

Gleaning information from the spiritual residue requires the vampire to hold the object and enter a shallow trance. She is only marginally aware of her surroundings while using The Spirit's Touch, but a loud noise or jarring physical sensation breaks the trance instantly.

System: The player rolls Perception + Empathy. The difficulty is determined by the age of the impressions and the mental and spiritual strength of the person or event that left them. Sensing information from a pistol used for murder hours ago may require a 5, while learning who owned a set of keys found days ago might be a 9.

The greater the individual's emotional connection to the object, the stronger the impression he leaves on it — and the more information the Kindred can glean from it. Also, events involving strong emotions (a gift-giving, a torture, a long family history) likewise leave stronger impressions than does short or casual contact. Assume that each success offers one piece of information. While one success tells the character only that "a man held this pocket watch last," three reveal that he was petty, middle-aged and afraid. Four successes discover his name, and five or more reveal his connection to the watch as well as some of the things he did with it in his possession.

•••• TELEPATHY

The vampire projects a portion of her consciousness into a nearby mortal's mind, creating a mental link through which she can communicate wordlessly or even read the target's deepest thoughts. The Kindred "hears" in her own mind the thoughts plucked from a subject as if they were spoken to her.

This is one of the most potent vampiric abilities, since, given time, a Kindred can learn virtually anything from a subject without him ever knowing. The Tremere and Tzimisce in particular find this power especially useful in gleaning secrets from others, or for directing their mortal followers with silent precision.

System: The player rolls Intelligence + Subterfuge (difficulty of the subject's Willpower). Projecting thoughts into the target's mind requires one success. The subject recognizes that the thoughts come from somewhere other than his own consciousness, although he cannot discern their actual origin.

To read minds, one success must be rolled for each item of information plucked or each layer of thought pierced. Deep secrets or buried memories are harder to obtain than surface emotions or unspoken comments, requiring five or more successes to access.

Telepathy does not commonly work upon the undead mind. A character may expend a Willpower point to make the effort, making the roll normally afterward. Likewise, it is equally difficult to read the thoughts of other supernatural creatures.

Storytellers are encouraged to describe thoughts as flowing streams of impressions and images, rather than as a sequence of prose. Instead of making flat statements like "He's planning on killing his former lover's new boyfriend," say "You see a fleeting series of visions: A couple kissing passionately in a doorway, then the man walking alone at night; you suddenly see your hands, knuckles white, wrapped around a steering wheel, with a figure crossing the street ahead; your heart, mortal now and hammering with panic as you hear the engine rev wildly; and above all, a blazing anger coupled with emotional agony and a panicked fear of loss."

Such descriptions not only add to the story, they also force the player to decide for herself what her character reads. After all, understanding minds — especially highly emotional or deranged minds — is a difficult and often puzzling task.

●●●●● Psychic Projection

The Kindred with this awesome ability projects her senses out of her physical shell, stepping from her body as an entity of pure thought. The vampire's astral form is immune to physical damage or fatigue, and can "fly" with blinding speed anywhere across the earth — or even underground — so long as she remains below the moon's orbit.

The Kindred's material form lies in a torpid state while her astral self is active, and the vampire isn't aware of anything that befalls her body until she returns to it. An ephemeral silver cord connects the Kindred's psyche to her body. If this cord is severed, her consciousness becomes stranded in the astral plane, the realm of ghosts, spirits and shades. Attempting to return to the vampire's physical shell is a long and terrifying ordeal, especially since there is no guarantee that she will accomplish the journey successfully. This significant danger keeps many Kindred from leaving their bodies for long, but those who dare can learn much.

System: Journeying in astral form requires the player to expend a point of Willpower and make a Perception + Occult roll. Difficulty varies depending on the distance and complexity of the intended trip; 7 is average, with 10 reflecting a trip far from familiar territory (a first journey from North America to the Far East; trying to shortcut through the earth). The greater the number of successes rolled, the more focused the character's astral presence is and the easier it is for her to reach her desired destination.

Failure means the character is unable to separate her consciousness from her body, while a botch can have nasty consequences — flinging her astral form to a random destination on Earth or in the spirit realm, or heading for the desired destination so forcefully that the silver cord snaps.

Changing course or continuing to another destination requires another point of Willpower and a new roll. Failure indicates that the vampire has lost her way and must retrace the path of her silver cord. A botch at this stage means the cord snaps, stranding the character's psychic form in the mysterious astral plane.

An astral form may travel at great speeds (the Storyteller can use 1000 miles per hour as a general guide) and carries no clothing or material objects of any kind. Some artifacts are said to exist in the spirit world, and the character can try to use one of these tools if she finds one. The character cannot bring such relics to the physical world when she returns to her body, however.

Seeing the Unseen

Auspex enables Kindred to perceive many things beyond mortal ken. Among its many uses, Auspex can detect the presence of a supernatural being who is hidden from normal sight (a vampire using Obfuscate, a mage cloaked with invisibility, a wraith) or pierce illusions created by the Discipline of Chimerstry.

• **Obfuscate:** When a vampire tries to use her heightened perceptions to notice a Kindred hidden with Obfuscate, she detects the subject's presence if her Auspex rating is higher than his Obfuscate. Conversely, if the target's Obfuscate outranks her Auspex, he remains undiscovered. If the two scores are equal, both characters make a resisted roll of Perception + Subterfuge (Auspex user) against Manipulation + Subterfuge (Obfuscate user). The difficulty for both rolls is 7, and the character with the most successes wins.

• **Chimerstry:** Likewise, vampires with Auspex may seek to penetrate illusions created with Chimerstry. The Auspex-wielder must actively seek to pierce the illusion (i.e., the player must tell the Storyteller that his character is trying to detect an illusion). Auspex-wielder and Chimerstry-wielder then compare relative scores, per Obfuscate, above. The process is otherwise identical to piercing Obfuscate.

• **Other Powers:** Since the powers of beings like mages and wraiths function differently from vampiric Disciplines, a simple comparison of relative ratings isn't applicable. To keep things simple, both characters make a resisted roll. The vampire rolls Perception + Subterfuge, while the subject rolls Manipulation + Subterfuge. Again, the difficulty is 7, and the character with the most successes wins.

Interaction with the physical world is impossible while using Psychic Projection. At best, the character may spend a Willpower point to manifest as a ghostlike shape. This apparition lasts one turn before fading away; while she can't affect anything physically during this time, the character can speak. Despite lacking physical substance, an astral character can use Auspex normally. At the Storyteller's discretion, such a character may employ any Animalism, Dementation, Dominate, Necromancy, Obtenebration, Presence and/or Thaumaturgy powers she has, though this typically requires a minimum of three successes on the initial Psychic Projection roll.

If two astral shapes encounter one another, they interact as if they were solid. They may talk, touch and even fight as if both were in the material world. Since they have no physical bodies, astral characters seeking to interact "physically" substitute Mental and Social Traits for Physical ones (Wits replaces Dexterity, Manipulation supplants Strength, and Intelligence replaces Stamina). Due to the lack of a material form, the only real way to damage another psychic entity is to cut its silver cord. When fighting this way, consider Willpower points to be health levels; when a combatant loses all of her Willpower, the cord is severed.

Although an astrally projected character remains in the reflection of the mortal world (referred to as the Penumbra in other World of Darkness games), she may venture further into the spirit realms, especially if she becomes lost. Other beings, such as ghosts, werewolves and even rare magi, travel the astral plane as well, and can interact with a vampire's psychic presence normally. Storytellers are encouraged to make trips into the spirit world as bizarre, mysterious and dreamlike as possible. The world beyond is a vivid and fantastic place, where the true nature of things is stronger and often strikingly different from their earthly appearances.

Note: For Storytellers familiar with White Wolf's other games, the "astral plane" to which the vampire travels is a reflection of the Umbra in general, not one specific level.

CELERITY

The Embrace gifts some vampires with startling speed and reflexes. They can use Celerity to move with amazing swiftness in times of stress. Mortals, and even Kindred lacking this Discipline, move as if in slow motion compared to the astonishing blur the vampire becomes.

Celerity is common among the Assamite, Brujah and Toreador clans. The Assamites use this ability to strike down their foes before the victims are even aware of the attack. Brujah delight in the advantage this Discipline gives them against superior numbers of opponents. Toreador are more likely to use Celerity to lend preternatural grace to live performances such as dance or extraordinary speed when creating sculptures or paintings — however, they can be as terrifying as any Assamite or Brujah when angered.

System: The character spends a single blood point. The next turn, she gains a number of additional full actions equal to her Celerity rating. These additional actions must be physical (e.g., the vampire cannot use a mental Discipline like Dominate multiple times in one turn). So a vampire with Celerity 4 who spends a blood point may perform a total of five physical actions in her next turn. The actions occur at the end of the turn (the vampire's regular action still takes place per her initiative roll).

Normally, a character without Celerity must apply a dice pool penalty if she wants to take multiple actions in a single turn. A character using Celerity performs his extra actions (including full movement) without penalty, gaining a full dice pool for each separate action. Extra actions gained through Celerity may not in turn be split into multiple actions.

CHIMERSTRY

The Ravnos are heirs to a legacy of illusion, and none can say exactly why. The elders of their clan, when properly approached, speak cryptically of *ghuls* and rakshasas, and the shapeshifting antics of their Antediluvian founder are the subject of many a dark campfire tale among the clan. But whatever the source, the nomadic Ravnos have a potent weapon in the form of their Discipline of Chimerstry.

Chimerstry is an art of conjuration; the vampire may draw upon her inner reserves to bring phantoms to life. These false images can confound mortal senses and sensory equipment alike. If the Cainite's power is strong enough, illusions created by Chimerstry may even baffle the heightened senses of the vampire. The Ravnos are fond of using this power to seduce, swindle or enslave mortals, effectively purchasing their victims' souls in exchange for a sack of bouillon that isn't there.

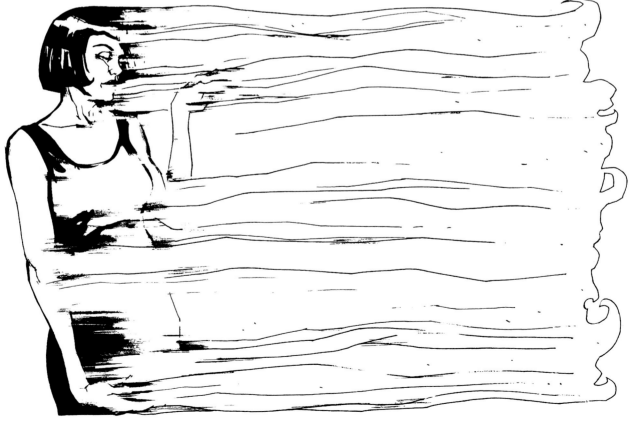

Illusions created by Chimerstry may be detected by Auspex (see "Seeing the Unseen," p. 152). They may also be seen for what they are by a victim who "proves" the illusion's falsehood (e.g., a person who walks up to an illusory wall, expresses his disbelief in it, and puts his hand through it effectively banishes the illusion).

• Ignis Fatuus

The vampire may conjure a minor, static mirage that confounds one sense. For instance, he may evoke a sulfurous stench, the image of a curtain, or the feel of raw silk. Note that although tactile illusions can be felt, they have no real substance; an invisible but tactile wall cannot confine anyone, and invisible razor-wire causes no real damage.

System: The player must spend a point of Willpower to create this illusion. It lasts until the Ravnos leaves its vicinity (such as stepping out of the room) or until another person sees through it somehow. The Cainite may also end the illusion at any time; this requires no effort, only the merest whim.

•• Fata Morgana

The Cainite can now create illusions that appeal to all the senses, although they remain static. For example, the vampire could throw a mirage over a dank basement, making it appear to be a sumptuous boudoir, although she could not create flickering candles or a flowing fountain. Again, the dweomer has no solid presence, although it's easy enough to make a filthy mattress on two sawhorses feel like a four-poster bed.

System: The player spends a Willpower point and a blood point to create the dweomer. These static images remain until dispelled, in much the same way that an Ignis Fatuus illusion does.

••• Apparition

Not really a power unto itself, Apparition allows a vampire to give motion to an illusion created with Ignis Fatuus or Fata Morgana. Thus, the Ravnos could create the illusion of a living being, running water, fluttering drapes or a roaring fire.

System: The creator spends one blood point to make the illusion move in one specific way. She may change the image's movement only if she has done nothing but concentrate on the mirage since creating it.

•••• Permanency

This power, also used in conjunction with Ignis Fatuus or Fata Morgana, allows a mirage to persist even when the vampire cannot see it. In this way, Ravnos often cloak their temporary havens in false trappings of luxury, or ward off trespassers with illusory guard dogs.

System: The vampire need only spend a blood point, and the illusion becomes permanent until dissolved.

••••• Horrid Reality

Rather than create simple illusions, the vampire can now project hallucinations directly into a victim's mind. The target of these illusions believes completely that the images are real; a hallucinatory fire can burn him, an imaginary noose can strangle him, and an illusory wall can block him. This power affects only one person at a time; although other people can try to convince the victim that his terrors are not real, he won't believe them.

System: A Horrid Realty costs two Willpower points to set in motion and lasts for an entire scene (although its effects may last longer; see below). If the vampire is trying to injure his victim, his player must roll Manipulation + Subterfuge (difficulty of the victim's Perception + Self-Control). Each success inflicts one health level of damage on the victim; if the player wishes to inflict less damage, he may announce a maximum amount of damage before rolling the dice. This power cannot actually kill its victims (although a target with a heart condition may well die from fright); a victim "killed" by an illusory attack loses consciousness or enters torpor. All injuries disappear once the victim is truly convinced that she wasn't actually harmed by the Horrid Reality. Of course, such a cure may take a long time, or even psychological therapy. The nightmarish power of Chimerstry is nothing to take lightly.

DEMENTATION

The special legacy of the Malkavian clan, Dementation allows the vampire to channel madness, focus it, and pour it into the minds of those around him. Though in former nights this power was practiced primarily by the Malkavians of the Sabbat, in recent years it has spread throughout the clan. Some Kindred speculate that this "infection" might be yet another move in the Jyhad; a few vampires, of particularly paranoid bent, even whisper that the Malkavians are to be harbingers of the Final Nights.

The practitioner of Dementation need not actually be mad himself — at least initially — although madness seems to grant a certain insight into the key tenets of this Discipline. Few vampires ask the Malkavians to teach them this Discipline, although the Lunatics are almost always eager to "enlighten" others. In fact, some say that one cannot learn the secrets of Dementation without eventually going mad.

Eerily enough, Dementation doesn't seem to inflict insanity on its victims *per se*. Rather, it seems to catalyze madness, breaking down doors into the hidden reaches of the mind and releasing whatever it finds there. The Malkavians claim that this is because insanity is the next step in the evolution of the mind — a necessary progression if one is to behold the truths of the universe. As such, they say, it is inherent to all minds, and evident only in the more highly evolved specimens of human or vampiric thought. Other Kindred pray the Malkavians are wrong, but find it difficult to dismiss such thoughts out of hand, particularly because Dementation works as well on vampires as it does on mortals....

• PASSION

The vampire may stir his victim's emotions, either heightening them to a fevered pitch or blunting them until the target is completely desensitized. The Cainite may not choose which emotion is affected; she may only amplify or dull emotions already present in the target. In this way, a vampire can turn mild irritation into frothing rage or dull true love into casual interest.

System: The player rolls Charisma + Empathy (difficulty of the victim's Humanity score). The number of successes determines the duration of the altered state of feeling. Effects of this power might include one- or two-point additions or subtractions to difficulties of frenzy rolls, Virtue rolls, rolls to resist Presence powers, etc.

1 success	One turn
2 successes	One hour
3 successes	One night
4 successes	One week
5 successes	One month
6+ successes	Three months

•• THE HAUNTING

The vampire may stir the sensory centers of his victim's brain, flooding the victim's senses with visions, sounds, scents or feelings that aren't really there. The images, regardless of the sense to which they appeal, are only fleeting "glimpses," barely perceptible to the victim. The vampire using Dementation cannot control what the victim perceives, but may choose which sense is affected.

The "haunting" effects occur mainly when the victim is alone, and mostly at night. They may take the form of the subject's repressed fears, guilty memories, or anything else that the Storyteller finds dramatically appropriate. The effects are never pleasant or unobtrusive, however. The Storyteller should let her imagination run wild when describing these sensory impressions; the victim may well feel as if she is going mad, or as if the world is.

System: The player spends a blood point and rolls Manipulation + Subterfuge (difficulty of his victim's Perception + Self-Control). The number of successes determines the length of the sensory "visitations." The precise effects are up to the Storyteller, though particularly eerie or harrowing apparitions can certainly reduce dice pools for a turn or two after the manifestation.

1 success	One night
2 successes	Two nights
3 successes	One week
4 successes	One month
5 successes	Three months
6+ successes	One year

••• EYES OF CHAOS

This peculiar power allows the vampire to take advantage of the fractured wisdom hidden in insanity. She may scrutinize the "patterns" of a person's soul, the convolutions of a vampire's inner nature, or even random events in nature itself. The Kindred with this power can discern the most well-hidden psychoses, or gain insight into a person's true self. Malkavians with this power often have (or claim to have) knowledge of the moves and countermoves of the great Jyhad.

System: This power allows a vampire to determine a person's true Nature, among other things. The vampire concentrates for a turn, then her player rolls Perception + Occult. The difficulty depends on the intricacy of the pattern. Discerning the Nature of a stranger would be difficulty 9; a casual acquaintance would be an 8, an old friend a 6. The Malkavian could also read the message locked in a coded missive (difficulty 7), or even see the doings of an invisible hand in such events as the pattern of falling leaves (difficulty 6). Almost anything might contain some hidden insight, no matter how trivial or meaningless. The patterns are present in most things, but are often so intricate they can keep a vampire spellbound for hours while she tries to understand their "message."

•••• VOICE OF MADNESS

By merely addressing his victims aloud, the Malkavian can drive targets into fits of blind rage or fear, forcing them to abandon reason and higher thought. Victims are plagued by hallucinations of their subconscious demons, and try to flee or destroy their hidden shames. Tragedy almost always follows in the wake of this power's use, although offending Malkavians often claim that they were merely encouraging people to act "according to their natures." Unfortunately for the vampire concerned, he runs a very real risk of falling prey to his own voice's power.

System: The player spends a blood point and makes a Manipulation + Empathy roll (difficulty 7). One target is affected per success, although all potential victims must be listening to the vampire's voice.

Affected victims fly immediately into frenzy or a blind fear like Rötschreck. Kindred or other creatures capable of frenzy, such as Lupines, may make a frenzy check or Rötschreck test (Storyteller's choice as to how they are affected) at +2 difficulty to resist the power. Mortals are automatically affected and don't remember their actions while berserk. The frenzy or fear lasts for a scene, although vampires and Lupines may test as usual to snap out of it.

The vampire using Voice of Madness must also test for frenzy or Rötschreck upon invoking this power, although his difficulty to resist is one lower than normal.

••••• TOTAL INSANITY

The vampire pulls the madness from the deepest recesses of her target's mind, focusing it into an overwhelming wave of insanity. This power has driven countless victims, vampire and mortal alike, to unfortunate ends.

System: The Malkavian must gain her target's undivided attention for at least one full turn to enact this power. The player spends a blood point and rolls Manipulation + Intimidation (difficulty of her victim's Willpower). If successful, the victim is afflicted with five derangements of the Storyteller's choice (see p. 222). The number of successes determines the duration.

1 success	One turn
2 successes	One night
3 successes	One week
4 successes	One month
5+ successes	One year

DOMINATE

This Discipline involves influencing the very thoughts and actions of others through the vampire's own force of will. Use of Dominate requires that the Kindred capture his victim's eye; as such, it may be used against only one subject at a time. The extent of this control depends on the particular power being applied.

While truly potent, Dominate powers can be exacting to perform. Commands must be issued verbally; after all, direct mind-to-mind contact is the purview of Auspex. Still, some simple orders may be made with signs — for example, a pointed

finger and forceful expression to indicate "Go!" If the subject doesn't understand the vampire (she doesn't speak the same language, the order doesn't make sense, she cannot hear his words), she won't comply with the directive, no matter how mighty the Kindred's supernatural will.

Not surprisingly, Kindred who use Dominate were often willful, controlling individuals in mortal life. Indeed, it's quite possible that this is what drew the vampires' sires to them in the first place. After all, the Giovanni, Lasombra, Tremere and Ventrue clans who specialize in this Discipline consider strong will a definite benefit. Due to this tendency toward control, characters with high Dominate scores may be unable to spend experience points to increase Abilities such as Empathy.

● COMMAND

The vampire locks eyes with the subject and speaks a one-word command which must be obeyed instantly. The order must be clear and straightforward — run, cough, fall, yawn, jump, laugh, sneeze, stop, belch, follow. If the command is at all confusing or ambiguous, the subject may respond slowly or perform the task poorly. The subject cannot be ordered to do something directly harmful to herself, so a command like "die" is ineffective.

The command may be included in a sentence, thereby concealing the power's use from others. This effort at subtlety still requires the Kindred to make eye contact at the proper moment and stress the key word slightly. An alert bystander — or even the victim — may notice the emphasis; still, unless she's conversant with supernatural powers, the individual is likely to attribute the utterance and the subsequent action as bizarre coincidence.

System: The player rolls Manipulation + Intimidation (difficulty of the target's permanent Willpower). More successes force the subject to act with greater vigor or for a longer duration (continue running for a number of turns, go off on a laughing jag, sneeze uncontrollably).

●● MESMERIZE

With this power, a vampire can verbally implant a false thought or hypnotic suggestion in the subject's subconscious mind. Both Kindred and target must be free from distraction, since Mesmerize requires intense concentration and precise wording to be effective. The vampire may activate the imposed thought immediately or establish a stimulus that will trigger it later. The victim must be able to understand the vampire, although the two need to maintain eye contact only as long as it takes to implant the idea.

Mesmerize allows for anything from simple, precise directives (handing over an item) to complex, highly involved ones (taking notes of someone's habits and relaying that information at an appointed time). A subject can have only one suggestion implanted at any time.

System: The player rolls Manipulation + Leadership (difficulty equal to the target's permanent Willpower). The number of successes determines how well the suggestion takes hold in the victim's subconscious. If the vampire scores one or two successes, the subject cannot be forced to do anything that seems strange to her (she might walk outside, but is unlikely to act like a chicken). At three or four successes, the command is effective unless following it endangers the subject. At five successes or greater, the vampire can implant nearly any sort of command.

No matter how strong the Kindred's will, his command cannot force the subject to harm herself directly or defy her innate Nature. So, while a vampire who scored five successes could make a 98-pound weakling attack a 300-pound bouncer, he could not make the mortal shoot herself in the head.

If a vampire tries to Mesmerize a subject before the target fulfills a previously implanted directive, compare the successes rolled to those gained during the implanting of the first suggestion. Whichever roll had the greater number of successes is the command that now lodges in the target's subconscious; the other suggestion is wiped clean. If the successes rolled are equal, the newer command supplants the old one.

●●● THE FORGETFUL MIND

After capturing the subject's gaze, the vampire delves into the subject's memories, stealing or re-creating them at his whim. The Forgetful Mind does not allow for telepathic contact; the Kindred operates much like a hypnotist, asking directed questions and drawing out answers from the subject. The degree of memory alteration depends on what the vampire desires. He may alter the subject's mind only slightly — quite effective for eliminating memories of the victim meeting or even being fed upon by the vampire — or utterly undo the victim's memories of her past.

The degree of detail used has a direct bearing on how strongly the new memories take hold, since the victim's subconscious mind resists the alteration the vampire imposes. A simplistic or incomplete false memory ("You went to the movies last night.") crumbles much more quickly than does one with more attention to detail ("You went to the nine o'clock showing of the new Leonardo DiCaprio movie. You thought about getting some popcorn, but the line was too long so you went right into the theater. The couple next to you kept whispering through the film until someone else shushed them. You liked the movie well enough, but the plot seemed weak. You were tired after it ended, so you went home, watched a little late-night television, and went to bed.").

Even in its simplest applications, The Forgetful Mind requires tremendous skill and finesse. It's a relatively simple matter to rifle through a victim's psyche and rip out the memories of the previous night, without even knowing what the subject did that evening. Doing so leaves a gap in the victim's mind, though, a hole that can give rise to further problems down the road. The Kindred may describe new memories, but these recollections seldom have the same degree of realism that the subject's true thoughts held.

As such, this power isn't always completely effective. The victim may remember being bitten, but believe it to be an animal attack. Greater memories may return in pieces as dreams, or through sensory triggers like a familiar odor or spoken phrase. Even so, months or years may pass before the subject regains enough of her lost memories to make sense of the fragments.

A vampire can also sense when a subject's memories were altered through use of this power, and even restore them like a hypnotist draws forth psychologically suppressed thoughts. However, the Kindred cannot use The Forgetful Mind to restore his own memories if they were stolen in such a way.

System: The player states what sorts of alteration he wants to perform, then rolls Wits + Subterfuge (difficulty of the target's Willpower score). Any success pacifies the victim for the amount of time it takes the vampire to perform the verbal alteration, provided the vampire does not act aggressively toward the victim. The table below indicates the degree of modification possible to the subject's memory, depending on the number of successes gained. If the successes rolled don't allow for the extent of change the character desired, the Storyteller reduces the resulting impact on the victim's mind.

1 success	May remove a single memory; lasts one day.
2 successes	May remove, but not alter, memory permanently.
3 successes	May make slight changes to memory.
4 successes	May alter or remove entire scene from subject's memory.
5 successes	May reconstruct entire periods of subject's life.

To restore removed memories or sense false ones in a subject, the character's Dominate rating must be equal to or higher than that of the vampire who made the alteration. If so, the player must make a Wits + Empathy roll (difficulty equal to the original vampire's permanent Willpower) and score more successes than his predecessor did.

•••• Conditioning

Through sustained manipulation, the vampire can make a subject more pliant to the Kindred's will. Over time, the victim becomes increasingly susceptible to the vampire's influence while simultaneously growing more resistant to the corrupting efforts of other immortals. Gaining complete control over a subject's mind is no small task, taking weeks or even months to accomplish.

Kindred often fill their retainers' heads with subtle whispers and veiled urges, thereby ensuring these mortals' loyalty. Yet vampires must pay a high price for the minds they ensnare. Servants Dominated in this way lose much of their passion and individuality. They follow the vampire's orders quite literally, seldom taking initiative or showing any imagination. In the end, such retainers become like automatons or the walking dead.

System: The player rolls Charisma + Leadership (difficulty of the target's permanent Willpower). Conditioning is an extended action; the Storyteller secretly determines the number of successes required. It typically requires between five and 10 times the subject's Self-Control score. Targets with more empathic Natures may require a lower number of successes, while those with willful Natures require a higher total. Only through roleplaying may a character discern whether his subject is conditioned successfully.

A target may become more tractable even before becoming fully conditioned. Once the vampire accumulates half the required number of successes, the Storyteller may apply a lower difficulty to the vampire's subsequent uses of Dominate. After being conditioned, the target falls so far under the vampire's influence that the Kindred need not make eye contact or even be present to retain absolute control. The subject does exactly as she is told, so long as her master can communicate with her verbally. No command roll is necessary unless the subject is totally isolated from the vampire (in a different room, over the

---

RESISTING DOMINATE

Most victims cannot stand against the effects of Dominate. Still, there are situations where this Discipline is powerless to sway the subject.

• **Mortals:** Few mortals can hope to resist Dominate, their strength of will nothing compared to the supernatural magnetism of a vampire. Still, there are extremely rare individuals who, due to strong religious faith, unique psychic talent or simple mental resolve, can shrug off this Discipline's effects. Beyond these scattered few, a select number of organizations like the Inquisition know certain rituals to render a mortal immune. Only a foolish vampire ignores the potential threat such human beings represent.

• **Vampires:** It is impossible to Dominate another Kindred who is of stronger Blood — the vampire must be of an equal or higher generation than the target for the powers to be effective.

• **Nature:** A character's Nature can have a distinct impact on how easily Dominate influences her. A vampire might control subjects with inherently empathic Natures (Caregiver, Child, Conformist) more easily, while those whose Natures denote a great degree of inner strength (Bravo, Director, Rebel) can be more of a challenge. The Storyteller may reduce the required difficulty or number of successes by one or two when the player rolls against those subjects with "weaker" Natures, or raise them by a similar amount for "stronger" Natures. On the other hand, "strong" Natures might be *more* easily influenced to take aggressive actions — for example, coaxing a Rebel to denounce the prince is likely easier than goading a Conformist to do the same thing. Ultimately, the Storyteller must adjudicate this.

• **Botches:** If a Dominate roll botches, the target is rendered immune to future attempts by the same vampire for the rest of the story.

---

phone). Even if a command roll fails, the target will still likely carry out part of the orders given.

After the subject is fully conditioned, other Kindred find her more difficult to Dominate. Such conditioning raises others' difficulties by two (to a maximum of 10).

It is possible, though difficult, to shake conditioning. The subject must be separated entirely from the vampire to whom she was in thrall. This period of separation varies depending on the individual, but the Storyteller may set it at six months, less a number of weeks equal to the subject's Willpower score (so a person with 5 Willpower must stay away from the vampire for just under five months). The subject regains her personality slowly during this time, although she may still lapse into brief spells of listlessness. If the vampire encounters the target before that time passes, a single successful Charisma + Leadership roll (difficulty of the target's Willpower score) on the part of the vampire completely reasserts the dominance.

If the subject makes it through the time period without intervention by her master, the target regains her former individuality. Even so, the vampire may reestablish conditioning more easily than the first time, since the subject is forever after

POLY

predisposed to falling under the Kindred's mental control. New attempts require half the total number of successes that the last bout of conditioning did.

••••• POSSESSION

At this level of Dominate, the force of the Kindred's psyche is such that it can utterly supplant the mind of a mortal subject. Speaking isn't required, although the vampire must capture the victim's gaze. During the psychic struggle, the contestants' eyes are locked on one another.

Once the Kindred crushes the subject's mind, the vampire moves his own consciousness into the victim's body and controls it as easily as he uses his own. The mortal falls into a mental fugue while under possession. She is aware of events only in a distorted, dreamlike fashion. In turn, the vampire's mind focuses entirely on controlling his mortal subject. His immortal body lies in a torpid state, defenseless against any actions made toward it.

Vampires cannot possess one another in this fashion, as even the weakest Kindred's mind is strong enough to resist such straightforward mental dominance. Only through a blood bond can one vampire control another to this degree.

System: The vampire must completely strip away the target's Willpower prior to possessing her. The player spends a Willpower point, then rolls Charisma + Intimidation, while the

subject rolls Willpower in a resisted action (difficulty 7 for both). For each success the vampire obtains over the victim's total, the target loses a point of temporary Willpower. Each success the subject gains over the vampire's total equals another die she adds to her roll on the next turn. It's often only a matter of time before the victim falls under the vampire's power. Only if the attacker botches can the subject escape her fate, since this makes the target permanently immune to any further Dominate attempts by that vampire.

Once the target loses all her temporary Willpower, her mind is open to the vampire. The vampire rolls Manipulation + Intimidation (difficulty 7) to determine how fully he assumes control of the mortal shell. Similar to the Animalism power Subsume the Spirit, multiple successes allow the character to utilize some mental Disciplines, noted on the chart below.

1 success	Cannot use Disciplines
2 successes	Can use Auspex
3 successes	Can also use Dominate, Presence
4 successes	Can also use Chimerstry, Dementation
5 successes	Can also use Necromancy, Thaumaturgy

The character may travel as far from his body as he is physically able while possessing the mortal. The vampire may also venture out during the day, albeit in the mortal form. However, the vampire's own body must be awake to do so, requiring a successful roll to remain awake (see p. 204). If the vampire leaves the mortal shell (by choice, if his body falls asleep, through supernatural expulsion, after sustaining significant injury), his consciousness returns to his physical form in an instant.

Once freed from possession, the mortal regains mental control of herself. This can happen in an instant, or the victim may lie comatose for days while her psyche copes with the violation.

The vampire experiences everything the mortal body feels during possession, from pleasure to pain. In fact, any damage the victim's body sustains is also applied to the character's body (although the Kindred may soak as normal). If the mortal dies before the vampire's soul can flee from the body, the character's body falls into torpor. Presumably this is in sympathetic response to the massive trauma of death, although some Kindred believe that the vampire's soul is cast adrift during this time and must find its way back to the body.

The Kindred can remain in the mortal's body even if his own torpid form is destroyed, though such a pathetic creature is not likely to exist for long. At each sunrise, the vampire must roll Courage (difficulty 8) or be expelled from the body. If forced from the mortal body, the vampire tumbles into the astral plane, his soul permanently lost in the spirit world. Nor may a vampire trapped in a mortal body be "re-Embraced"; if the Embrace occurs to such a creature, he simply meets Final Death.

FORTITUDE

All vampires possess a preternatural constitution that makes most normal damage inconsequential. Fortitude bestows a resilience and vigor far beyond even normal vampiric toughness. Kindred with this power ignore the mightiest punches and barely feel hails of bullets. This Discipline also helps protect against sources of damage even vampires fear, such as sunlight, fire and terminal falls.

Gangrel, Ravnos and Ventrue possess this potent ability. Gangrel enjoy the benefit of Fortitude as a matter of course, but Ravnos and especially Ventrue delight in the power's psychological effects. It's not unusual for a Ventrue to take a "fatal" blow, giving his opponent just enough time to register the vampire's smile before the Ventrue finishes off the shocked victim.

System: A character's rating in Fortitude adds to his Stamina for the purposes of soaking normal damage (bashing and lethal). A character with this Discipline may also use his dots in Fortitude to soak aggravated damage (Kindred cannot normally soak things like vampire bites, werewolf claws, magical effects, fire, sunlight or massive physical trauma). So a vampire with Fortitude 3 has three dice to soak aggravated damage.

See Chapter Six, pp. 208-209, for further details on soaking and damage.

Necromancy

Necromancy is at once a Discipline and a school of magical learning, all dedicated toward the command of the souls of the dead. It has some similarities to Thaumaturgy in that, rather than being a strict linear progression of powers, Necromancy consists of several "paths" and accompanying "rituals." Well-trained and puissant vampiric necromancers can summon the dead, banish or imprison souls, and even reinsert ghosts into living — or unliving — bodies. Needless to say, the study of Necromancy is not widespread among the Kindred, and its practitioners — primarily Giovanni Kindred — are shunned or ignored whenever possible.

Over the centuries, the various schools of vampiric Necromancy have diversified, leaving three distinct paths of necromantic magic available to Cainites. All necromancers first learn the so-called Sepulchre Path, then extend their studies to the Bone Path or the Ash Path as time and opportunity permit. The Sepulchre Path is always considered the character's "primary" path; it increases automatically as the character increases her overall Necromancy rating. The Bone and Ash Paths must be bought separately, using the experience costs for secondary paths.

Like Thaumaturgy, Necromancy has also spawned a series of rituals. While not nearly so immediate in effect as the basic powers of Necromancy, Necromantic rituals can have impressive long-term effects. Unsurprisingly, the elements of Necromantic ritual are things like long-buried corpses, hands from the cadavers of hanged men, and so on, and so obtaining suitable materials can be quite difficult. Scarcity of supply limits the frequency of Necromantic rituals, giving cause for many other Kindred to breathe a metaphorical sigh of relief.

System: A Cainite necromancer must learn at least three levels in the Sepulchre Path before learning his first level in either the Bone Path or the Ash Path. He must then achieve mastery in the Sepulchre Path (five levels) before acquiring any knowledge of the third path.

As with Thaumaturgy, advancement in the primary path (in this case, the Sepulchre Path) costs the normal experience amount, while study of secondary Necromantic paths incurs an additional experience-point cost (see p. 143). Because Necromancy is not quite so rigid a study as Thaumaturgy is, the rolls required to use Necromantic powers can vary from path to path and even within individual paths.

Statistics for wraiths may be found in Chapter Nine, pp. 282-283.

The Sepulchre Path

• Insight

This power allows a necromancer to stare into the eyes of a corpse and see reflected there the last thing the dead man witnessed. The vision appears only in the eyes of the cadaver and is visible to no one except the necromancer using Insight.

System: This power requires a roll of Perception + Occult (difficulty 8 for formerly living creatures, 10 for unliving ones such as vampires) as the vampire stares into the target's eyes. The number of successes on the roll determines the clarity of the vision; a botch shows the necromancer his own Final Death, which can induce Rötschreck.

This power cannot be used on the corpses of vampires who have reached Golconda, or those in whom advanced decomposition has already set in.

1 success	A basic sense of the subject's death
2 successes	A clear image of the subject's death and the seconds preceding it
3 successes	A clear image, with sound, of the minutes preceding death
4 successes	A clear image, with sound, of the half-hour before the subject's demise
5 successes	Full sensory perception of the hour leading up to the target's death

•• Summon Soul

The power of Summon Soul allows a necromancer to call a ghost back from the Underworld, though for conversational purposes only. In order to perform this feat, the Giovanni must meet certain conditions:

• The necromancer must know the name of the wraith in question, though an image of the wraith obtained via Psychometry will suffice.

• An object with which the wraith had some contact in life must be in the vicinity. If the object is something of great importance to the ghost, the chances for success in the summoning increase dramatically (-2 difficulty). **Note:** This bonus applies for all powers on the Sepulchre Path.

Certain types of ghosts cannot be summoned with this power. Vampires who achieved Golconda before their Final Deaths, or who were diablerized, are beyond the reach of this summons. Likewise, many ghosts of the dead cannot be called — they are destroyed, unable to return to the mortal plane, or lost in the eternal storm of the Underworld.

System: To use Summon Soul, the vampire's player must roll Perception + Occult (difficulty 7, or the ghost's Willpower if the Storyteller knows it). The number of successes on the roll indicates the tractability of the summoned spirit and how long the summoned wraith remains in the vicinity of her summoner. Summoned ghosts are visible and audible to the vampire who summoned them, and remain so up until the time the summoning wears off. Ghosts who wish to be summoned can voluntarily appear.

For each question the vampire asks the summoned spirit, the Storyteller should roll one die per summoning success. At least one success is needed on this second roll (difficulty 6) in order to keep the wraith around long enough to answer the question.

If a vampire botches a summoning roll, she calls forth a malevolent ghost (known as a spectre), which immediately sets about tormenting its summoner.

••• Compel Soul

With this power, a vampire can command a ghost to do his bidding for a while. Compel is a perilous undertaking and, when used improperly, can endanger vampire and wraith alike.

System: In order to compel a wraith, the vampire must first successfully summon it. Before the wraith has left the scene of the summoning, the vampire's player must roll Manipulation + Occult (difficulty equal to the target's Willpower). The wraith can spend Pathos (the ghostly equivalent of blood; assume a pool of 7 for all ghosts or consult Chapter Nine) to combat the compulsion; each point spent removes one of the vampire's successes. The vampire may attempt to compel a wraith multiple times during a single summoning.

For each success achieved on the Manipulation + Occult roll, the necromancer achieves a greater degree of control over the wraith. The breakdown is as follows:

Failure: The compulsion of the summoning ends and the wraith is free to leave. Many wraiths take the opportunity to assault their would-be masters as they depart.

One success: The wraith must remain in the vicinity and refrain from attacking any creature without the necromancer's consent.

Two successes: The wraith is bound to remain and answer any questions truthfully, though the questions had best be phrased carefully.

Three successes: The wraith is forced to remain and answer any questions truthfully, without evasion or omission.

Four successes: The wraith must remain, answering truthfully any questions asked of it. It must also perform any services commanded by its new master, though it is bound only by the letter of the command, not the spirit.

Five successes: The wraith is trapped, obeying the spirit of the vampire's commands to the best of its ability.

Compel holds a ghost for one hour per success rolled. If the vampire wishes, she can expend a temporary Willpower point to keep the wraith under the compulsion for an extra night. The expenditure of a permanent point of Willpower on the vampire's part binds the wraith for a year and a day.

•••• Haunting

Haunting binds a summoned ghost to a particular location or, in extreme cases, an object. The wraith cannot leave the area to which the necromancer binds it without risking self-destruction. A wraith attempting to leave the area of a haunting must make a Willpower roll (difficulty 10, two successes necessary) or take a level of aggravated damage; if the wraith runs out of health levels, it is hurled deep into the Underworld to face destruction.

System: The player rolls Manipulation + Occult (difficulty is target's Willpower if she resists; otherwise it is 4). Each success ties the wraith to a particular spot of the necromancer's choosing for a night; with the expenditure of a Willpower point, that becomes a week. Expenditure of a point of permanent Willpower extends the duration to a year.

••••• Torment

It is through the use of this power that elder Giovanni convince bound ghosts to behave — or else. Torment allows the vampire to strike a wraith as if he himself were in the lands of the dead, inflicting damage on the wraith's ectoplasmic form. The vampire remains in the real world, however, so he cannot be struck in return by the wraith.

System: The player rolls Stamina + Empathy (difficulty is the wraith's Willpower), and the vampire reaches out to "touch"

the wraith. Each success inflicts a level of lethal damage on the wraith. Should the wraith lose all health levels, it immediately vanishes into what appears to be a doorway to some hideous nightmare realm. Ghosts "destroyed" thus cannot reappear near the real world for a month.

The Bone Path

The Bone Path is concerned primarily with corpses and the methods by which dead souls can be restored to the living world — temporarily or otherwise.

• Tremens

Tremens allows a necromancer to make the flesh of a corpse shift once. An arm might suddenly flop forward, a cadaver might sit up, or dead eyes might abruptly open. Needless to say, this sort of thing tends to have an impressive impact on people who aren't expecting a departed relative to roll over in his coffin.

System: To use Tremens, the necromancer spends a single blood point, and the player must succeed on a Dexterity + Occult roll (difficulty 6). The more successes achieved, the more complicated an action can be inculcated into the corpse. One success allows for an instantaneous movement, such as a twitch, while five allow the vampire to set up specific conditions under which the body animates ("The next time someone enters the room, I want the corpse to sit up and open its eyes."). Under no circumstances can Tremens cause a dead body to attack or cause damage.

•• Apprentice's Brooms

With Apprentice's Brooms, the necromancer can make a dead body rise and perform a simple function. For example, the corpse could be set to carrying heavy objects, digging, or just shambling from place to place. The cadavers thus animated do not attack or defend themselves if interfered with, but instead attempt to carry out their given instructions until such time as they've been rendered inanimate. Generally it takes dismemberment, flame or something similar to destroy a corpse animated in this way.

System: A roll of Wits + Occult (difficulty 7) and the expenditure of a point of both blood and Willpower are all that is necessary to animate corpses with Apprentice's Brooms. The number of corpses animated is equal to the number of successes achieved. The necromancer must then state the task to which he is setting his zombies. The cadavers turn themselves to their work until they finish the job (at which point they collapse) or something (including time) destroys them.

Bodies energized by this power continue to decay, albeit at a much slower rate than normal.

••• Shambling Hordes

Shambling Hordes creates exactly what you think it might: reanimated corpses with the ability to attack, albeit neither very well nor very quickly. Once primed by this power, the corpses wait — for years, if necessary — to fulfill the command given them. The orders might be to protect a certain site or simply to attack immediately, but they will be carried out until every last one of the decomposing monsters is destroyed.

System: The player invests a point of Willpower, then spend a point of blood for each corpse the necromancer ani-

---

---

mates. The player then must succeed on a Wits + Occult roll (difficulty 8); each success allows the vampire to raise another corpse from the grave. Each zombie (for lack of a better term) can follow one simple instruction, such as "Stay here and guard this graveyard against any intruders," or "Kill them!"

Note: Zombies created by Shambling Hordes will wait forever if need be to fulfill their functions. Long after the flesh has rotted off the mystically animated bones, the zombies will wait…and wait…and wait — still able to perform their duties.

•••• Soul Stealing

This power affects the living, not the dead. It does, however, temporarily turn a living soul into a sort of wraith, as it allows a necromancer to strip a soul from a living — or vampiric — body. A mortal exiled from his body by this power becomes a wraith with a single tie to the real world: his now-empty body.

System: The player spends a point of Willpower and then makes a contested Willpower roll against the intended victim (difficulty 6). Successes indicate the number of hours during which the original soul is forced out of its housing. The body itself remains autonomically alive but catatonic.

This power can be used to create suitable hosts for Daemonic Possession.

••••• Daemonic Possession

Daemonic Possession lets a vampire insert a soul into a freshly dead body and inhabit it for the duration. This does not turn the reanimated corpse into anything other than a reanimated corpse, and one that will irrevocably decay after a week, but it does give either a wraith or a free-floating soul (say, that of a vampire using Psychic Projection) a temporary home in the physical world.

System: The body in question must be no more than 30 minutes dead, and the new tenant must agree to inhabit it — a ghost or astral form cannot be forced into a new shell. Of course, most ghosts would gladly seize the opportunity, but that's a different matter. Should the vampire, for whatever reason, wish to insert a soul into another vampire's corpse (before it crumbles to ash), the necromancer must achieve five successes on a resisted Willpower roll against the original owner of the body. Otherwise, the interloper is denied entrance.

Note: The soul can use whatever physical abilities (Dodge, Brawl, Potence) his new home possesses, and whatever mental abilities (Computer, Law, Presence) he possesses in his current existence. He cannot use the physical abilities of his old form, or the mental abilities of his new one.

THE ASH PATH

The Ash Path allows necromancers to peek into the lands of the dead and even to affect things there. Of the three Paths of Necromancy, the Ash Path is the most perilous to learn, because many of the Path's uses increase a necromancer's vulnerability to wraiths.

• SHROUDSIGHT

Shroudsight allows a necromancer to see through the Shroud, the mystical barrier that separates the living world from the Underworld. By using this power, the vampire can spot ghostly buildings and items, the landscape of the so-called Shadowlands, and even wraiths themselves. However, the odds are that an observant wraith will notice when a vampire suddenly starts staring at him, which can lead to unpleasant consequences.

System: A simple roll of Perception + Alertness (difficulty 7) allows a necromancer to utilize Shroudsight. The effects last for a scene.

•• LIFELESS TONGUES

Where Shroudsight allows a necromancer to see ghosts, Lifeless Tongues allows her to converse with them effortlessly. Once Lifeless Tongues is employed, the vampire can carry on a conversation with the denizens of the ghostly Underworld without spending blood or causing the wraiths to expend any effort.

System: To use Lifeless Tongues requires a roll of Perception + Occult (difficulty 6) and the expenditure of a Willpower point. This power also grants the effects of Shroudsight, so the vampire can see with whom, or what, she is conversing.

••• DEAD HAND

Similar to the Sepulchre Path power Torment, Dead Hand allows a necromancer to reach across the Shroud and affect a ghostly object as if it were in the real world. Ghosts are solid to necromancers using this power, and can be attacked. Furthermore, the necromancer can pick up ghostly items, scale ghostly architecture (giving real-world bystanders the impression that he's climbing on air!) and generally exist in two worlds. On the other hand, a necromancer using Dead Hand is quite solid to the residents of the Underworld — and to whatever weapons they might have.

System: The player spends a point of Willpower and makes a successful Wits + Occult roll (difficulty 7) for the vampire to activate Dead Hand. For each scene the vampire wishes to remain in contact with the Underworld, he must spend a point of blood.

•••• EX NIHILO

Ex Nihilo allows a necromancer to enter the Underworld physically. While in the lands of the dead, the vampire is essentially an extra-solid ghost. He maintains his normal number of health levels, but can be hurt only by things that inflict aggravated damage on ghosts (weapons forged from souls, certain ghostly powers, etc.). A vampire physically in the Underworld can pass through solid objects (at the cost of one health level) and remain "incorporeal" thus for a number of turns equal to his Stamina rating. On the other hand, vampires present in the Underworld are subject to all of the Underworld's perils, including ultimate destruction. A vampire killed in the Deadlands is gone forever, beyond even the reach of other necromancers.

System: Using Ex Nihilo takes a tremendous toll on the necromancer. To activate this power, the vampire must first draw a doorway with chalk or blood on any available surface. (**Note:** Doors can be drawn ahead of time for exactly this purpose.) The player must then expend two points of Willpower and two points of blood, then make a Stamina + Occult roll (difficulty 8) as the vampire attempts to open the chalk door physically. If the roll succeeds, the door opens and the vampire steps through into the Underworld.

When the vampire wishes to return to the real world, he needs merely to concentrate (and the player spends another Willpower point and rolls Stamina + Occult, difficulty 6). At Storyteller discretion, a vampire who is too deeply immersed in the Underworld may need to journey to a place close to the lands of the living in order to cross over. Vampires who wander too far into the lands of the dead may be trapped there forever.

Vampires in the Underworld cannot feed upon ghosts; their only sustenance is the blood they bring with them.

● ● ● ● ● SHROUD MASTERY

A bit of an exaggeration, Shroud Mastery is the ability to manipulate the veil between the worlds of the living and the dead. By doing so, a necromancer can make it easier for bound wraiths in his service to function, or make it nearly impossible for ghosts to contact the material world.

System: To exercise Shroud Mastery, the necromancer expends two points of Willpower, then states whether he is attempting to raise or lower the Shroud. The player then makes a Willpower roll (difficulty 9). Each success on the roll raises or lowers the difficulties of all nearby wraiths' actions by one, to a maximum of 10 or a minimum of 3. The Shroud reverts to its normal strength at a rate of one point per hour thereafter.

NECROMANTIC RITUALS

The rituals connected with Necromancy are a hodgepodge lot. Some have direct relations to the paths; others seem to have been taught by wraiths themselves, for whatever twisted reason. All beginning necromancers gain one Level One ritual, but any others learned must be gained through in-game play. Necromantic rituals are otherwise identical to Thaumaturgy rituals (pp. 182-185) and are learned in similar fashion, though the two are by no means compatible.

System: Casting times for necromantic rituals vary widely; see the description for particulars. The player rolls Intelligence + Occult (difficulty 3 + the level of the ritual, maximum 9); success indicates the ritual proceeds smoothly, failure produces no effect, and a botch often indicates that certain "powers" notice the caster, usually to her detriment.

CALL OF THE HUNGRY DEAD (LEVEL ONE RITUAL)

Call of the Hungry Dead takes only 10 minutes to cast and requires a hair from the target's head. The ritual climaxes with the burning of that hair in the flame of a black candle, after which the victim becomes able to hear snatches of conversation from across the Shroud. If the target is not prepared, the voices come as a confusing welter of howls and unearthly demands; he is unable to make out anything intelligible, and might well go briefly mad.

EYES OF THE GRAVE (LEVEL TWO RITUAL)

This ritual, which takes two hours to cast, causes the target to experience intermittent visions of her death over the period of a week. The visions come without warning and can last up to a minute. The caster of the ritual has no idea what the visions contain — only the victim sees them, after all. Each time a vision manifests, the target must roll Courage (difficulty 7) or be reduced to quivering panic. The visions, which come randomly, can also interfere with activities such as driving, shooting and so on.

Eyes of the Grave requires a pinch of soil from a fresh grave.

RITUAL OF THE UNEARTHED FETTER (LEVEL THREE RITUAL)

This ritual requires that a necromancer have a fingerbone from the skeleton of the particular wraith he's interested in. When the ritual is cast, the fingerbone becomes attuned to something vitally important to the wraith, the possession of which by the necromancer makes the casting of Sepulchre Path powers much easier. Most necromancers take the attuned fingerbone and suspend it from a thread, allowing it to act as a sort of supernatural compass and following it to the special item in question.

Ritual of the Unearthed Fetter takes three hours to cast properly. It requires both the name of the wraith targeted and the fingerbone already mentioned, as well as a chip knocked off a gravestone or other marker (not necessarily the marker of the bone's former owner). During the course of the ritual the stone crumbles to dust, which is then sprinkled over the fingerbone.

CADAVER'S TOUCH (LEVEL FOUR RITUAL)

By chanting for three hours and melting a wax doll in the shape of the target, the necromancer turns a mortal target into a corpselike mockery of himself. As the doll loses the last of its form, the target becomes cold and clammy. His pulse becomes weak and thready, his flesh pale and chalky. For all intents and purposes, he becomes a reasonable facsimile of the walking dead. Needless to say, this can have some adverse effects in social situations (+2 difficulty on all Social rolls). The effects of the ritual wear off only when the wax of the doll is permitted to resolidify. If the wax is allowed to boil off, the spell is broken.

GRASP THE GHOSTLY (LEVEL FIVE RITUAL)

Requiring a full six hours of chanting, this ritual allows a necromancer to bring an object from the Underworld into the real world. It's not as simple as all that, however — a wraith might well object to having his possessions stolen and fight back. Furthermore, the object taken must be replaced by a material item of roughly equal mass, otherwise the target of the ritual snaps back to its previous, ghostly existence.

Objects taken from the Underworld tend to fade away after about a year. Only items recently destroyed in the real world (called "relics" by wraiths) may be recaptured in this manner. Artifacts created by wraiths themselves were never meant to exist outside the Underworld, and vanish on contact with the living world.

Obfuscate

This uncanny power enables Kindred to conceal themselves from others' sight. By simply wishing to remain unseen, a vampire can disappear, even if he stands in full view of a crowd. The immortal doesn't actually become invisible; he simply deludes any observers into thinking he has vanished. Additional uses of Obfuscate include changing the Kindred's features and concealing other people or objects.

Unless the vampire purposefully makes himself seen, he can remain obscured indefinitely. At higher levels of power, the vampire may fade from view so subtly that those nearby never register the point at which he "left."

Under most circumstances, few mortals or supernaturals can penetrate Obfuscate's cloaking fog. Animals, operating on a more instinctual level, often perceive (and fear) the vampire's presence even if they can't detect him with their normal senses. Children and other innocents to whom deception is foreign might also be able to pierce the deception, at the Storyteller's discretion.

The Auspex Discipline enables Kindred to see through Obfuscate. Even that is not guaranteed, however; refer to "Seeing the Unseen," p. 152, for more details.

Since Obfuscate affects the viewer's mind, Kindred cannot use this Discipline to cloak their presence from mechanical devices. Video recordings and photographs capture the vampire's image faithfully. Even so, such is Obfuscate's ability to bend the mind that someone using a recording device will not see the immortal's image until she views the footage at a later date, if even then.

Several clans — Assamites, Followers of Set, Malkavians, Nosferatu — use this power, but it stands as the hallmark of the Nosferatu. A number of elder Kindred believe Caine, or perhaps Lilith, bestowed the clan with this Discipline to compensate for the hideous physical deformities its members suffer.

Most Obfuscate powers last for a scene or so, or until the vampire ceases maintaining them. Once evoked, they require very little mental effort to keep in place.

• Cloak of Shadows

At this level, the vampire must rely on nearby shadows and cover to assist in hiding his presence. He steps into an out-of-the-way, shadowed place and eases himself from normal sight. The vampire remains unnoticed as long as he stays silent, still, under some degree of cover (curtain, bush, door frame, lamppost, alley) and out of direct lighting. The immortal's concealment vanishes if he moves, attacks or falls under direct light. Furthermore, the vampire's deception cannot stand concentrated observation without fading.

System: No roll is required as long as the character fulfills the criteria described above. So long as he remains quiet and motionless, virtually no one but another Kindred with a high Auspex rating will see him.

•• Unseen Presence

With experience, the vampire can move around without being seen. Shadows seem to shift to cover him, and others automatically avert their gaze as he passes by. People move unconsciously to avoid contact with the cloaked creature; those with weak wills may even scurry away from the area in unacknowledged fear. The vampire remains ignored indefinitely unless someone deliberately seeks him out or he inadvertently reveals himself.

Since the vampire fully retains his physical substance, he must be careful to avoid contact with anything that may disclose his presence (knocking over a vase, bumping into someone). Even a whispered word or the scuffing of a shoe against the floor can be enough to disrupt the power.

System: No roll is necessary to use this power unless the character speaks, attacks or otherwise draws attention to himself. The Storyteller should call for a Wits + Stealth roll under any circumstances that might cause the character to reveal himself. The difficulty of the roll depends on the situation; stepping on a squeaky floorboard might be a 5, while walking through a pool of water may require a 9. Other acts may require a certain number of successes; speaking quietly without giving away one's position, for instance, demands at least three successes.

Some things are beyond the power of Unseen Presence to conceal. Although the character is cloaked from view while he smashes through a window, yells out or throws someone across the room, the vampire becomes visible to all in the aftermath. Bystanders snap out of the subtle fugue in which Obfuscate put them. Worse still, each viewer can make a Wits + Alertness roll (difficulty 7); if successful, the mental haze clears completely, so those individuals recall every move the character made up until then as if he were visible the entire time.

••• Mask of a Thousand Faces

The vampire can influence the perception of others, causing them to see someone different from the immortal himself. Although the Kindred's physical form does not change, any observer who cannot sense the truth sees whomever the vampire wishes her to see.

The vampire must have a firm idea of the visage he wishes to project. The primary decision is whether to create an imaginary face or to superimpose the features of another person. Manufactured features are often more difficult to compose in believable proportions, but such a disguise is easier to maintain than having to impersonate someone else. Of course, things get simpler if the Kindred borrows the face but doesn't bother with the personality.

System: The player rolls Manipulation + Performance (difficulty 7) to determine how well the disguise works. If the character tries to impersonate someone, he must get a good look at the subject before putting on the mask. The Storyteller may raise the difficulty if the character catches only a glimpse. The chart below lists the degrees of success in manufacturing another appearance.

Actually posing as someone else carries its own problems. The character should know at least basic information about the individual; especially difficult deceptions (fooling a lover or close friend) require at least some familiarity with the target in order to succeed.

1 success	The vampire retains the same height and build, with a few slight alterations to his basic features. Nosferatu can appear as normal, albeit ugly, mortals.
2 successes	He looks unlike himself; people don't easily recognize him or agree about his appearance.
3 successes	He looks the way he wants to appear.
4 successes	Complete transformation, including gestures, mannerisms, appearance and voice.
5 successes	Profound alteration (appear as the opposite sex, a vastly different age, extreme change of size).

•••• VANISH FROM THE MIND'S EYE

This potent expression of Obfuscate enables the vampire to disappear from plain view. So profound is this vanishing that the immortal can fade away even if he stands directly before someone.

While the disappearance itself is quietly subtle, its impact on those who see it is anything but. Most kine panic and flee in the aftermath. Especially weak-willed individuals wipe the memory of the Kindred from their minds. Although vampires are not shaken so easily, even Kindred may be momentarily surprised by a sudden vanishing.

System: The player rolls Charisma + Stealth; the difficulty equals the target's Wits + Alertness (use the highest total in the group if the character disappears in front of a crowd). With three or fewer successes, the character fades but does not vanish, becoming an indistinct, ghostlike figure. With more than three, he disappears completely. If the player scores more successes than an observer's Willpower rating, that person forgets that the vampire was there in the first place.

Tracking the character accurately while he appears ghostlike requires a Perception + Alertness roll (difficulty 8). A successful roll means the individual can interact normally with the vampire (although the immortal looks like a profoundly disturbing ghostly shape). A failed roll results in +2 difficulties (maximum 10) when attempting to act upon, or interact with, the vampire. The Storyteller may call for new observation checks if the vampire moves to an environment in which he's difficult to see (heads into shadows, crosses behind an obstacle, proceeds through a crowd). When fully invisible, the vampire is handled as described under Unseen Presence, above.

A person subject to the vanishing makes a Wits + Courage roll (mortals at difficulty 9, immortals at difficulty 5). A successful roll means the individual reacts immediately (although after the vampire performs his action for that turn); failure means the person stands uncomprehending for two turns while her mind tries to make sense of what she just experienced.

••••• CLOAK THE GATHERING

At this degree of power, the vampire may extend his concealing abilities to cover an area. The immortal may use any Obfuscate power upon those nearby as well as upon himself, if he wishes.

Any protected person who compromises the cloak exposes himself to view. Further, if the one who invokes the power gives himself away, the cloak falls from everyone. This power is particularly useful if the vampire needs to bring his retinue through a secure location without drawing the notice of others.

System: The character may conceal one extra individual for each dot of Stealth he possesses. He may bestow any single Obfuscate power at a given time to the group. While the power applies to everyone under the character's cloak, his player need only make a single roll. Each individual must follow the requirements described under the relevant Obfuscate power to remain under its effect; any person who fails to do so loses the cloak's protection, but doesn't expose the others. Only if the vampire himself errs does the endowment drop for everyone.

OBTENEBRATION

The bailiwick of the Lasombra, the Obtenebration Discipline grants its users power over darkness. The precise nature of the "darkness" invoked is a matter of debate among the Keepers. Some believe it to be shadows, while others, perhaps more correctly, believe the power grants a Kindred control over the stuff of her soul, allowing her to coax it tangibly forth.

In any event, the effects of Obtenebration are terrifying, as waves of enveloping blackness roil out from the vampire, washing over their targets like an infernal tide. Blatant uses of this power are obvious breaches of the Masquerade — of course, as Obtenebration is proprietary to the Sabbat, any Camarilla neonate or ancilla caught using the Discipline had better have an *impeccable* explanation.

Note: Lasombra vampires can see through the darkness they control, though other Lasombra cannot. Dreadful tales of rival Keepers struggling to blind and smother each other with the same

wisps of darkness circulate among young members of the clan, though no elders have come forth to substantiate these claims.

• SHADOW PLAY

This power grants the vampire a limited control over shadows and other ambient darkness. Though the vampire cannot truly "create" darkness, she can overlap and stretch existing shadows, creating patches of gloom. This power also allows Kindred to separate shadows from their casting bodies and even shape darkness into the shadows of things that are not truly there.

Once a Kindred takes control of darkness or shadow, it gains a mystical tangibility while under the vampire's manipulation. By varying accounts cold or hellishly hot and cloying, the darkness may be used to aggravate or even smother victims. Certain callous Lasombra claim to have choked mortals to death with their own shadows.

System: This power requires no roll, but a blood point must be spent to activate it. Shadow Play lasts for one scene and requires no active concentration. Kindred cloaking themselves in shadow gain an extra die in their Stealth dice pools and add one to the difficulties of ranged weapon attacks against them. Vampires who use the darkness to make themselves more terrifying add one die to Intimidation dice pools. Opponents plagued by flapping shadows and strangling darkness subtract one die from soak and Stamina dice pools. Mortals, ghouls and other air-breathers reduced to zero Stamina in this manner begin to asphyxiate; vampires lose all appropriate dice but are otherwise unaffected. Only one target or subject may be affected by this

power at any given time, though some modicum of concealment is offered to a relatively motionless group.

The unnatural appearance of this power proves extremely disconcerting to mortals and animals (and, at the Storyteller's discretion, Kindred who have never seen it before). Whenever this power is invoked within a mortal's vicinity, that individual must make a Courage roll (difficulty 8) or suffer a one-die penalty to all dice pools for the remainder of the scene, due to fear of the monstrous shadows.

•• SHROUD OF NIGHT

The vampire can create a cloud of inky blackness. The cloud completely obscures light and even sound to some extent. Those who have been trapped within it (and survived) describe the cloud as viscous and unnerving. This physical manifestation lends credence to the tales of those Lasombra who claim that the darkness is something other than mere shadow.

The tenebrous cloud may even move, if the creating Kindred so wishes, though willing this requires complete concentration.

System: The player rolls Manipulation + Occult (difficulty 7). Success on the roll generates darkness roughly 10 feet in diameter, though the amorphous cloud constantly shifts and undulates, sometimes even extending shadowy tendrils. Each additional success doubles the diameter of the cloud (though the vampire may voluntarily reduce the area she wishes to cover). The cloud may be invoked at a distance of up to 50 yards, though creating darkness outside the vampire's line of sight adds two to the difficulty of the roll and requires a blood point's expenditure.

The tarry mass actually extinguishes light sources it engulfs (with the exception of fire), and muffles sounds to the point of indistinguishability. Those within the cloud lose all sense of sight and feel as though they've been immersed in pitch. Sound also warps and distorts within the cloud. Even those possessed of Heightened Senses or Eyes of the Beast suffer +2 difficulty penalties for most actions. Additionally, being surrounded by the Shroud of Night reduces Stamina-based dice pools by two dice, as the murk smothers and agitates the victims (this effect is not cumulative with Shadow Play). More than one unfortunate mortal has "drowned" in darkness.

Mortals and animals surrounded by the Shroud of Night must make Courage rolls per Shadow Play, above, or panic and flee.

••• ARMS OF THE ABYSS

Refining his control over darkness, the Kindred can create prehensile tentacles that emerge from patches of dim lighting. These tentacles may grasp, restrain and constrict foes.

System: The player spends a blood point and makes a simple (never extended) Manipulation + Occult roll (difficulty 7); each success enables the creation of a single tentacle. Each tentacle is six feet long and possesses Strength and Dexterity ratings equal to the invoking vampire's Obtenebration Trait. If the vampire chooses, she may spend a blood point either to increase a single tentacle's Strength or Dexterity by one or to extend its length by six feet. Each tentacle has four health levels (and is affected by fire and sunlight as a vampire) and soaks bashing and lethal damage using the vampire's Stamina + Fortitude. Aggravated damage may not be soaked.

Tentacles may constrict foes, inflicting Strength +1 lethal damage per turn. Breaking the grasp of a tentacle requires the victim to win a resisted Strength roll against the tentacle (difficulty 6 for both).

All tentacles need not emanate from the same source — so long as there are multiple patches of suitable darkness, there are sources for the Arms of the Abyss. Controlling the tentacles does not require complete concentration; if the Kindred is not incapacitated or in torpor, she may control tentacles while carrying out other actions.

•••• BLACK METAMORPHOSIS

The Lasombra calls upon his inner darkness and infuses himself with it, becoming a monstrous hybrid of matter and shadow. His body becomes mottled with spots of tenebrous shade, and wispy tentacles extrude from his torso and abdomen. Though still humanoid, the Lasombra takes on an almost demonic appearance, as the darkness within him bubbles to the surface.

System: The player spends two blood points and makes a Manipulation + Courage roll (difficulty 7). Failure indicates the vampire cannot undergo the Black Metamorphosis (though he spends the blood points nonetheless); a botch inflicts two unsoakable health levels of lethal damage on the vampire, as darkness ravages his undead body.

While under the effects of the Black Metamorphosis, the vampire possesses four tentacles similar to those evoked via Arms of the Abyss (though their Strength and Dexterity ratings are equal to the vampire's own Attributes). These tentacles, combined with the bands of darkness all over the Lasombra's body, subtract two dice from the Stamina and soak dice pools of opponents physically touched in combat, for as long as the vampire remains in contact with the victim. The vampire may make an additional attack without penalty by using the tentacles (for a total of two attacks, not one additional attack per tentacle). Additionally, the vampire can sense his surroundings fully even in pitch darkness.

The vampire's head and extremities sometimes appear to fade away into nothingness, while at other times they seem swathed in otherworldly darkness. This, combined with the wriggling tentacles writhing from his body, creates an unsettling sight. Mortals, animals and other creatures not accustomed to this sort of display must make Courage rolls (difficulty 8) or succumb to a panic that amounts to Rötschreck (though it is inspired by the darkness rather than fire). Many Lasombra cultivate this devilish aspect, and the Black Metamorphosis adds three dice to the invoking Kindred's Intimidation dice pools.

••••• TENEBROUS FORM

At this level, the Kindred's mastery of darkness is so extensive that she may physically *become* it. Upon activation of this power, the vampire becomes an inky, amoeboid patch of shadow. Vampires in this form are practically invulnerable and may slither through cracks and crevices. In addition, the shadow-vampire gains the ability to see in utter darkness.

System: The transformation costs three blood points and occurs over three turns. The vampire is immune to physical attack while in the tenebrous form (though she still takes aggravated damage from fire and sunlight), but may not herself

physically attack. She may, however, envelop and ooze over others, affecting them in the same manner as a Shroud of Night, above, in addition to using mental Disciplines. Vampires in Tenebrous Form may even slither up walls and across ceilings or "drip" darkness upward — they have no mass and are thus unaffected by gravity. Rötschreck difficulties from fire and sunlight do increase by one for vampires in this form, as the light is even more painful to their shadowy bodies.

Mortals and others not used to such displays who witness the vampire transform into unholy shadow require Courage rolls (difficulty 8) in order not to suffer the debilitating terror described under Black Metamorphosis.

POTENCE

Vampires endowed with this Discipline possess preternatural strength. Potence enables vampires to leap tremendous distances, lift massive weights and strike opponents with terrifying force. Even the lowest ranks of this power gift the Kindred with physical might beyond mortal bounds. More powerful immortals have been known to leap so far they seem to be flying, toss cars aside like tin cans, and punch through concrete as if it were cardboard. While the mental Disciplines are awe-inspiring, Potence's brute effectiveness is formidable in its own right.

Clans Brujah, Giovanni, Lasombra and Nosferatu are the primary possessors of this Discipline. Still, members of other clans often make a point to search out someone who can enlighten them in the ways of Potence.

System: The player rolls all Strength-related tests normally, but then adds an automatic success for each point he has in Potence. Thus, the character succeeds at most Strength feats without needing to make a roll at all. In melee and brawling combat, the automatic successes are applied to the damage roll results.

PRESENCE

This is the Discipline of supernatural attraction. Kindred who develop Presence can inspire zealous fervor, devoted passion or unspeakable terror in mortal and immortal alike. This subtle power is one of the most useful Disciplines a vampire can have.

Presence is notable since, unlike virtually all other Disciplines, some of its powers can be used on entire crowds at a time. The vampire may bring large groups under her sway, so long as her face is visible to those she wishes to affect — Presence doesn't even require eye contact. Further, this Discipline transcends race, religion, gender, class and (most importantly) supernatural nature. In theory, the powers have the same chance of affecting a Methuselah as they do a cab driver. In practice, while Presence can sway virtually any immortal, older and more canny Kindred are much more likely to notice the influence and resist with preternatural will.

Quite aside from its deliberate uses, Presence conveys upon the vampire an indescribable mystique. She stands out in any crowd, drawing the interest (and often desire) of those around her even when she's merely standing still. The higher the vampire's Presence, the greater this allure and the more powerful its impact on others.

Anyone can resist Presence for one turn by spending a Willpower point and succeeding on a Willpower roll (difficulty 8), but the affected individual must keep spending points until he can no longer see the vampire (or, in the case of Summon, until the effect wears off). The simplest way to deal with this is to turn around and stop looking. Those who don't understand that they're dealing with supernatural influences (as is the case with most mortals) seldom think of this tactic, but it's a simple assumption for clever vampires. Vampires three or more generations lower than the wielder need only spend a single Willpower to ignore the Presence for an entire scene and need not roll Willpower to do so.

The major drawback of Presence is that it controls only the emotions. It causes others to feel a certain way toward the vampire, but does not give her outright control over them. While people weigh strongly the orders that the vampire declares, their minds are still their own. Suicidal or ridiculous directives don't sound any more sensible just because the person giving them is unusually fascinating. Still, inspired eloquence or significant wealth used in combination with this Discipline can enable the vampire to urge others along a desired course.

The Brujah, Followers of Set, Toreador and Ventrue clans are all adept in this Discipline. The Ventrue are arguably the most skilled with its application, however, due to their ability to use Presence and Dominate in efficient combination.

• Awe

Awe amplifies the sublime magnetism this Discipline gives the vampire. Those near the vampire suddenly desire to be closer to her and are very receptive to her point of view. Awe is extremely useful for mass communication. It matters little what is said — the hearts of those affected lean toward the vampire's opinion. The weak want to agree with her; even if the strong-willed resist, they soon find themselves outnumbered. Awe can turn a chancy deliberation into a certain resolution in the vampire's favor almost before her opponents know that the tide has turned.

Despite the intensity of this attraction, those so smitten do not lose their sense of self-preservation. Danger breaks the spell of fascination, as does leaving the area. Those subject to Awe will remember how they felt in the vampire's presence, however. This will influence their reactions should they ever encounter her again.

System: The player rolls Charisma + Performance (difficulty 7). The number of successes rolled determines how many people are affected, as noted on the chart below. If there are more people present than the character can influence, Awe affects those with lower Willpower scores first. The power stays in effect for the remainder of the scene or until the character chooses to drop it.

1 success	One person
2 successes	Two people
3 successes	Six people
4 successes	20 people
5 successes	Everyone in the vampire's immediate vicinity (an entire auditorium, a mob)

Those affected can use Willpower points to overcome the effect, but must continue spending Willpower every turn for as long as they remain in the same area as the vampire. As soon as an individual spends a number of Willpower points equal to the successes rolled, he shakes off the Awe completely and remains unaffected for the rest of the scene.

•• Dread Gaze

While all Kindred can frighten others by physically revealing their true vampiric natures — baring claws and fangs, glaring with malevolence, hissing loudly with malice — this power focuses these elements to insanely terrifying levels. Dread Gaze engenders unbearable terror in its victims, stupefying them into madness, immobility or reckless flight. Even the most stalwart individual will fall back from the vampire's horrific visage.

System: The player rolls Charisma + Intimidation (difficulty of the victim's Wits + Courage). Success indicates the victim is cowed, while failure means the target is startled but not terrified by the sight. Three or more successes means he runs away in abject fear; victims who have nowhere to run claw at the walls, hoping to dig a way out rather than face the vampire. Moreover, each success subtracts one from the target's action dice pools next turn.

The character may attempt Dread Gaze once per turn, though she may also perform it as an extended action, adding her successes in order to subjugate the target completely. Once the target loses enough dice that he cannot perform any action, he's so shaken and terrified that he curls up on the ground and weeps. Failure during the extended action means the attempt falters. The character loses all her collected successes and can start over next turn, while the victim may act normally again.

A botch at any time indicates the target is not at all impressed — perhaps even finding the vampire's antics comical — and remains immune to any further uses of Presence by the character for the rest of the story.

••• Entrancement

This power bends others' emotions, making them the vampire's willing servants. Due to what these individuals see as true and enduring devotion, they heed the vampire's every desire. Since this is done willingly out of love (albeit a perversion of it) instead of through sapping the subjects' wills, these servants retain their creativity and individuality.

While these obedient minions are more pleasant and spirited than the mind-slaves created by Dominate, they're also somewhat unpredictable. Further, since Entrancement is of a temporary duration, dealing with a lapsed servant can be troublesome. A wise Kindred either disposes of those she entrances after they serve their usefulness, or binds them more securely by a blood bond (made much easier by the minion's willingness to serve).

System: The player rolls Appearance + Empathy (difficulty of the target's permanent Willpower); the number of successes determines how long the subject is entranced (see the chart below). The Storyteller may wish to make the roll instead, since the character is never certain of the strength of her hold on the victim. The vampire may try to keep the subject under her thrall, but can do so only after the initial Entrancement wears off. Attempting this power while Entrancement is already in operation has no effect.

1 success	One hour
2 successes	One day
3 successes	One week
4 successes	One month
5 successes	One year

•••• SUMMON

This impressive power enables the vampire to call to herself any person whom she has ever met. This call can go to anyone, mortal or supernatural, across any distance within the physical world. The subject of the summons comes as fast as he is able, possibly without even knowing why. He knows intuitively how to find his summoner — even if the vampire moves to a new location, the subject redirects his own course as soon as he can. After all, he's coming to the vampire herself, not to some predetermined site.

Although this power allows the vampire to call someone across a staggering distance, it is most useful when used locally. Even if the desired person books the next available flight, getting to Kyoto from Milwaukee can still take far longer than the vampire needs. Obviously, the individual's financial resources are a factor; if he doesn't have the money to travel quickly, it will take him a far greater time to get there.

The subject thinks mainly of reaching the vampire, but does not neglect his own well-being. This is less of a consideration if he only has to cross a room, unless he must get through a gang of gun-wielding punks to do so. The individual retains his survival instincts, and while he won't shirk physical violence to reach the vampire's side, he won't subject himself to suicidal situations.

The summoning dissipates at dawn. Unless the subject is trained to continue toward the vampire after the first call, the immortal must summon each night until the target arrives. Still, as long as the vampire is willing and able, she is assured to greet her desired subject some night — as long as nothing happens to him along the way, of course.

System: The player rolls Charisma + Subterfuge. The base difficulty is 5; this increases to difficulty 7 if the subject is virtually a stranger. If the character used Presence successfully on the target in the past, this difficulty drops to 4 — however, if the attempt was unsuccessful, then the difficulty is 8.

The number of successes indicates the subject's speed and attitude in responding:

1 success	Subject approaches slowly and hesitantly.
2 successes	Subject approaches reluctantly and is easily thwarted by obstacles.
3 successes	Subject approaches with reasonable speed.
4 successes	Subject comes with haste, overcoming any obstacles in his way.
5 successes	Subject rushes to the vampire, doing anything to get to her.

••••• MAJESTY

At this stage, the vampire can augment her supernatural mien a thousandfold. The attractive become paralyzingly beautiful; the homely become hideously demonic. Majesty inspires universal respect, devotion, fear — or all those emotions at once — in those around the vampire. The weak scramble to obey her every whim, and even the most dauntless find it almost impossible to deny her.

People affected find the vampire so formidable that they dare not risk her displeasure. Raising their voices to her is difficult; raising a hand against her is unthinkable. Those few who shake off the vampire's potent mystique enough to oppose her are shouted down by the many under her thrall, before the immortal need even respond.

Under Majesty's influence, hearts break, power trembles, and the bold shake. Wise Kindred use this power with caution against mortal and immortal alike. While Majesty can cow influential politicians and venerable primogen, the vampire must be careful that doing so doesn't come back to haunt her later. After all, a dignitary brought low before others loses his usefulness quickly, while a humiliated Kindred has centuries to plan revenge.

System: No roll is required on the part of the vampire, but she must spend a Willpower point. A subject must make a Courage roll (difficulty of the character's Charisma + Intimidation) if he wishes to be rude or simply contrary to the vampire. Success allows the individual to act normally for the moment, although he feels the weight of the vampire's displeasure crushing down on him. A subject who fails the roll aborts his intended action and even goes to absurd lengths to humble himself before the vampire, no matter who else is watching. The effects of Majesty last for one scene.

PROTEAN

This Discipline allows the vampire to manipulate his physical form. Some Kindred view this power as a heightened connection to the natural world, while others see it as a magnification of the mark of Caine. Whatever its basis, vampires who develop this Discipline can grow bestial claws, assume the forms of wolves and bats, transform into mist and meld into the earth.

Vampires can generally use other Disciplines while transformed — Kindred in wolf form can still read auras and communicate with other animals. However, there are some situations in which the Storyteller may decide that the immortal cannot use a certain Discipline. After all, a vampire in mist form cannot use Dominate, since he has no eyes with which to make contact. The vampire's clothes and personal items also change when he transforms, presumably absorbed within his very substance. Kindred cannot transfigure large objects or other beings; Protean is a very personal expression of undead power.

A vampire who has been staked, thereby trapping his soul within the mortal coil, cannot transform. Some Kindred claim that truly powerful Gangrel — those who have mastered the highest levels of Protean — can deny even this limitation.

Clan Gangrel lays claim to this Discipline, although other individual vampires have learned some of Protean's secrets from these bestial Kindred.

• EYES OF THE BEAST

The vampire sees perfectly well in pitch darkness, not requiring a light source to notice details in even the darkest basement or cave. The vampire's Beast is evident in his red glowing eyes, a sight sure to disturb most mortals.

System: The character must declare his desire to call forth the Eyes. No roll is necessary, but the change requires a full turn to complete. While manifesting the Eyes, the character suffers a +1 difficulty to all Social rolls with mortals unless he takes steps to shield his eyes (sunglasses are the simplest solution).

A vampire without this power who is immersed in total darkness suffers difficulty penalties of +2 to perform most feats. At the Storyteller's option, ranged attacks, extended actions and precision tasks (those requiring more than one success to succeed) cannot be performed successfully at all.

• • FERAL CLAWS

The vampire's nails transform into long, bestial claws. These talons are wickedly sharp, able to rend flesh with ease and even carve stone and metal with little trouble. The Beast is prominent in the claws as well, making them fearsome weapons against other immortals. It's rumored that some Gangrel have modified this power to change their vampiric fangs into vicious tusks.

System: The claws grow automatically in response to the character's desire, and can grow from both hands and feet. The transformation requires the expenditure of a blood point and takes a single turn to complete.

The character attacks normally in combat, but the claws inflict Strength + 1 aggravated damage. Other supernaturals cannot soak this damage, although a power such as Fortitude may be used. Additionally, the difficulties of all climbing rolls are reduced by two.

• • • EARTH MELD

One of the most prized powers the Gangrel possess, Earth Meld enables the vampire to become one with the earth. The immortal literally sinks into the bare ground, transmuting his substance to bond with the earth.

Though a vampire can immerse himself fully into the ground, he cannot move around within it. Further, it is impossible to meld into earth through another substance. Wood slats, blacktop, even artificial turf blocks Earth Meld's effectiveness — of course, it's a relatively simple matter for a vampire at this level of power to grow claws and rip apart enough of the flooring to expose the raw soil beneath.

By interring himself in the ground, the vampire gains full protection from daylight when outdoors. It is also the method of choice for those Kindred who wish to sleep away the centuries; these vampires lock themselves in the earth's embrace, gaining strength and power as they rest. Superstitious and paranoid Kindred whisper that thousands of Ancients sleep within the ground and will awaken on the night of Gehenna.

While so interred, the vampire is in a transitional state between flesh and earth. His physical presence exists between the physical world and the astral plane. As such, the vampire is difficult to sense, even through supernatural means. However, a disruption to the soil that the immortal occupies, or to his presence on the astral realm, returns him immediately to the physical world (and to full wakefulness), showering dirt outward as his body displaces the soil.

System: No roll is necessary, although the character must spend a blood point. Subsuming into the earth is automatic and takes a turn to complete. The character falls into a state one step above torpor during this time, sensing his surroundings only distantly. The player must make a Humanity roll (difficulty 6) for the character to rouse himself in response to danger prior to his desired time of emergence.

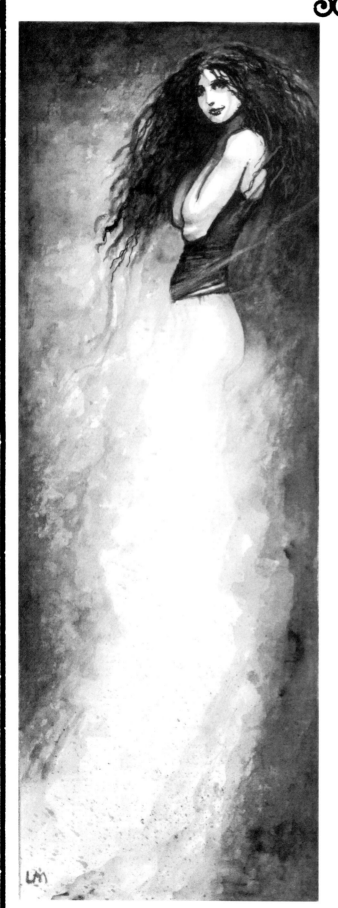

Since the character is in an in-between state, any attempts to locate him (catching his scent, scanning for his aura, traveling astrally) are made at +2 difficulty. Astral individuals cannot affect the vampire directly, instead meeting with a kind of spongy resistance as their hands pass through him. Similarly, digging in the material world encounters incredibly hard-packed earth, virtually as dense as stone.

Attempts at violence upon the submerged vampire from either side return him to his physical nature, expelling the soil with which he bonded in a blinding spray (all Perception-based rolls are at +2 difficulty for the turn). The character himself subtracts two from his initiative for the first turn after his restoration, due to momentary disorientation. Once expelled from the earth, the vampire may act normally.

•••• SHAPE OF THE BEAST

This endows the vampire with the legendary ability to transform into a wolf or bat. A Kindred changed in this way is a particularly imposing representative of the animal kingdom. Indeed, he is far superior to normal animals, even ones possessed by Subsume the Spirit. He retains his own psyche and temperament, but can still call upon the abilities of the beast form — increased senses for the wolf and flight for the bat.

Some vampires are reputed to change to other animal forms better suited to their environment — jackals in Africa, dholes in Asia, even enormous rats in urban environments.

System: The character spends one blood point to assume the desired shape. The transformation requires three turns to complete (spending additional blood points reduces the time of transformation by one turn per point spent, to a minimum of one). The vampire remains in his beast form until the next dawn, unless he wishes to change back sooner. Clothing and small personal possessions transform with the vampire.

While in the animal's shape, the vampire can use any Discipline he possesses except Necromancy, Serpentis, Thaumaturgy or Vicissitude. Furthermore, each form gives the character the abilities of that creature. In wolf form, the vampire's teeth and claws inflict Strength + 1 aggravated damage, he can run at double speed, and the difficulties of all Perception rolls are reduced by two. In bat form, the vampire's Strength is reduced to 1, but he can fly at speeds of up to 20 miles per hour, difficulties for all hearing-based Perception rolls are reduced by three, and attacks made against him are at +2 difficulty due to his small size.

The Storyteller may allow a vampire to assume a different animal shape, but should establish the natural abilities it grants the character.

••••• MIST FORM

This truly unsettling power enables the vampire to turn into mist. His physical shape disperses into a hazy cloud, but one still subject entirely to the immortal's will. He floats at a brisk pace and may slip under doors, through screens, down pipes and through other tiny openings. Although strong winds can blow the vampire from his chosen course, even hurricane-force winds cannot disperse his mist shape.

Some Kindred feel that this power is an expression of the vampire's ultimate control over the material world, while others believe that it is the immortal's soul made manifest (damned though it may be).

System: No roll is required, although a blood point must be spent. The transformation takes three turns to complete, although the character may reduce this time by one turn for each additional blood point spent (to a minimum of one turn). Strong winds may buffet the character about; only his rating in Potence (if any) may be used to resist this influence.

The vampire is immune to all mundane physical attacks while in mist form, although supernatural attacks affect him normally. Also, the vampire takes one fewer level of damage from fire and sunlight. The character may not attack others physically while in this state — this includes encountering another vampire in mist form. He may use Disciplines that do not require physical substance, however.

QUIETUS

Quietus, the Discipline of silent death, is practiced by the assassins of Clan Assamite. Using the principles of poison, vitae control and pestilence, this blood-based Discipline focuses on the destruction of its target through varying means. Quietus does not always cause a *quick* death; the Assassins rely upon its secret lethality to hide their involvement with their victims.

• SILENCE OF DEATH

Many Assamites claim never to have heard their targets' death screams. Silence of Death imbues the Assamite with a mystical silence that radiates from her body, muting all noise within a certain vicinity. No sound occurs inside this zone, though sounds originating outside the area of effect may be heard by anyone in it. Rumors abound of certain skilled Assamite viziers who have the ability to silence a *location* rather than a circumference that follows them, but no proof of this has been forthcoming.

System: This power costs one blood point to activate, which maintains a 20-foot radius of utter stillness around the Assamite for one hour.

•• SCORPION'S TOUCH

By changing the properties of her blood, an Assamite may create powerful venom that strips her prey of his resilience. This power is greatly feared by other Kindred, and all manner of hideous tales concerning methods of delivery circulate among trembling coteries. Assamites are known to deliver the poison by coating their weapons with it, blighting their opponents with a touch, or spitting it like a cobra. An apocryphal account speaks of a proud prince who discovered an Assamite plotting her exsanguination and began to diablerize her would-be assassin. Halfway through the act, she learned that she had ingested a dire quantity of tainted blood and was then unable to resist the weakened *hashashiyyin's* renewed attack.

System: To convert a bit of her blood to poison, the Assamite's player spends at least one blood point and rolls Willpower (difficulty 6). If this roll is successful, and the Assamite successfully hits (but not necessarily damages) her opponent, the target loses a number of Stamina points equal to the number of blood points converted into poison. The victim may resist the

poison with a Stamina + Fortitude roll (difficulty 6); successes achieved on the resistance roll subtract from the Assamite's successes to affect the target. The maximum number of blood points an Assamite may convert at any one time equals her Stamina. The number of successes scored indicates the duration of the Stamina loss.

1 success	One turn
2 successes	One hour
3 successes	One day
4 successes	One month
5 successes	Permanently (though Stamina may be bought back up with experience)

If a mortal's Stamina falls to zero through use of Scorpion's Touch, she becomes terminally ill and loses immunity to diseases, her body succumbing to sickness within the year unless she somehow manages to increase her Stamina again. If a Kindred's Stamina falls to zero, the vampire enters torpor and remains that way until one of her Stamina points returns. If a Kindred is *permanently* reduced to zero Stamina, she may recover from torpor only through mystical means.

To afflict her target with the poison, the Assamite must touch her target's flesh or hit that target with something that carries the venom. Many Assamites lubricate their weapons with the excretion, while others pool the toxin in their hands (or fleck their lips with the poison, for a "kiss of death") and press it to their opponents. Weapons so envenomed must be of the melee variety — arrows, sling stones, bullets and the like cannot carry enough of the stuff to do damage, and it drips off in flight. Players whose Assamites wish to spit at their targets must make a Stamina + Athletics roll (difficulty 6). No more than two blood points' worth of poison may be expectorated, and a Kindred may spit a distance of 10 feet for each point of Strength and/or Potence the character possesses. Assamites are immune to their own poison, but not the blood-venom of other Assamites.

••• Dagon's Call

This terrible and recently rediscovered power allows an Assamite to drown her target in his own blood. By concentrating, the Assamite bursts her target's blood vessels and fills his lungs with vitae that proceeds to strangle him from within. The blood actually constricts the target's body from the inside as it floods through his system; thus, it works even on unbreathing Kindred. Until the target collapses in agony or death throes, this power has no visible effect, and many Assamites prefer it because it leaves no trace of their presence.

System: The Assamite must touch her target prior to using Dagon's Call. Within an hour thereafter, the Assamite may issue the call, though she need not be in the presence or even in the line of sight of her target.

Invoking the power costs one Willpower point. The Assamite's player makes a contested Stamina roll against the target's Stamina; the difficulty of each roll is equal to the opponent's permanent Willpower score. The number of successes the Assamite achieves is the amount of damage, in health levels, the victim suffers. For an additional point of Willpower spent in the next turn, the Assamite may continue using Dagon's

Call by engaging in another contested Stamina roll. Damage from Dagon's Call is considered lethal. So long as the Assamite's player continues to spend Willpower, the character may continue rending her opponent from within.

•••• Baal's Caress

The penultimate use of blood as a weapon (short of diablerie itself), Baal's Caress allows the Assamite to transmute her blood into a virulent ichor that destroys any living or undead flesh it touches. In nights of yore, when Assamites led the charges of Saracen legions, the Assassins were often seen licking their blades, slicing open their tongues and lubricating their weapons with this foul secretion.

Baal's Caress may be used to augment any bladed weapon; everything from poisoned knives and swords to tainted fingernails and claws has been reported.

System: Baal's Caress does not increase the damage done by a given weapon, but that weapon inflicts aggravated damage rather than normal. No roll is necessary to activate this power, but one blood point is consumed per hit. For example, if an Assamite poisons his knife and strikes his opponent (even if he inflicts no damage), one blood point's worth of lubrication disappears. For this reason, many Assamites choose to coat their weapons with a significant quantity of blood. If the Assamite misses, no tainted blood is consumed.

••••• Taste of Death

A refinement of Baal's Caress, Taste of Death allows the Assamite to spit caustic blood at her target. The blood coughed forth with this power burns flesh and corrodes bone; some Assamites have been reported to vomit voluminous streams of vitae that reduce their targets to heaps of sludge.

System: The vampire may spit up to 10 feet for each dot of Strength and/or Potence he possesses. Hitting the target requires a Stamina + Athletics roll (difficulty 6). Each blood point spewed at the target inflicts two dice of aggravated damage, and there is no limit (other than the vampire's capacity and per-turn expenditure maximum) to the quantity of blood with which a target may be deluged.

Serpentis

Serpentis is the legacy of Set, his gift to his children. The Followers of Set carefully guard this Discipline's secrets, teaching the reptilian art only to those they deem worthy (almost never outsiders). Most Cainites fear the Setites purely because of this Discipline, the way of the serpent and the tempter. Serpentis can evoke an almost primordial fear in others, particularly those who recall the tale of Eden. After all, hiss the Setites, the serpent was an evil older than even Caine himself.

• The Eyes of the Serpent

This power grants the Setite the legendary hypnotic gaze of the serpent. The Setite's eyes become gold with large black irises, and mortals in the character's vicinity find themselves strangely attracted to him. A mortal who meets the vampire's beguiling gaze is immobilized. Until the character takes his eyes off his mortal victim, the person is frozen in place.

System: No roll is required, but this power can be avoided if the mortal takes care not to look into the Setite's eyes. Vampires and other supernatural creatures (Lupines, mages, *et al.*) can also be affected by this power if the Setite's player makes a Willpower roll (difficulty 9). If attacked or otherwise harmed, supernatural creatures can spend a point of Willpower to break the spell.

•• The Tongue of the Asp

The Setite may lengthen her tongue at will, splitting it into a fork like that of a serpent. The tongue may reach 18 inches, and makes a terrifyingly effective weapon in close combat.

System: The tongue's razor fork opens aggravated wounds (difficulty 6, Strength damage). If the Setite wounds her enemy, she may drink blood from the target on the next turn as though she had sunk her fangs into the victim's neck. Horrifying though it is, the tongue's caress is very like the Kiss, and even strikes mortal victims helpless with fear and ecstasy. Additionally, the tongue is highly sensitive to vibrations, enabling the vampire to function effectively in the darkness the clan prefers. By flickering her tongue in and out of her mouth, the vampire can halve any penalties relating to darkness (p. 209).

••• The Skin of the Adder

By calling upon her Blood, the vampire may transform her skin into a mottled, scaly hide. A vampire in this form becomes more supple and flexible. The Path of the Warrior (a line of

Setites who adhere to the ancient warrior-codes of Egypt) makes much use of this power.

System: The vampire spends one blood point and one Willpower point. The vampire's skin becomes scaly and mottled; this, combined with the character's increased flexibility, reduces soak difficulties to 5. The vampire may use her Stamina to soak aggravated damage from claws and fangs, but not from fire, sunlight or other magical energies. The vampire's mouth widens and fangs lengthen, enabling her bite to inflict an extra die of damage. Finally, the vampire may slip through any opening wide enough to fit her head through.

The vampire's Appearance drops to 1, and she is obviously inhuman if observed with any degree of care, though casual passersby might not notice if the vampire is in darkness or wearing heavy clothing.

•••• The Form of the Cobra

The Setite may change his form into that of a huge black cobra. The serpent weighs as much as the vampire's human form, stretches over 10 feet long, and is as thick as a woman's thigh. The Form of the Cobra grants several advantages, including a venomous bite, the ability to slither through small holes, and a greatly enhanced sense of smell. The character may use any Disciplines while in this form save those that require hands (such as Feral Claws).

System: The Setite spends one blood point; the change is automatic, but takes three turns. Clothing and small personal possessions transform with the vampire; the vampire remains in serpent form until the next dawn, unless he desires to change back sooner. The Storyteller may allow the Setite bonus dice on all Perception rolls related to smell, but the difficulties for all hearing rolls are increased by two. The cobra's bite inflicts damage equal to the vampire's, but the vampire does not need to grapple his victim; furthermore, the poison delivered is fatal to mortals.

●●●●● The Heart of Darkness

The Setite with mastery of Serpentis may pull her heart from her body. She can even use this ability on other Cainites, although this requires several hours of gruesome surgery. Only the new moon, the invisible moon, may grant this power success. If performed under any other moon, the rite fails. Upon removing her heart, the Setite places it in a small clay urn, and then carefully hides or buries the urn. She cannot be staked by any wood that pierces her breast, and finds it easier to resist frenzy. The heart is the seat of emotion, after all, and so the difficulties of all rolls to resist frenzy are two lower.

Setites are careful to keep their hearts safe from danger. If someone seizes her heart, the Setite is completely at that person's mercy. The Setite heart can be destroyed only by casting it into a fire or exposing it to sunlight. If this happens, however, the Setite dies where she stands, boiling away into a blistering heap of ash and blackened bone. Plunging a wooden stake into an exposed heart drives the Setite into instant torpor.

A Setite may carry her heart with her, or have several false hearts buried in different places. A Setite often avoids her heart's hiding place, to deter discovery. Those wise in Setite lore whisper that the corrupt elders of the clan often hold their underlings' hearts, the better to control the errant hatchlings.

System: This power requires no roll. Those who witness a Setite pull his heart from his breast (or cut the heart from another vampire) must make Courage rolls. Failure indicates anything from strong uneasiness to complete revulsion, possibly even Rötschreck.

Thaumaturgy

The Discipline of Thaumaturgy encompasses blood magic and other sorcerous arts. Thaumaturgy is the unique possession of the Tremere and one of its most jealously guarded secrets. Certain Kindred rumors even speak of mystic cabals of Tremere that hunt down those thaumaturges who are not members of the Warlocks' clan.

Clan Tremere created this Discipline by combining mortal wizardry with the power of vampiric vitae. Though its existence is not widely known by mortal mages and wizards, it is seen as a disreputable aberration of true magick by those familiar with it.

Thaumaturgy is a versatile and powerful Discipline. Like Necromancy, its practice is divided into two parts: paths and rituals. Thaumaturgical paths are applications of the vampire's knowledge of blood magic, allowing her to create effects at her whim. Rituals are more formulaic in nature, most akin to the ancient magical "spells" of bygone nights. Because so many different paths and rituals are available to the arcane Tremere, one never knows what to expect when confronted with a practitioner of this Discipline.

When a character first learns Thaumaturgy, the player selects a path for the character. That path is considered the character's primary path, and she automatically receives one dot in it, as well as one Level One ritual. Thereafter, whenever the character increases her level in Thaumaturgy, her score in the primary path increases by one as well. Rituals are learned separately, as part of a story; players need not pay experience points for their characters to learn rituals, though they must find someone to teach the rituals in question.

Path ratings never exceed Level Five, though the overall Thaumaturgy score may (higher levels of Disciplines will be covered in future products). If a character reaches Level Five in her primary path and increases her Thaumaturgy score afterward, she may allocate her "free" path dot to a different path. Thaumaturges may create their own paths (through player and Storyteller collaboration) once they achieve the sixth level of Thaumaturgy.

Many vampires (wisely) fear the Discipline of Thaumaturgy. It is a very potent and mutable Discipline, and almost anything the Kindred wishes may be accomplished through its magic.

Thaumaturgical Paths

Paths define the types of magic a vampire can perform. A vampire typically learns his primary path from his sire, though it is not unknown for some vampires to study under many different tutors and learn all their secrets.

As mentioned before, the first path a character learns is considered her primary path and increases automatically as the character advances in the Discipline itself. Secondary paths may be learned once the character has acquired two or more dots in her primary path, and they must be raised separately with experience points. Furthermore, a character's rating in her primary path must always be at least one dot higher than any of her secondary paths until she has mastered her primary path. Once the character has achieved mastery of the fifth level of her primary path, secondary paths may be increased to that level.

Each time the character invokes one of the powers of a Thaumaturgical path, the thaumaturge's player must spend a blood point and make a Willpower roll against a difficulty of the power's level +3. Only one success is required to invoke a path's effect—path levels, not successes, govern the power of blood magic. Failure on this roll indicates that the blood magic fails, while a botch signifies that the character loses a *permanent* Willpower point. Obviously, Thaumaturgy is not an art in which one merely "dabbles."

The Path of Blood

Almost every Tremere studies the Path of Blood as her primary path. It encompasses some of the most fundamental principles of Thaumaturgy, based as it is on the manipulation of Kindred vitae. If a player wishes to select another path as her character's primary path, she'd better have a good reason (though choosing a different path is by no means unheard of).

● A Taste for Blood

This power was developed as a means of testing a foe's might —an extremely important ability in the tumultuous early nights of Clan Tremere. By merely tasting the blood of his subject, the thaumaturge may determine how much vitae remains in the

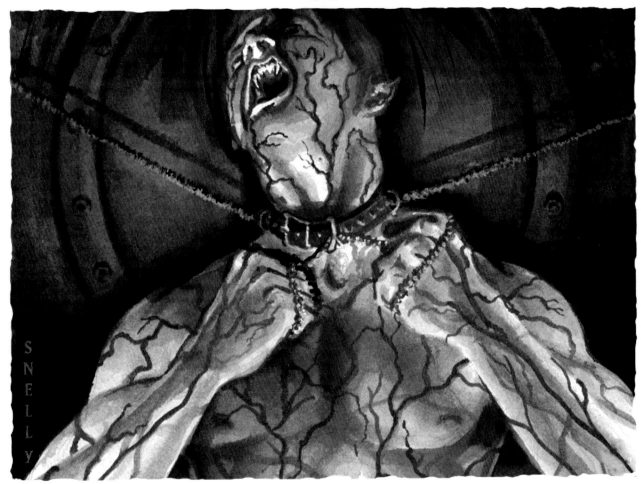

subject and, if the subject is a vampire, how recently he has fed, his approximate generation and, with three or more successes, whether he has recently committed diablerie.

System: The number of successes achieved on the roll determines how much information the thaumaturge gleans and how accurate it is.

●● BLOOD RAGE

This power allows a vampire to force another Kindred to expend blood against his will. The thaumaturge must touch her subject for this power to work, though only the lightest contact is necessary. A vampire affected by this power might feel a physical rush as the thaumaturge heightens his Physical Attributes, or may even find himself on the brink of frenzy as his stores of vitae are mystically depleted.

System: Each success forces the subject to spend one blood point immediately in the way the thaumaturge desires. Note that blood points forcibly spent in this manner may exceed the normal "per turn" maximum indicated by the victim's generation. Each success gained also increases the subject's difficulty to resist frenzy by one.

●●● BLOOD OF POTENCY

The thaumaturge gains such control over his own blood that he may effectively "concentrate" it, making it more powerful for a short time. In effect, he may temporarily lower his own generation with this power. This power may be used only once per night.

System: Successes earned on the Willpower roll must be spent both to decrease the vampire's generation and to maintain the change. One success allows the character to lower his generation by one step for one hour. Each success grants the Kindred either one step down in generation *or* one hour of effect. If the vampire is diablerized while this power is in effect, it wears off immediately and the diablerist gains power appropriate to the thaumaturge's actual generation. Furthermore, any mortals Embraced by the thaumaturge are born to the generation appropriate to their sire's original generation (e.g., a 10th-generation Tremere who has reduced his effective generation to eighth still produces 11th-generation childer).

Once the effect wears off, any blood over the character's blood pool maximum dilutes, leaving the character at his regular blood pool maximum. Thus, if a 12th-generation Tremere (maximum blood pool of 11) decreased his generation to ninth (maximum blood pool 14), ingested 14 blood points, and had this much vitae in his system when the power wore off, his blood pool would immediately drop to 11.

●●●● THEFT OF VITAE

A thaumaturge using this power siphons vitae from her subject. She need never come in contact with the subject — blood literally streams out in a physical torrent from the subject to the Kindred (though it is often mystically absorbed and need not enter through the mouth).

System: The number of successes determines how many blood points the Tremere transfers from the subject. The subject must be visible to the thaumaturge and within 50 feet. Using this power is like drinking from the subject — used three times on the same Kindred, it creates a blood bond on the part of the thaumaturge! This power is obviously quite spectacular, and Camarilla princes justifiably consider its public use a breach of the Masquerade.

● ● ● ● ● CAULDRON OF BLOOD

A thaumaturge using this power boils her subject's blood in his veins like water on a stove. The Kindred must touch her subject, and it is this contact that simmers the subject's blood. This power is always fatal to mortals, and causes great damage to even the mightiest vampires.

System: The number of successes gained determines how many blood points are brought to boil. The subject suffers one health level of aggravated damage for each point boiled (individuals with Fortitude may soak this damage *using only their Fortitude dice*). A single success kills any mortal, though some ghouls are said to have survived.

THE LURE OF FLAMES

This path grants the thaumaturge the ability to conjure forth mystical flames — small fires at first, but skilled magicians may create great conflagrations. The Lure of Flames is greatly feared, as fire is one of the surest ways to bring Final Death upon a vampire. See "Fire" (p. 227) for more information on how vampires suffer from flame.

Fire created by this path is not "natural." In fact, many vampires believe the flames to be conjured from Hell itself.

Fire conjured by The Lure of Flames must be released for it to have any effect. Thus, a "palm of flame" does not burn the vampire's hand and cause an aggravated wound — it merely produces light. Once the flame has been released, however, it burns normally and the character has no control over it.

System: The number of successes determines how accurately the thaumaturge places the flame in his desired location. One success is all that is necessary to conjure a flame in one's hand, while five successes place a flame anywhere in the Kindred's line of sight.

Individual descriptions are not provided for each level of this path — fire is fire, after all. The chart below describes the path level required to generate a specific amount of flame. To soak the damage at all, of course, a vampire must have the Fortitude Discipline.

- ●   Candle (difficulty 3 to soak, one health level of aggravated damage/turn)
- ● ●   Palm of flame (difficulty 4 to soak, one health level of aggravated damage/turn)
- ● ● ●   Campfire (difficulty 5 to soak, two health levels of aggravated damage/turn)
- ● ● ● ●   Bonfire (difficulty 7 to soak, two health levels of aggravated damage/turn)
- ● ● ● ● ●   Inferno (difficulty 9 to soak, three health levels of aggravated damage/turn)

MOVEMENT OF THE MIND

This path gives the thaumaturge the ability to move objects telekinetically through the mystic power of blood. At higher levels, even flight is possible (but be careful who sees you…). Objects under the character's control may be manipulated as if she held them — they may be lifted, spun, juggled or even "thrown," though creating enough force to inflict actual damage requires mastery of the fourth level or greater. Some thaumaturges skilled in this path even use it to guard their havens, animating swords, axes and firearms to ward off intruders.

This path may frighten and disconcert onlookers. Many people are quite put off when the pages of a book turn by themselves!

System: The number of successes indicates the duration of the thaumaturge's control over the object (or subject). Each success allows one turn of manipulation, though the Kindred may attempt to maintain control after this time by making a new roll (she need not spend additional blood to maintain control). If the roll is successful, control is maintained. If a thaumaturge loses or relaxes control over an object and later manipulates it again, her player must spend another blood point, as a new attempt is being made.

If this power is used to manipulate a living being, the subject may attempt to resist. In this case, the thaumaturge and the subject make opposed Willpower rolls each turn the control is exercised.

Like The Lure of Flames, individual power levels are not provided for this path — consult the chart below to see how much weight a thaumaturge may control. Once a Kindred reaches Level Three, she may levitate herself and "fly" at approximately running speed, no matter how much she weighs, though the weight restrictions apply if she manipulates other objects or subjects. Once a Kindred achieves Level Four, she may "throw" objects at a Strength equal to her level of mastery.

•	One pound
••	20 pounds
•••	200 pounds
••••	500 pounds
•••••	1000 pounds

THE PATH OF CONJURING

Invoking objects "out of thin air" has been a staple of occult and supernatural legend since long before the rise of the Tremere. This Thaumaturgical path enables powerful conjurations limited only by the mind of the practitioner.

Objects summoned via this path bear two distinct characteristics. They are uniformly "generic" in that each object summoned, if summoned again, would look exactly as it did at first. For example, a knife would be precisely the same knife if created twice; the two would be indistinguishable. Even a *specific* knife — the one a character's father used to threaten her — would appear identical every time it was conjured. A rat would have repeated "tiled" patterns over its fur, and a garbage can would have the exact same fluted texture over its surface. Additionally, conjured objects bear no flaws: Weapons have no

dents or scratches, tools have no distinguishing marks, and computers have featureless casings.

The limit on the size of conjured objects appears to be that of the conjurer; nothing larger than the thaumaturge can be created. The conjurer must also have some degree of familiarity with the object he wishes to call forth. Simply working from a picture or imagination calls for a higher difficulty, while objects with which the character is intimately familiar (such as the knife described above) may actually lower the difficulty, at the Storyteller's discretion.

When a player rolls to conjure something, the successes gained on the roll indicate the quality of the summoned object. One success yields a shoddy, imperfect creation, while five successes garner the thaumaturge a nearly perfect replica.

• SUMMON THE SIMPLE FORM

At this level of mastery, the conjurer may create simple, inanimate objects. The object cannot have any moving parts and may not be made of multiple materials. For example, the conjurer may summon a steel baton, a lead pipe, a wooden stake or a chunk of granite.

System: Each turn the conjurer wishes to keep the object in existence, another Willpower point must be spent or the object vanishes.

•• PERMANENCY

At this level, the conjurer no longer needs to pay Willpower costs to keep an object in existence. The object is, as this level's name suggests, permanent, though simple objects are still all that may be created.

System: The player must invest three blood points in an object to make it real.

••• MAGIC OF THE SMITH

The Kindred may now conjure complex objects of multiple components and with moving parts. For example, the thaumaturge can create guns, bicycles, chainsaws or cellular phones.

System: Objects created via Magic of the Smith are permanent items and cost five blood points to conjure. Particularly complex items often require a Knowledge roll (Crafts, Science, etc.) in addition to the basic roll.

•••• REVERSE CONJURATION

This power allows the conjurer to "banish" into nonexistence any object previously called forth via this path.

System: This is an extended success roll. The conjurer must accumulate as many successes as the original caster received when creating the object in question.

••••• POWER OVER LIFE

This power cannot create true life, though it can summon forth some truly impressive simulacra. Creatures (and people) summoned with this power lack the free will to act on their own, instead mindlessly following the simple instructions of their conjurer.

System: The player spends 10 blood points. Imperfect and impermanent, creatures summoned via this path are too complex to exist for long. Within a week after their conjuration, the simulacra vanish into insubstantiality.

HANDS OF DESTRUCTION

This Path is practiced almost exclusively by the thaumaturges of the Sabbat. Though it is not widely seen outside that sect, a few Camarilla Tremere have managed to learn the secrets of this path over the centuries. The Hands of Destruction has an infamous history, and some Tremere refuse to practice it due to rumors that it is demonic in origin.

Brutal and painful, this path provides thaumaturges with offensive capabilities not found in other, less martial paths. It embodies the violent nature of its Sabbat wielders, existing solely to cause entropy and decay.

• DECAY

This power accelerates the decrepitude of its target, causing it to wither, rot or otherwise break down. The target must be inanimate, though dead organic matter can be affected.

System: If the roll is successful, the inanimate object touched by the thaumaturge ages 10 years for every minute the Kindred touches it. If the vampire breaks physical contact and wishes to age the object again, another blood point must be spent and another roll must be made.

•• GNARL WOOD

This power warps and bends wooden objects. Though the wood is otherwise undamaged, this power often leaves the objects completely useless. This power may also be used to swell or contract wood, in addition to bending it into unwholesome shapes. Unlike other powers of this path, Gnarl Wood requires merely a glance rather than physical contact.

System: Fifty pounds of visible wood may be gnarled for each blood point spent on this power (the thaumaturge may expend as much blood as she likes on this power, up to her per-turn generational maximum). It is also possible to warp multiple visible objects — like all the stakes an opposing team of vampire-hunters wields.

••• ACIDIC TOUCH

The thaumaturge secretes a bilious, acidic fluid from any portion of his body. The viscous acid corrodes metal, destroys wood and causes horrendous chemical burns to living tissue.

System: The player spends blood to create the acid — the blood literally transmutes into the volatile secretion. One blood point creates enough acid to burn through a quarter-inch of steel plate or three inches of wood. The damage from an acid-augmented hand-to-hand attack is aggravated and costs one blood point per turn to use. A thaumaturge is immune to her own acidic touch.

•••• ATROPHY

This power withers a victim's limb, leaving only a desiccated, almost mummified husk of bone and skin. The effects are instantaneous; in mortals, they are also irreversible.

System: The victim may resist the effects of Atrophy by scoring three or more successes on a Stamina + Athletics roll (difficulty 8). Failure means the limb is permanently and completely crippled. Partial resistance is possible: One success indicates that difficulties involving the use of the arm increase by two, though these effects are still permanent with regard to mortals. Two successes signify that difficulties increase by one. Vampires afflicted by this power may spend five blood points to rejuvenate atrophied limbs. Mortals are permanently crippled. This power affects only limbs (arms and legs); it does not work on victims' heads, torsos, etc.

••••• TURN TO DUST

This fearsome power accelerates decrepitude in its victims. Mortals literally crumble to dust at the mere touch of a skilled thaumaturge, aged beyond death and into putrefaction.

System: Each success on the roll ages the victim by 10 years. A potential victim may resist with a Stamina + Courage roll (difficulty 8), but must accumulate more successes than the thaumaturge's activation roll — it's an all-or-nothing affair. If the victim succeeds, he does not age at all. If he does not acquire more successes than the thaumaturge, he ages the full amount. Obviously, this power, while it affects vampires, has no detrimental effect on them (they're immortal). At most, a Kindred victim withers slightly (-1 to Appearance) for one night.

RITUALS

Rituals are Thaumaturgical formulas, meticulously researched and prepared, that create powerful magical effects. Rituals are less versatile than paths, as their effects are singular and straightforward, but they are better suited toward specific ends.

All thaumaturges have the ability to use rituals, though each individual ritual must be learned separately. By acquainting herself with the arcane practice of blood magic, the thaumaturge gains the capacity to manipulate these focused effects.

Thaumaturgical rituals are rated from 1 to 5, each level corresponding to both the level of mastery of Thaumaturgy the would-be caster must possess and the relative power of the ritual itself. Unless stated otherwise, a ritual requires five minutes per level to cast. For example, Andreas the Tremere wishes to cast Ward Versus Ghouls, a Level Two Ritual. Invoking this ritual requires 10 minutes, and Andreas must know Thaumaturgy at 2 or greater.

Casting rituals requires a successful Intelligence + Occult roll, for which the difficulty equals 3 + the level of the ritual (maximum 9). Only one success is required for a ritual to work, though certain spells may require more successes or have variable effects based on how well the caster's roll goes. This uncertainty of effect is a recent development; Tremere rituals formerly worked infallibly, so long as the caster executed them successfully. Many thaumaturges fear that the movements of awakening Antediluvians have caused imbalance in the flow of magic, making the success of rituals more precarious than in previous nights. Should a roll to activate a ritual fail, the Storyteller is encouraged to create strange occurrences or side effects, or even make it appear that the ritual was successful, only to reveal its failure at a later time. A botched ritual roll may even indicate a catastrophic failure or summon an ill-tempered demon....

Rituals sometimes require special ingredients or reagents to work — these are noted in each ritual's description. Common components include herbs, animal bones, ceremonial items, feathers, eye of newt, tongue of toad, etc. Acquiring magical components for a powerful ritual may form the basis for an entire story.

At the first level of Thaumaturgy, the vampire automatically gains a single Level One ritual. To learn further rituals, the thaumaturge must find someone to teach him, or learn the ritual from a scroll, tome or other archive. Learning a new ritual can take anywhere from a few nights (Level One ritual) to months or years (Level Five ritual). Some dread Warlocks have studied individual rituals for decades, or even centuries. Precisely what these rituals do is unknown, but their effects are surely grave.

Level One Rituals

Defense of the Sacred Haven

This ritual prevents sunlight from entering an area within 20 feet of this ritual's casting. A mystical darkness blankets the area, keeping the baneful light at bay. Sunlight reflects off windows or magically fails to pass through doors or other portals. The caster draws sigils in her own blood on all the affected windows and doors, and the ritual lasts as long as the Tremere stays within the 20-foot radius.

System: This ritual requires one hour to perform, during which the thaumaturge recites incantations and inscribes glyphs. One blood point is required for this ritual to work.

Wake with Evening's Freshness

This ritual allows a Tremere to awaken at any sign of danger, especially during the day. If any potentially harmful circumstances arise, the Tremere immediately rises, ready to face the problem. This ritual requires the ashes of burned feathers to be spread over the area in which the Kindred wishes to sleep.

System: This ritual must be performed immediately before the Tremere settles down to slumber for the day. Any interruption to the ceremonial casting renders the ritual ineffective. If danger arises, the Tremere awakens and may ignore the Humanity dice pool limit rule for the first two turns of consciousness. Thereafter, the penalty takes effect, but the Tremere will have already risen and will be able to address problematic situations.

Communicate with Kindred Sire

By enacting this ritual, a Tremere may join minds with her sire, speaking telepathically with him over any distance. The communication may continue until the ritual expires or until either party ends the conversation. The caster must possess an item once owned by her sire for the ritual to work.

System: The caster must meditate for 30 minutes to create the connection. Conversation may be maintained for 10 minutes per success on the activation roll.

DEFLECTION OF WOODEN DOOM

This ritual protects the Tremere from being staked, whether or not she is resting or active. While this ritual is in effect, the first stake that would pierce the Tremere's heart disintegrates in the attacker's hand. A stake merely held *near* the Tremere is unaffected; for this ritual to work, the stake must actively be used in an attempt to impale the vampire.

System: The thaumaturge must surround herself with a circle of wood for a full hour. Any wood will work: furniture, sawdust, raw timber, 2' x 4's, whatever. The circle must remain unbroken, however. At the end of the hour, the vampire places a wooden splinter under her tongue. If this splinter is removed, the ritual is nullified. This ritual lasts until the following dawn or dusk.

DEVIL'S TOUCH

The Tremere use this ritual to place curses upon mortals who earn their ire. Using this ritual marks an individual invisibly, causing all those who come in contact with him to receive him poorly. The mortal is treated as the most loathsome individual conceivable, and all who deal with him do anything in their power to make him miserable. Even bums spit at an afflicted individual, and children taunt him and barrage him with vulgarities.

System: The effects of this ritual last one night, disappearing as the sun rises. The mortal (it doesn't work on vampires) must be present when the ritual is invoked, and a penny must be placed somewhere on his person (in a pocket, shoe, etc.).

LEVEL TWO RITUALS

WARD VERSUS GHOULS

Wary Tremere created this ritual to protect themselves from the minions of vengeful rivals. By invoking this ritual, the Tremere creates a glyph that causes great pain to any ghouls who come in contact with it. The Kindred pours a point's worth of blood over the object he wishes to ward (a piece of parchment, a coin, a doorknob, etc.), and recites the incantation, which takes 10 minutes. In 10 hours, the magical ward is complete, and will inflict excruciating pain on any ghoul unfortunate enough to touch the warded object.

System: Ghouls who touch warded objects suffer three dice of lethal damage. This damage occurs again if the ghoul touches the object further; indeed, a ghoul who consciously wishes to touch a warded object must spend a point of Willpower to do so.

This ritual wards only *one* object — if inscribed on the side of a car, the ward affects only that door or fender, not the whole car. Wards may be placed on weapons, even bullets, though this usually works best on small-caliber weapons. Bullets often warp upon firing, however, and for a ward to remain intact on a fired round, the player needs five successes on the Firearms roll.

PRINCIPAL FOCUS OF VITAE INFUSION

This ritual imbues a quantity of blood within the object upon which the ritual is cast. The object must be small enough for the vampire to carry in both hands, and it may be as small as a dime. After the ritual is conducted, the object takes on a reddish hue and becomes slick to the touch. At a mental command, the thaumaturge may release the object from its enchantment, causing it to break down into a pool of blood. This blood may serve whatever purpose the vampire desires; many Tremere wear enchanted baubles to ensure they have emergency supplies of vitae.

System: An object may store only one blood point of vitae. If a Kindred wishes to make an infused focus for an ally, she may do so, but the blood contained within must be her own (and if the ally then drinks the blood, he is one step closer to the blood bond). The ally must be present at the creation of the focus.

LEVEL THREE RITUALS

INCORPOREAL PASSAGE

Use of this ritual allows the thaumaturge to make herself insubstantial. The caster becomes completely immaterial and thus is able to walk through walls, pass through closed doors, escape manacles, etc. The caster also becomes invulnerable to physical attacks for the duration of the ritual. The caster must follow a straight path through any physical objects, and may not draw back. Thus, a Kindred may walk through a solid wall, but may not walk down through the earth (as it would be impossible to reach the other side before the ritual lapsed). This ritual requires that the caster carry a shard from a shattered mirror to hold her image as she moves insubstantially.

System: This ritual lasts a number of hours equal to the number of successes scored on a Wits + Survival roll (difficulty 6). The thaumaturge may prematurely end the ritual (and, thus, her incorporeality) by turning the mirror shard away so that it no longer reflects her image.

PAVIS OF FOUL PRESENCE

The Tremere joke privately that this is their "ritual for the Ventrue." Kindred who invoke the Presence Discipline on the subject of this ritual find the effects of their Discipline reversed, as if they had used the power on *themselves*. For example, a vampire using Presence to instill utter fear in a Kindred under the influence of this ritual feels the fear herself. This ritual is an unbroken secret among the Tremere, and the Warlocks maintain that its use is unknown outside their clan. The magical component for this ritual is a length of blue silk, which must be worn around the neck of the person protected by the magic.

System: This ritual lasts until the sunrise after it is enacted. Note that the Presence Discipline power must actually *succeed* before being reversed by the ritual.

LEVEL FOUR RITUAL

BONE OF LIES

This ritual enchants a mortal bone so that anyone who holds it must tell the truth. The bone in question is often a skull, though any part of the skeleton will do — some Tremere use strings of teeth, necklaces of finger joints or wands fashioned from ribs or arms. The bone grows blacker as it compels its holder to tell the truth, until it has turned completely ebony and has no magic left.

This ritual binds the spirit of the individual to whom the bone belonged in life; it is this spirit who wrests the truth from the potential liar. The spirit absorbs the lies intended to be told by the bone's holder, and as it compels more truth, it becomes more and more corrupt. If summoned forth, this spirit reflects the sins it has siphoned from the defeated liar (in addition to anger over its unwilling servitude). For this reason, anonymous bones are often used in the ritual, and the bone is commonly buried after it has been used to its full extent. A specific bone may never be used twice for this ritual.

System: The bone imbued with this magical power must be at least 200 years old and must absorb 10 blood points on the night that the ritual is cast. Each lie the holder wishes to tell consumes one of these blood points, and the holder *must* speak the truth immediately thereafter. When all 10 blood points have been consumed, the bone magic ceases to work any longer.

LEVEL FIVE RITUAL

BLOOD CONTRACT

This ritual creates an unbreakable agreement between the two parties who sign it. The contract must be written in the caster's blood and signed in the blood of whoever applies their name to the document. This ritual takes three nights to enact fully, after which both parties are compelled to fulfill the terms of the contract.

System: This ritual is best handled by the Storyteller, who may bring those who sign the blood contract into compliance by whatever means necessary (it is not unknown for demons to materialize and enforce adherence to certain blood contracts). The only way to terminate the ritual is to complete the terms of the contract or to burn the document itself. One blood point is consumed in the creation of the document, and an additional blood point is consumed by those who sign it.

VICISSITUDE

Vicissitude is the signature power of the Tzimisce and is almost unknown outside the clan. Similar in some respects to Protean, Vicissitude allows the Fiends to shape and sculpt their own or others' flesh and bone. When a Tzimisce uses Vicissitude to alter mortals, ghouls and vampires of higher generation, the effects of the power are permanent; vampires of equal or lower generation may heal the effects of Vicissitude as though they were aggravated wounds. Naturally, a wielder can always reshape her own flesh.

Note that while this Discipline permits powerful and horrific effects, the wielder must obtain skin-to-skin contact and must often physically sculpt the desired result. This even applies to the use of the power on oneself. Tzimisce skilled in Vicissitude are often inhumanly beautiful; those less skilled are simply inhuman.

Note: Nosferatu *always* "heal" back Vicissitude alterations, at least the ones that make them better-looking. The ancient curse of the clan may not be circumvented through Vicissitude, except possibly by the Antediluvian of the Tzimisce clan (who is rumored to have been destroyed anyway).

• MALLEABLE VISAGE

A vampire with this power may alter her own bodily parameters: height, build, voice, facial features and skin tone, among other things. Such changes are cosmetic and minor in scope — no more than a foot of height gained or lost, for example. She must physically mold the alteration, literally shaping her flesh into the desired result.

System: The player must spend a blood point for each body part to be changed, then roll Intelligence + Body Crafts (difficulty 6). To duplicate another person or voice requires a Perception + Body Crafts roll (difficulty 8), and five successes are required for a flawless copy; fewer successes leave minute, or not-so-minute, flaws. Increasing one's Appearance Trait is difficulty 10, thus usually requiring Willpower expenditure for even minimal success, and a botch permanently reduces the Attribute by one.

•• FLESHCRAFT

This power is similar to Malleable Visage, above, but allows the vampire to perform drastic, grotesque alterations on other creatures. Tzimisce often use this power to transform their servitors into monstrous guards, the better to frighten foes. Only flesh (skin, muscle, fat and cartilage, but not bone) may be transformed.

System: The vampire must grapple the intended victim, while her player makes a successful Dexterity + Body Crafts roll (difficulty variable: 5 for a crude yank-and-tuck, up to 9 for precise transformations). A vampire who wishes to increase another's Appearance Trait does so as described under Malleable Visage; reducing the Attribute is considerably easier (difficulty 5), though truly inspired disfigurement may dictate a higher difficulty. In either case, each success increases/reduces the Attribute by one.

A vampire may use this power to move clumps of skin, fat and muscle tissue, thus providing additional padding where needed. For each success scored on a Dexterity + Body Crafts roll (difficulty 8), the vampire may increase the subject's soak dice pool by one, at the expense of either a point of Strength or a health level (vampire's choice).

••• BONECRAFT

This terrible power allows a vampire to manipulate bone in the same manner that flesh is shaped. In conjunction with Fleshcraft, above, this power enables a Vicissitude practitioner to deform a victim (or herself) beyond recognition. This power should be used in conjunction with the flesh-shaping arts, unless the vampire wants to inflict injury on the victim (see below).

BODY CRAFTS

Vicissitude is as much an art as it is a power, and vampires who wish to use it well must learn a particular version of the Crafts Skill (p. 124), known as Body Crafts. This Skill enables its possessor to make all manner of alterations to living and dead flesh and bone. The Skill also gives insight into more mundane techniques; many Tzimisce are skilled at flaying, bone-carving, embalming, taxidermy, tattooing and piercing.

System: The vampire's player makes a Strength + Body Crafts roll (difficulties as above). Bonecraft may be used without the flesh-shaping arts, as an offensive weapon. Each success scored on the Strength + Body Crafts roll (difficulty 7) inflicts one health level of lethal damage on the victim, as his bones rip, puncture and slice their way out of his skin.

The vampire may utilize this power (on herself or others) to form spikes or talons of bone, either on the knuckles as an offensive weapon or all over the body as defensive "quills." If bone spikes are used, the vampire or victim takes one health level of lethal damage (the vampire's comes from having the very sharp bone pierce through his skin — this weaponry doesn't come cheaply). In the case of quills, the subject takes a number of health levels equal to five minus the number of successes (a botch kills the subject or sends the vampire into torpor). These health levels may be healed normally. Knuckle spikes inflict Strength +1 lethal damage, while defensive quills inflict a hand-to-hand attacker's Strength in lethal damage unless the attacker scores three or more successes on the attack roll (the defender still takes damage normally). Quills also enable the vampire or altered subject to add two to all damage inflicted via holds, clinches or tackles.

A vampire who scores five or more successes on the Strength + Body Crafts roll may cause a rival vampire's rib cage to curve inward and pierce the heart. While this does not send a vampire into torpor, it does cause the affected vampire to lose half his blood points, as the seat of his vitae ruptures in a shower of gore.

●●●● HORRID FORM

The Tzimisce use this power to become hideous monsters; naturally, this provides great advantages in combat. The vampire's stature increases to a full eight feet; the skin becomes a sickly greenish-gray or grayish-black chitin; the arms become apelike and ropy, tipped with ragged black nails; and the face warps into something out of a nightmare. A row of spines sprouts from the vertebrae, and the external carapace exudes a foul-smelling grease.

System: The Horrid Form costs two blood points to awaken. All Physical Attributes (Strength, Dexterity, Stamina) increase by three, but all Social Attributes drop to zero, save when dealing with others also in Horrid Form. However, a vampire in Horrid Form who is trying to intimidate someone may substitute Strength for a Social Attribute! Damage inflicted in brawling combat increases by one due to the jagged ridges and bony knobs creasing the creature's hands.

●●●●● BLOODFORM

A vampire with this power can physically transform all or part of her body into sentient vitae. This blood is in all respects identical to the vampire's normal vitae; she can use it to nourish herself or others, create ghouls or establish blood bonds. If all this blood is imbibed or otherwise destroyed, the vampire meets Final Death.

System: The vampire may transform all or part of herself as she deems fit. Each leg can turn into two blood points worth of vitae, as can the torso; each arm, the head and the abdomen convert to one blood point. The blood can be reconverted to the body part, provided it is in contact with the vampire. If the blood has been utilized or destroyed, the vampire must spend a number of blood points equal to what was originally created to regrow the missing body part.

A vampire entirely in this form may not be staked, cut, bludgeoned or pierced, but can be burned or exposed to the sun. The vampire may ooze along, drip up walls and flow through the narrowest cracks, as though she were in Tenebrous Form (p. 169).

Mental Disciplines may be used, provided no eye contact or vocal utterance is necessary — and if a vampire in this form "washes" over a mortal or animal, that mortal must make a Courage roll (difficulty 8) or fly into a panic.

"It's not over, and it's not that easy."

Lisé sat in the gutter, trying to shove her windpipe back into her throat. Janelle squatted on the hood of the '74 Cadillac next to her, claws still out and dripping. There was blood on her jacket, too, but it didn't show against the black. She smiled a long, thin smile down at Lisé, the sort of smile a cat makes when it sees a broken-backed mouse still trying to get away.

"You're done, Lisé," she said. "But not right away. You get to last the night." Lisé made a noise deep in the wreck of her throat. It might have been "Go to hell." Janelle ignored her mumble, ignored the sound of sirens off in the distance. "But tomorrow night, I'm going to find you again, and I'm going to do the exact same thing to you. And I'm going to keep doing it every night until I get bored, or until the bishop tells me it's time. But try to leave the city, I'll find out and I'll kill you. Try to get help, and I'll find out and I'll kill you. Your choice — now or later."

Lisé spat blood and tried to stand. Idly, Janelle slapped her back down into the gutter, then stretched and slid down off the car's hood. "Tomorrow. Sundown. It's a date," she purred, and walked unhurriedly away from the light.

CHAPTER FIVE: RULES

The only reason to have rules in a game, especially a storytelling game like **Vampire**, is to more or less level the playing field. The Storyteller can adjudicate most things in her **Vampire** game, deciding on her own whether or not the characters accomplish the actions they attempt. But truly unbiased rulings need some sort of standard or precedent, just so everybody knows that everyone's getting the same treatment.

Hence, rules.

Vampire uses only a few basic rules to get things done, but these rules can have countless permutations in the context of the game. This chapter covers the very basics, such as rolling dice; more specific, detail-oriented rules can be found throughout the book. Don't worry about mastering all the permutations at once — learn these basic rules first, and then everything else will come naturally.

TIME

Over the course of the game, time is presumed to pass as it would in the normal world — Tuesday follows Monday, month after month, and so on. However, there's no need to roleplay out every second ticking away. There's a huge difference between the speeds at which "game" time and real time pass. Over a four-hour game session, a week, month or even year might pass in the setting of the game — or the entire session might be spent detailing the events of an action-packed half-hour. You can play out a combat turn by turn, taking it in three-second increments, or you can let months pass away in a few minutes of real time. (The passage of time without players taking any real actions is called "downtime"; learning to use this little trick can help the pacing of your game immensely.)

To help maintain a sense of the passage of time without resorting to tedious charts and the like, **Vampire** uses six basic units to describe game time:

• Turn — The amount of time you need to take a fairly simple action; this can range anywhere from three seconds to three minutes, depending on the pace of the current scene.

• Scene — Like the basic division of plays and movies, a scene is a compact period of action and interaction that takes place in a single location. This could be the storming of a Tremere chantry, or a moonlit conversation on a park bench. There are exactly as many turns in a scene as the scene requires — there might not even be any turns if the scene consists of nothing but dialogue and character interaction.

• Chapter — An independent part of a story, virtually always played out in one game session. It consists of a number of scenes interconnected by downtime (see below); essentially, like a chapter in a novel or an act in a play.

• Story — A full tale, complete with introduction, rising action and climax. Some stories can take several chapters to complete; others can be finished in one.

• Chronicle — A series of stories connected by the characters themselves and their ongoing narrative, possibly even by a common theme or overarching plot.

• Downtime — Time that is "glossed over" with description rather than played out turn by turn or scene by scene. If the Storyteller says, "You wait in the foyer for four hours before the prince's ghoul summons you," rather than actually letting the characters play out their wait, the Storyteller is considered to be invoking downtime. Downtime allows trivial or tedious passages of time to be played through quickly.

ACTIONS

Over the course of a game, your character will do many things. Some of these tasks are considered *actions*, while others aren't. Speeches and conversations aren't considered actions as such — but just about everything else, from throwing a punch at your sire to trying to decipher a code, is probably an action. One action typically takes one turn (see above) of game time to complete.

It's easy enough to attempt an action — just tell the Storyteller what your character's trying to do and how she plans to go about it. And most actions — crossing the street or loading a pistol, for instance — are easy enough to be considered automatically successful. However, if you're trying to cross a four-lane highway full of speeding trucks, or trying to reload while you're hanging from a fire escape by one hand, there's a chance you might fail. So when there's reasonable doubt whether an action will succeed or not, you may have to roll dice to determine the results.

ROLLING DICE

Although the Storyteller is within perfect rights to declare whether a given action succeeds or fails (usually for dramatic purposes), in many cases chance enters into the equation. Therefore, **Vampire** uses a simple, portable form of "chance in a pocket" — dice. To be specific, **Vampire** uses 10-sided dice; you can find these in any game store or even many bookstores. The Storyteller may need quite a few; players need plenty as well, but can share among themselves. Ten dice are all that a beginning character will need at a given time.

You roll dice whenever the outcome of an action is in doubt or the Storyteller thinks there's a chance your character might fail. Your character's strengths and weaknesses affect the number of dice you roll, and thus directly affect your chances of success.

RATINGS

Although your character's personality is limited only by your imagination, his capabilities are defined by his Traits — all of his innate and learned aptitudes and abilities. Each Trait is described by a rating of 1 to 5; a 1 in a Trait is barely competent, while a 5 is the pinnacle of human achievement. Most people's Traits range from 1 to 3; a 4 in a Trait indicates an exceptional person, while a 5 is nearly incomparable — among humans, at any rate. Think of this as similar to the "star" rating system of

movies and restaurants — a 1 is barely passable while a 5 is superb. It's also possible to have a zero in a Trait — this usually represents a skill that the character never learned, but some exceptions (such as the hideous Nosferatu's lack of an Appearance Trait) do occur.

x   Abysmal
•   Poor
••   Average
•••   Good
••••   Exceptional
••••• Superb

Whenever you roll dice, you roll one die for every dot in the appropriate Trait; for instance, if your character is trying to find something and he has three dots in Perception, you would roll three dice. However, you almost never simply roll the number of dice you have in an Attribute; raw potential is modified by skill, after all. The most common rolls in the game involve adding the dice gained from an Attribute (p. 115) to the dice gained from an Ability (p. 119).

For instance, if Veronica were trying to find a specific file in a cluttered clerk's office, the Storyteller might have her player Lynn roll Perception + Finance — an Attribute plus an Ability. In this case, Lynn would take two dice for Veronica's Perception of 2, plus as many dice as she had in Finance; Veronica has Finance 4, so Lynn gets four more dice from that. Veronica has a total of six dice to attempt her task. These dice are called the *dice pool* — in other words, the total number of dice you roll in a single turn. Most often, you'll calculate a dice pool for only one action at a time, although you can modify it to be able to perform multiple tasks in a turn (for more information, see the "Multiple Actions" sidebar).

Of course, you might not need to add an Ability to an Attribute for some rolls; for instance, there's no skill that will help Veronica heft a small safe. In such cases, Lynn would use only the dice from the Attribute — in this case, Strength.

There is absolutely no situation in which more than two Traits can add to a dice pool. What's more, if your dice pool involves a Trait whose maximum rating is 10 (such as Humanity or Willpower), you can't add any other Traits to your dice pool. It's effectively impossible for a normal human being to have more than 10 dice in a dice pool.

Elder vampires, on the other hand....

DIFFICULTIES

There's no point in rolling dice unless you know what results you're looking for. Whenever you try to perform an action, the Storyteller will decide on an appropriate *difficulty number* and tell you her decision. A difficulty is always a number between 2 and 10. Each time you score that number or higher on one of your dice, you're considered to have gained a *success*. For example, if an action's difficulty is a 6 and you roll a 3, 3, 8, 7 and 10, then you've scored three successes. The more you get, the better you do. You need only one success to perform most actions successfully, but that's considered a marginal success. If you score three or more, you succeed completely.

<hr>

REFLEXIVES

Not everything that your character actually *does* counts as an action. For instance, spending a blood point to increase an Attribute is considered to take less than a second of game time — no dice are rolled, and your character can do this while doing something else. Such a "free action" is called a *reflexive* — in essence, a feat that doesn't require taking an action to accomplish.

Reflexives include such activities as spending blood points to increase Attributes, soaking damage, making a Virtue check, or activating Celerity to take extra actions. They aren't considered actions in any real way — you don't have to subtract from your dice pool to soak damage while you're firing a gun, for example. Of course, you still have to be conscious to perform many reflexives, but they don't get in the way of anything else you want to do in a turn.

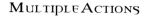

MULTIPLE ACTIONS

Occasionally, a player will want her character to perform more than one action in a turn — for example, firing a gun at two different targets, or climbing a ledge while kicking at pursuers below. In such situations, the player can attempt actions normally, though all actions suffer a penalty.

The player declares the total number of actions he wishes his character to attempt. He then subtracts a number of dice from his first dice pool equal to the total number of actions. Additional actions lose an extra die from their pools, cumulative; if a dice pool is reduced to zero or below in this manner, the action may not be attempted.

Example: Justin wishes his character, Hall the Nosferatu, to throw a punch while simultaneously dodging two incoming blows. Hall has Dexterity 3, Brawl 4 and Dodge 3. Justin calculates the dice pool for the punch (Dexterity 3 + Brawl 4 = 7 dice pool), then subtracts three dice from it (because of the three actions total), for a final dice pool of 4. The first dodge has a base dice pool of 6 (Dexterity 3 + Dodge 3), minus four (three for the number of actions, plus one for being the second multiple action), for a final dice pool of 2. The final dodge has a dice pool of 1 (6, minus three for the number of actions, minus an additional two for being the third action attempted). Hall had better be pretty lucky.

Vampires with the Discipline of Celerity (p. 153) may take multiple actions without subtracting dice from their dice pools. These extra actions may not themselves be divided into multiple actions.

Naturally, the lower the difficulty, the easier it is to score successes, and *vice versa*. Six is the default difficulty, indicating actions neither exceptionally tricky nor exceptionally easy to accomplish. *If the Storyteller or rulebook ever calls for you to make a roll, but doesn't give you a specific difficulty number, assume the task is difficulty 6.*

The Storyteller is the final authority on how difficult attempted actions are — if the task seems impossible, he'll make the difficulty appropriately high, while if the task seems routinely easy, the difficulty will be low (if the Storyteller decides you even have to roll at all). Particularly easy or difficult tasks might even demand difficulty numbers of 2 or 10; however, these should be extremely rare. A difficulty 2 task is so easy that's it's not really worth the trouble of a die roll, while a difficulty 10 action is almost impossible — you have an equal chance of botching (see below) as you do of succeeding, no matter how many dice you're rolling.

And, in case it needs to be said, a result of a 10 is always a success, no matter the difficulty number.

FAILURE

If you score no successes on a die roll, your character fails his attempted action. He misses his punch. His pitch is a ball instead of a strike. His attempt to persuade the prince falls flat. Failure, while usually disappointing, is not so catastrophic as a botch (below).

Example: Feodor, a Nosferatu, is attempting to spy on some suspicious-looking activities in one of the galleries of the sewers, and

The following charts should give you a good idea of how to combine difficulties and degrees of success. Italics indicate the average.

DIFFICULTIES

Three	Easy (installing software on a Macintosh)
Four	Routine (changing a tire)
Five	Straightforward (seducing someone who's already "in the mood")
Six	*Standard (firing a gun)*
Seven	Challenging (replacing a car's sound system)
Eight	Difficult (rebuilding a wrecked engine block)
Nine	Extremely difficult (repairing a wrecked engine block without parts)

DEGREES OF SUCCESS

One Success	Marginal (getting a broken refrigerator to keep running until the repairman arrives)
Two Successes	Moderate (making a handicraft that's ugly but useful)
Three Successes	Complete (fixing something so that it's good as new)
Four Successes	Exceptional (increasing your car's efficiency in the process of repairing it)
Five or More Successes	Phenomenal (creating a masterwork)

is perching precariously on an overhead pipe to do so. Justin the Storyteller tells Feodor's player, John, to roll his Dexterity + Stealth (difficulty 7). John rolls and gets 2, 5, 6, 6, 4, 3 — no successes. Justin rules that as Feodor attempts to shift position on the pipe, his foot slides on something slimy, and he loses his balance. The thugs below don't see Feodor, but he is definitely in trouble....

BOTCHES

Bad luck can ruin anything. One more basic rule about rolling dice is the "rule of one," or (spoken in a despairing tone) "botching." Whenever one of the dice comes up as a "1," it cancels out a success. Completely. Take the die showing "1" and one of the dice showing a successful number and set them aside. In this manner, an otherwise successful action may be reduced to failure.

Occasionally, truly bad fortune strikes. If a die roll garners no successes whatsoever, and one or more "1s" show up, a botch occurs. In other word, if none of your dice comes up a success, and there are dice showing "1s" (no matter how many), the roll is a botch. If you score at least one success, even if that success is canceled out and additional "1s" remain, it's just a simple failure.

A botch is much worse than a normal failure — it's outright misfortune. For instance, rolling a botch when trying to gun down a hunter might result in your gun jamming. Botching a Computer roll when hacking into a system will probably alert the authorities, while botching a Stealth roll is the proverbial

"stepping on a dry twig." The Storyteller decides exactly what goes wrong; a botch might produce a minor inconvenience or a truly unfortunate mishap.

Of course, some Storytellers may find that botches are cropping up a little too frequently in their chronicles (the laws of probability often warp around dice, as any veteran roleplayer can attest). In that case, it's the Storyteller's privilege to give everyone, player and Storyteller character alike, one botch "free" — in other words, the first botched roll of the session doesn't count. This rule tends to make unlife a little easier on the players — but then again, there's less chance of their enemies suffering a run of bad luck either....

Example: Alexandra, a Tremere played by Merida, is desperately firing a gun through the windows of the chantry, which are being shot out by a marauding Sabbat pack. Merida rolls Alex's Dexterity + Firearms (difficulty 8), and gets 9, 1, 1, 8, 1. The "1s" more than cancel out the successes, but because she rolled successes to begin with, the action simply fails.

She's not so lucky next turn. The dice come up 1, 3, 4, 3, 7. This time, not only did a "1" occur, but no successes were scored at all, so the action is a botch. The Storyteller rules that Alexandra's gun jams, and as she tries to force it, something crucial breaks, rendering the gun worthless. Alexandra starts to crawl for the back door, hoping that the pack hasn't found it yet....

AUTOMATIC SUCCESS

Let's face it—sometimes rolling dice gets tiresome, particularly when your character could perform a given action in his sleep. And anything that streamlines play and reduces distractions is a good thing. Thus, **Vampire** employs a simple system for automatic successes, allowing you to skip rolling for tasks that your character would find frankly mundane.

Simply put, if the number of dice in your dice pool is equal to or greater than the task's difficulty, your character automatically succeeds. No dice roll is necessary. Mind you, this does *not* work for all tasks, and *never* works in combat or other stressful situations. Furthermore, an automatic success is considered marginal, just as if you'd gotten only one success on the roll; if quality is an issue, you might want to roll dice anyway to try for more successes. But for simple and often-repeated actions, this system works just fine.

There's another way to get an automatic success on a roll: Simply spend a Willpower point (p. 136). You can do this only once per turn, and since you have a limited supply of Willpower you can't do this too often, but it can certainly help when you're under pressure to succeed.

TRYING IT AGAIN

Failure often produces stress, which often leads to further failure. If a character fails an action, he may usually try it again (after all, failing to pick a lock does not mean the character may never try to pick the lock again). In such cases, though, the Storyteller has the option to increase the difficulty number of the second attempt by one. If the attempt is failed yet again, the difficulty of a third attempt goes up by two, and so on. Eventually, the difficulty will be so high that the character has no chance of succeeding (the lock is simply beyond her ability to pick).

Examples of when to use this rule are: climbing a wall, hacking into a computer system, or interrogating a prisoner. After all, if you couldn't find a handhold, defeat the security program, or get the prisoner to talk the first time, there's a reasonable chance you might not be able to do it at all.

Sometimes the Storyteller shouldn't invoke this rule. For example, failing to shoot somebody with a gun, detect an ambush, or keep on another driver's tail are to be expected in stressful situations. Such failure does not automatically lead to frustration and failed future attempts.

Example: Winters, a diplomat for the Prince of Atlanta, is not having a good night. He's at the table with a Nosferatu envoy in some critical negotiations, and things aren't going well. When Winters wishes to add a little witty Elizabethan repartee to smooth things over with the lady, the Storyteller craftily suggests that Winter's player, Edward, roll Wits + Etiquette (difficulty 6) in addition to roleplaying his banter. Edward does so — and Winters fails to realize that his antiquated compliment insults the Nosferatu (she, however, has no difficulty informing him of the fact). He attempts to make amends, but this time the Storyteller tells Edward the difficulty is 7; Winters is under the gun, and another insult could break negotiations off entirely.

COMPLICATIONS

The preceding rules should be enough to get you going, and for chronicles that favor storytelling over dice-rolling, they might be all you ever need. However, they don't necessarily cover all instances — for example, what if you're trying to do something while a Storyteller character is actively trying to stop you? What if your friend tries to help you break a code?

The various ways to complicate matters below are intended to bring extra color to games. You certainly don't have to use them, but they might add more realism and suspense to your game.

The following complications are relatively simple and generic, usable to describe a wide variety of actions. For plenty of situation-specific complications, see Chapter Six.

EXTENDED ACTIONS

Sometimes you need more than one success to accomplish a task fully. For example, you might have to spend all night tracking down obscure newspaper articles in a library, or climb a cliff face that's impossible to scale in a turn. If you need only one success to accomplish an action, the action in question is called a *simple action*. But when you need multiple successes to score even a marginal success, you're undertaking an *extended action*. Simple actions are the most common in **Vampire**, but you will have ample opportunity to perform extended actions.

In an extended action, you roll your dice pool over and over on subsequent turns, trying to collect enough successes to succeed. For example, your character is trying to dig a temporary haven in the forest floor, using only his bare hands. The Storyteller tells you that you need 15 successes to hollow out a den that provides sufficient protection from the sun. You'll eventually succeed, but the longer you go, the more chance there is of you botching and collapsing the tunnel. What's more, if you have only so many turns before dawn, the speed with which you finish your task becomes doubly important. The Storyteller in all cases is the final authority on which tasks are extended actions and which aren't.

You can usually take as many turns as you want to finish an extended action (but situations being what they are in **Vampire**, you won't always have that luxury). If you botch a roll, however, you may have to start over again from scratch. Depending on what you're trying to do, the Storyteller may even rule that you can't start over again at all; you've failed and that's that.

Because extended actions are often quite *apropos* for describing certain feats, they're used frequently in Chapter Six. However, because of the amount of dice-rolling involved, extended actions should probably be kept out of the more intense sessions of roleplaying.

RESISTED ACTIONS

A simple difficulty number might not be enough to represent a struggle between characters. For instance, you may try to batter down a door while a character on the other side tries to hold it closed. In such a case, you'd make a *resisted roll* — each of you rolls dice against a difficulty often determined by one of your opponent's Traits, and the person who scores the most successes wins.

However, you're considered to score only as many successes as the amount by which you exceed your opponent's successes; in other words, the opponent's successes eliminate your own, just as "1s" do. If you score four successes and your opponent scores three, you're considered to have only one: a marginal success. Therefore it's difficult to achieve an outstanding success on a resisted action. Even if your opponent can't beat you, he can still diminish the effect of your efforts.

Some actions (arm-wrestling contests, debates, car chases) may be both extended and resisted. In such cases, one or the other of the opponents must achieve a certain number of

---

EXAMPLE OF EXTENDED ACTION

Veronica Abbey-Roth is trying to work up a large portion of capital for a certain upcoming project of hers. Even though she has Resources 4, the Storyteller rules that she'd have to liquidate much of her belongings to get the money she wants. So Veronica decides to play fast and dirty with her money, running a number of illegal operations and playing a very intricate game with the stock market to raise the money she needs. The Storyteller decides that for Veronica to reach her goal, Lynn will have to score 18 successes on an extended Wits + Finance roll (difficulty 7 — this is an intrinsically tricky way to earn money). What's more, since this sort of thing takes time, she can make only one roll per night of game time.

Veronica has Wits 3 and Finance 4, so Lynn rolls seven dice each night. She gets three successes on her first roll — things are opening up nicely. On her second roll, she gets two successes, for a total of five. Unfortunately, luck isn't with her on the third roll. She gets 3, 4, 1, 6, 4, 1, 6 — a botch! The Storyteller rules that one of Veronica's brokers has gone sour, and she's actually lost money on the transaction. But the efforts of three nights' work have been neatly condensed into five minutes or so of real time. As the game continues, Veronica is left with a tighter budget for a while, and the choice of trying again (and running the risk of attracting the Justice Department's attention) or abandoning her grandiose plot....

EXAMPLE OF RESISTED ACTION

Veronica, prowling for trouble at the latest Camarilla soiree, has determined by night's end to spite her rival, a Ventrue by the name of Giselle. Giselle arrived at the *fête* with her latest childe in tow: Tony, a talented and delicious young man with a medical license and a much-vaunted pedigree. Veronica decides that there would be nothing more amusing than stealing Giselle's childe away from her for the evening — of course, that'll take some doing, as Giselle will be watching him like a hawk.

Lynn (Veronica's player) and the Storyteller roleplay out much of the initial three-way conversation (as well as the covert knife-edged glances) between Veronica, Giselle and Tony. Finally, the Storyteller has Lynn roll Veronica's Manipulation (3) + Subterfuge (3), resisted by Giselle's Manipulation (3) + Subterfuge (4). Lynn rolls six dice versus a difficulty of 7 (Giselle's Manipulation + Subterfuge); the Storyteller rolls Giselle's seven dice versus difficulty 6 (Veronica's Manipulation + Subterfuge). Lynn manages to score four successes, while Giselle remarkably manages only three. Giselle's successes subtract from Lynn's, leaving Lynn with one success. Tony opts to make the rounds with Veronica, although her marginal success means he casts a few longing glances back Giselle's way....

successes to succeed. Each success above the rival's total number in a given turn is added to a running tally. The first to achieve the designated number of successes wins the contest.

TEAMWORK

You don't always have to go it alone. If the situation warrants (usually during an extended action such as researching a family tree or decoding an Aramaic inscription), characters can work together to collect successes. If the Storyteller decides that teamwork is possible for the task in question, two or more characters can make rolls separately and add their successes together. They may never combine their Traits into one dice pool, however.

Teamwork can be effective in many situations — dogpiling on the prince's pet enforcer, shadowing a hunter or doing research in the library, for instance. However, it can actually prove to be a hindrance in certain situations (including social interaction such as fast-talking or seducing a subject), and one person's botch can bollix the whole attempt.

THE GOLDEN RULE

This is the most important rule of all, and the only real rule worth following: *There are no rules.* This game should be whatever you want it to be, whether that's a nearly diceless chronicle of in-character socialization or a long-running tactical campaign with each player controlling a small coterie of vampires. If the rules in this book interfere with your enjoyment of the game, *change* them. The world is far too big — it can't be reflected accurately in any set of inflexible rules. Think of this book as a collection of guidelines, suggested but not mandatory ways of capturing the World of Darkness in the format of a game. You're the arbiter of what works best in your game, and you're free to use, alter, abuse or ignore these rules at your leisure.

TRY IT OUT

Well, that's it. Those are the basic rules — everything else is just clarification or expansion, the icing on the cake. If you understand these rules, you should be able to play the game with no problem. If you don't yet understand them, reread the section. Better yet, try a couple of rolls yourself.

Let's say that Veronica has finally gotten cause to use that snub-nosed revolver in her handbag — a carjacker is threatening Marcus, her chauffeur. The difficulty for hitting someone at short range is 6 (see Chapter Six for more details on combat). Take three dice for Veronica's Dexterity Attribute of 3, and one for her Firearms Skill of 1. You have four dice in your dice pool — fair, but not great. Now go ahead and roll. Count up your successes, but don't forget to take away a success for every "1" you roll. Did you make it? Did you botch? The more successes you get, the more accurately placed the bullet (and the better the odds that the carjacker won't be merely grazed and start returning fire).

Now try an extended and resisted action — we'll say a debate. (It might not sound that interesting at first, but consider that a debate held before the primogen council has some *very* high stakes....) This will be an indefinite series of rolls, each one perhaps using a different Trait and requiring different difficulties. You need to accumulate five more successes than your opponent to prove your point and sway the council. A botch eliminates all of your accumulated successes (you've made yourself look like a fool somehow).

• First roll: Each player rolls Charisma + Expression, difficulty of the opponent's Wits + 3 (those opening remarks are very important).

Action	Example	Description
Simple	Dodging a bullet, Sensing an ambush	Task is completed with one roll. The Storyteller announces the difficulty and the players roll dice. Automatic success is possible.
Extended	Mountain climbing, Research	Task is completed when a given number of successes are obtained, which may require more than one roll (which provides more chances of botching).
Resisted	Shadowing	A contest of skill between two individuals. They compare their number of successes; the character with the most successes wins.
Extended & Resisted	Arm wrestling	As a resisted action; the contest requires a given number of successes and may take more than one turn to complete.

• Second and third rolls: As the debate heats up, each player rolls Intelligence + Expression, difficulty of the opponent's Intelligence + Expression.

• Fourth roll (and any subsequent rolls): Each player rolls Manipulation + Expression (difficulty of the opponent's Wits + Expression) to put the final spin on his argument.

Examples of Rolls

This rules system is designed with flexibility in mind, and as a result, there are about 270 combinations of Attributes and Abilities. This daunting number is just the beginning, too — you can certainly devise more Talents, Skills or Knowledges if you think there's need. In this manner, you have a huge variety of rolls to simulate actions — whatever you think is most appropriate. The following examples of rolls are meant to give you some idea of the possibilities that might come up in a game.

• You want to conduct yourself flawlessly at the governor's formal dinner (and you can't actually eat anything). Roll Dexterity + Etiquette (difficulty 8).

• You're miles from your haven, and the sun will be up soon. Roll Wits + Survival (difficulty 7) to find shelter for the day.

• You try to distract the bodyguard with your left hand while surreptitiously slipping your knife back into your belt with your right. Roll Dexterity + Subterfuge (difficulty of the bodyguard's Perception + Alertness).

• You lock gazes with the gang leader, trying to cow him into submission before his gang — of course, he wants to do the same to you. Make a Charisma + Intimidation roll, resisted by his Charisma + Intimidation.

• The ritual requires three days of nonstop chanting. Can you stay awake even through the daylight hours to finish it? Roll Stamina + Occult (difficulty 9).

• You need to board up the door to your haven in record speed — and it needs to be durable, too. Roll Wits + Crafts (difficulty 7).

• You've got access to the chantry library for exactly one night — you'd better find the name you want quickly, but there are a *lot* of books here. Roll Wits + Occult (difficulty 8) every hour; you need to achieve 15 successes.

• It's not the message of the song, it's how good you look singing it. Roll Appearance + Performance (difficulty 6) to have your choice of groupies.

• How long can you remain motionless in the bushes while the guards chat about the game? Roll Stamina + Stealth (difficulty 7). Each success allows you to hold still for one hour.

• It would be foolish to threaten your rival openly while in the confines of Elysium. Roll Manipulation + Intimidation (difficulty 8) to properly veil your threat without leaving her in doubt as to your intentions.

• Suddenly, a man pushes a crate out of the van you've been chasing — roll Wits + Drive (difficulty 6) to swerve out of the way in time.

• Can you distract the guard dogs while you slip in? Roll Manipulation + Animal Ken (difficulty 8).

• Did she just threaten you? Roll Perception + Intimidation (difficulty 5) to figure out what that Lick meant by that comment.

• You try to get his attention by driving your knife through his hand and into the oak bar. Roll Strength + Melee (difficulty 6).

• You try to pull alongside the fleeing Mercedes so your friends can leap aboard. Make an extended Dexterity + Drive roll, resisted by the Mercedes driver's Wits + Drive. If you accumulate five total successes more than his total successes, you're in position. If he accumulates a total of five more successes than you get, he escapes.

• The new gang in town's been awfully good at picking out Kindred-run operations to take over. Roll Charisma + Streetwise (difficulty 8) to see what people know about them. The more successes you get, the more information you receive, but the legwork will take an entire night regardless.

• What sort of alarm system does this place have? Roll Perception + Security (difficulty 6).

• Whose story will the prince believe — yours or your enemy's? Roll Manipulation + Expression, resisted by your rival's Manipulation + Expression.

• You try convincing the clerk of the court that you're an IRS auditor and that you need to see the court records. Roll Manipulation + Finance (difficulty 8).

• Can you read the German translation of *The Book of Nod* without losing something in the transition? Roll Intelligence + Linguistics (difficulty 8).

• You have to keep running if you're going to outdistance your pursuers. Make an extended Stamina + Athletics roll (difficulty 7); if you collect 15 successes, you've outlasted them.

• You need to convince the judge to release you before the sun rises. Roll Charisma + Law (difficulty 8) to make a plea eloquent enough.

Game Terms

Here we define a number of terms used in the rules that first-time players and new Storytellers might not be familiar with.

• **Ability:** These are Traits that describe what a character knows and has learned, rather than her physical and psychological make-up. Abilities are Traits such as Intimidation, Firearms and Occult.

• **Action:** An action is the performance of a deed, which is a consciously willed physical, social or mental activity. When players announce that their characters are doing something, they are taking an action.

• **Advantage:** This is a catchall category that describes the mystical Disciplines and Backgrounds of a character.

• **Attribute:** These are Traits that describe what a character inherently is. Attributes are such things as Strength, Charisma and Intelligence.

• **Botch:** 1) A naturally rolled "1," which cancels out a success die. 2) A disastrous failure, indicated by rolling one or more "1s" and no successes on the 10-sided dice rolled for an action.

• **Character:** Each player creates a character, an individual he roleplays over the course of the chronicle. Though "charac-

ter" could imply any individual, we use it here to describe the players' characters.

• **Dice Pool:** This describes the dice you have in your hand after adding together your different Traits. It is the number of dice you can roll for that action.

• **Difficulty:** This is a number from 2 to 10 measuring the difficulty of an action a character takes. The player needs to roll that number or higher on at least one of the dice in his dice pool.

• **Downtime:** The time spent between scenes, where no roleplaying is done and turns are not used. Actions might be made, and the Storyteller might give some descriptions, but generally time passes quickly.

• **Extended Action:** An action that requires a certain number of successes, accumulated over several turns, for the character to actually succeed.

• **Health:** This is a measure of the degree to which a character is wounded or injured.

• **Points:** The temporary score of a Trait such as Willpower and blood pool — the squares, not the circles.

• **Rating:** A number describing the permanent value of a Trait — most often a number from 1 to 5, though sometimes a number from 1 to 10.

• **Reflexive:** A situation in which dice might be rolled, but that does not count as an action for the purpose of calculating dice pools. Examples of reflexives are soak rolls and Willpower rolls to resist mind control.

• **Resisted Action:** An action that two different characters take against each other. Both compare their number of successes, and the character with the most wins.

• **Scene:** A single episode of the story; a time and place in which actions and events take place moment by moment. A scene is often a dramatic high point of the story.

• **Score:** The temporary value of a Trait or combination of Traits used in a single roll.

• **Simple Action:** An action that requires the player to get only one success to succeed, though more successes indicate a better job or result.

• **Storyteller:** The person who creates and guides the story by assuming the roles of all characters not taken by the players and determining all events beyond the control of the players.

• **System:** A specific set of complications used in a certain situation; rules to help guide the rolling of dice to create dramatic action.

• **Trait:** Any Attribute, Ability, Advantage or other character index that can be described as a number (in terms of dots).

• **Troupe:** The group of players, including the Storyteller, who play **Vampire: The Masquerade**, usually on a regular basis.

• **Willpower:** A measure of a character's self-confidence and internal control. Willpower works differently from most Traits — it is often spent rather than rolled.

Blood drips onto paper with a sound like a snare drum. Rat — tat — tat it goes. I'm using those drops they way I used to use my heartbeat, as a way to count out a few seconds when I'm trying to be calm. But my heart doesn't beat anymore, so I need to find something else to use.

Right now, it's the sound of my blood dripping from my girlfriend's mouth onto the newspaper on the floor. She's supposed to be swallowing it, drinking it and letting it turn her into a vampire so we can be together, but nothing's happening. I don't know why.

I did it the way Riki told me you have to do it. I took all of her blood first, then I cut my wrist open and let everything drizzle into her mouth the way she used to drizzle chocolate syrup onto her ice cream. Then I sat down and I waited for her to open her eyes again.

That was an hour ago. It's not supposed to take that long. The blood keeps dripping out of her mouth and I keep putting more in, and it's not working. The sun's coming up, and it's not working, and the blood keeps on spilling on the floor. Honey, you've got to drink. Please drink, honey. Don't be dead. Please, don't be dead.

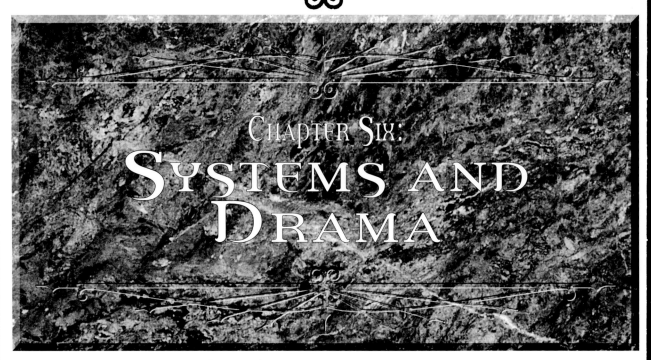

Chapter Six:
Systems and Drama

While **Vampire**'s focus is on roleplaying and character interaction, dramatic scenes often involve some element of die rolling. As Chapter Five shows, the basic Storyteller rules are designed to streamline this process as much as possible, allowing you to pay attention to the story. To assist you and the Storyteller further, this chapter covers more specific dice mechanics, including general dramatic systems, combat, injury and recovery.

We reiterate that the following systems are suggestions for how we think situations can be best handled. If, in your chronicles, you come up with a way you like better, by all means use it. Also — particularly when dealing with social actions like seductions and speeches — the dice should *never* get in the way of roleplaying. If a player has his character make a particularly inspired (or painful) speech, deliver a particularly smooth (or cheesy) opening line, or come up with a brilliant (or laughable) alibi, feel free to let the character succeed (or fail) automatically, regardless of what the dice and Traits say.

Dramatic Systems

The only things limiting your actions are your imagination and your character's skill. During a game session, characters — both player and Storyteller personalities — may attempt numerous diverse and complicated activities. The Storyteller is responsible for keeping all of this action organized while determining success or failure for all characters.

Dramatic systems simplify the Storyteller's job by supplying rules for a number of common activities. Generally, a character attempting to accomplish a task adds together an Attribute and an Ability. If a task falls within a character's specialty (p. 117), that character may be able to roll extra dice if the player scores one or more "10s" on his roll.

Storytellers should, and will undoubtedly have to, invent their own dramatic systems for new situations. The list of systems below is in no way exhaustive, but provides a solid foundation on which to base events. Bear in mind that for rolls involving Talents and Skills, characters lacking a specific Ability may default to the Attribute on which the Ability is based (albeit at +1 difficulty for Skill-based actions).

Most of these systems involve taking one or more actions (p. 190) over one or more turns. A number of these systems may be tried again if the first attempt is unsuccessful. Subsequent efforts may suffer a difficulty penalty, at the Storyteller's discretion (see "Trying It Again," p. 193).

Automatic Feats

Automatic feats require the character to take an action, but don't involve a die roll under most circumstances. The following are common automatic feats; Storytellers may decide that other feats are automatic, at their discretion.

• **Blood Use (Healing, Augmenting Attributes, etc.):** Vampire characters may spend blood to heal themselves. To do so, the character must concentrate and do nothing else for one full turn. A character may attempt to heal while performing other actions, but this requires success on a Stamina + Survival reflexive roll (difficulty 8). Failing this roll means the vampire loses all expended blood points with no effect, while a botch causes the vampire to lose both an additional blood point and an additional health level. Spending blood to raise Physical Attributes or power Disciplines may be done automatically, without the need for concentration. A character may spend an amount of vitae equal to her per-turn rating, as dictated by her generation (p. 139).

• **Getting to Feet:** Characters may rise from the ground in one turn without making a roll. If a character wishes to get to her feet while doing something else in the same turn, she must take a multiple action (see "Multiple Actions," p. 192) with a Dexterity + Athletics roll (difficulty 4) to rise successfully.

• **Movement:** Characters may choose to walk, jog or run. If walking, a character moves at seven yards per turn. If jogging, a character moves at (12 + Dexterity) yards per turn. If all-out running, a character moves at (20 + [3 x Dexterity]) yards per turn.

Characters may move up to half maximum running speed, then subsequently attack or perform another action; see p. 209 for particulars. Characters may also wish to move *while* taking another action. This is possible, but each yard moved subtracts one from the other action's dice pool.

Note that injured characters (p. 216) cannot move at maximum speed.

• **Readying Weapon:** This can involving drawing a weapon or reloading a gun with a prepared clip. In most cases, no roll is required, so long as the character takes no other action that turn. If the character wishes to ready a weapon while doing something else in the same turn, the player must reduce his dice pool (see "Multiple Actions," p. 192) and roll Dexterity + Melee or Firearms (difficulty 4) for the readying attempt.

• **Starting Car:** This takes an action, but requires no roll.

• **Yielding:** The character allows the character with the next-highest initiative (p. 207) to act. She may still act at the end of the turn. If all characters (player and Storyteller) yield during a turn, no one does anything that turn.

Physical Feats

These systems cover actions involving the three Physical Attributes (Strength, Dexterity and Stamina). These feats typically require a die roll.

• **Climbing [Dexterity + Athletics]:** When your character climbs an inclined surface (rocky slope, side of building), roll Dexterity + Athletics. Climbing is typically an extended roll. For an average climb with available handholds and nominal complications, your character moves 10 feet for every success. The Storyteller adjusts this distance based on the climb's difficulty (easier: 15 feet per success; more difficult: five feet per success). The number of handholds, smoothness of the surface and, to a lesser extent, weather can all affect rate of travel. A short, difficult climb may have the same difficulty as a long, easy climb. The extended action lasts until you've accumulated enough successes to reach the desired height. Botching a climbing roll can be bad; your character may only slip or get stuck, or she may fall.

If the character activates the Protean power of Feral Claws or constructs bone spurs with the Vicissitude power of Bonecraft, all climbing difficulties are reduced by two.

• **Driving [Dexterity/Wits + Drive]:** A Drive roll isn't needed to steer a vehicle under normal circumstances — assuming your character has at least one dot in the Drive Skill. Bad weather, the vehicle's speed, obstacles and complex maneuvers can challenge even the most competent drivers. Specific difficulties based on these circumstances are up to the Storyteller, but should increase as the conditions become more hazardous.

For example, driving in heavy rain is +1 difficulty, but going fast while also trying to lose pursuers increases the difficulty to +3. Similarly, maneuvering in heavy traffic is +1, but adding a breakneck pace while avoiding pursuit bumps the difficulty to +3. A failed roll indicates trouble, requiring an additional roll to avoid crashing or losing control. Characters in control of a vehicle, and who have no dots in the appropriate Ability, need a roll for almost every change in course or procedure. On a botch, the vehicle may spin out of control or worse.

Because different cars handle differently — some are designed for speed and handling while others are designed for safety — a chart is provided to help calculate the difficulty for any maneuver. Generally, for every 10 miles over the safe driving speed of a vehicle, the difficulty of any maneuver is increased by one. Exceedingly challenging stunts and bad road conditions should also increase the difficulty accordingly. The *maximum* number of dice a driver can have in her dice pool when driving is equal to the maneuver rating of the vehicle. Simply put, even the best driver will have more trouble with a dump truck than she will with a Ferrari.

Vehicle	Safe Speed	Max Speed	Maneuver
6-Wheel Truck	60	90	3
Tank (modern)	60	100	4
Tank (WWII)	30	40	3
Bus	60	100	3
18-Wheeler	70	110	4
Sedan	70	120	5
Minivan	70	120	6
Compact	70	130	6
Sporty Compact	100	140	7
Sport Coupe	110	150	8
Sports Car	110	160	8
Exotic Car	130	190+	9
Luxury Sedan	85	155	7
Midsize	75	125	6
SUV	70	115	6
Formula One Racer	140	240	10

• **Encumbrance [Strength]:** The temptation to carry loads of equipment to satisfy every situation can be overwhelming. The Storyteller should make life difficult for players whose characters pack arsenals everywhere they go. A character can carry/tote 25 pounds per point of Strength without penalty. The Potence Discipline adds to the character's effective Strength.

Should a character exceed this total, every action involving physical skills incurs an automatic +1 difficulty due to the added weight. Also, every 25 pounds over the allocation halves the character's base movement. A character bearing a total weight of double her Strength allocation can't move. This system is a guideline, and should not call for an inventory check every time your character picks up a pen.

• **Hunting [Perception]:** It is the nature of the vampire that she must hunt. For each hour the vampire spends searching for human prey, allow the player to make a Perception roll against a difficulty based on the area in which the vampire hunts.

Area	Difficulty
Slum neighborhood/The Rack	4
Lower-income/bohemian	5
Downtown business district	6
Warehouse district	6
Suburb	7
Heavily patrolled area	8

Success on this roll indicates that the vampire has found and subdued prey, in a manner appropriate for the vampire and the area (perhaps she has seduced a vessel, crept into a house of sleepers, or simply ambushed and assaulted a victim). She may now ingest one die's worth of blood points. Failure indicates that the hour is spent looking fruitlessly, while a botch indicates a complication (perhaps the character accidentally kills a vessel, picks up a disease, enters the domain of a rival Kindred or suffers assault from a street gang). If a botch does occur, go into roleplaying mode and let the character try to work her way out of trouble.

If the character catches prey, but currently has fewer blood points in her body than [7 minus Self-Control], a frenzy check (p. 228) is necessary to see if she can control her hunger. If the player fails this roll, the character continues to gorge on the vessel until she is completely sated (at full blood pool), the victim dies from blood loss, or she somehow manages to regain control of herself. If a tragedy occurs, the vampire might well lose Humanity.

The Fame Background reduces difficulties of hunting rolls by one per dot (to a minimum of 3), while the Herd Background adds one die per dot in the Background (so long as one's herd could conceivably be in the area). However, Storytellers may increase hunting difficulties for particularly inhuman vampires (Nosferatu, some Gangrel, vampires with Humanity scores of 4 or below), as such monsters find it difficult to blend in with a crowd.

• **Intrusion [Dexterity/Perception + Security]:** Intrusion covers breaking and entering, evading security devices, picking locks, cracking safes — and preventing others from doing the same. When bypassing active security, your roll must succeed on the first attempt; failure activates any alarms present (opening manual locks may be attempted multiple times, though). Intrusion rolls can range from 5 [standard lock] to 10 [Fort Knox], depending on a security system's complexity (the Storyteller decides the actual difficulty). Certain tasks might require a minimum level of Security Skill for the character to have any chance of succeeding (e.g., Security 1 might let you pick a simple lock, but not crack a safe). Also, most intrusion tasks require lockpicks or other appropriate tools. On a botch, the character's clumsy break-in attempt goes horribly awry.

Setting up security measures is a standard action, but multiple successes achieved in the effort increase the system's quality (essentially adding to its difficulty to be breached).

• **Jumping [Strength, or Strength + Athletics for a running jump]:** Typically, jump rolls are made versus a difficulty of 3. Each success on a jump roll launches your character two feet vertically or four feet horizontally. To jump successfully, a character must clear more distance than the distance between her and her destination. On a failure, the character fails to clear the required distance, but the player may make a Dexterity + Athletics roll (typically versus difficulty 6) to allow the character to grab onto a ledge or other safety as she falls. On a botch, your character may trip over her own feet, leap right into a wall or fall to her doom.

If the player makes a Perception + Athletics roll (difficulty 6, three successes required) before attempting a jump, he may gauge exactly how many successes are needed to make the leap.

• **Lifting/Breaking [Strength]:** The chart below provides the minimum Strength needed to deadlift or break various weights without a die roll. Characters of lower Strength may roll to affect heavier weights than their Strength scores allow for. The roll is made not with Strength, but with Willpower, and is difficulty 9. Each success advances the character by one level on the chart. The Potence Discipline also adds its dots to the character's effective Strength.

Strength	Feats	Lift
1	Crush a beer can	40 lbs.
2	Break a wooden chair	100 lbs.
3	Break down a wooden door	250 lbs.
4	Break a 2'x4' board	400 lbs.
5	Break open a metal fire door	650 lbs.
6	Throw a motorcycle	800 lbs.
7	Flip over a small car	900 lbs.
8	Break a 3' lead pipe	1000 lbs.
9	Punch through a cement wall	1200 lbs.
10	Rip open a steel drum	1500 lbs.
11	Punch through 1" sheet metal	2000 lbs.
12	Break a metal lamp post	3000 lbs.
13	Throw a station wagon	4000 lbs.
14	Throw a van	5000 lbs.
15	Throw a truck	6000 lbs.

Characters can work together to lift an object. This is simply a teamwork roll with the individual players rolling separately and combining any resulting successes.

Lifting is all or nothing — if you fail the roll, nothing happens. At the Storyteller's discretion, your character's effective Strength may be raised if all she wants to do is drag something a short distance instead of pick it up. On a botch, your character may strain something or drop the object on her own foot.

• **Opening/Closing [Strength]:** Opening a door with brute force calls for a Strength roll (difficulty 6 to 8, depending on the material of the door). A standard interior door requires only one success to bash open or slam shut. A reinforced door generally takes five successes. A vault door might take 10 or more successes. These successes may be handled as an extended action. While teamwork is possible (and recommended), a door can still be forced open through a single individual's repeated hammering. Obviously, a door not held in some way can be opened without resorting to force. A botch causes a health level of normal damage to your character's shoulder.

Certain doors (metal vault doors and the like) may require a Strength minimum even to make an attempt. The Potence Discipline adds automatic successes to the roll.

• **Pursuit [Dexterity + Athletics/Drive]:** Vampires must often pursue their terrified prey, and sometimes they themselves must flee. Generally, pursuit can be resolved automatically by using the formulas for calculating movement (p. 200); if one party is clearly faster than another, the faster party catches or avoids the slower party eventually. However, if two characters are of equal or nearly equal speed, or if one character is slower but might lose the faster character or make it to safety before she catches him, use the system below.

Basic pursuit is an extended action. The target starts with a number of free extra successes based on his distance from the pursuer. This breaks down as follows: on foot, one for every two yards ahead of pursuers; in vehicles, one for every 10 yards ahead of pursuers. For chases involving vampires and mortals, remember that mortals tire, but the undead do not.

The target and pursuers make the appropriate roll (depending on the type of pursuit) each turn, adding new successes to any successes rolled in previous turns. When the pursuer accumulates more total successes than the target has, she catches up and may take further actions to stop the chase. As the target accumulates successes, he gains distance from his pursuers and may use that lead to lose his opponents. Each success that the quarry accumulates beyond the pursuer's total acts as a +1 difficulty to any Perception roll a pursuer has to make to remain on the target's tail. The Storyteller may call for the pursuer to make a Perception roll at any time (although not more than once each turn). If the pursuer fails this roll, her target is considered to have slipped away (into the crowd, into a side street). On a botch, the pursuer loses her quarry immediately. If the quarry botches, he stumbles or ends up at a dead end.

• **Shadowing [Dexterity + Stealth/Drive]:** Shadowing someone requires that your character keeps tabs on the target without necessarily catching her — *and* while not being noticed by her! The target's player can roll Perception + Alertness whenever she has a chance to spot her tail (the Storyteller decides when such an opportunity arises); the pursuer's player opposes this with a Dexterity + Stealth roll (or Dexterity + Drive, if the shadower is in a vehicle). The difficulty for both rolls is typically 6, but can be modified up or down by conditions (heavy crowds, empty streets, etc.). The target must score at least one more success than her shadow does to spot the tail; if so, she may act accordingly.

Shadowers who have trained together can combine their separate rolls into one success total.

• **Sneaking [Dexterity + Stealth]:** Rather than fight through every situation, your character can use stealth and cunning. A sneaking character uses Dexterity + Stealth as a resisted action against Perception + Alertness rolls from anyone able to detect her passing. The difficulty of both rolls is typically 6. Unless observers score more successes than the sneaking character does, she passes undetected. Noise, unsecured gear, lack of cover or large groups of observers can increase Stealth difficulty. Security devices, scanners or superior vantage points may add dice to Perception + Alertness rolls. On a botch, the character stumbles into one of the people she's avoiding, accidentally walks into the open, or performs some other obvious act.

Note that vampires using the Obfuscate Discipline (p. 166) may not have to make rolls at all.

• **Swimming [Stamina + Athletics]:** Assuming your character can swim at all (being able to do so requires one dot of Athletics), long-distance or long-duration swimming requires successful swimming rolls versus a difficulty determined by water conditions. After all, although vampires can't drown, they are corpses and thus have little buoyancy. The first roll is necessary only after the first hour of sustained activity; only one success is

needed. If a roll fails, the character loses ground — perhaps pulled out of her way by a current. If a roll botches, she starts to sink, or perhaps stumbles upon a less-than-finicky shark.

Vampires caught in shallow water during the day will take damage from sunlight (assume that a submerged vampire has protection equivalent to being under cloud cover).

• **Throwing [Dexterity + Athletics]:** Objects (grenades, knives) with a mass of three pounds or less can be thrown a distance of Strength x 5 in yards. For every additional two pounds of mass that an object has, this distance decreases by five yards (particularly heavy objects don't go very far). As long as the object's mass doesn't reduce throwing distance to zero, your character can pick up and throw it. If an object can be lifted, but its mass reduces throwing distance to zero, the object can be hurled aside at best — about one yard's distance. Obviously, if an object can't be lifted, it can't be thrown at all (refer instead to "Lifting/Breaking," p. 202).

The Storyteller may reduce throwing distances for particularly unwieldy objects or increase them for aerodynamic ones. Throwing an object with any degree of accuracy requires a Dexterity + Athletics roll versus difficulty 6 (to half maximum range) or 7 (half maximum to maximum range). This difficulty can be adjusted for wind conditions and other variables at the Storyteller's whim. On a botch, your character may drop the object or strike a companion with it.

MENTAL FEATS

These systems cover tasks involving the three Mental Attributes (Perception, Intelligence and Wits), as well as tasks using the Virtues, Humanity and Willpower. Mental tests can provide you with information about things your character knows but you, the player, don't. Still, you should depend on your creativity when solving problems — not on die rolling.

• **Awakening [Perception, Humanity]:** Vampires are nocturnal creatures and find it difficult to awaken during the day. A vampire disturbed in his haven while the sun is in the sky may roll Perception (+ Auspex rating, if the vampire has it) versus difficulty 8 to notice the disturbance. Upon stirring, the vampire must make a Humanity roll (difficulty 8). Each success allows the vampire to act for one turn. Five successes mean the vampire is completely awake for the entire scene. Failure indicates the vampire slips back into slumber, but may make the Perception roll to reawaken if circumstances allow. A botch means the vampire falls into deep sleep and will not awaken until sundown.

While active during the day, the vampire may have no more dice in any dice pool than his Humanity rating.

• **Creation [variable]:** Some vampires were artists, musicians, writers or other creative types in life; others spend centuries trying to rekindle the spark of passion that undeath has taken from them. Certainly, the society of the Damned has gazed upon many wondrous (and horrific) works of art never seen by human eyes.

When trying to create something, a variety of rolls can be used, depending on just what it is the character wishes to create. Perception (to come up with a subject worthy of expression) + Expression or Crafts (to capture the feeling in an artistic medium) is a common roll. In all cases, the player must decide the general parameters of what she wants her character to create (a haiku about roses, a portrait of the prince, an epigram for the christening of a new Elysium site). The difficulty is variable, depending on the nature of the creation (it's easier to write a limerick than a villanelle). The number of successes governs the quality of the creation: With one success, the character creates a mediocre, uninspired but not terrible work, while with five successes the character creates a literary or artistic masterpiece. Some works (novels, large sculptures) might require extended success rolls. On a botch, the character creates the greatest work ever known to Kindred or kine (of course, everyone else who sees it immediately realizes what crap it actually is).

At the Storyteller's discretion, a vampire who creates a particularly inspired masterwork might be eligible for a rise in Humanity, via experience points.

• **Hacking [Intelligence/Wits + Computer]:** Most business and political transactions involve the use of computers, which can give neonates a surprising advantage in the Jyhad. A would-be hacker's player rolls Intelligence or Wits + Computer versus a variable difficulty (6 for standard systems, up to 10 for military mainframes and the like). Successes indicate the number of dice (up to the normal dice pool) that can be rolled to interact with the system once it's been breached.

Actively blocking a hacker is a resisted action; the adversary with the most successes wins. On a botch, the character may trip a flag or even reveal her identity to the system she's trying to breach.

• **Investigation [Perception + Investigation]:** Any search for clues, evidence or hidden contraband involves Investigation. The Storyteller may add to the difficulty of investigations involving obscure clues or particularly well-concealed objects. One success reveals basic details, while multiple successes provide detailed information and may even allow deductions based on physical evidence. On a botch, obvious clues are missed or even destroyed accidentally.

• **Repair [Dexterity/Perception + Crafts]:** Depending on the precise specialty, the Crafts Skill allows for repairs of everything from pottery to automobile engines. Before repairing a device that's on the fritz, your character must identify its problems (accomplished as a standard research roll; see below). The Storyteller then sets the difficulty of the repair roll, if any. This difficulty depends on the problems' severity, whether the proper tools or any replacement parts are on hand, and if adverse conditions exist. An inspired research roll may offset these factors somewhat. A simple tire change is difficulty 4, while rebuilding an entire engine might be difficulty 9. Basic repairs take at least a few turns to complete. More complex repairs are extended actions that last 10 minutes for each success needed. On a botch, your character may simply waste time and a new part, or may make the problem worse.

• **Research [Intelligence + Academics/Occult/Science]:** Research is performed when searching computer databases for historical facts, when looking for obscure references in ancient documents, or when trying to learn the true name of a Methuselah. In all cases, the number of successes achieved determines the amount of information discovered; one success gives you at least basic information, while extra successes provide more details.

The Storyteller may assign a high difficulty for particularly obscure data. On a botch, your character may not find anything at all or may uncover completely erroneous information.

• **Tracking [Perception + Survival]:** Unlike shadowing, tracking requires you to follow physical evidence to find a target. Discovering footprints, broken twigs, blood trails or other physical signs leads the tracker right to the subject. Following such a trail is a standard action; multiple successes provide extra information (subject's rate of speed, estimated weight, number of people followed). The quarry can cover her tracks through a successful Wits + Survival roll. Each success on this roll adds one to the difficulty of tracking her. Abnormal weather, poor tracking conditions (city streets, Elysium) and a shortage of time also add to tracking difficulty. On a botch, your character not only loses the trail, but destroys the physical signs of passage.

SOCIAL FEATS

These systems cover tasks involving the three Social Attributes (Appearance, Manipulation and Charisma). Roleplaying usually supersedes any Social skill roll, for better or worse. Storytellers may ignore the Social systems when a player exhibits particularly good, or excruciatingly bad, roleplaying.

• **Carousing [Charisma + Empathy]:** You influence others (particularly potential vessels) to relax and have fun. This might include showing a potential ally a good time, loosening an informant's tongue or making instant drinking partners who come to your aid when a brawl starts. The difficulty is typically 6 (most people can be persuaded to loosen up, regardless of intellect or will), though it might be higher in the case of large (or surly) groups. Certain Natures (Bon Vivant, Curmudgeon) can also influence the roll's difficulty. On a botch, your character comes off as an obnoxious boor, or people begin to question why your character hasn't touched her own food and drink....

• **Credibility [Manipulation/Perception + Subterfuge]:** The Subterfuge Talent is used with Manipulation when perpetrating a scam or with Perception when trying to detect one (a scam can range from impersonating the authorities to using forged papers). All parties involved, whether detecting the lie or perpetrating it, make an appropriate roll (typically difficulty 7). The scam's "marks" must roll higher than the perpetrator to detect any deception. False credentials and other convincing props may add to the difficulty of uncovering the dupe, while teamwork may help reveal the scam. Hacking and/or intrusion rolls may be called for to pull off an inspired scam successfully. If your character perpetrates the scam and you botch, the entire plan falls apart.

• **Fast-Talk [Manipulation + Subterfuge]:** When there's no time for subtlety, baffle them with nonsense. The target can be overwhelmed with a rapid succession of almost-believable half-truths. Hopefully, the subject believes anything she hears just to get away from the babble — or becomes so annoyed that she ignores your character completely. This is a resisted action — your character's Manipulation + Subterfuge against the target's Willpower. The difficulty of both rolls is typically 6, and whoever scores more successes wins. On a tie, more babbling is needed. On a botch, your character goes too far, angering the target and rambling without effect.

• **Interrogation [Manipulation + Empathy/Intimidation]:** Anyone can ask questions. With the Interrogation Ability, you ask questions and have leverage. Interrogating someone peacefully (Manipulation + Empathy) involves asking strategic questions designed to reveal specific facts. This method is a resisted action between your character's Manipulation + Empathy and the subject's Willpower. Both actions are typically made against a difficulty of 6. Rolls are made at key points during questioning, probably every few minutes or at the end of an interrogation session.

Violent interrogation (Manipulation + Intimidation) involves torturing the victim's mind and/or body until she reveals what she knows. This is a resisted action between your character's Manipulation + Intimidation and the target's Stamina + 3 or Willpower (whichever is higher). Rolls are made every minute or turn, depending on the type of torture used. The subject loses a health level for every turn of physical torture, or one temporary Willpower point per turn of mental torture. The combined effect of physical and mental torture has devastating results. A botched roll can destroy the subject's body or mind.

Two or more interrogators can work together, combining successes; this works even if one interrogator is using Empathy while another is using Intimidation (the classic "good cop/bad cop" ploy).

Whatever the interrogation method used, if you roll more successes in the resisted action, the target divulges additional information for each extra success rolled. If your extra successes exceed the victim's permanent Willpower score, she folds completely and reveals everything she knows. The extent and relevancy of shared information are up to the Storyteller (details are often skewed to reflect what the subject knows or by what she thinks her interrogator wants to hear).

• **Intimidation [Strength/Manipulation + Intimidation]:** Intimidation has two effects. Intimidation's passive effect doesn't involve a roll; it simply gives your character plenty of space — whether on a bus or in a bar. The higher your Intimidation rating, the wider the berth that others give him.

Intimidation's active application works through subtlety or outright threat. Subtlety is based on a *perceived* threat (losing one's job, going on report, pain and agony later in life). Roll Manipulation + Intimidation in a resisted action against the subject's Willpower (difficulty 6 for both rolls); the target must get more successes or be effectively cowed.

The blatant form of intimidation involves direct physical threat. In this case, you may roll Strength + Intimidation in a resisted roll (difficulty 6) against either the subject's Willpower or her Strength + Intimidation (whichever is higher). On a botch, your character looks patently ridiculous and doesn't impress anyone in attendance for the rest of the scene.

• **Oration [Charisma + Leadership]:** From a general's rousing speeches to a politician's slick double-talk, the capacity to sway the masses emotionally creates and destroys empires. When your character speaks to an audience, from a small board meeting to a large crowd, roll Charisma + Leadership. Difficulty is typically 6; the Storyteller may increase the difficulty for a huge, cynical, dispassionate or openly hostile audience. Oration is hit or miss — your character either succeeds or fails. On a botch, your character may damage her reputation or even be assaulted by the audience.

If the character has time to prepare a speech beforehand, the Storyteller may roll the character's Intelligence + Expression (difficulty 7). Success on this roll reduces the subsequent Charisma + Leadership difficulty by one. Failure has no effect, while a botch actually increases the Charisma + Leadership difficulty (the character inserts a gaffe into the speech).

• **Performance [Charisma + Performance]:** Vampires are certainly egotistical creatures, and some among their number are actors, poets, musicians or other sorts of entertainers. When a character performs live before an audience, roll Charisma + Performance (difficulty 7). As with oration, the audience's mood can increase the difficulty, as can the performance's complexity. One success indicates an enjoyable, if uninspired, effort, while additional successes make the performance a truly memorable event to even the most surly crowd. On a botch, your character forgets lines, hits the wrong chord or otherwise flubs.

• **Seduction [variable]:** Vampires are master seducers, for their very sustenance often depends on coaxing potential prey into an intimate liaison. The particular situation and style of the seduction determine which Ability is used.

Seduction is an involved process involving several different rolls and Abilities:

• First roll (approach/opening remarks): The player rolls Appearance + Subterfuge versus a difficulty of the subject's Wits + 3. Each success above the initial one adds one die to the vampire's dice pool for the second roll. A failure means the subject expresses his disinterest; a botch means the subject might grow disgusted or angry.

• Second roll (witty repartee): The player rolls Wits + Subterfuge versus a difficulty of the subject's Intelligence + 3. Again, each success above the initial one adds one die to the dice pool for the final roll. If the roll fails, the subject breaks off the contact, but might prove receptive at a later date (after all, the first impression was good).

• Third roll (suggestive/intimate conversation): The player rolls Charisma + Empathy versus a difficulty of the subject's Perception + 3. If the third roll succeeds, the subject is enamored with the character and agrees to depart with her to a private spot. What happens next is best handled with roleplaying, but can certainly involve the drinking of blood, as well as other complications.

On a botch, the vampire likely ends up with a drink in her face.

COMBAT SYSTEMS

Combat in **Vampire** attempts to capture the drama of violent conflict without downplaying its grim reality. Every effort has been made to create a system true to the dynamics, limitations and viciousness of real combat while still leaving room for the unique (and often spectacular) elements that vampires bring to it.

The Storyteller should be flexible when arbitrating combat situations; no rules can fully reflect the variety of situations encountered in warfare. If these systems slow the game or cause bickering, don't use them. Combat systems are meant to add depth to the game, not create conflict between the players and the Storyteller.

DESCRIBING THE SCENE

Before each turn, the Storyteller should describe the scene from each character's perspective. Sometimes this will be a wrap-up of the last turn, making what occurred clear to all players. This constant description is essential to avoid confusion.

This is the Storyteller's chance to organize and arrange events so that all goes smoothly when the players interact with the environment she has created. The Storyteller should make her descriptions as interesting as possible, leaving open all sorts of possibilities for characters' actions.

TYPES OF COMBAT

There are two types of combat, each involving the same basic system with minor differences:

• **Close Combat:** This covers unarmed combat (Dexterity + Brawl) and melee (Dexterity + Melee). Unarmed combat can involve a down-and-dirty Pier Six brawl or an honorable test of skill. Opponents must be within touching distance (one meter) to engage in unarmed combat. Melee involves hand-held weapons, from broken bottles to swords. Opponents must be within one or two meters of each other to engage in melee.

• **Ranged Combat:** Armed combat using projectile weapons — pistols, rifles, shotguns, etc. Opponents must normally be within sight (and weapon range) of each other to engage in a firefight.

COMBAT TURNS

In combat, many things happen at virtually the same time. Since this can make things a bit sticky in a game, combat is divided into a series of three-second turns. Each combat turn has three stages — *Initiative*, *Attack* and *Resolution* — to make it easier to keep track of things.

STAGE ONE: INITIATIVE

This stage organizes the turn and is when you declare your character's action. Various actions are possible — anything from leaping behind a wall to shouting a warning. You must declare what your character does, in as much detail as the Storyteller requires.

Everyone, player and Storyteller character alike, rolls one die and adds it to their *initiative rating* [Dexterity + Wits]; the character with the highest result acts first, with the remaining characters acting in decreasing order of result. If two characters get the same total, the one with the higher initiative rating goes first. If initiative ratings are also the same, the two characters act simultaneously. Wound penalties subtract directly from a character's initiative rating.

Although you declare your character's action now, including stating that your character delays her action to see what someone else does, you wait until the *attack* stage to implement that action. At this time, you must also state if any multiple actions will be performed, if Disciplines will be activated, and/or if Willpower points will be spent. Characters declare in reverse order of initiative, thus giving faster characters the opportunity to react to slower characters' actions.

All of your character's actions are staged at her rank in the order of initiative. There are three exceptions to this rule. The first is if your character delays her action, in which case her maneuvers happen when she finally takes action. Your character may act at any time after her designated order in the initiative, even to interrupt another, slower character's action. If two characters both delay their actions, and both finally act at the same time, the one with the higher initiative score for the turn acts first.

The second breach of the initiative order occurs in the case of a defensive action (see "Aborting Actions," and "Defensive Maneuvers," on the next page), which your character may perform at any time as long as she has an action left.

Finally, all multiple actions (including actions gained through activating the Discipline of Celerity) occur at the end of the turn. If two or more characters take multiple actions, the actions occur in order of initiative rating. An exception is made for defensive multiple actions, such as multiple dodges, which happen when they need to happen in order to avert attack.

Stage Two: Attack

Attacks are the meat of the combat turn. An action's success or failure and potential impact on the target are determined at this stage. You use a certain Attribute/Ability combination depending on the type of combat in which your character is engaged:

• **Close Combat:** Use Dexterity + Brawl (unarmed) or Dexterity + Melee (armed).

• **Ranged Combat:** Use Dexterity + Firearms (guns) or Dexterity + Athletics (thrown weapons).

Remember, if your character doesn't have points in the necessary Ability, simply default to the Attribute on which it's based (in most cases, Dexterity).

In ranged combat, your weapon may modify your dice pool or difficulty (due to rate of fire, a targeting scope, etc.); check the weapon's statistics for details.

Most attacks are made versus difficulty 6. This can be adjusted for situational modifiers (long range, cramped quarters), but the default attack roll is versus 6. If you get no successes, the character fails her attack and inflicts no damage. If you botch, not only does the attack fail, but something nasty happens: The weapon jams or explodes, the blade breaks, an ally is hit.

Stage Three: Resolution

During this stage, you determine the damage inflicted by your character's attack, and the Storyteller describes what occurs in the turn. Resolution is a mixture of game and story; it's more interesting for players to hear "Your claws rip through his bowels; he screams in pain, dropping his gun as he clutches his bloody abdomen" than simply "Uh, he loses four health levels." Attacks and damage are merely ways of describing what happens in the story, and it's important to maintain the narrative of combat even as you make the die roll.

Normally, additional successes gained on a Trait roll simply mean that you do exceptionally well. In combat, each success above the first you get on an attack roll equals an additional die you add automatically to your damage dice pool! This creates fatal and cinematic combat.

Damage Types

All attacks have specific damage ratings, indicating the number of dice that you roll for the attack's damage (called the *damage dice pool*). Some damage dice pools are based on the attacker's Strength, while others are based on the weapon used. *Damage dice rolls are made versus difficulty 6.* Each success on the damage roll inflicts one health level of damage on the target. However, the damage applied may be one of three types:

• **Bashing:** Bashing damage comprises punches and other blunt trauma that are less likely to kill a victim (especially a vampire) instantly. All characters use their full Stamina ratings to resist bashing effects, and the damage heals fairly quickly. Bashing damage is applied to the Health boxes on your character sheet with a "/."

• **Lethal:** Attacks meant to cause immediate and fatal injury to the target. Mortals may not use Stamina to resist lethal effects, and the damage takes quite a while to heal. Vampires may resist lethal damage with their Stamina. Like bashing damage, lethal damage is applied to the Health boxes on your vampire's character sheet with a "/."

• **Aggravated:** Certain types of attacks are deadly even to the undead. Fire, sunlight, and the teeth and claws of vampires, werewolves and other supernatural beings are considered aggravated damage. Aggravated damage cannot be soaked except with Fortitude, and it takes quite a while to heal. Aggravated damage is applied to the Health boxes on your character sheet with an "X."

Damage dice pools can never be reduced to lower than one die; any attack that strikes its target has at least a small chance of inflicting damage, at least before a soak roll is made. Moreover, damage effect rolls cannot botch; a botched roll simply means the attack glances harmlessly off the target. Specifics on applying damage effects are described on pp. 216-218.

Combat Summary Chart

Stage One: Initiative

• Roll initiative. Everyone declares their actions. The character with the highest initiative performs her action first. Actions can be delayed to any time later in the order of initiative.

• Declare any multiple actions, reducing dice pools accordingly. Declare Discipline activation and Willpower expenditure.

Stage Two: Attack

• For unarmed close-combat attacks, roll Dexterity + Brawl.

• For armed close-combat attacks, roll Dexterity + Melee.

• For ranged combat, roll Dexterity + Firearms (guns) or Dexterity + Athletics (thrown weapons).

• A character can abort to a defensive action (block, dodge, parry) at any time before her action is performed, as long as you make a successful Willpower roll (or a Willpower point is spent).

Stage Three: Resolution

• Determine total damage effect (weapon type or maneuver), adding any extra dice gained from successes on the attack roll.

• Targets may attempt to soak damage, if possible.

Soak

Characters can resist a certain degree of physical punishment; this is called *soaking* damage. Your character's soak dice pool is equal to her Stamina. A normal human can soak only against bashing damage (this reflects the body's natural resilience to such attacks). A vampire (or other supernatural being) is tougher, and can thus use soak dice against lethal damage. Aggravated damage may be soaked only with the Discipline of Fortitude. Against bashing or lethal damage, Fortitude adds to the defender's soak rating (so a character with Stamina 3 and Fortitude 2 has five soak dice against bashing and lethal damage, two soak dice against aggravated damage).

After an attack hits and inflicts damage, the defender may make a soak roll to resist. This is considered a reflexive; characters need not take an action or split a dice pool to soak. *Unless otherwise stated, soak rolls are made versus difficulty 6.* Each soak success subtracts one die from the total damage inflicted. As with damage rolls, soak rolls may not botch, only fail.

Example: Liselle the Gangrel has Stamina 3 and Fortitude 1. She is attacked with a knife, and the attacker scores three levels of lethal damage. Liselle may soak this attack with four dice (Stamina 3 + Fortitude 1). She rolls 1, 9, 9, 7. The "1" cancels out one of the successes, leaving Liselle with two. She thus ignores two of the three health levels inflicted by the knife, taking only one level of damage.

Had Liselle been merely human, she would not have been able to soak the (lethal) knife wound at all, and would have taken the full three health levels.

Armor

Simply put, armor adds to your character's soak. The armor's rating combines with your base soak for purposes of reducing damage. Light armor offers a small amount of protection, but doesn't greatly hinder mobility. Heavy armor provides a lot of protection, but can restrict flexibility.

Armor protects against bashing, lethal and aggravated damage from teeth and claws; it does not protect against fire or sunlight. Armor is not indestructible. If the damage rolled in a single attack equals twice the armor's rating, the armor is destroyed.

Armor types, their ratings and other specifics are described on p. 214.

Combat Maneuvers

These maneuvers give you a variety of choices in combat. Roleplaying combat is more entertaining if you can visualize your character's moves instead of simply rolling dice. Most of these maneuvers take one action to execute.

General Maneuvers

• **Aborting Actions:** You can abandon your character's declared action in favor of a defensive action as long as your character hasn't acted in the turn. Actions that can be aborted to include block, dodge and parry. A successful Willpower roll versus difficulty 6 (or the expenditure of a Willpower point) is required for a character to abort an action and perform a defensive one instead. When spending Willpower for an abort maneuver, a character may declare the Willpower expenditure

at the time of the abort. A Willpower roll to abort is considered a reflexive, not an action. (See "Defensive Maneuvers," below, for descriptions of block, dodge and parry.)

• **Ambush:** Ambushes involve surprising a target to get in a decisive first strike. The attacker rolls Dexterity + Stealth in a resisted action against the target's Perception + Alertness. If the attacker scores more successes, she can stage one free attack on the target and adds any extra successes from the resisted roll to her attack dice pool. On a tie, the attacker still attacks first, although the target may perform a defensive maneuver. If the defender gets more successes, he spots the ambush, and both parties roll initiative normally. Targets already involved in combat cannot be ambushed.

• **Blind Fighting/Fire:** Staging attacks while blind (or in pitch darkness) usually incurs a +2 difficulty, and ranged attacks cannot be accurately made at all. The powers of Heightened Senses (p. 149) and Eyes of the Beast (p. 173) partly or fully negate this penalty.

• **Flank and Rear Attacks:** Characters attacking targets from the flank gain an additional attack die. Characters attacking from the rear gain two additional attack dice.

• **Movement:** A character may move half of her running distance (see "Movement," p. 200) and still take an action in a turn. Other maneuvers such as leaping or tumbling may be considered separate actions, depending on their complexity.

• **Multiple Actions:** If you declare multiple actions, subtract dice from the first dice pool equal to the total number of actions taken. Each subsequent action loses an additional die (cumulative). If a character performs *only* defensive actions in a turn, use the appropriate block, dodge or parry system.

The Discipline of Celerity allows vampires to take multiple actions without this penalty. See the Discipline description for particulars.

• **Targeting:** Aiming for a specific location incurs an added difficulty, but can bypass armor or cover, or can result in an increased damage effect. The Storyteller should consider special results beyond a simple increase in damage, depending on the attack and the target.

Target Size	Difficulty	Damage
Medium (limb, briefcase)	+1	No modifier
Small (hand, head, computer)	+2	+1
Precise (eye, heart, lock)	+3	+2

Defensive Maneuvers

It's a given that your character tries to avoid being hit in combat — that's why everyone makes attack rolls. Sometimes, though, all your character wants to do is avoid attacks. You may announce a *defensive action* at any time before your character's opponent makes an attack roll, as long as your character has an action left to perform. You can declare a defensive action on your character's turn in the initiative, or can even *abort* to a defensive maneuver. You must make a successful Willpower roll (or may simply spend one point of Willpower) to abort. If the Willpower roll fails, your character must carry out the action that you declared originally.

There are three types of defensive actions: block, dodge and parry. Your character can defend against virtually any kind of attack with these three maneuvers. However, your character may not be able to avoid every single attack that's directed at her. She can't dodge when there's no room to maneuver, and she can't block or parry if she doesn't know an attack is coming.

Each defensive maneuver uses the same basic system: The defensive action is a resisted roll against the opponent's attack roll. Unless the attacker gets more total successes, he misses. If the attacker gets more successes, those that he achieves in excess of the defender's successes, if any, are used to hit (the attacker doesn't necessarily use *all* the successes he rolled). So if the defender has fewer successes than the attacker does, the defender's maneuver can still reduce the effectiveness of the attack, even if the maneuver can't counteract it completely.

• **Block:** A Dexterity + Brawl maneuver using your character's own body to deflect a hand-to-hand bashing attack. Lethal and aggravated attacks cannot be blocked unless the defender has Fortitude or is wearing armor.

• **Dodge:** A Dexterity + Dodge maneuver useful for avoiding attacks of all types. Your character bobs and weaves to avoid Melee or Brawl attacks (if there's no room to maneuver, she must block or parry instead). In firefights, your character moves at least one yard and ends up behind cover (if there's no room to maneuver and/or no cover available, she can drop to the ground). If your character remains under cover or prone thereafter, cover rules apply against further Firearms attacks (see "Cover," p. 212).

• **Parry:** A Dexterity + Melee maneuver using a weapon to block a Brawl or Melee attack. If a character makes a Brawl attack and the defender parries with a weapon that normally causes lethal damage, the attacker can actually be hurt by a successful parry. If the defender rolls more successes than the attacker does in the resisted action, the defender rolls the weapon's base damage plus the parry's extra successes as a damage dice pool against the attacker.

Block, dodge and parry can be performed as part of a multiple action in your character's turn (punching then blocking, shooting then dodging, parrying then striking). Using a multiple action to act and defend is advantageous because your character can still accomplish something in a turn besides avoiding attacks.

Example: Liselle wants to claw a ghoul, then dodge two attacks — a multiple action. This is considered three separate actions using her Dexterity (3) + Brawl (2) for the claw slash, and her Dexterity (3) + Dodge (3) two separate times for dodging. The claw slash is reduced by three dice (giving her two dice in her dice pool) because Liselle performs three actions. The first dodge is reduced by four dice (for another dice pool of two), per the multiple-action rules. The final dodge is reduced by five dice (leaving one die).

Rather than make defensive maneuvers a part of a multiple action, you may declare that your character spends an entire turn defending. The normal multiple-action rules are not used in this case. Instead, you have a full dice pool for the first defensive action, but lose one die, cumulatively, for each subsequent defense action made in the same turn. It is difficult to avoid several incoming attacks.

Remember that any actions, including defensive ones, versus multiple attackers still suffer difficulty penalties (see "Multiple Opponents," p. 211).

Example: Liselle spends a whole turn dodging. With a Dexterity of 3 and a Dodge of 3, she can dodge up to six attacks. Liselle's player rolls six dice against the first attack, five dice against the second, four dice against the third, three dice against the fourth, two dice against the fifth and a single die against the sixth attack. Liselle can't do anything else that turn but dodge.

CLOSE COMBAT MANEUVERS

This is simply a listing of the common maneuvers used in close combat; feel free to develop your own moves (with the Storyteller's approval). All hand-to-hand attacks inflict bashing damage unless stated otherwise. The damage inflicted by melee attacks depends on the weapon type (see the Melee Weapons Chart, p. 214). It is typically lethal, though clubs and other blunt instruments inflict bashing damage.

Difficulty and damage for these maneuvers may be modified at the Storyteller's discretion, depending on the combat style the character uses. As always, drama and excitement take precedence over rules systems.

• **Bite:** This maneuver is available only to vampires (or other supernatural creatures with sharp teeth, such as werewolves). A bite maneuver is a "combat" bite, intended to cause damage rather than drain blood. Bite damage is aggravated. To use a bite attack, the vampire must first perform a successful clinch, hold or tackle maneuver (see below). On the turn following the successful attack, the player may declare the bite attempt and make a roll using the modifiers below.

Alternatively, a player can declare her vampire's bite to be a "Kiss" attack. A Kiss is resolved in the same way as a normal bite, but inflicts no health levels of damage. Upon connecting with a Kiss, the vampire may begin to drain the victim's blood at the normal rate, and the victim is typically helpless to resist (see p. 139 for specifics). Following the Kiss, a vampire may, if she chooses, lick the puncture wound of the Kiss closed, thereby removing any evidence that she has fed.

Traits: Dexterity + Brawl   **Difficulty:** Normal

Accuracy: +1   **Damage:** Strength +1

• **Claw:** This attack is available only to vampires with the Protean power of Feral Claws or who construct bone spurs with the Vicissitude power of Bonecraft. A few other supernatural creatures, such as werewolves, also have claws. A claw attack

inflicts aggravated damage (if Feral Claws) or lethal damage (if a Vicissitude-constructed weapon).

Traits: Dexterity + Brawl **Difficulty:** Normal
Accuracy: Normal **Damage:** Strength +1

• **Clinch:** On a successful attack roll, the attacker goes into a clinch with the target. In the first turn, the attacker may roll Strength damage. In each subsequent turn, combatants act on their orders in the initiative. A combatant can inflict Strength damage automatically or attempt to escape the clinch. No other actions are allowed until one combatant breaks free. To escape a clinch, make a resisted Strength + Brawl roll against the opponent. If the escaping character has more successes, she breaks free; if not, the characters continue to grapple in the next turn.

Traits: Strength + Brawl **Difficulty:** Normal
Accuracy: Normal **Damage:** Strength

• **Disarm:** To strike an opponent's weapon, the attacker must make an attack roll at +1 difficulty (typically 7). If successful, the attacker rolls damage normally. If successes rolled exceed the opponent's Strength score, the opponent takes no damage but is disarmed. A botch usually means the attacker drops her own weapon or is struck by her target's weapon.

Traits: Dexterity + Melee **Difficulty:** +1
Accuracy: Normal **Damage:** Special

• **Hold:** This attack inflicts no damage, as the intent is to immobilize rather than injure the subject. On a successful roll, the attacker holds the target until the subject's next action. At that time, both combatants roll resisted Strength + Brawl actions; the subject remains immobilized (able to take no other action) until she rolls more successes than the attacker does.

Traits: Strength + Brawl **Difficulty:** Normal
Accuracy: Normal **Damage:** None

• **Kick:** Kicks range from simple front kicks to aerial spins. The base attack is at +1 difficulty and inflicts the attacker's Strength +1 in damage. These ratings may be modified further at the Storyteller's discretion, increasing in damage and/or difficulty as the maneuver increases in complexity.

Ability: Brawl **Difficulty:** +1
Accuracy: Normal **Damage:** Strength +1

• **Multiple Opponents:** A character who battles multiple opponents in close combat suffers attack and defense difficulties of +1, cumulative, for each opponent after the first (to a maximum of +4).

• **Strike:** The attacker lashes out with a fist. The base attack is a standard action and inflicts the character's Strength in damage. The Storyteller may adjust the difficulty and/or damage depending on the type of punch: hook, jab, haymaker, karate strike.

Traits: Dexterity + Brawl **Difficulty:** Normal
Accuracy: Normal **Damage:** Strength

• **Sweep:** The attacker uses her own legs to knock the legs out from under her opponent. The target takes Strength damage and must roll Dexterity + Athletics (difficulty 8) or suffer a knockdown (see "Maneuver Complications," p. 213).

The attacker can also use a staff, chain or similar implement to perform a sweep. The effect is the same, although the target takes damage per the weapon type.

Traits: Dexterity + Brawl/Melee **Difficulty:** +1
Accuracy: Normal   **Damage:** Str; knockdown

• **Tackle:** The attacker rushes her opponent, tackling him to the ground. The attack roll is at +1 difficulty, and the maneuver inflicts Strength +1 damage. Additionally, both combatants must roll Dexterity + Athletics (difficulty 7) or suffer a knockdown (see "Maneuver Complications," p. 213). Even if the target's Athletics roll succeeds, he is unbalanced, suffering +1 difficulty to his actions for the next turn.

Traits: Strength + Brawl   **Difficulty:** +1
Accuracy: Normal   **Damage:** Strength +1

• **Weapon Length:** It is difficult to get in range with a punch or knife if someone else is wielding a sword or staff. A character being fended off with a longer weapon must close in one yard, then strike, losing a die from her attack roll in the process.

• **Weapon Strike:** A slashing blow, thrust or jab, depending on the weapon used. See the Melee Weapons Chart, p. 214, for particulars.

Traits: Dexterity + Melee   **Difficulty:** Normal
Accuracy: Normal   **Damage:** Per weapon type

RANGED COMBAT MANEUVERS

Many physical conflicts involve ranged weapons. The following maneuvers allow for a number of useful actions during a firefight, but don't feel limited by this list. If the need arises, try developing a new maneuver (at the Storyteller's discretion). Refer to the Ranged Weapons Chart, p. 214, for specific information.

• **Aiming:** The attacker adds one die to her attack dice pool on a single shot for each turn spent aiming. The maximum number of dice that can be added in this way equals the character's Perception, and a character must have Firearms 1 or better to use this maneuver. A scope adds two more dice to the attacker's pool in the first turn of aiming (in addition to those added for Perception). The attacker may do nothing but aim during this time. Additionally, it isn't possible to aim at a target that is moving faster than a walk.

• **Automatic Fire:** The weapon unloads its entire ammunition clip in one attack against a single target. The attacker makes a single roll, adding 10 dice to her accuracy. However, the attack roll is at a +2 difficulty due to the weapon's recoil. Extra successes add to the damage dice pool, which is still treated as equivalent to one bullet. An attacker using automatic fire may not target a specific area of the body.

Example: Kincaid unloads a full AK-47 clip at the advancing elder. His player rolls Dexterity (4) + Firearms (3) + 10 (for the maneuver). The roll is made versus difficulty 8 (6 for short range +2 for recoil). He scores a total of six successes, and the elder doesn't dodge. Kincaid's player now rolls 12 dice of damage — 7 (the base damage for an assault rifle) + 5 (for the successes). The clip is completely emptied.

This attack is permissible only if the weapon's clip is at least half-full to begin with.

Traits: Dexterity + Firearms   **Difficulty:** +2
Accuracy: +10   **Damage:** Special

• **Cover:** Cover increases an attacker's difficulty to hit a target (and often the target's ability to fire back). Difficulty penalties for hitting a target under various types of cover are listed below. A character who fires back from behind cover is also at something of a disadvantage to hit, as he exposes himself and ducks back under protection. Firearms attacks made by a defender who is under cover are at one lower difficulty than listed below. (If a listed difficulty is +1, then the defender suffers no penalty to make attacks from under that cover.) If your character hides behind a wall, attackers' Firearms rolls have a +2 difficulty. Your character's attacks staged from behind that wall are at +1 difficulty.

Note that difficulties for combatants who are both under cover are cumulative. If one combatant is prone and one is behind a wall, attacks staged by the prone character are at +2 difficulty, while attacks staged by the character behind the wall are also at +2 difficulty.

Cover Type	Difficulty Increase
Light (lying prone)	+1
Good (behind wall)	+2
Superior (only head exposed)	+3

• **Multiple Shots:** An attacker may take more than one shot in a turn by declaring a multiple action (the first shot's dice pool is reduced by the total number of shots fired, and each subsequent shot is reduced by an additional die, cumulative). The attacker can fire a number of shots up to the weapon's full rate of fire.

Ability: Dexterity + Firearms   **Difficulty:** Normal
Accuracy: Special   **Damage:** Weapon type

• **Range:** The Ranged Weapons Chart lists each weapon's short range; attacks made at that range are versus difficulty 6. Twice that listing is the weapon's maximum range. Attacks made up to maximum range are versus difficulty 8. Attacks made at targets within two meters are considered *point blank*. Point-blank shots are made versus difficulty 4.

• **Reloading:** Reloading takes one full turn and requires the character's concentration. Like any other maneuver, reloading can be performed as part of a multiple action.

• **Strafing:** Instead of aiming at one target, full-automatic weapons can be fired across an area. Strafing adds 10 dice to accuracy on a standard attack roll, and empties the clip. A maximum of three yards can be covered with this maneuver.

The attacker divides any successes gained on the attack roll evenly among all targets in the covered area (successes assigned to hit an individual are added to that target's damage dice pool, as well). If only one target is within range or the area of effect, only half the successes affect him. The attacker then assigns any leftover successes as she desires. If fewer successes are rolled than there are targets, only one may be assigned per target until they are all allocated.

Dodge rolls against strafing are at +1 difficulty.

Ability: Dexterity + Firearms   **Difficulty:** +2
Accuracy: +10   **Damage:** Special

• **Three-Round Burst:** The attacker gains two additional dice on a single attack roll, and expends three shots from the weapon's clip. Only certain weapons may perform this maneuver; see the Ranged Weapons Chart for particulars. Attacks are made at +1 difficulty due to recoil. As with full-auto fire, the damage dice pool is based on one bullet from the weapon in question.

Ability: Dexterity + Firearms   **Difficulty:** +1

Accuracy: +2   **Damage:** Weapon type

• **Two Weapons:** Firing two weapons gives the attacker a distinct advantage, but has its share of complications. Doing so is considered performing a multiple action, complete with reduced dice pools for total shots taken and for any recoil. Additionally, the attacker suffers +1 difficulty for her off-hand (unless she's ambidextrous). The attacker can fire a number of shots up to each weapon's rate of fire.

Ability: Dexterity + Firearms   **Difficulty:** +1/off-hand

Accuracy: Special   **Damage:** Weapon type

MANEUVER COMPLICATIONS

The following are common combat complications. The Storyteller should add any others as the situation warrants.

• **Blinded:** Add two dice to attack rolls made against a blinded target. Furthermore, blind characters are at +2 difficulty on all actions.

• **Dazed:** If, in a single attack, the attacker rolls a number of damage successes greater than the target's Stamina (for mortals) or Stamina + 2 (for vampires and other supernatural beings), the victim is dazed. The target must spend her next available turn shaking off the attack's effects. Only damage successes that penetrate the defender's soak attempt count toward this total.

• **Immobilization:** Add two dice to attack rolls made on an immobilized (i.e., held by someone or something) but still struggling target. Attacks hit automatically if the target is completely immobilized (tied up, staked or otherwise paralyzed).

• **Knockdown:** Quite simply, the victim falls down. After suffering a knockdown, the subject makes a Dexterity + Athletics roll. If successful, she may get back on her feet immediately, but her initiative is reduced by two in the next turn. On a failed roll, the subject spends her next action climbing to her feet, if she chooses to rise. On a botch, she lands particularly hard or at a severe angle, taking an automatic health level of normal damage.

Maneuvers like tackle and sweep are intended to knock an opponent down. However, an especially powerful attack of any kind may send the target to the ground. Such instances are best left to the Storyteller's discretion, and should occur only when appropriately cinematic or suitable to the story.

• **Stake Through Heart:** A vampire can indeed be incapacitated by the classic wooden stake of legend. However, the legends err on one point: A Kindred impaled through the heart with a wooden stake is not destroyed, but merely paralyzed until the stake is removed.

To stake a vampire, an attacker must target the heart (difficulty 9). If the attack succeeds and inflicts at least three health levels of damage, the target is immobilized. An immobilized victim is conscious (and may use the Auspex Discipline), but may not move or spend blood points.

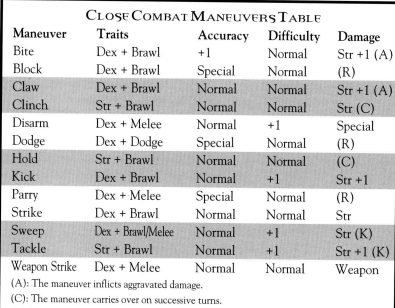

CLOSE COMBAT MANEUVERS TABLE

Maneuver	Traits	Accuracy	Difficulty	Damage
Bite	Dex + Brawl	+1	Normal	Str +1 (A)
Block	Dex + Brawl	Special	Normal	(R)
Claw	Dex + Brawl	Normal	Normal	Str +1 (A)
Clinch	Str + Brawl	Normal	Normal	Str (C)
Disarm	Dex + Melee	Normal	+1	Special
Dodge	Dex + Dodge	Special	Normal	(R)
Hold	Str + Brawl	Normal	Normal	(C)
Kick	Dex + Brawl	Normal	+1	Str +1
Parry	Dex + Melee	Special	Normal	(R)
Strike	Dex + Brawl	Normal	Normal	Str
Sweep	Dex + Brawl/Melee	Normal	+1	Str (K)
Tackle	Str + Brawl	Normal	+1	Str +1 (K)
Weapon Strike	Dex + Melee	Normal	Normal	Weapon

(A): The maneuver inflicts aggravated damage.

(C): The maneuver carries over on successive turns.

(K): The maneuver causes knockdown.

(R): The maneuver reduces an opponent's attack successes.

RANGED COMBAT MANEUVERS TABLE

Maneuver	Traits	Accuracy	Difficulty	Damage
Automatic Fire	Dex + Firearms	+10	+2	Weapon
Multiple Shots	Dex + Firearms	Special	Normal	Weapon
Strafing	Dex + Firearms	+10	+2	Weapon
3-Round Burst	Dex + Firearms	+2	+1	Weapon
Two Weapons	Dex + Firearms	Special	+1/off-hand	Weapon

ARMOR CHART

Class	Armor Rating	Penalty
Class One (reinforced clothing)	1	0
Class Two (armor T-shirt)	2	1
Class Three (Kevlar vest)	3	1
Class Four (flak jacket)	4	2
Class Five (full riot gear)	5	3

Armor adds its rating to the character's soak dice pool against bashing damage, lethal damage, and aggravated damage from fangs and claws. It does not protect against fire or sunlight. However, armor also subtracts a number of dice from dice pools related to bodily coordination and agility (most Dexterity-based dice pools). This is reflected in the penalty listing. Attackers may make targeting rolls to hit unprotected portions of a defender and thus ignore the armor (Storyteller assigns difficulty penalty — typically +1 or +2).

MELEE WEAPONS CHART

Weapon	Damage	Conceal
Sap+	Strength +1	P
Club+	Strength +2	T
Knife	Strength +1	J
Sword	Strength +2	T
Axe	Strength +3	N
Stake*	Strength +1	T

+ Denotes a blunt object. Blunt objects inflict bashing damage unless targeted at the head (see "Targeting," p. 209). If so, they inflict lethal damage.

* May paralyze a vampire if driven through the heart. The attacker must target the heart (difficulty 9) and score three damage successes.

RANGED WEAPONS CHART

Type	Damage	Range	Rate	Clip	Conceal
Example					
Revolver, Lt.	4	12	3	6	P
SW M640 (.38 Special)					
Revolver, Hvy.	6	35	2	6	J
Colt Anaconda (.44 Magnum)					
Pistol, Lt.	4	20	4	17+1	P
Glock 17 (9mm)					
Pistol, Hvy.	5	30	3	7+1	J
Sig P220 (.45 ACP)					
Rifle	8	200	1	5+1	N
Remington M-700 (30.06)					
SMG, Small*	4	25	3	30+1	J
Ingram Mac-10 (9mm)					
SMG, Large*	4	50	3	32+1	T
Uzi (9mm)					
Assault Rifle*	7	150	3	42+1	N
Steyr-Aug (5.56mm)					
Shotgun	8	20	1	5+1	T
Ithaca M-37 (12-Gauge)					
Shotgun, Semi-auto	8	20	3	8+1	T
Fiachi-Law 12 (12-Gauge)					
Crossbow**	5	20	1	1	T

Damage: Indicates the damage dice pool. Versus mortals, firearms are considered lethal damage. Versus vampires, firearms are considered bashing damage unless the head is targeted (see "Targeting," p. 209), in which case the damage is considered lethal.

Range: This is the practical shot range in yards. Weapons may be fired at twice this distance, but the attacks are considered long range (difficulty 8).

Rate: The maximum number of bullets or three-round bursts the gun can fire in a single turn. This rate does not apply to full-auto or spray attacks.

Clip: The number of shells a gun can hold. The +1 indicates a bullet can be held in the chamber, ready to fire.

Concealment: P = Can be carried in the pocket; J = Can be hidden in a jacket; T = Can be hidden in a trenchcoat; N = Cannot be concealed on the person at all.

*Indicates the weapon is capable of three-round bursts, full-auto and sprays.

**The crossbow is included for characters who wish to try staking an opponent. Crossbows require five turns to reload. Unless the crossbow is aimed at the head or heart, it inflicts bashing damage on Kindred. It inflicts lethal damage versus mortals.

HEALTH

As mentioned in Chapter Three, your character has a Health Trait comprising seven health levels. Although vampires are immortal and do not die naturally, sufficient injury can incapacitate them, drive them into lengthy periods of dormancy, or even kill them once more (this time for good).

THE HEALTH CHART

The Health chart on the character sheet helps you track your character's current physical condition. It also lists the penalty imposed on your dice pool for each level of injury that your character sustains. As your character suffers more injuries, her health declines until she becomes incapacitated — or dead.

Every character has seven health levels, ranging from Bruised to Incapacitated. Characters can also be in full health (with no health levels checked off), in torpor, or dead. When an attacker scores a success on a damage roll, your character takes one health level of damage. This is marked on your character sheet in the appropriate box, although the mark you make depends on the type of damage inflicted (see "Applying Damage," below).

The number to the left of the lowest marked box indicates your current dice penalty. As your character gets more and more battered, it's increasingly difficult for him to perform even the simplest of tasks. The dice penalty is subtracted from your dice pool for every action (not reflexives such as soak) until the wound heals.

The penalty also indicates impaired movement. For convenience, we reprint the Health chart from Chapter Three.

HEALTH CHART

Health Level	Dice Pool Penalty	Movement Penalty
Bruised		Character is only bruised a bit and suffers no dice pool penalties due to damage.
Hurt	-1	Character is superficially hurt and suffers no movement hindrance.
Injured	-1	Character suffers minor injuries and movement is mildly inhibited (halve maximum running speed).
Wounded	-2	Character suffers significant damage and may not run (though he may still walk).
Mauled	-2	Character is badly injured and may only hobble about (three yards/turn).
Crippled	-5	Character is catastrophically injured and may only crawl (one yard/turn).
Incapacitated		Character is incapable of movement and is likely unconscious. He may do nothing except spend blood points. Incapacitated vampires with no blood in their bodies enter torpor.
Torpor		Character enters a death-like trance. He may do nothing, not even spend blood, until a certain period of time has passed.
Final Death		Character dies again, this time forever.

• **Incapacitated:** The stage immediately before torpor, incapacitation differs from unconsciousness in that your character collapses from the combined effects of physical trauma and pain. She falls to the ground and may do nothing except spend blood points to heal damage. Further damage suffered by an incapacitated vampire sends her into torpor or, if the damage is aggravated, inflicts Final Death on her.

• **Torpor:** *Torpor* is the deathlike sleep common to the undead, particularly among ancient vampires. Torpor may be entered voluntarily (certain undead, weary of the current age, enter torpor in hopes of reawakening in a more hospitable time) or involuntarily (through wounds or loss of blood). Once in torpor, a character remains dormant for a period of time depending on her Humanity rating.

As mentioned, characters with zero blood points in their blood pools begin to lose health levels each time the rules call for them to spend blood. When a vampire falls below Incapacitated in this fashion, she enters torpor. There she will remain until someone feeds her at least a blood point. If this happens, she may rise, regardless of Humanity rating. This sort of revivification works only for vampires who enter torpor from blood loss.

Vampires who enter torpor due to wounds must rest for a period depending on their Humanity rating:

Humanity	Length of Torpor
10	One day
9	Three days
8	One week
7	Two weeks
6	One month
5	One year
4	One decade
3	Five decades
2	One century
1	Five centuries
0	Millennium+

Following this period of rest, the player may spend a blood point and make an Awakening roll (p. 204) for her character to rise. If the vampire has no blood in her body, she may not rise until she is fed; if the player fails the Awakening roll, she may spend another blood point and make an Awakening roll the following night. If the vampire rises successfully, she is considered Crippled and should either spend blood or hunt immediately.

A character may enter torpor voluntarily. This state resembles the character's normal daily rest, but is a deeper form of slumber and should not be entered into lightly. A vampire in voluntary torpor may rise after half the mandatory time period for involuntary torpor, but must make an Awakening roll to do so. A torpid vampire may ignore the nightly need for blood; she is effectively in hibernation.

Mortals have no torpor rating; if reduced below Incapacitated, they simply die.

• **Final Death:** If a vampire is at the Incapacitated health level or in torpor and takes one more level of aggravated damage, he dies permanently and finally. A player's character who meets Final Death is out of the game; the player must create a new character if she wishes to continue play.

An incapacitated or torpid vampire may also be sent to Final Death through massive amounts of bashing or lethal trauma (decapitated, trapped under a 10-ton rock, fed into a wood chipper, caught at ground zero of an explosion, crushed by deep-sea pressure, etc.). Typically, this damage must be enough to destroy or dismember the corpse beyond repair.

APPLYING DAMAGE

There are three damage types in **Vampire**. Bashing damage includes all forms of temporary injury — from punches, clubs and other blunt trauma. Vampires, and only vampires, consider firearms attacks to be bashing damage as well — unless the bullets are aimed at the head (difficulty 8), in which case they are considered lethal. Vampires can suffer bashing damage, but consider it more of an annoyance than anything else. Lethal damage covers permanent, killing wounds. Humans die easily from lethal injury, and even the undead can be traumatized by massive amounts of lethal damage. Finally, aggravated damage includes those forces even other vampires fear — fire, sunlight, and the teeth and claws of their own kind.

All types of injuries are cumulative, and the combined injury determines your character's current health level. Specifics on each type of damage are provided below.

Bashing and lethal damage differ in their effects, but, for vampires, both types of damage are considered *normal*. Normal damage is recorded as a slash ("/") in the appropriate Health chart box. Aggravated damage is marked with an "X" for each level inflicted. Aggravated damage always gets marked above normal (whether bashing or lethal). So if you mark a level of normal damage in the Bruised box, and take one aggravated health level later on, "move down" the bashing level to the Hurt box by marking that box with a "/." The aggravated level is then noted by simply drawing another slash through the Bruised box, turning it into "X." Normal levels taken after aggravated levels are simply drawn in on the next open box. Normal damage isn't as severe as aggravated, so it's always marked last and healed first (see below).

—HEALTH—

Bruised		☒
Hurt	-1	☑
Injured	-1	☐
Wounded	-2	☐
Mauled	-2	☐
Crippled	-5	☐
Incapacitated		☐

Example: Veronica Abbey-Roth, trapped in a witch-hunter's sanctum, has already taken a level of bashing (normal) damage from an Inquisitor's punch (Veronica's Health chart is noted with "/" in the Bruised box). Another witch-hunter blasts Veronica with a propane torch, scoring three aggravated health levels. Veronica's chart is marked with "X" in the Bruised, Hurt and Injured health levels, and "/" in the Wounded box (essentially moving the punch's damage down the chart). The combined damage puts Veronica at -2 dice to all her action dice pools. On the verge of frenzy, Veronica beats her way through the Inquisitors and stumbles out of the ancient cathedral.

BASHING DAMAGE

Bashing damage covers all forms of injury that aren't likely to kill instantly and that fade relatively quickly. Most forms of hand-to-hand combat — punches, clinches, kicks, tackles and the like — inflict bashing damage. Bashing damage generally impairs less than lethal damage does, and heals faster.

Vampires are relatively unaffected by bashing damage — a punch to the gut has little effect on the undead. However, massive concussive trauma can send a vampire into torpor.

Mortals may soak bashing damage with their Stamina, while vampires may also soak bashing damage with their Stamina (+ Fortitude, if they have that Discipline). However, any bashing damage applied to a vampire *after* the soak roll is halved (round fractions down) — the Kindred's corpselike bodies simply don't bruise and break like the kine's.

Example: Veronica has been cornered by her enemy, the Sabbat vampire Kincaid (it's just not Veronica's lucky night!). Kincaid takes a swing at Veronica. He strikes her, and his player calculates damage. Kincaid has a Strength 4 and two levels of Potence. His damage roll is a very good 8, 6, 7, 9, plus two automatic successes for Potence — a full six health levels of damage. Veronica tries to soak (versus the standard difficulty of 6), using her Stamina of 2. Her player rolls a 3 and 8 — one success. Kincaid inflicts five health levels of bashing damage — but, because Veronica is undead, she halves the final result and rounds down. She suffers only two health levels of damage.

Veronica, in desperation, swings back, and manages to hit the Sabbat. She has a Strength of 1, so only one die is rolled. Luckily, it comes up 9, inflicting one health level of damage, and Kincaid fails his soak roll (Stamina 4 and Fortitude 1 allow him to roll five dice, which come up 4, 5, 1, 9, and 3). However, because the damage is bashing, the one health level of damage is halved and rounded down to zero! Veronica flails frantically at Kincaid, who laughs at her pathetic efforts to hurt him.

If your character falls to Incapacitated due to bashing (or lethal) damage, then takes another level of bashing (or lethal) damage, she enters torpor. If your character falls to Incapacitated due to bashing damage but then takes a level of aggravated damage, she meets Final Death.

LETHAL DAMAGE

Lethal damage is just that — lethal, at least to mortals. Even vampires take a sword-wielder seriously — a vampire who is hacked to bits or decapitated will die the Final Death, though not as readily as a mortal. Knives, bullets, swords and the like all cause lethal wounds. At the Storyteller's option, blunt attacks aimed at a vital body part (difficulty 8 or 9 to target) can cause lethal damage, particularly versus mortals.

Lethal damage is intended to cause immediate and grievous injury. For the kine, lethal injuries take a long time to heal and usually require medical attention for any hope of recovery. For well-fed vampires, knife wounds, shotgun blasts and the like are simply…annoying.

Mortal characters may not soak lethal damage at all — all such damage is applied directly to their health levels. Kindred characters may soak lethal damage normally with Stamina (+ Fortitude, if they have it). Lethal damage that penetrates the soak roll is applied normally to their health levels. However, lethal damage is considered normal for the purpose of healing, so vampires may easily nullify lethal damage by spending blood points.

When your character's Health boxes fill to Incapacitated, and she takes a further level of lethal damage, she enters torpor (p. 216). If your character is reduced to Incapacitated via lethal damage, and she takes a further level of aggravated damage, she meets Final Death.

Aggravated Damage

Certain attacks are anathema to the undead. Fire and the rays of the sun inflict terrible wounds on the undead, as can the teeth and claws of other vampires (as well as the attacks of werewolves or other supernatural creatures).

As mentioned, each level of aggravated damage should be marked with an "X" on the Health chart. Aggravated damage may not be soaked except with the Discipline of Fortitude. Moreover, aggravated damage is far more difficult to heal. A level of aggravated damage may be healed only with a full day of rest and the expenditure of five blood points (though a vampire may, at the end of the full day's rest, cure additional aggravated health levels by spending an additional five blood points *and* one Willpower point per extra aggravated health level to be healed). Worst of all, a vampire who loses his last health level due to aggravated damage meets Final Death — his eternal life ends at last, and he goes to whatever reward awaits him beyond the grave.

Mortals may ignore sunlight, but obviously take damage from fire, fangs and claws. If a mortal is susceptible to a type of aggravated damage (fire, for example), that damage is treated as lethal.

States of Being

The World of Darkness is a hostile place. The dangers inherent to such an uncivilized environment are many, and they inflict the same kinds of harm that combat does. As well, a vampire's greatest enemy lies within, in the form of the Beast. Whether a vampire suffers the fiery grip of frenzy or the slow descent into monstrousness, the Beast is ever willing to batten on the Damned.

The following systems present a variety of ways that characters can suffer injury, whether physical, mental or emotional. As well, this section presents a couple of rare and precious ways whereby the Damned can hope to rise above their state.

Blood Bond

One of the most wondrous and terrible properties of Kindred vitae is its ability to enslave nearly any being who drinks of it three times. Each sip of a particular Kindred's blood gives the Kindred in question a greater emotional hold over the drinker. If a being drinks three times, on three separate nights, from the same Kindred, she falls victim to a state known as the *blood bond*. A vampire who holds a blood bond over another being is said to be that victim's *regnant*, while the being subordinate to the bond is called the *thrall*.

Put simply, blood bond is one of the most potent emotional sensations known. A blood bound victim is absolutely devoted to her regnant and will do nearly anything for him. Even the most potent uses of Dominate cannot overcome the thrall's feelings for her regnant; only true love stands a chance against the bond, and even that is not a sure thing.

MORTALS' HEALING TIMES

Though the power of their Blood enables vampires to heal most wounds instantly, mortal "licksticks" are not so fortunate. The following systems allow Storytellers to simulate the effects of damage on vampires' mortal foes, friends…and prey.

Like vampires, mortals have seven health levels and suffer dice pool penalties for wounds. Unlike vampires, mortals can heal their wounds only through time, rest and medical care. Moreover, mortals have no "torpor" state; any amount of damage below the Incapacitated level kills them. Mortals can soak bashing damage, but cannot soak lethal or aggravated damage (though obviously mortals take no damage from sunlight).

Each level of damage to a mortal (whether bashing or lethal) must be healed individually. Thus, if a mortal takes enough bashing damage to reduce him to Incapacitated, he spends a full 12 hours in a delirious state before healing to Crippled. Healing that level takes six hours, and so on.

HEALING BASHING DAMAGE

Bashing damage up to the Wounded level can be cared for without medical skill; these wounds heal on their own, without treatment. Bashing damage beyond Wounded may have deeper consequences. A mortal's vision or hearing may be altered due to a concussion, she may suffer excruciating pain from internal bruising or experience some other extreme discomfort. These effects can be negated if the mortal receives adequate medical attention.

Health Level	Recovery Time
Bruised to Wounded	One hour
Maimed	Three hours
Crippled	Six hours
Incapacitated	12 hours

Once bashing levels reach Incapacitated, mortals fall unconscious, but do not sink below Incapacitated… yet. However, any further bashing wounds are X'd over previous bashing ones, making them lethal. At that point, recovery is handled as lethal damage. In this way, a mortal can be slowly beaten to death.

HEALING LETHAL DAMAGE

Lethal damage of any sort can be deadly — that's why it's called lethal. Lethal wounds that go unattended may continue to bleed until the mortal passes out and dies from blood loss. Other dangers can also arise from infection, cellular damage or broken limbs.

Any lethal damage past Hurt requires medical treatment to prevent further harm. Untreated lethal wounds worsen by one level of lethal damage per day. When a mortal sustains lethal damage down to Incapacitated, he's one health level away from death. If he takes one more wound (whether bashing or lethal), he dies.

If the individual is at Maimed or higher, he may recover with rest over the times listed below. However, if the mortal is Crippled or Incapacitated, no recovery is possible unless he receives medical attention. Indeed, at Incapacitated the individual is comatose at worse and delirious at best, and could still die.

Health Level	Recovery Time
Bruised	One day
Hurt	Three days
Injured	One week
Wounded	One month
Maimed	Two months
Crippled	Three months
Incapacitated	Five months

The blood bond is most commonly used to ensnare mortals and ghouls, but Kindred can bind each other as well. Such is the blood bond's power that a mighty elder can be bound to a lowly neonate; in this respect, the blood of a 13th-generation fledgling is (presumably) as strong as that of Caine himself. As such, the blood bond forms an essential strategy in the Jyhad; some Ancients are said to hold dozens of influential Kindred in secret thralldom.

• **First drink:** The drinker begins to experience intermittent but strong feelings about the vampire. She may dream of him, or find herself "coincidentally" frequenting places where he might show up. There is no mechanical effect at this stage, but it should be roleplayed. All childer have this level of bond toward their sires, for the Embrace itself forces one drink upon the childer; they may love their "parents," hate them, or both, but are rarely indifferent toward them.

• **Second drink:** The drinker's feelings grow strong enough to influence her behavior. Though she is by no means enslaved to the vampire, he is definitely an important figure in her life. She may act as she pleases, but might have to make a Willpower roll to take actions directly harmful to the vampire. The vampire's

influence is such that he can persuade or command her with little effort (Social rolls against the thrall are at -1 difficulty).

• **Third drink:** Full-scale blood bond. At this level, the drinker is more or less completely bound to the vampire. He is the most important person in her life; lovers, relatives and even children become tertiary to her all-consuming passion.

At this level, a regnant may use the Dominate Discipline on a thrall, even without the benefit of eye contact. Merely hearing the regnant's voice is enough. Additionally, should the thrall try to resist the Dominate for some reason, the difficulty of such resistance is increased by two. Naturally, a higher-generation vampire still cannot use Dominate on a lower-generation thrall.

The blood bond is true love, albeit a twisted and perverse version of it. Ultimately, we can't reduce the vagaries of love down to a simple "yes/no" system. Some thralls (particularly people with Conformist or other dependent Natures or with Willpower 5 or less) will commit any act, including suicide or murder, for their beloved; other characters have certain core principles that they will not violate.

A full blood bond, once formed, is nearly inviolate. Once bound, a thrall is under the sway of her regnant and her regnant only. She cannot be bound again by another vampire unless the first blood bond wears away "naturally." A vampire can experience lesser (one- and two-drink) bonds toward several individuals; indeed, many Kindred enjoy such bonds, as they create artificial passion in their dead hearts. Upon the formation of a full blood bond, though, all lesser sensations are wiped away. Vampire lovers occasionally enter into mutual blood bonds with each other; this is the closest thing the undead can feel to true love. Even this sensation can turn to disgust or hate over the centuries, though, and in any event few Kindred are trusting enough to initiate it.

A blood bond is a mighty force, but it is at its most potent when perpetually reinforced with further drinks. Feeding a thrall often reinforces the bond, while depriving a thrall of vitae may cause the bond to grow tepid over time. As well, like any other relationship, treatment and courtesy play a part in the dynamics of the bond. A thrall who is treated well and fed often will likely fall even more deeply in love, while a thrall who is degraded and humiliated may find resentment and anger eating away at the bond.

It is possible, though difficult, for a vampire to temporarily resist a blood bond. Doing so requires the player to make a Willpower roll (difficulty is typically 8, though this can be modified depending on the regnant's treatment and the thrall's Nature) and accumulate a number of successes equal to the number of times the thrall has partaken of the regnant's blood. The thrall must then spend a Willpower point. Upon doing so, the bond is negated for a variable amount of time: from one scene (if the thrall merely wishes to plot against the regnant, deliver confidential information to an enemy, etc.) to one turn (if the thrall wishes to attack the regnant physically). The thrall can continue to expend Willpower to extend the duration of "freedom," but once she ceases doing so, the blood bond resumes at full force.

A blood bond can be broken, though this requires the thrall to not only avoid the regnant entirely for an extended period of time, but also spend great amounts of Willpower to overcome the "addiction." As a general rule, a thrall who neither sees nor feeds from her regnant for a period of (12 - Willpower) months finds her bond reduced by one level (so, a fully bound thrall with a Willpower of 5 has her blood bond reduced to the equivalent of two drinks if she goes seven straight months without any contact with the regnant). If the bond is reduced to zero in this fashion (a feat typically accompanied by the expenditure of a great deal of Willpower on the thrall's part, as she resists the gnawing urge to seek out her sire), it is nullified entirely.

Another, though somewhat less certain, way to be rid of the bond is to kill the regnant. Such a choice is extremely perilous on many levels, and makes no guarantees that everything will go smoothly. Those who have been released by such means claim the bond shatters like spun glass upon the moment of the regnant's Final Death. The thrall's Nature may play a large part in whether the control is completely ended, though, and such aftermath is best left in the hands of the Storyteller.

DEGENERATION

Let's face it: Despite all efforts to the contrary, a vampire is going to succumb to moral failure sooner or later in his unlife. Willfully or otherwise (ethics are particularly hard to maintain in frenzy), a vampire occasionally commits atrocity and risks losing his Humanity to the Beast. If the character feels remorse for his actions, he knows that his Humanity is still intact. If he commits a wrongful act and callously disregards it, however, his Humanity is obviously waning.

One of the most important themes of **Vampire: The Masquerade** is the Kindred's struggle to retain their souls and avoid the clutches of the Beast. Thus, it is extremely important to use morality and Humanity in a consistent, dramatic manner. If the Storyteller allows the players to (sometimes literally) get away with murder, the story will suffer, as one of the tragedies of vampiric existence vanishes. If the Storyteller is too strict with Humanity rules, though, all the characters will be ravening, blood-gorged maniacs by the end of the first session. Keeping a handle on Humanity is a hard thing to do, but the Degeneration system is designed to help that.

The system is simple: Whenever a character takes an action that the Storyteller decides is morally questionable, the character may suffer degeneration — a permanent loss of Humanity. If degeneration is a possibility, the player whose character commits the act should make a Conscience roll for that character. The difficulty is 8 — reprehensible acts are hard to justify — though the Storyteller may modify this. Willpower may not be spent for an automatic success on this roll — all the ego in the world won't protect a character from guilt.

If the player makes the roll with even one success, the character loses no Humanity — he feels enough remorse or somehow manages to justify his transgression. If he fails the roll, the character loses a point of Humanity. If the player botches, the character loses a point of both Humanity and Conscience, and also gains a derangement, decided upon by the Storyteller (who should make it appropriate). Obviously, morality is not something a Kindred can afford to take lightly. Remember that a vampire whose Humanity drops to zero is no longer suitable to be a player's character. (To be perfectly honest, Kindred with low Humanity

scores aren't particularly appropriate either, but can be enjoyably tragic figures in comparison to their nobler counterparts.)

ON THE BRINK

A Storyteller should always warn a player before she takes an action that may cause degeneration. Players should understand the consequences of their characters' actions, and should have the opportunity to enjoy making the decision. Likewise, a player whose character is in frenzy should be told when the character is about to do something heinous — and can only watch in impotent horror as the character casts her morals to the winds at the Beast's command. (Remember, though, that a player may spend a point of Willpower in order to stave off the pangs of frenzy for a turn.) Players should not be allowed to think they can get away with anything. Make it obvious that a roll may become necessary if vicious characters persist in committing self-centered deeds. Likewise, don't bait and switch. If you warn them that a roll is imminent, go through with it, or you risk ruining the mechanic's usefulness.

USING HIERARCHIES OF SIN

Degeneration checks may seem arbitrary or ill defined. To some degree, they are, but this is intentional. Moreover, degeneration checks are not random so much as they are subjective. A Storyteller has *carte blanche* to monitor character morality in her chronicle. This is a huge responsibility for the Storyteller, but one that ultimately makes for a great deal of tragedy and horror, as the characters gradually descend into a state of utter monstrosity though they desperately rail against it. Storytellers, beware — players should never feel that you are screwing them out of Humanity or, consequently, their characters. Use degeneration checks consistently but sparingly, lest the tragedy erode to an incessant series of failed die rolls. Because this mechanic is so heavily entrenched in the Storyteller's line of duty, her own morality is often reflected in how she applies the rule. This is encouraged, as it illustrates literally what **Vampire** may do only in allegory.

To lend a sense of order to degeneration checks, consult the Hierarchy of Sin here. (**Note:** Other Paths use Hierarchies of Sin as well, though their ideas of "sin" are different. See the Appendix

HIERARCHY OF SIN — HUMANITY	
Humanity	Moral Guideline
10	Selfish thoughts
9	Minor selfish acts
8	Injury to another (accidental or otherwise)
7	Theft
6	Accidental violation (drinking a vessel dry out of starvation)
5	Intentional property damage
4	Impassioned violation (manslaughter, killing a vessel in frenzy)
3	Planned violation (outright murder, savored exsanguination)
2	Casual violation (thoughtless killing, feeding past satiation)
1	Utter perversion or heinous acts

for other Paths and their ethical codes.) Whenever a character commits a dubious act, see how that action relates to the hierarchy. If the action is *at or below* the level of the character's Humanity score, a roll is warranted — as a character falls further down the Humanity scale, she becomes increasingly callous, and minor peccadilloes cease to bother her. The use of the term *violation* in the hierarchy is deliberately vague, to aid the Storyteller. A violation may be anything questionable, and is presented to avoid inclining the scale toward any single transgression. Violation may be killing, callous injury, rape (what do you think taking blood by force is?) or any other villainy the Storyteller considers wrong.

It seems hard to slide to the lowest echelons of the scale, but consider the prominence of the Beast as Humanity falters. Sooner or later, the character will be committing depravity outside her own volition. The Storyteller is free to decree that characters of low Humanity (4 or less) occasionally act according to various urges and impulses that must be resisted with Conscience rolls or Willpower expenditure. This is the critical crux of **Vampire: The Masquerade** — how closely can the character skirt the Beast before it drags her into damnation?

DERANGEMENTS

Derangements are behaviors that are created when the mind is forced to confront intolerable or conflicting feelings, such as overwhelming terror or profound guilt. When the mind is faced with impressions or emotions that it cannot reconcile, it attempts to ease the inner conflict by stimulating behavior such as megalomania, bulimia or hysteria to provide an outlet for the tension and stress that the conflict generates.

Vampires or mortals receive derangements under conditions of intense terror, guilt or anxiety. If a player botches a Virtue or Willpower roll (for example, when confronted with Rötschreck), the Storyteller may decide that the experience causes a derangement in the character. Other examples of derangement-inducing events include killing a loved one while in a frenzy, being buried alive, or seeing hundreds of years of careful scheming dashed in an instant of bad luck. Generally, any experience that causes intense and unpleasant emotion or thoroughly violates a character's beliefs or ethics is severe enough to cause a derangement. The Storyteller alone determines which derangement a character receives, choosing (or creating) one appropriate to the character's personality and the circumstances of the event that caused the disorder.

It must be noted that people who are "crazy" are neither funny nor arbitrary in their actions. Insanity is frightening to those who are watching someone rage against unseen presences or hoard rotten meat to feed to the monsters that live next door; even something as harmless-sounding as talking to an invisible rabbit can become disturbing to observers. The insane, however, are only responding to a pattern known to them, stimuli that they perceive in their own minds. To their skewed perceptions, what's happening to them is perfectly normal — *to them*. Your vampire's derangement is there for a reason, whether he's a Malkavian who resided at Bedlam before his Embrace or a Ventrue who escaped from five months of torture at the hands of an Inquisitor. What stimuli is his insanity inflicting on him, and how is he reacting to what's happening? The player should work with his Storyteller to create a pattern of provocations for his derangement, and then decide how his character reacts to such provocation.

Derangements are a challenge to roleplay, without question, but a little time and care can result in an experience that is dramatic for all involved.

OBSESSIVE/COMPULSIVE

The trauma, guilt or inner conflict that causes this derangement forces the individual to focus nearly all of her attention and energy onto a single repetitive behavior or action. Obsession relates to an individual's desire to control her environment — keeping clean, keeping an area quiet and peaceful, or keeping undesirable individuals from an area, for example. A compulsion is an action or set of actions that an individual is driven to perform to soothe her anxieties: for example, placing objects in an exact order, or feeding from a mortal in a precise, ritualistic fashion that is never allowed to vary.

Vampires with an obsessive or compulsive derangement must determine a set of specific actions or behaviors, as described above, and follow them to the exclusion of all else. The effects of obsessive/compulsive behavior can be negated for the course of one scene by spending a temporary Willpower point. The difficulty of any attempt to coerce or Dominate a vampire into ceasing her behavior is raised by one. If a vampire is forcibly prevented from adhering to her derangement, she automatically frenzies.

MULTIPLE PERSONALITIES

The trauma that spawns this derangement fractures the victim's personality into one or more additional personas, allowing the victim to deny her trauma or any actions the trauma causes by placing the blame on "someone else." Each personality is created to respond to certain emotional stimuli — an abused person might develop a tough-as-nails survivor personality, create a "protector," or even become a murderer in order to deny the abuse she is suffering. In most cases none of the personalities is aware of the others, and they come and go through the victim's mind in response to specific situations or conditions.

When a vampire suffers this derangement, the Storyteller and the player must agree upon how many and what kind of personalities develop, and the situations that trigger their dominance in the victim. Each personality should be relevant to the trauma that causes it. Not only is each personality distinct, but in the case of Kindred, the different personalities might believe themselves to be from different clans and sires.

Kindred with multiple personalities can manifest different Abilities and even Virtues for each of their personalities, but it is the Storyteller's responsibility to determine the specific details.

SCHIZOPHRENIA

Conflicting, unresolveable sets of feelings and impulses can cause a victim to develop schizophrenia, which manifests as a withdrawal from reality, violent changes in behavior, and hallucinations. This is the classical sort of derangement, causing victims to talk to walls, imagine themselves to be the King of Siam, or receive instructions from their pets telling them to murder people.

Roleplaying this derangement requires careful thought, because the player must determine a general set of behaviors

relevant to the trauma that caused the derangement. The hallucinations, bizarre behavior and unseen voices stem from a terrible inner conflict that the individual cannot resolve. The player needs to establish a firm idea of what that conflict is and then rationalize what kind of behavior this conflict will cause.

Kindred with this derangement are unpredictable and dangerous. In situations that trigger a vampire's inner conflict, the difficulties of all rolls to resist frenzy increase by three, and the vampire loses three dice from all Willpower rolls.

PARANOIA

The victim of paranoia believes that her misery and insecurity stem from external persecution and hostility. Paranoids obsess about their persecution complexes, often creating vast and intricate conspiracy theories to explain who is tormenting them and why. Anyone or anything perceived to be "one of them" is often subjected to violence.

Kindred who suffer from paranoia have difficulty with social interaction; the difficulties of all dice rolls involving interaction are increased by one. They are distrustful and suspicious of everyone, even their own blood bound progeny. The slightest hint of suspicious behavior is enough to provoke a frenzy roll, with the difficulty relative to the degree of the behavior. This paranoia may even extend to complex and rigorous feeding practices, to keep "them" from contaminating the vampire's food supply.

MEGALOMANIA

Individuals with this derangement are obsessed with accumulating power and wealth, salving their insecurities by becoming the most potent individuals in their environment. Such individuals are invariably arrogant and supremely sure of their abilities, convinced of their own inherent superiority. The means of achieving their status can take many forms, from devious conspiracies to outright brutality. Any individual of equal or higher status than the victim is perceived to be "competition."

Kindred with this derangement constantly struggle to rise to the height of power and influence, by whatever means necessary. In a megalomaniac's view, there are only two classes of people: those who are weaker, and those who do not deserve the power they have and must be made weaker. This belief extends to everyone around the vampire, including members of her own coterie. This derangement lends an extra die to all of the victim's Willpower rolls, due to her towering sense of superiority.

If a megalomaniacal vampire is presented with the chance to diablerize a more potent Kindred, she will be sorely tempted. A Willpower roll (difficulty 10) is needed for the vampire to avoid taking "what is rightfully hers."

BULIMIA

Individuals with bulimia assuage their guilt and insecurity by indulging in activities that comfort them — in this case, consuming food. A bulimic will eat tremendous amounts of food when subjected to stress, then empty her stomach through drastic measures so she can eat still more.

In the case of vampires with this derangement, the need to feed is a means of relieving the fear and anxiety endemic to the World of Darkness. A bulimic vampire may feed four or more times a night — gorging herself, burning the blood in pointless (or not so pointless) activity, then starting the cycle again.

A vampire with bulimia gets hungry much more quickly than other vampires do. When feeding, a bulimic vampire must make a Conscience roll (difficulty 7). If she fails the roll, she feeds until her blood pool is full, whether the vampire needs the extra blood or not. A vampire who is forcibly kept from feeding risks frenzy (make a frenzy roll, difficulty 6). The difficulty increases by one for every 15 minutes that she is prevented from drinking.

Hysteria

A person in the grip of hysteria is unable to control her emotions, suffering severe mood swings and violent fits when subjected to stress or anxiety.

Hysterical Kindred must make frenzy checks whenever subjected to stress or pressure. The difficulties of these rolls are normally 6, increasing to 8 if the stress is sudden or especially severe. Additionally, any action that results in a botch causes the vampire to frenzy automatically.

Manic-Depression

Manic-depressives suffer from severe mood swings, sometimes resulting from severe trauma or anxiety. Victims may be upbeat and confident one moment, then uncontrollably lethargic and pessimistic the next.

Kindred with this derangement are constantly on a hair trigger, never knowing when the next mood swing will strike. Whenever the vampire fails a task, the Storyteller has the option of secretly making a Willpower roll (difficulty 8) for the character. If the character fails the roll, she lapses into depression. Additionally, the vampire will go into depression whenever one of her rolls is botched, or if her blood pool ever drops below 2. The Storyteller should roll a die to determine how many scenes the character remains depressed, keeping the number a secret.

Vampires in a depressive state have their Willpower ratings halved (minimum 1). In addition, the vampire may not access her blood pool to raise Attributes. Upon emerging from the depressive state, the character is energetic, relentlessly upbeat and active (obsessively so) for a number of scenes proportionate to the time spent in depression. When a vampire is in this manic state, the difficulty of all rolls to resist frenzy is raised by one.

Fugue

Victims suffering from fugue experience "blackouts" and loss of memory. When subjected to stress, the individual begins a specific, rigid set of behaviors to remove the stressful symptoms. This differs from multiple personalities, as the individual in the grip of a fugue has no separate personality, but is on a form of "autopilot" similar to sleepwalking.

Kindred suffering from this derangement require a Willpower roll when subjected to extreme stress or pressure (difficulty 8). If the roll fails, the player must roleplay her character's trancelike state; otherwise, control of the character passes to the Storyteller for a number of scenes equal to the roll of a die. During this period, the Storyteller may have the character act as she sees fit to remove the source of the stress. At the end of the fugue, the character "regains consciousness" with no memory of her actions.

Sanguinary Animism

This derangement is unique to the Kindred, a response to vampires' deep-seated guilt regarding the act of feeding on the blood of mortals. Kindred with this derangement believe that they do not merely consume victims' blood, but their souls as well, which are then made a part of the vampire's consciousness. In the hours after feeding, the vampire hears the voice of her victim inside her head and feels a tirade of "memories" from the victim's mind — all created by the vampire's subconscious. In extreme cases, this sense of possession can drive a Kindred to carry out actions on behalf of her victims. Obviously, diablerie would be unwise for an animist to perform....

Whenever a vampire with this derangement feeds on a mortal, a Willpower roll is needed (difficulty 6, or 9 if she drains the mortal to the point of death). If the roll succeeds, she is tormented by the "memories" of the person whose soul she has partially consumed, but is still able to function normally. If the roll fails, then the images in her mind are so strong that it is akin to having a second personality inside her, an angry and reproachful personality that seeks to cause harm to the vampire and her associates. The player must roleplay this state; otherwise, control of the character passes to the Storyteller, who runs the character as if the mind of her victim is in control. During the moments just before dawn, control automatically reverts to the vampire.

Deterioration

A vampire who is staked or otherwise paralyzed continues to spend blood at the rate of one point per night. If the vampire is further deprived of blood, the decaying process that unlife has held at bay begins again. A vampire with no blood begins consuming all excess moisture within his body, at a rate of one health level per day. As the process continues, the vampire begins to resemble a mummified corpse. At first the vampire appears merely emaciated, but as the body is completely dehydrated, the meat and ligaments, along with the mostly useless organs within the body, begin to wither. By the seventh day, when the character has reached Incapacitated on the Health chart, the character's eyes shrivel within his skull, the tendons and ligaments within the body draw painfully tight, the gums recede from the teeth, and the lips draw back in a death-rictus. At this point, the character enters torpor.

Once in torpor, the character cannot rise unless supplied with enough blood to bring him back to Injured on the Health chart (at least four blood points). A vampire emerging from this state is ravenous to the point of insanity, and will attack whatever source of blood is closest, regardless of any emotional ties.

Leaving a vampire staked until he reaches this near-death state, then reviving him with just enough blood to prolong the agony, is a favorite method of torture for both the Inquisition and the Sabbat. Most vampires undergoing this form of torture suffer permanent mental damage as a result.

Diablerie

There is one thing that elder Kindred dread even more than fire or the light of the sun. This is the sin known as *diablerie*, or the *Amaranth*. Among Camarilla society, diablerie is the ultimate crime; those who practice it are subject to the harshest punishments imaginable. It is as loathed and feared as cannibalism is among mortal society. The vampires of the Sabbat, as well as the warriors of Clan Assamite, are said to indulge in diablerie freely, which is yet another reason why the elders hate them so.

Quite simply, diablerie is the act of feeding on a vampire in the way that a vampire feeds on a mortal. In so doing, not only does the murderer consume the victim's blood (and vampire blood is far, far sweeter than even the tastiest mortal's), but the victim's power as well. By stealing the life of a vampire closer to Caine, the vampire can permanently enrich his own vitae. In this manner can even the youngest vampire gain the power of the elders, should he have the strength and daring to wrest it from them.

Elders know the crime as the Amaranth; in olden nights, it is said, an amaranth flower was presented to the victim a week before he was to be hunted. Kindred legend tells many dark tales of murderous childer betraying and cannibalizing their own sires, and it is for this reason more than any other that elder Kindred harbor such distrust for the neonates among them. Indeed, the great Jyhad itself may well have its roots in this eternal and savage struggle for ultimate power.

COMMITTING DIABLERIE

A vampire seeking to commit diablerie must drain all the blood from his Kindred victim. Following this act, the vampire must continue to suck, for (according to Kindred legend) the very soul is withdrawn from the victim's body and taken into the diablerist's. The effort involved in diablerie is monumental, for the vampiric soul is a greedy thing and clings tenaciously to unlife, hoping to regenerate its body and rise once again.

Once a vampire's body has been drained of all blood, the true struggle begins. The diablerist's player makes an extended Strength roll (difficulty 9). Each success inflicts one automatic health level on the victim (the victim cannot soak, and damage is considered aggravated). When all the victim's health levels have been drained, the victim's essence is taken into the attacker and the emptied body begins decaying immediately.

A vampire committing diablerie is quite vulnerable to attack. Total concentration goes into the struggle to draw forth the essence of the victim, and stopping for even a moment ruins the chance of capturing the spirit. All attacks against a vampire attempting diablerie are made versus a difficulty of 2.

THE REWARDS OF DIABLERIE

Upon successful completion of diablerie, the diablerist is overwhelmed by euphoria, and a Self-Control roll is necessary (difficulty 10 minus the character's Humanity) to avoid frenzy. The sensation is akin to orgasm, but much more powerful — so powerful, in fact, that certain Kindred are addicted to the sensation. All other Kindred fear these vampires, known as "rogues," for their addiction to the pleasures of Amaranth makes them a threat to everyone. Even vampires too weak to provide additional power are devoured for the simple pleasure of the act.

The true benefit of diablerie becomes evident if the diablerist feeds on the vitae of a vampire of lower generation (e.g., if a ninth-generation vampire commits diablerie on a seventh-generation vampire). The diablerist literally steals the power and potency of the victim's own blood, and thus permanently lowers her own generation by one, bringing her closer to the mythical power of Caine. All benefits of the lowered generation — a larger and more potent blood pool, the ability to Dominate more Kindred and, in some cases, the ability to increase Traits above 5 — are bestowed upon the vampire.

If the victim was of much greater power (five or more generation levels) than the diablerist, the Storyteller may rule that the predator lowers her generation by more than one step. This is particularly likely if the victim was ancient (2000+ years of age). It would not be unreasonable for a 12th-generation neonate who drank the blood of a 3000-year-old member of the Fifth Generation to advance three or even more generation steps. Ultimately, this decision rests in the Storyteller's hands.

Moreover, drinking the vitae of elder vampires can induce a temporary increase in the diablerist's Discipline levels (by one, two or even more dots), as the potent blood augments the predator's own mystic arts. If the elder vampire was several generations removed from the diablerist's own generation, the effects can seem miraculous, even if they are short lived. These increased powers last for a single scene, unless the Storyteller decides otherwise.

To commit diablerie, the diablerist must take blood directly and immediately from the victim; the blood may not be stored and used later. Moreover, only one diablerist may commit the act on a given victim; a pack of neonates cannot swarm around an elder like hungry sharks, no matter how potent the victim's blood. The Tremere and Assamite clans are rumored to have developed mystic means of bypassing one or both of these prohibitions.

THE PERILS OF DIABLERIE

Committing diablerie seems like the perfect crime to many power-hungry neonates. There is no body left when the deed is done, as most vampires over a decade old quickly rot into unrecognizable mounds of carrion. Without solid evidence, it's difficult for even the most despotic prince to make an outright accusation of murder. But those who commit the atrocity soon learn that diablerists wear the evidence of their crime on their very souls. Vampires with the Auspex Discipline can detect a diablerist by using Aura Perception. The stolen energies of the victim mingle with the energies of the diablerist, leaving thick black marks running across the diablerist's aura. These marks stand out as clearly as motor oil on a crystal-clear pond, covering the softer colors of the vampire's own aura and betraying the crime beyond question.

Not all vampires know of diablerie or the stains it leaves behind. Many younger Kindred might simply question the odd discoloration on the vampire's aura. Most elder vampires understand what the stains mean, though, and could well call for the diablerist's immediate punishment or use the information as blackmail at a later date.

These marks remain in evidence a number of years equal to the difference between the victim's generation and the diablerist's original generation (mimimum one year, even if the victim was higher generation). In example, if a 12th-generation vampire drinks the blood of a ninth-generation vampire (becoming 11th generation in the process), the evidence remains on his aura for three years. Additionally, practitioners of Thaumaturgy can use the Path of Blood to detect the diablerist's sin, even centuries

after the crime was committed. For that reason, and for many others, practitioners of the Amaranth fear the Tremere.

Even those without special perceptions often sense a "taint" about the diablerist. For one month per generation removed from the victim, a diablerist gives off a "vibe" that leaves more sensitive Kindred unsettled. The Kindred in question may not actually know what the diablerist did, but they'll feel uncomfortable around him just the same. A player whose vampire comes in contact with a diablerist may make a Perception roll (difficulty of 12 minus the sensing vampire's Humanity rating — vampires with high Humanity are more aware of such things) to notice that something about the diablerist just "doesn't feel right." Followers of alternate paths of morality (see the Appendix) generally fail to notice the unusual sensation, as they are no longer attuned to their emotions in the same way. The Storyteller has final say in these matters.

A few rumors speak of diablerists displaying certain mannerisms of their late victims, particularly if the victims were of great psychic fortitude (Willpower 10) and of much stronger Blood than their murderers. If this is true, and the soul of a particularly mighty undead can manifest in the body of its killer, the implications are frightening, particularly in light of the Jyhad.

Such is the horror of diablerie that, according to most elders, even a blood hunt is no grounds for its practice. Hunters may drink a victim's blood, even to the last drop, but may not continue the process of diablerie once the victim is drained. Indeed, by decree of the Inner Circle, only a sire is permitted to diablerize her childe, and then only during a blood hunt. In

practice, many younger Kindred take the opportunity of a blood hunt's chaos for kinslaying, and princes often look the other way if the criminal was heinous enough.

Lastly, for Camarilla vampires and others who adhere to the way of Humanity, there is the loss of Humanity to consider. Diablerie is worse than murder: The Amaranth literally absorbs the victim's soul, destroying any chance of the victim finding peace in the afterlife. Such a heinous crime strips a minimum of one Humanity from the character's Humanity rating. Additionally, for extremely vicious attacks, the Storyteller might require a Conscience roll (difficulty 8). Failure means the loss of an additional Humanity point, while a botch could well mean the loss of even more.

DISEASE

There are certain advantages to being a walking corpse. One of the biggest is a natural immunity to most diseases. AIDS, cancer, influenza and other illnesses mean little or nothing to the undead.

But immunity to disease doesn't mean the vampires can ignore diseases. Any illness that can be transmitted by the blood is a potential problem for vampires, because they can carry the illness and transmit it from victim to victim. Indeed, several Kindred in Haiti and the US have become active carriers for the HIV virus. By drinking from someone infected with the HIV virus and then feeding on different victims, these vampires have helped to spread an already rampant infection.

In some fiefdoms any vampire found carrying HIV is locked away for the good of the herd. In rare cases such carriers have even been put to Final Death for spreading the disease. Such plague-dogs are frowned upon heavily in the Camarilla, for not only does disease threaten the human populace, but victims of the disease might speak of their affiliation with vampires, putting the Masquerade in grave danger.

Vampires with the Medicine Knowledge are sometimes recruited by the primogen in major cities to regulate the spread of disease through the Kiss. In the past decade, such vampires have been invited to speak before conclaves, alerting elder and neonate alike about noticeable signs of drug abuse and obvious physical symptoms that vampires should try to avoid. Even the vampires of the Sabbat, with their lack of concern for the herd, have begun to consider regulations regarding disease carriers.

An Intelligence + Medicine roll (difficulty 7) will allow characters to detect the presence of HIV, hepatitis or other blood-related diseases. If the roll is failed, the vampire does not notice the symptoms and exposes himself to disease (Stamina roll, difficulty 6, to avoid). A botch indicates the character feeds sloppily and automatically becomes a carrier for the disease.

Kindred legends speak of certain plagues potent enough to affect vampires. Very few vampires have any knowledge of such ailments, and those who do are highly prized. Despite the Kindred's formidable powers, they are ill prepared to handle the occasional illness that can cause them harm.

ELECTROCUTION

Vampires are not nearly so affected by simple electricity as are mortals. Nonetheless, electrocution might occasionally prove a danger. The strength of the electrical flow determines the amount of lethal damage a character takes from electrocution. She suffers the damage effect noted below each turn until contact with the source is severed (Strength roll to pull away — difficulty 5 for vampires, 9 for mortals). Vampires may soak this damage normally — but, if a soak roll is botched, the damage is considered aggravated, as the vampire's bloodstream and brain are fried.

Electrical damage is a lethal effect, and armor doesn't protect against it (depending on the subject's defenses, the circumstance and the Storyteller's decision).

Health Levels/Turn	Electrical Source
One	Minor; wall socket
Two	Major; protective fence
Three	Severe; vehicle battery, junction box
Four	Fatal; main feed line, subway rail

If a mortal character is subjected to significant amounts of electrical damage (that reduce her to Incapacitated), she may suffer permanent damage. This can be physical impairment (reduced Physical Attributes), permanent memory loss, brain damage (reduced Mental Attributes) or disfigurement (reduced Appearance). Specifics are up to the Storyteller.

FAITH

According to Kindred legend, the Curse of Caine has made all vampires forever outcast in the eyes of God. This might or might not be the case, but it is quite true that symbols or persons of great religious faith can cause discomfort or even harm to the Damned.

Most mortals, even supposedly devout ones, lack the ability to affect the Kindred with faith alone. However, certain mortals, those

with the True Faith Trait, can use their devotion as a defense or weapon against vampires. See Chapter Nine for further information.

FALLING

Even vampires can suffer great damage from falling significant distances. The Storyteller rolls one die of bashing damage for every 10 feet (rounded down) that your character falls before hitting something solid.

Falling damage may be soaked normally. Landing on sharp objects can change the damage from bashing to lethal at the Storyteller's discretion.

If your character plummets 30 meters or more, she reaches terminal velocity. The damage effect reaches a maximum of 10 dice at this point, and it is considered lethal damage. Additionally, any armor your character wears in a terminal-velocity fall functions at only half its rating (rounded down), since it's not designed for this sort of punishment.

FIRE

Vampires fear fire, for it is one of the few things that can end their immortal existences. Fire damage is aggravated and ignores armor; it may be soaked only with Fortitude. A fire's size determines the levels of aggravated damage a character endures per turn, while its heat determines the difficulty of the Fortitude soak roll. A character suffers the full damage effect for each turn that she's in contact with the flames; she must leave the area and/or put out any fire on her to stop taking damage. All damage inflicted by fire is automatically successful unless soaked (i.e., a character trapped in a bonfire takes two *automatic* health levels of damage per turn, not the results of two damage *dice* per turn).

Soak Difficulty	Heat of Fire
3	Heat of a candle (first-degree burns)
5	Heat of a torch (second-degree burns)
7	Heat of a Bunsen burner (third-degree burns)
8	Heat of an electrical fire
9	Heat of a chemical fire
10	Molten metal

Health Levels/Turn	Size of Fire
One	Torch; a part of the body is exposed to flame
Two	Bonfire; half of the body is exposed to flame
Three	Raging inferno; entire body is engulfed in flame

Note: Electricity in and of itself does not cause aggravated damage to vampires, but the heat generated by lightning or high-voltage electrical current can cause internal burns which are aggravated. Electrical damage may be soaked normally, using a character's Stamina + Fortitude. Damage is considered "normal" damage unless the character botches her soak roll, in which case the injury is considered aggravated as a result of internal burns.

If your character falls to Maimed, she is scarred temporarily by the flames (reduce Appearance by one until her wounds recover to Bruised). If she is reduced to Crippled or Incapacitated by the fire, the burns cover the majority of her body, reducing Appearance by two.

FRENZY AND RÖTSCHRECK

There is, trapped within the false civility of the Camarilla and the alleged camaraderie of the Sabbat, a hidden truth. Vampires are monsters, possessed of an inner Beast. Though, like humans, they have the capability of overruling their baser instincts, sometimes they fail. When this occurs, the Hunger and the Beast become uncontrollable, and no one is safe from their excesses. Older vampires refer to the ensuing savage fits as "succumbing to the Beast Within." Younger Kindred refer to these outbursts simply as *frenzies*.

THE NATURE OF THE BEAST

During a frenzy, a character literally — and usually unwillingly — gives into the darkest instincts of the vampiric nature. The character is consumed with rage or hunger, unable — or unwilling — to consider the effects of any action. Friends, foes, lovers, ethics: None of these things matter to a vampire in frenzy. If a vampire in frenzy is hungry, he will feed from whoever is closest without regard for the vessel's well-being. If the vampire is angry, he will do everything in his power to destroy the cause of his anger. A vampire struck by fear will commit any atrocity to remove himself from the source of his terror, regardless of the consequences. The character completely surrenders to the basest aspects of his Nature, shunting aside the Demeanor most commonly presented to those around him. He is, in short, the Beast.

Among the Camarilla, succumbing to frenzy is seen as weakness, a humiliating loss of control. Vampires who frenzy often, and especially in public, run the risk of social rejection or worse. Though many among the Camarilla Kindred are monsters through and through, the laws of the Masquerade and simple civility require that the Beast be kept in check; those who cannot do so are not vampires, but animals, and should be put down for the good of all. Among the Sabbat, frenzy is seen as a natural urge, like mortals' needs for food and sex. Sabbat vampires deride the Camarilla's attitude toward frenzy as that of weak-willed fools who cannot accept their true predatory nature. Accordingly, Sabbat typically seek not to prevent frenzy, but to control it and use it to their advantage.

A frenzy can be induced by many things, but great rage or hunger are the most common provocations. It is dangerous to deny or humiliate the undead. For this reason, vampires of the Camarilla commonly veil slights and threats in webs of double-talk and subtlety, that they not suddenly trigger an outburst in Elysium or conclave. Ultimately, the Storyteller can call for a vampire to make a frenzy roll at any time, whenever he feels the character might have cause to lose control.

A vampire in frenzy gains several temporary benefits from the state. Vampires in frenzy completely ignore all dice pool penalties inflicted by injury until the frenzy ends. Once the frenzy is finished, the pain comes back and the crippling effects of the wounds take hold again. All difficulties to Dominate a frenzied character are increased by two, and all difficulties to resist the effects of Dominate are reduced by two. The character never needs Willpower rolls to accomplish a feat, because the rage fueling the vampire's actions is both a catalyst to heightened state of mind and a barrier against unwanted intrusions. Lastly, characters in frenzy are immune to the detrimental effects of Rötschreck.

SYSTEMS

The rules for handling a frenzy are deliberately vague, and the Storyteller is encouraged to make whatever changes she deems necessary to accommodate her chronicle.

In some cases, Kindred can manage to overcome the urge to frenzy. A vampire on the verge of frenzy must make a Self-Control roll against a variable difficulty. The difficulty is often 6 to 8, but if trying to overcome the urge to commit a blatantly evil act, the vampire's player can roll against a difficulty of (9 minus Conscience) instead. The character must score five successes to completely overcome the desires for violence, but even one success halts the frenzy temporarily. For each success below five, the character can resist the urge to frenzy for one turn. After this duration expires, the character may try again to gain extra successes and thus continue to resist the frenzy. Once five successes are acquired, over a greater or lesser period, the vampire resists the Beast's urges.

Failure means the character goes into an emotional rampage, doing exactly what she wants to do with no worries of later repercussions. Botching the Self-Control roll means the character remains in a frenzy until the Storyteller decides otherwise, and (at the Storyteller's discretion) she may gain a derangement related to the frenzy.

The following list shows common stimuli that can incite a frenzy, and the typical difficulty for a character to resist. Remember, if the frenzy has the potential to cause the vampire to commit an atrocity (killing a child or other innocent, for example), the Storyteller can rule that the difficulty is (9 minus Conscience) instead.

Provocation	Difficulty
Smell of blood (when hungry)	3 (or higher in extreme cases)
Sight of blood (when hungry)	4 (or higher in extreme cases)
Being harassed	4
Life-threatening situation	4
Malicious taunts	4
Physical provocation	6
Taste of blood (when hungry)	6 (or higher in extreme cases)
Loved one in danger	7
Outright humiliation	8

Note: The Storyteller has final say in what can or cannot provoke a frenzy. In some cases the Storyteller might completely ignore what the players feel should send their characters into a rage, and instead have some minor event cause a frenzy. This is commonly done in situations where the Storyteller feels a frenzy can make a point about a character's personality, or enhance the events of a story.

ROLEPLAYING FRENZY

Characters in a frenzy are not themselves — or, more accurately, reveal more of themselves than they normally would. They will do anything to sate their hunger or destroy the source of the frenzy, even attacking other players' characters. Characters in a frenzy generally attack their enemies first, but if no enemies are present, friends are perfectly acceptable fodder for their baser instincts. Even lovers and family can fall victim to vampires in frenzy. The character might feel remorse and hideous guilt later, but while the frenzy occurs, nothing matters save the immediate gratification of the character's desires. This can often lead to subsequent degeneration checks (p. 221). Therefore, repeated frenzies can prove very detrimental to a vampire's Humanity.

Some players might feel hesitant about roleplaying a frenzy, but such is the nature of the vampire. Players should be encouraged to portray the frenzy effectively. If they cannot do so, the Storyteller should feel free to take over control of the character, running it as he deems appropriate until the frenzy ends.

A player whose character is in the midst of frenzy may choose to spend a Willpower point. This enables him to control one action of his character for one turn. In this manner, a vampire may give her victim-to-be a chance to run, or an offending mortal the chance to stammer out an apology. This moment of self-control lasts for only a turn, possibly two; it does not stop the frenzy, merely allows the character to control it slightly. As Storyteller, if a frenzied character takes an action you deem inappropriate, you may allow the action, but rule that the character has just spent a Willpower point to take the action.

The Storyteller decides how long any frenzy lasts, but one scene typically suffices. If a character is knocked unconscious or trapped alone for an extended period, the odds are good she will eventually regain control of herself.

RÖTSCHRECK: THE RED FEAR

Though there are few things that can kill a vampire — and though many among the Damned claim to loathe their immortality — certain sources of injury frighten all vampires. Sunlight and fire can bring about a panicked flight-or-fight mentality. While under the spell of this *Rötschreck*, a vampire flees in blind panic from the source of her fear, frantically lashing out at anything in her way regardless of any personal attachments or affiliations. Rötschreck is in most ways similar to any other frenzy; just as the Beast sometimes seizes control in times of anger, so too in times of great fear.

Relatively innocuous stimuli, or stimuli directly under the character's control, are unlikely to induce Rötschreck. For example, a character who sees a lit cigarette in a nightclub, or a screened-in fireplace in an ally's home, might grow uneasy, but is unlikely to succumb to the Red Fear. If that same cigarette is pointed threateningly at the vampire, though, or the fireplace suddenly flares up in a draught....

A vampire seeking to avoid Rötschreck requires a Courage roll. As with frenzy, five successes must be accumulated to ignore the Beast completely, though fewer successes enable the vampire to overcome her fear for a greater or lesser period of time. Failure means the vampire flees madly from the danger, making a beeline for safety and tearing apart anything or anyone that gets in her way. Any attempt to restrain a vampire suffering from the Red Fear results in an immediate attack, just as if the character were suffering from a frenzy. One Willpower point may be spent to maintain control for one turn.

A character who is the victim of a botched Courage roll immediately frenzies and remains in a frenzy until the Storyteller decides otherwise.

Provocation	Difficulty
Lighting a cigarette	3
Sight of a torch	5

Bonfire	6
Obscured sunlight	7
Being burned	7
Direct sunlight	8
Trapped in burning building	9

GOLCONDA AND OTHER MEANS OF SALVATION

For most Kindred, to be vampire is to be eternally Damned. Many legends speak of vampirism as the curse not only of Caine, but of the Devil himself. To become vampire means being forever forsaken by God and man, and so an unlife of horror leads, at last, to an afterlife in Hell. Even those vampires who scorn such "superstition" nonetheless see a secular hell of sorts in their Beast, their Hunger and the simple ennui that comes with centuries of existence.

It is not surprising, then, that some Kindred speak of a state of being whereby they may transcend their eternal hunger and rage. Vampires who attain this state, which is called *Golconda*, are said to have mastered the Beast to such an extent that it no longer controls their actions. While still tied to the need for blood, vampires in Golconda need far less of it than their ravenous kin. Moreover, they are able to quell the urges of the Beast to such an extent that they need never fear losing control to it. They are no longer properly Kindred, but a different, higher species of creature entirely.

As the stories go, Golconda is known only to a few among the undead, and these no longer participate in the Jyhad or the society of their kind. They live in the wild places, as one with the beasts of the field and the birds of the sky. Even the werewolves leave the masters of Golconda be, for they are not Damned, but Hallowed. Vampires in Golconda occasionally enter the larger society of undead, seeking disciples whom they can guide along the path to Golconda — but only in secret, for the Jyhad displeases them and they wish nothing to do with it. A few stories say that one of the Antediluvians has found the path to Golconda, and that this being seeks both to bring other Damned into Golconda's grace and to frustrate the schemes of its rivals. In truth, none can — or will — say.

Among the Camarilla, Golconda is seen as a pleasant but ultimately whimsical fable — an allegory for maintaining one's Humanitas, but nothing more than that. Some among the Inconnu are said to possess the secrets of Golconda, and to aid actively in its attainment — then again, there are many rumors concerning these recluses. The Sabbat, by contrast, scorn Golconda and its seekers as unworthy of true vampires. Wolves, they say, should not seek to emulate sheep.

Storytellers are free to include Golconda in their chronicles, and players may pursue it if they choose. Attaining Golconda, though, cannot be simulated with charts or experience points. It is as ephemeral, yet as powerful, as love or self-acceptance, and its attainment should be the focus of an entire chronicle. In general, characters learn of Golconda only after spending some time among the undead, for Golconda lore is spread in puzzling riddles and whispered from seeker to seeker. Many vampires never hear of it at all.

Pursuit of Golconda entails not only seeking out cryptic lore, but also seeking the truth in the vampire's own being. It is certain that vampires who wish to attain Golconda must feel — and display — remorse. The greater a vampire's sins, the greater the penance neces-

sary. Vampires wishing to enter Golconda must seek out the families of old victims and make amends, protect those weaker than they, and try to make the World of Darkness a better place. This inevitably entails maintaining one's Humanity and spending Willpower to commit good deeds (and avoid monstrous ones) whenever possible.

As mentioned, attaining Golconda should come only at the end of a long (months, if not years, of real time) and arduous chronicle. During this chronicle, characters must meet certain criteria. They must attain Humanity ratings of 7 or higher and Conscience ratings of 4 or higher, and they must maintain those ratings over lengthy periods. They must seek always to overcome the worst effects of frenzy, fighting the urge and spending Willpower points if necessary to avoid committing atrocities. Moreover, they must, over dozens of stories, consistently display penitent, abstinent and honorable behavior. Power, indiscriminate feeding and the games of the Jyhad are to be avoided by vampires seeking the higher path.

Typically, at about the midpoint of the chronicle, prospective Golconda-seekers travel in search of a mentor reputed to harbor the secrets of Golconda. Having found this mentor, the vampires must prove themselves worthy through the undertaking of quests and answering of riddles. Such tasks often lead the questers through grave perils to both body and soul.

The culmination of the chronicle comes when a worthy vampire undergoes a ritual called the *Suspire*. Sometimes the vampire is approached by others already in Golconda, who guide the vampire through the test; other times, the mentor conducts the Suspire; still other times, the vampire travels into the wilderness and undergoes the Suspire alone. The precise effects of the ritual are unknown (and in the Storyteller's hands), save that it involves a perilous journey into the world of dreams and, ultimately, into the vampire's own soul. It is extraordinarily difficult, and many vampires fail to survive it with unlives or sanity intact. Still others return from the Suspire whole, but having forever failed to gain Golconda. There are no second chances, and so perhaps the lot of the latter is the most bitter of all.

Should a vampire actually gain this legendary state, the effects are most miraculous. Foremost among them is a total immunity to frenzy or Rötschreck. The vampire will never again commit an evil act at the Beast's urging (though the player can still choose to sin, the dice will never again force a character to do wrong). Though a vampire in Golconda must drink vitae, nevermore need he fear inadvertently taking too much from a victim.

As well, the character does not need to drink blood as often. The character loses only one blood point per week rather than one blood point per night. He must still spend blood normally to power Disciplines, heal wounds, etc.

Furthermore, a vampire in Golconda partly transcends the Curse binding his own Blood to the fount of Caine. In so doing, he may increase any Trait to as high as 10, regardless of generation. His blood pool remains as it was, though.

A vampire in Golconda must maintain rigid standards of physical and mental purity. Should his Humanity rating ever slip below 7, or his Conscience rating ever fall below 4, the vampire loses all benefits of Golconda, including heightened Traits.

BECOMING MORTAL

Besides the tales of Golconda, certain legends among the Kindred speak of vampires who have thrown off the Curse of Caine and become mortal once more. No vampire seems actually to know any of their kind who has done such a thing; all such tales involve "the lover of my grandsire's ally" or "the childe of a distant prince" or some other indeterminate figure. The catalysts behind such a change can be anything from slaying one's sire to finding true love to sacrificing oneself unselfishly for another (and becoming mortal in the dying). Most Kindred, cynical and jaded as they are, scoff at such tales — then again, acts of true love or unselfish sacrifice in the world of the Damned are rare indeed. Ultimately, the truth of such things is up to the Storyteller.

POISONS AND DRUGS

As undead, vampires have little fear of conventional poisons. However, they may succumb to poisons or drugs contained within the bloodstream of their victims. Indeed, certain vampires, known as "lushes" or "heads," actively seek out victims under the influence of alcohol or drugs, that they might receive a vicarious buzz.

Obviously, we cannot present the effects of every drug and poison in a work of this size. Following are some examples of what might happen if a vampire drinks the blood of a poisoned or drugged victim. A vampire with low Willpower (4 or less) and/ or an appropriate Nature (Bon Vivant, Child) might risk addiction to a certain substance, but this is unlikely. In general, the effects of most drugs on vampires are far less than their effects on the humans in whose bloodstreams the substances run.

- **Alcohol:** The vampire subtracts one from Dexterity and Intelligence dice pools for every two drinks' worth of alcohol in his victims' blood. This effect fades at the rate of one die per hour, as the alcohol purges itself from the bloodstream.

- **Marijuana:** The vampire experiences slightly altered perception of time, as well as a one-die reduction to Perception dice pools. Difficulties of frenzy rolls are decreased by one, due to the calming effect of the drug. The effects last for about an hour.

- **Hallucinogens:** The vampire lowers all dice pools by one to three (inability to concentrate). He suffers effects similar to the Level Two Dementation power The Haunting. Depending on the precise nature of the "trip," he may gain extra dice in one particular Ability or find his Auspex Discipline raised by a dot or more. The effects last for (8 minus Stamina) hours.

- **Cocaine/crack/speed:** Vampires with the Celerity Discipline gain an extra level of the Discipline for (10 minus Stamina) minutes after drinking. Difficulties to resist frenzy are increased by one.

- **Heroin/morphine/barbiturates:** The vampire subtracts two from Dexterity and all Ability dice pools for (10 minus Stamina) minutes, and experiences a dreamlike state for (12 minus Stamina) hours. Difficulties of frenzy rolls are decreased by one.

- **Salmonella (food poisoning):** The vampire becomes nauseated, unable to consume more blood (roll Stamina, difficulty 6, to overcome), and suffers one health level of bashing damage. The effects last about a day.

- **Poison:** The vampire subtracts one from all dice pools and takes from one to three levels of normal damage per scene or even turn, depending on the intensity of the poison. Few poisons have any real effect on the undead, and most inflict a fixed

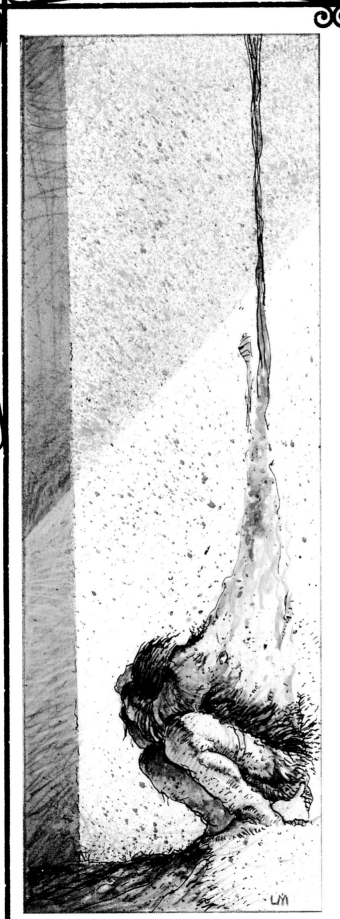

maximum amount of damage before wearing off. The vampire may purge the blood at his normal expenditure rate, and the effects heal automatically within minutes to hours after purging the blood.

SUNLIGHT

Sunlight, even more than fire, is deadly to vampires. Even diffuse sunlight running through a heavy curtain can cause burns, and direct sunlight sears all but the most powerful vampires. Unless a character has Fortitude, the rays of the sun cause burns, no matter how weak they are. Characters with Fortitude (and only characters with Fortitude) may attempt to soak sun damage, using a soak dice pool equal to the level of the Discipline. The difficulty to soak the damage depends on the intensity of the light, while the amount of damage taken depends on the amount of protection between the vampire's skin and the sunlight.

No part of a vampire is immune to the rays of the sun. Any character looking into direct sunlight is blinded instantly, her retinas burned by the illumination. Fortunately for vampires, the light reflected from the moon is not strong enough to inflict any serious damage, though some suffer the equivalent of mild sunburn if they are exposed to the light of a full moon and aren't wearing any protective gear.

As with fire, sunlight inflicts *automatic* damage per turn unless soaked.

Soak Difficulty	Intensity of Light
3	Faint light coming through a closed curtain; heavy cloud cover; twilight
5	Fully protected by heavy clothes, sunglasses, gloves and a wide-brimmed hat
7	Indirect light coming through a window or light curtains
9	Outside on a cloudy day; hit by one ray of direct light; catching the sun's reflection in a mirror
10	Direct rays from an unobscured sun

Health Levels/Turn	Exposure
One	Small part of body exposed — a hand or part of the face
Two	Large part of body exposed — a leg, an arm or the whole head
Three	Fifty percent or more of the body exposed — wearing thin clothing

TEMPERATURE EXTREMES

Vampires, being undead, suffer little from the privations of temperature. However, high (200°F+) temperatures might have the same effects as fire, at the Storyteller's discretion. Vampires suffering from extreme cold might be forced to spend additional blood points or suffer from the effects of frostbite (-1 or more to Dexterity-based dice pools). In general, though, vampires should not suffer greatly from most "normal" temperature fluctuations.

Example of Play

[Justin has gathered Rob, Cynthia and Allison together for a **Vampire** story. Justin is the Storyteller. Rob plays Jillian Brand, a Toreador dilettante; Cynthia plays DMZ, a Gangrel gangbanger/would-be anarch; and Allison plays MortyxX, a loathsome Nosferatu ex-coroner. The three have gathered to investigate strange activities in the barrens of the inner city, activities which have led to the disappearance of Jillian's sire Miranda, open warfare among DMZ's gangsta allies, and the firebombing of a Nosferatu tenement-aerie. The three characters, realizing that fate has thrown them together for the nonce, have agreed to meet at a popular Kindred hotspot.]

[Rob arrives a few minutes before the other players, so, to pass the time, he and Justin launch into a one-on-one storytelling exercise involving Jillian's interaction with her herd.]

An hour after sundown. Jillian lies pale and languorous on velvet sheets, entwined in the romance-novel arms of Miguel, her latest doll. His mouth on her neck is simultaneously enticing and vaguely irritating, his breath pungent and mammalian; she twists her head about to dislodge him, presses her lips to his waiting ones, nibbles at his lower lip and then slowly sinks her teeth into the fleshy bit.

A sharp intake of breath — from him, not her, of course — as she sucks. Muttered exclamation of pain.

"There, there, sweetness," she mutters abstractedly, kissing the wound closed. "Such a brave lad you are. See. Just a love bite." She rolls up, assuming a sitting position. This wasn't distracting her. Images of Miranda superimposed themselves over the kine's vapid features. "Now, M, lie back. Jill has errands to attend to this evening. Perhaps we should rendezvous at…no, I might be out a while. Sleep, dearest, then go home, and I'll call you sometime." Miguel gives a bovine grunt of half-conscious assent, already sinking into slumber.

Humming tunelessly, she dresses quickly — something eye-catching yet practical, yes? — and steps out into the secret world.

[Cynthia and Allison arrive, so Justin and Rob cut their freestyle roleplay short and begin the game as a whole.]

Jillian drives herself — even with all eternity ahead of her, there's nothing like effortlessly whipping a Beamer down a busy thoroughfare — to the agreed-upon spot, valet-parks, and waves to the bouncer in lieu of paying. Even by mortal standards, this club has seen an absurd number of incarnations, so it's a perfect rendezvous for younger Licks seeking to avoid the attentions of their change-wary elders. Now it plays techno, or electronica, or D&B, or whatever the children are listening to this week. There's the amusingly named DMZ, uncharacteristically early, face set in that sullen pout that signifies vulnerability hidden under faux indifference. It's only a so-so hunting mechanism for mortals, better when coupled with the ability to eviscerate prey with a backhand swat.

[Justin sits back, sets the scene at the club, and watches as Rob, Cynthia and Allison guide their characters through a little roleplaying and one-upsmanship.]

Jillian saunters over as DMZ sneers. Normally, she loves baiting the shrill little anarch, but she's too anxious about Miranda. Besides, a cursory aura-glance reveals that the Gangrel's not in the mood to lose a duel of repartee, so Jillian decides to come right to the point. "Any news on what's up?"

"Shit." DMZ dry-spits in disgust at the dance floor. "Not a goddamn one of the motherfuckers is saying anything. All anybody knows is that some motherfuckers with extreme firepower are setting up shop, no connections to anyone known, and fuck any boundaries." DMZ sniffs at the air, in the manner of a dog. "I smell a bad time rising in this city. Maybe time to move on."

"Werewolves'd make sushi of you, flavor it with that chip on your shoulder." It's MortyxX, creeping up on them as usual, presumably just crawled up out of whatever hellhole he rested in during the day. Jillian can barely make him out; shadows mercifully cloak the patchwork thing he calls a body, revealing only the odd lump or appendage bent in decidedly unnatural fashion.

"Ahh…I thought the place smelled of formaldehyde," Jillian mutters.

"What you smell, sweetie, is a lead as to what's going on, which is more than any of the rest of you've got. But if you're going to cop an attitude…" MortyxX seems to shrug in the shadows, then turn his bulk away.

"Go on, then, Rat," Jillian says. "Who'll help you? The prince? Unlikely! The rest of your foul brood? You're doing this to earn status with your sewermates, not toady to 'em. Why don't you just spit out what you've got so we can move on?"

[Last session, Allison had MortyxX dig around (by phone) through his network of contacts. Since he has a major contact in the shipping industry, MortyxX is privy to many comings and goings in the city.]

"Well, then. A little bird in a certain shipping company tells me that, while all this hubbub's been going on, trucks have been driving over to, and unloading crates at, the Devil's Playground. Yep. That place — the abandoned tenement turned squatter zone. Now what use would a bunch of crackheads and derelicts have for crates full of stuff — right on the borders of a war zone in your turf, anarch?"

"Crates of what?"

"Don't know. Mysterious how the invoices just up and disappeared. I caught a glimpse of some of the boxes in a temporary — sunproof — storage facility. Big enough for weapons — or your sire, Jill, or maybe just pieces of her."

"That's all you've got? Strictly circum—" Jillian halts in midsentence as MortyxX holds up a distinctive purple scarf. "Interesting how things get left lying around," MortyxX says. "I seem to recall your sire wearing this little trinket to one of those high-society soirees I wasn't invited to but crashed anyway. What's it doing in a rundown and dirty warehouse? And why are Kindred being moved through the middle of a gangland battleground — unless someone's got a decided use for something they've got — like their blood?"

There's no more to say. The three leave the club and hop in Jillian's car. Jillian spins the BMW intown, taking care to avoid the Avenue — where their movements will be plain as day to gossiping harpies — and discreetly circumventing the Five Bowers region — de facto territory of Candlemas, a Lunatic of great age and uncertain humors.

[Because the players state that they wish to avoid notice from the Kindred community as a whole, the Storyteller has Jillian roll Wits + Stealth (difficulty 5) to avoid scrutiny. She rolls three dice for her Wits, plus one for her Stealth rating of 1, and gets one success.]

The neighborhoods deteriorate around them — prime anarch hunting grounds. Jillian, not wanting to park her car close to the Devil's Playground or alert anyone within the building, parks the Beamer on a deserted side street, praying that no one trashes the vehicle while she's away. The three Kindred get out, walking through an urban version of purgatory. Sirens wail in the distance, groans echo from nearby alleyways, and once a chopper swoops over the blighted zone.

"Nice neighborhood you live in, Z," Jillian mutters.

"Fuck you, you skanky bitch!" DMZ retorts. "What the fuck would you know about having a neighborhood, since you get handed everything on both sides of life?!?"

"Oh, spare me the—" Jillian's rebuttal is interrupted as the disgusted MortyxX, eschewing subtlety, walks out right under a flickering streetlight — an action, Jillian notes, that flouts the prince's law more meaningfully than all of DMZ's posturing — and brazenly snatches a woman off the street.

[While they walk through the adjoining tenements to the Devil's Playground, Allison, realizing that MortyxX is low on blood, asks Justin if she can make a hunting roll. Justin says okay, but decides to raise the difficulty by one — after all, MortyxX's attention is elsewhere. The difficulty is 5 — they're more or less in red-light central — and MortyxX has a Perception rating of 3. He rolls 1, 9, 8 — one success total. Prey is in the area, and Justin decides to act out the hunt.]

The woman, an obvious whore, screeches and beats at MortyxX's implacable talon. "Get yer damn hands off me, asshole. You want a blow job, it's gonna be—" The glassy-eyed woman catches a glimpse of MortyxX's lump of a face under the streetlight. "What the fuck is that, some kinda mask, or are you just—"

"It isn't a mask, you stupid, dead bitch," MortyxX hisses, and wrenches her neck with one hand. The vertebrae separate with a crack that would have churned Jillian's

stomach in her breathing days. Pressing the spasming body against the alley wall and the horrified face to his own, MortyxX gnaws away at the corpse's skin in a parody of passion, then sucks luridly at the tatters of the face. In the nearby buildings, lights flicker prudently off.

"Damn, that is cold," DMZ mutters, while Jillian turns away. They come to me, she tells herself, and I give them pleasure in return. And if one dies, it's like an angel taking them to Heaven.

[Because MortyxX so greatly overpowers his victim, the Storyteller dispenses with combat rolls and the like, simply allowing MortyxX to kill the girl. MortyxX still retains Humanity, though, and murder is a gross violation of the Hierarchy of Sins. Justin calls for Allison to make a Humanity roll, using MortyxX's Conscience rating (2) versus a difficulty of 8. Allison scores 3 and 9 — one success. MortyxX is gripped with a sense of the pointlessness of the slaughter, and will probably dream of the girl for days afterward. He does not lose a point of Humanity — this time.

[Figuring the woman might be on drugs or have a disease, Justin decides to secretly roll a die — 1 to 5, she's sick or on something, 6 to 10, she's clean. The roll comes up 8, so MortyxX is no filthier than usual.]

Leaving the corpse twisted in a dumpster, MortyxX leads the trio two more blocks, then motions them around a corner. In front of them, the edifice known as the Devil's Playground looms against the dead gray sky. Fires crackle on the rooftop, and laughter reverberates from broken doorways whose gaping interiors dance with fireflies of blue flame.

DMZ gives a long, low whistle. "My sire told me that when the Black Hand came to his city, in the '50s, they lit fires everywhere. Burned the damn primogen hall down under cover of a race riot. Bastards love to burn shit."

The three Kindred carefully begin walking around the sides of the tenement, staying close to the shadows. As Jillian walks, though, her foot crunches on something that hisses and squirms at her — a huge rat! Jillian yelps, startled, and answering shouts echo from one of the tenement's broken doorways.

[The coterie decides to sneak around the sides of the building, looking for an entrance or anything else of relevance. MortyxX, not wishing to be invisible to his companies, eschews Obfuscate. Justin calls for the trio to make Dexterity + Stealth rolls versus difficulty 7. Allison rolls MortyxX's Dexterity (3) + Stealth (3) and scores 2, 8, 4, 8, 4, 5 — two successes. Cynthia rolls DMZ's Dexterity (4) and Wits (2) and scores 9, 1, 7, 5, 5, 5 — one success. Rob, though, after totaling Jillian's Dexterity (2) and Stealth (1), rolls 1, 5, 4 — a botch!]

Three figures emerge from the doorway, knives in hand. The huge, shambling shapes lumber toward the vampires, and Jillian's Heightened Senses smell the distinctive scent of augmented vitae characteristic of ghouls.

[Justin calls for Rob, Cynthia and Allison to make initiative rolls for their characters. Rob adds Jillian's Dexterity (2) to her Wits (3) and rolls a die, scoring 5, for a total of 10. Allison totals MortyxX's Dexterity (3) and Wits (3), then rolls a very high 9, for an exceptional 15. Cynthia does the same thing for DMZ's Dexterity (4) and Wits (3), then rolls a 7, scoring 14. Justin, rolling for all the ghouls at once, scores a 6 and adds it to the ghouls' Dexterity (3) + Wits (2). The ghouls will go on 11.

[Now actions are declared, in reverse order of initiative. Rob, speaking for Jillian, decides that she will spend a blood point to raise her Stamina to 3 (a reflexive), then use her Presence power of Dread Gaze on the ghoul closest to her. Justin decides that the ghouls will split up, one ghoul for each player's character. Cynthia, for her part, says that DMZ will spend a blood point to extrude his Talons of the Beast — an automatic action — then launch himself at the ghoul closest to him. Finally, Allison declares MortyxX's intent to run back into a nearby alley, at which point he hopes to be able to use his Obfuscate power of Unseen Presence.]

MortyxX springs back toward the shadows of the alley whence he'd just emerged, leading a ghoul in pursuit. Snarling with fury, DMZ pounces toward another ghoul, baring fangs and claws as he leaps. Jillian, meanwhile, composes herself, doing her best to evoke her unearthly powers of Presence as her assailant balls a meaty fist and shambles toward her, grinning.

DMZ and the ghoul meet in the middle of the deserted street. Ducking beneath the ghoul's swing, DMZ slashes frantically, and disembowels the ghoul in one blow. The ghoul wails, a high, piercing shriek, and drops to the ground. DMZ snarls, a predator's cry, and dips his fanged maw toward his fallen foe…then thinks better of it, and shakes off the haze of bloodlust.

The ghoul chasing MortyxX runs into the alley after the Nosferatu, but sees only empty shadows. Meanwhile, Jillian stands firmly as the last creature cocks a fist and slams it into her gut. She staggers back, but the undead are little hindered by such blows. "Is that the best you can do, sweetness?" she purrs, then contorts her face into a mask of rage and hisses at the ghoul. Like a building hit by a wrecking ball, the creature falls to the ground, sobbing, in front of his much smaller assailant.

[Now the resolution phase of the turn begins. MortyxX is fastest, and he's simply moving, so Justin allows the action to take place unhindered. Next goes DMZ, who activates his Protean power, moves into combat range — without penalty, since the ghouls are less than half his movement maximum away — and slashes at his opponent. Cynthia takes seven dice for DMZ's Dexterity (4) + Brawl (3) and rolls versus difficulty 6,

scoring a 3, 1, 10, 9, 7, 4 and 6. The "1" cancels out the "10," but that still leaves a respectable three successes. Because the ghoul was not attempting to dodge, Cynthia rolls DMZ's damage pool — 3 (for Strength) + 1 (for a claw) + 2 (for the extra successes over the one needed to hit). Furthermore, because Talons of the Beast inflict aggravated damage, the ghoul cannot hope to soak the damage unless he has the Fortitude Discipline (he doesn't). The dice come up 10, 8, 8, 9, 6, 6! Six successes — enough to drop the ghoul from Healthy to Crippled in one strike. Though technically the ghoul is still in the fight, Justin decides that such damage more than suffices to dispatch the lowly minion. The ghoul sinks to his feet, dead or soon to be.

[However, Justin does decide that such a quick kill might be enough to provoke a blood-frenzy in the vampire. He tells Cynthia to roll DMZ's Self-Control score (2) versus a difficulty of 5. Cynthia rolls a 2 and 5 — one success, and barely that. DMZ manages to rein in his Beast, but only just.

[The ghoul chasing MortyxX continues his pursuit. Because MortyxX reaches shadow, and Justin thinks it would be dramatic for him to turn the tables on his pursuers, he tells Allison that he'll allow the Obfuscate power's use if she makes a successful Wits + Stealth roll (difficulty 8). Allison takes six dice (for MortyxX's Wits of 3 + Stealth of 3) and rolls 2, 1, 10, 9, 8, 6. The "1" cancels the "10," but Allison still scores two successes. The ghoul chases MortyxX into the alley's mouth…and sees no one.

[Meanwhile, the ghoul swings at Jillian, who elects not to dodge (in hopes of making her Dread Gaze all the more intimidating). The ghoul has a Dexterity of 3 and a Brawl of 2, so he rolls five dice versus difficulty 6 to hit. He rolls 5, 1, 9, 6, 5 — because the "1" cancels out the "9," the ghoul scores only one success, not enough to add damage successes to the punch. Still, he's a strong fellow (3) and has a dot of Potence, so he rolls three dice for a punch. His damage roll (versus difficulty 6) comes up 7, 3, 8, and he adds an automatic Potence success — three successes, pretty good. Jillian attempts to soak and fails outright, rolling 4, 1, 9. However, because Jillian is undead and concussive trauma means relatively little to her, she halves the result to one level. The punch drops her to Bruised, but doesn't cause her to suffer any wound penalties. Rob says that Jillian laughs in the ghoul's face, then hisses menacingly.

[Because Jillian basically shrugged off a strong man's full-on punch, Justin elects to reduce the difficulty of her Dread Gaze roll by one. Rob rolls Jillian's Charisma (3) + Intimidation (2) versus a difficulty of only 4. She scores 3, 10, 10, 9, 6 — easily, easily enough to cow the ghoul. The ghoul shrieks, then drops into a fetal ball, sobbing.

[And so the combat continues, until one side or the other wins. Are the ghouls indeed minions of the Sabbat? Will Jill find her sire, or are they being led into an elaborate trap? Is MortyxX trustworthy at all, or is he stringing them along? Only a continuation of the story will answer any of these questions.]

Whereas the Cainite known as Dylan has committed grievous acts which threaten both the Camarilla and the survival of our kind entire

and

Whereas he has committed numerous acts in violation of the Traditions, such that he has breached the Masquerade, assaulted and killed other Kindred in express violation of the laws of our kind and consorted with the Kindred of the Sabbat

and

Whereas he has confessed to these acts without repentance, and sworn blood-oaths to the effect that he intends to repeat these crimes

Be it noted that

By the will of Clan Tremere, he is hereby declared Anathema. His name is to be placed on the Red List, and a blood hunt against him is to be declared in all our domains. Any who grant him succor are likewise guilty and shall likewise be punished. Let there be no penalty or censure against any who drinks the blood of Dylan, for he has declared himself outlaw and enemy of the Children of Caine.

So be it decreed this 23rd night of June, 1987

Quaestor
Johannes Dee

Domina
Gabrielle di Righetti
(Justicar)

Witness
Petrodon
(Justicar)

CHAPTER SEVEN:
A HISTORY OF THE KINDRED

Renauld, you know that I am a being of exquisite discernment; I consider writing for posterity an exercise in ego gratification and unworthy of our species. Therefore, I was somewhat piqued by your request that I annotate this vulgar bit of history. Oh, fret not — my irritation is well spent by now. You have nothing to fear from me.

In fact, I would be remiss to omit the fact that I actually gained some enjoyment from this gurgling Warlock's regurgitated opinions. It is both vexing and refreshing to watch the pretense to "humanity" that some Camarilla babes practice — vexing because they still refuse to admit to what they are, and refreshing in the sense that watching a farce is refreshing.

So, here, then. When all is said and done, this rather abbreviated recounting of our history has provided me with some divertissement. I hope that it suits your expectations. But do not ask such a favor of me again, for I cannot guarantee that I shall always be in as generous a humor.

Vykos

To Dr. Paul Frazier:

Let me be the first to welcome you to the Chantry of the Five Boroughs. I trust your journey was a safe one, and that your trip from JFK was not particularly hazardous. Hopefully your tour of New York's docks was reasonably picturesque. There is something to be said for allies with names that end in vowels, no?

I was sent your résumé prior to your arrival, and I can see why you were chosen to join us. You may feel that your place is uncertain among members of the higher echelons. While I would normally say that time clears up everything, we don't have time. As you've no doubt been told, we are in the middle of a war, and you've been drafted to join us. Suffice to say, we need you and here you are.

According to your previous regent, you are unfamiliar with the history of our kind as a whole. It's unusual to receive one with so scant an education, but I've been told your Embrace was a hasty one, and study time was considered too precious a commodity prior to sending you here. The papers enclosed contain a history of the Kindred as a whole, one that I've updated over the years as my knowledge increased and modern times came upon us. Don't worry about absorbing it all the first night — try to understand the meat of the text, and we'll deal with the finer details later. Pay particular attention to anything regarding the Sabbat. They're the reason you're out here. If you don't understand, then ask! I would rather answer a few questions than pick up the pieces from a bad guess based on ignorance. The former takes time; the latter takes much more valuable resources.

Settle in and start reading — tomorrow will be a very busy night.

Aisling Sturbridge
Regent of the Five Boroughs

IN THE BEGINNING

Most of what we know about our origins comes from fragments of *The Book of Nod*, and even that is couched in legends, for all that many of our kind consider it gospel. We all know about Caine and the murder of Abel (I hope). God exiled Caine from mortal company for the crime, and Caine went as an exile into the "Land of Nod," wherever that is. There, according to the *Book*, he met Lilith, the first wife of Adam according to Hebraic folklore. She alone among mortals succored him, and he took a long refuge with her, during which he was supposedly approached by the angels Uriel, Raphael and Michael. Each angel told Caine that he need only beg God's forgiveness and his exile would be ended. Each time he refused, and was thereby cursed, little by little, into the being that would be called the first vampire. With Lilith's assistance, he learned the abilities and arts that we call "Disciplines," finally leaving her when he believed she had no more to teach him.

THE FIRST CITY

For an undetermined amount of time, Caine wandered, miserable and alone in the wastes, until one night he reached a dwelling of men. The First City, according to the most ancient literature in *The Book of Nod*, was a wonder of antiquity. Realistically, it could hardly have been anything grandiose — probably a primitive town made up of clay huts with a surrounding wall — but it was Caine's first human contact in years. The people, amazed by Caine's abilities, made him as their king, and for a while Caine was content. As the years passed, though, loneliness began to plague him. He fell prey to one of the most common reasons for the Embrace — companionship. Few things change, particularly one like this.

Despite omens that his childer would eventually slay each other, even as he had murdered his brother, he persisted, even-

Ah, I see we have read The Book of Nod! How clever these usurping would-be magi are! How voluminous their libraries of antiquity!

The passages that our fledgling abridges in such inelegant fashion are engraved on the heart of every true Noddist. In fact, our Tremere seems to have caught all of the words but none of the essence, if you follow me. I have argued these passages several times with my colleagues, and could quote you a panoply of theories concerning the symbolism and true meaning of the Book's first part. For instance, some crass folk prefer to interpret "Caine the herdsman" as symbolizing an agrarian society forced to destroy a competing hunter-gatherer tribe (who had stolen the former's crops). But I fear that our theories, although certainly elaborate, are no more concrete than what is recorded here.

tually creating three — Enoch (for whom the city would eventually be named), Zillah and Irad, according to the stories. They would become known as the Second Generation. This arrangement would have been fine except the three childer now wished for childer of their own. They Embraced without thinking, until Enoch was nearly overrun, in spite of Caine's wishes. Humans and vampires lived side by side, each aware of the other, but the humans were meant to serve vampires, not coexist with them.

The Great Flood (the same Flood of Noah's story) wiped out many mortals and a number of the weaker vampires. When the waters receded at last, though, none could have imagined what happened next.

The Second City

Caine hid himself away from his grandchilder, hating the sight of them. He believed the Flood was a punishment from God for having Embraced, and he decided to remove himself from the temptation. He didn't want to be found, and those who went looking for him were told to depart and leave him to his self-imposed exile. While he was hidden, however, the Third Generation (now known as the Antediluvians, for they had survived the Flood) slew the Second Generation.

Enoch the city had been destroyed in the Flood, true, but a new city soon rose in its place, what we today call the Second City. The mortals, bereft of their king, set his childer in his place. It was not a wise choice. As time went on, the Antediluvians began to fight among themselves, setting their own progeny at each other's throats. The quarrel consumed all, including the mortals, and the city soon fell. This marks the beginning of the Jyhad, although what event started the whole thing none seems to be able to answer. *The Book of Nod* insists that the Jyhad was a curse from Uriel to Caine for creating progeny when he had been forbidden to do so. Others believe it was some petty matter between two Kindred (just like it is today) that blossomed out of control.

Just because Caine was hidden did not mean that he didn't take an interest in his grandchilder. Legend has it that he cursed the founder of the Nosferatu with ugliness for some ugly practices (the legends, as usual, are closemouthed about what) and Malkav with madness for defacing an image of him. He mourned the loss of the Second Generation, still cursing his grandchilder for the ruin they brought on themselves and the world. However, the Third Generation truthfully did not care. Once the Jyhad had begun, they became more concerned with matters that would occupy them for the next several thousand years.

The Ancient World

After the Second City's destruction, many vampires chose to scatter, finding their own ways and making their own destinies. The Kindred walked in ancient Britain, Greece and Rome as gods, inspiring poets and warriors much as they would for the next 2000 and some years, and those poets and warriors would remember those they had encountered in stories of *lamia* and the occasional lycanthrope.

However, wherever the Kindred laired, rivalries flared up. In Greece, it was the Kindred of Athens against their enemies in Sparta. They goaded the Peloponnesian Wars and left both cities as near-husks when the dust settled; Sparta humbled, and Athens' resources mostly exhausted. When the Kindred of Macedonia poured in, the invasions drove the combatants out. Of particular note is the rivalry between the Kindred of Rome and Carthage. Indeed, Carthage deserves special mention for the role it played in Kindred history, both as a whole and for the vampires involved.

Carthage

Depending on whom you ask, the vampire colony of Carthage is either one of the Kindred's greatest achievements or a stunning example of hubris. In the end that's for history to decide. But one thing is certain — Carthage has cast a long shadow down through the ages. Some Kindred squabble and fight with each other to this night because of what happened there over two millennia ago.

Carthage, the capital of Phoenicia, was something to see in the mortal world. Phoenician traders crossed the Mediterranean, bartering for riches to adorn their city and others. Phoenician sailors were some of the finest in the Greco-Roman world, and their ships plied the waters from the Fertile Crescent to Iberia. For many years, Carthage even surpassed Rome for beauty, something Rome didn't take very well. But while the mortals quarreled over trading rights, and Rome's heart burned with envy to see Carthage so prosperous, there was more going on in the shadows of both cities. For Carthage had been set up by the vampires of Clan Brujah to be a grand experiment, an attempt both to re-create Enoch and to prove once and for all that mortals and Kindred could live openly together.

I've heard so many differing stories about the success of this that I'm not sure which is true. By all accounts, Carthage's vampire inhabitants managed to make things work for at least a little while. Those mortals who lived beside vampires apparently understood their neighbors' "differences," and allowances were made for them. For instance, the blood in the slaughterhouses

You will note that the superstitious reverence with which the Camarilla lapdogs hold their Antediluvian forebears is in no shortage here. I am hardly one to doubt the mysticism inherent in our own lineage — there were sorcerers in my homeland long before the accursed Tremere reared their juvenile heads — but really! Curses, spread by Caine to his grandchilder? A wrathful deity curses Caine, who becomes the wrathful deity to the Antediluvians, who then play said role to us? I have learned much of the clans' strengths and weaknesses in my own centuries of observation, and am unwilling to accept such near-religious explanations. Godlike power does not a god make; nor do I believe that such power cannot be wrested away from its keepers. I have enjoyed my hubris for some time, and have not yet felt a thunderbolt.

was given to them, plus there were servants designated for feeding. In spite of the Brujah propensity for temper, there are no records of the city being turned into an abattoir because someone insulted a vampire's descendant or the like. Of course, right beside these accounts are stories that blood sacrifices and devil-worship were rampant — whom do you want to believe tonight? At any rate, there was at least a façade of order, and Carthage seemed to be holding its own among both vampires and mortals.

Yes, there's a "but" in there. The "but" was in Rome — Rome's vampires, primarily Malkavians and Ventrue if the records are true, apparently coveted the wealth of Carthage, and found the Brujah's "experiment" to be outrageous. Perhaps for the superstitious Malkavians, Carthage directly flouted Caine's law that the Children of Caine and the Children of Seth should have nothing but enmity for each other. If nothing else, the thought that others of their kind could enjoy greater success and happiness than they was intolerable to them. In the end, they demanded to see Carthage destroyed.

Two Punic Wars and a lot of elephants later, the Kindred of Rome had their wish. The city was razed and burned, killing those vampires who didn't get out of the city. In the fields, the earth was salted, and those who had hidden in the ground to escape the flames were shriveled into husks, the blood leached from their bodies. The vampires who escaped carried their tale (and their bitterness) with them for years afterward. To this night, many Brujah despise the Ventrue for their role in destroying what some call "The Greatest Society."

> Carthage. What a pathetic, water-blooded symbol this has become for the Camarilla. We grow nightly nearer to re-creating such a city, such an existence, in every Sabbat holding across the globe — and yet, our rivals' vision has been so blurred by time that they do not recognize the dark Utopia which our efforts shall bring to pass. What feeble excuses for historians the Camarilla must sport that they do not recognize patterns unfolding again before their very eyes.

THE DARK AGES

According to some, this was one of our greatest eras, or at least one of the best times to have been a vampire. In consideration, it was certainly one of the more liberal times. The Masquerade had not yet been formalized; many vampires ruled cities and manors, or held high position in the mortal courts of Church and state, often quite openly. Mortals lived in terror of the supernatural, believing wholeheartedly in witches, lycanthropes, faeries and vampires. The Kindred took great advantage of this, and in a world of long, dark nights, they truly were its masters. The Camarilla and Sabbat as we know them didn't exist — everyone was as independent as they imagined themselves to be.

It was during this time that our clan, the Tremere, joined the vampires. Our records claim we began as a cabal of mortal wizards, and our leaders, the Master and curséd Goratrix, sought immortality to give themselves and the rest of the House the necessary time to work on their magic. To this end, they studied the "life" processes of the Kindred, then sought to duplicate them. The Master's plan worked perfectly — but, realizing they had put themselves in serious danger, the cabal's leaders set out to make themselves a place in the night's hierarchy before they were destroyed. The culmination of this effort was the elimination of Saulot, an Ancient of the late-lamented Clan Salubri.

How I wish that this chronicler had fallen into our hands as well as her work! This uneducated hatchling of this benighted century has clearly eaten her spoonfuls of Tremere propaganda like a good infant! No mention of the noble reputation of the wise and well-traveled Saulot, or that of his inoffensive childer? No reference to the experiments wrought on our kind by Tremere pretenders to Caine's throne? No citations of the wars fought across the Carpathians to scourge this upstart pestilence of a clan from the face of Europe? Clearly history is written by the victor, and it is obvious that the Tremere "elders" (if one can call them that, for I doubt any exist that are older than myself by even a century) fancy themselves victors for the nonce.

Still, here we arrive at a time in history which I can detail from experience rather than conjecture. Apart from the eruption of the aforementioned Tremere boil, the Dark and Middle Ages were a lordly time to be a vampire. We ruled the torchlit cities with none to tell us otherwise, and the peasants dutifully cowered before us, their dread lords. The kine remained deliciously ignorant, while we spent our nights learning the true midnight ways of the world. As enjoyable as the modern age is, I think I would not weep overlong if those distant times had lasted forever. Of course, such things never do.

THE BURNING TIMES

Unfortunately, the openness of vampire society started to have some serious consequences. Not everyone was afraid of the vampire ruling as lord from the castle on the hill. The Church, using the weapons of courage and Faith, began to strike back at the night. Some were mortal pawns whose greed or rage finally overcame their fear enough to betray their masters. Some were driven by righteousness and religious fervor, believing that they were cleansing the world of evil. A few actually had good intentions, driven by tales or sights of vampire arrogance and atrocities during the so-called "Long Night."

Vampires of today might not think this so much — most think that the Inquisition is just an empty threat the elders use to keep the whelps in line, or that it was as tired and toothless as the men who were said to make up its ranks. Neither could be further from the truth. Imagine a world where the Church has its fingers in everything — from medicine, to education, to politics. It has the power to order wars fought in its name, to dethrone kings, and to command obedience from just about everyone in society. And it has started to turn its might on the whole of vampirekind.

Frightened yet? Neither were the vampires of 1200 — until the Church started to win.

THE WITCH-FIRES AND THE ANARCH REVOLT

The Crusades finally ended — badly — for the mortals of Europe. They wanted someone to blame, and the Church turned inward on itself, seeking out the "corrupt." For the next 200 years, the Inquisition and its allies practiced the scorched-earth policy on Europe, spreading outward from Switzerland and into Germany, France, Hungary, Spain and England. These people took whoever they could find who might be sending Europe and God's people to Hell, whether they were Jews, Muslims, Cathars, women, political enemies, heretics, vampires.... The total list would take up too much space, but you understand.

A number of vampires were found and sent to the fires — some caught off guard in their havens, some betrayed, some even murdered. Yes, "murdered," and don't try to change the subject. Some elders, in their rush and struggle to escape, decided to throw the neonates and ancillae of the age like so much cannon fodder in the path of the oncoming Inquisitors. Not everyone went quietly — the self-preservation instinct doesn't end with the Embrace. A number of these "throwaways" escaped and began to band together for safety, finding common cause. This was the beginning of the rabble that would call themselves the

One thing I've come to understand in creating this is that we Kindred have two strikes against us with regards to history: 1) Most times, we react to what the mortals do, not the other way around, no matter how much we might boast otherwise; and 2) No matter how cruel or depraved some of our kind fancy themselves to be, humans will always have something new to teach us. Most of the heinous acts we read about in the history books were mortal-inspired and mortal-executed, not vampiric.

anarchs. What's a shame is that, for all the movement was begun for an understandable cause, it's become a stew of howling younglings, ranting without reason, selling themselves to the highest bidder who can push their cause and meet their price.

At the apex of the turmoil, with the elders struggling to hold onto their reins of power, the anarchs decided they were ready to throw off those reins once and for all. The timing was impeccable — between the Inquisition and the Crusades, the elders' resources were devastated. There was almost no formal organization, no system of protection against the marauding anarchs beyond simply banding together, and the elders were by and large too independent and paranoid of each other to consider it. Then about two dozen elders from many clans came together and presented a case for the founding of a shadow society that would become the Camarilla. It was well received, according to most accounts, but the elders were still nervous about banding together with centuries-old rivals. Then things escalated — news began to circulate of anarch-developed magicks that, some said, could throw off the shackles of the blood bond. The anarchs' numbers swelled, and rumors claimed that the anarchs had begun to absorb entire clans; some found it suspicious that the ritual for breaking the blood bond seemed to have roots in Eastern Europe (long known as Tzimisce country). In Italy, a new clan arose from apparently nowhere, and many elders were quite concerned as to how that could have come about (but whatever their suspicions, they kept entirely their own counsel — I've yet to find anything on it that doesn't have the ring of "friend of a friend"). There's no telling which was the final

catalyst, but whatever it was, the elders of Europe's seven great clans abruptly fell in, and pulled together the first official meeting of the Camarilla in 1450.

Sprenger and Kramer only fed the fires with their *Malleus Maleficarum* (The Witches' Hammer). In fact, after its publishing, we Tremere found ourselves in even greater danger, if that's possible. Our historical associations with sorcerers and other magicians ensured that we were guilty by association when those groups were being hunted. In spite of our allies and "kin," we lost inordinate numbers compared to other Kindred during this time.

How the Kindred survived at all, I'm not sure. Some went into torpor, but forgot to tell anyone where they were and thus were never awakened; they might well still be sleeping somewhere in Europe. Some died at the hands of enemies who took advantage of the chaos. Many burned in the witch-fires, their true natures discovered, either as a result of trying to protect their herds or by dint of other associations having nothing to do with their vampirism. Others languished in dungeons or were seared by the power of zealous Faith. In the end, survival became partially a matter of chance and more a matter of strategy. A few survived by barricading themselves behind massive resources — for example, creating childer to put in harm's way. Some, perhaps possessed of precognition or just smelling trouble on the wind, sought quiet places away from the worst uproar or even out of Europe proper. Lastly, and most importantly, the Masquerade (long considered to be more of a cautionary measure than a matter of life or death) was adopted and enforced on a wide scale. Never again would the vampire lords ride through the night, frightening peasants and openly ruling manor and abbey. It was the beginning of unlife as most of us know it — walking in the shadow between worlds, never revealing ourselves to the eyes of the masses.

Now let's add in the middle of all this the Anarch Revolt, still going on. Now that the Camarilla had organization, it had a means by which to mass its strength and bring the wrath of Caine down on the offending anarchs. For the Tremere, the war was personal — we had a long-running feud with the thrice-damned Tzimisce, and here they were on the other side of the fence. Naturally we gave no quarter. After some 40 years of

nightly battle, the Camarilla finally gained the upper hand. The anarchs, realizing that it would be suicidal to continue, raised the white flag. The first conclave was called in 1493, and the Convention of Thorns treaty ended the war. For most. A number of anarchs refused to surrender, choosing instead to run and regroup. When they reemerged, they had become the abomination known as the Sabbat. One hundred years of bloody fighting to give us two sides, and the guarantee of even more fighting through the years.

The Inquisition. A curse on our kind, yes, but it also had something of the air of a blessing. We lost much in those times. Castles fell; libraries went up in flames, and their precious lore is gone forever. Good friends (and noble rivals) died the Final Death in the mortals' fires. But we Cainites lost something else during those times that I would not have back for all the world.

We lost our complacency.

As the ignorant and weak were rooted out and put to the stake and torch, the clever among us did what was necessary to survive. In strife came opportunity; many elders, including two whom I need not name here (but ah! what a matchless victory that was!), perished in an ignoble but fitting manner when we childer decided that we would, at last, take control of our own destinies.

I remember the call to sign the Convention of Thorns. I tell you frankly that I would rather have burned in the Inquisition's fires than become a lapdog to the cancerous Tremere and their contemptible allies, and there were many — oh, many, indeed — who felt as I did. How is it that Donsanto put it? "If the Camarilla would hunt their own in response to the humans' crusades, then let us show them that these witches will not burn so easily! Come, storm our Sabbath — and see how you fare against victims who will never bow their heads to the headsman's axe!"

Trite, yes. But his sentiment is preserved today.

The Black Plague

Kindred today will tell you that we are immune to sickness, that we only carry it around and spread it when we feed, that sickness has never posed a threat. Think again.

Most vampires have conveniently forgotten the Black Death, probably because most vampires of today didn't live through it. True, I didn't, but I've met those who have. Any who think that sickness doesn't affect us should let one of them instruct otherwise.

There are three forms of plague — bubonic, pneumonic and septimatic. Bubonic gave the victim those ugly swellings all over; pneumonic primarily affected a victim with coughing and symptoms most would think to be a severe cold; septimatic caused a victim to spit blood and die within as little as two hours. Of these, septimatic passed through the blood and was extremely contagious. An unsuspecting vampire fed on septimatic victims, and became an instant plague dog. Worse, the vampire himself would begin to feel sick: losing blood through coughing and spitting, achy joints that turned into searing pain when the body tried to cleanse itself, and a strange inclination to torpor.

Not only did Europe lose many of its priests, we Cainites lost nearly our entire priestly order: many became sickened when they leaned over the dying to give Last Rites and the victims had bleeding buboes or were aspirating blood. The Black Plague made feeding a nightmare, according to the writers of the times. Many vampires turned to feeding on each other, leading to blood bonds or diablerie. Some elder vampires began to create childer simply to cannibalize them. Those who attempted to travel beyond the reaches of the Plague, up into Scandinavia and Latvia, ended up taking the disease with them in the fleas that rode in their clothes.

The Plague broke out again in England in the 1600s, about the same time as the Great Fire. The more I look at the evidence, the more I'm convinced that some torpid vampire, carrying the Plague unawares, woke up, fed and began the cycle again. Luckily it didn't spread far — the Great Fire took care of cleaning up the city very nicely.

THE RENAISSANCE

By all accounts, this was one of the greatest times to be supernatural and undead. With the fires of the witch-hunts either banked or cooling, a lot of people were so happy to be alive that they went a little crazy. On the mortal side of things, you had the poets, the playwrights, the romantics, the inventors. On the supernatural side, you had…well, the poets, the playwrights, the romantics, the inventors. Mortals and Kindred interacted regularly, even if the mortals didn't know whom they interacted with. So long as the person could talk a good game, most people were willing to accept her.

Learning, some of it preserved through the years by Kindred, came back into the world; certainly there had to be vampires teaching young impressionable minds about the Greeks and Romans as though they'd been there (chances are they were). I wouldn't be a bit surprised to hear that some vampires replenished the stores of lost Greek and Roman literature from their own libraries. Castiglione's *The Courtier* and Machiavelli's *The Prince* made leadership and diplomacy an art form, no doubt where many of our "modern" forms of Kindred government arose from. Mortal artists of all kinds seeking patronage gave many vampires a chance to rejoin the games of mortal society, and to reach for that promise of humanity regained. I would even suspect that the Elysiums we're so familiar with found new incarnations during this time, in performances at the Globe, the courts of the Medicis and Elizabeth the First, or the palazzos and chateaux of the wealthy new middle class.

Yes, it was in many ways a party for Europe, whether vampire or human or something else. After years of a Church run amuck, of enemies wielding flame and steel, many were ready for a little time to "catch their breath" and remember the good things in unlife.

Was everything wine and roses? Hardly — the Camarilla and Sabbat were still fighting the last gasps of the Anarch Revolt, and that move of the Jyhad took up about 200 years. Finally, the Camarilla forced the Sabbat to start backing down. Whether the Sabbat made a strategic retreat or simply ran out of time and forces, they did indeed withdraw from most of Europe. According to one of my better resources, the Sabbat went north into Scandinavia to lick their wounds and wait for the opportunity to sneak back in. Apparently they had many wounds, since the next 50 years or so passed in relative calm.

I will not speak such praise of the Renaissance. It was a space of time, nothing more, nothing less. Yes, art and history and philosophy and theatre blossomed; and I'm certain that such Kindred as preferred to think of themselves as still "human" at heart enjoyed themselves immensely. For those of us without such pretty delusions, it was somewhat less awe-inspiring.

The 18th Century

As the New World was colonized, the Sabbat must have gotten the jump on the Camarilla and moved out there first, since they were there to greet the boats in America and Hispaniola when other vampires made the trip (if the stories my "uncle" told were true). At the time, most European Kindred thought, "Let them have it. It's a wilderness, full of savages and animals, like themselves." They thought that the Sabbat would burn themselves out, and no one's hands got dirty.

How and why the elders didn't know that the Sabbat was out there I don't know. A number of European Kindred influenced colonial ventures and representatives of the crowns, which were by and large successful. Surely they would realize that there was something going on…. Over time, this information has been so thoroughly covered in rumor and hearsay that I can't tell what's fact anymore. What I can safely venture is that the Kindred guiding these ventures probably started to get greedy, particularly those in England. They were apparently surprised by the Revolution, and promptly claimed that the Sabbat had been at work. I'm inclined to think it was a matter of some "uppity" mortals getting the drop on the vampires. In all my time of reading war journals and dealing with them nightly, I have rarely seen the Black Hand use mortals as their pawns in the Camarilla-Sabbat wars, even today; they are too proud to make use of "inferior" weapons.

At any rate, recall that the European Kindred back in the Old Country controlled a number of crowns and colonial ventures, and for the American mortals (and the few American vampires) to rise up and go to war risked a number of delicately arranged trading agreements and treaties, not to mention that it was "highly impertinent," according to one Toreador prince of the time. I'm sure the few American vampires, who were enjoying being out of reach of the Old Country's stifling formality and hoary elders, took pains to make sure the colonies had assistance, even if it came from the Sabbat. The Revolution provided a nice cover for yet another Sabbat-Camarilla skirmish, this one quickly burning out because of numbers.

Across the ocean in France, probably encouraged by the success of the Americans, another revolution began, this one far more bloody and with less motive. Who was to blame in this one? Well, there's always the Sabbat — they do make handy boogeymen, don't they? My sire, who lived through Robespierre's little tea party as a mortal, believed in hindsight that Brujah and Nosferatu were more likely culprits, while one of my former regents (who also lived through the Revolution, but as a vampire) insists that the Malkavians were to blame. I've decided to compromise — I think it was once again vampires of every sort getting caught up in existing mortal affairs on one end or another. I doubt the Sabbat had too much involvement, because there's no record of Kindred war or invasion (they were apparently too busy in the colonies). Whatever the cause, it didn't preclude a number of vampires from taking advantage of the chaos — or dying in it. Since many Kindred typically hobnobbed with the royalty, it wasn't too hard to convince the mobs to find them guilty and have them beheaded; Madame Guillotine apparently rarely slept. Thankfully, my own grandsire and sire managed to escape the rush as the Reign of Terror spiraled out of control.

The fools in the Camarilla had no idea what potential the New World offered. Some among us journeyed there long before our anemic rivals, and there learned to subsist on the less numerous kine. It was an unglamorous existence, or so I understand. But not one without rewards. Our presence, once rooted in the fertile soil of the Americas, could not be torn out.

As for the revolutions of the time — how tedious it must be to search for a Cainite hand in every little altercation in which the humans indulge themselves! Perhaps the Camarilla elders maintain their delusions about our involvement because it suits them to believe that anarchy and revolution are not concepts integral to the "sane," "orderly" mind. Oh, those unstable Sabbat hobgoblins must have been responsible, eh? Never mind that we were too occupied with rooting out the incompetent and worthless among ourselves at the time to bother with directing a human war — as if a forest fire could be harnessed and made to pull a plow.

I do hope they continue to reason in such a fashion. It will be all the sweeter when their own childer rise up against them and drag them neatly into whatever hell awaits our ilk.

AGE OF STEAM —
CENTURY OF PROGRESS

This was a time of exploration and industry. Mortals leaped forward in a quest for progress, and the Kindred were there to patronize the brilliant and reap the fruits of civilization. In a time of gentility and manners, many elders enjoyed the propriety demanded of the age, and even tonight they continue to maintain traditions to which they were first introduced at this time. Wherever mortals went, we were there. I would say that "lucrative" doesn't begin to describe our ventures.

What's above is the textbook version, what is normally told to apprentices. For as much went on in the 19th century, I think it deserves a little more than a paragraph. If nothing else, it tends to gloss over a few important points.

As vampires in search of new domains and herds pressed into continents where they had rarely gone, they found themselves running into enemies and wonders the likes of which they had never encountered before. For many vampires, this was their first real contact with the vampires of the Far East, of the subcontinent, and of Africa. Many got quite a shock when they realized that these vampires were vastly different from those of Europe and America. Like the rest of the explorers, the vampires decided to push their agendas for colonization. Instead of rolling over like the mortal natives did, these strange vampires re-sponded with full force. Powers that none had ever seen before were loosed on the invaders. The fight went on in the shadows as the Europeans fought to colonize and "civilize the savages." At one point, mortal and supernatural (on both sides) ended up as allies against the other. In the end, the Kindred withdrew and waited for the humans to get the job mostly done before trying it again. Even then, those who returned didn't press their luck, but stayed very firmly within the "civilized" areas — Hong Kong, Madagascar, Bombay, Cairo — places where the white man was definitely in charge. I'll freely admit that we don't know nearly as much as we'd like about the Far East and Africa, except for some really strange stories that I'm not sure I want to believe.

Africa has also proved a thorn in the collective side of the Tremere — all attempts to establish a chantry there have ended in failure for reasons few can explain. Asia has also remained something of a mystery to us. The only chantry that has maintained any stability or longevity is in highly Westernized Hong Kong, and its future is currently in debate in the wake of the handover. It would be folly for us to break off our one inroad into the East, but the place desperately needs those who are more schooled in Eastern culture and mysticism (or who at least speak some Chinese) to take advantage of the vast opportunities or make any inroads with the Eastern Brethren.

Steam ushered in enormous developments in manufacturing, travel, industry — whatever it was, steam somehow improved it. For the Kindred, steam brought about a number of advances that most were very happy to take advantage of. Steamships and locomotives meant that vampires could actually consider travel and make a go of it — fewer stopping points, quicker progress, sunproof conveyances, the sorts of things that ensured you would probably arrive at your destination in one piece. Steam in the factories brought in capital, and many Kindred made money hand over talon when they realized that steam was in fact the wave of the future. The best example of such success is Michael Vanderbilt, who rode both his name and his business acumen to a mansion, a herd of New York's finest socialites, and a set of factories up and down the East Coast.

The 19th century was also a time of social upheaval and change. Not every Kindred of the clans was involved with this, but some generalizations can be made regarding who did what. With the factories came exploited workers, and the Brujah were after those like flies on shit. Muckraking reporters, social workers and labor organizers gained prominence, often through dint of mysterious (Nosferatu?) informants, but the elders' interference ensured that they never got as far as they wanted. Factories took the people away from the small country towns and into crowded city slums — good, if filthy, hunting. Textile, mining and other industries also wreaked havoc on the landscape, pouring smog into the air, clear-cutting forests and poisoning the water, no doubt to the rage of our Lupine foes.

In an era of causes and social activism, a number of vampires found mortals whose efforts dovetailed nicely with their own, albeit with far different and certainly not always benign reasons. Malkavians, I am certain, watched Nellie Bly go undercover in mental hospitals to report on the abuses of the insane. Some Nosferatu, especially in London and New York, occasionally steered the burgeoning social workers to look after their herds.

Brujah Rabble fraternized with Socialists, labor unions and social workers to "bring more to the underdogs" — a euphemism, I am sure, for finding easy blood. More refined Kindred patronized whatever cause was fashionable at the moment; nothing made quite the fashion statement for mortals like how many "charities" one was aiding. If nothing else, it was taking care of the herds, in the same way that a farmer takes care of his animals. Healthy cows give good milk, if you follow my line.

I've been told that, socially speaking, Elysiums and parties ran like pages out of Edith Wharton. It was one thing to have money in these nights, but unless you had someone telling you where to spend it and what to spend it on, the harpies had a field day with you. The ideal of Elysium, unchanged since the Renaissance, was taken out of mothballs, dressed up with a few new frills, and proved that it could still take a turn around the ballroom floor. A clansman tells me that during these days, Elysium could be anything from the intellectual (a lecture on Socialism) to the artistic (a drawing-room recital) to the transcendent (exercises to open oneself to "transcendental possibilities" — whatever that was). I occasionally wonder how many vampires were actually delighted to discover they were still human enough to be bored to sleep in Elysium.

The Sabbat decided to make another attempt to throw the Camarilla out of the Americas, and, according to a rather unpopular scholar of our kind, the elders actually came damn close to losing. Thank the Sabbat who fell through on their end of things — if not for that, you wouldn't be reading this. The werewolves in the American frontier decided that they weren't interested in sharing it with the rest of us — so much for "manifest destiny." As for the rest, if even half the accounts I've read or heard from elders are true, the red-light districts and drug trades owed a large part of their briskness to certain enterprising vampires, particularly Setites.

Most Kindred I've talked to are positive that there must have been something in the water around this time. How else to account for all the supernatural events cropping up all over the landscape? From photographed faeries to rapping tables, haunted rectories and occultism, the 20th century followed the 19th as if by clinging to its shroud.

A note about the Whitechapel Murders — I've looked through every book available in the library and through a number of other places, and I can't find anything on this Lord Fianna. Like a boogeyman, he appears long enough to have a reign of terror as Jack, then vanishes without a trace. Are you convinced of his vampirism? Personally, I think Lord Fianna is hogwash, an attempt for Prince Mithras to hide his embarrassment when even he couldn't find out who Jack was with all the resources of the Camarilla put at his disposal. There is still an outstanding blood hunt for Fianna, which I don't think will ever come due. Truthfully, I believe it was a mortal — a very sick mortal that not even Malkavians would touch — but mortal all the same. Mortals have taught me enough times that they understand cruelty and evil in ways that make even us flinch.

AGE OF SPIRITS

The Age of Spiritualism deserves a little more than a throwaway line or two, straddling two centuries as it does and playing a role in Kindred history far greater than most give it credit for. Having seen it from both sides (as a mortal in its heyday, then as a vampire watching it sputter and die), I can say that this was a time rich with strangeness and the supernatural.

We Tremere were busy, much more than usual. This was the age of table-rappings, séances, mediums, channelers…and frauds, fakes, showmen and debunking that would wound us for years to come. Ghosts and mediumship was something that we had had trouble getting into with any depth, and this era seemed to have been all but made for us to finally do so. Even Kindred who traditionally avoided occultism (primarily out of respect for our long-held stake in the matter) made ventures into the field, and gave us some surprising undiscovered treasures.

Having endured more than enough fraudulent séances that purported to contact my late mother, I can easily understand what it was that drove Houdini to expose these charlatans. Over the years, I've heard a number of stories from Tremere and some other vampires regarding this time, and few have spoken about it with aught save bitterness — tales of lost lovers, children and sires they had hoped to contact, only to be bilked and blinded. Part of the bitterness stemmed from being taken for fools, but even the Damned did not care to have such fragile hopes and emotions so casually used and exploited. In that regard, we were no different from the kine, and I think that may have bothered some more than they wanted to reveal. Perhaps enough to sponsor debunkers and bribe assistants into revealing their tricks for a spectacular fall.

Some have suggested the rather high amount of supernatural instances that took place during this era were signs that the Masquerade was weak. That was only part of the equation. The supernatural became a desirable thing to discuss and study, and even the shyest people came forward with stories of their encounters with ghosts and other night creatures, knowing they would be received with a modicum of seriousness. Supernatural literature likewise reached a rather respectable spot, particularly stories regarding vampires. And lastly, serious inquiry and study of ghosts, mediumship and other paranormal events and denizens came into its own, particularly with the founding of the Society for Psychical Research (SPR) and its American counterpart.

According to my sire, who spent most of this time in London, certain busybody vampires insinuated themselves in the publishing industry after vampire and ghost stories started appearing in great numbers. Nonetheless, the publication of *Dracula* sent the Camarilla into a tailspin. Some found it amusing, but not all did. A few elders believed that it might instigate widespread breaches of the Masquerade and bring inordinate curiosity from mortals, or a backlash from angry Tzimisce. A number of cities suddenly found themselves hosting archons, who were waiting to bring the hammer down on *any* erring Kindred. Strangely enough, the Fiends were remarkably quiet; I would have thought that they would be out burning every copy they could get their hands on for its portrayal of "The Dragon."

Between *Dracula*, the Cottingley photos and table-rappings, the hunters didn't know which way to go. Unfortunately for us, they increased in numbers as time went on — fraud and greed from the paranormal brokers, a World War, deluded serial killers and general world-weariness had begun to take their toll on mortal belief and tolerance of the supernatural. Encouraged by Houdini's own crusade, recruited by the Inquisition, mortals attempted to turn on us, but could not find the footholds that had supported them in the Burning Times. The Sabbat decided to see about launching some incursions into American cities then, thinking the Inner Circle distracted, but were rudely surprised to find the princes prepared and itching for a fight. As the world tossed fitfully in its final dreams, the revolutionaries and zealots decided to wake it up once and for all.

Again, the romanticism of this feeble-minded newborn shows through. I suppose if she had read Upton Sinclair in her youth, she might have had some idea of the sorts of opportunities that industrialism offered. The densely packed populations of the rapidly expanding cities allowed a delicious assortment of delights to our kind — and I do not list involvement in various humanitarian causes among them. Roses and wine, indeed. How soft and malleable the minds of childer have become in recent years.

REVOLUTION

As the centuries turned from the 19th to the 20th, the discontent started by revolutionaries began to boil, and then boiled over. All over Europe, old monarchies toppled and were thrown aside in favor of "new orders" that supposedly favored the proletariat.

One of the prime examples was the October Revolution led by Lenin in Russia. Out with the oppressive monarchy and in with the people's government. In my research, even the most ardent conspiracy theorists haven't been able to find Kindred involvement with the fall of the Romanovs. Their execution at Ekaterinberg shocked many vampires, and not just the Blue Bloods. It was the death knell of the age of monarchy; never again would there be kings and emperors and sovereignty such as Czar Nicholas and his mortal contemporaries had known. Since then, at least three clans claim to have Embraced Anastasia into their ranks. None show any signs of being remotely related to the Romanovs; I think it was done as a status symbol that's since backfired on their poor suckered clans. And Rasputin — let's not even talk about *that*.

France, Germany, Spain, Serbia — all over the continent, mortals tested the bonds of freedom. Some won, some lost, some didn't get anywhere except back where they started. The Kindred, as usual, watched and placed bets on the winners. Some elders claim that certain vampires encouraged the discontent of the mortals, risking instability in the cities in the name of shaking the status quo. Certainly, many Sabbat incursions into Camarilla cities were synchronized with revolutionary turmoil. So were a number of anarch-led *coup d'etats* and attempts at same.

A World at War

I think most Kindred believed themselves completely jaded to the notion of war and its brutality when the World Wars came in. But I know a number of complacent vampires suddenly sat up and took notice when tanks rolled across the fields of France, mustard gas turned men into blistered meat, and rapid-fire guns demonstrated the ability to mow down dozens at a time. Before then, brutality had meant something else — swords and axes, looting and pillaging, and on a relatively smaller scale. But this time the destruction was more widespread, more were taking up arms and those arms were capable of dealing massive amounts of damage. While a few young vampires plunged headlong into the fray, many elders ran for the hills. Even if one doesn't breathe, mustard gas can get really hard on the lungs. And brutality aside, the sheer scope of the event amazed many. World War I was called the Great War for a reason; at the time it was the biggest event most had ever seen — literally entire nations pitting themselves against each other. Telephones, telegraph, radio — all assured that no matter where one was, he got the latest news on the war.

The Camarilla still fought with the Sabbat, even during this time. Our wars with them never went completely out, just smoldered like embers under ashes before bursting into flame again. Whether Camarilla Kindred were rumrunning in Chicago, feeding on the shattered population of Russia, overseeing the fledgling movie industry or just surviving, the Sabbat was there.

Just after the Depression, though, Sabbat activity all but ceased. The war packs still ventured out for a little street-to-street fighting, but all seemed strikingly quiet. I still don't know what it was that pulled the Black Hand underground. Maybe a Caine sighting. At any rate, with all the Camarilla's Kindred had before them, a Sabbat war was the last thing anyone wanted.

Very few vampires of today like to talk about their involvement with WWII in Europe, and I suppose I can't blame them, not with my own record before me. In retrospect it's easy to say, "We didn't know, we kept ourselves out of mortal affairs, we were misled, etc." This sounds like a lot of excuses to me. We who are all in some way living relics cannot claim that this was a first in history, because it wasn't. Ignorance is no excuse for allowing genocide, which, besides being distasteful, was a foolish culling of the herds. As for the rest of the war, it was the Great War Take Two, with a few changes. Mustard gas might have been outlawed, but blitzkriegs spreading fires all over a city isn't exactly an improvement. Kindred trying to flee the hellhole that Europe had become retreated to the States, straining many power structures within established cities and stretching resources to the limits. Those of us who stayed behind watched cities being bombed while in the "safety" of the cellars, fought off looters with our bare hands or drank from anything wearing a German uniform.

I have seen too many wars in my time to believe that the World Wars were somehow "different" from other conflicts. The sole difference was scale; with a world newly united by radio, telephone and other ingenious devices, humankind's penchant for slaughter could simply be played out on a much grander stage. Even the charnel houses erected by the Third Reich were only moderately novel; man has been doing such things to his neighbor since — why, since the murder of Abel, I daresay. Still, such innovations in efficiency have not gone unnoticed. Hitler and his pack were a dangerously clever mob. I am glad they are dead.

The Modern Age

After the bombing of Hiroshima and Nagasaki, the world seemed to turn over again, as if trying to reinvent itself. This time, it didn't do quite so well.

Reconstruction was long and arduous, even more for vampires than for mortals. For many elders and ancillae, it meant actually seeing their world, their havens, their treasures lying in rubble. Many of the prudent (and lucky) had managed to move their greatest prizes (childer, books, relics) to safer locations, but not everyone was so fortunate. The old world literally had been ripped apart, and was being put back together, and for elder Kindred, it was a difficult time. A few simply couldn't handle seeing the destruction of their worlds, and chose to enter torpor or stayed up to watch the sun rise.

The McCarthy era — I was sent out to watch this with a few others, primarily to make sure no important pawns ended up on the stands. Many of the elders who had started to reemerge after the World Wars went right back into their cellars and coffins; most of them had been European at one time or another, and saw too many similarities between the Burning Times and the hearings for comfort. They were probably right; while those found "guilty" couldn't be burned alive in the town square, they could be publicly pilloried and humiliated, which could be just as bad. Well, nearly as bad.

The Age of Aquarius — Believe it or not, we Tremere accomplished little during the '60s. While there was a resurgent interest in magic (a welcome change after the cold, sterile '50s), it offered relatively little to us. In truth, the orgies, psychedelics and music were meant for those who still had living flesh. Yes, I tried blood-borne psychedelics, but not on purpose — a mistake in feeding that I will never forget. If nothing else, between the fashions, the music and the people, it had to be one of the most absurd eras I've ever seen.

Now here we are, in an age that has seen mortals land on the moon, the Iron Curtain rise and fall, and some of the most destructive weaponry imaginable developed for the purpose of "defense." Ever since the bomb came down on Hiroshima, this technology has spread like wildfire; literally every night seems to bring some new gadget or discovery. I know of elder vampires who have fallen so far behind the times that they won't accept a telephone call, much less use this marvelous email, mostly because they are fearful of using such things. I must admit, it's rather disturbing to find that the machines and ideas I once read about in H.G. Wells or Jules Verne when I was a mortal adolescent in 1904 are coming into common use. Occasionally I have to struggle with learning something new or throw myself on the mercy of a neonate for assistance, but it's part of being what we are — we may "stop," but the world does not. If you don't keep up, you'll be left by the wayside. What is frightening is that these same vampires sometimes destroy the younger ones who do know how to use technology because the elders are equally frightened of them. And they're supposed to be leading us into the next millennium?

Most of the violent crime occurring today isn't vampire-committed, but it's great cover for other things to take place. When I first arrived, Milos Kilar (the previous regent) told me that the Sabbat attacks had shown a pattern of growing steadily more frenzied over the past decade. This sounds like of one of two things: Either they're going for the "last swing before the fall," or they're desperately trying to make a difference with what's coming. My guess is the former, although I couldn't be certain what they're swinging at.

With one millennium changing to the next, the Gehenna cults and elder doomsayers (you'll meet them — the ones who publicly scoff at the notion of Antediluvians, then whisper their fears and blasphemy in their chambers when they think they can't be heard) are even more anxious and desperate as the years tick ever closer. I know of a certain pontifex who is increasingly obsessed with finding the "woman with the crescent moon birthmark" talked about in *The Book of Nod*, to the point of ignoring other, more pressing concerns. Some claim that the Sabbat is going into its last frenzy and hurrah because its leaders believe the Antediluvians will rise sometime near, or shortly after, the beginning of the millennium. Already, they've taken back several domains from the princes, and have claimed a few more that the Camarilla has traditionally held. We hold the line in New York, but only by hanging on with our claws like cats desperate to avoid getting wet. If New York falls, the East Coast crumbles.

As for the Camarilla itself, see my above comment. We stand fast, but — and speak not of this outside the chantries — we're starting to show the wear and tear of the centuries. Unless something finally gives way — our leaders come to their senses, the Sabbat vanishes, the Master awakens — we may find ourselves starting to crumble like an old tombstone. And then it won't matter what cities we hold, because without the Camarilla to hold things together in any reasonable fashion, the Kindred will fall apart.

And this is where we stand, after 5000 years of history.

Aisling Sturbridge

Updated 5/23/98

Here, much as it pains me to do so, I must concur — conditionally — with this mongrel's conclusions. Where once the changes to a society were measured by the century, now they occur by the decade, if that infrequently. I know of Cainites who once prided themselves on their adaptability, but have now chosen to sink beneath the ground and wait for a more sedate era to arrive.

More fools they, for Gehenna will surely be upon us before they wake again.

Our war is far from over. In fact, the portents are among us — there is a frenzy among the Noddist circles I frequent, a berserk scrabbling to unlock the secrets of the Book before it is too late to utilize their wisdom. Yes, prophecies can be forged; look at the babblings of Nostradamus, and try to tell me that he was a person of true insight. However, too many of the Book of Nod's revelations ring of truth, even to the most refined vampiric prescience. And with the portents comes a renewed vigor. Even the lowliest Cainite can sense that all the centuries of waiting will soon be at an end, and that the events that shall remake the world are at hand. I would be terrified, if I still had the mortal blood for it. My bones would be chilled with dread, if the marrow within them had not cooled lifetimes ago.

But fear is no longer my way, and all I feel now is anticipation.

Yours in the Age to Come,

Vykos

It's three in the morning and I'm in the process of figuring out how good it feels to be dead. The streets are slick with rain, and the streetlights are reflecting off the pavement like God wants every manhole cover to have a halo. A block down Locust Street, I can see a car pulling out from a turn. I can read the license plate from here — I never could have done that when I was alive. At the end of the street I can see the trees in Rittenhouse Square, and I swear I can count every leaf and every bead of water on each one.

I can see it all, and it's so beautiful.

I can see him, too. He's wearing a tan trenchcoat and carrying a closed-up black umbrella. I start walking toward the Square, timing my pace so that I'll bump into him at the crosswalk. Now I can see the streaks of gray in his hair, the lines on his face. He looks about 40, a little tired of life but still chugging along in his rut. His pace is steady, mechanical. I move faster.

He suddenly stops and looks up at the clearing sky. Maybe he's looking for an answer through the bare branches of the park's trees. Maybe he's just got the animal instinct that screams "Predator!" It doesn't matter. I'm close now...20th Street, 19th —

He turns from the sky and starts walking again. His eyes meet mine from a block away, and I think he knows. He doesn't stop again, though. He doesn't turn away. And I see the pain and the hope and the history written on his face, every last moment of a life that's about to end, and I fall in love with him.

I fall in love this way every night, and every evening I wake up with a broken heart again. There's no one to blame but me, though. No one to blame but me.

Chapter Eight: STORYTELLING

Forget about the pages of rules and the handfuls of dice. Close the book, turn out the lights, and tell me a story about dark desires and relentless hunger. I'll tell you about a vampire, about her talents and her weaknesses, and you tell me what kind of challenges she faces, what rewards or perils come her way. You plan the twists and turns the story will take, and I will tell you how the vampire navigates them. Only you know how the story ultimately ends, but only I know how the vampire will arrive there. Along the way, the work you put into the story gives my vampire the chance to grow and develop, and her actions breathe life into the world you have created.

That is the challenge of storytelling. **Vampire** is about the inner struggle between humanity and monstrosity in the face of unfettered power and eternal life. No mortal law binds the Kindred, no moral code restrains them — only fading passions or ideals nurtured in mortal life keep a vampire from indulging her horrific nature, and those memories become harder and harder to recall as the years stretch into centuries. In short, **Vampire** is about the characters and how they develop — or wither — in the face of tragedy and temptation. Can a mortal steeped in religious faith reconcile her deeply held beliefs with her lust for blood? Can a vampire resist the temptation to Embrace her lover rather than face an eternity of loneliness? The Beast awaits any Kindred who surrenders herself completely to her predatory urges. The Storyteller must draw on the characters' backgrounds, hopes, and ambitions to create stories that challenge their — and their players' — convictions and beliefs. As a result, taking on the role of a Storyteller in a **Vampire** game is very demanding, requiring careful thought and background work to build character-driven chronicles and stories. You must create a world that is a nightmare reflection of our own, enticing and repellent, exhilarating and horrifying. You must evoke the thrill of inhuman power and a fear of what might happen if the character ever loses control. And you can't let the characters just

keep to themselves and survive off daring thefts from the local blood bank. The night air is thick with the intrigues of the elders as Gehenna draws nigh, and the ancillae manipulate neonates as they see fit, promising great rewards — and even greater risks.

Storytelling sounds like a lot to manage all at once, and it is at first. Fortunately, the Storyteller doesn't have to do it all herself. The secret to successful storytelling is, ironically, the work of the players. Fulfilling the expectations and interests of a chronicle's players is the first trick to creating the game's setting. Then — if the chronicle and its overall story have been carefully developed — the actions of the characters, both good and bad, will have consequences that in turn spawn further stories. Never forget: The more the players are involved with what happens in a chronicle, the less work you, the Storyteller, must take upon yourself. You aren't supposed to do it all alone. The Storyteller should have as much fun with the game as the players, and this chapter details how.

This chapter illustrates the process of creating and running a **Vampire** chronicle, and offers advice for making the most out of the individual stories that carry the chronicle along. Building a detailed and cohesive background, a world for your players to hunt in, begins with input from your players and your own ideas for what kind of an overall story you would like to tell. Once you have decided on the details of the setting, the next step is creating characters to fill it, again keeping in mind the kind of chronicle you want to tell. After the characters are in place, you can then get to writing the chronicle in earnest, working out the intrigues and events that move the overall story along and draw on each character's goals and motivations. Each step builds upon the next, giving you more and more background to make each story enjoyable and easy to manage. If you have never run a roleplaying game before, don't be intimidated by the big picture. Take it a step at a time, do it for fun, and let your imagination run wild.

The First, Fleeting Glimpse

It starts with a couple of ideas. You read through the book, and some things jump out at you. Maybe it's the image of a haughty prince ruling a city with an oppressive hand, or perhaps you like the idea of a band of anarchs making their own rules and living like wolves in the urban wilderness. Something catches your eye and sets off a spark in your mind, and you think, "This could make a cool chronicle." The question is, how do you turn these nebulous ideas into a well-rounded foundation for the stories you want to tell?

The first step begins with the players. Before you can really develop the foundation for your chronicle, you must have a strong grasp on what sorts of characters they want to play and how their concepts relate to your ideas. Suppose you are considering a chronicle set against the backdrop of a prince's meteoric rise and fall in a large, important city. You might envision stories of intrigue, treachery and the corrupting influence of great power. But what if one player has her heart set on playing a Nosferatu anarch, and another wishes to be an apolitical, narcissistic Toreador, neither of which is compatible with your overall concept? It's never a good idea to force a character concept on a player, because you want players to feel like they are contributing to the game and playing characters in whom they are really interested. At this point comes some amount of negotiation and compromise; perhaps you can interest them in your backdrop of political conflicts and double-dealing, but shift the focus of the chronicle to center instead on the characters' struggles to *avoid* the plots of their elders while pursuing their individual agendas. The important point is to make sure that your ideas and the players' expectations are in synch before you even begin to develop the chronicle. This way the players can add their ideas to your own and make your job much easier in the long run.

Once everyone agrees on the general idea of the chronicle, the players can begin to create their characters and you can begin to create the world in which they will hunt. It's worthwhile to do this simultaneously because it allows your ideas and theirs to play off one another, and might point you in directions that you could have missed otherwise. Suppose, for example, that a player wants her character to have been a government agent prior to her Embrace. You could then take this idea and expand upon it: The character worked for a covert division within the FBI, performing counterintelligence work that specifically investigates high-level corporate executives and politicians. This division has in fact been subverted by a powerful vampire who uses it as a resource to gather influential information and hinder the activities of her rivals. To add yet another level of conflict, you might decide that this primogen is now eyeing another member of the division for the Embrace, someone whom the character had a friendship with (or perhaps loved) as a mortal. You can then encourage the player to further develop the agency her character worked for, letting her provide details such as a history and important personalities that you blend into your world. This lets her flesh out her character, allows her to contribute to the game as a whole, and gives you valuable resource material for your chronicle. Get your players to go into a lot of detail when creating their characters. Sit in with them during the creation process, and brainstorm about their backgrounds, then make the most of the information they come up with. They can provide you with a whole host of characters, situations and conflicts that will be of use to you later.

It is important to take the characters' Backgrounds into account and develop them in detail, because as neonates these newly Embraced vampires still have very strong ties to the lives they have left behind. Encourage the purchase of allies, contacts, influence and the like, then brainstorm with the player to flesh them out. Where do a character's resources come from? Is she an heiress? Did she win the lottery? Did she stumble onto a drug deal gone sour and steal the bloodstained cash? What effect do these circumstances have on who the character is and her place in the chronicle? Likewise, allies or contacts are more than just dots on the character sheet — they are people with their own feelings and emotions. For instance, suppose a player wants her character to have a midlevel contact in the police department. Who is this contact, and how did the character establish this relationship? The contact might be the character's uncle, a veteran homicide detective who has a habit of asking pointed questions about the character's lifestyle and activities (particularly if he catches her at the scene of a recent murder!).

Each Background is an added dimension to the character concept, containing a wealth of ideas to inspire a Storyteller. How do the characters handle the sudden and irrevocable separation from everything they have ever known or loved? Do they fake their deaths, or simply walk away from their mortal lives? Do the characters leave loved ones who simply will not accept their disappearance and go to any lengths to find them? Can the characters stay away from spouses or children, torn by love yet knowing what might happen one night when the Hunger overtakes them? These situations are some of the first dilemmas that the characters must face, and can influence their actions in many subtle ways. While it is always tempting to just gloss over the particulars of each character's Embrace and get on with "being a vampire," this leaves out a vital dimension in the character's struggle to maintain her humanity, and provides you with a fertile field to draw ideas and supporting characters.

Once you have determined a general direction for your chronicle and incorporated elements of the players' characters, you can make some decisions about the world in which their stories will take place. Having detailed the setting for the chronicle (usually a city, but it is possible to run small-town or even wilderness chronicles) and peopled it with supporting characters that add to your overall concept, you can begin shaping the chronicle in earnest.

A World Dark and Deadly

Before your chronicle can be written, there must be a stage where its actions can be played out. You need to create a setting for your stories, a world that supports the themes and ideas you want to explore in your chronicle and starkly illustrates the glories and terrors of undead existence. The world of the vampire is dark, dangerous, enigmatic and rich in imagery. Consider these guidelines when inventing the details of your world:

• **The Extinction of Virtue:** There are few illusions left in the World of Darkness. Centuries of greed and deceit (on the part of humans as well as Kindred) have eroded humanity's innocence. Cynicism and despair permeate everything, from the tags on city walls to the movies in theaters. No one dares to believe in much of anything, because virtues like compassion and charity are just invitations to be victimized. A gentle soul and a loving heart are rare as diamonds, and as precious.

• **Blood and Money:** Life is cheap, and desperate people resort to violence out of frustration, fear, hatred and greed. Crime is ever-present, and many families and neighborhoods adapt a siege mentality against the rest of the world. It's us or them.

• **No More Good Guys:** The world has lost its heroes. They were caught in sex scandals or taking bribes, or perhaps they fell victim to endemic urban violence. There is no strong leadership, no faith in politicians or belief in building a better tomorrow. People know better.

• **Haunted Houses:** Humanity is rotting from within, continuing a sad, slow decline, and symbols of its decay are everywhere in the weathered façades of great, Gothic churches and granite office buildings. Amid soulless towers of steel and glass might sit an abandoned cathedral whose stained glass is rich with color and beauty from a time now lost. Such a place serves as a haunting reminder of what might have been, or could be again.

• **The Rage of the Millennium:** The end of an age draws nigh, and already the rumors and prophecies fly. Will it be a new beginning, or the end of the world? Many Kindred and mortals alike fear for what is to come and preach of apocalyptic doom, while others take to the streets with savage, desperate abandon, determined to make their mark on the world before it all goes up in flames.

These points illustrate the essence of the World of Darkness, and they are important because they heighten the dilemmas that your characters face as they grapple with their fading humanity. Despair and resignation are all around them; violence and death are common. What is one more killing, one more lie? How much difference can one person, even a vampire, make? Virtues like courage and compassion are hard to find and even harder to maintain, but it is the struggle for them that is important. This struggle is the source of the game's triumph and tragedy, and the decisions you make in developing your setting should take this into account. It is important to point out that you don't have to adhere religiously to these concepts, and the degree to which you emphasize them is strictly a matter of personal taste. The only truly important thing to remember is that your environment should be one in which doing the right and honorable thing is difficult and daunting.

There is, of course, no limit to the possible physical locations you can choose for your chronicle — with enough imagination and forethought, a **Vampire** chronicle can be set anywhere from Washington, DC to the Amazon Basin. The best locations, of course, are major cities, because they allow for a large population of vampires and are focal points for the money and power that most Kindred seek. If you wish to locate your chronicle in a large city that you are unfamiliar with, your local library can provide useful information and maps, which you can then reinterpret to suit your purposes. Remember, though, that you aren't constrained to be faithful in every detail; this is the World of Darkness, and you can shape it any way you choose. Consider the guidelines above, and where necessary alter the details in favor of your own ideas, or to build the proper mood. Many Storytellers prefer to set their chronicles in dark reflections of their own hometowns, which allows them and their players to draw upon everyday knowledge to help envision the places that their characters visit.

As you map out the length and breadth of your locale, draw ideas from important city features, combining function with symbolism to make interesting images. For instance, an abandoned and decaying train station in the center of the city might make an ideal site for Elysium, with its high, vaulted halls and faded grandeur. A little-used cathedral might become a haven for the city's Caitiff, who are drawn to its symbolism of sanctuary and redemption. A half-built zoo could serve as the anarchs' playground, or a block of skeletal construction sites could give the Nosferatu an aerie to look out over the streets. Vampires are territorial creatures, and the places they claim invariably mirror their individual character and attitudes. Again, don't let hard reality dissuade you from going with a cool idea; if you want your prince to rule from a Victorian mansion but your city doesn't have one, make one and put it where you want. In **Vampire**, details always take a back seat to mood and imagery.

So at this point you have three sources to draw on to build the setting of your chronicle: You have your own general ideas, you have all the details provided by your players during character creation, and you have at least some knowledge of the locale you have chosen. Now comes the time to develop your chronicle in detail.

WRITTEN IN BLOOD

The *chronicle* is the overall story that the Storyteller wishes to tell. It is made up of a series of smaller stories in which the player characters are the central figures. Think of a chronicle as a collection of books that tell a long, complicated tale. Each book is a story unto itself, which is further broken up into chapters, and then into scenes. What happens in each individual story depends a lot on the course of the chronicle as a whole. It's this stage of development that is the most demanding and time-consuming for the Storyteller. Unlike many other open-ended RPG "campaigns," **Vampire** chronicles have a definite beginning, middle and end. Accordingly, you need to detail this structure in advance, in order to organize your thoughts, show you when to pick up the pace, and provide tension over the course of individual stories. A chronicle loses its focus and energy if there is no real end in sight. After all this work, you want to close things off with a bang, not a whimper, right? Get a journal or disk and set it aside to hold notes and ideas as you outline the course of events in your chronicle. Don't try to keep it all in your head.

At this point, you have a pretty large amount of information to help guide your development of the chronicle; now you have to flesh out the course the stories will take and blend all of the details into a workable whole. The first step is to choose a governing theme. A theme is the central idea that describes the basic plotline of the overall story. Some suitable themes for **Vampire** chronicles include:

• **The Jyhad:** Though the Antediluvians' very names have been lost to antiquity, it is whispered that their Byzantine intrigues still permeate and direct the course of Kindred events. Crusades have been fought, nations have risen and fallen, whole clans have been destroyed, all to further their inhuman agendas in a struggle where perhaps even the players have forgotten what the game is all about. As the end of the age draws nigh, some believe that an apocalyptic endgame is at hand. The Storyteller can use this theme to draw the characters into a chronicle of secret societies or desperate, ambitious elders who perhaps believe that they see the threads of the Antediluvians' schemes and struggle to prevent their completion. Alternatively, the characters might find themselves pursuing their individual agendas, only to discern a pattern emerging that ties all of the events together. Have they become pawns in the Great Game? If so, what are they being used to accomplish, and by whom are they being used?

• **Bound by Invisible Chains:** Unlife brings power and freedom beyond the scope of anything mortals can imagine. A vampire is a law unto herself — or is she? For all that the Kindred are the immortal masters of their world, they are still victims of obligations, intrigue and their own passions. A vampire might master a city, but is she truly the master of her own fate? This theme works best when the chronicle centers around a group of ambitious vampires who seek to establish themselves as powerful and influential figures in a city or sect, to become powers in their own right and answerable to no one. From the beginning, they must scheme and struggle to escape the influence of their sires, their equally ambitious peers, and later the elders whose roles the characters eventually wish to supplant. But along the way deals must be made, alliances forged and broken, friends won and enemies made, and by the time the characters reach the pinnacle that they seek, they find that they are no more masters of their fates than they were before. The stakes have simply gotten higher.

• **Cold Redemption:** Many among the newly Embraced react with horror at what they have become and struggle to redeem themselves and their lost humanity at every turn. Characters turn their powers to helping the homeless or the poor, acting like modern Robin Hoods or simply defending the helpless from the predations of other Kindred. This theme not only pits the characters against other vampires who reject and scorn such "misplaced" altruism, but also against the wild urges of the Beasts within themselves. One moment of frenzy can turn a mission of mercy into a horrific tragedy.

• **The Birth of a New Age:** Many vampires familiar with *The Book of Nod* speak of an imminent cataclysm, the end of one cycle and the beginning of another. The old order will be swept away, and many idealists and madmen among the Kindred increasingly espouse visions of the new order which will take its place. As the end of the millennium passes and talk turns to increasingly hysterical visions of upheaval, the characters choose for themselves whether to resist the tides of revolution or be swept up in them. Will they fight to maintain the old order against anarchy, or will they join (or form) an idealistic crusade to reshape the world?

• **The Shadows or the Shackle:** The struggle between the Camarilla and the Sabbat is fundamentally a matter of philosophy: Are vampires meant to give humans their due and coexist alongside them, or are the Kindred the next evolutionary step and meant to rule humanity as mortals control their cattle? A Camarilla-dominated city under siege provides a powerful setting for this theme, as the characters find themselves caught in a war of ideology. Which sect is right? The characters might be a dissenting voice amid the Camarilla, or see "Sabbat sympathizers" in every shadow. An especially challenging variation on this theme leads the characters on a noble and tragic crusade to bridge the differences between the two sects.

• **Home Lies the Heart:** The undead existence of a vampire is lonely and full of horrors; it is no surprise, then, that many neonates try desperately to cling to the relationships and normalcy of their mortal lives. Can vampires truly go home, or are they simply setting the stage for tragedy? This theme emphasizes the vampire's irrevocable separation from humankind. For all that they prowl the night, surrounded by unknowing kine, the fact remains that the sunlit world is forever denied to them, and the Hunger that they feel is a constant danger to their loved ones. Characters unwilling to leave their mortal lives behind must risk the Masquerade, their Hunger, and the safety of those they care about. Are they selfishly clutching at the warmth and affection that they may have taken for granted in life? Or are they desperately trying to hold onto their humanity by focusing on the only things in life that truly matter?

Themes are important because they let you focus the events and actions along a central idea. This gives your chronicle consistency and emotional resonance, which you can build to a climactic finale. It is entirely possible to have more than one theme; you might want to create a chronicle that explores the mortal ties of neonate vampires as they are ensnared in the schemes of their elders, who themselves frantically prepare for the Gehenna to come. While the characters become the willing or unwilling agents of these schemes, they are torn between building a new order and preserving the world they once knew. Multiple themes can build a rich chronicle for a troupe as a whole, or each character can embody a theme all her own, separate and distinct from her fellows. The only limit is how much effort you, as the Storyteller, wish to devote in developing and smoothly integrating multiple themes.

Once you have chosen a theme, you can begin to develop the course of events that your chronicle will take, from beginning to end. Like any good story, a chronicle must have a conclusion to be truly effective, and if you know where the chronicle is going, you will have much more confidence in, and control over, your stories. Consider the your initial ideas, the characters and the themes you have chosen, then flesh out the details of your chronicle as a rough outline of events. For example:

Let's go back to the initial idea of a group of characters whose Embrace and unlife begin against the backdrop of a charismatic vampire's rise and fall as prince of a city. You might decide on two themes for your chronicle: *The Shadow or the Shackle*, and *Bound by Invisible Chains*. You like the idea of giving the characters a vision of the freedom and power that elder Kindred possess, then drawing them into an ever-tightening mesh of intrigue and deceit as they find themselves in a position to grab power and status by the side of the would-be prince. But once in power, the façade of idealism and enlightenment falls away, and the new prince proves to be every bit the despot that her predecessor was. The characters, for all their newfound influence, are trapped in a web of obligations and allegiances to the prince and her other allies, no more free to do as they please than they were as neonates. As events worsen, rumbles of dissent spread throughout the city, and the characters must question not only their loyalty to the current regime, but also the worthiness of the Camarilla's philosophies as a whole. You want the chronicle to end in a blazing finale, during which the characters must decide whether to hold true to their loyalties for the sake of honor and principle, or to bring down the prince they helped raise to power and choose a new course for the city. Now you need to determine a rough outline sequence of events to get the characters to that point.

Things should start out simply, because the characters will need some time to get acquainted with the city and its denizens. You decide that the first stories will center on the characters' Embrace and their relationship to their sires, challenging the characters to reconcile their new existences with the ties of their mortal lives. How the characters react to their new situation can spawn conflicts and goals that you can expand upon as subplots over the course of the chronicle. Along the way, the characters come into contact with some of the other Kindred in the city, then they are presented before the city's current prince. You want to emphasize the atmosphere of unrest in the city as the Kindred chafe under the iron hand of a tyrant, so as the characters explore the city you plan for several encounters which will give them firsthand experience with the prince's tyranny. They might witness the brutal excesses of primogen who support the prince, or their sires might call upon them to carry messages of dissent to other powerful elders. Perhaps they might even become involved in a blood hunt, called upon a hapless Kindred for a highly dubious offense. Over the course of these incidents, the characters acquaint themselves with another Kindred — an ancilla who is cautious but eloquent in his opposition to the current order. The characters might listen and sympathize, or they might denounce him, or the coterie might be torn along conflicting lines of loyalty and philosophy. As time passes, it becomes clear that this Kindred seeks to claim the title of prince for himself. The characters stand to gain status and power by supporting the usurper, or lesser rewards from the current regime by exposing the rebellion. You choose to leave these events open-ended. The players are the central figures in the chronicle and should make their own decisions, according to their individual concepts and agendas.

Ultimately the rebellion must come to a head, and you choose, for the interests of the story, that the rebellion succeeds, thanks to or in spite of the characters' actions. Depending on the choices that they made, the characters must meet the challenges of the aftermath. Either they are powerful and influential members of the new order, or they are hounded and reviled as supporters of the old regime. How the characters cope with these changes occupies the latter half of the chronicle, as time progresses and the new prince sheds his noble pretensions and is revealed as no less a tyrant than his predecessor. Now the characters have assumed the roles of the elders whom they envied as neonates, but find that such lofty heights are no less fraught with peril and constraints. In the end, the chronicle brings the characters full circle; depending on which choices they made in the beginning, they may find themselves part of the oppressive regime, or charismatic firebrands seeking support among the neonates to stage a rebellion of their own.

You now have a basic outline of the overall events in your chronicle. In addition to these major points, smaller plotlines will be spawned by the characters' personal goals and backgrounds. These subplots can be tied to the overall plot, or they may be entirely unconnected, contributing to the whole through character development and added conflict. For example, while the would-be usurper gathers his support to overthrow the prince, he may have designs on Embracing a mortal in a key position of power at a company the prince controls. This mortal in question happens to be a friend of one of the characters, or perhaps the characters might find themselves opposed to the Embrace on grounds of principle or personal philosophy, though in the main they support the plans for rebellion. Some ideas for subplots suggest themselves at the beginning of your chronicle, provided by the characters' backgrounds and personalities. Others arise over the course of the game, as relationships and important decisions influence the course of events. Incorporate as many of these subplots into your chronicle as you feel comfortable with, because they provide alternate storylines that add dimension to the characters and the chronicle as a whole.

Other possibilities for chronicles and the themes they can explore include:

• **To Search for Hidden Secrets:** Gehenna fast approaches, and many Kindred fear that the world may soon go up in flames. The characters could be the brood of a single sire, or a coterie of individuals who must search out the millennia-old secrets of the Antediluvians and identify their schemes before it's too late. Themes conducive to this kind of chronicle revolve around the quest for power and the manipulations of unseen forces, or the temptations that vast powers make upon the soul. The Storyteller can add elements of terror and suspense, as the characters draw closer to horrible secrets that perhaps no one, mortal or Kindred, was ever meant to know.

• **Live Free or Die:** The characters are a gang of anarchs rebelling against the dictates of an overbearing, authoritarian prince. Perhaps their sires are outspoken in their defiance of the prince's rule, actively fomenting disobedience and an end to the established order. The prince counters this by claiming that her law alone keeps the Sabbat from the city. Her rule brings order and stability, which the characters gravely threaten. Relevant themes for this kind of chronicle can include self-will versus an imposed order, or freedom of thought and expression in the face of oppression.

• **The Cold Company of Sharks:** The characters are high-society vampires scheming to gain power and status among the ancillae and elders of a city. Power politics, intrigue and betrayal are the order of the day, as rivals welcome one another with cordial smiles while their underlings wage a silent, ruthless war on the city streets. This chronicle explores the potent themes of trust, friendship, loyalty and the corrupting taste of power.

• **No Place Called Home:** The characters are refugees from a city taken by the Sabbat or torn apart by the intrigues of the Jyhad. They must find a new existence in a different city, choosing to return to the heights of power they formerly enjoyed, or perhaps to exist in seclusion and shun the intrigues of the prince's court. Then come indications that this city, too, is about to suffer the same fate as their former home. Do the characters attempt to take a stand and avert another disaster, or will they flee again? This chronicle can explore themes like courage and honor, or friendship, or betrayal.

• **Conquistadors:** This chronicle tells of the triumph or tragedy of founding a new fiefdom in a distant city. At the bidding of either the Sabbat or the Camarilla (or acting without the blessing of either sect), the characters must attempt to wrest the city from the forces, both human and supernatural, who might already claim it. Suitable themes for such a chronicle can be anything from the Jyhad to complex ideas revolving around the value of "progress" versus the value of an indigenous culture.

• **The Free City:** An ambitious council of primogen declare a city to be free and open to Kindred and kine alike, a place of peace where all can coexist. But can the dream work? The characters can be the agents working to build this daunting dream, making friends and allies out of former enemies. Then tragedy strikes — a misunderstanding (or outright sabotage) breaks the truce, and friend turns against friend. Themes of this chronicle can range from the poison of prejudice to themes of honor, courage and compassion.

• **Golconda:** Rumors emerge of a mysterious stranger, newly arrived in the city, claiming to be a Methuselah who has found the way to Golconda. Does she speak the truth, or is she an agent of the Jyhad sent to divide the city at the bidding of her masters? The characters must find out, and along the way face the temptations of what the mysterious figure offers. Suitable themes for this chronicle can center on redemption, humanity, greed, loyalty and compassion.

• **Angels of Mercy, Angels of Death:** The characters rebel against the teachings of their sires, horrified at what they have become and the means by which they were Embraced. Defiant and headstrong, they declare their own personal war against the creatures who spawned them, fighting for the sake of people who would see little difference between the Dark Angels and the forces they do battle with. Suitable themes for this chronicle may include honor, humanity, courage, prejudice and betrayal.

• **Tale of Two Cities:** The characters are a coterie/pack of vampires who decide to defect to the opposing camp, either Camarilla to Sabbat or *vice versa*. The characters must somehow make their way to their former enemies, show their interests are genuine, and overcome whatever challenges are necessary to be accepted into the new sect. Then they are enlisted in a campaign to conquer their former home. Themes for this chronicle can include greed, love, friendship, betrayal, truth and deceit.

COURTS OF CRIMSON AND ALABASTER

Once you have created your central themes and detailed the course of the chronicle, you are ready to get down to specifics about your setting and the Storyteller characters who exist there. The outline you have developed should give you a guideline as to which characters you need and when they will come into play. For instance, in the example of the usurper prince developed previously, the Storyteller would initially develop the major vampires of the city and their holdings, as well as details of the city's Elysium and the current prince. As play progresses, the

Storyteller can fill in details of the rest of the city's Kindred, from the up-and-comers to the disenfranchised Caitiff, as well as mortals who might play roles in the chronicle. The point is that you, as the Storyteller, should not feel like you have to generate a whole world in a single day. Figure out what you will need for the immediate point in the chronicle, develop those elements in detail, then work ahead to address your future needs.

More than any other roleplaying game, **Vampire** demands well-crafted Storyteller characters to make the chronicle potent and challenging. Mortal life is transitory; cities come and go. But the Kindred remain, immortal, outwardly unchanging, the only constant in an ever-changing world. Storyteller characters are the heart and soul of a chronicle, giving your landscape life, action and energy. Paint them in vivid detail and act through them to evoke emotions and ideas in your players.

The first Storyteller characters you are likely to create will be those generated by your players' character Backgrounds. This is a good place to start, because the players will help you brainstorm their affiliates' histories and characteristics. When creating your first Storyteller characters, work along the following guidelines:

Envision the role: Each character performs a role in your chronicle, even down to the accountant who crosses a dark parking lot and falls prey to a character's hunger. Establish what role the character is to play, then determine what qualities are necessary for the character to fulfill the role effectively. A victim (yes, put some detail into as many victims as possible; make the players feel that their characters are preying on *people*, not cardboard cutouts) embodies qualities of sympathy, terror and pathos. An antagonist, on the other hand, evokes qualities of ruthlessness, or cleverness, or even brute belligerence.

Paint a picture: Envision what the character looks like, taking into account the qualities you have chosen. Pick out one or two characteristics that make the character interesting to you. If you are envisioning one of the characters' herd, for instance, the image of a tall, broad-shouldered man with a prominently broken nose offers a memorable picture, and suggests other interesting images which have appeal. The picture of a powerfully built man, an obvious brawler, helpless in a smaller Kindred's Embrace evokes the power and horror of the vampire.

Choose a name: This sounds obvious, but carefully chosen names enhance characters, while poor ones detract from the character image and can even lessen the overall mood of the scenes in which the character appears. If we took the brawler from the example above and named him Poindexter, the players would have a hard time getting past the name, much less appreciating the character and his plight.

Age: A character's age is of great significance when creating vampire characters for your chronicle. Immortality wears away at all the ties that connect vampires to the mortal life they once knew. Friends and family wither away, homes fall to ruin — the idea of finding warmth and comfort in human company loses all value as the years stretch into centuries. For the Kindred, each year separates them further from mortal society, as their experiences and ambitions broaden and their perspectives become increasingly alien. What value are a 30-year-old human's in-

sights to one who has watched nations rise and fall? After a few hundred years of existence, a vampire regards a mortal as something akin to a domesticated animal — useful, perhaps even worthy of some affection, but still a creature of very limited lifespan and awareness. A vampire who has existed and schemed for millennia has no more regard for the mortal societies she coldly manipulates than a beekeeper has for his hives.

Personality: Choose one or two words that embody the character's personality. In the beginning, you may wish to fall back on the Natures and Demeanors provided for character creation, then expand your repertoire of archetypes as you become more experienced. To make interesting characters, consider choosing personality types that seem to run counter to the "role" that you intend them to play in your chronicle. For example, if you are envisioning a master villain who will haunt the player characters at every turn, you could challenge the players' expectations and make the character friendly, outgoing, even compassionate — someone who believes that destroying the characters is a regretful necessity, but one that will benefit everyone in the long run.

Past History: Every significant character in your chronicle benefits from some amount of past history. What conflicts has the character faced; whom has she loved or hated? Are there enemies or former lovers out there who might cross paths with the players' characters at some point? Did the character have a mentor, and how did the relationship affect the character? Establish a character's past history in as much detail as you deem relevant to the chronicle. A character who performs very limited roles, like a street contact or a mortal family member, might not merit as much detail, whereas the course of a 300-year-old primogen's existence would certainly benefit from a record of the Kindred's past experiences.

Quirks: Everyone is an individual, and everyone, mortal or Kindred, has quirky habits accumulated over time. Whether it's drinking milk right out of the carton or feeding on a mortal to the music of *Die Fledermaus*, individual quirks further define characters and make them memorable.

Flaws/Weaknesses: Nobody is perfect. All people have weaknesses or character flaws against which they struggle. This is especially important with regards to major adversaries. Villains who do nothing wrong, make no mistakes, and are afraid of nothing are not only discouraging but boring as well. Blind spots or flaws provide chinks in a villain's armor that the characters can exploit, or give an extra level of pathos to a heroic character who must battle not only external demons, but internal ones as well.

Statistics/Skills: Do this last. They're just numbers. Storyteller characters do not have to be constructed along the careful lines of a player's character. You can assign a Storyteller character whatever levels and skills you wish. If the characters aren't unique and interesting, the best set of numbers in the world won't do any good for your chronicle.

The key element to making characters memorable is to avoid stereotypes. It is easy to get lazy and just describe a roving character as a "Brujah anarch," in which case the players fall back on a single well-worn image and set of mannerisms to describe what they encounter. Pretty soon every "Brujah anarch" the characters encounter looks the same, sounds the same, and

acts the same. Defy your players' expectations. With a little thought you can give a character a quirky spin that makes her unique and engages your players' imaginations. Suppose the players encounter a Ventrue who controls one of the city's major corporations. Now a stereotypical Ventrue would be cool and arrogant, refined and cultured. Ho hum. But what if this vampire had been a surfer for most of his mortal life, dragged back to chair Daddy's company and then later made into a vampire to strengthen one Kindred's stranglehold on local industry? What kind of Ventrue would this person be? Sometimes stereotypes have value (especially to mislead the players), but for the most part they should be avoided.

INTO THE FIRE

For weeks you have spent your time outlining the chronicle you want to tell, as well as building the world and detailing the characters who inhabit it. You have watched your players create their characters, and enmeshed their ideas with your own to give the players their own stake in your creation. Now it's time to begin the tale. Here is where all that background work will pay off and let you concentrate on telling your stories in the best way you can.

With your chosen themes and the outline of your chronicle in mind, you need to establish the events that bring each character into the Embrace, and eventually into the coterie, pack or brood. This is by no means mandatory, and in fact many Storytellers prefer simply to talk over these details, make some assumptions with the

players, and then get right to the action. Unfortunately this means losing an opportunity for some powerful storytelling, and a way for both player and Storyteller to explore what might be the most significant event in a character's development.

One does not become a vampire through a secret oath and a handshake. It begins in blood and an instant of hot pain. Terror turns to ecstasy, wiping away any resistance. Was the character a willing participant, seduced into the Embrace, or was he taken by force, a violation as traumatic and scarring as a rape? Either way, the character is *killed*, yet does not die. He awakens, hollow and hungry, his insides dead and his skin like ice. Then he senses blood in the air, and he makes his first kill…. Telling the story of the Embrace and claiming that first victim is an excellent way to highlight the conflicts and urges that set the vampire apart from mortals.

After the characters have been given their unlives, it remains to be seen how they are all brought together into a group. Introducing the characters to one another and watching their relationships forged over the course of the first story can give the players greater insight into the chemistry of the group and set the stage for possible conflicts. The way in which a group of characters can be brought together depends in part on the type of coterie that they are to form. Some examples are:

• **The Sire's Ready Hand**: A powerful vampire has carefully chosen the characters to form a group of talented and efficient agents. Each individual is chosen for her talents and mortal connections, then brought into the brood, though sometimes Kindred from other clans can be "adopted" into the coterie if their abilities are particularly useful. Members of such a coterie are sometimes brought into the group against their wishes, usually through coercion or manipulation, which can be the nucleus of a beginning story.

• **Spirits of Like Mind:** Vampires are by nature territorial and solitary creatures, but this doesn't mean that they cannot form relationships based on common interests and shared experiences. Such a coterie could comprise very diverse characters and clans, linked together by a common belief or crisis. Suppose a group of neonates find themselves thrown together when their territories are raided by the Sabbat? Conversely, the characters might be relatively weak vampires who decide to ally themselves to carve out hunting grounds of their own in opposition to more powerful but solitary Kindred. More ambitious possibilities include banding together to supplant the city's primogen, resisting the perceived influence of the Jyhad, or protecting mortal society from the depredations of vampire manipulation. The storytelling advantages of such a coterie include possible conflicts and tensions stemming from the characters' sense of loyalty and friendship in the face of clan/brood ties.

• **The Wild Ones:** This is the classic coterie of neonate vampires who band together under a charismatic leader and defend their hunting grounds from all comers. Most such coteries are anarchs who are giving the finger to the prince, but this doesn't necessarily have to be the case.

These coteries also lend themselves to chronicles in which the characters are diablerists, gaining power by criminally stalking and slaying the city's elders. Diablerie can be a ticket to vast power, but exacts a cost on the characters' safety and souls.

• **At the Prince's Command:** The characters are bound together at the behest of the prince or archbishop of the city, ostensibly to perform a specific task or responsibility. The ties that bind them together can be as informal as a promise and a handshake or as powerful as shared blood. With the exception of this unifying element, though, the characters can be entirely opposed to one another, even mortal foes. This is easily the most difficult kind of coterie to play, requiring hard work from players and Storyteller to find ways for the characters to put aside their differences and work together, but it can also make for some excellent storytelling.

• **The Outcasts:** The characters are pariahs, because of their actions or their status in society, and are thrown together simply because there is safety in numbers, and they have less reason to be haughty. This is the typical coterie for Caitiff, but it can apply to characters from any clan. Perhaps the characters were set up by a powerful and mysterious rival, and they must come together to clear their names.

When uniting characters in a brood or coterie, some thought must be given beforehand as to whether or not conflict between characters will be permitted, or if mutually agreed-upon loyalty and good relations will be allowed to prevail. Vampires are creatures of ambition and manipulation, and even within a coterie each Kindred is likely to have her own personal agenda based upon individual backgrounds and goals. When the individual agendas

within a group are at cross-purposes, treachery and deception are powerful themes that the Storyteller can draw upon to starkly illustrate the ultimately solitary nature of each vampire. Treachery within a coterie should not be forced upon the characters simply for the sake of the chronicle; instead, by forming a group of vampires with potentially opposing personal goals, the Storyteller can set out the conditions to engender treachery and deception amongst the coterie, and then let events take their course. For example, consider a coterie containing a character who is a diablerist, feeding on the vitae of more powerful Kindred out of a sense of revenge, while another character in the same group is a Toreador who believes herself to be in love with a powerful primogen. Yet another character in the coterie might have political aspirations and is eager to court allies among the city's elders. Will the diablerist manipulate the Toreador to ambush and destroy the primogen? Conversely, might the Toreador be forced to betray the diablerist out of love for the primogen? Or will the political aspirant manipulate them both, assisting in the destruction of the primogen, then betraying the diablerist in hopes of filling the void left by the primogen's destruction?

CREATING STORIES

There are several key elements to the storytelling process which you should consider when developing your stories. These are: *plot*, *conflict*, *setting* and *mood*.

The plot is what the story is about; it is the sequence of events and actions that the characters follow from beginning to end. The first question you should ask yourself when sitting down to design a story is what the plot will be. Like your chronicle, you need to have a clear idea of where the story will go and how you will build the action to a satisfying end. There are two types of plots: Main plots are stories which are integral parts of your chronicle and move the overall story along, while secondary plots are unconnected stories which may or may not have anything to do with the chronicle, but provide entertaining diversions. The best way to run a chronicle is to intersperse secondary plots in between your main plots to give you some breathing room between major events, and to allow you to try out interesting ideas without jeopardizing the integrity of your main story.

For your main plots, refer back to your chronicle outline and use it to suggest the next step that your story needs to take. Are the characters still getting their bearings in the city and meeting its inhabitants? Perhaps they should be sent as an envoy from their sire to another powerful vampire, where they might detect the first hints of unrest under the oppressive hand of the city's prince, setting the stage for the themes you wish to explore. The outline that you created for the chronicle is there to give you guideposts in creating and directing the flow of your main plots.

With secondary plots, anything goes. If your players have been sweating through a series of grim and difficult main plots, maybe it's time to throw in something darkly funny to break the tension. Perhaps they encounter a band of vampire-hunters who make up for skill and knowledge with a little reckless enthusiasm and a lot of homemade weapons? If the characters are becoming a little cavalier about their undead existence, you can create a story involving a mortal family member or lover who has run afoul of the Kindred. Secondary plots are good for experimentation and as transition pieces between one major plot and another.

Any plot should be able to have its central idea summed up in a few short sentences:

• The coterie is sent to negotiate terms with the Prince of Atlanta, but the Nosferatu primogen will attempt to capture them along the way.

• The characters are approached by a mysterious Caitiff who seeks their help to investigate some disappearances among the homeless herds.

• The characters' sire makes his move to depose the current prince.

If you cannot explain the main idea of the story in a couple of sentences, you are probably trying to do too much at one time. Focus your ideas into one or two central actions, and then develop the course of these events.

It is entirely possible to have a plot within a plot, a side story that runs parallel to the main story you are telling and concerns one or more of the characters. These subplots are good for character development, providing extra conflicts or obstacles that complicate the resolution of the main story. Subplots might include the appearance of a character's former lover, who is in thralldom to the coterie's main antagonist. Or a member of the coterie may be called upon to act against members of his own clan, then must decide where his loyalties lie. If enough detail has been devoted to the creation of the players' characters, many of the stories you create can have additional complications for individual members of the coterie. Make use of these subplots whenever possible, so long as they do not detract from the main story as a whole. By working a character's background (or current relationships) into your stories, you further enmesh the player's ideas into the chronicle and actively involve that player in telling the story.

After determining the plot for your story, you then must concentrate on the central conflict. Conflict represents obstacles or opposing forces that the characters must overcome to resolve the plot. Conflict can stem from many sources, both within and without the player group. Suppose the characters' sire has ordered the coterie to eliminate several key mortal servants of a rival Kindred. The characters must overcome the mortals' bodyguards and other security measures, working all the while within the restrictions of the Masquerade — and then there are ethical considerations. Characters with high Humanity could object to what is essentially a series of cold-blooded assassinations, thus creating conflict both within the character group and without. Whenever possible, Storytellers should encourage this kind of internal dilemma, More than any other kind of conflict, moral conflict presents the characters with an obstacle that they can't simply overcome with brute force. It makes them think, and that is the best kind of challenge there is.

Conflict can be created in any number of combinations. Some obvious sources include:

• **The Clash of Kindred:** Vampires are ever at odds with one another, competing for hunting grounds, political influence, etc.

• **The Feuds of Clans:** On a greater scale, the clans of a city often come into conflict over territory, resources or simply prejudice. Internecine struggles within a sect can be as vicious as any war between sects.

• **The Onus of Authority:** Younger generations fear and resent the power of their elders, and anarchs with attitude but little wisdom chafe under the rule of prince or primogen.

• **Trials of Tyranny:** Power corrupts; what, then, of the prince of a major city? All too often these powerful vampires abuse their authority for their own ends, causing all manner of tragedy.

• **The War of Worlds:** The Camarilla and the Sabbat represent different visions of the world, and the two are locked in a bitter battle for supremacy. Cities across Europe and America are battlegrounds for these longtime enemies.

• **The Terror of the Wilds:** The Kindred are not the only creatures to hunt the night. The wilderness is home to the werewolves, a race of shapeshifters whose rage is terrible to behold. From time to time their campaign against the Kindred finds its way onto their enemies' home streets.

• **The Weight of the Mask:** Maintaining the Masquerade is the one iron law of the Camarilla, one which even the most despotic prince would not dare to break. Sometimes action must be taken to keep the secrets of the Kindred, and while the risks are great, the rewards can be greater.

• **Hounds and the Hunter:** Certain agencies, within the government and without, suspect the existence of vampires and are determined to hunt them down.

• **The Soul of the Beast:** The Beast is real, raging and wearing away at every vampire's self-control. The battle against the monster within is central to every vampire's existence, and is a universal conflict that should permeate every chronicle to some degree.

With the plot and its conflicts firmly in mind, you can consider the elements of the setting and mood for your story. Setting is as important a consideration for each story as it is for the chronicle as a whole; well-chosen details can evoke images and impressions that enhance the impact of the tale you want to tell. Try to make the setting echo the feelings which you find to be appropriate to the story. For instance, suppose you wish to have the characters enter the lair of a powerful Nosferatu. The way you envision the lair and the creature who lives there, you want the players to feel a sense of helplessness and despair:

The steps of the shelter are crowded, even at midnight. Homeless derelicts sit singly or in small groups, muttering to one another and watching the street with furtive, glassy eyes. Past the weathered wooden doors is a wide hall filled with silent, still forms. Some sleep, clutching trash bags filled with their worldly belongings and wrapped in layers of grimy clothes. Others sit on the cots or against the walls, staring into space, their expressions lost, as if struggling to remember who they were and how they came to this cheerless existence. Across the room, past the cold and empty pots of the soup line, lies a dark doorway and the stairs that lead down into the vampire's chambers.

Creating the mood for the story goes hand-in-hand with choosing your setting, because it relates again to the kind of atmosphere you want to convey to the players. If the setting consists of evocative surroundings for the story, the mood is the way in which you choose to describe the surroundings, and the actions of the characters in them. The secret to evoking a proper mood is to emphasize details that paint the picture you want to convey, while minimizing others. For example:

Fear: To evoke a mood of fear, emphasize images of helplessness, vulnerability and horror. *The children stare at you with eyes that are glassy and round from shock. They scamper away as you approach, whimpering as they retreat into the shadows. All of them avoid the iron door looming at the other end of the cellar.*

Anger: To evoke anger, emphasize details of violence, frustration and outrage. *Someone in the crowd screams, a sound of pure rage, and then a bottle smashes against the side of a car. A storefront window shatters, and then the sounds of fists and clubs thudding into flesh echo down the street.*

Loneliness: Loneliness is evoked by images of abandonment and solitude. *The theater has once seen days of glory; now its grand marquee is dark, and the windowpanes in the ticket booth are long since broken. Along one wall, yellowed posters linger under grimy glass panes, celebrating the premiere of blockbusters and sultry starlets now lost to time.*

Despair: A common mood in **Vampire** stories, despair and angst spring from images of helplessness, dashed hopes and loss of innocence. *They built the boardwalk at the turn of the century for lovers and children, with brightly painted carnival rides and seaside stands selling candy and confections, or offering prizes to tempt an eager suitor. Now the rides are rusted and dull, their skeletons creak in the cold sea air, and the only souls haunting the graffiti-stained shacks are the derelicts, caring for nothing more than a little shelter and a place to drink.*

A carefully chosen setting and details hit the players in the gut, getting under their skin and giving them memorable images that make the gaming experience more tangible and immediate.

Once you have a strong grasp of these elements, you have to put them together into individual scenes that hook the players, set the stage for the action, build the action to a climax, then resolve the story in a way that ties up any loose ends and sets the stage for the next story.

The Hook: The first step in any story is to involve the characters and pique their curiosity and interest. The hook can be a stranger appealing to the characters for help, or a sudden summons to the court of the prince, or the witnessing of a sudden and startling event. Storytellers should create their story hooks to appeal directly to the characters' personality and backgrounds. For instance, a character who was a detective in her mortal life can be drawn into a story by a baffling murder or theft that sets the events of the story in motion. If a character has political ambitions, she would be drawn into a story that hints at opportunities for advancement or leverage against her competition.

Setting the Stage: Once you have the characters interested, you have to draw them into the story and set out the challenges that lie ahead. Don't lay all your cards on the table at once; the best way to keep players curious is to give them only a piece of the puzzle at a time. Let them have a sense of what they need to accomplish, an immediate objective toward achieving their goal, and give them hints of what might lie beyond. If the players are smart, they will try to look ahead and figure out where their characters' actions will lead them. If not, they will be open to all sorts of plot twists and complications to make their unlives interesting.

For example, suppose the characters learn of a child who has been kidnapped by an unknown Kindred. The characters might be drawn to save the child for diverse personal reasons (one character might feel strongly about protecting children, another might be obsessed with feeding on the child, still another might want to rescue the child simply to thwart the plans of the kidnapper), but in the beginning, all the information they have is the child's identity and accounts describing the kidnapping. From there they must learn the identity of the kidnapper and the kidnapper's motives, which can add whole new implications to the story. What if the kidnapper is a powerful primogen whose favor the characters have been courting for some time? Do they thwart his plans and forfeit their previous efforts?

Building the Action: As the players progress, the challenges the characters face should become increasingly difficult, with perhaps a few surprises thrown in to complicate things. When you design a story, throw in some hidden complications that the players don't know anything about and can be learned only with a little initiative and forethought. For example, the man the characters want to kidnap might have recently invested in several highly paid bodyguards, or the Kindred who is supposed to be providing the characters with information and assistance might be blood bound to someone else. Try to pull the rug out from under the players at least once during the story, though allow them the chance to head off the problem if they use their heads and are resourceful. As the difficulties increase and the tensions mount, you can build the action to a dramatic finale.

The Climax: Your ultimate finale must be worth the effort the characters went through to get there. This is a golden rule of storytelling. Anticlimaxes work fine in books, but not when a group of people have put in hours of effort to reach a goal. The more the players and their characters have to endure, the more dramatic the climax has to be, or they will come away disappointed.

Resolution: Also known as cause and effect, this is the point in the story where the characters see the effects of their actions and resolve any loose ends or questions which came up along the way. This is a step in the storytelling process where it is easy to put aside any real roleplaying and just have a question-and-answer session with the players. If possible, try to play out the aftermath of a story, letting the players see the effects of their characters' work. This denouement helps build the sense of a bigger picture while sustaining players' interest and curiosity.

DANCING WITH THE DEAD

It is not enough to design a good story — it must be well told, presented with detail and energy. When you tell your story, strive to make the most of the following qualities:

Description: Make each scene vivid with detail. The quality of your descriptions affect everything from the mood you want to convey to the action of a brutal firefight. Describe people, places and activities in a way that engages all of your players' senses. It isn't enough to say, "After a few hours stalking the streets, you feed on a mortal leaving from work." Instead, say

"The streets are rimed with patches of dirty gray ice, and a knife-sharp December wind howls between the tall buildings. You keep to the shadows, stalking the alleys and the silent parking garages — anywhere that a lone mortal might stray. You force your lungs to draw in great gusts of air, wincing at the reek of car exhaust and rotting trash while you search for the telltale hint of warm flesh and blood. Hunger sharpens your senses, narrowing your focus to one single set of impressions — the sight, sound and smell of your prey. Suddenly you hear the hollow echo of footsteps, a single pair of feet crossing the concrete floor of a garage. The Hunger claws at you as you start to run." The more detail you can give, the easier the scene is to envision, and the more alive it becomes.

Characterization: Make your Storyteller characters individuals. This is 10 times harder for you than for the players, because they only have one character to concentrate on, while you have an entire city. The amount of attention you can give to each character depends, naturally, on how important she is to your chronicle. Major characters should be treated with all the depth and detail of a player's character. Get inside their heads, use their histories to determine what kind of personality that they might have. Give them hates, fears and hobbies. For minor characters, single out a few distinguishing characteristics. Make them absent-minded, or abrasive, or neurotic. Don't be afraid to use little quirks that you might observe about people in everyday life. Also, make your Kindred characters *vampires*. They are

undead, their bodies pale and cold, and their personalities flavored by their origins in civilizations that are hundreds, even thousands of years old. The older a vampire, the more introverted and alien her personalities. Incorporate manners of speech, modes of dress or customs that the character would have had ingrained into her in her mortal life.

Dialogue: This goes hand-in-hand with characterization, and it is possibly the most important skill a Storyteller must master. When characters talk to one another in the game, whether within the coterie or between a player and Storyteller character, act out the conversation. You can bring out more depth to your characters and make the experience more immediate with dialogue, expression and body language. Give each character a distinctive voice and mannerisms appropriate to her personality. Acting out dialogue doesn't come easily — it takes a quick mind and some improvisational skills, and a little bit of courage if you are self-conscious. Don't get stressed — you're playing a game with friends. Encourage the players to participate, even give an extra experience point at the end of each session for good interplay if you want. Conversation is an art and a skill, and it gets better with practice.

Action: The World of Darkness is cold and brutal, and vampires are the epitome of the human predator. Make your action scenes dynamic and explosive — bones crunch, blood sprays, guns thunder and objects blow apart under a hail of bullets. Keep the dice-rolling in combat scenes to a minimum, interpret the results quickly and then launch into pulse-pounding description. (Storyteller rolls dice for an enemy attack) "The Brujah leaps over the bar with a howl and swings the bat one-handed at Clive. The aluminum club hits him in the mouth with a crunch of bone and a spray of blood and enamel, knocking Clive off his feet." The key element is the intensity of the experience. Don't be afraid to fudge results sometimes to keep the action and pace at a fever pitch.

Mystery: Keep the players guessing. Never show them the full picture of what is going on. One of the fundamental facts of Kindred existence is that knowledge is power and the key to survival. Nothing in the World of Darkness is quite what it appears to be, and it is good to emphasize this point with plot twists, betrayals and hidden complications to your stories.

Influencing Events: Vampire is about telling a good story, which requires careful planning and an idea of where the events of your chronicle are leading. The problem is that sometimes the players will throw you a curve. Perhaps they will miss the obvious clue that will expose the central mystery of the chronicle, or maybe they will go in a totally unexpected direction and stumble onto a part of the story that they weren't supposed to deal with yet. Worse yet, one of them gets a lucky hit in battle and kills off the major villain whom you had planned to be their major adversary for the next 12 stories. There are no easy solutions to these situations, but basically you have two courses of action to choose from: Roll with the punches and adapt to the changes, or use your godlike powers to avoid the problem entirely. The best rule of thumb is to fudge events directly only if it enhances the game as a whole. If the characters miss a vital piece of data, steer them back to it. If you would rather see your major villain killed off in a more dramatic way, fudge his soak rolls and let him limp away. Still, use this sparingly. It is your privilege as the Storyteller, but if you abuse it you will convince the players that their characters can't really succeed at anything, which ruins the game.

The Commandments

The art of storytelling is a process, like any artistic endeavor, and at first it seems like an overwhelming task. The main elements to remember, though, can be broken down into five "musts" and five "must-nots":

• **Involve the Players Whenever Possible:** Incorporate their ideas and backgrounds into your city and chronicle. This will take some of the burden of world-building off your shoulders and give the players more of a stake in the story you are telling. Ultimately, the players should be the most important — though not necessarily the most powerful — denizens of your chronicle.

• **Accommodate the Players' Expectations:** It's their game too, remember. You need to have some idea of what kind of game the players want to play before developing your chronicle.

• **Work Things Out in Advance:** The more you have worked out before game time, the more attention you will be able to devote to telling the story. If you've taken the time to think through the story's various twists and turns, you will be better able to roll with the inevitable player curve ball.

• **Story First, Rules Second:** Do not let the tale you want to tell get held back by the rules. You can make them or break them as you see fit, if doing so enhances the story and makes it more enjoyable for the players.

• **Description, Dialogue, and Action:** Make your world come alive with vibrant description, involving sights, smells, taste and touch. Encourage roleplaying by acting out conversations, using different voices to individualize your characters. Keep the pace and intensity high with dynamic action.

Conversely—

• **Avoid Stereotypes:** Nothing drains the life out of your chronicle faster than an endless parade of identical, cardboard characters.

• **Don't Forget the Payoff:** If the players work hard and make smart decisions, their characters' success must be in proportion to the challenges they have faced, or they will feel cheated.

• **Don't Tell Them Everything:** Much of the challenge in a game is in the mystery, the parts of the story that you hold back for the players and their characters to discover on their own.

• **Don't Abuse Your Power:** You are the final arbiter of events. Your word is law, but you cannot use this authority to beat the characters into doing what you want them to do. It is a game, it's for fun, and everyone should have a good time, whether it follows the script or not.

• **Don't Panic:** If the players pull the rug out from under you, don't be afraid to call a break and take some time to collect your thoughts. It will happen a lot at first, but after a while you will be able to handle anything they throw at you.

The archbishop, bloated with the blood of centuries, seems almost to be a part of his throne. His robes drape over the hoary wood of the furniture, making it impossible to tell where one ends and the other begins. In his fat fingers he holds a chess piece, exquisitely carved from ivory.

"Beautiful, is it not?" he asks, and I realize with a start he is speaking to me. He motions me forward, to inspect his toy.

It is indeed a beautiful piece of work. The ivory has a slight yellowish tinge to it, and an unusual heft, and it is as cool to the touch as the day it was carved. I look down at it and am impressed. A woman's face, proud and defiant, stares back at me. Her features are sharp and aristocratic, her hair long, her garments rich. It is as if any second she might come to life in my hand and demand an accounting for my rudeness in holding her thus.

"A…queen?" I ask.

"Of course. My childe, Lucita. Disobedient, but beloved nonetheless." He wheezes his bulk forward and smiles paternally. "It has been decades since I've seen her, but Vykos was kind enough to create this for me. She took down her portraits," he says apologetically, "the last time she was here."

I frown. "Vykos is the Tzimisce, yes?"

Archbishop Monçada nods serenely. "And a Noddist scholar, and a gentleman, for a fiend."

"He bonecrafted this for you, did he not?"

"Of course. And the rest of the set. We even played a game." He motions at a table nearby. On it rests an inlaid board, ebony and gold, with a bare handful of pieces on it. I walk over to the set, examine it. The first piece I heft is a black pawn. It has my face.

"It is a pity," Monçada murmurs from very close behind me, "that most of the pieces had to be swept from the board."

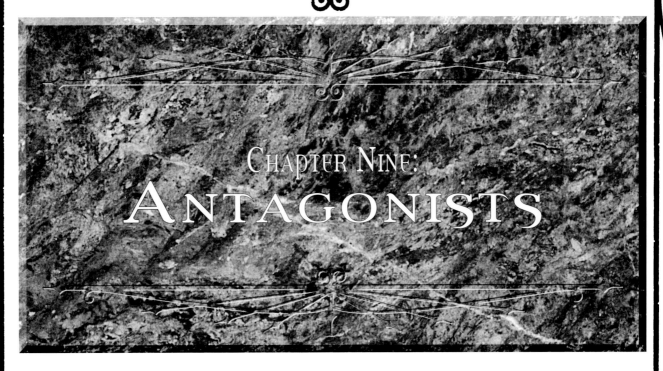

Chapter Nine: Antagonists

The World of Darkness holds many other terrors besides the Kindred. Though it is the vampires who are most inextricably intertwined with mortal society (and, given their appetites, how could it be otherwise?), there are other monsters in the Earth's darker corners. Few are friendly to the Kindred, some are outright enemies, and the Kindred, despite their immortality, know little of the others' ways or customs.

This chapter presents basic information on the Kindred's most common foils and foes, including templates representing archetypal examples of the creatures.

Witch-Hunters

It is tempting, upon the Embrace, to run amuck in mortal society, heedless of the mortal insects all around. Elder vampires know better, and thus the lords of the Camarilla enforce the Masquerade above all. In the Middle Ages, an Inquisition-led population alerted to vampires' depredations nearly wiped out the Kindred's millennia-old society. How much more easily, the Inner Circle shudderingly wonders, could a human population of six billion, armed with napalm, phosphorus rounds and nuclear weapons, dispose of the parasites in its midst?

Most mortals, enshrouded in superstition and science, remain blind to the vampires in their midst — but some do know, and fear. Mortals who hunt the Kindred are known as witch-hunters, after the Inquisitors of old. Most are just that — agents of a hostile Church. A few kine in government agencies, secret societies and criminal organizations also deal, at varying levels of depth and hostility, with the Kindred.

The Inquisition

Historians think of the Inquisition as that frightening face the Catholic Church showed the world from 1231 to 1834. But Kindred who have any sense of self-preservation whatsoever know that the Inquisition didn't end in the 19th century, that it endures to the present night and is more fearsome than ever. Indeed, few mortals conjure dread among knowledgeable vampires the way modern Inquisitors do.

The public at large, historians in general and even some of the Church's highest officials — including the Pope — know nothing of the Inquisition's current activities, due to the organization's intense secrecy. The Society of Leopold, as it's properly called nowadays, comprises Catholics primarily but no longer exclusively. The Inquisition's "interfaith" membership devotes itself to the eradication of vampires and other supernatural entities, an agenda the Society pursued vigorously for 17 years under the guidance of Monsignor Amelio Carpaccio. When the monsignor suffered a fatal stroke a year ago, though, the Society had to deal with an internal crisis that had loomed gradually during the previous decade.

During that time, the godlessness of 20th-century existence had led all but the most fervid Inquisitors to conclude that the Apocalypse was *not* imminent — surely not at the close of the second millennium, anyway, and perhaps not even after the *thousand*-and-second millennium. Yet every member of the Society felt certain that the Adversary's earthly forces would attach tremendous importance to this calendrical turning point and possibly carry out some devastating worldwide sacrilege. And while some Leopolders feared the Savior might never return (though none ever said so), all of them recognized the real and present threat that creatures of the darkness posed to humanity. Worse, the very populace that Inquisitors risked their lives to protect seemed ready to emulate, even embrace, these evil beings. Morale in the Society also suffered because of the mounting controversy over torture, which Carpaccio himself had banned officially as an unacceptable Inquisitorial tool. Of course, unofficial and clandestine torture was the rule for some

of the Society's members, who saw their war as unwinnable otherwise.

All this fear and uncertainty combined to pave the way for a leader who was sure of herself and her techniques (especially all 212 of those agonizing methods she "unbanned" in her first act as Inquisitor General): onetime Austrian Provincial Ingrid Bauer, known behind her back as "The Original Iron Maiden."

Vampires never realized how relatively easy their unlives were during Carpaccio's tenure. Granted, through the years the venerable old witch-hunter presided, directly or indirectly, over the destruction of many, many Cainites and ghouls; thus, the prevalent Kindred attitude toward the Inquisition then was general wariness. Still, there were always a few vampires brazen (or stupid) enough to antagonize the Society purposely, plus a tinier number bold and clever enough to make it their catspaw in the Jyhad. Now, elders trade rumors of turncoat Inquisitors who betrayed their Cainite masters, a high-ranking Ventrue and her Lasombra rival. Supposedly, both Kindred still languish in an unknown dungeon where they suffer tortures at witch-hunters' hands. Neonates whisper tales of coteries routed by sword-wielding Leopolders who display previously unglimpsed fierceness and skill. Most troubling to the Children of Caine are recent reports of napalm assaults against longtime havens, some of them lairs that had remained inviolate for decades.

Bauer, of course, was the force behind such activities. Only a handful of Kindred elders had enough information to make that link, however, as an exhaustive purge of disloyal elements from the Inquisition's ranks coincided with the new Inquisitor General's rise to power. The Society's Censors carted off nearly every member who was actively spying for the Kindred, a sizable percentage of individuals "sympathetic" to the plight of the Damned, and a few entirely innocent Leopolders who learned the true meaning of suffering for a cause. Only a handful of moles survived this "Inquisitors' Inquisition," and they now live in fear of their comrades and of belated discovery. For the most part, these spies' Cainite masters, fearing traps that might lead to the Society's oubliettes, have abandoned their secret servitors.

A new vigor prevails among most Inquisitors, but a familiar malaise endures as well — in a slightly different guise. Even as Bauer sees to it that braziers are lit, racks are oiled, and molten lead is at hand in Inquisition dungeons on five continents (Asia continues to defy the organization), the use of torture again becomes a thorny issue. Whereas before there was a vocal majority that wanted such methods reinstated, now there is a silent minority that agonizes over such practices. The real problem here is that these moral qualms are actually eroding one of the Inquisition's most powerful weapons against vampires: True Faith. This quality, inherent to certain individuals, can repel a vampire without resorting to crosses, holy water or any other sacred emblem — in fact, in the hands of nonbelievers such items are useless against Kindred. Monsignor Carpaccio understood intimately the soul-deadening, faith-damping effects of using torture against any creature, even an undead one. He saw the speedy destruction of vampires not as killing ("*Sono già morti,*" he liked to say. "They're already dead."), but as a mercy; torture, however, he considered a descent into the enemy's repulsive cruelty. Alas, Inquisitor General Bauer, con-

vinced as she is of the rightness of her crusade and her methods alike, is immune to such qualms. Interestingly, she is one of the rare Inquisitors with extensive experience as a torturer *and* impressive True Faith. The two things are not always exclusive, just generally so.

The Society of Leopold may pay a steep price for choosing Bauer as its leader. True, she is waging the holy war against the Kindred and their ilk (she sees werewolves, among others, as vampires' tools) that most Inquisitors wanted — and needed — to fight. With the combat colleges she has established in Nevada's Black Rock Desert and in the Spanish Pyrenees, she is also improving the organization's readiness for that war. Now, every Inquisitor carries a sword-cane and is quite adept in its use. Bauer even personally instructs her subordinates in the proper techniques for organizing congregations into witch-hunting mobs. Unfortunately, she is unable to address her troops' spiritual woes, which are substantial. Alcoholism, depression and addiction to pornography are rife among Leopolders. Plus, it's not inconceivable that significant numbers of the Society's ethical elite may split from their fellows over the torture issue, although these highly moral individuals also tend to be extremely loyal. As for Bauer herself, she could have the shortest tenure of any Inquisitor General this century if she really gets the Kindred worried — and they should be.

Then again, she *is* the Original Iron Maiden.

Inquisitor

Attributes: Strength 2, Dexterity 3, Stamina 3, Charisma 4, Manipulation 3, Appearance 2, Perception 3, Intelligence 3, Wits 3

Abilities: Alertness 2, Brawl 2, Dodge 2, Drive 1, Expression 2, Leadership 3, Melee (sword-cane) 3, Occult 3, Stealth 2, Theology 3

Humanity: 5 to 10 (Inquisitors can be holy or as depraved as the monsters they fight), **Willpower:** 9

Equipment: Sword-cane, rosaries, crucifix, stakes, Bible, propane torch

Note: A few Inquisitors have ratings of 1 or higher in the True Faith Trait. Such individuals usually, though not necessarily, have Humanity ratings of 9 or above.

Government

Anything the kine's government manages to accomplish in the World of Darkness borders on the miraculous, given the influences exerted by conspirators, secret societies and assorted cabals too numerous to list — and these schemers are *in addition* to the manifold vampire factions that fancy themselves masters of the puppetmasters. To some extent, the efforts of all these manipulators cancel each other out or run afoul of things as mundane as bureaucratic incompetence or unswerving greed.

Miracles sometimes do occur in the midst of such chaos, though — or, as with the National Security Agency's "recent discovery" of the Kindred menace, through a literal mechanism of chaos. By tortuous paths, the NSA, an information-monitoring arm of the US intelligence community, obtained devices that can distinguish vampires and ghouls from mortals. With astonishing alacrity and utter secrecy, the organization deployed these

TRUE FAITH

True Faith is a special Trait that only a few people in the World of Darkness possess. While many mortals are more or less devoted to a belief in some form of higher being or purpose, only a small number have the burning zeal, the profound conviction that can protect them against creatures like vampires. Note that, while most vampire legends portray the Damned being repelled by crosses and the like, Faith can manifest in any religious form. A devout Jew might be able to ward off vampires with her Star of David, or a Taoist might be able to intone special prayers, while a Christian lacking True Faith finds his crucifix impotent against the undead.

This Faith is not necessarily increased through experience. Certainly, it may rise as a result of a person's experience, but it is more vital than that, more a measure of conviction and strength of mind. Nor is it something that comes from outside the individual, from some God or angel. Whether or not their beliefs are correct, these people believe so fervently that their own conviction protects them. At the Storyteller's discretion, Faith should rise or fall to reflect a person's religious certainty and zeal.

The Faith Trait, like any other, has a rating of 1 to 5. Exactly what protection is afforded to the individual by the Trait depends on this rating, as described below. Of course, these are just guidelines. Storytellers should amend them as required to fit the tone or add drama to their stories.

• Any character with Faith may attempt to ward off vampires by brandishing a holy symbol or uttering prayers. (This is the Hollywood cliché of the vampire being held back by a crucifix.) The person rolls Faith against a difficulty equal to the vampire's Willpower. The number of successes indicates the number of steps backward the vampire is forced to take. If no successes are scored, the vampire need not step back but may not advance. A botch indicates that the vampire may advance unhindered. Further, if the cross, Bible or other symbol is placed against the vampire's body, each success causes an aggravated health level of damage, burning into the flesh.

•• A mortal with a Faith rating of 2 or more may resist vampiric Dominate by spending Willpower (one point typically protects for a few turns).

••• A person with a Faith of 3 or more may sense the presence of a vampire. She need not consciously try to sense a vampire's presence, but must be in peaceful, quiet surroundings — perhaps alone in thought, praying, reading Torah, meditating on the Bible, etc. The person will not sense the vampire's presence if she is preoccupied (e.g., arguing) or in a crowded, noisy place (jostled by a mob, in the midst of a raucous banquet, etc.). This ability need not be infallible; the Storyteller should let the person sense the vampire only when it is dramatically convenient. Note that the person cannot know exactly what she senses through her Faith; all that she will know is that something unclean or evil is nearby.

•••• The mortal may not be turned into a ghoul and is unaffected by any mind-altering Disciplines like Presence and Obfuscate.

••••• The person is so pure, so holy, that she can fill a vampire with self-loathing, disgust, terror, even physical pain. Any vampire hearing the person pray, preach or recite psalms, or being touched by the person, may be forced to flee immediately by any available means. A vampire who is unable to flee is reduced to a gibbering wreck, flailing on the floor and screaming, sobbing or begging forgiveness. To avoid fleeing, the vampire must either expend one Willpower point per turn or must make a Stamina roll each turn (difficulty of 5 + her own Intelligence). That's right — the higher the vampire's Intelligence, the higher the difficulty, because the more tortured and guilty she will feel.

In theory, a mortal might have a Faith rating of greater than 5, but these people are one in a billion — the sort of people who are venerated as saints. They are unlikely to enter a chronicle (and certainly no more than once), but their powers would be enormous.

There is actually one easy way for a vampire to detect a person with a Faith rating, other than bitter experience — Aura Perception always shows it up. A mortal with Faith has her aura permanently altered so that she has a silver/gold "halo" around her body. The strength of the Faith determines the brightness of the halo. Note that the halo is not normally visible; only Auspex reveals it.

Remember that Faith represents a person's total commitment to her beliefs. That person will act accordingly. Those with high Faith ratings may seem fanatical, even insane to those not of their religion.

Note that Cainites will not normally have Faith ratings. They consider themselves the Damned, after all. Think very, very carefully before letting any vampire have this power.

"chaoscopic scanners" in locations including Dulles International Airport, the Pentagon, the Old Executive Office Building, the Capitol and the White House, all behind the façades of new metal detectors. Significantly, no one outside the NSA is privy to the true nature of these added checkpoints, including the operators of the various metal detectors, which are real and working. Not even the president is aware that he and his staff are monitored daily by NSA operatives looking for so-called "black-bodies," a reference to Cainites' appearance when viewed through a chaoscope. Of the NSA's own personnel, only three people in decision-making positions know the truth: General Rex Shivers, Colonel Alec Riley and Colonel George Johnstone. Add to them the actual monitoring staff, and the total comes to two dozen.

The NSA's discretion in this matter stems, in part, from established procedure. Spymasters, canny in their paranoia, trust no one, *especially* not their fellow agencies. Shivers' people aren't even sharing with their civilian counterparts at the NSA any information about governmental encroachment by these mysterious black-body entities. Plus, there's the natural question of just how influential these inhuman infiltrators may be: Do they

already control the FBI, the CIA, Congress, the president? Most important, however, is the larger uncertainty implicit in that question: The NSA knows its discoveries aren't quite human, but the organization's members don't yet understand exactly what the black-bodies are.

Hobbling these covert watchers is the very rationality that spurred them to use the chaoscope, and that has plagued them since the first time NSA brass saw one of these machines demonstrated at the headquarters of the Paranormal Research Wing, a Vermont-based think tank. After General Shivers got a glimpse of wraiths cavorting in the Underworld, he suggested that PRW scientists had actually discovered some parallel dimension rather than an afterlife existence. He then ordered the PRW's security clearances hiked and, on a hunch, a streamlined version of the chaoscope to be installed at the White House. Four months and a billion dollars later, the old Cold Warrior was watching for things like the ones he'd seen at PRW. What he saw ultimately were ghouls and a vampire attending a state dinner, but viewed chaoscopically these creatures were easy to mistake for the disembodied dead Shivers had already glimpsed. The conclusion he reached was entirely reasonable — that his transdimensional entities were possessing Washington officials to manipulate the government. He also happened to be wrong, but, weirdly, not so far off the mark.

To some extent, the NSA's military triumvirate is "reinventing the wheel" with its expensive new toys. Also, a great deal of money could have been saved if anyone had bothered to train infrared cameras on a few of those chilly Cainites. Even without

such tools, General Arthur Clifford, Shivers' predecessor, had a far more accurate understanding of what the Kindred are. Unfortunately, that knowledge was mutual, and unknown Cainite elements were able to discredit Clifford and have him ousted. Thus, Shivers, Riley and Johnstone rose to the top at NSA because they were skeptics regarding the supernatural — in contrast with the deluded, utterly credulous figure Clifford was made to seem at his downfall. Nevertheless, Clifford's replacements now know a lot of the same things he knew — and then some — but they're interpreting the data quite differently. They're aware, for example, of their organization's traitors, operatives Bruce Higgins and Felicity Price. More importantly, the NSA has also identified the vampires who control these two pawns. The agency is already cataloging what it dubs "known extradimensionals" and their "normal" contacts. As the extent of Kindred influence in world commerce, media and governance becomes clear to General Shivers and his staff, the "war of reconnaissance" the NSA is waging will seem ever more of a luxury. When that time comes, the NSA operatives who've been training in armored moon suits with aural inhibitors and mirrored faceplates will learn firsthand what they've been prepared to fight. And when that time comes, the Children of Caine will learn the folly of dismissing technology, just as the masters of that technology will discover that the world is full of stranger things than science and rationality can ever explain.

Of course, the other federal intelligence-gathering and law-enforcement agencies (and even out-of-the-loop civilian personnel within the NSA) are carrying on largely as they did before the advent of the chaoscope, given the covert nature of the device. At the FBI and the CIA, only scattered handfuls of agents (some of them moles placed years ago by the NSA's General Clifford) have the vaguest clue about supernatural activity. The Bureau's secret Special Affairs Department (also known as SAD), for example, lingers on only because of the undying support of Senator Jesse Grubbholb. After all, Arthur Clifford's fall hasn't made it any easier to get any above-board federal money for pursuing supernaturals.

More's the pity, because the hunting in and around the bureaucracy alone would be incredible. At the Centers for Disease Control in Atlanta, several strategically placed individuals, most of them under vampiric mind control, keep the lid on incidents that involve "suspicious" (i.e., Cainite) blood or corpses. The lack of blood-bound servitors here was a conscious effort by various Kindred masters to avoid entanglements with nosy epidemiologists, as vitae remains chemically distinct from human blood even in ghouls. However, that dodge also insulates these conspirators from chaoscopic detection. The devices are useless in identifying victims of Dominate. Still, it wouldn't take much for a key piece of evidence to slip past these guardians and allow the agency's legitimate disease detectives to glimpse the full picture. At the state, county and municipal levels of law-enforcement, things look much like they do at the top: vast numbers of common cops, sheriffs and state troopers trying to do their jobs, most of them utterly oblivious of the various factions that struggle nightly to co-opt, deflect or otherwise influence the police. Ghoul cops exist, but they're pretty much beneath the NSA's radar, so to speak. And, as at the top, the myriad efforts to preserve the Masquerade, uncover it, detain this one or arrest that one often end in a wash, and the cops carry out their business as intended.

Sample Government Agent

Attributes: Strength 3, Dexterity 2, Stamina 3, Charisma 2, Manipulation 3, Appearance 2, Perception 3, Intelligence 3, Wits 3

Abilities: Alertness 3, Athletics 2, Brawl 3, Computer 1, Dodge 3, Drive 3, Firearms 3, Investigation 4, Melee 2, Occult 1, Politics 2, Stealth 2

Humanity: 6 to 8, **Willpower:** 7

Equipment: Heavy pistol, black suit, cool sunglasses, badge and ID card, electronic surveillance devices

The Arcanum

This secret society's members are among the foremost mortal pursuers of supernatural knowledge in the World of Darkness. They are scholars, bibliothecaries and archaeologists, epopts, Hermetics and herbalists, Kabbalists, cryptographers and students of the occult. Since the Victorian era, the Arcanum's 300 academics and explorers have ventured into the world's oddest, most remote corners to learn everything they can about the unseen and the unknown.

Long ago, these mortals learned that, sometimes, the unseen and the unknown have very sharp teeth and most unsavory appetites. Arcanists also learned that vampires do not like being the objects of investigation, a fact harshly emphasized by Cainites' torching of the group's Boston Chapter House in 1910. The resulting loss of life and destruction of irreplaceable books (the latter perhaps more than the former) left the Arcanum wary of delving into Kindred secrets. Nonetheless, vampires remained a focus for the group's curiosity — and for its collective guilt. Various members argued over the years that turning a blind eye to the activities of vampires was complicity to genocide.

Lately, unbeknownst to most of their fellows, several Arcanists have taken action in this area. None of the organization's members qualify as fools, however, and few consider themselves warriors, so "action," in this context, means the judicious synthesis and redirection of information. Thus, several recent strikes by the Inquisition (which Arcanists also learned about long ago) against Kindred lairs had their secret origins in the Arcanum's archives. Similarly, the Reverend Jebediah Brown, an independent witch-hunter and former Arcanist, still believes his ongoing theft of intelligence from Arcanum chapter houses goes unnoticed — but, in truth, he is but another tool in an intricate armchair war.

Not even all of the Arcanum participants in these "campaigns" are aware of one another's efforts. Because of the intense danger vampiric investigation might pose to the entire organization, such activity is grounds for dismissal. Thus, Arcanists engage in "siccing the witch-hunters" singly or in groups of two or three at most, and always with extreme care to preserve their anonymity. No member risks more with these clandestine pursuits than Sandeep D'Souza, Chancellor of the New Delhi Chapter House and heir apparent to the Arcanum's Grand Chancellorship. Yet, since finding himself amidst rioting Sabbat vampires a year ago in Frankfurt and witnessing their depredations up close, D'Souza has been a changed man. He doesn't understand why he was spared, which further fanned his guilt and ultimately propelled the Arcanist onto his current course. D'Souza is uncomfortable with using people as pawns against the Kindred, but he now finds inaction to be unthinkable.

Most of the organization's seekers of mysteries continue to encounter vampires in the same sorts of ways and places they always have: unexpected ones. It was through analyzing accounts by Arcanists who were looking for other things entirely (including the Grail) that D'Souza and his ilk have been able to pinpoint many Kindred havens. Of course, some of their suppositions are based on where missing colleagues are thought to have vanished.

Arcanum Scholar

Attributes: Strength 2, Dexterity 2, Stamina 2, Charisma 2, Manipulation 2, Appearance 2, Perception 4, Intelligence 4, Wits 3

Abilities: Academics 4 (or higher), Computer 3, Dodge 1, Drive 1, Etiquette 2, Expression 2, Investigation 3, Linguistics 2 (or higher), Melee 1, Occult 4, Science 3

Humanity: 8, **Willpower:** 7

Equipment: Laptop, extensive library, sedan, collected occult paraphernalia, sizable bank account

Criminals

Kindred long ago cemented their influence over parts of *La Cosa Nostra*, the Russian Mafiya, the Cali and Medellín drug cartels, plus assorted ethnic, biker and street gangs. Vampires use such criminals as cannon fodder, as obstacles for the authorities, as scapegoats when the Jyhad's skirmishes draw the attention of any media not under vampiric sway, and even as sustenance that goes largely unmissed should a Cainite get greedy while feeding. Given the superstition and ignorance common to so many criminals, there's some advantage to be gained from rumors that the "Big Boss" can see through walls, laugh at bullets, etc. Most vampires choose to exert their will from total secrecy, however, and so most crooks have no idea of the Kindred's existence or agendas.

Lately, someone has been altering this equation. Some carefully chosen midlevel thugs, including several Mafia lieutenants, Organizatsiya chiefs, a Cali Cartel street boss and others with a range of affiliations, have been hearing lectures on Cainite history, morphology and power structures. The informants in question are knowledgeable and calculating. They share kernels of wisdom that are likely to incite an individual boss or gang against a specific vampire or Kindred in general. By playing on mortal fears and ambitions, these mysterious visitors have already ignited what promises to be a gang war of epic — if not apocalyptic — proportions.

In several New York City boroughs, for example, street violence is at an all-time high. After a dreadlocked stranger presented himself to the members of the Montego Bay drug posse, demonstrated supernatural powers, claimed to be a messenger from Jah and tricked the crew's Cainite leader into revealing his true nature, things got ugly fast. Intergang conflict quickly followed as Brooklyn *mafioski*, armed with stakes and AK-47s, joined the party. In Manhattan, Giovanni vampires reacted harshly after some of their normally civil Colombian colleagues raided a clan haven and chainsawed apart a few ghouls. Similar strife grips Miami, Los Angeles and Chicago.

Most of the affected Kindred reacted swiftly enough to avoid harm in the first wave of violence. In fact, its sole vampire casualty was Red Simon, the Montego Bay posse's unlucky chief. Quelling the gang warfare has thus far defied both individual efforts and concerted ones. The ongoing violence and pervasive Sabbat presence have hampered investigations by Camarilla justicars in the targeted cities, but neither factor has prevented widespread realization among the Kindred that these events were a patently orchestrated assault. One consistent detail about the informants has surfaced: While they vary by race, gender and description in the reports assembled thus far, all consistently identified themselves as "Caitiff."

Of course, this tidbit met with both consternation and skepticism among Cainites. It seemed too transparent an attempt at further dividing their ranks, and rather a stupid, pointless ploy for these dispossessed vampires to attempt anyway. Nevertheless, whoever committed this act of war (in every sense) clearly knew Kindred culture. The culprits — or perhaps culprit, as some vampires suspect a lone metamorph of some sort — surely must be supernatural, as many of the informants claimed to be angels helping to redeem gangsters' "immortal souls" and displayed unearthly abilities. Unfortunately for the Cainites, many of the criminals so approached were susceptible to such arguments.

Immediate consequences of this enemy action include the reduced usefulness of organized criminals for the Kindred and the unsavory possibility that rogues may have to be purged from a variety of gangs. The long-range alternative is less pleasant, as some Kindred worry that bounties for vampires could become popular among crooks very quickly indeed. The mood on the streets of the major metropolitan centers is decidedly edgy, and only the most powerful (or foolhardy) Cainites now supervise criminal organs directly. Whether the situation could worsen still — especially given the anonymity of the perpetrator(s) — remains to be seen.

CRIMINAL ENFORCER/BOSS

Attributes: Strength 4, Dexterity 3, Stamina 3, Charisma 3, Manipulation 4, Appearance 1, Perception 2, Intelligence 2, Wits 3

Abilities: Alertness 2, Athletics 1, Brawl 3, Dodge 3, Drive 2, Finance 2, Firearms 3 (or higher), Melee 2, Security 3, Stealth 2, Streetwise 3 (or higher), Subterfuge 2

Humanity: 6 (often lower), **Willpower:** 6

Equipment: SMG, bulletproof vest, midsized car, knife, hidden computer disks detailing operations

This template represents a reasonably tough, savvy member of the underworld. Typical thugs and gangbangers will be much less threatening, while a Mafia Don or similar fellow will have higher Mental Attributes and extra Knowledges.

GHOULS

A vampire's blood has great power, power that can be passed on. Long ago, the Kindred discovered that mortals who drank vampiric blood would become possessed of supernatural abilities and dark appetites. Soon it became common practice for vampires to keep certain favored servants, battening them on vitae — and blood bonding them in the process — all the better to have undying, hellishly loyal servitors — ghouls.

Most ghouls exist at the whim of their domitors (masters), serving loyally in exchange for vitae. As they are as susceptible to the blood bond as anyone, ghouls are almost without exception unfailingly devoted to their masters — and if the domitor has more than one ghoul servant, the result may be a jealous struggle between them for the domitor's favor. A ghoul's emotions run to extremes with the heady drug of vitae in his veins — such a creature often falls prey to great rages and disturbing cravings. The name "ghouls" was not chosen at random....

The following characteristics are shared by all ghouls:

• A ghoul does not age as long as he has Kindred blood in his system. However, once the ghoul has passed his natural lifespan, he must always have vitae in his body, or he will swiftly age to the point of death and decomposition. This decomposition might occur within days or (for very old ghouls) within minutes.

• Ghouls may use the vitae in their systems to heal themselves, as do vampires, or to increase their Physical Attributes in similar fashion. Ghouls soak bashing damage like other mortals (i.e., they do not divide net damage in half). However, while they have vitae in their bodies, they may soak lethal damage. A ghoul who does not use vitae to heal wounds heals as per mortal healing rates (p. 219).

• All ghouls learn Potence 1 within minutes of ingesting blood for the first time, and can also learn Fortitude. Most ghouls can progress no farther than the first level in a Discipline, but some can learn higher levels of Disciplines; the upper limit of a ghoul's Discipline levels is usually decreed by his domitor's generation.

• A ghoul might be capable of learning other Disciplines that his domitor knows, but the learning process is very long and arduous.

• The vampiric blood in their system affects ghouls psychologically as well as physically. They are capable of entering frenzy, although their difficulty numbers to resist are two lower.

• Some long-term ghouls eventually develop side effects resembling their domitor's clan weakness. For instance, a ghoul who drinks too much Nosferatu vitae may begin sprouting unsightly boils and buboes, while a Ventrue's vassal might find his dark appetites even more demanding than before.

For more information on ghouls of all stripes (including the possibility of playing ghoul characters), see **Ghouls: Fatal Addiction**.

TRUSTED VALET

Attributes: Strength 2, Dexterity 3, Stamina 2, Charisma 3, Manipulation 3, Appearance 4, Perception 3, Intelligence 3, Wits 3

Abilities: Academics 2, Alertness 2, Computer 1, Crafts 2, Dodge 2, Drive 2, Empathy 3, Etiquette 4, Finance 2, Firearms 2, Leadership 2, Linguistics 1, Medicine 2, Melee 2, Occult 1, Subterfuge 3

Disciplines: Potence 1, possibly one other Discipline at 1
Humanity: 7, **Willpower:** 4

GHOUL BODYGUARD

Attributes: Strength 4, Dexterity 4, Stamina 4, Charisma 2, Manipulation 2, Appearance 2 (possibly higher), Perception 4, Intelligence 2, Wits 3

Abilities: Alertness 4, Athletics 2, Brawl 4, Dodge 3, Drive 2, Firearms 4, Intimidation 3, Investigation 2, Medicine 1, Melee 3, Occult 1, Stealth 3, Streetwise 2

Disciplines: Fortitude 1, Potence 1, possibly one other Discipline at 1

Humanity: 5, **Willpower:** 5

WEREWOLVES

Vampires are urban creatures, and have always been. However, it is more than easy access to prey that keeps them sequestered in their city domains. Many vampires that try to cross the open land perish without seeing their destinations. They die at the claws of the Cainites' ancient enemies: the Lupines — the werewolves.

Even the eldest Cainite historians cannot say when the war between the vampires and the Lupines began. As far as anyone can tell, the hatred between the two species has lasted for as long as both have existed. And like any feud, each death fuels the fire into an inferno.

No vampire can emerge from a battle with a pack of werewolves unscathed; legend has it that even Methuselahs have fallen to Lupine claws (or to the fangs of their own kind soon after, weakened as they were after even a victory).

To date, the war between Kindred and Lupine continues. The vampires hate, resent, even fear the werewolves and their berserk attacks. As for the werewolves' perspective on the war — few can say. Some scholars of occult lore postulate that the werewolves strive to tear down modern civilization, reducing humanity to primitive tribalism so that they can rule the uncivilized world once more. If this were true, the vampires, as lords of the urban territories, would seem to be "in the way." Other scholars counter that Lupines seem to be able to "scent" vampires, and that they hunt the Kindred as part of some religious Jyhad of their own. For their part, the Lupines have refused to explain their actions — and the Kindred would rather see the Lupines extinct than reach any belated peace, so the bloodshed continues.

In some areas of the world, there are rumors of other werebeasts — jaguar-people in the Amazon Basin, fox-spirits in the East, even an urban society of wererats that boils below the Nosferatu's tunnels. However, if such creatures exist, they are even more elusive than the Lupines, and have yet to show themselves in any sort of numbers. Considering as much trouble as the Cainites have with the wolves at their doors, the Kindred are in no hurry to deal with shapeshifters of other bloods.

(For the werewolves' perspective on things, as well as an indepth look at their society and capabilities, see **Werewolf: The Apocalypse**.)

Powers and Weaknesses

• Lupines can take the forms of humans and wolves, as well as some forms that combine the traits of both. Most terrifying of all is their "wolfman" battle form, a wolf-headed, nine-foot killing machine that inspires a supernatural terror in humans. In this form, all their Physical Attributes are doubled, but they cannot use Social Attributes in connection with creatures other than werewolves and wild beasts (save to intimidate or terrify, of course).

• Werewolves can attack several times each turn, often taking two to six actions in a single turn (as Celerity, save with no blood point restriction). They also fly into frenzy as readily as any Brujah, and in this killing state they suffer no health level penalties for wounds.

• Lupines heal incredibly rapidly, regenerating a health level each turn. Only fire, silver, or the teeth and claws of other supernatural creatures (such as a vampire's fangs) can cause lasting injuries to a werewolf — and a werewolf can even heal these wounds as a normal human can. Worse, werewolves can soak such damage with ease. Consider all damage — bashing, lethal and aggravated — to be soakable with the werewolf's normal Stamina. However, because they are living beings, werewolves do not halve bashing damage applied to them, as the undead do.

• Werewolves fuel their supernatural powers with Gnosis, a measure of their innate spiritual energy. This Gnosis is a "battery" of sorts, like vampires' blood points. They regain Gnosis through long meditation or from bargaining with spirits.

• Lupines are apparently able to travel invisibly through the "spirit world," sometimes appearing from nowhere to attack their foes.

• Wolfsbane avails nothing against the Lupines; however, silver is indeed their Achilles' heel. Werewolves cannot soak damage from silver weapons, and cannot regenerate such wounds as quickly as they normally could.

• Lupines can call on strange mystical powers, not entirely dissimilar to Cainite Disciplines, and given time, can work certain rituals in the manner of Thaumaturgy. These powers depend on the werewolf's area of specialization, and can be represented by

Disciplines — presume that a scout has something akin to Obfuscate, a shaman Thaumaturgy, and so on.

Adolescent Werewolf

Attributes (human): Strength 3, Dexterity 3, Stamina 3, Charisma 2, Manipulation 2, Appearance 2, Perception 3, Intelligence 2, Wits 3

Abilities: Alertness 3, Animal Ken 2, Athletics 2, Brawl 3, Crafts 2, Dodge 2, Firearms 2, Intimidation 3, Investigation 2, Leadership 1, Linguistics 1, Melee 2, Occult 1, Stealth 3, Survival 3

Equivalent Disciplines: Celerity 3, Potence 1, Protean 4

Humanity: 7, **Willpower:** 5, **Gnosis:** 4

Veteran Lupine

Attributes (human): Strength 4, Dexterity 3, Stamina 4, Charisma 3, Manipulation 2, Appearance 3, Perception 4, Intelligence 3, Wits 4

Abilities: Alertness 3, Animal Ken 3, Athletics 2, Brawl 4, Crafts 2, Dodge 2, Expression 1, Firearms 2, Intimidation 3, Investigation 2, Leadership 1, Linguistics 1, Medicine 1, Melee 3, Occult 3, Stealth 3, Survival 4

Equivalent Disciplines: Celerity 4, Potence 2, Protean 4

Humanity: 6, **Willpower:** 7, **Gnosis:** 6

Elder Shapeshifter

Attributes (human): Strength 5, Dexterity 4, Stamina 5, Charisma 5, Manipulation 3, Appearance 3, Perception 5, Intelligence 3, Wits 4

Abilities: Alertness 4, Animal Ken 4, Athletics 4, Brawl 5, Crafts 2, Dodge 4, Expression 3, Firearms 2, Intimidation 4, Investigation 2, Leadership 4, Linguistics 1, Medicine 1, Melee 5, Occult 4, Stealth 4, Survival 5

Equivalent Disciplines: Celerity 5, Dominate 2, Fortitude 2, Obfuscate 3, Potence 3, Protean 4, one other Discipline at 4

Humanity: 5, **Willpower:** 9, **Gnosis:** 8

MAGI

Nothing terrifies an immortal like something he cannot understand. And no vampire, regardless of age, truly understands the magi. Even those Kindred who once belonged to that arcane fraternity are puzzled by their demented ways. Enlightened by unintelligible wisdom, wizards make creation dance to their tune. That mad waltz eludes the Kindred, and while they won't admit it, it frightens them, too.

The origins of sorcery are lost in legend. It has been said that Mother Lilith herself learned the secret Arts, and that she passed them to favored mortals. If such tales are true, then magi are both cousins and enemies of the Kindred: cousins through their shared tie to Lilith, and enemies because of that same heretical lineage.

Whatever its origins, magick is real, and it takes many forms. In the hands of a high magician, it calls forth the elements in ways that would please an I.L.M. artist. Most magi command subtler Arts, however — unnatural coincidences, shifts of passion and strange turns of fate. More often than not, a magus hides in plain sight; no physical match for a Kindred, he places his toys, calls his gods, and conjures small but significant phenomena.

Dangerous Draughts

Lupine blood is potent stuff, and a powerful allure to the Kindred. A werewolf's blood is so rich that, although its body holds the equivalent volume of 10 blood points, a vampire can draw 25 actual blood points from the Lupine before its veins run dry. Even if a Cainite has time to guzzle only a blood point's worth, he gains two points for his pool. However, the supernatural power of werewolf blood can also be dangerous wine.

A vampire who feasts on werewolf blood is far more susceptible to frenzy and Rötschreck while the Lupine blood remains in her system. Every blood point of werewolf blood increases the difficulty to resist frenzy by one — yes, if a character drinks only two blood points worth of volume from a Lupine, her difficulties to resist frenzy are two higher. Even if the vampire successfully staves off her Beast, she becomes paranoid and short-tempered for as long as the blood remains in her system. In some cases, vampires have even gained temporary derangements from feasting on particularly volatile werebeasts.

There are rumors that Lupine blood can even temporarily grant levels of Potence or Celerity. However, this isn't always the case. It seems to have something to do with the werewolf's own bloodline, and how pure its heritage is. Unfortunately for would-be hunters, the more purely bred Lupines are often in positions of leadership in their packs, and it is a deadly proposition to go through the rank and file to catch the alpha.

When pressed, however, a master sorcerer can literally turn a vampire to stone or burn him to a crisp. These wizards are indeed subtle and quick to anger.

Try as they might, vampires cannot attain the secrets of the magi; centuries — no, *millennia* — of blood bonds, Embraces, pacts and mind-rape have produced mere shadows of mortal magick. The essence of life itself fuels these mysteries, and that essence is lost to the ranks of the Damned.

The disciplines and intrigues of *le magiciens* divide their kind into several distinct (and hostile) camps:

Wizards, Witches and Miracle-workers

The most obvious magi practice the arts of sorcery and witchcraft. Surrounded by ritual trappings, the wizards and witches of the Old World drape themselves in "New Age" garb. Many neonates mistake such folk for frauds, but a blast of lightning or withering curse assures an errant childe that some myths are real.

Warlocks of Clan Tremere proudly point to their long association with high magicians; one sect, the Order of Hermes, has a love/hate relationship with the Tremere that goes back nearly 1,000 years, to the founder of the clan himself. After a millennium of wars, truces and alliances, the two cabals reached an uneasy compromise: namely, to avoid each other whenever possible. Still, the clan and the Order spy on each other almost habitually, and often lay traps when the other side isn't looking.

Other cults are less predictable, and far more hidden; the so-called Verbena family preserves the pagan ways of their forbears, and practices a body-warping form of blood-magick. Shapeshifters, healers and sybarites, these witches make love and war in equal measure. Like the Order of Hermes, the witch-folk lair in the shadow-side of Kindred affairs. Rare is the elder who has not at least *heard* of their gory rites, though few have attended personally.

In the Church (or the shadow of it, at least), miracle-workers and Satanic priests tend faithful herds. Among the children of God, these shepherds command vast, almost Biblical powers — prophecy, curing, purification and, of course, fire. Their opposites revel in the nights, profaning anything remotely sacred and conspiring to bring about the End of Time. These demon-bound sell-souls conjure foul things and curse their enemies with plague. Many Setites consider these deviants their kin and feed their appetites with loving care.

Shamans and Yogi

Mastery of mind, body and ghostly powers hone these folk into enigmas. Some specialize in strange martial arts; others meditate quietly while their spirits wander in astral form; still others make offerings to dead gods and ghosts, parlaying primitive rituals into disturbing powers.

As a whole, such magi tend toward secrecy; they favor the dress and speech of bygone cultures, or mingle it with "modern primitive" fashions. The latter seem especially appealing to young Kindred — they possess a cool that neonates occasionally emulate. Unlike the wizards or their ilk, modern shamans avoid "showy" magick; their Arts call up disturbing phenomena, or focus human potential to superhuman extremes, but the shamans rarely do so. While they can manipulate emotions, thoughts or elements, such magi often want to be left alone. With the exception of Setites and the occasional Gangrel, most Kindred grant them that wish.

Techno-freaks

Frighteningly incomprehensible to most Kindred, these hypertech magi meld machines, magick and human flesh in bizarre, horrific ways. Some command computer databases like mortal viruses, wiping out reams of valuable information; other search those self-same databases, uncovering things no prince wants discovered. Worst of all are the freaks who "customize" themselves with mechanical parts; these last acquire Discipline-like powers — lethal strength, unfaltering stamina, omniscient senses and built-in weaponry. Some have become so deeply attached to their machines that their vitae literally becomes toxic to the Kindred. Such *things* are Final Death on two legs, and even elders fear them.

These weird factions appear to be locked in a shadow struggle; elders speak of wizard-wars which literally shook the earth during the Dark Ages and Renaissance. These days, things play out at a slightly lower hum; magick appears to have lost much of its sting in the modern age — or has it transformed into something more dangerous? The techno-freaks bear out this troubling possibility, but the elders remain unconvinced. Whatever the truth may be, the magi remain a mysterious lot. Any Kindred who wants to savor immortality avoids such mortals as if they were walking sunlight.

SYSTEMS

Magickal powers are diverse; to simulate a magician's repertoire, the Storyteller may assign a pack of Disciplines as his "arsenal." Common Disciplines include Thaumaturgy, Auspex, Dominate, Presence, Protean, Obfuscate and Obtenebration; uncommon powers include Animalism, Celerity, Fortitude, Potence and Chimerstry. A young magician would command five or so dots, an experienced one 10 or more, and a powerful wizard might have 20+.

A few other things are worth remembering:

• Magi are mortal. While they can attempt to soak bashing attacks, they cannot soak lethal or aggravated damage without conjuring some sort of armor or utilizing cybernetic protection. Magi do not heal damage unless some medicinal spell is employed (curing one health level per success). While a rare few possess a Celerity-like power, most magicians act only once per turn. Wizards are not immune to the blood bond, and the Embrace destroys their power forever.

• Magick demands will; hence, magicians often have Willpower ratings between 6 and 10.

• Although the magi do not depend on age for their Arts, powerful ones may have effective "Generation" Backgrounds (8-12) to reflect their arcane prowess. The more powerful the magus, the higher her effective "generation."

• An odd syndrome — Paradox — attacks magi whose spells are too overt. A naturally rolled "1" on an exceedingly obvious spell (flight, a fireball, shapechanging, a chain-gun rising from the mage's back, etc.) causes things to go horribly wrong. Paradoxed wizards find their spells backfiring or their bodies exploding; some are swept off to Hell by demonic forces. Thus, magi are wary about using magick openly, even around the Kindred. Better safe than sorry!

• A vampire with Thaumaturgy can try to counter a magickal spell directed at her; a Wits + Occult roll (difficulty 6) "soaks" such spells, reducing the attack's potency by one level (or die) per success. A Tremere who eliminates a mage's successes neutralizes his spell.

• Magicians gather into orders for mutual protection; several of these sects have infiltrated mortal cults, survivalist groups, New Age fellowships, churches, and local and national governments. Wizards and their associates are rare, but they lurk at the fringes of Kindred politics. A magician does not have to weave a spell to cross a vampire's plans, nor will he be obvious unless he wants to be....

YOUNG CULTIST

Attributes: Strength 3, Dexterity 3, Stamina 3, Charisma 3, Manipulation 4, Appearance 3, Perception 2, Intelligence 4, Wits 4

Abilities: Academics 2, Alertness 3, Athletics 2, Brawl 2, Dodge 2, Drive 2, Empathy 2, Firearms 3, Intimidation 2, Melee 2, Occult 4, Streetwise 3, Subterfuge 3

Equivalent Disciplines: Auspex 2, Dominate 2, Presence 1, Protean 1, Thaumaturgy 3 (one or two paths)

Blood Pool: 10, **Willpower:** 5

Equipment: Knife, several guns, ritual instruments (candles, rope, chalk, robes, chalice), intimidating clothes, friends

HIGH WIZARD

Attributes: Strength 2, Dexterity 2, Stamina 2, Charisma 3, Manipulation 5, Appearance 2, Perception 4, Intelligence 4, Wits 4

Abilities: Academics 5, Alertness 3, Dodge 2, Drive 1, Empathy 4, Etiquette 3, Finance 2, Firearms 1, Intimidation 4, Investigation 3, Leadership 2, Linguistics 4, Medicine 2, Occult 5, Subterfuge 3

Equivalent Disciplines: Auspex 4, Chimerstry 3, Dominate 2, Fortitude 2, Obfuscate 4, Presence 3, Thaumaturgy 5 (many paths and rituals)

Blood Pool: 12, **Willpower:** 9

Equipment: Sanctuary, extensive library, ritual instruments (books, blades, chalk, candles, potions, incense), sword-cane, tailored clothing

TECHNOLOGICAL ABOMINATION

Attributes: Strength 5, Dexterity 4, Stamina 5, Charisma 2, Manipulation 2, Appearance 2, Perception 4, Intelligence 3, Wits 4

Abilities: Alertness 3, Athletics 3, Brawl 3, Computer 4, Crafts (Mechanical Repair) 4, Drive 3, Firearms 4, Intimidation 4, Investigation 4, Law 2, Melee 3, Occult 4, Science 3, Security 5, Stealth 2, Streetwise 2

Equivalent Disciplines: Auspex 2, Dominate 2, Fortitude 4, Potence 3, Presence 3

Blood Pool: 10 (poisonous — one aggravated health level per blood point consumed), **Willpower:** 8

Equipment: Automatic weapons, body armor, mini-computer, communications devices, black armored sedan, black trenchcoat, mirrorshades

FAERIES

These strange and enigmatic beings exist among both mortals and supernaturals without leaving a trace of their presence. Modern fae differ greatly from the tiny sprites and mighty tree-lords known in ages past. They are beings of magic and illusion, and exactly why they have chosen to take human form and walk among mortals is unknown.

Though the fae have changed in appearance, Kindred who have interacted with them claim that they have changed little — if any — in nature. They are still creatures of the wild, and are best avoided by the Children of Caine. Few who have dealings with them come out ahead in the bargain; even then most vampires are left changed, and occasionally driven mad. The very presence of these creatures of Dream can cause a vampire to suffer pangs of acute loss and agony. Faeries' physical and spiritual beauty can awaken long-dead feelings in a vampire — a yearning to believe in magic, or a poignant sense of his lost innocence — feelings that may drive the vampire to despair or madness.

Most of the time fae are invisible to mortals, their true faerie selves masked in human form. Only those familiar with their ways are able to pierce the glamours that conceal them, and even then it is neither easy nor necessarily safe. The fae enjoy their privacy and do not take kindly to those who attempt to unmask them. Yet when they choose to reveal themselves, their powers can be as terrible as they are beautiful.

Faeries take many forms. Some, like the sidhe, are exquisitely beautiful, while others, like the redcaps, are hideous and gruesome. Even when they do make their presence known, the encounter is usually quickly forgotten by anyone present, as though it were a fading dream.

A few Cainites, primarily Malkavians and Ravnos, hunt the fae for their blood, believing the rumors that it is far more potent than mortal blood. Tremere have been known to seek out fae blood as well, for various unwholesome purposes. Among those who claim to have tasted this sweet nectar, the experience is quite varied. Some vampires say that fae blood tastes little or no different from mortal blood; others speak of rapturous bliss, hallucinatory qualities or transcendent experiences. Some compare it to feeling the morning sun shining upon one's face once more — both in its exhilaration and in its excruciating pain.

Little is known of faerie customs or society. One thing that is known about them is that fae activity increases greatly during certain times of the year, such as the equinoxes and solstices. It is during these times and during festivals, such as Mardi Gras, that the vast majority of known encounters with faeries take place. Vampires may encounter fae at any time, they just aren't aware of it.

Even less is understood about their magic. Their powers seem to be fueled from a source they call Glamour, though how this Glamour is used and how it is restored remain mysteries. Some Kindred theorize that faeries restore their Glamour during special times of the year, and it is for that reason that they are most active then. Others claim that they draw their energy from secret places of natural beauty. Certain members of Clan Toreador believe that faeries gain their power through a connection to mortal art and artists. More than one Toreador has come into conflict with a changeling over a particularly talented artist or musician.

• Faeries heal as mortals, though many know healing magic. They may soak lethal damage, but do not halve net bashing damage. They take aggravated damage only from fire.

• They find the presence of vampires distasteful, and tend to avoid the undead. They may conceal their faerie forms from a vampire's sight, but Auspex often allows a vampire to pierce the disguise.

SAMPLE FAERIES

The following are several examples of faeries that a vampire might encounter. Those described here are only a few of the myriad possibilities — faeries come in as many shapes and sizes as there are dreams. Fae encountered in a **Vampire** story should remain distant and mysterious. Even if a vampire somehow befriends one of these beings, the alienation should be constantly reinforced. Additionally, the fact that the fae are so vibrant and full of life will serve as a constant reminder of what

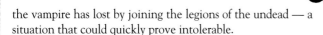

the vampire has lost by joining the legions of the undead — a situation that could quickly prove intolerable.

Pooka Trickster

This trickster often resembles an animal, at least when she reveals her faerie self. Kindred scholars of fae lore believe that pooka can shift into the form of the animal that they represent, in a manner similar to the Lupines, though this has never been observed. The pooka take delight in teasing and tormenting others.

Attributes: Strength 2, Dexterity 5, Stamina 2, Charisma 4, Manipulation 5, Appearance 2, Perception 3, Intelligence 2, Wits 2

Abilities: Alertness 3, Animal Ken 2, Brawl 3, Dodge 5, Performance 3, Occult 2, Security 2, Stealth 5, Subterfuge 4

Equivalent Disciplines: Animalism 2, Auspex 2, Chimerstry 3, Celerity 2, Obfuscate 4, Protean 4

Blood Pool: 10, **Willpower:** 6, **Glamour:** 6

Redcap Warrior

This brutish faerie thrives on carnage. His bloodlust can be as fierce as that of a vampire in blood-frenzy. In ancient times, redcaps delighted in dipping their caps in the blood of freshly fallen victims — thus their name.

Attributes: Strength 3, Dexterity 4, Stamina 4, Charisma 1, Manipulation 3, Appearance 1, Perception 3, Intelligence 2, Wits 4

Abilities: Alertness 3, Athletics 3, Brawl 4, Dodge 2, Intimidation 4, Melee 4, Streetwise 3, Security 2, Stealth 2

Equivalent Disciplines: Celerity 3, Fortitude 2, Obfuscate 3, Potence 2

Blood Pool: 10, **Willpower:** 5, **Glamour:** 5

Sidhe Enchantress

To look upon one of these magnificent beings is to look upon Heaven itself. The beauty of a sidhe is enough to overwhelm even the most jaded vampire. She can weave glamours and illusions that astound the senses and leave victims paralyzed with fear or awe.

Attributes: Strength 2, Dexterity 4, Stamina 3, Charisma 4, Manipulation 4, Appearance 7, Perception 3, Intelligence 3, Wits 4

Abilities: Alertness 2, Athletics 2, Dodge 2, Empathy 3, Etiquette 4, Expression 4, Intimidation 3, Leadership 4, Occult 4, Performance 4, Subterfuge 2

Equivalent Disciplines: Celerity 1, Chimerstry 5, Dominate 4, Obfuscate 4, Presence 5

Blood Pool: 15, **Willpower:** 7, **Glamour:** 10

WRAITHS

Ghosts. Phantoms. The restless dead. Call them what you like, these malingering spirits of departed mortals have been around as long as Cainites have, perhaps longer. Many call themselves wraiths, and they are bound to the living world by some Passion, some unfinished business in the warm realms. Not every dead mortal manifests as one of the Restless, but all who do so retain links to

people, places or things from their lives. Such physical anchors can sway the emotion-driven existences of wraiths, who sustain themselves with strong emotions much as Kindred do with blood.

As any victim of a haunting can attest, wraiths, though normally incorporeal, can appear among the living in a variety of guises and through a range of powers similar to vampiric Disciplines. The invisibly hurled plate, the sourceless whisper, the worm-riddled visage that flickers at the edge of perception — all are in a wraith's bag of tricks, and Cainites are not immune to such magics. Haunted vampires are doubly damned, and such unfortunates typically find themselves shunned by Kindred society. But wraiths can't howl and rattle their way around the Skinlands — the warm world, where people still *have* skin — with impunity. Impeding them is the Shroud, a spiritual wall that separates the living from the dead.

Most Cainites, save the Giovanni clan, manage to elude any entanglement with wraiths. Vampires who do otherwise sometimes regret their actions. A dead person with a grudge against a vampire can be an annoyance (by frightening off prey) or a threat (by directing wraithly powers at the target of his ire).

• Wraiths "feed" on emotion; this recharges their passion pool, which is used to power their magical abilities. Kindred in frenzy may actually find themselves strengthening a ghostly opponent.

• Wraiths manifest most effectively in "haunted" sites and places where great suffering or trauma has left a psychic residue (battlefields, torture chambers, the bridge where a suicide leapt, etc.). In such places, the Shroud between the worlds of the living and the dead is weak.

• Cainites' physicality and wraiths' incorporeality make conventional fights between them out of the question. Vampires can influence one of the Restless by manipulating her fetters (objects or persons important to the ghost in life), or they can affect a wraith directly with Thaumaturgy, Necromancy or other Disciplines. Conversely, wraiths can possess mortals in order to attack a Cainite, or they can invisibly propel inanimate objects.

• Wraiths are normally invisible unless they choose to be seen. Vampires can perceive them through Auspex, however.

• Some Giovanni have encountered ghosts of true malice and hatred, who set about making their would-be masters' lives an absolute misery. These dark spirits seem to "live" only for inflicting pain, and indeed seem to thrive on it. Other ghosts seem to fear them, and refer to them as *spectres*.

• Wraiths can affect the lands of the living, albeit with great effort. In the Shadowlands, however, they can easily inflict damage to the foolish who invade their home turf. (Stats to the right of the "/" reflect the wraith in the Shadowlands.)

Recently Deceased

This newly made wraith is most likely quite cocky and still has significant ties with the mortal world. However, he is inexperienced about the ways of the Underworld and the supernatural, often leading to a few rude surprises.

Attributes: Strength 0/2, Dexterity 3, Stamina 3, Charisma 2, Manipulation 3, Appearance 2, Perception 3, Intelligence 2, Wits 3

Abilities: Academics 1, Alertness 3, Brawl 1, Bureaucracy 2, Computer 2, Dodge 2, Empathy 3, Intimidation 2, Investigation 1, Law 2, Melee 1, Occult 2, Politics 1, Stealth 1, Streetwise 1, Subterfuge 2

Equivalent Disciplines: Auspex 1, Chimerstry 1, Dementation 2, Dominate 1, Vicissitude 1

Willpower: 5, **Passion Pool:** 5

Spectre

Death and time have not improved this wraith in the least. Perhaps he died with such rage and hate in his heart that his dark side consumed him utterly upon death, or perhaps his bitterness slowly drove him into darkness. Whatever the reason, he now keeps fear and pain as his companions. Spectres seem to communicate by way of a shared consciousness, and if one requires aid, at least three more will answer his summons.

Attributes: Strength 0/3, Dexterity 3, Stamina 5, Charisma 2, Manipulation 3, Appearance 1, Perception 2, Intelligence 4, Wits 3

Abilities: Alertness 3, Brawl 4, Dodge 4, Intimidation 3, Melee 3, Occult 2, Stealth 2, Streetwise 3, Subterfuge 3

Equivalent Disciplines: Auspex 2, Chimerstry 4, Dementation 4, Obfuscate 2, Obtenebration 3, Presence 2, Protean 2, Vicissitude 4

Willpower: 7, **Passion Pool:** 9

Old Soul

She may have been dead for a decade or centuries. Those of such power are not often seen in the Shadowlands, as time has worn away some of their connections to the mortal world. Those who do appear are considered some of the strongest and most feared wraiths.

Attributes: Strength 0/4, Dexterity 5, Stamina 5, Charisma 3, Manipulation 4, Appearance 1, Perception 5, Intelligence 3, Wits 3

Abilities: Academics 2, Alertness 3, Brawl 2, Bureaucracy 4, Computer 3, Dodge 3, Empathy 3, Intimidation 3, Investigation 1, Law 2, Linguistics 1, Melee 2, Occult 2, Politics 1, Stealth 3, Streetwise 1, Subterfuge 3

Equivalent Disciplines: Auspex 2, Chimerstry 1, Dementation 4, Dominate 3, Presence 2, Thaumaturgy 3 (The Lure of Flames 3, Movement of the Mind 3), Vicissitude 3

Willpower: 9, **Passion Pool:** 10

The sun is in the sky, and we have nowhere to go, and they are routing us with fire.

The damn fools will burn down all of London to get us, I think. Never mind that with the wind whipping up from the south, these fires will take the whole city in a matter of hours — they will have caught their vampires. Not a building will be left standing this side of the Thames, but they'll be happy, having destroyed the "monsters."

The scent of smoke has wafted down to my haven. It is so hard to move when the sun is in the sky, so hard to force blood into my limbs. I am sluggish, confused, and the smoke smell is forcing its way into my nostrils. Underneath it I can taste other scents — charred flesh, old ash. Some of the things that are roasting are rats. Others are my childer.

My haven is stone, yes, but the ceiling is shored with heavy beams. Those will burn, no doubt, and I will burn with them if I do not move. Fortunately, I have foreseen such contingencies. There is an iron ring in the floor, attached to a stone door. With the help of the blood, I lift it, and see blackness below. Behind me, I can hear one of my childer pounding on the door to my haven, pleading for entrance as the flames take him. But there is no time, and he is already doomed. With a silent farewell, I descend into the sewers and close the trap door behind me. With the thunder of the stone coming down, the screams abruptly cease. For that, I am thankful.

Here, all is darkness surrounded by cool stone. I shall rest here, and sleep. Then, when the sun sets, I will rise and walk among the huddled mortals, who have burned their homes to destroy my childer. I will exact from them the same price they have exacted from me. The difference is this: Unlike me, they have no place to run.

APPENDIX

ALTERNATE VIRTUES AND PATHS OF ENLIGHTENMENT

Some vampires forgo the petty mortal concerns embodied by the concept of Humanity. These Kindred reason that they are no longer human, thus they have no need to apply the sentiments of the living to themselves.

Whether or not a Kindred chooses to follow the moral tenets of Humanity, some sort of behavioral system must exist. To accept utter randomness is to court the Beast, and no vampire wishes to sink into the clutches of mindless depravity. Even those vampires who plumb the depths of immorality have some ethical bulwark they use to anchor themselves against the Beast.

Kindred who voluntarily abandon Humanity follow behavioral codes known as *Paths of Enlightenment*. While mechanically similar to Humanity, these codes have very little — in fact, sometimes *nothing* — to do with the mores of mortal culture. Adopting a Path of Enlightenment means giving up everything that matters to a "normal" person or, indeed, many Kindred.

So You Want to Follow a Path

Many Kindred loan themselves especially well to certain Paths. By all means, if your character concept fits a Path better than Humanity — and if the Storyteller permits — take it! It is important to know a few things before you commit to a Path of Enlightenment, however.

• **Paths are advanced concepts:** For beginning players and Storytellers, it's best to stick with Humanity. Not only do most vampires still maintain vestiges of their mortal beliefs, it's less difficult to portray a character who knows and believes similar things as the player.

• **Paths are exclusive:** Few Kindred are initiated into the secrets of the Paths. Most vampires — even those of the independent clans and the Sabbat — follow the ways of Humanity; they simply tend to degenerate to very low levels over time. Not just anyone can follow a Path; becoming such an inhuman creature requires discipline and spiritual strength, albeit of a distinctly alien sort. A person seeking to join a Path must have the capacity to discard her human nature, as well as the fortitude to survive the process.

• **Paths are utterly inhuman:** Players wishing their characters to adopt Paths of Enlightenment are in for *extremely* demanding roleplaying experiences. Absolutely nothing the player believes in will be reflected by any of these Paths. These are codes of immortal ethics that Kindred have spent hundreds of years, if not millennia, studying. It's fine and good to have an Assamite character following the Path of Blood, but the player will have to devote an enormous amount of energy toward thinking how that character really thinks.

As a corollary to this, a Path follower is treated as though he has a Humanity score of 3 when using the rules for interacting with mortals. If the Path follower's Path rating is less than 3, use that score instead.

• **Paths shock conventional moralities:** This cannot be stressed enough. Paths use game systems similar to Humanity, but the codes that constitute these ideas emphasize such alien ideals that anyone observing them is likely to be put off. Look over the Hierarchies of Sin for the Paths — some of them accord prestige, honor or righteousness to behavior that would cause the gods to strike a human dead in his tracks. Some codes espouse killing, while others cannot be bothered with it. Indeed, some codes are so selfish that even *thinking* about helping others constitutes a moral failure.

To put it plainly, this is some heavy shit. These Paths are here to illustrate how utterly inhuman and removed the Kindred are from humankind, and to give them spiritual protection from the talons of the Beast. Use the Paths when the story or character demands them, not to free the characters from penalties for wanton murder or perversion.

Systems

Characters on Paths of Enlightenment use the same systems for degeneration as characters who still subscribe to Humanity. Each Path has its own Hierarchy of Sin, which functions the same as the one on p. 221. To recap, any time the Storyteller feels that the character is about to act in a manner contrary to morality *as her Path defines it* (i.e., she wishes to do something proscribed at her Path level or below), he should warn her that persistence will require a degeneration check. If the character undertakes the action anyway, have the player make the degeneration check (alternatively, the Storyteller may do this in secret) and apply the proper consequences, if any.

Some Paths are so far removed from conventional human morality that concepts like Conscience and Self-Control do not apply to them at all. For these codes of ethics, different Virtues apply. Depending upon which Path a character follows, Conscience may be replaced by the Virtue of Conviction, while Self-Control may be replaced by the Virtue of Instinct. No character may have both Conscience and Conviction or Self-Control and Instinct. Which Virtues the character actually possesses depends upon which Path he follows. Remember, however, that all characters have Courage, regardless of Path.

Conviction

The Conviction Virtue quantifies a character's ability to maintain a sense of reason when faced with desire, suffering or need. Utterly inhuman, Conviction represents the reconciliation of the predatory urge with the character's capacity for atrocity.

As opposed to Conscience, which deals with remorse and atonement for Path transgressions, a character with Conviction recognizes his failure and plans to overcome it. Conviction is completely inhuman; the character who has this Trait can no longer pass for human under anything but the most cursory of scrutiny. Creatures who can sense the Beast (vampires, werewolves, etc.) immediately recognize someone with the Conviction Virtue for what he truly is: a monster. Like Conscience, Conviction comes into question when a character must check for degeneration.

- •   Steady
- ••   Determined
- •••   Driven
- ••••   Brutal
- •••••   Completely self-assured

Instinct

The Instinct Virtue refers to a character's ability to control the Beast by familiarity rather than denial. It allows characters to "ride the wave" of frenzy and emotional excess by keeping a close rein on their passion, rather than letting passion control *them*. As atavistic as Conviction, Instinct is the Virtue of a monster who accepts his nature rather than maintaining a sense of human compassion.

Instinct allows the character to harness the Beast's destructive power; a character with high Instinct is primal and turbulent. A player rolls Instinct when attempting to control a character's existing frenzy. When a character who possesses the Instinct Virtue faces frenzy, she *always* enters the frenzy, unless the difficulty to avoid it is less than her Instinct Trait, in which case she may choose whether or not to frenzy. Thereafter, for the duration of the frenzy, the character is wholly under the Beast's sway, and must be run by the player (or controlled by the Storyteller) in an appropriate fashion. Any time the player wishes the character to consciously take an action (known as "riding the wave"), she must roll Instinct against the difficulty to avoid the frenzy. Frenzies affect the character normally (including ignoring wound penalties, etc.), though she may sometimes exert a bit of control while so enraged.

- •   Intuitive
- ••   Feral
- •••   Bestial
- ••••   Visceral
- •••••   Primal

Creating a Path Follower

If a player wishes to create a beginning character on a Path, a few changes in the character-creation rules take place.

• **Alternate Virtues begin at zero:** While every human (and thus every recently Embraced Kindred) has a modicum of their "natural" Virtues, vampiric Virtues must be inculcated from the ground up. So, while a character with Conscience, Self-Control and Courage is created with one free dot in each Virtue, then has seven points to spend on Virtues, a character with Conviction, Self-Control and Courage begins with only two free dots (in Self-Control and Courage). A character with Conviction, Instinct and Courage begins with only one free dot (in Courage). All characters receive seven points to spend, but must use points to buy the inhuman Virtues to at least 1. This may seem unfair, but shunting off one's human nature is not undertaken lightly. Even monsters are not created overnight.

• **A vampire following a Path of Enlightenment must begin the game with a Willpower Trait of 5, minimum:** This can be achieved by spending points on Courage or raising Willpower with freebie points. Beings of lesser ego simply do not have the spiritual vigor needed to break down their very souls and rebuild them from the ground up.

• **Beginning characters may not start the game with Path scores above 5:** If the combination of the character's Virtues would indicate a Path score of higher than 5, simply record "5." Likewise, freebie points may not be spent to increase a beginning character's Path rating above 5, either. Beginning character vampires who subscribe to these codes still have only 25 or fewer years of experience as Kindred — hardly enough time to master the rigors of inhuman codes of behavior.

• **In all other ways, unless otherwise specified, inhuman Paths and Virtues are used like their human counterparts.** So, if a roll calls for the player to use Perception + Self-Control, and the character has Instinct, roll Perception + Instinct.

SWITCHING FROM HUMANITY TO A PATH

A character may also elect to eschew his human nature in favor of a Path. This is exceedingly difficult, and those who fail find themselves permanently soul-scarred as a result.

A character seeking to switch from Humanity to a Path must have a Humanity rating of 3 or below, as well as ratings of 1 in whichever Virtue or Virtues are to change to their counterparts. For example, a vampire seeking to follow a Path espousing Conviction and Instinct must have Conscience and Self-Control ratings of 1.

During the chronicle, a "deserving" candidate is typically approached by a Kindred already on the Path; in this sense, Paths resemble secret fraternal orders, approaching candidates they deem worthy rather than being open to solicitation. This process should always be roleplayed. If the character chooses to initiate himself toward the Path, he begins a program of rigorous study, and a vampire already on the Path is assigned as the initiate's mentor. An initiate spends at least a year in contemplation and study of the Path's ways. During this time, the initiate must forcibly degenerate his human Virtues, dropping them to "acceptable" levels (Humanity 3 or below, ratings of 1 in appropriate Virtues), if he has not done so already. Again, this should be accomplished by roleplaying.

The vampire then undertakes a test, which must be roleplayed by the player and Storyteller. This test can involve study of forbidden lore, answering of riddles, completion of ordeals and tasks, or whatever else the Storyteller deems appropriate for the given Path. However, part of the test always involves the vampire committing an act that, in human terms, would be viewed as an atrocity. Such a deed is undertaken not for the sake of mindless evil, but rather to impart a lesson about the character's nature in relation to the Path.

Following the completion of the test, the character makes a Willpower roll. If the character's Humanity is 3, the difficulty of the roll is 10. If the character's Humanity is 2, the difficulty is 8, and if the character's Humanity is 1, the difficulty is 6. Willpower may not be spent to gain automatic successes on this roll. If the character succeeds, he sheds his human nature and the Virtues that accompany it, gains ratings of 1 in all appropriate Path Virtues, and gains a Path rating of 1. If the character scores three or more successes, he experiences a profound, if twisted, enlightenment, gaining a Path rating of 2.

If the character fails the roll, he commits a stupid, pointless atrocity without gaining any corresponding understanding. He loses a point of Humanity, fails to attain the rudiments of the Path, but may reattempt the test (at a difficulty appropriate to his lowered Humanity Trait) in a month's time. If the character botches the roll, he loses a point of Humanity and may not reattempt the test for an entire year.

Should a character be driven to Humanity zero in this fashion, his soul is lost to the Beast, and the character is permanently taken over by the Storyteller.

THE PATH OF BLOOD

Hail the call of Haqim, and speak his message.
The blood of the kafir belongs in our veins; it is our right — our duty — to take it.
Restraint has no place in the heart of the killer.
— *The Parables of Blood*

Nickname: Dervishes

Basic Beliefs: This Path is practiced almost exclusively by the diablerist assassins of Clan Assamite, although only vampires who demonstrate true loyalty to the clan learn its harsh code. The founding principle of this Path explains that the children of Caine (or Khayyin, as the Assamites refer to him) are wicked failures, fit primarily to bring the brood of Haqim (the Assamites' name for their own clan founder) closer to "the One," a state of mystical transcendence. Haqim instructs his childer to salvage or strike down Khayyin's other childer, drinking their blood in an effort to destroy the taint they inflict on the world.

Assamites on this Path follow two basic precepts. First and foremost, the clan seeks to convince other Kindred of their flawed, cursed nature, and thus convert them to the service of those on the Path. Kindred as a whole are a blight upon the earth, and only by upholding Haqim's righteous code can they redeem themselves. Should vampires resist attempts at conversion, the Assamites kill and diablerize them, using the blood of the victims to lower their generations and thus return to Haqim's bounty. Although they are not inherently psychotic murderers, Assamites on the Path of Blood place little value on the unlives of other Kindred, and must have good reason not to slay most vampires with whom they come in contact. Vampires on this Path pose serious threats to other Kindred around them, and do not frequently associate with non-Assamite Kindred. Blood is blood, however, and Assamites are not so fatuous as to disregard the value of the vast web of Kindred society. Thus, many Assamites offer their martial expertise as murderers and bodyguards in return for payments of vitae — provided that they may harvest blood from those whom they bring down in combat.

Few young Assamites follow this Path or even know of its existence — Clan Assamite conspires to keep its beliefs secret from most other Kindred of the world. Hundreds of years ago, the Assamites' bloodthirsty ways united all other Children of Caine against them, and they are loath to face the concerted opposition of Khayyin's bastard brood again. As such, only the most accomplished and able Assamites learn this Path's tenets; young Assamites who face dire odds may jeopardize the clan's nominally covert vitae crusade.

THE ETHICS OF THE PATH

• Faithfully follow the teachings of Haqim.

• Mortals are beneath the notice of vampires. Feed from them only when necessary.

• Lose no opportunity to sate the Beast with the vitae of other Kindred.

• Withstand the Beast's fury — failing to master oneself results in lessened prowess.

• Seek knowledge that may aid the clan in its war on the cursed spawn of Khayyin.

PATH OF BLOOD HIERARCHY OF SINS

Score	Moral Guideline	Rationale
10	Killing a mortal for sustenance	Human blood is nourishing to the body, but the murder of lessers is poison to the soul.
9	Breaking a word of honor to a clanmate	Solidarity is important to the Assamites' holy cause.
8	Refusing to offer a non-Assamite an opportunity to convert	The childer of Khayyin are a curse and must be saved.
7	Failing to destroy an unrepentant Kindred outside the clan	Those who do not accept Haqim's teachings forfeit their unlives.
6	Succumbing to frenzy	Haqim teaches ascendance, not indulgence.
5	Failing to pursue the lore of Khayyin	To oppose one's enemies successfully, one must learn all about them.
4	Failing to pursue lesser blood	Other members of the clan may benefit from such vitae, no matter how diluted.
3	Refusal to aid a more advanced member of the Path	To act selfishly is to fall into the snares of Khayyin's spawn.
2	Failing to take an opportunity to lower one's generation	Haqim has decreed this as paramount to his childer's cause.
1	Acting against another Assamite	This is treason to the Path and the clan.

• Extend the glory of Haqim's cause to other Kindred. Should they refuse, use them to further your own journey back to Khayyin's grace.

VIRTUES

Vampires on the Path of Blood subscribe to the virtues of Conviction and Self-Control.

HISTORY

The Assamites practiced an early version of this Path for hundreds of years before the formations of the Camarilla and Sabbat. Their bloodlust led them into open conflict with powerful elder Kindred, who desperately sought to stifle the marauding diablerists. The Assamites found themselves in the same situation as the anarchs during the time of the Anarch Revolt, and the Camarilla levied a curse on the clan, making it impossible for the Assamites to consume Kindred vitae. For centuries, the clan followed a debased version of the Path, crippled by its members' inability to commit diablerie directly. Since breaking the blood curse, the Assamites have renewed their support of the old Path, and pursue diablerie with deadly vengeance.

CURRENT PRACTICES

The fatal nature of this Path with regard to other Kindred stands behind much of the fear and mistrust of Clan Assamite. Predominantly practiced by proven ancillae and elders of the clan, the Path of Blood leads these beings into direct conflict with non-Assamite vampires. Kindred on the Path of Blood gracefully attempt to convince other Kindred of their "one true way," so a few individuals from other clans also support this Path.

Practitioners of little understanding seek merely to follow the teachings of Haqim, doing so with little question. However, those of greater wisdom seek to explore just what "becoming One" entails. By taking the cursed blood of the Antediluvians and their spawn, the followers of the Path hope to concentrate the curse of Khayyin in the hands of those who will use it responsibly. In such a way, according to Path doctrine, can the great endgame of Gehenna be averted. Accordingly, Assamite Ancients practice rigorous purity and meditation, and rumors of a Golconda-like state among these beings have recently trickled into the larger Kindred community.

DESCRIPTION OF FOLLOWERS

Study, diablerie, proselytizing and selective strikes against the rest of the Kindred world occupy the nights of Kindred on this Path, for it is a course of righteous justice — at least to the minds of Assamites. Fanatical in their quest, the Assassins bring Final Death to those who would make the difference between growing closer to Khayyin and not. Even those of higher generation fall prey to the Kindred on this Path, for it is rumored that certain followers of the Path may preserve a victim's essence in his vitae, then send the blood back to the Assamite stronghold at Alamut to aid other members of the clan. Mostly, however, Assamites seek to convert those of high generation, as they are farther removed from their progenitors and, thus, the taint of evil.

FOLLOWING THE PATH

This Path espouses liberal practice of diablerie, and followers should pursue that end should other recourse fail. More enlightened Kindred on the Path of Blood also seek to uncover lore and knowledge that may lead them to foes possessed of ancient and powerful blood. As such, vampires who follow the Path of Blood are not mindless monsters gorging on Kindred vitae, but would-be saviors of the entire world. All Kindred on the Path of Blood strive to attain "Oneness" with the mythical Haqim, though few who have reached this lofty goal deign to explain its nature. Most Dervishes believe that Oneness resembles Golconda, or another state wherein vampires can cast off their curse and revel in their Cainite natures.

Common Abilities: Combat and occult Abilities aid followers in their pursuit of the Path's principles. Brawl, Melee, Dodge, Intimidation and Occult are among the Abilities prized by Path of Blood supporters.

Preferred Disciplines: This Path lends itself to the refinement of Quietus, Obfuscate and Celerity. Some followers cultivate knowledge of Thaumaturgy to aid them in their bloody quests.

THE PATH OF THE BONES

The body is a shell; the mind a cell.
The soul is chaff. Death is the purpose: inevitable death.

— Alessandre Giovanni, *Thanatopsis IV*

Nickname: Gravediggers

Basic Beliefs: The Path of the Bones, it is believed, grew out of a warped code upheld by the morbid vampires who sired the Giovanni. Human, Kindred or otherwise, every being sooner or later ends up in death's arms. The most ardent followers of this Path espouse "giving oneself over to the comprehension of life's inevitable end." Vampires who follow this Path seek the knowledge of precisely what death is: Is it simply the end of life? The transition of the soul to what lies after life? Is it the end of the soul's desire to be? These questions haunt the followers of the Path of the Bones each night.

Many vampires believe that the Path of the Bones is a degenerate Path that encourages followers to participate in all manner of murder and deviance. Those who uphold the Path and those who are familiar with it, however, know that it involves itself with a pursuit of life's and unlife's meaning. Followers of the Path seek to understand death's nature and purpose, and thus the roles individuals play in the greater scheme of the world. Mortality is inevitable, except for vampires, who have somehow managed to cheat the cycle.

Kindred nature, however, is generally outside the avenues this Path explores. It is truly a scholar's code, as the Kindred who follow it forsake even their own comfort to advance their understanding of mortality's mysteries. These Kindred are not necessarily cruel — they merely value comprehension more than human life.

At its simplest, the Path of the Bones seeks to define not only what death *is*, but also its meaning to those who have escaped it. It is a Path of knowledge and power, and many who support it learn to wield great influence over the living and dead alike. Many among the Path become quite erudite in the ways of ghosts, but even these odd beings fail to answer many of the Gravediggers' questions — what, for example, happens to a ghost that resolves its psychic struggle or discorporates into the void?

THE ETHICS OF THE PATH

- Study death in all its permutations.
- Determine when death occurs; define it.
- Search for a purpose for death and the life that prefaces it.
- Quantify the differences of death by various causes.
- Achieve a comfort with death and unlife — distinguish between damnation and salvation.
- Hasten death's arrival, should it seem to be unnaturally delayed.

VIRTUES

Vampires on the Path of the Bones observe the virtues of Conviction and Self-Control.

HISTORY

This Path grew out of a moral code upheld by the vampires whom the Giovanni destroyed in their bid for greater power. A select few Giovanni saw more than a means to an end in their practice of Necromancy, and upheld the rituals and studies of their forebears. Although the Path is not widely practiced among the clan, followers of its precepts pioneered most of the Giovanni's advances in Necromancy.

CURRENT PRACTICES

Elder members of Clan Giovanni follow this Path, as do those with a sincere interest in improving their necromantic knowledge for a purpose other than temporal power. Giovanni who uphold the Path of the Bones rarely deal with mortals, as their grim inquisitiveness often proves fatal for mortals with whom they come in contact.

DESCRIPTION OF FOLLOWERS

Vampires on this Path are genuinely curious, wishing to learn exactly what purpose individuals serve. Thanatology is more a science than a philosophy to Kindred on the Path of the Bones. This Path is quite introspective, and greedy Giovanni rarely follow it, preferring the more materially comfortable outlook of Humanity. Gravediggers support the Giovanni family primarily through the knowledge they bring it, rather than through advancing the political aims of the clan.

PATH OF THE BONES HIERARCHY OF SINS

Score	Moral Guideline	Rationale
10	Showing a fear of death	Fear inhibits learning.
9	Failing to study an occurrence of death	Refusal to learn indicates refusal to understand.
8	Accidental killing	There is no opportunity to gain insight.
7	Postponing feeding when hungry	Denial of the self serves no greater purpose.
6	Succumbing to frenzy	The Beast is irrational, and emotion serves little to advance understanding.
5	Refusing to kill when an opportunity presents itself	Experimentation proves theory, and without proof, there is no conclusion.
4	Making a decision based on emotion rather than logic	Vampires are dead; so, too, are their emotions.
3	Inconveniencing oneself for another's benefit	Death is inevitable; what meaning does easing another's doomed discomfort have?
2	Needlessly preventing a death	One must not prevent the cycle, but should learn from it.
1	Actively preventing a death	Such emotional ties befit humans, not Kindred.

FOLLOWING THE PATH

Vampires who subscribe to the tenets of the Path of the Bones should be detached yet inquisitive. Although they are not cavalier about death, Gravediggers seldom aid one about to slough off the mortal coil, preferring to watch and learn. Less fatalistic vampires may take issue with this, and the Kindred on this Path will not act against them should they seek to aid the dying individual. Obviously, their time has not yet come, though were their benefactor absent....

Common Abilities: Kindred on this Path naturally specialize in those proficiencies that advance their macabre research. Knowledges are favored, particularly in the realms of Medicine, Occult and Science.

Preferred Disciplines: Followers of this Path obviously favor Necromancy, and also refine their aptitude with Auspex. As well, certain elders of the Path are rumored to have developed unique mystic arts related to the study of death.

THE PATH OF NIGHT

The only blasphemy one may commit is failing to acknowledge one's darkest passions. Unlife is a curse, surely, though its purpose is to master the evil within — and deliver it to the world without.

— Alexei Guylaine, Sabbat Templar

Nickname: Nihilists

Basic Beliefs: Those vampires who follow the Path of Night wholly accept their damnation; indeed, they believe that, as vampires, it is their preordained role to act as agents of damnation. Unlife is nothing without pain, and misery enjoys company. This Path is practiced largely by young Kindred of Clan Lasombra, who gladly mortify their own souls in the interests of bringing atrocity to the world.

The Path of Night borrows heavily from Catholic dogma, though it concerns itself more with abandonment and damnation than redemption. The vampire's purpose in unlife, according to this Path, is to scourge the Earth, to act as an agent of evil and, thus, ultimately to do the bidding of the greater powers that dictate good and evil alike. None lives without original sin, and those who follow this Path are beholden to expose and exacerbate that sin. Life and unlife are varying states of damnation; those who fail to realize their full potential are lost sheep, suitable only for slaughter.

This is one of the most terrible Paths in existence, as it concerns itself with the outright and intentional discomfort of others. Its followers are more than mere bullies or sadists, however, in that they are sincere in their beliefs. One who receives the curse of Caine is bound by fate and duty to wreak vengeance upon the Children of Seth. In so doing, vampires on this Path hope that, by fulfilling the roles meant for them, they can transcend those roles and find ultimate peace. This final goal aside, though, the Path of Night is a Path of hostility and antagonism, and the company of those who follow it is extremely hard to abide.

For many Kindred, this is also a desperate Path, but one accessible to self-loathing vampires who seek a sense of purpose in the final nights of looming Gehenna.

THE ETHICS OF THE PATH

- Leave no being untouched by your taint.
- Tempt and horrify those around you; the weak will fall, while the strong will be tempered by your testing of them.
- Inspire others to accept their inner darkness.
- Experience every sensation imaginable, and then some.
- Death is a means, not an end.
- Kindred, as souls damned by God, fulfill their purpose by preying upon mortals.

VIRTUES

Vampires on the Path of Night observe the virtues of Conviction and Instinct.

HISTORY

Few, if any, have certifiably chronicled this Path's inception or evolution. By varying accounts the outgrowth of medieval death cults, Satanic cabals, debased Methuselahs or the practices upheld by Adam's first wife Lilith and her children, the Path of Night has been forsaken by most Kindred with any sense of Humanity at all. Some suspect a coterie of Lasombra known as the Black Angels foment dissension among the clan, turning impressionable Keeper neonates down the Path's unwholesome trail.

CURRENT PRACTICES

No sin is too vile for a follower of this Path to indulge, and no trust is too sacred to break. Kindred on the Path of Night tie their fates very closely to mortals, who bear the brunt of their depredations. As harbingers of damnation, the Nihilists cull the secret fears and sorrows of humans around them, inflicting these terrors upon the kine as the whim takes them.

Ironically, vampires on this Path often have great reverence for those whom they perceive as truly "good" or "blessed." Indeed, one infamous Keeper, who plagued a family of witch-hunters down three generations and was finally destroyed by a scion of the line, is rumored to have praised his destroyer for her resolve.

DESCRIPTION OF FOLLOWERS

This Path is upheld almost exclusively by Lasombra, though the Keepers find occasional converts among other clans. Lasombra who follow this Path are held in low regard by many other Keepers, as there is no room for nobility on this Path. While most Lasombra maintain other codes of morality drawn from the Sabbat, the ones who follow this Path are true fiends of the night.

FOLLOWING THE PATH

Vampires on the Path of Night terrorize their victims, a term which may apply to anyone to whom the Nihilist is drawn. Kindred on this Path are loath to kill — that removes potential targets, though they are not above doing so if the death may cause great grief to others or if preventing it would inconvenience their own existence. To some degree, the Nihilists ironically shepherd the kine, showing them what may await them if they are unrepentant. However, no follower of this Path would openly admit such a thing. They are devils, pure and simple, in their own minds.

Common Abilities: Kindred on this Path specialize in Abilities that allow them to torment others. Brawl, Intimida-

PATH OF NIGHT HIERARCHY OF SINS

Score	Moral Guideline	Rationale
10	Killing a mortal for food	Dead mortals feel no dread.
9	Acting in the interests of another	Gehenna is nigh — there is no time to fulfill petty agendas.
8	Failing to be innovative in one's depredations	Familiarity for one's vile acts breeds contempt for them in others, and they may soon fail to shock.
7	Asking aid of another	Those who cannot provide for themselves fulfill their ends poorly.
6	Accidental killing	God has made Kindred horrors, not murderers.
5	Bowing to another Kindred's will	The games of the Jyhad are diversions from the Damned's true purpose.
4	Intentional or impassioned killing	Death serves no one; it merely deprives one of a victim.
3	Aiding another	Compassion has no place in a vampire's undead heart.
2	Accepting the superiority of another	All Kindred are equal under God's plan.
1	Repenting one's behavior	The Kindred's purpose is to cause repentance, not to practice it.

tion, Melee and Medicine (for physiological knowledge) all have their place among the Nihilists.

Preferred Disciplines: Followers of this Path cultivate Obtenebration for the sheer terror it inspires, as well as Potence for the pain it allows one to inflict.

THE PATH OF METAMORPHOSIS

We are ever in between until the chrysalis overtakes us.
— Laika, Tzimisce *koldun*

Nickname: Metamorphosists

Basic Beliefs: The world is made up of evolutionary chains. Animals are below humans, who are below the Kindred, who themselves are below something. The metaphysical, arcane members of Clan Tzimisce follow this Path, which focuses on defining and attaining the state of being beyond the curse of vampirism. Citing their use of the transformative Discipline of Vicissitude, the Tzimisce believe they have the potential to transcend the constraints of the flesh. Hearing Metamorphosist Fiends speak, however, reveals the true monstrosity of their philosophy; they believe that the next step is a state akin to apotheosis, and they will do anything — *anything* — to achieve it.

Some Metamorphosists believe that their ideology corresponds closely with the concepts of the enigmatic mages. Although their means are different — the Path of Metamorphosis leans heavily toward the passage from life into undeath and onward — it seems that both groups seek some sort of supernatural "ascension."

The Tzimisce are characteristically thorough in their study of this Path's ideals. By coordinating their experiments on living, dead and undead subjects (as well as other curiosities they may come across, like werewolves or the errant ghost), the Fiends have formed complex theories as to precisely what the next step in vampiric transcendence is. The solitary and suspicious Tzimisce rarely compare notes, however, and the Path suffers as each follower spends much of her unlife learning the rudiments that other Kindred have already deciphered.

THE ETHICS OF THE PATH

• Learn the characteristics of all stages of life and death.

• One should not concern oneself overly with mortals — they are a step below the Kindred, not above them.

• Do not share knowledge with others, as it is too valuable to trust to a flawed creature like oneself.

• Indulge the Beast *and* deny it; true comprehension of unlife requires a broad range of experience.

• One should alter and augment one's body — changing the flesh may pave the way toward changing the soul.

• Do not heed the needs or desires of others, as their lack of introspection may distract even the keenest intellect.

VIRTUES

Vampires on the Path of Metamorphosis subscribe to the Virtues of Conviction and Instinct.

HISTORY

The Tzimisce have researched this Path in their solitary way for literally thousands of years. The Tzimisce have always been creatures of tremendous mystical potential; the followers of this Path seek to realize that potential. Followers of this Path relate very little to the world outside themselves, and many relate this fact to the inexorable decline of the clan itself.

CURRENT PRACTICES

Most Metamorphosists claim membership in the Sabbat but pay it little more than lip service, involved as they are in more esoteric pursuits. In truth, this Path long predates any sect, and Kindred committing themselves to it subscribe to beliefs and creeds far older than petty notions of Kindred politics.

DESCRIPTION OF FOLLOWERS

Followers of the Path of Metamorphosis are truly some of the most alien creatures any Kindred could hope (or have the misfortune) to meet. Metamorphosists are cold, utterly inhuman and exactingly scientific. Their concerns are metaphysical rather than legitimately ethical, and it is precisely this frame of mind that leads many to believe that the Metamorphosists have literally begun their transformation into something else. Some

Score	Moral Guideline	Rationale
10	Postponing feeding when hungry	Hunger causes distraction.
9	Indulging in pleasure	Hedonism deters one from greater ends.
8	Imploring another for knowledge	The lessons of Metamorphosis are secrets that must be uncovered, not copied.
7	Sharing knowledge with another	Knowledge must be learned, not simply illustrated.
6	Refusing to kill when knowledge may be gained from it	Before superseding death, the Metamorphosist must understand the phenomenon.
5	Failing to ride out a frenzy	A Kindred must know the Beast to transcend it.
4	Considering the needs of others	Those who cannot be bothered to attain Metamorphosis are beneath one's attention.
3	Failure to experiment, even at risk to oneself	The Path may be understood only through empirical research.
2	Neglecting to alter one's own body	Physical change must be attained before any more significant metamorphosis.
1	Exhibiting compassion for others	The fates of others drag one into devolution, not transcendence.

take this a step further by altering their flesh in various means until they no longer have a recognizable gender or look even remotely human.

FOLLOWING THE PATH

Metamorphosists conduct all manner of bizarre experiments, most of which take place far from others' eyes. It is a distant, lonely philosophy, removed from any needs other than the matter of sustenance. Followers should be heedless of others around them, existing only to satisfy their personal concerns.

Common Abilities: This Path concerns itself almost exclusively with Knowledges, particularly those of Occult, Medicine and Science. Many Metamorphosists also pursue more specialized Knowledges such as Philosophy, Theology and sundry supernatural lores in hopes of uncovering secrets unexplored in larger fields of study.

Preferred Disciplines: The Tzimisce Metamorphosists favor attention to their unique powers of Vicissitude. Thaumaturgy and Auspex are also highly prized.

THE PATH OF PARADOX

Although we are locked outside the cycle, we may not forsake it.
— Raj, *Blood Diaries*

Nickname: Shilmulo (a Romani word for vampire)

Basic Beliefs: Upheld exclusively by vampires of the Ravnos clan, the Path of Paradox concerns itself with the vampires' karmic duty to continue the grand cycle of ages. The Path of Paradox pays a heavy debt to certain tenets of Hinduism and, some whisper, to the indecipherable codes upheld by the Cathayan vampires of the Orient.

According to the Path of Paradox, Kindred are locked perpetually outside the illusory cycle of the universe (*maya*). Whereas most beings are reincarnated through *samsara*, a continual "entanglement" in the cycle of rebirth, Kindred have eluded that cycle. Every individual has his own purpose, or *svadharma*, according to the Path of Paradox, although vampires, excluded from the cycle, have lost theirs. In place of the *dharma* they once followed, each Kindred must now try to advance *maya*,

hopefully understanding it in the process and finally penetrating the great illusions that shroud Ultimate Truth from their eyes.

The means by which the Ravnos undertake this cyclical advancement, however, is by selective deception. Other vampires look upon the Ravnos as untrustworthy, and can hardly be expected to take the advice of the Gypsy Kindred. As such, the Ravnos have had to resort to elaborate ruses in order to get other vampires — or, indeed, anyone with whom they come in contact at all — to undertake a course of action. Ravnos vampires see their undead state as a curse, like many other Kindred do. However, the Ravnos believe this *shruti* (what has been learned from the gods) to be due to their failure to understand *maya*. Other Kindred, also removed from the karmic wheel, often fail to realize the necessity of their return to the cycle. The Ravnos understand this — and expedite their return by destroying them.

THE ETHICS OF THE PATH

• Embrace only if absolutely necessary, and then only from the *jati* (family line, also referred to as the Rom in one specific case).

• Interpret the *svadharma* of others and aid them in their fulfillment of it.

• Destroy other Kindred, for they are unnatural to *maya*.

• Erase karmic debt, dispel *maya*'s illusions and return to the *samsara*.

• Use deception to achieve your ends, as others bear the fault of distrust.

• Confuse the Antediluvians by returning their childer to the cycle.

VIRTUES

Vampires on the Path of Paradox uphold the Virtues of Conviction and Self-Control.

HISTORY

This Path arose among the Ravnos during the latter nights of the Roman Empire. The deceit the Ravnos command is even believed by some to have played a major role in the collapse of the empire. The Path, according to many Ravnos, had become debased shortly after Rome's collapse and had remained so for hundreds of years until a stirring (and secret) event contrived to

Score	Moral Guideline	Rationale
10	Embracing a woman	Males traditionally make better offerings to the gods.
9	Embracing outside the *jati*	Many others fail to comprehend the depth of the Paradox philosophy.
8	Destroying another Shilmulo	Charity does *not*, as is widely believed, begin at home.
7	Killing a mortal for sustenance	Death robs a person of the ability to fulfill their *svadharma*.
6	Failing to destroy another vampire	Those who cannot see the true way should be returned to a productive role in the cycle.
5	Killing a mortal for reasons other than survival	A person may not have achieved her *svadharma*, and preventing such is anathema.
4	Failure to aid another's *svadharma*	The *shruti* defines this as the Shilmulo's purpose.
3	Allowing one's sect affairs to precede one's *dharma*	One's allegiance should be to the gods, not one's companions.
2	Becoming blood bound	One may never destroy one's regnant, which is the whole purpose of this Path.
1	Embracing needlessly or out of personal desire	One must return others to the cycle, not extract them from it.

encourage the Ravnos to rethink their ways. Ravnos on this Path once had reputations as lighthearted tricksters, though recent reconsideration of where the clan was headed has cast a grim new light on the Ravnos and their philosophies.

CURRENT PRACTICES

It is too simple a conceit to say that the Ravnos destroy vampires and burn karma. In fact, the Path of Paradox is arduous and demanding, since, to truly uphold the code, one must glean important grains of information from those with whom one conspires, in order to understand their *svadharma* better. Many of the Ravnos' deceptions are, in reality, complicated tests purveyed to cause the subject to reveal hidden aspects of herself. Thus, the Ravnos travel the world, ousted by ignorant Kindred who fail to realize the necessity of the Shilmulo's duties.

DESCRIPTION OF FOLLOWERS

Most followers of this Path are Ravnos, though certain lines of Malkavians and Gangrel adhere to the Path. Increasingly cosmopolitan Kindred have surfaced among the Ravnos clan, indicating that either the Ravnos pay little heed to their code or that *jati* are more extended than one would think otherwise.

FOLLOWING THE PATH

Kindred on the Path of Paradox commonly hold other vampires in contempt, believing that they ignorantly or arrogantly refuse to seek their reintroduction to the cycle. As such, the Ravnos have taken the responsibility upon their shoulders to do it *for* others. This may require concocting complex webs of deception in order to ascertain what a given person's *svadharma* is, or simply destroying a vampire and placing her back in the cycle, where a new *svadharma* awaits.

Common Abilities: Kindred on this Path focus on Abilities that allow them to gain advantage over others, such as Alertness, Empathy, Subterfuge, Stealth and Investigation.

Preferred Disciplines: Followers of this Path practice Chimerstry in order to dupe their subjects and as a means of manipulating the illusions intrinsic to *maya*. Shilmulo favor Fortitude as well, to protect themselves from their subjects' ire. Many also master Auspex, with which they may better divine hidden secrets.

THE PATH OF TYPHON

It is these secrets which warp our souls, these very enigmas which mark us with our master's venom.

Typhon is not a loving father.

— Khamala Bey, *The Thousand Nights of Sutekh*

Nickname: Theophidians (only among themselves; the outside world knows them as Corrupters or by the Followers of Set nickname, Serpents)

Basic Beliefs: Vampires who follow the Path of Typhon have a truly sinister purpose in mind. Theophidians seek the resurrection of their patron and father, Set. Though most vampires view Set simply as a mythical member of the Third Generation, Theophidian doctrine teaches that Set was, in fact, a divine being even before his Embrace. Indeed, Theophidians view Caine as a lesser being than Set, and claim that Set in fact allowed Caine to Embrace him so that he might use the descendants of Caine to strike at his divine counterparts, such as the mythical Gaia and Lilith. In this manner does Set, and through him the Setites themselves, fulfill their place in the universe, acting as agents of entropy and breaking down the old so that the new may blossom.

Accordingly, this Path preaches the importance of influence and control. Many Setites on the surface appear to be little more than pimps, pushers and fixers; in truth, they are much more. Setites commonly view other individuals as tools or founts of information — they are resources for the Setites either way. By gaining control over others, the Setites may use them to fulfill their own ends. Thus, rather than owing those who provide them with information or services, the Setites reverse the role, and instead have their marks come to *them* first.

Followers of this Path revere Set as something more than a vampire — Set is attributed a deified status, almost a literal translation of the Egyptian god of the underworld. Ways and means for achieving this reincarnation differ, and for this reason, the Followers of Set extend their influence far and wide in hopes of finding information wherever it resides.

THE ETHICS OF THE PATH

• Gather information, secret or otherwise, and learn how it applies to the resurrection of Set.

- Contribute to the clan's greater goal of reviving its slumbering master.
- Bring others under your sway, thereby increasing your influence and capability.
- Subjugate the Beast, as its reckless wiles serve only itself.
- Maintain a veil of secrecy, for other look ill upon this Path's means and ends.
- Look for Set's hidden signs and act upon them.

VIRTUES

Vampires on the Path of Typhon uphold the virtues of Conviction and Self-Control.

HISTORY

Theophidians claim a history dating back to nights before the First City. Whether or not this is true is a matter of much debate, especially among detractors, but the widespread presence of human myths that mimic the relationship between Set and Osiris lends credence to its longevity. For millennia, the Theophidians have plied their degenerate trade from ill-lit alleys to holy temples and everywhere in between. Many leaders among the Kindred and kine alike owe their acquisition of power to the followers of this Path, though the prices they have paid are surely high.

CURRENT PRACTICES

Theophidians support no sect other than their own clan, though some members have forsaken the resurrection of Set and actually oppose his quest from the ranks of the Sabbat. Many followers of this Path cultivate blood cults of devout followers and indenture legions of desperate individuals to themselves. While the Theophidians are not averse to doing "dirty work" themselves — quite the contrary — they reason that with others serving their purposes, they can accomplish much more than they would ever be able to by themselves. Thus, followers of this Path play many roles: seekers, fixers, scholars, courtesans and harvesters of souls.

DESCRIPTION OF FOLLOWERS

The Theophidians are frequently social chameleons, given their need to move through many different circles. They are smooth, ingratiating and wholly inspired by their greater cause. Followers of this Path rarely ask favors of others — they prefer to help satisfy the desires of others, and then call in favors based on what they have already done for those others. It is this side that non-Setite Kindred see most frequently and despise; they publicly decry the vice-peddling and corruption of the Followers of Set as breaches of the Masquerade or the puppetry of the Ancients. The Setites know the truth, however: Other Kindred are loath to acknowledge the desires in themselves that a canny Theophidian can satisfy. Clever Setites have even managed to convince non-Setite Kindred to follow this Path after long periods of corruption, dependency and debasement.

FOLLOWING THE PATH

Followers of the Path of Typhon are first and foremost seekers of arcane lore, though their keen social graces also make them silver-tongued diplomats. These Kindred are also insidious, working their way into existing vampire societies with serpentine façades of false identities and cadres of loyal followers. The eldest Theophidian in a given locale often erects a temple to Set in some out-of-the-way place, to better serve the slumbering god.

Common Abilities: Any Ability that helps the Kindred achieve her end is prized by the followers of this Path. As such, the Theophidians have very diverse and capable members. Abilities of particular favor among the Setites include Empathy, Intimidation, Streetwise, Subterfuge, Performance, Academics, Investigation and Politics.

Preferred Disciplines: Theophidians are masters of the reptilian Discipline of Serpentis, though their dealings with others inspire them to pursue the Setite clan Disciplines of Presence and Obfuscate.

MERITS AND FLAWS

Merits and Flaws are optional Traits that a Storyteller may choose to include, or prohibit, in her chronicle. Properly used, Merits and Flaws help players create and individualize their characters. *Merits* are special abilities or advantages that are rare or unique in the general Kindred population, while *Flaws* are liabilities or disadvantages that pose challenges to a character's nightly existence. These Traits can provide player characters with added depth and personality, but Storytellers should be careful to ensure that any Traits chosen will not adversely influence the course of the chronicle or give one character an unfair advantage over the rest.

PATH OF TYPHON HIERARCHY OF SINS

Score	Moral Guideline	Rationale
10	Pursuing one's own indulgences instead of another's	The slide into vice is a tool, not a recreation.
9	Refusing to aid another follower of the Path	Teams work efficiently to raise Set.
8	Failing to destroy a vampire in Golconda	Those who have transcended their desires cannot brought under sway.
7	Failing to observe Setite religious ritual	This is akin to denying Set.
6	Failing to undermine the current social order in favor of the Setites	Other Kindred are purposeless or misled, and this indolence delays Set's revival.
5	Failing to do whatever is necessary to corrupt another	The more individuals in the Setites' debt, the better.
4	Failing to pursue arcane knowledge	The mysteries of Set's resurrection may be hidden anywhere.
3	Obstructing another Setite's efforts	The ranks of the righteous are no place for petty power plays.
2	Failing to take advantage of another's weakness	Compassion has no place in Set's greater plans.
1	Refusing to aid in Set's resurrection	This is the purview of unbelievers.

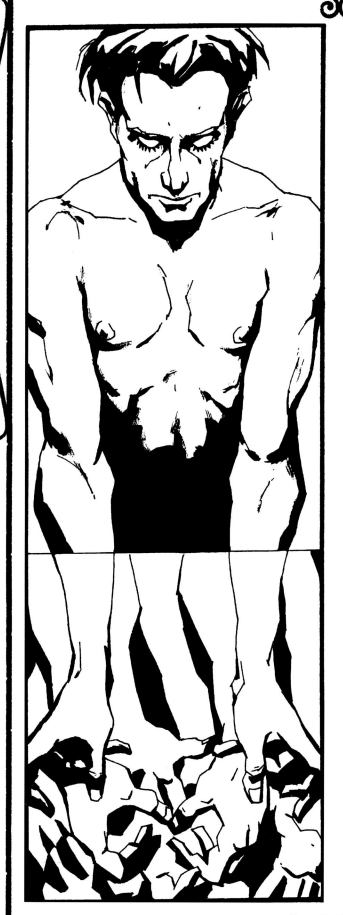

Merits and Flaws can be selected only during character creation and are purchased using freebie points. Each Merit has its own point cost, while each Flaw has a point value which *adds* to the amount of freebie points a player can spend during the creation process. A character may take as many Merits as the player can afford, but no character may have more than seven points' worth of Flaws (which would give a character a total of 22 freebie points to spend in other areas).

Merits and Flaws are divided into four categories: physical, mental, social and supernatural. The physical category describes Merits or Flaws that deal with a character's physical makeup or abilities, while the mental category addresses intellectual abilities or patterns of behavior. The social category comprises relationships and individual status in Kindred or mortal society, while supernatural Merits and Flaws concern the paranormal abilities of vampires and the way they interact with the physical world. Storytellers are encouraged to create their own Merits or Flaws, ones appropriate to their chronicles.

Physical

Acute Sense (1-pt. Merit)

One of your senses is exceptionally sharp, be it sight, hearing, smell, touch or taste. The difficulties for all tasks involving the use of this particular sense are reduced by two. This Merit can be combined with the Discipline Auspex to produce superhuman sensory acuity.

Ambidextrous (1-pt. Merit)

You have a high degree of off-hand dexterity and can perform tasks with the "wrong" hand at no penalty. You must still use the rules for taking multiple actions, but will not suffer a difficulty penalty if, say, you use two weapons or are forced to use your off hand.

Eat Food (1-pt. Merit)

You have the capacity to eat food and even savor its taste. While you cannot derive any nourishment from eating regular foods, this ability will serve you well in maintaining the Masquerade. Of course, you can't digest what you eat, and there will be some point during the evening when you must force yourself to heave it back up.

Catlike Balance (1-pt. Merit)

You possess an innately perfect sense of balance. Characters with this Merit reduce difficulties of all balance-related rolls (e.g., Dexterity + Athletics to walk along a narrow ledge) by two.

Blush of Health (2-pt. Merit)

You look more hale and healthy in appearance than other vampires, allowing you to blend with human society much more easily. You still retain the color of a living mortal, and your skin feels only slightly cool to the touch.

Enchanting Voice (2-pt. Merit)

There is something about your voice that others cannot ignore. When you command, they are cowed. When you seduce, they swoon. Whether thunderous, gentle, persuading or simply talking, your voice commands attention. The difficulties of all die rolls involving the use of the voice to persuade, charm or command are reduced by two.

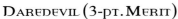

DAREDEVIL (3-PT. MERIT)

You are good at taking risks, and even better at surviving them. When attempting exceptionally risky actions (such as leaping from one moving car to another), characters with this Merit add an additional three dice to their rolls, and negate a single botch die that may result from such a roll. Generally, such actions must be at least difficulty 8 and have the potential to inflict at least three health levels of damage if failed.

EFFICIENT DIGESTION (3-PT. MERIT)

You are able to draw more than the usual amount of nourishment from blood. When feeding, you gain an additional point to your blood pool for every two points of blood you consume. This does not allow you to exceed your blood pool maximum.

HUGE SIZE (4-PT. MERIT)

You are abnormally large in size, at least 6'10" and 300 pounds in weight. Aside from making you extremely noticeable in public, this extra mass bestows an additional Bruised health level. Characters with this Merit may also gain bonuses to push objects, open barred doors, avoid being knocked down, etc.

SMELL OF THE GRAVE (1-PT. FLAW)

You exude an odor of dampness and newly turned earth, which no amount of scents or perfumes will cover. Mortals in your immediate presence become uncomfortable, so the difficulties of all Social rolls to affect mortals increase by one.

SHORT (1-PT. FLAW)

You are well below average height — four and a half feet tall or less. You have difficulty reaching or manipulating objects designed for normal adult size, and your running speed is one-half that of a normally proportioned human.

HARD OF HEARING (1-PT. FLAW)

Your hearing is defective. The difficulties of any die rolls involving the use of hearing are increased by two.

14TH GENERATION (2-PT. FLAW)

You were created five or fewer years ago by a member of the 13th generation. Though you have 10 blood points in your body, only eight of them may be used to heal wounds, power Disciplines, raise Attributes, etc. Obviously, taking this Flaw precludes you from taking the Generation Background, and you may not start with Status, either. You are likely a clanless Caitiff, for your blood is probably too thin to pass down the distinguishing characteristics of a clan. Most 14th-generation vampires should also take the *Thin Blood* Flaw.

INFECTIOUS BITE (2-PT. FLAW)

You lack the enzymes that allow most Kindred to seal the wounds caused by their feeding. You may not automatically lick the wounds of your feeding closed. In fact, your bites have a one in five chance of becoming infected and causing mortal victims to become seriously ill. The precise nature of the infection is determined by the Storyteller.

BAD SIGHT (1- OR 3-PT. FLAW)

Your sight is defective. The difficulties of any die rolls involving the use of your eyesight are increased by two. As a one-point Flaw, this condition can be corrected with glasses or contacts; as a three-point Flaw, the condition is too severe to be corrected.

ONE EYE (2-PT. FLAW)

You have only one eye — which eye is missing is up to you. The difficulties of all Perception rolls involving eyesight are increased by two, and the difficulties of all die rolls requiring depth perception are increased by one (this includes ranged combat).

DISFIGURED (2-PT. FLAW)

A hideous disfigurement makes your appearance disturbing and memorable. The difficulties of all die rolls relating to social interaction are increased by two. You may not have an Appearance rating greater than 2.

CHILD (3-PT. FLAW)

You were a small child (between five and 10 years old) at the time of your Embrace, leaving your Physical Attributes underdeveloped and making it difficult to interact with some aspects of mortal society. You may not have more than two dots in Strength or Stamina, except when raising Physical Attributes with blood points, and the difficulties of all die rolls when attempting to direct or lead mortal adults are increased by two. Characters with this Flaw must also purchase the *Short* Flaw.

DEFORMITY (3-PT. FLAW)

You have some kind of deformity — a misshapen limb, hunchback, clubfoot, etc. — which affects your physical abilities and interactions with others. A hunchback, for instance, would lower a character's Dexterity by two dots and increase the difficulty of die rolls relating to social skills by one. It is the responsibility of the Storyteller to determine the specific effects of the deformity chosen.

LAME (3-PT. FLAW)

Your legs are damaged, which prevents you from running or walking easily. You are forced to walk with a cane or possibly leg braces, and have a pronounced limp to your stride. Your walking speed is one-quarter that of a normal human, and running is impossible.

MONSTROUS (3-PT. FLAW)

Your physical form was twisted during the Embrace, and now reflects the Beast that rages inside you. Characters with this Flaw appear to be savage monsters and have Appearance ratings of zero. Even Nosferatu have difficulty interacting with such individuals.

PERMANENT WOUND (3-PT. FLAW)

You suffered injuries during your Embrace which your transformation somehow failed to repair. At the beginning of each night, you rise from sleep at the Wounded health level, though this may be healed by spending blood points.

SLOW HEALING (3-PT. FLAW)

You have difficulty healing wounds. It requires two blood points to heal one health level of normal damage, and you heal one health level of aggravated damage every *five* days (plus the usual five blood points and Willpower expenditure).

ADDICTION (3-PT. FLAW)

You suffer from an addiction to a substance, which must now be present in the blood you drink. This can be alcohol, nicotine, hard drugs or simply adrenaline. This substance always impairs you in some fashion (see "Poisons and Drugs," p. 231, for particulars).

MUTE (4-PT. FLAW)

You cannot speak. You may communicate with the Storyteller and describe your actions, but cannot talk to player or Storyteller characters unless everyone concerned uses Linguistics dots to purchase a commonly understood sign language or you write down what you wish to say.

THIN BLOOD (4-PT. FLAW)

Your blood is thin, weak and does not sustain you well. All blood point costs are doubled (e.g., using blood-related Disciplines or healing damage), and you are unable to create a blood bond. Furthermore, efforts to sire other vampires succeed only 20% of the time.

DISEASE CARRIER (4-PT. FLAW)

Your blood carries a lethal and highly contagious disease. The disease can be anything from rabies to HIV, and Kindred who drink your blood have a 10 percent chance of becoming a carrier as well. You must spend an extra blood point each night on awakening, or you will begin manifesting symptoms of the disease (increased chance to frenzy for rabies, reduced soak rolls for HIV, etc.).

DEAF (4-PT. FLAW)

You cannot hear. While you may ignore some applications of Dominate, you may not listen to electronic or vocal media, and the difficulties of many Alertness rolls are increased by three.

FLESH OF THE CORPSE (5-PT. FLAW)

Your flesh does not fully regenerate itself once it is damaged. While you are able to heal yourself to the point of regaining full functionality, your skin still retains the cuts, tears, bullet holes, etc., which you have incurred. Depending on the nature of the damage, this Flaw will make social dealings exceedingly difficult.

BLIND (6-PT. FLAW)

You cannot see. Characters can compensate for the loss of vision by becoming more sensitive to other sensory input, but visual cues and images are lost to them. Actions involving hand-eye coordination are very difficult to perform, especially under stressful conditions. Difficulties of all Dexterity-based rolls are increased by two. Oddly, vampires with Level Two Auspex (Aura Perception) are still able to use this ability, thought the information is interpreted via the other senses.

MENTAL

COMMON SENSE (1-PT. MERIT)

You have a significant amount of practical, everyday wisdom. Whenever the character is about to act in a way contrary to common sense, the Storyteller can make suggestions or warnings about the implications of said action. This is a very useful Merit to give to beginning players unfamiliar with the game.

CONCENTRATION (1-PT. MERIT)

You have the ability to focus your mind and shut out any distractions or annoyances. Characters with this Merit are unaffected by any penalties stemming from distracting circumstances (e.g., loud noises, strobe lights, hanging upside down).

Time Sense (1-pt. Merit)

You have an innate sense of time and are able to estimate the passage of time accurately without using a watch or other mechanical device.

Code of Honor (2-pt. Merit)

You have a personal code of ethics to which you adhere. The specifics of this code must be worked out with the Storyteller prior to play, and the character must follow it strictly. Characters with this Merit gain two additional dice to all Willpower or Virtue rolls when acting in accordance with their code (e.g., defending the helpless) or when attempting to avoid situations that might force them to violate their code.

Eidetic Memory (2-pt. Merit)

You remember, with perfect detail, things seen and heard. Documents, photographs, conversations, etc., can be committed to memory with only minor concentration. Under stressful conditions involving numerous distractions, you must make a Perception + Alertness roll (difficulty 6) to summon enough concentration to absorb what your senses detect.

Light Sleeper (2-pt. Merit)

You can awaken instantly at any sign of trouble or danger, and do so without any sleepiness or hesitation. You may ignore rules regarding how Humanity/Path restricts the number of dice available during the day.

Natural Linguist (2-pt. Merit)

You have a flair for languages. You may add three dice to any dice pool involving written or spoken languages.

Calm Heart (3-pt. Merit)

You are naturally calm and do not easily fly off the handle. You receive two extra dice when attempting to resist a frenzy. Brujah may not take this Trait.

Iron Will (3-pt. Merit)

When you are determined and your mind is set, nothing can thwart you from your goals. When you are affected by a Dominate power, you may spend a point of Willpower to shake off the effects. In addition, you receive three extra dice to resist the effects of any mind-altering magic, spell or Thaumaturgy path. This Merit does not affect Presence or other powers dealing with the emotions.

Deep Sleeper (1-pt. Flaw)

When you sleep, it is very difficult for you to awaken. The difficulty of any die roll to awaken during the day is increased by two.

Nightmares (1-pt. Flaw)

You experience horrendous nightmares every time you sleep, and memories of them haunt you during your waking hours. Upon awakening, you must make a Willpower roll (difficulty 7) or lose a die on all actions for that night. A botched Willpower roll indicates that, even when awake, you still believe that you are locked in a nightmare.

Phobia (2-pt. Flaw)

You have an overpowering fear of something. Spiders, snakes, crowds and heights are examples of common phobias. You must make a Courage roll every time you encounter the object of your fear. The difficulty of the roll is determined by the Storyteller, and if you fail the roll you must retreat from the object.

Prey Exclusion (1-pt. Flaw)

You refuse to hunt a certain class of prey. You might refuse to feed upon drug dealers, or policemen, or accountants, or rich people — if you accidentally feed upon such an individual, you automatically frenzy and must make a roll to prevent Humanity loss (difficulty 7). Witnessing other Kindred feeding on the object of your exclusion might also provoke a frenzy, at the Storyteller's discretion. Ventrue, owing to the limitations imposed on their feeding by their clan weakness, may not take this Flaw.

Shy (1-pt. Flaw)

You are distinctly ill at ease when dealing with people and try to avoid social situations whenever possible. Difficulties for all rolls involving social interaction with strangers are increased by two. If the character becomes the center of attention in a large group, difficulties are increased by three.

Soft-Hearted (1-pt. Flaw)

You cannot stand to watch others suffer. You avoid any situation that involves causing someone physical or emotional pain, unless you make a Willpower roll (difficulty 8). You must have a Humanity rating of 7 or above to take this Flaw.

Speech Impediment (1-pt. Flaw)

You have a stammer or other speech impediment that hampers verbal communication. The difficulties of all die rolls involving verbal communication are increased by two. You must roleplay this Flaw whenever possible.

Short Fuse (2-pt. Flaw)

You are easily angered. Difficulties to avoid frenzy are two greater. Brujah vampires cannot take this Flaw, as they already suffer from a similar malady.

Territorial (2-pt. Flaw)

You are extremely territorial, staking out a particular area as your hunting ground and reacting aggressively to trespassers. If another vampire enters your territory uninvited, you must make a frenzy roll. If you fail, you immediately attack the interloper and continue attacking until the intruder is dead or has left your hunting grounds. You are reluctant to leave your territory except in desperate circumstances.

Vengeful (2-pt. Flaw)

You have a score to settle, incurred either during your mortal days or after the Embrace. You are obsessed with taking your revenge on an individual or group, and it is your overriding priority in any situation where you encounter the object of your revenge. You may temporarily resist your need for vengeance by spending a Willpower point.

Amnesia (2-pt. Flaw)

You are unable to remember anything about your past, yourself or your family, though your past might well come back to haunt you. Your origins and the circumstances behind your amnesia are for the Storyteller to determine, and she is encouraged to make it as interesting as possible.

LUNACY (2-PT. FLAW)

You are affected by the phases of the moon, increasing your chances to frenzy. Under the crescent moon, difficulties to avoid frenzy increase by one. Under the half or gibbous moon, difficulties rise by two. When the moon is full, difficulties increase by three.

WEAK-WILLED (3-PT. FLAW)

You are highly susceptible to Dominate and intimidation by others; Dominate attempts automatically affect you unless the Discipline wielder is of higher generation, and your difficulties to resist Social abilities such as Intimidation or Leadership, as well as mind-altering spells or magic, are increased by two. Your Willpower Trait may never rise above 4.

CONSPICUOUS CONSUMPTION (4-PT. FLAW)

It is not enough for you to draw nourishment from the blood of mortals — you believe you must also consume your victim's heart, liver and other blood-rich tissue. Of course, this will necessitate the deaths of all of your victims (unless you are extremely creative), which might lead to numerous problems with the Masquerade and maintaining Humanity. Characters with this Flaw must additionally purchase the *Eat Food* Merit.

SOCIAL

PRESTIGIOUS SIRE (1-PT. MERIT)

Your sire has or had great status in her sect or clan, and this has accorded you with a certain amount of prestige. Though your sire may no longer have any dealings with you, the simple fact of your ancestry has marked you forever. This prestige might aid you greatly in dealings with your elders or other neonates, or it might engender jealousy or contempt.

NATURAL LEADER (1-PT. MERIT)

You are gifted with a certain magnetism to which others naturally defer. You receive two extra dice when making Leadership rolls. You must have a Charisma rating of 3 or greater to purchase this Merit.

DEBT OF GRATITUDE (1-3-PT. MERIT)

An elder owes you gratitude because of something either you or your sire did for her. The depth of gratitude the elder owes depends on how many points the player wishes to spend. One point might mean the elder owes the character a favor; three points might mean that she owes the character her unlife.

DARK SECRET (1-PT. FLAW)

You have some sort of secret that, if uncovered, would be of immense embarrassment to you and would make you a pariah in the local Kindred community. This could be anything from having murdered an elder to being a member of the Sabbat.

INFAMOUS SIRE (1-PT. FLAW)

Your sire was, and perhaps still is, distrusted and disliked by many of the city's Kindred. As a result, you are distrusted and disliked as well.

MISTAKEN IDENTITY (1-PT. FLAW)

You look similar to descriptions of another Kindred, which cause cases of mistaken identity. This can prompt numerous awkward or even dangerous situations, especially if your "twin" has a terrible reputation or is wanted for some crime.

SIRE'S RESENTMENT (1-PT. FLAW)

Your sire dislikes you and wishes you ill. Given the smallest opportunity, she will actively seek to do you harm. Your sire's allies also work against you, and many elders may resent you.

ENEMY (1-5-PT. FLAW)

You have an enemy, or perhaps a group of enemies, who seek to harm you. The power of the enemy depends upon how many points the player wishes to spend (five points indicate the wrath of a Methuselah, archmage or other potent supernatural foe).

HUNTED (4-PT. FLAW)

You are pursued by a fanatical witch-hunter who believes (perhaps correctly) that you are a danger to humanity. All those with whom you associate, be they mortal or Kindred, may be hunted as well.

PROBATIONARY SECT MEMBER (4-PT. FLAW)

You are a defector. You turned traitor to the Camarilla, Sabbat, Followers of Set or other vampiric order, and you still have much to prove before you are accepted by the Kindred you have defected to. Elders, ancillae and even neonates treat you with distrust and even hostility, and your reputation might even sully those whom you regularly associate with.

SUPERNATURAL

MEDIUM (2-PT. MERIT)

You possess the natural affinity to sense and hear spirits, ghosts, and shades. Though you cannot see them, you can sense them, speak to them and, through pleading or cajoling, draw them to your presence. You may call upon them for aid or advice, but there will always be a price.

MAGIC RESISTANCE (2-PT. MERIT)

You have an inherent resistance to the rituals of the Tremere and the spells of the mages of other creeds and orders. The difficulty of all such magic, both malicious and beneficent, is two higher when directed at you. You may never learn the Discipline of Thaumaturgy.

ORACULAR ABILITY (3-PT. MERIT)

You can see and interpret signs and omens. You are able to draw advice from these omens, for they provide hints of the future and warnings of the present. When the Storyteller feels that you are in position to see an omen, you will be required to make a Perception + Occult roll, with the difficulty relative to how well the omen is concealed. If successful, you may then roll Intelligence + Occult to interpret what you have seen, the difficulty again relative to the complexity of the omen.

SPIRIT MENTOR (3-PT. MERIT)

You have a ghostly companion and guide. The identity and exact powers of this spirit are up to the Storyteller, but it can be called upon in difficult situations for help and guidance.

UNBONDABLE (3-PT. MERIT)

You are immune to being blood bound.

LUCKY (3-PT. MERIT)

You were born lucky—or else the Devil looks after his own. Either way, you may repeat any three failed rolls per story, including botches, but you may try only once per failed roll.

TRUE LOVE (4-PT. MERIT)

You have discovered, perhaps too late, a true love. He or she is mortal, but is the center of your existence, and inspires you to keep going in a world of darkness and despair. Whenever you suffer, the thought of your true love gives you the strength to persevere. This Merit grants you one automatic success on all Willpower rolls, which can be negated only by a botch die. This can be a great gift and also a hindrance, for your true love may require protection and occasionally rescue.

NINE LIVES (6-PT. MERIT)

Fate has granted you the opportunity to come as close to Final Death as anyone can get and still survive. When a roll occurs that would result in your death, the roll is made again. If the next roll succeeds, then you live—and one of your nine lives is used up. If that subsequent roll fails, then another reroll is made, until either a successful roll occurs or your nine lives are used up. The Storyteller should keep careful count of how many lives the character has remaining.

TRUE FAITH (7-PT. MERIT)

You have a deep-seated faith in and love for God, or whatever name you choose to call the Almighty. You begin the game with one point of True Faith (see p. 272); this Trait adds one die per point to all Willpower and Virtue rolls. You

must have a Humanity of 9 or higher to choose this Merit, and if you lose even a single point, all your Faith points are lost and may be regained only when the lost Humanity is recovered. Individuals with True Faith are capable of performing magical acts akin to miracles, but the exact nature of those acts is up to the Storyteller.

TOUCH OF FROST (1-PT. FLAW)

Plants wither as you approach and die at your touch. Your touch leeches heat from living beings, as though you are made of ice.

REPULSED BY GARLIC (1-PT. FLAW)

You cannot abide garlic, and the smallest whiff of its scent will drive you from a room unless you make a successful Willpower roll (difficulty based on the strength of the odor).

CURSED (1-TO 5-PT. FLAW)

You are the recipient of a supernatural curse. The strength and pervasiveness of the curse depend upon how many points you wish to incur. Examples follow:

• If you pass on a secret you were entrusted with, your betrayal will come back to harm you in some way. (1 pt.)

• You stutter uncontrollably when you try to describe what you have seen or heard. (2 pts.)

• Tools break or malfunction when you try to use them. (3 pts.)

• You are doomed to make enemies of those whom you most love or admire. (4 pts.)

• Every one of your accomplishments or triumphs will eventually become soiled or fail in some way. (5 pts.)

Cast No Reflection (1-pt. Flaw)

You actually cast no reflection, just like the vampires of legend. This can have a very detrimental effect when trying to pass as a human. Vampires of Clan Lasombra automatically have this Flaw (and you may be mistaken for one of them if you possess this).

Eerie Presence (2-pt. Flaw)

Mortals have an unconscious awareness of your undead nature, which makes then anxious and ill at ease in your presence. Because of this, difficulties of all die rolls relating to social interaction with mortals are increased by two.

Repelled by Crosses (3-pt. Flaw)

You are repelled by the sight of ordinary crosses, believing them to be symbols of holy might. When confronted by a cross, you must make a Willpower roll (difficulty 9) or flee from the symbol for the duration of the scene. If you botch the roll, not only must you attempt to flee, but the touch of the cross can cause aggravated damage (one health level of damage per turn that the cross touches your skin). This damage cannot be soaked, even if the vampire possesses Fortitude.

Can't Cross Running Water (3-pt. Flaw)

You believe in the old folklore, and cannot cross running water unless you are at least 50 feet above it. Running water is considered to be any body of water at least two feet wide in any direction and not completely stagnant.

Haunted (3-pt. Flaw)

You are haunted by an angry and tormented spirit, most likely one of your first victims. This spirit actively attempts to hinder you, especially when feeding, and does its utmost to vent its anguish upon you and anyone in your presence. The Storyteller determines the exact nature of the spirit, its powers, and whether or not it can eventually be laid to rest.

Grip of the Damned (4-pt. Flaw)

There is no ecstasy in your Embrace — only terror and pain. Mortals upon whom you feed struggle and shriek all the while as you attempt to feed, requiring you to grapple with them for as long as you wish to take their blood. For vampires with high Humanity, this experience may require a Humanity roll, at the discretion of the Storyteller.

Dark Fate (5-pt. Flaw)

You are doomed to experience Final Death or, worse, suffer eternal agony. No matter what you do, you cannot avoid this terrible fate. At some point during the chronicle, your Dark Fate will come upon you. Even more ghastly is the fact that you occasionally have visions of this fate, and the malaise these images inspire requires an expenditure of a temporary Willpower point to avoid, or else you lose a die from all of your actions for the remainder of the night. It is up to the Storyteller to determine the exact nature of this fate, and when it will occur. This is a difficult Flaw to roleplay; ironically, though it may seem as though it removes all free will, the knowledge of one's death can be quite liberating.

Light-Sensitive (5-pt. Flaw)

You are even more sensitive to sunlight than other vampires are. Sunlight causes double normal damage, and the light of the moon can cause lethal damage in a manner similar to the sun, though it must shine directly upon you. Even bright lights hurt your eyes, requiring the use of sunglasses.

Bestiary

Vampires are creatures of the cities and rarely interact with the beasts of the wild. Indeed, most animals fear the Children of Caine, hissing or snarling as the unnatural creatures approach. Nonetheless, certain vampires, particularly those with the Animalism Discipline, employ animals as companions, spies or soldiers. Then, too, animals are occasionally changed into ghouls, particularly by the vampires of Clans Gangrel and Nosferatu.

For the most part, normal animals are best described with only Physical Traits. Few have Intelligence scores higher than 2, or Perception scores lower than 3. Social Traits, of course, are purely subjective. Damage inflicted by animals is lethal, although small creatures might inflict bashing damage at the Storyteller's discretion. Any of the beasts below can be turned into ghoul retainers with occasional meals of vampire blood; such companions gain Willpower, a dot of Potence, a blood pool of 10, and some "trained" Abilities that wild animals lack. Assume that any Trait in parentheses is instilled through human contact and training; an animal in the wilderness does not have these Abilities unless there's something magical about it. Animals whose health levels include Incapacitated can survive longer than those without it — others die when they run out of health levels. The Blood Pool Trait reflects how many points a feeding Cainite can drain from a beast. Note that animal blood is far less satisfying than human vitae; some animals that have more blood than a human actually have lower blood pool ratings.

Alligator

Strength 4, Dexterity 2, Stamina 4
Willpower: 3, Health Levels: OK, OK, OK, -1, -1, -1, -2, -5, Incapacitated
Attack: Bite for seven dice; tail slap for six dice
Abilities: Alertness 2, Athletics 2, Brawl 2, Stealth 3
Blood Pool: 5

Note: Alligators and crocodiles have one soak die of armor, usable against bashing or lethal damage. Big reptiles (Nile or estuarine crocs) might have higher Strength, Stamina and damage scores.

Bat

Strength 1, Dexterity 3, Stamina 2
Willpower: 2, Health Levels: OK, -1,-3
Attack: Bite for one die
Abilities: Alertness 3, Dodge 3, Stealth 2
Blood Pool: 1/4 (1 blood point equals four bats)

Note: Bats can fly at 25 mph. Vampires who employ the Protean Discipline to transform into bats are larger and more aggressive than normal bats.

BEAR

Strength 5, Dexterity 2, Stamina 5

Willpower: 4, Health Levels: OK, OK, OK, -1, -1, -1, -3, -3, -5, Incapacitated

Attack: Claw for seven dice; bite for five

Abilities: Alertness 3, Brawl 3, Intimidation 2, Stealth 1

Blood Pool: 5

BIG CAT

Strength 4/5, Dexterity 3, Stamina 3/4

Willpower: 5, Health Levels: OK, -1, -1, -2, -2, -5, Incapacitated

Attack: Claw for four/five dice; bite for five/six dice

Abilities: Alertness 3, Athletics 2, Brawl 3 (Intimidation 4, Stealth 3)

Blood Pool: 5

Note: This template represents a leopard, panther, jaguar or other "smaller" big feline. Traits to the right of the slash represent a tiger or lion.

BIRD (LARGE)

Strength 2, Dexterity 3, Stamina 3

Willpower: 3, Health Levels: OK, -1, -1, -2, -5

Attack: Claw for two dice; bite for one (desperation)

Abilities: Alertness 3, Athletics 2, Brawl 1, Dodge 2, Intimidation 2 (Brawl 3, Empathy 4, Intimidation 4)

Blood Pool: 1/2 (1 blood point equals two large birds)

Note: This template can represent a hawk, crow, raven, owl or even vulture. A bird can typically fly at 25 to 50 mph.

CAT

Strength 1, Dexterity 3, Stamina 3

Willpower: 3, Health Levels: OK, -1, -2, -5, Incapacitated

Attack: Claw or bite for one die

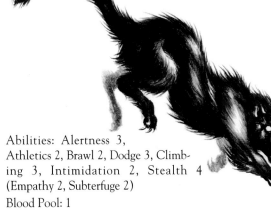

Abilities: Alertness 3, Athletics 2, Brawl 2, Dodge 3, Climbing 3, Intimidation 2, Stealth 4 (Empathy 2, Subterfuge 2)

Blood Pool: 1

DOG

Strength 4, Dexterity 3, Stamina 3

Willpower: 5, Health Levels: OK, -1, -1, -2, -2, -5

Attack: Bite for five dice; claw for four

Abilities: Alertness 3, Athletics 2, Brawl 3 (Dodge 3, Empathy 2, Intimidation 3, Stealth 2)

Blood Pool: 2

Note: These Traits reflect a large hound, such as a mastiff or hunting dog. Smaller, domestic canines will not be as formidable.

HORSE

Strength 4/6, Dexterity 2, Stamina 3/5

Willpower: 2/4, Health Levels: OK, OK, -1, -1, -2, -2, -5, Incapacitated

Attack: Trample or kick for six/seven dice; bite for three

Abilities: Alertness 3, Athletics 2, Brawl 1 (Brawl 3, Empathy 2, Intimidation 2)

Blood Pool: 3/4

Note: Horses typically fear the undead, but can be trained as mounts. The Traits to the right of the slash or in parentheses represent a Clydesdale or similar large stallion.

Pig/Boar
Strength 2/4, Dexterity 2, Stamina 4/5
Willpower: 3, Health Levels: OK, OK, -1, -1, -2, -4, Incapacitated
Attack: Bite for two/four dice; boars gore for five
Abilities: Alertness 2, Athletics 2, Brawl 2 (Intimidation 2)
Blood Pool: 3/4

Note: Traits to the right of the slash or in brackets represent boars.

Rat
Strength 1, Dexterity 2, Stamina 3
Willpower: 4, Health Levels: OK, -1, -5
Attack: Bite for one die
Abilities: Alertness 2, Brawl 1, Dodge 3, Stealth 3
Blood Pool: 1/4 (1 blood point equals 4 rats)

Note: Rats are often turned into ghouls and used as spies and guards by Nosferatu. They often attack in swarms (see the rules below).

Wolf
Strength 3, Dexterity 3, Stamina 3
Willpower: 3, Health Levels: OK, -1, -1, -3, -5, Incapacitated
Attack: Bite and claw for four dice
Abilities: Alertness 2, Athletics 1, Brawl 3, Dodge 1, Stealth 2
Blood Pool: 2

Note: Vampires who turn into wolves move at double normal running speed.

Packs and Swarms
Although the Traits listed above detail individual creatures, some animals attack *en masse*. Also, it's quite atmospheric for a vampire elder to overwhelm his victims with rodent or canine minions. If a swarm of hornets or horde of rats accosts the characters, use the rules that follow.

Instead of trying to determine what each and every member of a pack or swarm does, simply roll to see if the swarm itself harms a character. Narrate the results from there.

Each beast type is given a listing on the chart, below. Roll the damage dice pool listed once per turn (difficulty 6), and allow the characters to try to dodge or soak the result. This damage is lethal, or possibly bashing in the case of small or weak creatures. Packs attack once per turn per target, and act on the initiative given on the chart.

If a character dodges, he can move normally for the remainder of the turn. Otherwise, his attackers slow him down to half his usual movement. If they score more than three health levels' worth of damage in one turn (after the target soaks), or if the player botches an appropriate roll, the character is knocked down and overrun. He can only move a yard or two per turn and the swarm's damage difficulty falls to 5. Efforts to get back up and continue moving have higher than normal difficulties (typically difficulty 7 or 8).

The health levels listed reflect the amount of damage it takes to disperse a pack or swarm. An additional two health levels destroy the attackers completely. Pistols, rifles and small melee weapons (knives, brass knuckles, bottles, claws, bare hands) inflict a single health level per strike, no matter how many attack or damage successes are rolled (that is, the

strike hits only one creature). Shotguns, submachine guns and large melee weapons (swords, staves, boards, chainsaws) do normal damage (each damage success rolled eliminates one health level of the swarm as a whole), as do large-area attacks (Molotov cocktails, frost storms, gusts of wind, explosions). Swarms and packs don't soak.

Depending on the size of the pack, two or more characters might be affected by it and can attack it in return. Anyone who helps an overrun character can be attacked as well. A human can outrun some packs or swarms (those consisting of rats or bugs), but can't hope to outrun others (those consisting of hyenas or birds).

Animal	Damage	Health Levels	Initiative
Small bugs	1	5	2
Large bugs	2	7	3
Flying bugs	2	5	4
Birds, bats	4	9	5
Rats	3	7	3
Large rats (one or more feet long)	4	9	3
Feral cats	4	6	6
Wild dogs	6	15	4

Epilogue:
Under the
Horns of Blood

"Everything I have told you, even this, is a lie."

Those were Alisdair's last words to me, wheezed out while I rammed a broken-off chair leg between his ribs, and they might have been the only true thing I ever heard him say. I mean, he told me that a stake to the heart would immobilize a vampire, and yet there he was, still talking to me even as I stuck two feet of cherrywood through his chest. I don't think he should have been able to do that.

I don't understand it. I don't understand any of this. But I do understand that I've done something I probably shouldn't have.

Drifting lazily through the half-opened window, the last flecks of Alisdair's ashes are fluttering out into the night. From where I'm sitting on the floor, I can see the moon just barely crawling above the skyline. It's a crescent with the horns pointed up, fat and bloody orange through the smog. My roommate Carol would say that a moon like that is a symbol of female power, and that the color represents the magic inherent in menstruation, and so on. I just look at it and think that the air's got to be utterly filthy if it turns the moon that shade of red. I'm even vaguely thankful that in my new condition, I don't have to breathe that crap anymore.

The breeze curls through the room, bringing with it the stench of the streets below. Underneath it I can still smell the burned-paper smoke that Alisdair crumbled into once I finished with him. I don't think that smell's ever going to leave this place. If I stay, it's going to drive me insane sooner or later. Even though he's dead, even though I drank every last drop of his blood, he's somehow not gone yet. There's an echo of him in my head now, and if I stay here that echo's just going to get louder and louder.

Right. I need to get out, need to get away from the place where I murdered Alisdair. I'm not even sure why I did it, though God knows he must have deserved it for something or other that he'd done over the years. I could lie and say he deserved it for turning me into a vampire, but that would be a disservice to whatever memory I have of him. The more I think about it, the more certain I am that something told me to find him; I'm sure that same something told him to Embrace, rather than kill, me.

Maybe that something is what told me that I needed to stick that pole in his ribs, then drain him dry, too. I almost could have sworn I heard someone else in here while I did the deed, telling me what I needed to do but not why I needed to do it. That's not a bad little rationalization for murder, is it?

Still, let's face it, even with the element of surprise there is no way I should have been able to inconvenience Alisdair, never mind kill him. In the three weeks since he Embraced me, I've seen him outrun police cars and lift his piano with his off hand. I, on the other hand, can turn my cheeks pink — and only if I try really *really* hard. He should have been able to stop me without thinking about it. Why didn't he?

Did someone keep him from defending himself? Or did he just want someone to kill him already? It's not like I can ask him now.

Leave this place. Now. His money is in the center drawer of the desk — you'll have to smash the wood to reach it.

There's no one else here. No one else saw me murder Alisdair; no one's come in since. The neighbors never bothered us, so it can't be them.

I said leave now.

There's still no one here, but screw it, I'm not taking chances. I walk over to the desk, frowning at what I'm about to do. It's a beautiful piece; Alisdair once told me he'd rescued it from a marquis' Paris manor during the Terror. Then again, he told me he'd been made a vampire two centuries ago in England, and never set foot in France. Everything is a lie, indeed. I wonder if I can trust any of what he said about what being a vampire really means.

Expecting resistance, I pull on the bronze handle of the center drawer. It doesn't budge.

Hurry!

Whoever my unseen patron is, he's feeling rushed. I close my eyes and try to imagine the blood flowing into my arms, giving me strength. It was a trick that Alisdair showed me, one I honestly haven't picked up too well.

Like this, Celeste. Suddenly I hear Alisdair's voice, feel his will guiding the power of the blood through me. This can't be happening. He's dead. He's gone. I killed him, drank him down. *I'm here, and I'm with you forever now, my darling. You're going to need my help — you've got oh so much to do, and you'll never make it without me. Your other friend agrees — that's why he had you kill me the way you did.*

The front face of the overstuffed drawer rips off with a sharp crack, and then it drops to the floor amidst a blizzard of papers and bills. I hurriedly stuff handfuls of cash into my bag, then reach into the drawer one last time and take Alisdair's Glock pistol. I'm counting on Alisdair's paranoia here — thank God I'm right and the gun is loaded.

It's worthless, the not-Alisdair voice says. I stop for a second, startled, and look up…

…and there's a face at the window. We're 15 stories up, and there's a face at the window, a pale, fanged, ugly face. It's screaming something at me about diablerie and the End Times, but I don't waste time listening.

I raise the gun and fire, putting six shots into the thing outside the window. It explodes into a mess of blood on broken glass, and falls away. Inside I can hear Alisdair exulting;

outside there's only the wet screaming of the vampire falling a hundred feet to the pavement.

If you rush, you can make it to your car before he heals.

I don't stop this time, don't debate a thing. I just sprint from the apartment, slamming the door behind me for the last time. As I turn the corner to the stairwell, I can distantly hear more things being smashed inside. The ugly guy brought friends, I guess.

They're afraid of you. They're afraid of what you're going to do.

"Who the hell are you?" I scream into the air, even as I take the steps down four at a time. "Where's Alisdair?"

I'm a friend. And Alisdair is part of you now. His strength is yours. You'll need it in the nights ahead. Your enemies have been waiting for you since before you were born.

And with that I'm out the door and through the lobby, nearly running over Abe the doorman in the process. Down the block I can hear sirens, presumably cops and an ambulance headed this way to investigate the flattened body on the sidewalk and the gunshots. I turn the other way, heading down King, and keep running. My side hurts. The hand I used to rip open Alisdair's desk drawer hurts. My arm hurts, especially right above my elbow where I've got that ugly birthmark that Carol kept cooing over. There's an empty gun in my hand, and I'm wheezing out of sheer reflex, and I wish I could just sit down and rest.

Not yet. Drop the gun, but keep running. You'll be able to rest soon.

"Yeah?" I pant as I run out in front of a taxi. The Pakistani driver starts to yell but then shouts something in fear as he sees Alisdair's dried blood on my face. "When's soon?"

After you've killed me, too.

And I can hear Alisdair's laughter mix with the screams of distant sirens as I plunge deeper and deeper into the night. It's a sound that's going to haunt me until the end of the world.

Which, if my hunch is right, won't be long.

INDEX

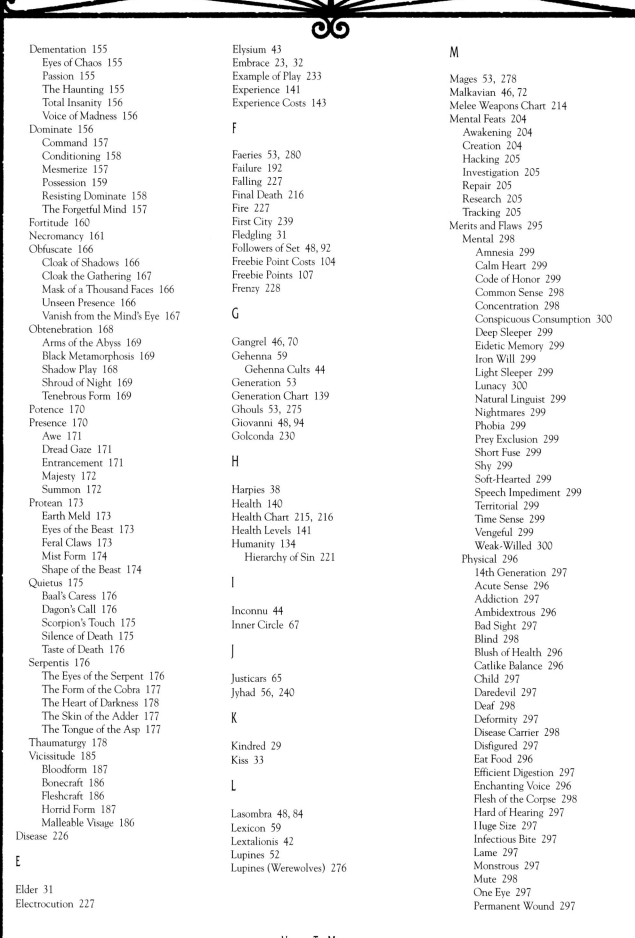

VAMPIRE
THE MASQUERADE

NAME: NATURE: GENERATION:
PLAYER: DEMEANOR: HAVEN:
CHRONICLE: CLAN: CONCEPT:

ATTRIBUTES

PHYSICAL	SOCIAL	MENTAL
Strength ●OOOO	Charisma ●OOOO	Perception ●OOOO
Dexterity ●OOOO	Manipulation ●OOOO	Intelligence ●OOOO
Stamina ●OOOO	Appearance ●OOOO	Wits ●OOOO

ABILITIES

TALENTS	SKILLS	KNOWLEDGES
Alertness OOOOO	Animal Ken OOOOO	Academics OOOOO
Athletics OOOOO	Crafts OOOOO	Computer OOOOO
Brawl OOOOO	Drive OOOOO	Finance OOOOO
Dodge OOOOO	Etiquette OOOOO	Investigation OOOOO
Empathy OOOOO	Firearms OOOOO	Law OOOOO
Expression OOOOO	Melee OOOOO	Linguistics OOOOO
Intimidation OOOOO	Performance OOOOO	Medicine OOOOO
Leadership OOOOO	Security OOOOO	Occult OOOOO
Streetwise OOOOO	Stealth OOOOO	Politics OOOOO
Subterfuge OOOOO	Survival OOOOO	Science OOOOO

ADVANTAGES

BACKGROUNDS	DISCIPLINES	VIRTUES
_____ OOOOO	_____ OOOOO	Conscience/Conviction ●OOOO
_____ OOOOO	_____ OOOOO	
_____ OOOOO	_____ OOOOO	
_____ OOOOO	_____ OOOOO	Self-Control/Instinct ●OOOO
_____ OOOOO	_____ OOOOO	
_____ OOOOO	_____ OOOOO	
_____ OOOOO	_____ OOOOO	Courage ●OOOO

MERITS/FLAWS

_____
_____
_____
_____
_____
_____
_____
_____
_____

HUMANITY/PATH

O O O O O O O O O O

WILLPOWER

O O O O O O O O O O
☐ ☐ ☐ ☐ ☐ ☐ ☐ ☐ ☐ ☐

BLOOD POOL

☐ ☐ ☐ ☐ ☐ ☐ ☐ ☐ ☐ ☐
☐ ☐ ☐ ☐ ☐ ☐ ☐ ☐ ☐ ☐

HEALTH

Bruised		☐
Hurt	-1	☐
Injured	-1	☐
Wounded	-2	☐
Mauled	-2	☐
Crippled	-5	☐
Incapacitated		☐

EXPERIENCE